FROMMER'S

COMPREHENSIVE TRAVEL GUIDE

DELAWARE, MARYLAND, PENNSYLVANIA & THE NEW JERSEY SHORE '92-'93

by Patricia Tunison Preston
and John J. Preston

PRENTICE HALL TRAVEL

NEW YORK • LONDON • TORONTO • SYDNEY • TOKYO • SINGAPORE

Dedicated to Thomas F. Preston,
beloved brother, great writer,
and enthusiastic traveler

FROMMER BOOKS

Published by Prentice Hall General Reference
A division of Simon & Schuster Inc.
15 Columbus Circle
New York, NY 10023

ISBN 0-13-334608-0
ISSN 1055-5382

Manufactured in the United States of America

CONTENTS

LIST OF MAPS

ACKNOWLEDGMENTS

With special thanks to our family and friends for all their encouragement to us in the writing of this book.

We would also like to acknowledge the tremendous help and enthusiasm of the many dedicated people who work long and hard for the various state and local tourist organizations in the mid-Atlantic states. In particular, we extend a big "thank you" to the following:

In Pennsylvania Deb Hickok, Cheryl Slavinsky, R. C. Staub, Marilyn Kane, Corinne Laboon, Pamela Matt, Terese Wallack, M. Susan Breen, Marguerite Foster, Norma Bigham, Martina Witmer, Eileen McGinley, Anne Case, Maryann Harrington, David Yonki, Barbara Groce, Philip Magaldi, Jr., Pam Collins, Dan Park, Joanne Craig, Karen Harvey, Wendy Cox, Bob Chandler, Kitty Felion, Lisa Feinstein, Sam Rogers, and many more.

In Delaware Gigi Dux Windley, Ivy Allen, Sara Brownlowe, Dorothy Hipple, Sandra Ardis, Sandra Dale, Kay Anderson, and many more.

In Maryland Jane White, Cheryl Todd, Shirley Wisenburg, Marty Batchelor, B. J. Bupp, Herman Schieke Jr., Dorothy Briscoe, Winnie Belle LeCompte, Sandie Marriner, Lewis Carmen, and Barbara Ortt.

In New Jersey Eileen Thornton, Susan Safire Ricciardi, Bernard W. Groff, and Blair Learn.

And at Amtrak Patricia Duricka.

INVITATION TO THE READER

In this guide to the mid-Atlantic states, we describe what we regard as the best of the many wonderful establishments that we came across while conducting our research. You, too, in the course of your travels, may come across hotels, inns, restaurants, shops, or attractions that you feel should be included here; or you may find that some of the places we selected have since changed for the worse. Let us know about them. Address your comments to:

Patricia and John Preston
Delaware, Maryland, Pennsylvania & the New Jersey Shore
c/o Prentice Hall Travel
15 Columbus Circle
New York, NY 10023

A DISCLAIMER

We have made every effort to ensure the accuracy of the prices as well as of the other information contained in this guide. Yet we advise you to keep in mind not only that prices fluctuate over time but that some of the other information herein also may change as a result of the various volatile factors affecting the travel industry.

The authors and the publisher cannot be held responsible for the experiences of the reader while traveling.

SAFETY ADVISORY

Whenever you are traveling in an unfamiliar city or country, stay alert. Be aware of your immediate surroundings. Wear a moneybelt and keep a close eye on your possessions. Be particularly careful with cameras, purses, and wallets—all of which are favorite targets of thieves and pickpockets.

CHAPTER 1

GETTING TO KNOW DELAWARE, MARYLAND, PENNSYLVANIA & THE NEW JERSEY SHORE

1. GEOGRAPHY

2. HISTORY

• DATELINE

3. SPORTS & RECREATION

4. RECOMMENDED BOOKS

Delaware, Maryland, Pennsylvania, and the New Jersey Shore—four great vacation destinations. Each is distinctive and different in its own right, yet all are an integral part of an historic and diverse 60,000-square-mile travel corridor in the heart of America's east coast.

Comprising the largest chunk of the region commonly known as the "mid-Atlantic states," these four destinations are an exciting blend of cities and countryside, mountains and monuments, beaches and byways—the best of both the north and south.

For the most part, they are bordered by the Atlantic Ocean, which means a collage of beaches, each with its own personality and attractions—from America's number-one destination, Atlantic City, and Victorian Cape May, both in New Jersey, to the white sands of Ocean City on Maryland's eastern shore, or Delaware's "quiet resorts," which dominate the Delmarva peninsula. Not to be outdone, Pennsylvania has its own beaches along the Lake Erie shorefront.

These four states are also rimmed and divided by picturesque rivers and bays, such as the Delaware, Lehigh, Allegheny, Susquehanna, Brandywine, Chesapeake, and Potomac. Swimming, boating, and white-water rafting are just a few of the sports that draw visitors. Vacationers also come to pay homage to the heroes of history, commemorated on the cobblestone streets of Philadelphia, the brick-lined pathways of Annapolis, or the grassy fields of Gettysburg and Valley Forge in Pennsylvania; Antietam in Maryland; Brandywine in Delaware/Pennsylvania; and Monmouth in New Jersey.

Much of what is great about our country has evolved from these states—from Philadelphia's Constitution Hall, where our government was founded, to Baltimore's Fort McHenry, which inspired the words of the "Star Spangled Banner." Even little

Delaware played a crucial role in forging the new nation by being the first state to ratify the constitution.

Best of all, this region is a medley of places that are synonymous with happy vacation dreams—from the honeymoon resorts of the Pocono Mountains in Pennsylvania to the dockside crab restaurants of Maryland, the museums that rim Wilmington, the gaming tables of Atlantic City, the chocolatey aromas of Hershey, the antique shops of Bucks County, the outlet stores of Reading, and so much more.

1. GEOGRAPHY

REGIONS IN BRIEF

PHILADELPHIA The "City of Brotherly Love," this is largest city in Pennsylvania and the second-largest city on the east coast. Rimmed by the Delaware and Schuylkill Rivers and the bucolic byways of Fairmount Park, it is an exciting blend of old and new—from the Colonial architecture of "America's most historic square mile" to the futuristic museums, trendy hotels, and glassy skyscrapers of today. It is also the setting of the Liberty Bell, Independence Hall, and the riverfront promenade known as Penn's Landing, as well as the home of such diverse attractions as the U.S. Mint, the marching Mummers, and the tasty "cheese steak."

> ✪ **The mid-Atlantic region contains scenes of spectacular natural beauty and a wealth of historical attractions.**

BUCKS COUNTY Less than 20 miles north of Philadelphia, Bucks County is the epitome of the best of William Penn's sylvan countryside—meandering rivers, glistening lakes, grassy towpaths, wooded hillsides, and wildflower-filled fields. This peaceful setting is also home to authentic historic districts, welcoming country inns, unique museums, and a flourishing literary and artistic tradition.

LANCASTER COUNTY Situated beside the Susquehanna River, this fertile county is the heartland of rural Pennsylvania farm life. It is home to a large community of Amish people, often referred to as "Pennsylvania Dutch." A gentle and religious people, they cling to the traditions of their ancestors, using horse-drawn buggies for transport and mule-powered machinery to farm the land. This area is a haven for wholesome home-cooked foods and freshly made baked goods, roadside stands and country markets, handmade quilts and colorful hex signs.

READING Founded by two of William Penn's sons, this historic city is nestled along the banks of the Schuylkill River and rimmed by the Blue Mountains. It has many claims to fame, including being the birthplace of Daniel Boone and the nucleus of a prime mushroom-growing region, but, most of all, it is acclaimed as a shopping mecca, with more than 250 outlet stores.

THE POCONOS Wedged in the northeast corner of Pennsylvania and rimmed by the Delaware and Lehigh Rivers, this popular mountain resort area is spread over four rural counties (Monroe, Pike, Carbon, and Wayne). It is a year-round outdoor paradise, for skiing, whitewater rafting, horseback riding, biking, hiking, and boating. Thanks to an array of "couples only" hotels with heart-shaped pools and champagne baths, it is also known as the "honeymoon capital" of the world.

THE LEHIGH VALLEY With the Lehigh River as its backbone, this picturesque and productive valley revolves around a trio of busy cities. The largest is Allentown, an industrial hub and the setting for Dorney Park. Bethlehem, home of Bethlehem Steel, is acclaimed as "America's Christmas City," thanks to its Moravian traditions and symbolic white star that sits on a nearby hillside. The smallest of the three

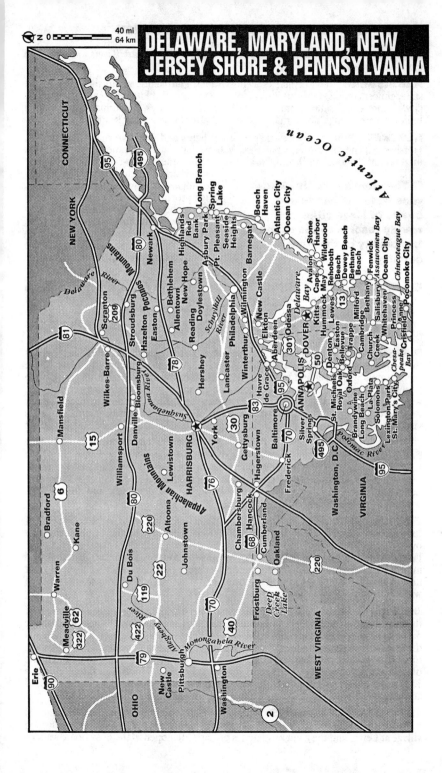

cities—Easton—is at the junction of the Lehigh and Delaware Rivers and is rich in canal-era traditions.

HARRISBURG The capital of Pennsylvania, Harrisburg sits in the heart of the state, almost equidistant from Philadelphia to the east and Pittsburgh in the west. The city's impressive skyline, rimmed by the Susquehanna River, is dominated by a capital building with a huge dome that is patterned after St. Peter's in Rome.

HERSHEY With candy-kiss-shaped street lights and sweet aromas filling the air, Hershey is a chocolate-lover's paradise. Visitors can watch the candy-making process in action at "Chocolate World," and enjoy many other candy-related attractions at Hersheypark and the Hershey Museum. The highly acclaimed Hershey Hotel, which provides all of its guests with candy bars on check-in, sits on a hillside overlooking the town, surrounded by 23 acres of rose-filled gardens. For those seeking more than chocolates, there's an 11-acre zoo and Indian caves dating back from the 1600's.

> ✪ **The contrast in life-styles runs from the hustle and bustle of large cities and trendy resorts to the rustic tranquillity of the Amish country.**

CENTRAL PENNSYLVANIA This vast core of Pennsylvania, almost 200 miles in width and length, offers a wide variety of experiences, from the shady shorelines of the Susquehanna and the flat battlefield terrain of Gettysburg to the mountainous lumberlands of Williamsport and the rolling farmlands near Danville and Bloomsburg.

PITTSBURGH The metropolitan hub of western Pennsylvania, Pittsburgh sits at the confluence of three rivers: the Allegheny, the Monongahela, and the Ohio. Once synonymous with steel and pollution, Pittsburgh has worked hard in recent years to become a "Renaissance City," home of clean air and aesthically pleasing architecture, with parks, flowers, waterfalls, and trees at every turn. Although the downtown area is very compact, Pittsburgh's attractions reach out into the suburbs—to the hillside vistas of Mount Washington, the shopping meccas of Station Square and the South Side, and the great universities and museums of Oakland.

ERIE Pennsylvania's third-largest city, Erie is the state's only port on the Great Lakes. The waterfront is Erie's focal point, with 18 sandy beaches, hiking trails, bird-watching areas, and opportunities for boating, fishing, and other watersports. Lake Erie perch and Great Lakes yellow pike top local menus, and four nearby wineries supply a variety of local vintages.

WILMINGTON Delaware's largest city, Wilmington is located at the confluence of the Christina, Brandywine, and Delaware rivers. Founded by the Swedes, this city owes much to the French family of the du Ponts, who built a chemical empire here. Fueled by the success of the du Ponts, Wilmington today is a financial, banking, and industrial hub. It is also a cultural gateway to the Brandywine Valley's cluster of great museums and gardens—from Winterthur and The Hagley to Longwood, most of which were du Pont family estates in earlier days.

DOVER The capital of Delaware, Dover is also literally at the geographic center of the state. It is the setting for major historic buildings and museums, as well as a bucolic parklike square, simply called The Green. On the outskirts of the city, there are many diverse attractions, including Dover Downs International Speedway, a car-racing mecca; Dover Air Force Base, the largest aerial port facility on the east coast and home of the giant C-5 Galaxy airplanes; and the Bombay Hook Wildlife Refuge, a 15,000-acre haven for hundreds of species of migrating and resident waterfowl and animals.

THE DELAWARE BEACHES Hugging the Atlantic shoreline for more than 20 miles, these beaches offer a great variety of surfside scenery—from the historic fishing village at Lewes and the giant sand dunes of Cape Henlopen to the busy boardwalk of

Rehoboth. Tiny Dewey Beach, only two blocks wide, is nestled between the Atlantic and Rehoboth Bay, while Bethany Beach and Fenwick Island are usually referred to as "Quiet Resorts," with relatively little commercial activity amid wide stretches of sugary white sands.

BALTIMORE Maryland's largest city, Baltimore is situated on the Patapsco River off Chesapeake Bay. The birthplace of the famous clipper ships, it is an historic port with an Inner Harbor that has been dramatically rejuvenated in recent years. Radiating from its waterfront, the city is a thriving blend of futuristic skyscrapers, overhead walkways, cascading fountains, and open-air plazas. It also boasts a bustling harborside recreation area known as "Harborplace," a tourist mecca of restaurants, curiosity shops, and trendy boutiques, with musical entertainment.

> ○ **Some of the finest examples of Colonial architecture are preserved here, as part of the country's historical heritage.**

ANNAPOLIS Home of the U.S. Naval Academy, Annapolis is situated at the confluence of the Chesapeake Bay and Severn River. Boat tours and sailing schools beckon visitors to see the city from afloat. As the capital of Maryland, it is also rich in history and boasts a historic district of more than 1,500 buildings. A vista of 18th-century mansions, churches, inns, and public buildings, Annapolis is compact and easily walkable.

MARYLAND'S EASTERN SHORE Hugging the Chesapeake Bay, Maryland's eastern shore is a paradise of beaches and bayfront activities. This is the setting for some of Maryland's oldest towns, rich in Colonial architecture, such as Easton and Oxford; the former shipbuilding center of St. Michael's; and the crabbing center at Tilghman. Further south is Cambridge on the Choptank River, famed for its Victorian district, and the nearby Blackwater National Wildfowl Refuge. Next is the crabber's haven of Crisfield, known as the seafood capital of the world. Inland is Salisbury, home of Perdue Chickens and the North American Wildfowl Art Museum, while bustling Ocean City is Maryland's only beach-and-boardwalk resort on the Atlantic Ocean.

WESTERN MARYLAND Stretching for over 200 miles, this corridor of Maryland offers a diverse tableau of scenic attractions. Frederick, in the heart of horse country, contains a beautifully preserved historic district of 18th- and 19th-century buildings; while nearby New Market is the antiques capital of the state. Hagerstown is the "hub" of the Cumberland Valley, and home of the Maryland Theatre, a rococo landmark; nearby is the Antietam battlefield, scene of the bloodiest single day of the Civil War. Cumberland is the departure point for the new Western Maryland Scenic Railroad, and Deep Creek Lake is Maryland's premier ski resort and watersports haven.

ATLANTIC CITY With more than 30 million visitors a year, Atlantic City is the New Jersey Shore's prime destination. Although there is a wide sandy beach and well-maintained 60-foot-wide boardwalk, most visitors come to Atlantic City to "strike it rich" at one of the 12 major casino gambling resorts.

DATELINE

- **1492** Columbus discovers the New World.
- **1609** Henry Hudson explores the Delaware.
- **1610** Delaware is named for Lord de La Warre.
- **1620** Cape May is discovered.
- **1629** "First Town" is settled in Delaware.
- **1634** The founding of Maryland takes place.
- **1637** "New Sweden" settlement established at Wilmington.
- **1643** The foundations of Pennsylvania are set.
- **1649** Puritans find a home in Annapolis.
- **1682** William Penn establishes Pennsylvania.
- **1729** Baltimore is established.
- **1758** The establishment of Pittsburgh takes place.
- **1774–1800** Philadelphia serves as the Colonial capital.

(continues)

CAPE MAY At the southern tip of New Jersey, Cape May is unique in the endless chain of shore resorts. Although it has a fine beach and promenade, Cape May is much more—it's a beautifully restored Victorian district. Many of these buildings, rich in bright colors and flowery gingerbread trim, have been converted into bed-and-breakfast inns, and others are open for tours. Visitors can tour Cape May in Victorian style via horse-drawn carriages and trolleys. Fishing, boating, and bird-watching offer a change of pace from the Victoriana.

THE REST OF THE NEW JERSEY SHORE More than 50 beaches, and over two dozen boardwalks, too—that's the essence of the Jersey Shore, stretching for over 127 miles along the Atlantic Ocean. You can take your pick, from the serene charm of Spring Lake and the family-oriented appeal of Ocean City or Ocean Grove, to the back-to-back motels of the Wildwoods, or the wildlife havens of Avalon and Stone Harbor. This region also includes the Sandy Hook National Recreation Area, Monmouth Battlefield State Park, Monmouth Park racetrack, Garden State Arts Center, and the 172-foot Barnegat Lighthouse on Long Beach Island.

2. HISTORY

EARLY EXPLORATIONS

Although it is universally accepted that Christopher Columbus discovered the New World in 1492, more than 100 years passed before exploration reached northward into the area that now comprises Pennsylvania, Delaware, Maryland, and the New Jersey Shore.

Like most of the New World, this tiny area was settled initially by the Native Americans, specifically the Lenni Lenape and Nanticoke tribes. The first European to arrive was probably Henry Hudson in 1609, when he sailed in from the Atlantic and along the neighboring bay (now known as Delaware Bay). He might have stepped off the *Half Moon* to explore, but, as fate would have it, the sight of dangerous shoals spurred him to turn his ship northward—and eventually to discover the Hudson River in New York.

The following year, an English sea captain, Samuel Argall, sailed into the same waters by accident as he was en route to Virginia. It is said that he named the body of water in honor of Lord de La Warre, the governor of Virginia. And hence the name "Delaware" evolved to describe the bay and eventually the land.

FIRST SETTLEMENTS BY THE DUTCH & ENGLISH

After Hudson's initial efforts, the Dutch made their mark several more times in the New World. In 1620, Captain Cornelius Jacobson Mey explored the area that is now

Cape May on the southern tip of New Jersey. He bestowed his name on the land, calling it "Cape Mey" (which was eventually anglicized to "May").

Similarly, it is recorded that the Dutch West India Company purchased land in 1629 from the Native Americans in the area that is now Delaware. This was followed in 1631 by the arrival of a group of Dutch who sought to establish a whaling colony in what is now the port of Lewes in Delaware. This settlement, called "Zwaanendael" (meaning the "Valley of the Swans"), is usually credited as being Delaware's first European colony; in later years, Lewes came to be known as the "first town in the first state."

Within a year, however, a misunderstanding between the Lenni Lenape Indians and the Dutch resulted in the tragic massacre of the new colonists and the end of the settlement of Zwaanendael.

Meanwhile, on the southern rim of what is now Maryland, 140 colonists arrived from England in 1634 on two ships, *The Ark* and *The Dove*. These stalwart settlers set up a community, known as St. Mary's City, that served as the beginning of Maryland and the state's first capital until 1694. Among the achievements of this early city was the enactment of the first laws recognizing religious tolerance.

"NEW SWEDEN" & THE PURITANS

Three years after St. Mary's City was founded by the English, a new attempt at colonization was launched by yet another European country, Sweden. In 1637, two Swedish ships, the *Kalmar Nykel* and the *Vogel Grip,* entered Delaware Bay and sailed northward almost 60 miles, entering a smaller river. The people on board named this new body of water the Christina River, after their queen, and in time they built a fortress, also in her name, and called their settlement "New Sweden." It would eventually become Wilmington.

The Swedes adapted well, using local trees to build log cabins, said to be the first in the New World. They also raised livestock and grew crops including corn, a staple introduced to them by the Native Americans. The Swedes are also credited with laying the foundations of what was to become Pennsylvania, by establishing a small settlement at Tinicum Island in the Delaware River in 1643.

In 1649, yet another group, the Puritans from England, came on the scene. They landed first in Virginia, but encountered religious harassment, so they moved northward to what is now Annapolis, settling at the mouth of the Severn River, near Chesapeake Bay. These early inhabitants called it Anne Arundel Town, after the wife of the second Lord Baltimore, proprietor of the colony of Maryland, but in 1695 it was renamed Annapolis for Princess Anne of England, and the Colonial government of Maryland was moved here from St. Mary's City. It has been Maryland's capital ever since.

THE COMING OF THE QUAKERS

By 1664 the English had become the dominant force among the European colonists, winning most of the Eastern seaboard, with settlements stretching from New England to Virginia.

DATELINE

- **1862** The Battle of Antietam takes place.
- **1863** The Battle of Gettysburg is fought.
- **1903** The Hershey Chocolate Factory is founded.
- **1925** Deep Creek Lake is created.
- **1939** Little League baseball is inaugurated at Williamsport, Pa.
- **1952** The William Preston Lane Bridge opens up the eastern shore.
- **1976** Gambling is approved for Atlantic City.
- **1981** Harborplace debuts in Baltimore. Delaware enacts the Financial Center Development Act.

? DID YOU KNOW . . . ?

- **Delaware** is referred to as the First State, because it was the first of the 13 original colonies to ratify the Constitution, on December 7, 1878.

- Among the smallest of the 50 states, Delaware is only 96 miles long and 35 miles wide at its broadest point. Yet it contains 28 miles of Atlantic coastline, 11 state parks, and 12 wildlife areas.

- More than half of the Fortune 500 companies are incorporated in the state of Delaware.

- Three of America's oldest churches—Old Swedes (1698) in Wilmington, Old Welsh Tract near Newark (1703), and Barratt's Chapel (1780) at Frederica—are still in use in Delaware.

- In 1939 the Delaware-based du Pont Company first developed and produced nylon at its plant in Seaford, now known as the "nylon capital of the world."

- Delaware has no sales tax.

- Some 50% of Delaware's 28-mile Atlantic coastline is devoted to wildlife refuges and parks.

- Dover Air Force Base is the home of the giant C-5 Galaxy airplane, one of the world's largest operational aircrafts—equivalent to an eight-lane bowling alley.

- Sussex County, home of the Delaware beaches, is the number-one chicken broiler–producing county in the nation.

- In 1880 the first beauty contest was held in Rehoboth Beach to select "Miss United States." Thomas Edison was a judge.

- The northernmost public-owned stand of bald cypress in the United States is located at Trussom Pond near Laurel.

- The Nanticoke tribe, native to Delaware, still resides in Sussex County. Each September its members celebrate their heritage with a pow wow in Millsboro.

This position was accelerated in 1682 when William Penn crossed the Atlantic to claim extensive lands that were granted to him and his Quaker followers. Calling the territory "Penn's Silvania" or "Penn's Woods," he sought to establish a colony where friendship would be the code of life. To this end, he founded Philadelphia, a "green countrie towne," that would soon become known as the "City of Brotherly Love."

Calling his work a "Holy Experiment," Penn had one purpose in mind, religious freedom for all, so that no one group would dominate another. One of the first things he did was to sign a peace treaty with the local tribes, ensuring that both natives and newcomers would "live friendly together." Soon persecuted peoples from all parts of Europe flocked to the new land—Mennonites, Amish, Dunkards, Moravians, Methodists, and many others. This melding of many diverse peoples under the banner of friendship helped to shape and develop Pennsylvania into a model for the other colonies.

THE CITIES TAKE SHAPE

In subsequent years, the region's other great cities began to evolve, including Baltimore, named after Lord Baltimore of England and founded in 1729.

Pittsburgh developed in 1754 when it was settled by the French as Fort Duquesne at the confluence of the Monongahela, Allegheny, and Ohio Rivers. The British captured it in 1758 and renamed it in honor of their prime minister, William Pitt the Elder, and later the fort passed its name on to the city. Pittsburgh's importance was underscored in 1760 when a huge coal seam was discovered on the edge of the city.

As events propelled the American colonies toward the quest for independence from Great Britain, Delaware, Maryland, New Jersey, and Pennsylvania, were in the forefront of the struggle.

THE STRUGGLE FOR INDEPENDENCE

Philadelphia, in particular, played a key role as capital of the colonies, for most of the period 1774–1800. Among the most significant events to take place in Philadelphia were the First Continental Congress, which was convened at Carpenters' Hall in 1774, followed by the Second Continental Congress (1775–83), which met at the Pennsylvania State House, later to become Independence Hall. The most significant act of the

? DID YOU KNOW . . . ?

- **Maryland** is known as the Old Line State. This nickname can be traced to Colonial times, when Marylanders led the way in many Revolutionary War encounters.

- In southern Maryland, tobacco was once so prized that it served as legal tender.

- Centrally located among the original 13 colonies, Maryland donated the land on which the new nation's capital, Washington, D.C., was built.

- Maryland's state tree, the Wye Oak, in Talbot County, is more than four centuries old and spreads its massive crown to 165 feet, making it one of the world's largest white oaks.

- Maryland is home port to the largest fleet of private pleasure craft on the east coast.

- Just 199 miles wide and 125 miles from north to south, Maryland is one of the smallest of the 50 states.

- Maryland's most prominent feature, the Chesapeake Bay, gives the state a coastline of more than 3,000 miles.

- The Calvert Cliffs, unique to southern Maryland, are the home of 4-million-year-old fossils, brought to the surface by tides and constant erosion from the Patuxent River and Chesapeake Bay.

- Maryland's Pimlico Racetrack is the home of the Preakness Stakes, second jewel of the Triple Crown races. First run in 1873 and held continuously since 1909, the Preakness was named after a popular horse of the late 19th century.

Congress was, of course, the adoption of the Declaration of Independence on July 4, 1776. Four days later, on July 8, the Declaration of Independence was read publicly for the first time in the State House Yard.

Among the engagements of the seven-year war that were fought on the soil of these four states were the battles of Trenton (1776), Brandywine (1777), Germantown (1777), and Monmouth (1778). The encampment of George Washington's army at Valley Forge during the winter of 1777–78 was also a milestone, although no battle was fought there.

During the Revolutionary War period, Philadelphia remained the capital of the colonies except for nine months of British occupation September 30, 1777, to June 28, 1778, when the Continental Congress met at County Courthouse in York and adopted the Articles of Confederation, the first document to describe the colonies as the United States of America. As hostilities drew to a close, Philadelphia again relinquished its preeminence and Annapolis reigned as the first peacetime capital of the United States from November 26, 1783 until August 13, 1784. This city served as the site for the ratification of the Treaty of Paris, the document in which Britain formally recognized the independence of the United States, ending the Revolutionary War.

After almost nine months in Annapolis, the capital was once again firmly back in Philadelphia, and in 1787 a Federal Convention of 55 delegates gathered at Independence Hall. For four months they met, debated, and revised the Articles of Confederation and ultimately developed the Constitution of the United States. The seat of government remained in Philadelphia until 1800, except for a brief period when New York City held the honor.

STATEHOOD & EARLY GROWTH

When it came to approving the new Constitution, Delaware took the initiative on December 7, 1787, thus earning itself the title of "First State"—the first of the original 13 colonies to ratify the Constitution. It was followed by Pennsylvania on December 12, 1787, New Jersey on December 18, 1787, and Maryland on April 28, 1788.

The post–Revolutionary War era gave the new states a chance to grow and expand. Farming was pivotal to the growth of all four states, and Pennsylvania also produced great quantities of iron-ore and coal. Throughout the 19th century, new immigrants from Europe arrived daily, including a Frenchman, Eleuthère Irénée du Pont de Nemours, who started a black-powder mill on the banks of the Brandywine in 1802. This establishment proved to be the foundation of a family empire that was to

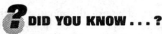

DID YOU KNOW . . . ?

- **Pennsylvania** is called the Keystone State, because it was the keystone, or pivot, in the development of the 13 original colonies into a nation.

- Pennsylvania is the birthplace of the 15th president, James Buchanan, as well as of such diverse personalities as pioneer Daniel Boone, inventor Robert Fulton, novelist James Michener, artist Andrew Wyeth, golfer Arnold Palmer, and singer Mario Lanza.

- Basically rectangular in size, Pennsylvania is 310 miles wide and 180 miles from top to bottom, for a total of 45,888 square miles. It has a population of about 12 million.

- Three-fifths of Pennsylvania is still forest.

- The number-one industry in Pennsylvania is agriculture; the second-largest industry is travel.

- The 400-mile Pennsylvania Turnpike opened in 1940 as the first high-speed, multi-lane highway in the United States.

- The highest point in Pennsylvania is Mt. Davis, in the Laurel Highlands, at 3,213 feet; the lowest point is the Delaware River.

- Pennsylvania has more than 50 natural lakes and 2,500 artificial lakes.

- In 1993 the Pennsylvania state park system will be 100 years old. It's the country's third-largest state park system, with 114 outdoor recreational areas and more than 276,000 acres of property.

- America's first pike, Route 30, runs from Philadelphia to west of Pittsburgh.

- For the 1876 World's Fair, a Pennsylvania pharmacist concocted a brew of herbs, bark, and roots that sold as the first root beer.

- Pennsylvania has more covered bridges than any other state in the country—a total of 221.

become the largest chemical company in America and a powerful influence on the entire Mid-Atlantic area.

Transportation avenues blossomed—the 19th century soon became the age of the railroad, the steamboat, and the canals, and rivers were harnessed for milling and industrial use. National roads were built and western Maryland and western Pennsylvania became gateways to the west. Transport was also aided in 1829 with the completion of the Delaware and Chesapeake Canal, a waterway that provides a short-cut from Chesapeake Bay to the Atlantic.

WAR YEARS: AN ANTHEM & A SPEECH

This was a relatively peaceful era for the region except for the War of 1812, which began with a British blockade of the Chesapeake and Delaware bays. By 1813 much of the action had shifted westward toward the Great Lakes. After losing the American frigate *Chesapeake* to the British, the American fleet on Lake Erie, led by Oliver Hazard Perry, defeated a British counterpart, giving the United States control of this strategic waterway. Perry's assessment of the situation, "We have met the enemy and they are ours" became legendary. The war's other notable event for this region happened in Baltimore in 1814 as the Americans were holding off a siege of Fort McHenry by the British. Francis Scott Key, a native Marylander, was inspired to write the words of the "Star-Spangled Banner," the song that would become our national anthem.

Maryland again brought the region into prominence in 1845, when the United States Naval Academy was founded at Annapolis on the grounds adjacent to the Severn River.

Less than 20 years later, the Civil War (1861–65) was to have a big effect on the entire Mid-Atlantic area, and especially Maryland and Pennsylvania. Although much of the initial fighting was confined to Confederate territory, two of the most significant battles took place in these two states. On September 17, 1862, the Battle of Antietam at Sharpsburg, Maryland, became the single bloodiest day of the war, with the dead and wounded exceeding 10,000 on both sides. This was followed almost a year later by the Battle of Gettysburg in Pennsylvania, July 1–3, 1863—three days of ferocious fighting that mark the turning point of the war. Confederate losses totaled 28,000 killed, wounded, or missing, effectively undermining the Confederate strength, while the Union's total was 23,000.

DID YOU KNOW . . . ?

- **New Jersey** is known as the Garden State, because it is home to more than 8,000 farms spread over nearly a quarter of its lands.

- New Jersey is 160 miles long and only 32 miles wide at its broadest point, yet it boasts 127 miles of Atlantic beach shoreline, 800 lakes and ponds, and more than 100 streams and rivers.

- New Jersey has the third-largest park system in the nation, with 35 state parks, 11 state forests, and five recreational areas.

- New Jersey's 1-million-acre Pinelands National Reserve, more commonly called the Pine Barrens, comprises the largest natural wilderness area east of the Mississippi and the largest tract of wilderness on the Mid-Atlantic coast.

- The world's largest blueberry plantation is at Hammonton, N. J., northwest of Atlantic City.

- Atlantic City's Convention Hall pipe organ is the largest musical instrument ever built. It has 33,000 pipes (ranging in length from 3/16 of an inch to 64 feet) and 1,225 speaking stops.

- Just off Sunset Beach at Cape May, you can see the remains of *The Cyclops*, an experimental concrete ship that sank in 1924.

- Asbury Park has its own Rock 'n Roll Museum, tracing the careers of such Jersey Shore–born musical stars as Bruce Springsteen, Jon Bon Jovi, Southside Johnny, and Little Steven.

Less than five months later, on November 19, 1863, Gettysburg was the scene of President Abraham Lincoln's Gettysburg Address, a speech designed to dedicate the cemetery at the scene of the battle and to offer some consolation and hope for the future, as the war continued to flare in other states. It became one of the most oft-quoted speeches in history.

MODERN MILESTONES

In the 35 years from the Civil War's end to the dawn of the 20th century, the United States moved quickly from a war-torn nation to a leading industrial power in the world. Other, lesser-known milestones were also coming to pass that would have local impact in the states of Delaware, Maryland, New Jersey, and Pennsylvania. These include the establishment of Atlantic City as an incorporated village in 1854, as well as the construction of the world's first oceanfront boardwalk there. In 1873, the Delaware resort of Rehoboth Beach had its beginning as a site for "camp meetings" of the Methodist Church and a few years later a similar use by the Christian Church Conference led to the formation of Bethany Beach as a resort. On July 4, 1875, Ocean City, Md., was officially opened as a beach resort.

Events of particular significance during the 20th century in the mid-Atlantic region include the founding of the Hershey Chocolate Factory by Milton Hershey in 1903, followed in 1907 by the establishment of Hersheypark. In 1925, the 12-mile-long artificial Deep Creek Lake was created as a year-round watersport and wintersport playground in western Maryland. In 1939, Williamsport, Pa., became the birthplace and the world headquarters of Little League baseball.

In Maryland, the William Preston Lane Bridge was built in 1952, from Annapolis to Kent Island, making the eastern shore truly accessible to the rest of the state. In 1976, the passage of the casino-gambling referendum marked the official rebirth of Atlantic City. Harborplace, the cornerstone of waterfront urban development of Baltimore, was opened in 1981. For Delaware, one of the most important milestones has been the passage of the Financial Center Development Act of 1981, a law that freed banks from restrictions on credit-card interest rates and provided tax advantages for banks moving assets to the state. This legislation drew many of the nation's largest banks to Delaware, as well as other businesses, earning Delaware the title of "corporate capital of the world." Currently, thousands of businesses are incorpo-

✪ **Many of the country's finest museums are located here, containing specimens of Early American art as well as contemporary works by American and European artists.**

rated in the state, including more than half of the Fortune 500 companies and more than a third of the companies listed on the New York Stock Exchange.

Some of the highlights for the future include a new midcity Convention Center for Philadelphia by 1994; a new baseball stadium and a new subway for Baltimore, both slated for completion in 1992–93; a new waterfront housing and recreation development for Erie in 1992–93; a new airport for Pittsburgh in 1992; a new airport and Convention Center for Atlantic City by 1994; and a newly enlarged boardwalk and fortified seawall at Ocean City by 1992.

3. SPORTS & RECREATION

With an ever-changing kaleidoscope of farmlands and natural vistas, the four states of Pennsylvania, Delaware, Maryland, and New Jersey offer many opportunities for outdoor recreation and sport. Two states—Pennsylvania and Maryland—are etched with mountains and hillsides suitable for skiing, while the Atlantic coast of Delaware and Maryland, and the entire New Jersey Shore offer miles of sandy beaches and oceanfront activities. All four areas are rich in rivers, lakes, and bays, as well as parks and picnic areas, hiking and biking trails, and wildlife. The state travel and tourism bureaus will provide excellent information in advance of your trip (see "Information" in Chapter 2). In addition, the following agencies provide specialized information.

○ **The region offers a vast variety of outdoor activities, from skiing and riding rapids for the more daring to fishing and bird-watching for the contemplative visitor.**

FISHING

Pennsylvania Fish Commission, P.O. Box 1673, Harrisburg, PA 17105–1673 (tel. 717/657-4518).

Delaware Division of Fish and Wildlife, 89 Kings Highway, P.O. Box 1401, Dover, DE 19903 (tel. 302/736-4431 or toll-free 800/345-4200 in Delaware and 800/736-4431 out of state).

Maryland Department of Natural Resources, Tidewater Administration, Fisheries Division, 580 Taylor Ave., Annapolis, MD 21401 (tel. 301/974-3765).

New Jersey Department of Fish, Game, and Wildlife, 501 E. State St., CN 400, Trenton, NJ 08625 (tel. 609/292-2965).

HUNTING

Pennsylvania Game Commission, 2001 Elmerton Ave., Harrisburg, PA 17110-9797 (tel. 717/787-4250).

Delaware Division of Fish and Wildlife, 89 Kings Highway, P.O. Box 1401, Dover, DE 19903 (tel. 302/736-4431).

Main Wildlife Office, Forest, Park, and Wildlife Service, B-2, Maryland Department of Natural Resources, 580 Taylor Ave., Annapolis, MD 21404 (tel. 301/974-3195).

New Jersey Department of Fish, Game, and Wildlife, 501 E. State St., CN 400, Trenton, NJ 08625 (tel. 609/292-2965).

STATE PARKS

Pennsylvania Bureau of State Parks, P.O. Box 1467, Harrisburg, PA 17105-1467 (tel. 717/787-8800 or toll-free 800/63-PARKS).

Delaware Division of Parks and Recreation, 89 Kings Highway, P.O. Box 1401, Dover, DE 19903 (tel. 302/736-4702).

Maryland Department of Natural Resources, Maryland Forest, Park, and Wildlife Service, Tawes State Office Building, Annapolis, MD 21401 (tel. 301/974-3195).

New Jersey Division of Parks and Forestry, 501 E. State St., Station Plaza 5, 4th floor, Trenton, NJ 08625 (tel. 609/292-2792).

HIKING AND WILDLIFE AREAS

Pennsylvania Department of Forestry, P.O. Box 1467, Harrisburg, PA 17105–1467 (tel. 717/783-7941).

Delaware Division of Fish and Wildlife, 89 Kings Highway, P.O. Box 1401, Dover, DE 19903 (tel. 302/736-4431).

Maryland Forest, Park, and Wildlife Service, Tawes State Office Bldg., Annapolis, MD 21401 (tel. 301/974-3195).

New Jersey Division of Parks and Forestry, 501 E. State St., Station Plaza 5, 4th floor, Trenton, NJ 08625 (tel. 609/292-2792).

4. RECOMMENDED BOOKS

Dille, Carolyn, *The Chesapeake Cookbook* (New York: Clarkson N. Potter, Inc., 1990).

Fitzgerald, S., *The Delaware Seashore* (Wilmington: Jared Company, 1989).

Granick, E. W., *The Amish Quilt* (Intercourse, Pa.: Good Books, 1990).

McCullough, David G., *The Johnstown Flood* (New York: Simon & Shuster, 1968).

McDonough, M., Emerson, J., Pennebaker, J., and Rainey, W. D., *Delaware— First Place* (Chatsworth, Canada: Windsor Publications, 1990).

Tanzer, Virginia, *Call It Delmarvelous* (McLean, Va.: EPM Publications, 1983).

Uzzell, S., *Maryland* (Portland, Ore.: Graphic Arts Center Publishing, 1983).

Vessels, J., *Delaware, Small Wonder* (New York: Harry N. Abrams Inc., 1984).

Ward, G. C. with Burns, R. and K., *The Civil War: An Illustrated History* (New York: Alfred A. Knopf, 1990).

Weslager, C. A., *New Sweden on the Delaware* (Wilmington: Middle Atlantic Press, 1988).

———, *Pennsylvania and the Bill of Rights* (University Park, Pa.: Pennsylvania Historical Association Press, 1987).

———, *Pennsylvania Architecture* (University Park, Pa.: Pennsylvania Historical Association Press, 1988).

———, *Pennsylvania Painters* (University Park, Pa.: Pennsylvania Historical Association Press, 1990).

———, *The Pennsylvania Germans: A Brief Account of their Influence in Pennsylvania* (University Park, Pa.: Pennsylvania Historical Association Press, 1990).

CHAPTER 2

PLANNING A TRIP TO DELAWARE, MARYLAND, PENNSYLVANIA & THE NEW JERSEY SHORE

1. INFORMATION

When planning your trip, you can obtain helpful brochures and information by contacting the state tourist offices in advance. For specific data on individual cities, resorts, and areas, see the appropriate chapter.

DELAWARE Delaware Tourism Office, Delaware Development Office, 89 Kings Highway, P.O. Box 1401, Dover, DE 19903 (tel. toll-free 800/441-8846 or in Delaware 800/282-8667).

MARYLAND Maryland Office of Tourism Development, 9th floor, 217 E. Redwood St., Baltimore, MD 21202 (tel. 301/333-6611 or toll-free 800/543-1036).

PENNSYLVANIA Bureau of Travel Development, Pennsylvania Department of Commerce, 453 Forum Building, Harrisburg, PA 17120 (tel. 717/787-5453 or toll-free 800/VISIT PA).

NEW JERSEY New Jersey Division of Travel and Tourism, 20 W. State St., CN 826, Trenton, NJ 08625 (tel. 609/292-2470 or toll-free 800/JERSEY-7).

2. WHEN TO GO

CLIMATE

Depending on your interests and vacation time, Delaware, Maryland, Pennsylvania, and the New Jersey Shore are always in season. The region has a moderate climate, with four distinct seasons, typical of the mid-Atlantic section of the United States.

The greatest extremes in temperature are found in Pennsylvania and Maryland. Both these states stretch over 200 miles in width, and have mountainous regions rising to over 3,000 feet as well as sea-level land, so they offer a mix of warm extremes in the summer and cold snowy temperatures in winter. Delaware and the New Jersey Shore, on the other hand, are slightly more temperate, with cool ocean breezes in summer and relatively mild winters.

In the period June through August, it is common for temperatures to reach the 90-degree level during the day. In the December through March period, temperatures average in the 30s. The spring and fall months are harder to predict, with temperatures likely to be anywhere from the 40s to the 70s, like most of the eastern seaboard states. Average temperatures along the Atlantic coast are about 10 degrees warmer in winter and 10 degrees cooler in summer than other parts of the states. Annual rainfall for all states averages 35 inches to 45 inches.

HOLIDAYS & EVENTS

In the chapters that follow on individual cities or resorts, we mention appropriate outstanding annual events. In some cases, if a festival or happening is of interest to you, you may want to plan a visit around the event. On the other hand, if an event means scarce hotel rooms and higher prices, you may want to avoid visiting at that time.

3. WHAT TO PACK

As a general rule, pack light. Except for the deluxe hotels in major cities like Philadelphia, Pittsburgh, Baltimore, Annapolis, and Wilmington, you'll probably be carrying your own bags. Services are limited at suburban hotels, country inns, and bed-and-breakfasts, and many of these do not have elevators.

Common sense will help you to pack—light clothing for the beach resorts and warm insulated wear for the ski areas. For general touring, comfortable sports clothes are best—slacks, sweaters, a blazer, windbreaker jacket, and some rainwear. Sturdy and comfortable walking shoes are a must. Don't forget boots or rubbers in winter.

For the big city restaurants and for many of the finer country inns, guests are often asked to dress up for dinner. Jackets (and sometimes ties) will be required for men, and cocktail dresses or stylish pantsuits for women. If in doubt, check in advance.

Sunglasses are always helpful, especially if you are heading to see a sunset on the Chesapeake, Rehoboth Bay, Deep Creek Lake, or Lake Erie. If you are fond of swimming or exercise, do bring a bathing suit or work-out clothes, since more and more hotels and inns are adding health facilities. And don't forget an umbrella—it comes in handy, especially in the mountainous areas when a sudden shower may surprise you.

4. GETTING THERE

Delaware, Maryland, Pennsylvania, and the New Jersey Shore are all easy to reach by air, rail, or road.

BY PLANE

No matter where you live, you'll have no problems getting a flight to the major city gateways and the smaller regional airports located here. There are over 15 airports from which to choose.

Delaware   Served by Philadelphia.

Maryland Baltimore, Ocean City, Salisbury, Easton, Cumberland, and Washington County Regional Airport.

Pennsylvania Philadelphia, Pittsburgh, Harrisburg, Erie, Allentown/ Bethlehem/Easton, Scranton/Wilkes-Barre, Lancaster, Reading, Williamsport.

New Jersey Shore Atlantic City.

Prices, of course, vary with your point of origin, destination, and the type of airfare you choose. To get the best deal, it is wise to consult a travel agent or several carriers, and compare the prices. At the moment, it costs anything from $159 to $1,000 to fly across the U.S.A. one-way, so airfares really depend on many factors.

The lowest prices are usually **APEX fares** (advance-purchase excursions), which require that you book and pay for your ticket at a certain time. You might also have to travel at off-peak times and perhaps during midweek, like Tuesday or Wednesday. Don't be put off by the restrictions, however, as such conditions can usually save you at least 50% off normal fares!

BY TRAIN

All four of these states are served daily by regular **Amtrak** rail service, with major stations as follows:

Delaware Wilmington.

Maryland Baltimore.

Pennsylvania Philadelphia, Pittsburgh, Harrisburg, Lancaster, and Erie.

New Jersey Shore Atlantic City.

Like airfares, train prices depend a lot on searching out the best deal. At the moment, **Amtrak** (tel. toll-free 800/USA-RAIL) offers a special "All Aboard America" fare of $259 for round-trip cross-country travel, while the regular coach fare can run as high as $700 or more. Fares change often, so be sure to consult a travel agent or Amtrak when you are planning a trip.

BY BUS

For those who prefer to travel by bus, **Greyhound/Trailways** serves the large cities and many smaller towns throughout the region:

Delaware Wilmington, Dover, Rehoboth Beach, Bethany Beach.

Maryland Baltimore, Frederick, Hagerstown, Cumberland, Easton, Cambridge, Salisbury, Ocean City.

Pennsylvania Philadelphia, Pittsburgh, Erie, Harrisburg, Lancaster, Reading, the Poconos, the Lehigh Valley, Gettysburg, York, Williamsport, and the counties of Bucks, Columbia, and Montour.

Fares depend on the time of travel, distance, and many other factors. Always ask for "**Moneysaver**" fares to get the lowest price. For more extensive travel, look into the "**Ameripass**," a ticket that allows unlimited travel over a certain period of time for a flat fee.

BY CAR

By car, you have a choice of 10 interstate roads to bring you to and within the region. Interstate 95, the east coast's major north-south route, passes through all four of the states. From the north or south, you can also follow I-87, I-81, or I-79. In an east-west direction, I-80, I-76, or I-78 crosses all or parts of Pennsylvania and New Jersey; I-70 and the new I-68 lead to the Maryland area; and I-84 travels into northeast Pennsylvania.

5. GETTING AROUND

This region is ideal for all types of sightseeing. In the case of the big cities, we recommend that you take a plane, train, or bus to the city of your choice, and leave your car at home. Cities like Philadelphia, Pittsburgh, and Baltimore have excellent local transport systems, and can easily be explored on foot as well.

For the smaller cities, the country towns, and the beaches, it is best to bring your own car or to rent a car when you arrive at a major gateway. In each chapter, we list local options.

If you don't drive, then a package tour or escorted group tour might be best for you. Some tour companies which currently specialize in itineraries of this region include **Casser Tours,** 46 W. 43rd St., New York, NY 10036 (tel. 212/840-6500 or toll-free 800/251-1411); **CIE Tours International,** 108 Ridgedale Ave., Morristown, NJ 07960-4244 (tel. 201/292-3438 or toll-free 800/CIE-TOUR and 800/447-0279 in NJ); **Colette Tours,** 162 Middle St., Pawtucket, RI 02860 (tel. 401/728-3805 or toll-free 800/832-4656 and 800/752-2655 in New England; **Cosmos and Globus-Gateway,** both at 95-25 Queens Blvd., Rego Park, NY 11374 (tel. 718/268-7000 or toll-free 800/221-0090); **Domenico Tours,** 751 Broadway, Bayonne, NJ 07002 (tel. 201/823-8687 or toll-free 800/554-TOUR); and **Peter Pan Tours,** 1776 Main St., P.O. Box 1776, Springfield, MA 01102 (tel. 413/739-TOUR or toll-free 800/237-8747). You can contact these operators and ask for their brochures, or go to your travel agent, who will probably have other suggestions as well.

6. SUGGESTED ITINERARIES

IF YOU HAVE 1 WEEK

Do Delaware   Start in Wilmington and spend half of the week seeing the city and the surrounding Brandywine Valley and New Castle; then move south and devote the rest of the week to Dover and one or two of the beaches.

Meander around Maryland   Spend 2 days in Baltimore exploring the Inner Harbor and downtown sights; then head west taking in Frederick, New Market, Hagerstown, and Cumberland.

Explore the Eastern Shore of Maryland   Start at Easton and spend a couple of days touring that historic city plus Oxford and St. Michaels; then a day in Crisfield, Cambridge, and Salisbury, before ending at Ocean City.

Savor the Southeast of Pennsylvania   Start in Philadelphia for a day or two and then branch out into Lancaster County and to Hershey, or concentrate on Bucks County and the Lehigh Valley.

Follow the Susquehanna River in Pennsylvania   Start at Harrisburg/Hershey and then go south to Gettysburg, York, and Chambersburg, or head north and see Columbia and Montour counties and Williamsport.

Wander around Western Pennsylvania   Spend 2 or 3 days in Pittsburgh and then a couple of days in the Laurel Highlands, ending at Erie for 2 days or more to explore the lake shore.

Combine a bit of Maryland with Pennsylvania   Visit Gettysburg and York in Pennsylvania, and Frederick and Baltimore in Maryland, all within short drives of each other.

See the Mountain Country of Pennsylvania and Maryland

Combine a visit to the Laurel Highlands region of Pennsylvania with some time in Deep Creek Lake, Cumberland, and western Maryland.

Bask at the Beaches Spend half the week beach-hopping along the New Jersey Shore, and then spend the remaining 3 days in Atlantic City or Cape May, or divide your time between both.

IF YOU HAVE 2 WEEKS

Hone in on the Highlights of Pennsylvania Start in Philadelphia for 2 or 3 days, and then explore the Pennsylvania Dutch Country for 2 days, northward to the Poconos for a couple of days, and then spend a week dividing your time between Harrisburg/Hershey, Gettysburg, and Pittsburgh.

Tour All of Maryland Start in Baltimore and do the central and western part of the state during the first week, and then head to Annapolis for a few days and spend the rest of the second week on the eastern shore.

Combine Delaware with Maryland's Eastern Shore Take the first week to travel the state of Delaware from north to south, ending at Fenwick Island. Cross the border into Ocean City, and then devote your second week to the Chesapeake Bay area of the eastern shore.

Follow the Rivers of Pennsylvania and the Seacoast of New Jersey Start in the Lehigh River Valley and explore Allentown, Bethlehem, and Easton; go over to Bucks County on the Delaware River, and then to Philadelphia, bordered by the Delaware and the Schuylkill; spend the second week along the seacoast exploring the New Jersey shore.

IF YOU HAVE 3 WEEKS

Sample a Bit of Everything Start in Philadelphia for a few days, then over to Atlantic City for a little gambling and glamour, to Cape May for a dose of Victoriana, and then take the ferry to Delaware. Spend the second week exploring the beaches of Delaware, Maryland's eastern shore, and Annapolis. The third week could start with a couple of days in Baltimore and then into southeastern Pennsylvania to enjoy Pennsylvania Dutch Country, Harrisburg/Hershey, Gettysburg, and, if time allows, ending in Pittsburgh.

Do Pennsylvania in Depth Start in Pittsburgh and Erie and then to the center of the state along the Susquehanna, and to Harrisburg for the first week. The second week could include Hershey, Gettysburg, York, and Pennsylvania Dutch Country, ending in Philadelphia. After a few days in the City of Brotherly Love, spend the remainder of the third week exploring Bucks County, the Lehigh Valley, and the Poconos.

Cover the Three Coastal States Explore Maryland from west to east, ending in Baltimore on the first week. Continue to Annapolis and the eastern shore during the second week, ending at the Delaware beaches. Relax at the beaches or go north to Wilmington and the Brandywine Valley. For the third week, take the ferry to New Jersey and spend a week wending your way up the New Jersey shore, with a couple of nights each in Cape May and Atlantic City.

THEMED ITINERARIES

Civil War Sites Combine visits to the battlefields of Gettysburg, Pa., and Antietam, Md.

Colonial Cities and Enclaves Walk the brick paths and cobblestone byways of Philadelphia, Pennsylvania, historic New Castle and Dover, Delaware, and Annapolis, Maryland.

Wineries Tour and taste at the vineyards and wineries of Bucks County, Lancaster County, the Brandywine Valley, and the New Jersey Shore. Or focus on the wineries along Lake Erie's shores at Northeast, Pa., near Erie.

Surf and Sand Beach-hop from the vibrant pace of Ocean City, Md., to the "quiet" Delaware beaches and the dozens of choices along the New Jersey shore.

Nature   The choices are many, from the Bombay Hook National Wildlife Refuge outside of Dover, Del., to the Blackwater National Wildlife Refuge near Cambridge, Md., as well as the Cape May Bird Observatory and the Stone Harbor Bird Sanctuary on the New Jersey Shore.

Vintage Railroad Rides   It's "All aboard!" on scenic railways at Jim Thorpe, Strasburg, Gettysburg, and New Hope, Pa., as well as at Wilmington, Del., and Cumberland, Md.

River Sports   For these active pursuits, combine a trip to Pennsylvania's Lehigh Valley, with time in the Poconos and along the river in Bucks County, or westward over to the Laurel Highlands near Pittsburgh.

7. PRICE GUIDELINES

Throughout this guide, we describe the region's best lodgings, restaurants, sightseeing attractions, and activities, with the latest prices. The prices listed are for all levels, from expensive to budget, with an emphasis on moderate choices.

These prices are correct now, as we go to press, but probably will go up, due to inflation and other factors, during 1992 and 1993. You may have to add 10% to 20% to the costs we list, as time passes, but, in the main, these prices reflect a range or barometer. While the cost of a room or a dinner may change by a few dollars, at least you can be guided by the general level of prices indicated.

CHAPTER 3

FOR THE FOREIGN TRAVELER

1. PREPARING FOR YOUR TRIP

2. GETTING TO THE U.S.

• FAST FACTS: FOR THE FOREIGN TRAVELER

Although American fads and fashions have spread across Europe and other parts of the world so that America may seem like familiar territory before your arrival, there are still many peculiarities and uniquely American situations that any foreign visitor will encounter. This chapter is meant to clue you in on what they are.

International visitors should also read the Introduction carefully.

---

1. PREPARING FOR YOUR TRIP

NECESSARY DOCUMENTS

Canadian nationals need only proof of Canadian residence to visit the United States. Citizens of Great Britain and Japan need only a current passport. Citizens of other countries, including Australia and New Zealand, usually need two documents: a valid **passport** with an expiration date at least six months later than the scheduled end of their visit to the United States and a **tourist visa** available at no charge from a U.S. embassy or consulate.

To get a tourist or business visa to enter the United States, contact the nearest American embassy or consulate in your country; if there is none, you will have to apply in person in a country where there *is* a U.S. embassy or consulate. Present your passport, a passport-size photo of yourself, and a completed application, which is available through the embassy or consulate.

You may be asked to provide information about how you plan to finance your trip or show a letter of invitation from a friend with whom you plan to stay. Those applying for a business visa may be asked to show evidence that they will not receive a salary in the United States.

Be sure to check the length of stay on your visa; usually it is six months. If you want to stay longer, you may file for an extension with the Immigration and Naturalization Service once you are in the country. If permission to stay is granted, a new visa is not required unless you leave the United States and want to reenter.

MEDICAL REQUIREMENTS

No inoculations are needed to enter the U.S. unless you are coming from, or have stopped over in, areas known to be suffering from epidemics, especially of cholera or yellow fever. Applicants for immigrants' visas (and only they) must undergo a screening test for AIDS under a law passed in 1987.

If you have a disease requiring treatment with medications containing narcotics or drugs, carry a valid, signed prescription from your physician to allay any suspicions that you are smuggling drugs. Do the same if you are carrying syringes.

TRAVEL INSURANCE

All such insurance is voluntary in the U.S.; however, given the very high cost of medical care, we cannot too strongly advise every traveler to arrange for appropriate coverage before setting out. There are specialized insurance companies that will, for a relatively low premium, cover: loss or theft of your baggage; trip-cancellation costs; guarantee of bail in case you are sued; sickness or injury costs (medical, surgical, and hospital); costs of an accident, repatriation, or death. Such packages (for example, "Europe Assistance" in Europe) are sold by automobile clubs at attractive rates, as well as by insurance companies and travel agencies.

2. GETTING TO THE U.S.

Travelers from overseas can take advantage of the **APEX (Advance Purchase Excursion) fares** offered by all the major U.S. and European carriers. Aside from these, attractive values are offered by **Icelandair** on flights from Luxembourg to New York and by **Virgin Atlantic** from London to New York/Newark.

Some large airlines (for example, TWA, American Airlines, Northwest, United, and Delta) offer travelers on their transatlantic or transpacific flights special discount tickets under the name **Visit USA,** allowing travel between any U.S. destinations at minimum rates. They are not on sale in the U.S., and must therefore be purchased before you leave your foreign point of departure. This system is the best way of seeing the U.S. at low cost. You should obtain information well in advance from your travel agent or the office of the airline concerned, since the conditions attached to these discount tickets can be changed without advance notice.

For further information about travel to and around Delaware, Maryland, Pennsylvania, and the New Jersey Shore, see "Getting There" in Chapter 2, and the "Getting Around" sections in individual city and region chapters.

FAST FACTS FOR THE FOREIGN TRAVELER

Accommodations   See "Philadelphia Accommodations" in Chapter 4, and the "Where to Stay" sections of Chapters 5–21.

Automobile Rentals   See "Getting Around" in appropriate chapters.

Business Hours   See "Fast Facts" in appropriate chapters.

Climate   See Chapter 2.

Currency and Exchange. The U.S. monetary system has a decimal base: one **dollar** ($1) = 100 **cents** (100¢).

The most common **bills** (all green) are the $1 ("a buck"), $5, $10, and $20 denominations. There are also $2 (seldom encountered), $50, and $100 bills (the two latter are not welcome when paying for small purchases).

There are six denominations of **coins:** 1¢ (one cent, or "penny"); 5¢ (five cents, or "nickel"); 10¢ (ten cents, or "dime"); 25¢ (twenty-five cents, or "quarter"); 50¢ (fifty cents, or "half dollar"); and the rare—and prized by collectors—$1 piece (both the older, large silver dollars and the newer, small Susan B. Anthony coin).

Traveler's checks denominated in *dollars* are accepted without demur at most hotels, motels, restaurants, and large stores. But as any experienced traveler knows, the best place to change traveler's checks is at a bank.

However, the method of payment most widely used is the **credit card:** VISA (BarclayCard in Britain), MasterCard (EuroCard in Europe, Access in Britain, Diamond in Japan), American Express, Diners Club, and Carte Blanche, in descending order of acceptance. You can save yourself trouble by using "plastic money" (that is, credit cards), rather than cash or traveler's checks, in 95% of all hotels, motels, restaurants, and retail stores (except for those selling food or liquor). A credit card can serve as a deposit for renting a car, as proof of identity (often carrying more weight than a passport), or as a "cash card," enabling you to draw money from banks that accept them.

Note: The "foreign-exchange bureaus" so common in Europe are rare even at airports in the U.S., and nonexistent outside major cities. Try to avoid having to change foreign money, or traveler's checks denominated other than in U.S. dollars, at a small-town bank, or even a branch bank in a big city; in fact, leave any currency other than U.S. dollars at home—it may prove more nuisance to you than it's worth. If you do bring foreign currency to the United States, there is a currency exchange desk at John F. Kennedy International Airport, and at most other international gateways. Most major banks exchange currency.

Customs and Immigration   Every adult visitor may bring in, free of duty: one liter of wine or hard liquor; 200 cigarettes or 100 cigars (but *no* cigars from Cuba) or three pounds of smoking tobacco; $400 worth of gifts. These exemptions are offered to travelers who spend at least 72 hours in the U.S. and who have not claimed them within the preceding six months. It is altogether forbidden to bring into the country foodstuffs (particularly cheese, fruit, cooked meats, and canned goods) and plants (vegetables, seeds, tropical plants, etc.). Foreign tourists may bring in or take out up to $10,000 in U.S. or foreign currency with no formalities, larger sums must be declared to Customs on entering or leaving.

The visitor arriving by air, no matter what the port of entry—New York, Boston, Miami, Honolulu, Los Angeles, or the rest—should cultivate patience and resignation before setting foot on U.S. soil. The U.S. Customs service is among the slowest and most suspicious on earth. On some days, especially summer weekends, you may wait two hours or more to have your passport stamped at major international airports. Add the time it takes to clear Customs and you will see that you should make very generous allowance for delay in planning connections between international and domestic flights—an average of two to three hours at least.

In contrast, for the traveler arriving by car or by rail from Canada, the border-crossing formalities have been streamlined to the vanishing point. And for the traveler by air from Canada, Bermuda, Shannon, and some points in the Caribbean, you can sometimes go through Customs and Immigration at the point of *departure,* which is much quicker and less painful.

Electric Current   U.S. wall outlets give power at 110–115 volts, 60 cycles, compared to 220 volts, 50 cycles, in most of Europe. Besides a 110-volt converter, small appliances of non-American manufacture, such as hair dryers or shavers, will require a plug adapter with two flat, parallel pins.

Embassies and Consulates   All embassies are located in the national capital, Washington, D.C.; some consulates are located in major cities, and most nations have a mission to the United Nations in New York City.

Listed here are the embassies and some consulates of the major English-speaking countries—Australia, Canada, Ireland, New Zealand, and the United Kingdom. If you are from another country, you can get the telephone number of your embassy by calling "information" in Washington, D.C. (tel. 202/555-1212).

Australia   The **embassy** is at 1601 Massachusetts Ave., NW, Washington, DC 20036 (tel. 202/797-3000). A **consulate** is located in New York, at International Building, 636 Fifth Ave., NY 10111 (tel. 212/245-4000).

Canada   The **embassy** is at 501 Pennsylvania Ave. NW, Washington, DC 20001 (tel. 202/682-1740). A **consulate** is located in New York, at 1251 Ave. of the Americas, NY 10020 (tel. 212/586-2400).

Ireland   The **embassy** is at 2234 Massachusetts Ave. NW, Washington, DC 20008 (tel. 202/462-3939). A **consulate** is located in New York, at 515 Madison Ave., NY 10022 (tel. 212/319-2555).

New Zealand   The **embassy** is at 37 Observatory Circle NW, Washington, DC 20008 (tel. 202/328-4800).

United Kingdom   The **embassy** is at 3100 Massachusetts Ave. NW, Washington, DC 20008 (tel. 202/462-1340). A **consulate** is located in New York, at 845 Third Ave., NY 10022 (tel. 212/752-8400).

Emergencies   In all major cities you can call the police, an ambulance, or the fire brigade through the single emergency telephone number **911.** Another useful way of reporting an emergency is to call the telephone-company operator by dialing **0** (zero, *not* the letter O). Outside major cities, call the county sheriff or the fire brigade at the number you will find in the local telephone book.

If you encounter such travelers' problems as sickness, accident, or lost or stolen baggage, it will pay you to call **Travelers Aid,** an organization that specializes in helping distressed travelers, whether American or foreign. Check the local telephone book for the nearest office, or dial 0 and ask the telephone operator.

Holidays   On the following legal national holidays, banks, government offices, post offices, and many stores, restaurants, and museums are closed:

New Year's Day (Jan 1)
Martin Luther King Day (third Mon in Jan)
Presidents Day (third Mon in Feb)
Memorial Day (last Mon in May)
Independence Day (July 4)
Labor Day (first Mon in Sept)
Columbus Day (second Mon in Oct)
Veterans (Armistice) Day (Nov 11)
Thanksgiving Day (last Thurs in Nov)
Christmas Day (Dec 25)

Election Day, which falls on the Tuesday following the first Monday in November, is a legal national holiday during presidential-election years.

Information   See Chapter 2.

Legal Aid   The foreign tourist, unless positively identified as a member of the Mafia or of a drug ring, will probably never become involved with the American legal system. If you are pulled up for a minor infraction (for example, of the highway code, such as speeding), never attempt to pay the fine directly to a police officer; you may wind up arrested on the much more serious charge of attempted bribery. Pay fines by mail, or directly into the hands of the clerk of the court. If accused of a more serious offense, it is wise to say and do nothing before consulting a lawyer. Under U.S. law, an arrested person is allowed one telephone call to a party of his choice. Call your embassy or consulate.

Liquor Laws   See "Fast Facts" in city chapters.

Mail   If you want your mail to follow you on your vacation, you need only fill out a change-of-address card at any post office. The post office will also hold your mail for up to one month. If you aren't sure of your address, your mail can be sent to you, in your name, **c/o General Delivery** at the main post office of the city or region where you expect to be. The addressee must pick it up in person, and produce proof of identity (driver's license, credit card, passport, etc.).

Generally to be found at intersections, mailboxes are blue with a red-and-white logo, and carry the inscription "U.S. MAIL." If your mail is addressed to a U.S. destination, don't forget to add the five-figure ZIP Code, after the two-letter abbreviation of the state to which the mail is addressed (PA for Pennsylvania, DE for Delaware, MD for Maryland, and NJ for New Jersey).

Measurements and Sizes   While most of the rest of the world is on the metric system, for nonscientific purposes the United States still adheres to its own units of measurement. For tables to help you with conversions, see the Appendix.

Medical Emergencies   See "Emergencies," above.

Post   See "Mail."

Radio and Television   Audiovisual media, with three coast-to-coast networks—ABC, CBS, and NBC—joined in recent years by the Public Broadcasting System (PBS) and the cable network CNN, play a major part in American life. In the big cities, televiewers have a choice of about a dozen channels (including the UHF channels), most of them transmitting 24 hours a day, without counting the pay-TV channels showing recent movies or sports events. In smaller communities the choice may be limited to four TV channels (there are 1,200 in the entire country), and a half dozen local radio stations (there are 6,500 in all), each broadcasting a particular kind of music—classical, country, jazz, pop, gospel—punctuated by news broadcasts and frequent commercials.

Safety   In general, the United States is safer than most other countries, particularly in rural areas, but there are "danger zones" in the big cities which should be approached only with extreme caution.

As a general rule, isolated areas such as gardens and parking lots should be avoided after dark. Elevators and public-transport systems in off-hours, particularly between 10pm and 6am, are also potential crime scenes. You should drive through decaying neighborhoods with your car doors locked and the windows closed. Never carry on your person valuables like jewelry or large sums of cash; traveler's checks are much safer.

Taxes   In the United States there is no VAT (value-added tax), or other indirect tax at a national level. Every state, as well as each city in it, is allowed to levy its own local tax on all purchases, including hotel and restaurant checks, airline tickets, etc. It is automatically added to the price of certain services such as public transportation, cab fares, phone calls, and gasoline. It varies from 4% to 10% depending on the state and city, so when you are making major purchases such as photographic equipment, clothing, or high-fidelity components, it can be a significant part of the cost.

For sales tax rates in the four mid-Atlantic states, see appropriate city chapters.

Telephone, Telegraph, and Telex   Pay phones are an integral part of the American landscape. You will find them everywhere: at street corners, in bars, restaurants, public buildings, stores, service stations, along highways, etc. Outside the metropolitan areas, public telephones are more difficult to find. Stores and gas stations are your best bet. Average cost of a three-minute local call is 25¢.

For **long-distance or international calls,** stock up with a supply of quarters; the pay phone will instruct you when, and in what quantity, you should put them into the slot. For direct overseas calls, first dial 011, followed by the country code (Australia, 61; Republic of Ireland, 353; New Zealand, 64; United Kingdom, 44; and so on), and then by the city code (for example, 71 or 81 for London, 21 for Birmingham) and the number of the person you wish to call. For long-distance calls in Canada and the United States, dial 1 followed by the area code and number you want.

Before calling from a hotel room, always ask the hotel phone operator if there are any telephone surcharges. These are best avoided by using a public phone, calling collect, or using a telephone charge card.

For **reversed-charge or collect calls,** and for **person-to-person calls,** dial 0 (zero, *not* the letter O) followed by the area code and number you want; an operator will then come on the line, and you should specify that you are calling collect, or person-to-person, or both. If your operator-assisted call is international, ask for the overseas operator.

For local **directory assistance** ("information"), dial 411; for long-distance information dial 1, then the appropriate area code and 555-1212.

Like the telephone system, **telegraph** and **telex** services are provided by private corporations like ITT, MCI, and above all, Western Union. You can bring your telegram in to the nearest Western Union office (there are hundreds across the country), or dictate it over the phone (a toll-free call, 800/325-6000). You can also telegraph money, or have it telegraphed to you, very quickly over the Western Union system.

Telephone Directory   See *Yellow Pages,* below.

Time   The U.S. is divided into six **time zones.** From east to west, these are: Eastern Standard Time (EST), Central Standard Time (CST), Mountain Standard Time (MST), Pacific Standard Time (PST), Alaska Standard Time (AST), and Hawaii Standard Time (HST). Always keep these changing time zones in mind if you are traveling (or even telephoning) long distances in the United States. For example, noon in New York City (EST) is 11am in Chicago (CST), 10am in Denver (MST), 9am in Los Angeles (PST), 8am in Anchorage (AST), and 7am in Honolulu (HST).

Daylight Saving Time is in effect from 1am on the first Sunday in April until 2am on the last Sunday in October except in Arizona, Hawaii, part of Indiana, and Puerto Rico.

Tipping: This is part of the American way of life, on the principle that you must expect to pay for any service you get. Here are some rules of thumb:

Bartenders: 10%–15%.
Bellhops: at least 50¢ per piece; $2–$3 for a lot of baggage.
Cab drivers: 15% of the fare (20% in large cities).
Cafeterias, fast-food restaurants: no tip.
Chambermaids: $1 a day; more in big-city hotels.
Cinemas, movies, theaters: no tip.
Checkroom attendants (restaurants, theaters): 50¢ a garment; $1 in large cities.
Doormen (hotels or restaurants): not obligatory, but $1 at top hotels.
Gas-station attendants: no tip.
Hairdressers: 15%-20%.
Parking-lot attendants: 50¢ ($1 in hotels).
Redcaps (airport and railroad station): at least 50¢ per piece; $2–$3 for a lot of baggage.
Restaurants, nightclubs: 15%–20% of the check.
Sleeping-car porters: $2–$3 per night to your attendant.

Toilets   Foreign visitors often complain that public toilets are hard to find in most U.S. cities. True, there are none on the streets, but the visitor can usually find one in a bar, restaurant, hotel, museum, department store, or service station—and it will probably be clean (although the last-mentioned sometimes leaves much to be desired). Note, however, a growing practice in some restaurants and bars of displaying a notice that "toilets are for the use of patrons only." You can ignore this sign, or better yet, avoid arguments by paying for a cup of coffee or soft drink which will qualify you as a patron. The cleanliness of toilets at railroad stations and bus depots may be more open to question, and some public places are equipped with pay toilets, which require you to insert one or two 10¢ coins (dimes) into a slot on the door before it will open.

Yellow Pages   There are two kinds of telephone directory available to you. The general directory is the "white pages," in which private and business subscribers are listed in alphabetical order. The inside front cover lists emergency numbers for police, fire, and ambulance, and other vital numbers (like the Coast Guard, poison control center, crime-victims hotline, etc.). The first few pages are devoted to community-service numbers, including a guide to long-distance and international calling, complete with country codes and area codes.

The second directory, the *Yellow Pages,* lists all local services, businesses, and industries by type, with an index at the back. The listings cover not only such obvious items as automobile repairs by make of car, or drugstores (pharmacies), often by geographical location, but also restaurants by type of cuisine and geographical location, bookstores by special subject and/or language, places of worship by religious denomination, and other information that the tourist might otherwise not readily find. The *Yellow Pages* also include city plans or detailed area maps, often showing postal ZIP codes and public transportation routes.

PHILADELPHIA

A "greene countrie towne" is the way that William Penn envisioned his new city on the Delaware River in 1682. And if this founding father could see his town today, he'd be mighty proud. Not only has this city retained and revitalized its original parks and historic buildings, but it has aesthetically blended them with gleaming new office skyscrapers and thriving commercial complexes. Cobblestone courtyards and broad tree-lined boulevards exist side by side with bustling transitways.

Years ago, it was true that Philadelphia bore the brunt of W. C. Fields's jokes, but in the 1970s this spunky settlement said, "No more." Spurred by the Bicentennial and other recent historic celebrations, concerned citizens stepped forward, and enlightened urban planning came to the fore. Neglected landmarks were restored, derelict halls turned into chic shopping malls, old inns were glamorized, new hotels with skylit atriums sprang up, and a culinary renaissance began that has literally cooked up hundreds of exciting new restaurants.

Most of all, Philadelphia is our nation's "Cradle of Liberty"—the home of the Liberty Bell, Independence Hall, and America's "most historic square mile." In many ways, this hub of 4 million people—the second largest city on the east coast—has influenced the lives of all Americans.

A BIT OF HISTORY

Philadelphia's history from 1774 until 1800 is inextricably linked to the lofty ideals of independence urged by our nation's founding fathers. The First Continental Congress convened in this city at Carpenters' Hall in 1774. The Second Continental Congress, which forged America's destiny, met in the Pennsylvania State House, later to become Independence Hall. It was there that the Congress made the fateful decision to prepare the Declaration of Independence, which was then read publicly for the first time in this city's State House Yard on July 8, 1776.

Except for 9 months during the British occupation, Philadelphia was the Revolutionary War capital, and later continued as the capital of the fledgling nation. In 1787, the Constitutional Convention met to revise the Articles of Confederation, and, for four months, 55 delegates secretly developed the Constitution of the United States. It was indeed fitting that Philadelphia remained the new nation's capital until 1800.

Although the city is no longer our nation's capital or even the capital of Pennsylvania, it still retains the landmarks and the aura of those early days. As you wander from building to building in the Independence National Historical Park, the cobblestones seem to echo with the footsteps of George Washington, Thomas Jefferson, John Adams, and Ben Franklin. Drop into the Betsy Ross House and see the workroom where the first "Stars and Stripes" flag pattern was sewn, and, of course, you can't miss paying your respects to the Liberty Bell.

Visitors to Philadelphia are often surprised that this city has also produced many "firsts" for America: the first hospital, the Philadelphia Hospital; the first university,

WHAT'S SPECIAL ABOUT PHILADELPHIA

Ace Attractions

☐ Independence National Historical Park, home of the Liberty Bell and Independence Hall.

☐ U.S. Mint, the largest money-making facility of its kind in the world.

☐ City Hall, beaux-arts landmark with a 37-foot statue of William Penn at its rooftop tower.

☐ Penn's Landing, the Delaware River spot where William Penn first arrived, now a promenade and recreation area.

Events/Festivals

☐ Philadelphia Open House, tours of private homes.

☐ Jambalaya Jam, a weekend of New Orleans–style food and music.

For the Kids

☐ Please Touch Museum, a special world designed for children aged 7 or younger.

Literary/Artistic Shrines

☐ Edgar Allan Poe National Historical Site, short-term home of the great American author.

☐ Norman Rockwell Museum, containing a complete set of the artist's cover drawings for the *Saturday Evening Post*.

Museums

☐ Franklin Institute Science Museum, home of the new Futures Center.

☐ Philadelphia Museum of Art, one of the world's largest collections of American paintings.

☐ Rodin Museum, containing the largest collection of Rodin works outside of France.

☐ Mummers Museum, home of the colorful marching band.

Parks

☐ Fairmount Park, the world's largest landscaped city park.

Zoos

☐ Philadelphia Zoo, the first in the United States (1874).

---

the University of Pennsylvania; the first mint, the United States Mint; the first stock exchange; and many more, including the nation's first zoo.

Philadelphia is also the gateway to some of the Mid-Atlantic region's most inviting countryside. Travel less than 20 miles outside this vibrant city and you are in the heart of three of the top visitor destinations on the east coast—Valley Forge, the Brandywine Valley (see Chapter 12), and Bucks County (see Chapter 5).

1. ORIENTATION

ARRIVING

BY PLANE **Philadelphia International Airport,** Penrose Avenue, off I-95 (tel. 215/492-3181), is 8 miles southwest of the city center. With more than 1,000 flights a day, this airport is an east coast gateway, serving arrivals and departures to over 100 U.S. cities as well as flights to Europe, Canada, Mexico, and the Caribbean, and connections to the Orient.

More than two dozen airlines serve this airport, including major transcontinental carriers, such as **American** (tel. 215/365-4000); **Continental** (tel. 215/592-8005);

Delta (tel. 215/928-1700); **Northwest** (tel. 215/492-2475); **Pan American Express** (tel. 215/244-5000); **TWA** (tel. 215/923-2000); **United** (tel. 215/568-2800); and **USAir** (tel. 215/563-8055), and foreign flag airlines such as **British Airways** (tel. 215/492-2460); **Air Jamaica** (tel. 215/545-5705); **Lufthansa** (tel. 215/668-9630); and **Mexicana** (tel. 215/972-5353).

Taxi and **limousine services** stop at all baggage-claim areas. Average cab fare between the airport and city is $18 to $20. Among the car-rental firms that maintain desks at the airport are **Avis, Budget, Dollar, Hertz, National,** and **Thrifty.**

If you prefer public transport, a rapid transit link between the airport and three major downtown points is operated by **Southeastern Pennsylvania Transportation Authority (SEPTA).** Known as **Philadelphia Airport Rail** (tel. 215/580-7800), this service operates daily from 6am to midnight, traveling between terminals A, B, C, D, or E, to the 30th Street Station at 30th and Market Streets (Gate B, Track 6, upper-level track area); Penn Center/Suburban Station at 16th Street and John F. Kennedy Boulevard (Gate 4B, Track 3); and Market East Station, located just north of Market Street between 10th and 12th Streets (Gates 2B and 4B, Track 3). Travel time is 25 minutes, and the one-way fare is $4.75 for adults and $2.40 for children under 12.

BY TRAIN   Philadelphia is the hub of transportation on **Amtrak's** Northeast corridor. Trains from points north, east, west, and south arrive and depart daily from Amtrak's 30th Street Station, 30th and Market Streets (tel. 215/824-1600 or toll-free 800/USA-RAIL). This station is located just west of the central downtown region, on the west side of the Schuylkill River. It is within walking distance of Drexel University and the University of Pennsylvania, but you will need a taxi to get to the major downtown hotels. *Note:* Some trains also stop at the North Philadelphia Station, Broad Street and Glenwood Avenue, all used mostly by those who live in that area. Do not be confused, however, and get off prematurely. Chances are you'll want the 30th Street Station if your destination is midcity.

BY BUS   Daily services are provided into Philadelphia by **Greyhound,** 1001 Filbert St. (tel. 215/931-4000). The depot is in the central downtown district, near to hotels and Philadelphia's major attractions.

BY CAR   Philadelphia is well served by interstate highways from all directions. From the north, I-95 leads into the northeastern section of the city, with several exits into midtown, including I-676 (Vine Street Expressway), which takes you into the historic district. I-95 is also the best route from points south. From the east, take I-295 or the New Jersey Turnpike, connecting to I-676, over the Benjamin Franklin Bridge, into the heart of the city. From the west, you can approach via Rte. 30 or I-76 to the Schuylkill Expressway into the city center. Traffic can be heavy and congested, particularly at morning or evening rush hours. If you are not familiar with the city, try to arrive in the late morning or early afternoon.

TOURIST INFORMATION

The **Philadelphia Convention and Visitors Bureau** operates a full-time **Visitors Center** at 1525 John F. Kennedy Blvd., at 16th Street, Philadelphia, PA 19102 (tel. 215/636-1666 or toll-free 800/321-9563). It's open daily from 9am to 6pm, Memorial Day through Labor Day, and from 9am to 5pm every other day of the year except Christmas. For news of what's happening in Philadelphia, you can also call the 24-hour Event Hotline (215/337-7777, ext. 2540); you'll be connected to a 2-minute taped message, updated three times a week.

CITY LAYOUT

Wherever you go in Philadelphia, you can usually look up and see the statue of William Penn proudly surveying his "greene countrie town" from 35 stories up atop

City Hall. Up until 1986, this was the highest mark on the city skyscape, and no other structure could be built taller than "Billy Penn's hat," but the recent additions of 50- and 60-story skyscrapers, especially along Market Street, have changed the city skyline dramatically. In many ways, reaching for new horizons symbolizes the essence of this city from its very first days.

MAIN ARTERIES AND STREETS

Philadelphia is laid out according to a grid system, with the Delaware River on the east and the Schuylkill River (pronounced *Scool*-kill) cutting through its western side. Most north-south streets, beginning with **Front** (1st Street) on the Delaware, are numbered; while east-west streets are named. **Broad Street,** which is the main artery in the north-south direction, is an exception, and is the equivalent of 14th Street. **Market** is the principal east-west artery, with north-south designations fanning out from this point.

All downtown north-south streets have alternate one-way traffic, with the exception of Broad, which has three lanes in each direction. Market Street is one-way eastbound between 20th and 15th Streets. Westbound motorists should use **John F. Kennedy Boulevard** above 15th Street. Otherwise, traffic patterns are orderly, except that **Chestnut Street** is closed to all traffic other than buses between 8th and 18th Streets, so Chestnut is best avoided as a crosstown artery.

THE NEIGHBORHOODS IN BRIEF

When William Penn designed his "greene countrie towne" over 300 years ago, he created an urban plan that has survived the centuries. The cornerstones of his layout, five parklike squares, still exist today, although the original names have been changed. They are **Penn** (formerly Centre) **Square; Washington** (originally Southeast) **Square; Franklin** (once Northeast) **Square; Logan** (first named Northwest) **Square** or more commonly called **Logan Circle** today; and **Rittenhouse** (which started as Southwest) **Square.** Once you get to know the squares and their surrounding areas, you have a firm grasp on the essence of Philadelphia today.

Extending east of Franklin and Washington Squares to the Delaware River, the **Olde City** is where Philadelphia began, a cobblestone street area now known as the **Independence National Historical Park.** Also known as America's most historic square mile, this is the home of the **Liberty Bell,** the symbol of our country's freedom; **Independence Hall,** where the Declaration of Independence was adopted and the U.S. Constitution was written; and dozens of other landmark buildings. Nearby, you can also visit **Penn's Landing,** the spot on the Delaware where William Penn first pulled up his ship to dock; as well as **Society Hill,** a charming old neighborhood of brick walks and Federal houses; and the adjacent SoHo-style area of **South Street,** which attracts visitors to its many trendy restaurants, art galleries, and boutiques.

Right in the heart of midtown where Broad Street crosses Market Street is **City Hall.** Standing in the space that was once Centre Square and now known as Penn Square because of the giant statue of William Penn that dominates the top of City Hall, this urban government complex is the focal point of the city's downtown area. Most businesses are located within five or six blocks of here, as are the leading theaters, department stores, shops, hotels, and restaurants.

A patch of greenery in the city's southwest corner, the tree-lined **Rittenhouse Square** is rimmed by a fashionable residential enclave, with graceful brick town houses, chic shops, and stylish restaurants.

Formerly called **Logan Square,** this parklet is in the center of the Benjamin Franklin Parkway, the wide, shady, and flag-lined boulevard usually compared to the Champs-Elysées. This roadway links City Hall to **Fairmount Park** and is surrounded by many of the town's foremost museums, making Logan Circle the cultural corner of Philadelphia. The adjacent Fairmount Park is full of beautiful old houses, gardens, monuments, and acres of recreational facilities.

Depending on your time, this may be all of Philadelphia that you will see.

However, if you are interested in the city's major educational institutions, then you'll want to cross the Schuylkill River westward from Market Street or John F. Kennedy Boulevard. Both the **University of Pennsylvania** and **Drexel University** are located here, and farther westward you'll find a cluster of colleges and top-name schools, ranging from **Villanova** to **Bryn Mawr.** This side of the river also holds the city's **Civic Center** and the main rail terminal, **30th Street Station.**

Other sections of the city that are of interest include **Chestnut Hill,** to the northwest, an elite village of revitalized and restored Colonial and 19th-century homes and storefronts; **Germantown,** founded in 1685, and today an area containing some of Philadelphia's oldest houses.

One of the most colorful ethnic neighborhoods is **South Philadelphia,** the part of the city that produced Mario Lanza, Joey Bishop, Fabian, Frankie Avalon, Bobby Rydell, and Chubby Checker. Today it is known for its open-air Italian Market, boccie courts, and a parade of pasta restaurants along Passyunk Avenue. Another popular tourist mecca is Philadelphia's **Chinatown,** located two blocks northwest of Independence Mall.

2. GETTING AROUND

BY PUBLIC TRANSPORTATION

SUBWAY Subway service runs in an east-west pattern along Market Street and in a north-south direction on Broad Street. It's particularly handy if you are traveling between downtown and 30th Street Station. For complete fare and schedule information, call SEPTA (tel. 215/580-7800).

BUS The Southeastern Pennsylvania Transportation Authority (SEPTA) operates a large fleet of buses throughout the city center area. The price on most routes is $1.50 and exact change or a token is required.

In addition, of particular interest to visitors, SEPTA runs a no. 76 bus (the "Ben FrankLine"), from Society Hill/South Street to the Philadelphia Museum of Art at the entrance to Fairmount Park. It travels through the historic district and along Chestnut Street and the Benjamin Franklin Parkway, convenient to over 50 places of interest. A short audio narration of the route's highlights is provided. The Ben FrankLine is a perfect orientation tour to downtown Philadelphia; the fare is $1.50.

If you'll be using the buses often, it pays to purchase the "SEPTA Visitor Key" for $7. It's a handy pocket guide that includes five tokens (worth $7.50 alone), maps, and discount coupons worth up to $450. For more information about where to purchase the Visitor Key, call 215/580-7800.

BY TAXI

There are numerous taxis operating throughout the city. You can hail available cabs as they cruise the street or go to areas where taxis frequently line up, such as hotels and the midcity suburban train station at 16th Street and John F. Kennedy Boulevard (across from the Visitor Center). If you prefer to order a cab by phone, call **Liberty Cab** (tel. 215/365-8414), **Metro Fleet** (tel. 215/423-3333), **Quality City Cab** (tel. 215/728-8000), **United Cab** (tel. 215/625-2881), or **Yellow Cab Co.** (tel. 215/922-8400).

BY CAR

RENTALS In addition to the car-rental desks at the airport, you can hire a car at the following downtown locations: **Avis,** 30th Street Station and 2000 Arch St.

(for either call toll-free 800/331-1212); **Budget,** 21st and Market Streets (tel. 215/492-9400); **Hertz,** 30th Street Station and 31 S. 19th St. (for either call toll-free 800/654-3131); **National,** 36 S. 19th St. (tel. 215/567-1760) and 36th and Chestnut Streets (tel. 215/382-6504); and **Thrifty,** 6915 Essington Ave. (tel. 215/365-3900).

Parking   Although some limited on-street parking is available, particularly after 6pm, it is best to park in one of the downtown parking lots or garages. Rates average $2 to $3 an hour, with a maximum of $6 to $8 in the evenings at most places.

FAST PHILADELPHIA

American Express   16th Street and John F. Kennedy Boulevard (tel. 215/587-2300); 615 Chestnut Street (tel. 215/592-9211).

Area Code   Unless indicated otherwise, all telephone numbers in this chapter have a 215 area code.

Baby-sitters   Call-A-Granni, Inc., 1133 East Barringer Street (tel. 215/924-8723.

Drugstores   CVS Pharmacy, 6501 Harbison Avenue (tel. 215/333-4300), is open 24 hours a day.

Emergencies   Dial 911 for the fire or police department, or an ambulance.

Eyeglasses   Pearl Vision Centre, Gallery 1 at 9th and Market (tel. 215/627-1626). American Vision Centers, 1616 Chestnut Street (tel. 215/564-0922).

Hairdressers/Barbers   Colonial-Deluxe Men's Hairstyling, 622 Market Street (tel. 215/627-1747).

Hospitals   Thomas Jefferson University Hospital, 11th and Walnut (tel. 215/928-6000); and Misericordia Hospital, 54th Street and Cedar Avenue (tel. 215/748-9100).

Information   See Orientation, above.

Laundry/Dry Cleaning   Crosstown Cleaners, 330 North Broad (tel. 215/563-8719).

Libraries   The Free Library of Philadelphia, Main Branch, Logan Circle (19th and Vine Streets). First lending library in the country (tel. 215/686-5320).

Liquor Laws   Closing time for most bars is 2am, 7 days a week. Legal drinking age is 21. Liquor is sold through package stores in quantity. Beer can be purchased from special distribution centers or over the counter in bars.

Lost Property   If lost at a hotel, restaurant, shop, or attraction, contact management. If lost or found in public areas, contact police (tel. 215/686-5230).

Police   Dial 911 in an emergency.

Post Office   B. Free Franklin Post Office, 316 Market Street (tel. 215/592-1289), open 9am to 5pm, Mon to Sun inclusive. Logan Branch, 6198 North Broad (tel. 215/549-3700), open 9am to 5pm, Mon to Sat inclusive.

Religious Services   For your convenience, the front desk of the hotels have a list of houses of worship, with the hours of services. You may also consult the *Yellow Pages* under "Churches," "Religious Organizations," and "Synagogues."

Restrooms   All hotels, restaurants, and attractions have restrooms available for customers and guests.

Safety   As large cities go, Philadelphia is generally safe. But there are precautions you should take. Stay alert and be aware of your immediate surroundings. Wear a moneybelt and keep a close eye on your possessions. Be particularly careful with cameras, purses, and wallets—all favorite targets of thieves and pickpockets. Be especially careful walking on dark streets and in parks after dark. Every society has its criminals. It's your responsibility to be aware and alert even in the most heavily touristed areas.

Shoe Repairs   Happy Cobbler, 2 Penn Center Concourse (tel. 215/751-9809) or ask at the front desk of your hotel.

Taxes   There is a state sales tax of 6% on most items like meals, etc., but not on clothes. There is an 11% tax on hotel rooms.

Telegrams   Western Union, 1618 North Broad Street (tel. **215/232-2299**); and 1107 Locust Street (tel. **215/351-4300**).
Transit Information   215/580-7800.
TV   WYW-TV Channel 3 (NBC), WPVI-TV Channel 6 (ABC), WCAU-TV Channel 10 (CBS), WHYY-TV Channel 12 (PBS), and WTAF-TV Channel 29 (FOX).

3. PHILADELPHIA ACCOMMODATIONS

Like most big cities, Philadelphia's lodgings are not cheap, especially during midweek, when business traffic is heavy. However, do not despair. If you can plan to come over a weekend, you'll find that almost all of Philadelphia's hotels offer very attractive weekend packages, with savings from 30% to 50% or more off normal weekday tariffs.

To help you acquaint yourself with the exact locations of the hotels listed below, we are grouping them according to the main sightseeing areas of the city.

Rates do not include taxes or breakfast, unless otherwise indicated.

CITY HALL AREA/MAIN BUSINESS DISTRICT

VERY EXPENSIVE

HOTEL ATOP THE BELLEVUE, 1415 Chancellor Court, Philadelphia, PA 19102. Tel. 215/893-1776, or toll-free 800/221-0833. Fax 215/732-8518. 120 rms, 40 suites. A/C MINIBAR TV TEL
$ Rates: $190–$230 single; $210–$250 double; $255–$1,250 suite. AE, CB, DC, MC, V. **Parking:** $13.

The newly restored Bellevue building, dating from 1904 and known for its French Renaissance facade, has long been a landmark in downtown Philadelphia, and now it is also the home of one of the city's most lavish hostelries. Managed by Cunard, this new hotel is located on the top seven floors of the Bellevue. About half of the spacious guest rooms have views of the city while the rest overlook an interior atrium courtyard. Rooms are decorated in a turn-of-the-century theme accenting the original high ceilings and all have a VCR. The public areas include a rooftop lounge, the Barrymore Room, on the 19th floor, with the building's original domed ceilings, stained glass, painted murals, and semicircular windows. It's the ideal spot to watch the sun set on the Philadelphia skyline. In addition, there is a gourmet restaurant, Founders, on the rooftop level, and a sidewalk-café eatery, the Conservatory, on the 12th floor.

Services: Full-time concierge, valet parking, 24-hour room service.
Facilties: Health club with indoor pool, racquetball, squash, basketball courts, exercise equipment, and indoor jogging track.

FOUR SEASONS, 1 Logan Square, Philadelphia, PA 19103. Tel. 215/ 963-1500, or toll-free 800/268-6282. Fax 215/963-9506. 371 rms. A/C MINIBAR TV TEL
$ Rates: $205–$255 single; $235–$285 double. AE, CB, DC, MC, V. **Parking:** $18.50.

Although relatively new (opened in 1983), the Four Seasons is a splendid example of ageless hotel grandeur, ideally located overlooking the fountains and sculptures of Logan Square and near the Philadelphia Museum of Art and the gold-domed Cathedral of Sts. Peter and Paul. The interior is a showcase of

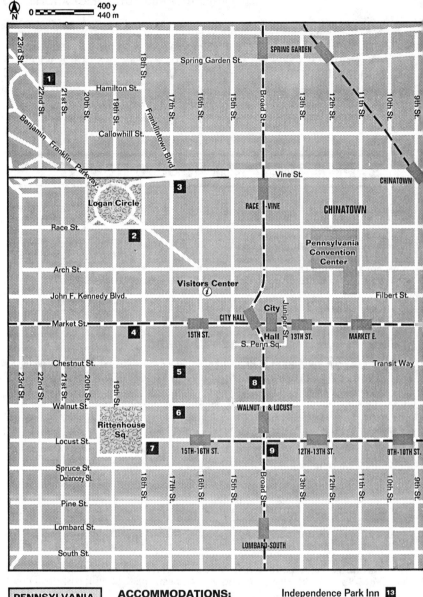

ACCOMMODATIONS:

PENNSYLVANIA

Harrisburg

Philadelphia

ACCOMMODATIONS:

The Barclay **7**
Comfort Inn at Penn's Landing **11**
Four Seasons **2**
Hershey Philadelphia Hotel **9**
Holiday Inn-Center City **4**
Holiday Inn-Independence Mall **10**
Hotel Atop the Bellevue **8**

Independence Park Inn **13**
Latham Hotel **6**
Omni Hotel at Independence Park **12**
Quality Inn-Center City **1**
Ritz-Carlton Hotel **5**
Sheraton Society Hill **14**
Thomas Bond House **15**
Wyndam Franklin Plaza **3**

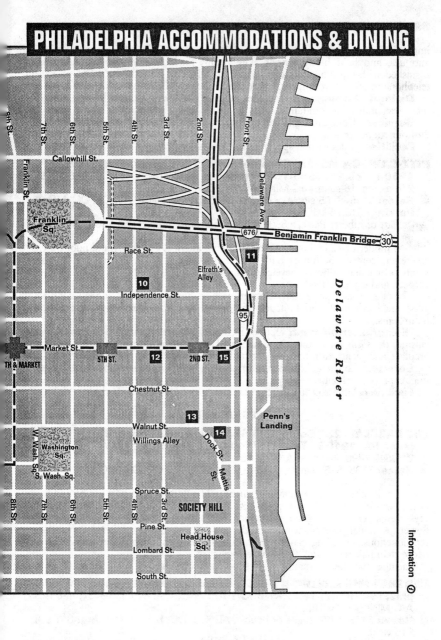

imported Italian marble, hand-sewn wool carpeting and Oriental rugs, one-of-a-kind antiques, and light blond woods. The rooms (including nonsmoking units) are furnished with reproductions of Philadelphia's Federal period; you'll find an extra telephone in the bathroom, plus thick terry robes and hair dryers.

Dining/Entertainment: Facilities include The Swann Café, a lounge, and the main restaurant, the Fountain.

Services: Complimentary shoeshine, valet parking, full-time concierge, and 24-hour room service.

Facilities: Indoor pool, spa, massage rooms, hair salon.

RITZ-CARLTON HOTEL, Chestnut and 17th Streets, Philadelphia, PA 19103. Tel. 215/563-1600 or toll-free 800/241-3333. Fax 215/564-9559. 274 rooms, 16 suite. A/C MINIBAR TV TEL

$ Rates: $195–$265 single or double; $425–$1,500 suites. AE, CB, DC, MC, V. **Parking:** $15.75 self, $18 valet.

Part of Liberty Place, a $600-million mixed-use project that also includes two office towers, 60 specialty retail shops, and underground parking, this hotel has a modern facade, but a warm traditional interior. The lobby and public areas are reminiscent of the homes built in Philadelphia during the Federal period, with wainscotting, fine millwork, beveled glass, antiques and original artworks, handwoven carpets, and crystal chandeliers.

The guest rooms are equally elegant, with mahogany furniture, designer fabrics, gilt-framed prints of Old Philadelphia, crystal and porcelain lamps, and marble bathrooms.

Dining/Entertainment: Options include the Dining Room for classical French cuisine, the Grill for traditional American fare, and the Lobby Bar with working fireplace and piano for a relaxing cocktail or tea.

Services: Concierge, 24-hour room service, valet, turndown, shoeshine, babysitting, express checkout.

Facilities: Fitness center, foreign exchange, notary public, gift shop.

EXPENSIVE

THE BARCLAY, 237 South 18th St., Rittenhouse Square East, Philadelphia, PA 19103. Tel. 215/545-0300, or toll-free 800/421-6662. Fax 215/545-2896. 240 rms. A/C TV TEL

$ Rates: $135–$155 single; $145–$165 double. AE, CB, DC, MC, V. **Parking:** $15.75.

Right on the city's most fashionable square is The Barclay, now part condo and part hotel. An old-world aura will greet you as you step inside the long lobby with its crystal chandeliers, marble floors, classic Oriental rugs, and vases with handmade silk flowers. A similar atmosphere reigns in the guest rooms, mostly furnished with antique reproductions, including canopy beds, four-posters, antique armoires, and chests. More than half the rooms also have refrigerators.

Facilities include a restaurant, gift shop, and concierge.

HERSHEY PHILADELPHIA HOTEL, Broad and Locust Streets, Philadelphia, PA 19107. Tel. 215/893-1600 or toll-free 800/533-3131. 428 rms. A/C MINIBAR TV TEL

$ Rates: $135–$170 single or double. AE, CB, DC, MC, V. **Parking:** $11 self, $15 valet.

Situated in the heart of the city's business and shopping districts, this modern, 25-story tower has a four-story atrium lobby and a modern, airy look. Each of the wide-windowed contemporary rooms is currently undergoing renovation.

Facilities include a restaurant/café, indoor swimming pool, outdoor sun deck, health club, sauna, and whirlpool.

LATHAM HOTEL, 17th and Walnut Streets, Philadelphia, PA 19103. Tel. 215/563-7474, or toll-free 800/528-4261. Fax 215/563-4034. 139 rooms, 3 suites. A/C MINIBAR TV TEL.

$ Rates: $130–$160 single; $150–$180 double; $325–$425 suites. AE, CB, DC, MC, V. **Parking:** $14.

A small, European-style hotel, this former apartment building was thoroughly refurbished and renovated in 1988–90. The guest rooms vary in size but feature quality reproduction furniture, designer bedspreads and draperies, bay windows, writing desks, and spacious bathrooms with hairdryer and phone. Facilities include a restaurant, a piano-bar lounge, concierge, valet laundry service, turndown, room service, and complimentary use of a nearby fitness club.

WYNDHAM FRANKLIN PLAZA, Two Franklin Plaza, Philadelphia, PA 19103. Tel. 215/448-2000, or toll-free 800/822-4200. Fax 215/448-2864. 758 rms, 38 suites. A/C TV TEL
$ Rates: $145 single; $165 double; $250–$1,000 suite. AE, CB, DC, MC, V. **Parking:** $13 self, $17 valet.

Built in the early 1980s, this modern hotel just off Logan Circle has a bright, airy four-story lobby with a 70-foot glass atrium, enlivened with leafy potted trees and flowers. The guest rooms are equipped with all the expected deluxe features, including floor-to-ceiling mirrors and contemporary furnishings.

Dining/Entertainment: There is a full-service restaurant, Between Friends, as well as a sidewalk café and coffee shop, and a lounge.

Facilities: Sports center, indoor swimming pool, squash, racquetball, tennis courts, jogging track.

MODERATE

HOLIDAY INN–CENTER CITY, 1800 Market St., Philadelphia, PA 19103. Tel. 215/561-7500, toll-free 800-HOLIDAY. Fax 215/561-4484. 443 rms. A/C MINIBAR TV TEL
$ Rates: $112–$139 single; $120–$147 double. AE, CB, DC, MC, V. **Parking:** $11.

Almost midway between Rittenhouse Square and Logan Circle is this handy up-to-date hotel built in 1971 and completely renovated in 1986. Each room offers either one or two double beds or a king-size bed, with light wood furnishings and pastel tones. Facilities include a restaurant, a cocktail lounge, outdoor swimming pool, and exercise room.

QUALITY INN–CENTER CITY, 510 North 22nd St., Philadelphia, PA 19130. Tel. 215/568-8300, toll-free 800-228-5151. Fax 215/557-0529. 278 rms, 3 suites. A/C TV TEL
$ Rates: $55–$65 single or double; $110–$180 suite. AE, CB, DC, MC, V. **Parking:** Free.

Located one block north of the Benjamin Franklin Parkway, at the entrance to Fairmount Park, this modern four-story hotel is in the heart of the museum district, four blocks from Logan Circle. Rooms are furnished in bright contemporary colors. Facilities include a restaurant, Poor Richard's Café, an outdoor pool, and a lounge.

HISTORIC AREA/RIVERFRONT

VERY EXPENSIVE

OMNI HOTEL AT INDEPENDENCE PARK, 4th and Chestnut Streets, Philadelphia, PA 19106. Tel. 215/925-0000, or toll-free 800/THE-OMNI. Fax 215/925-1263. 155 rms. A/C TV TEL
$ Rates: $205–$230 single or double. AE, CB, DC, MC, V. **Parking:** $17.50.

Opened in 1990, this is one of the newest hotels in the historic district. The lobby of this 15-story property sets the tone of luxury that prevails throughout, with brass and marble accoutrements, Oriental urns, crystal lamps, fresh floral arrangements and huge plants, and mirrored walls.

The guest rooms, accessible by computer card keys, are furnished with dark woods, traditional furniture, soft-toned designer fabrics, louvered closet doors, and marble bathrooms.

Dining/Entertainment: Choices include the Azalea restaurant and the Lobby Lounge.

Services: Concierge, valet service, 24-hour room service.

Facilities: Swimming pool, sauna, and health club.

EXPENSIVE

SHERATON SOCIETY HILL, 1 Dock St., Philadelphia, PA 19106. Tel. 215/238-6000, or toll-free 800/325-3535. Fax 215/922-2709. 365 rms. A/C MINIBAR TV TEL

$ Rates: $160–$185 single; $160–$220 double. AE, CB, DC, MC, V. **Parking:** $11 self, $17.50 valet.

Just a block from the Delaware River and four blocks from Independence Hall, this modern property has a brick town-house facade, designed to reflect the character of residential Society Hill. The entrance gives a hint of contemporary style, with a four-story atrium lobby, but the overall theme conveys the ambience of a Colonial courtyard. Each guest room features Early American decor with reproduction furnishings and fabrics.

Dining/Entertainment: There is a full-service restaurant, Hadley's, and a lounge, the Wooden Nickel Pub.

Services: Full-time concierge, laundry service, room service, notary public.

Facilities: Indoor skylit swimming pool, health club with exercise room.

MODERATE

HOLIDAY INN-INDEPENDENCE MALL, 400 Arch St., Philadelphia, PA 19106. Tel. 215/923-8660. or toll-free 800/THE BELL. Fax 215/923-8660, ext. 3369. 364 rms. A/C TV TEL

$ Rates: $99–$129 single; $119–$149 double; AE, CB, DC, MC, V. **Parking:** $9.

If you want to stay in the midst of the historic section, this is a good choice. It is within two blocks of the Liberty Bell, Betsy Ross's house, and most of the other top attractions. In keeping with the aura of this historic neighborhood, the lobby has a permanent American Revolutionary Navy exhibit, including 30 specially commissioned paintings. The guest rooms offer Colonial-style furnishings and draperies. Facilities include a restaurant, café, lounge, and a rooftop swimming pool.

INDEPENDENCE PARK INN, 235 Chestnut St., Philadelphia, PA 19106. Tel. 215/922-4443, or toll-free 800/624-2988. Fax 215/922-4487. 36 rms. A/C TV TEL

$ Rates: (including continental breakfast): $85–$115 single; $115–$130 double. AE, CB, DC, MC, V. **Parking:** $9.

This charming hotel in the heart of the historic district, two blocks from the Delaware riverfront, is a real find. Listed on the National Register of Historic Places, the five-story Victorian granite building dates from 1856, when it was opened as a dry-goods business. It was restored and converted into a hotel in 1988, and has an elevator.

Inside a historic atmosphere prevails, with a fireplace in the lobby, Colonial background music, and quill pens on the registration counter and in each room. The guest room furniture is a blend of Colonial reproductions and art deco pieces. Services include complimentary morning newspaper, afternoon tea, concierge, and turndown.

THOMAS BOND HOUSE, 129 South Second St., Philadelphia, PA 19106. Tel. 215/923-8523, or toll-free 800/854-2663. 10 rms, 2 suites (all with bath). A/C TV TEL

$ Rates: $80–$120 single or double; $150 suite. AE, CB, DC, MC, V. **Parking:** $9.

This bed-and-breakfast is tucked in a restored Federal building and is located within the Independence National Historic Park. Restored and maintained by the National Park Service, it was originally built as a residence in 1769 for Dr. Thomas Bond, a founder of the Pennsylvania Hospital; subsequent additions in 1824 and 1840 have made it into a three- and four-story structure. Guest rooms either have twin beds, a double bed, or a queen-size bed, and each is decorated individually with Colonial-style furnishings and accessories; two suites also have working fireplaces, whirlpool baths, sitting areas, and sofa beds.

BUDGET

COMFORT INN AT PENN'S LANDING, 100 North Delaware Ave., Philadelphia, PA 19106. Tel. 215/627-7900 or toll-free 800/228-5150. Fax 215/238-0809. 85 rms. A/C TV TEL

$ Rates: (including continental breakfast): $68 single; $75–$110 double. AE, CB, DC, MC, V. **Parking:** Free.

⑤ If you have a car, this riverfront hotel opposite Penn's Landing is an ideal choice. Half the rooms of the ten-story, art deco–style hotel have views of the water and the rest face the city skyline. Each unit has light contemporary furnishings with two double beds or one king-size bed. Two floors are for nonsmokers. There is a cocktail lounge/breakfast room in the lobby, but no dining room; the hotel operates a courtesy shuttle van to historic sites.

4. PHILADELPHIA DINING

For many years, Philadelphia cuisine was synonymous with the cheese steak. In case you have never indulged, this is an oversized sandwich, usually on a hot-dog bun, stuffed with quickly cooked lean beef slices, and smothered with fried onions and melted cheese (generally of the Cheez Whiz variety). According to your taste, you can also garnish your cheese steak with hot peppers, mushrooms, tomato sauce, provolone, or other cheeses.

While cheese steaks will always be a Philadelphia tradition, there has also been a happy renaissance in fine dining in this city within the last 15 years. Spurred on by the midtown Restaurant School and some of its more eager and talented alumni, the number of restaurants in and around Philadelphia has now mushroomed to over 500, with more on the way. Housed in Colonial row houses, converted storefronts, on rooftops, or by the harbor, the restaurants of Philadelphia offer a great variety of settings and menus. You'll find traditional seafood houses, restored Colonial taverns, ethnic enclaves, haute and nouvelle cuisine dining rooms, and a diversity of regional eateries, to name a few. Like the hotels, the Philadelphia restaurants are spread throughout the city, so we'll group them by area and at the same time try to give you a cross-section of menu types and price ranges.

Always keep in mind that parking can be a problem. Spaces on the street are hard to come by, and garages and parking lots can be costly. However, many restaurants offer free or reduced-rate parking, especially in the evening. Be sure to inquire about this when you make a reservation (you could save $5 to $10). If a restaurant does not offer parking facilities, then it might be cheaper and more convenient to leave your car wherever it is and use a taxi or public transportation.

CITY HALL AREA/MAIN BUSINESS DISTRICT

VERY EXPENSIVE

LE BEC FIN, 1523 Walnut St. Tel. 567-1000.
   Cuisine: FRENCH. **Reservations:** Required.

$ Prices: Fixed-price dinner $89; fixed-price lunch $31. AE, DC, MC, V.
Open: Lunch Mon–Fri seatings at 11:30am and 1:30pm; dinner Mon–Sat seatings at 6 and 9pm.

This establishment is best described as a French country mansion in the heart of downtown Philadelphia. Over the past 15 years, under the direction of owner-chef Georges Perrier, it has earned a worldwide reputation for fine cuisine. A Louis XVI decor predominates the gracious town-house dining room. Giant crystal chandeliers, damask-covered walls, and gilt-framed portraits highlight the setting, and the tables are set with fresh flowers, Cristofle silver, and fine Limoges china.

The menu changes seasonally, but the lunch usually includes sweetbreads and snow peas; filet of veal with mustard seeds; or sole sautéed with lemon, capers, and parsley. The dinner menu features pigeon served with ravioli of eggplant; filet of venison; filet of veal and lamb with two sauces; fricassee of lobster and oysters; and braided bands of salmon and sole. There are over 30 desserts, such as orange-chocolate mousse, Grand Marnier souffle, and Alsatian almond tart.

EXPENSIVE

BOOKBINDER'S SEAFOOD HOUSE, 215 South 15th St. Tel. 545-1137.
  Cuisine: SEAFOOD. **Reservations:** Required.
  $ Prices: Appetizers $3.95–$10.95; main course $14.95–$28.95; lunch $3.95–$12.95; AE, CB, DC, MC, V.
  Open: Lunch Mon–Fri 11:30am–3:30pm; dinner Mon–Fri 3:30–11pm, Sat 4pm–midnight, Sun 3–10pm.

And now we come to the "other" great seafood legend in this city, which celebrated its 50th year in 1985. Operated by the fourth generation of the Bookbinder family, this midtown restaurant is busy, crowded, and noisy, but the food and attentive service are worth it. Lunch features mainly sandwiches, raw bar selections, stews, and crab cakes; you can also order lobster, priced according to size, from $19.95. Lobsters are usually the focus at dinner, with four-pounders at $39.95, but such a large crustacean can, of course, feed two or more. Other choices include baked bluefish; whole Jersey flounder; stone crabs; lobster stew, Newburg, or thermidor; as well as steaks and chops. A favorite starter is the snapper soup laced with sherry.

DILULLO CENTRO, 1407 Locust St. Tel. 546-2000.
  Cuisine: ITALIAN. **Reservations:** Recommended.
  $ Prices: Appetizers $4–$10; main courses $14.50–$25.50; lunch $10–$16. AE, CB, DC, MC, V.
  Open: Lunch Mon–Fri 11:45am–1:45pm; dinner Mon–Sat 5:30–10:30pm.

A renovated theater between 14th and 15th Streets is the setting for this dazzling rendezvous, known for its gourmet northern Italian cuisine, in the heart of the theater district. Lavishly appointed with impressionist murals, mirrored walls, and imported marble, the restaurant has four dining rooms with decors that reflect their names, including the Vineyard, Garden, and Courtyard. A muraled elevator leads you to the lower-level Ferrari Lounge, which features piano music nightly.

Lunch offers unusual pastas (such as quill-shaped pasta or pasta filled with lobster), pan-roasted fish dishes, and light meat entrees. Dinner choices include marinated and grilled pheasant; medallions of salmon in creamy vermouth sauce; filet of Dover sole; and sautéed lobster with ginger.

GARDEN, 1617 Spruce St. Tel. 546-4455.
  Cuisine: AMERICAN. **Reservations:** Recommended.
  $ Prices: Appetizers $5–$10; main courses $14.95–$24.95; lunch $10.95–$19.95. AE, CB, DC, MC, V.
  Open: Lunch Mon–Fri 11:30am–1:45pm; dinner Mon–Sat 5:30–10pm.
  Closed: Sat–Sun in July–Aug.

✪ The Garden is an 1870s City Center town house (actually, two houses), originally the Philadelphia Musical Academy, with a tree-shaded outdoor brick courtyard and canopied deck. A delightful setting any time of year, this restaurant was started in 1974 by Kathleen Mulhern, who also owns Harry's Bar. The Garden is a favorite with local executives for "power lunches." Inside are five dining rooms, on two levels, with a variety of decors ranging from a candlelit Victorian parlor with floral wallpaper to an informal oyster bar. Lunch includes steaks, lobsters, gourmet salads, steak tartare, loin of veal, and chicken breast. A similar menu at dinner features rack of lamb, thin calves' liver, breast of duck with herb-scented oranges, and curried shrimp with chutney, as well as steaks and lobsters. All main courses are accompanied by salad and vegetable.

HARRY'S BAR AND GRILL, 22 South 18th St. Tel. 561-5757.

Cuisine: AMERICAN. **Reservations:** Recommended.
$ Prices: Appetizers $3.95–$8.95; main courses and lunch $10.95–$24.95. AE, CB, DC, MC, V.
Open: Lunch Mon–Fri 11:30am–2pm; dinner Mon–Fri 5:30–9:30pm.

A clubby ambiance prevails in this two-story restaurant off Chestnut Street, a favorite with neighborhood buisness executives. The decor is dominated by wood-paneled walls, beveled-edge mirrors, and gilt-framed oil paintings on the lower level, while upstairs features a gallery of horse and dog art.

The lunch and dinner menus are similar in selection and price, and offer aged prime steaks, sirloin steak tartare, a variety of grilled seafood, and seasonal game dishes, such as squab and pheasant. Jackets are required for men.

SUSANNA FOO, 1512 Walnut St. Tel. 545-2666.

Cuisine: CHINESE. **Reservations:** Recommended.
$ Prices: Appetizers $3–$9; main courses $15–$24; lunch $9–$16. AE, MC, V.
Open: Lunch Mon–Fri 11:30am–2:30pm; dinner Mon–Thurs 5–10pm and Fri–Sat 5–11pm.

✪ Presided over by the chef-owner of the same name, this serene art-deco dining room offers creative gourmet Chinese cuisine at its finest. The featured dishes include Mongolian lamb, sautéed filet mignon in Szechuan peppercorn sauce, Kung Pao chicken with roasted peanuts, crispy duck with five-spice sauce, pan-fried prawns with honey walnuts and herb cream sauce, sizzling grouper in carmelized sweet-and-sour sauce, and charcoal-grilled baby rack of lamb with ginger, lemon grass, and soy marinade.

MODERATE

HOFFMAN HOUSE, 1214 Sansom St. Tel. 925-2772.

Cuisine: GERMAN/AUSTRIAN. **Reservations:** Recommended.
$ Prices: Appetizers $3.95–$9.95; main courses $10.95–$24.95; lunch $6.95–$16.95. AE, CB, DC, MC, V.
Open: Lunch Mon–Fri 11:30am–2:30pm; dinner Mon–Sat 5–9pm.

This restaurant near 12th Street has been a midtown tradition for over 65 years. With German music in the background, the charm of Bavaria is much in evidence in the two dining rooms, from the mounted bear heads and porcelain plates on the walls, sturdy old sideboards, and stained-glass windows to the dark-paneled walls that came from the captain's cabin of a German freighter. Lunch choices range from sandwiches of sausage, sardine, or liverwurst to light dishes, such as smoked pork loin or filet of veal. Dinner entrées include sautéed loin of venison, braised saddle of rabbit, roast pork with sauerkraut, sauerbraten, wienerschnitzel, weisswurst, and chicken with sweet paprika.

TOP OF THE CENTRE SQUARE, 1500 Market St. Tel. 563-9494.

Cuisine: INTERNATIONAL. **Reservations:** Recommended.
$ Prices: Appetizers $3.95–$6.95; main courses $12.95–$21.95; lunch $5.95–$11.95. AE, CB, DC, MC, V.

Open: Lunch Mon–Fri 11:30am–3pm; dinner Mon–Thurs 5:30–10pm, Fri–Sat 5:30pm–midnight, Sun 4:30–9pm.

Situated on the 41st floor of an office building in the center of town, this modern restaurant with bilevel seating offers sky-high wraparound views of the city, the two rivers, and New Jersey. Lunch focuses on sandwiches, pastas, quiches, and light dishes. After dark, the city lights glow and the menu adds a continental flair. Dinner entrées include salmon, shrimp tempura, trout stuffed with crabmeat, veal Oscar, bouillabaisse, prime ribs, and steaks.

CAROLINA'S, 261 South 20th Street. Tel. 545-1000.

Cuisine: AMERICAN REGIONAL. **Reservations:** Recommended.

$ Prices: Appetizers $2.95–$7.95; main courses $8.95–$17.95; lunch $4.95–$8.95. AE, CB, DC, MC, V.

Open: Lunch Mon–Fri 11:45am–2:30pm; dinner Sun–Thurs 5:30–10pm, Fri–Sat 5:30–11pm; brunch Sun 11am–2:30pm.

A shopfront building with a "vintage Philadelphia" decor of tin ceiling, tapestry-covered chairs, and local artworks is the home of this trendy restaurant where the creative menu changes every day. Dinner entrées often include such dishes as grilled duck breast with homemade garlic duck sausage patties in an orange sauce; veal loaf with mashed bliss potatoes; grilled tuna on lemon pepper linguine with sweet red pepper sauce; and grilled salmon with black linguine and cream dill sauce. Lunch items include unusual sandwiches (eggplant with mozzarella, ham with apple, or smoked lamb) and regional specialties, such as a quesadilla tortillas and steamed pork dumplings.

SANSOM STREET OYSTER HOUSE, 1516 Sansom St. Tel. 567-7683.

Cuisine: SEAFOOD. **Reservations:** Not accepted.

$ Prices: Appetizers $2.95–$6.95; main courses $8.95–$16.95; lunch $3.95–$13.95. AE, DC, MC, V.

Open: Lunch Mon–Sat 11am–3pm; dinner Mon–Sat 3–10pm.

Ever since 1947, the Sansom Street Oyster House has been a good midtown choice for fresh seafood at moderate prices. Located between 15th and 16th Streets, this two-room restaurant is simple, with bare wood tables and hand-printed menus that change daily. Lunch fare, which tends to be light, includes sandwiches, seafood stews, and chowders. Dinner offers at least half a dozen types of oysters from the raw bar, and lobsters, cod steak, St. Peter's fish, tuna steak, blackened redfish, sea trout, oyster pan roast, and mixed seafood platters, plus chicken and steaks. Seafoods are prepared grilled, fried, sautéed, or baked, according to your wishes. There is a nonsmoking section.

TGI FRIDAYS, 18th Street at Benjamin Franklin Parkway. Tel. 665-TGIF.

Cuisine: AMERICAN. **Reservations:** Not accepted.

$ Prices: Appetizers $2.95–$6.95; main courses $6.95–$12.95; lunch $3.95–$7.95. AE, CB, DC, DISC, MC, V.

Open: Daily 11am–1am.

Part of a popular countrywide chain, this restaurant is fairly new to Philadelphia, but it has fast become a hub in the museum area. The bilevel atmosphere is relaxed and casual, and you can order a snack or a multi-course meal at any time. The same menu applies all day, offering a wide variety of sandwiches, burgers, pizzas, nachos, and salads. Main courses range from sweet and sour chicken and baby back ribs to fettuccine Alfredo, chicken Cordon Bleu, blackened Cajun-style seafoods, and steaks of all sizes and types. A second location, in the heart of the Olde City, is at 500 South Second St. (tel. 625-8389).

MARABELLA'S, 1420 Locust Ave. Tel. 545-1845.

Cuisine: INTERNATIONAL. **Reservations:** Not accepted for dinner.

$ Prices: Appetizers $2.95; main courses $7.95–$14.95; lunch $3–$6. AE, DC, MC, V.

Open: Mon–Thurs 11:30am–11:30pm, Fri–Sat 11:30am–12:30am, Sun 11:30am–11pm.

An art-deco atmosphere and big-band music from the 1950s set the tone at Marabella's, a trendy (and sometimes noisy) new restaurant between 14th and 15th Streets, in the heart of the theater district. The decor includes old-fashioned jukeboxes and lots of wall mirrors, but the real draw here is an all-day menu with moderate-to-budget prices. At lunchtime, you can get burgers and sandwiches. The dinner entrées include grilled swordfish, hot and spicy grilled chicken, and filet mignon with mushrooms.

BUDGET

CORNED BEEF ACADEMY, 1801 John F. Kennedy Boulevard. Tel. 568-9696.
    Cuisine: AMERICAN. **Reservations:** Not accepted.
$ **Prices:** Lunch $4.95–$6.95. No credit cards.
    Open: Breakfast daily 7–10am; lunch 11am–3pm.

Ⓢ Hearty, overstuffed sandwiches are the trademark at this lunch favorite. Service is fast (with paper plates and plastic cups) and the food is straightforward, with such deli specialties as lean and sliced-to-order corned beef, roast beef, brisket, and turkey, plus soups and salads.

DOCK STREET BREWING COMPANY, Two Logan Square. Tel. 496-0413.
    Cuisine: INTERNATIONAL. **Reservations:** Accepted, but usually not required.
$ **Prices:** Appetizers $4–$8; main courses $7–$10; lunch $4–$9. AE, CB, DC, DISC, MC, V.
    Open: Mon–Thurs and Sun 11am–10pm; Fri–Sat 11am–midnight.

Ⓢ This brew-pub restaurant houses a small copper brewhall, where six types of beer, ale, stout, and porter are produced daily. Visitors are welcome to watch the six-step brewing process—from roasted barley malts to beer. The restaurant also houses a bakery, where crusty five-grain and sourdough breads are baked for use in the dining room. The lunch menu offers soups, pub-style sandwiches, and burgers. Dinner entrées include many of the items available at lunch, as well as Welsh rarebit, Alsatian choucroute, and jerked pork.

OLDE CITY/RIVERFRONT AREA
VERY EXPENSIVE

OLD ORIGINAL BOOKBINDER'S, 125 Walnut St. Tel. 925-7027.
    Cuisine: AMERICAN. **Reservations:** Recommended.
$ **Prices:** Appetizers $4.95–$12.95; main courses $17.95–$40.95; lunch $5.95–$24.95. AE, CB, DC, MC, V.
    Open: Lunch Mon–Fri noon–2:45pm; dinner Mon–Fri 2:45–10pm, Sat noon–10pm; Sept–June Sun 1–9pm; July–Aug Sun 1–3pm.

Almost everyone has heard of the Old Original Bookbinder's, a legend in Philadelphia dining and the source for some confusion with its midtown rival, which is simply called Bookbinder's. The Bookbinder family opened their first seafood restaurant at this location in 1865; when they sold it to the Taxin family in the 1930s, the Bookbinder name was retained as part of the deal. To complicate matters, the Bookbinder family then opened a new restaurant on 15th Street, and also called it by their own family name. This particular "original" restaurant is larger and handy to the Independence Park sights.

    Lunch choices change daily and feature sandwiches, seafood entrées (such as lobster pot pie and New England cod cakes), and steaks. The dinner menu offers a huge selection, including lobsters of all sizes (up to five pounds), Dover sole, and Scottish finnan haddie. For meat eaters, there are generous steaks and veal dishes.

EXPENSIVE

CITY TAVERN, 2nd and Walnut Streets. Tel. 923-6059.
    Cuisine: AMERICAN. **Reservations:** Recommended.

$ Prices: Appetizers $4.50–$7.50; main courses $12.50–$22; lunch $4.50–$9.50. AE, MC, V.
Open: Lunch daily 11:30am–3:30pm; dinner daily 5–10pm.

✪ The first tavern on this site was built in 1773 and served as a rendezvous point during the drafting of the Constitution. Although the original structure was demolished in 1854, the National Park Service faithfully reconstructed it and opened the site as a restaurant in 1975. The decor includes flickering hurricane lamps, open fireplaces, and harpsichord music.

Even the recipes hearken back to 18th-century tastes. Lunch features salads (such as Colonial salamagundy), sandwiches, and light entrées (like turkey rarebit and Colonial pasty, a combination of meats and herbs in a pastry shell). The choices for dinner include sautéed duck with raspberry glaze, pheasant in a sauce of truffles and port, Cornish hen with cranberry-orange relish, flounder in puff pastry shell, and charbroiled steaks.

THE DICKENS INN, 421 South 2nd St. Tel. 928-9307.

Cuisine: BRITISH. **Reservations:** Recommended.
$ Prices: Appetizers $5.25–$7.25; main courses $16.50–$24.95; lunch $4.95–$7.95. AE, MC, V.
Open: Lunch daily 11:30am–2:30pm; dinner daily 5–10pm. AE, CB, DC, MC, V.

As its name implies, this three-story Federal town house conveys a Dickensian atmosphere—and much of the inn's period furnishings and bric-a-brac have been imported from London. The menu offers a fitting selection of dishes such as roast beef with Yorkshire pudding, steak and mushroom pie, roast duckling, braised rabbit, pork calvados, grilled loin of lamb, and seafood. Just to top it off, English ales are available and there's often a darts game in the tavern room.

CAFE NOLA, 328 South St. Tel. 627-2590.

Cuisine: CAJUN-CREOLE. **Reservations:** Recommended.
$ Prices: Appetizers $3.95–$7.95; main courses $13.95–$19.95; lunch $4.95–$9.95. AE, CB, DC, DISC, MC, V.
Open: Lunch Tues–Sat noon–3pm; dinner Sun–Thurs 5–11pm, Fri–Sat 5pm–midnight.

Between 3rd and 4th Streets you'll find Café Nola, a restaurant that blends Cajun-Creole cooking with Italian flair, in an art-deco setting. Lunch offerings concentrate on soups, stews, gumbos, and salads. The dinner menu includes jambalaya, rock shrimp étouffée, Cajun prime rib, Acadian crabmeat tart, and swordfish saltimbocca. Monday is "shrimp night," when all shrimp dishes are half price.

MEIJI-EN, Pier 19, North Delaware Ave. at Callowhill St. Tel. 592-7100.

Cuisine: JAPANESE. **Reservations:** Recommended.
$ Prices: Appetizers $4–$8; main courses $12–$18. AE, CB, DC, MC, V.
Open: Dinner Sun–Thurs 5–9pm, Fri–Sat 5–11pm.

Japanese cuisine and harborfront views are the dual draws at this restaurant, which juts out into the water at the end of a pier, surrounded by a marina and boating center. The interior is typically Japanese, with tranquil gardens and waterfalls. The menu includes tableside sukiyaki, shabu shabu, and teppanyaki choices, as well as sushi, sashimi, and tempura. You can also get New York steak, grilled swordfish, or lobster tail.

MODERATE

DI NARDO'S FAMOUS CRABS, 312 Race St. Tel. 925-5115.

Cuisine: ITALIAN. **Reservations:** Required for a party of six or more.
$ Prices: Appetizers $2.95–$6.95; main courses $8.95–$17.95; lunch $3.95–$7.95. AE, CB, DC, MC, V.

Open: Lunch Mon–Sat 11am–3pm; dinner Mon–Sat 5–11pm, Sun 4–9pm.

The freshest seafood at moderate prices is the keystone to success at this restaurant, located in an old neighborhood between 3rd and 4th Streets and within a block of Elfreth's Alley or the Betsy Ross House. This restaurant is younger than the eatery of the same name in Wilmington (started in 1938).

Lunch consists mainly of shellfish salads, pastas, platters, and crab and fish sandwiches. Crab is king at dinner, with a choice of steamed crabs, crab claws, crab imperial, sautéed crabmeat, and soft-shell crabs. If you don't mind using a mallet and a little effort, crack open the hard-shell variety yourself. If crab is not your passion, you can also get rainbow trout or flounder, cioppino (Italian seafood stew), and steaks. If you are really enamored of crabs, you can also have your crabs to go, for $90 a bushel or $2 each.

PHILADELPHIA FISH & COMPANY, 207 Chestnut St. Tel. 625-8605.
   Cuisine: AMERICAN. **Reservations:** Recommended.
$ Prices: Appetizers $2.95–$6.95; main courses $10.95–$24.95; lunch $5.95–$7.95. AE, MC, V.
   Open: Lunch Mon–Fri 11:30am–4pm, Sat noon–3pm; dinner Mon–Thurs 4–10pm, Fri–Sat 4pm–midnight, Sun 3–10pm.
Mesquite-grilled seafoods are the specialty of this restaurant in the historic area opposite the Independence Park Visitor Center. The simple contemporary setting is decorated with framed American wine posters; in the summer there is additional seating on an outside front deck.

Lunch features light entrées, sandwiches, and salads. Dinner offers entrées cooked over Texas woods and charcoal, such as mahi-mahi, mako shark, Atlantic swordfish, whole lobster, rainbow trout, and crab cakes.

PRIMAVERA, 146 South St. Tel. 925-7832.
   Cuisine: ITALIAN. **Reservations:** Recommended.
$ Prices: Appetizers $3.95–$5.95; main courses $11.95–$19.95. No credit cards.
   Open: Dinner Mon–Thurs 5:30–10:30pm, Fri–Sat 5:30–11pm, Sun 4–9pm.
On a strip known for fine restaurants, Primavera is a leader of fine Italian cuisine. Occupying the first floor of a restored row house between 1st and 2nd Streets, this small dining room serves dinner only. The house specialty is zuppa di pesce for two (clams, mussels, lobster, and filet of fish), but equally good are the scampi, saltimbocca, and sautéed lobster.

BUDGET

JIM'S STEAKS, 400 South St. Tel. 928-1911.
   Cuisine: AMERICAN. **Reservations:** Not required.
$ Prices: Lunch and main courses $3.50–$4.95. No credit cards.
   Open: Mon–Thurs 10am–1am; Fri–Sat 10am–3am; Sun noon–10pm.

Of the reputed 2,000 cheese-steak houses in Philadelphia, this landmark on the corner of South and 4th Streets has been a favorite since 1939. Here you can sample traditional Philadelphia cheese steaks and the submarine-type sandwiches called hoagies. You'll find a cheery art-deco tile setting and walls lined with signed photos of celebrities who have eaten here.

5. PHILADELPHIA ATTRACTIONS

SUGGESTED ITINERARIES

IF YOU HAVE 1 DAY Head for the Independence National Historical Park, "America's most historic square mile."

IF YOU HAVE 2 DAYS Take in the historic area plus the riverfront area of Penn's Landing, Society Hill, and South Street.

IF YOU HAVE 3 DAYS Do all of 2-day activities plus spend a day in the city's museums along the Benjamin Franklin Parkway and Fairmount Park.

IF YOU HAVE 5 DAYS Linger at the major museums, explore more of the neighborhoods, including Chinatown and Antique Row. Plan a day's outing to Valley Forge and take a sightseeing cruise aboard the *Spirit of Philadelphia*.

THE TOP ATTRACTIONS

INDEPENDENCE NATIONAL HISTORICAL PARK

The focal point of Philadelphia is **Independence National Historical Park,** an area often called "America's most historic square mile." Located just west of the Delaware River, between Walnut and Arch Streets, this four-block-square area is primarily administered by the National Park Service and encompasses over two dozen sites, with the prime attractions being the **Liberty Bell** and **Independence Hall,** two of our nation's greatest monuments of freedom.

Other attractions in this historic complex include the **City Tavern,** 2nd and Walnut Streets, a restaurant housed in a reconstruction of the famous Revolutionary War tavern where delegates to the First and Second Continental Congresses gathered (see "Philadelphia Dining"); **Carpenter's Hall,** where the first Continental Congress met in 1774 (open daily Tues–Sun 10am–4pm); **Old City Hall,** 5th and Chestnut Streets, home of the first U.S. Supreme Court, 1791–1800; and **Congress Hall,** 6th and Chestnut Streets, where the House and Senate met when Philadelphia was the newborn nation's first capital.

Perhaps the best place to start your visit in this historic complex is at the **National Park Service Visitor Center** at 3rd and Chestnut Streets (tel. 597-8974). Here you can pick up brochures that highlight the park's many historic attractions, and view an introductory film, *Independence,* directed by John Huston.

Among sights to see are:

LIBERTY BELL, Market St.

The Liberty Bell is housed in a special glass-enclosed pavilion between 5th and 6th Streets. Park rangers continually greet visitors and give short background talks on the history and significance of the bell.

Admission: Free.
Open: Daily 9am–5pm. **Bus:** 76.

INDEPENDENCE HALL, 5th and Chestnut Streets.

Across the street from the Liberty Bell is Independence Hall, where the Declaration of Independence was adopted and the U.S. Constitution was written. Originally intended as the State House for the province of Pennsylvania, this building can also be seen by joining one of the tours given throughout the day.

Admission: Free.
Open: Daily 9am–5pm. **Bus:** 76.

THE GRAFF HOUSE, 7th and Market Streets.

This is a reconstruction of the house where Thomas Jefferson lived when he wrote the Declaration of Independence. A short film about Jefferson is shown.

Admission: Free.
Open: Daily 9am–5pm. **Bus:** 76.

ARMY–NAVY MUSEUM, Chestnut Street between 3rd and 4th Streets.

Housed in a replica of the 18th-century home of Quaker merchant Joseph Pemberton, this museum depicts the development of the Army and Navy from 1775 to 1800.

Admission: Free.
Open: Daily 9am–5pm. **Bus:** 76.

MARINE CORPS MEMORIAL MUSEUM, Chestnut Street between 3rd and 4th Streets.

This attraction, housed in a reconstructed 1790 building, commemorates the early history of the Marine Corps.

Admission: Free.
Open: Daily 9am–5pm. **Bus:** 76.

BISHOP WHITE HOUSE, 309 Walnut St.

Built in 1786–87, this is the home of the first bishop of the Episcopal Diocese of Pennsylvania.

Admission: Free.
Open: Daily 9am–5pm. **Bus:** 76.

TODD HOUSE, 4th and Walnut Streets.

This is the 1775 home of Dolley Payne Todd, who later became Dolley Madison, wife of President James Madison.

Admission: Free.
Open: Daily 9am–5pm. **Bus:** 76.

FRANKLIN COURT, between 3rd and 4th Streets, Chestnut and Market Streets.

Franklin Court stands on the site that was once Benjamin Franklin's house, and has been developed as a tribute to him. Visit the underground museum, printing shop, and an archeological architecture exhibit. This site also includes the B. Free Franklin Post Office, open 7 days a week.

Admission: Free.
Open: Daily 9am–5pm. **Bus:** 76.

SECOND BANK OF THE U.S., 420 Chestnut St.

A fine example of Greek Revival architecture dating back to 1824, this building houses a unique portrait gallery and occasional special exhibits.

Admission: Free.
Open: Daily 9am–5pm. **Bus:** 76.

MORE ATTRACTIONS

BETSY ROSS HOUSE, 239 Arch St. Tel. 627-5343.

This is the restored Colonial home in which Elizabeth ("Betsy") Griscom Ross lived and operated an upholstery shop from 1773 to 1786. She is credited with making the first U.S. flag. Located between 2nd and 3rd Streets, the house is furnished with family artifacts associated with Betsy, who is buried in the adjacent garden.

Admission: Free.
Open: Tues–Sun 10am–5pm. **Closed:** Thanksgiving, Christmas, and New Year's Day. **Bus:** 76.

ELFRETH'S ALLEY, off 2nd St., between Arch and Race Streets.

Less than a block from the Betsy Ross House is this registered National Historic Landmark, reputed to be the oldest residential street in the nation. A narrow cobblestone path is lined with 30 houses that were built between 1728 and 1836. Originally occupied by craftspeople and shopkeepers, these homes reflect a variety of architectural styles, and some have Colonial courtyards. It is said that Ben Franklin visited friends at No. 122 often. A museum is located in No. 126 and may be visited, but all of the other buildings are privately owned today and not ordinarily open to the public. There is an annual "open house" in June, however, if you want to see more. For full details, contact the Elfreth's Alley Association, 126 Elfreth's Alley, Philadelphia, PA 19106 (tel. 574-0560).

Museum Admission: Free.
Open: Daily 10am–4pm. **Bus:** 76.

EDGAR ALLAN POE NATIONAL HISTORICAL SITE, 532 North 7th St. Tel. 597-8780.

The acclaimed American author lived here from 1843 to 1844. "The Black Cat," "The Gold Bug," and "The Tell-Tale Heart" were published during his residency.

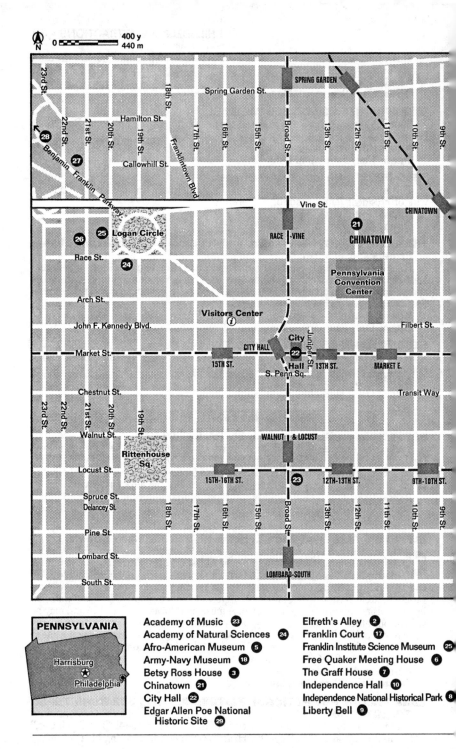

PENNSYLVANIA

Harrisburg ✪

Philadelphia

Academy of Music ㉓
Academy of Natural Sciences ㉔
Afro-American Museum ❺
Army-Navy Museum ⑱
Betsy Ross House ❸
Chinatown ㉑
City Hall ㉒
Edgar Allen Poe National
   Historic Site ㉙

Elfreth's Alley ❷
Franklin Court ⑰
Franklin Institute Science Museum ㉕
Free Quaker Meeting House ❻
The Graff House ❼
Independence Hall ❿
Independence National Historical Park ❽
Liberty Bell ❾

PHILADELPHIA ATTRACTIONS

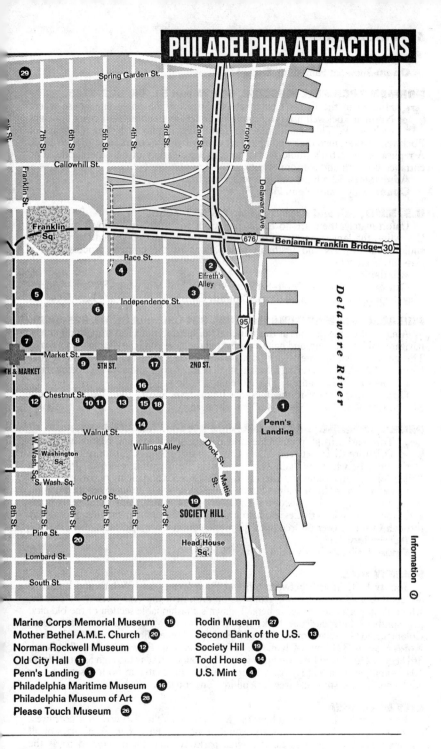

Marine Corps Memorial Museum (15)
Mother Bethel A.M.E. Church (20)
Norman Rockwell Museum (12)
Old City Hall (11)
Penn's Landing (1)
Philadelphia Maritime Museum (16)
Philadelphia Museum of Art (28)
Please Touch Museum (26)

Rodin Museum (27)
Second Bank of the U.S. (13)
Society Hill (19)
Todd House (14)
U.S. Mint (4)

Admission: Free.
Open: Tues–Sat 9am–5pm. **Bus:** 47.

NORMAN ROCKWELL MUSEUM, 601 Walnut St. Tel. 922-4345.

✪ Housed in the Curtis Center, at 6th Street, is the publishing house where Norman Rockwell used to submit his *Saturday Evening Post* cover drawings each week. This small museum features a display reflecting 47 years of Rockwell's works, including a complete set of his magazine covers from 1916 to 1963. A replica of the artist's studio is also here, as are a variety of his other works. The entrance is at 6th and Sansom Streets.

Admission: $2 adults, children under 12, free.
Open: Daily 10am–4pm. **Bus:** 76.

U.S. MINT, 5th and Arch Streets. Tel. 597-7350.

Unfortunately, there are no free samples, but you might still enjoy a tour of the U.S. Mint, the largest operation of its kind in the world. Self-guided tours include audio-visual displays and firsthand observations of the coinage process from a glass-enclosed gallery.

Admission: Free.
Open: Oct–Dec, Apr Mon–Sat 9am–4:30pm; Jan–Mar Mon–Fri 9am–4:30pm; May–Sept Mon–Sun 9am–4:30pm. **Closed:** Christmas, New Year's Day. **Bus:** 76.

PHILADELPHIA MARITIME MUSEUM, 321 Chestnut St. Tel. 925-5439.

A nautical theme prevails at this museum, with exhibitions featuring ship models, navigational instruments, and paintings that tell the story of Pennsylvania's waterways. This museum also operates Workshops on the Water, a barge at Penn's Landing boat basin (tel. 925-7589), featuring seasonal small craft exhibits and a boat-building shop.

Admission: $2.50 adults, $1 children and seniors.
Open: Museum year-round Tues–Sat 10am–5pm, Sun 1–5pm; Workshops early May to Oct Wed–Sun 9:30am–4:30pm. **Bus:** 76.

PENN'S LANDING, off I-95, Delaware Avenue. Tel. 923-8181.

✪ This harborfront promenade and park extends for ten blocks along the Delaware River between Market and Lombard Streets. Historically, it marks the spot where William Penn landed in Pennsylvania in 1682. Today it is Philadelphia's playground, with access from major roads and plenty of parking as well as a new footbridge from Walnut Street. The 37-acre site is home to a port museum, two permanently docked historic ships, and various visiting ships. Sightseeing boats and other waterside activities are also available in the summer months. From May through October, over 60 free open-air music concerts are held here.

Admission: Free.
Open: Daily, 24 hours a day. **Bus:** 76.

SOCIETY HILL

Society Hill, an area between 6th and Front Streets, and Walnut and Lombard Streets, takes its name from a group of businessmen, the Free Society of Traders, whom Penn persuaded to settle here. Today it's a fashionable section of the old city, just south of Independence Park, where you can stroll among restored Federal, Colonial, and Georgian homes. Two of Philadelphia's finest houses, the **Hill-Physick-Keith House**, 321 South 4th St. (tel. 925-7866), and the **Powel House**, 244 South 3rd St. (tel. 215/627-0364), are open for guided tours, Tuesday through Saturday from 10am–4pm; and on Sunday from 1–4pm. Admission charge in both cases is $3 for adults and $2 for students; free for children under age 6.

CITY HALL AREA

From City Hall, you can follow the Benjamin Franklin Parkway in a northwest direction through Logan Circle, and you'll be on "museum row." With flags of all nations waving in the breezes, this wide parkway, sometimes referred to as the

Champs-Elysées of Philadelphia, is a perfect setting for the grand institutions that are located here.

The Benjamin Franklin Parkway also leads you into **Fairmount Park,** the world's largest landscaped city park, with 8,700 acres of winding creeks, rustic trails, green meadows, and 100 miles of jogging, bike, and bridle paths. In addition, this park features more than a dozen historical and cultural attractions including some of the nation's finest early American homes, which were transferred here from their original sites. These include a Quaker farmhouse, and Federal, Georgian, and Greek Revival homes; as well as gardens, boathouses, America's first zoo (1874), and a Japanese teahouse.

CITY HALL, Penn Square at Broad and Market Streets. Tel. 568-3351.

Built between 1871 and 1901, this landmark Beaux Arts building is the seat of the municipal government and was the tallest structure in Philadelphia until the 1988 completion of the 60-story One Liberty Place office tower. City Hall is crowned by a giant 37-foot statue of William Penn, believed to be the largest single piece of sculpture on any building in the world; it stands atop a 548-foot tower that is visible for miles. Tour participants are asked to assemble in Conversation Hall at Room 201, North Broad Street entrance (near Masonic Temple). Starts at 12:30pm only.

Admission: Free.

Open: Tours, Mon–Fri 12:30pm. **Bus:** 76.

FRANKLIN INSTITUTE SCIENCE MUSEUM, 20th Street and Benjamin Franklin Parkway. Tel. 448-1200.

This four-floor complex has been a pioneer in the development of "hands-on" science experiences for all ages, with a variety of exhibits, ranging from a 350-ton locomotive to a Boeing 707, as well as a model of the largest walk-through heart in the world. This is also the home of the Benjamin Franklin National Memorial, housing a 30-ton marble statue of its namesake plus a collection of authentic Franklin artifacts and possessions.

The centerpiece of this museum, however, is the new Futures Center and Omniverse Theater, featuring eight exhibits on the future, inviting visitors to participate in a variety of experiences, from stepping inside a space suit and exploring a space station, to walking through a tropical rain forest or controlling a robot.

Lastly, there is a division of this museum devoted to the Fels Planetarium, with exhibits on astronomy and live constellation shows.

Admission: Museum/Futures center $7.50 adults, $6 children; Omniverse Theater, $6 and $5 extra, respectively, and requires advance reservations. Planetarium shows are $1.50 extra per person. Combination tickets for all exhibits and shows are $9.95 adults, $8.95 children.

Open: Mon–Sat 10am–5pm, Sun noon–5pm. The Future Center/Omniverse Theater is also open until 9pm except Mon. **Bus:** 76.

PHILADELPHIA MUSEUM OF ART, 26th St. and Benjamin Franklin Parkway. Tel. 763-8100.

Ever since the movie *Rocky,* most visitors recognize the famous steps that lead to this museum. Once you climb the steps (or take an easier access entrance), you'll see one of the largest and finest collections in the world of American paintings and decorative arts from Colonial times to the present; other galleries include works by Renoir, Van Gogh, Cézanne, Picasso, Duchamp, and Matisse. In addition, there are collections of tapestries, arms, and armor.

Admission: $5 adults, $2.50 children aged 5–18, free Sun 10am–1pm.

Open: Tues–Sun 10am–5pm. **Bus:** 76.

RODIN MUSEUM, 22nd St. and Benjamin Franklin Parkway. Tel. 787-5476.

The largest collection of Rodin sculptures and drawings outside France are on

display at this museum, including "The Thinker," the "Gates of Hell," and "The Burghers of Calais."
Admission: Donation.
Open: Tues–Sun 10am–5pm. **Bus:** 76.

ACADEMY OF NATURAL SCIENCES, 19th Street and Benjamin Franklin Parkway. Tel. 299-1000.

Founded in 1812, the Academy of Natural Sciences is the home of a $2.5 million permanent exhibition on dinosaurs; the nationally recognized children's "hands-on" nature museum, "Outside-In," featuring live animals; and "Exploring the Earth," an exhibit on earthquakes, volcanoes, gems, and minerals.
Admission: $5.50 adults, $4.50 children aged 3–12.
Open: Mon–Fri 10am–4:30pm, Sat–Sun 10am–5pm. **Bus:** 76.

MUMMERS MUSEUM, 2nd St. and Washington Ave. Tel. 336-3050.

A showcase for the colorful costumed dancers, this museum includes the New Year's suits from recent Mummers' parades, and a sound-and-light revue highlighting 300 years of origins, history, and achievements of the Mummers. In addition, there are print murals dating back to the 1880s, musical instruments, artifacts, and memorabilia, a hall of fame, and research library.
Admission: $2 adults, $1 children 12 and under.
Open: Tues–Sat 9:30am–5pm, Sun noon–5pm. **Closed:** Sun in July–Aug and all major holidays. **Bus:** 5.

KIDS' PHILADELPHIA

PLEASE TOUCH MUSEUM, 210 North 21st St. Tel. 963-0666.

Although there are many activities in Philadelphia that are of interest to children of all ages, this is one that is designed just for children seven years or younger. Among the activities children can participate in are role playing in a TV news set with camera and monitor, computer games, workshops, and theater events. Children should be accompanied by adults.
Admission: $4 per person.
Open: Tues–Sun 10am–4:30pm. **Bus:** 76.

ORGANIZED TOURS

BUS TOURS Grayline Tours, P.O. Box 5985 (tel. 569-3666), offers three different sightseeing tours of the Philadelphia area, ranging from a 3-hour historic tour and cultural tour to a combination of both tours lasting 4½ hours. Tours are scheduled from late spring through October and range from $16 to $32 for adults and $10 to $14 for children under 12. All tours depart from the Visitors Center at 16th Street and John F. Kennedy Boulevard and from most midtown hotels.

WALKING TOURS To explore the four-block historic district at your own pace with the benefit of a prerecorded commentary, you can rent an AudioWalk and Tour cassette player and tape. The narration describes each attraction as you walk from site to site; an illustrated souvenir map also comes with the tape. You can rent the lightweight player and cassette (adaptable for one to eight listeners) every day year round from the **AudioWalk and Tour** desk at the Norman Rockwell Museum, 6th and Sansom Streets (tel. 925-1234), located across from Independence Square. The charge is $8 for one person, $18 for two to six people (with a speaker/player). If you prefer to purchase the tape and use your own cassette recorder, the cost of the tape is $10.95.

CANDLELIGHT STROLLS From May through October, you can join in group candlelight walks of the historic district, organized by **Centipede Tours, Inc.,** 1515 Walnut St. (tel. 735-3123). Led by guides in Colonial costume, these walks cover the Olde City area (Friday) and Society Hill (Thursday and Saturday). All tours begin at 6:30pm from the City Tavern, 2nd and Walnut Streets. The charge is $5 for adults and $4 for children.

HORSE-AND-CARRIAGE TOURS To get the feel of Philadelphia as it was in days of old, you may wish to try a narrated horse-drawn carriage ride. Operated by the **76 Carriage Co.** daily, these tours begin at Independence National Historical Park, 5th and Chestnut Streets, from 10am to 5pm, with later hours in the summer months. The fares range from $10 for 15 minutes to $20 for a half-hour (maximum of four people per carriage). Reservations are not necessary, but if you wish further information, call 923-8516.

BOATING TOURS The Philadelphia skyline and harbor sights can best be seen from the *Spirit of Philadelphia,* docked at Pier 24, at the Philadelphia Marine Center (tel. 923-1419). This is a new 600-passenger ship, air-conditioned and fully carpeted, with two enclosed decks and two open-air decks, offering sightseeing cruises year round. The trips, which require reservations, run as follows:

   Lunch cruises, with buffet and entertainment, Monday through Friday, from noon to 2pm; the charge is $17.95 for adults, $8.75 for children. On Saturday and Sunday, a brunch cruise is operated from noon to 2pm and 1 to 3pm, respectively, at a cost of $19.95 for adults and $10.95 for children.

   Evening dinner cruises, featuring buffet, dancing, and entertainment, are scheduled daily from 7 to 10pm. The cost is $30.95 per person on weekdays and $34.95 on weekends.

   Moonlight party cruises, with dancing, snacks, and cocktail service, go out from 11:30pm to 2am on Friday and Saturday. The $15-per-person price includes the food but not the drinks.

6. PHILADELPHIA SPECIAL EVENTS

Among the major events scheduled each year are the Philadelphia Flower Show (early to mid-March); the Philadelphia Antiques Show (early April); The Book and the Cook, a weekend gathering at a cross-section of the city's restaurants of cookbook authors and chefs from around the country (mid-April); Philadelphia Open House, featuring tours of private homes (late April–early May); the AfricaAmericas Festival (early May); Penn's Landing Summer Season, featuring more than 60 free concerts and events along the river (May–October); and the Jambalaya Jam, a New Orleans–style food and music festival along Penn's Landing (Memorial Day weekend).

7. PHILADELPHIA SAVVY SHOPPING

In Philadelphia, some of the best shopping is in clusters—malls and galleries where everything is under one roof. This weatherproof shopping concept makes the City of Brotherly Love an attractive place to shop in all weather and all seasons of the year.

GREAT AREAS

THE GALLERY AT MARKET EAST, 9th and Market Streets. Tel. 925-7162.
   This is one of the nation's largest urban shopping complexes, with 200 stores and restaurants. Spread on four levels, the indoor shopping courtyard features everything from fashions to food shops, all under one glass roof. Open Monday, Tuesday, and Thursday through Saturday from 10am to 7pm, Wednesday from 10am to 9pm, and Sunday from noon to 5pm.

THE BOURSE, 5th and Market Streets. Tel. 625-0300.
   Across from Independence Hall, you'll find more than 50 shops and restaurants housed in this 10-story landmark constructed between 1893 and 1895 as Philadelphia's first merchant's exchange. Spread out over four levels, the interior

includes impressive Corinthian columns, brass and marble staircases, balconies embellished with marble, and wrought-iron and cast-iron rails. The wares for sale range from crafts to designer fashions, fast foods to vintage wines. Open daily, but hours vary among the shops or concessions.

THE SHOPS AT THE BELLEVUE, Broad and Walnut Streets. Tel. 875-8350.

Some of the world's most famous names in consumer goods and fashions are located in this 3.5-story atrium mall. Shops include Polo-Ralph Lauren, Gucci, Alfred Dunhill, Neuchatel Chocolates, and Tiffany and Co. Open Monday, Tuesday, and Thursday through Saturday from 10am to 6pm, Wednesday from 10am to 8pm.

THE SHOPS AT LIBERTY PLACE, Market and Chestnut Streets. Tel. 851-9050.

One of the newest shopping developments of this city, this cluster features over 60 shops, restaurants, and services on two levels surrounding a central rotunda. Choices include an artisan's cooperative as well as such leading names as J. Crew, Johnston & Murphy, Brentano's Booksellers, Rand McNally, Crabtree & Evelyn, Godiva Chocolatier. Open Monday, Tuesday, and Thursday through Saturday from 9:30am to 7pm, Wednesday from 9:30am to 9pm, and Sunday from noon to 6pm.

SHOPPING A TO Z
ANTIQUES

Philadelphia's haven for antique buffs is "Antiques Row," a three-block area on Pine Street, from 9th to 12th streets, which includes dozens of stores and curio shops.

DEPARTMENT STORES

JOHN WANAMAKER'S, 1300 Market St. Tel. 422-2648.

This department store is the oldest in the United States. John Wanamaker's was founded in 1861 and occupies an entire block in the heart of the city next to City Hall. As you traverse the main floor, you'll see the emblem of the store, a 2,500-pound bronze eagle in the middle of the center aisle. The world's largest pipe organ is also located here, and if you happen to stroll by at 11:15am or 5:15pm (except Sunday), you'll be treated to a short concert. Shopping hours are Monday, Tuesday, and Thursday through Saturday from 10am to 7pm, Wednesday from 10am to 9pm, and Sunday from 11am to 6pm.

STRAWBRIDGE AND CLOTHIER, 8th and Market Streets. Tel. 629-2000.

This is another Philadelphia shopping tradition, dating back to 1868. It is a full-line, eight-floor department store with everything from fashions to food and furniture. Open Monday, Tuesday, and Thursday through Saturday from 10am to 7pm, Wednesday from 10am to 9pm, and Sunday from 11am to 6pm.

DISCOUNT SHOPPING

FRANKLIN MILLS, 1455 Franklin Mills Circle. Tel. 632-1500.

One of the city's newest shopping attractions is this giant mall launched in May 1989. Located on 300 acres off I-95, it is touted as the world's largest regional specialty shopping mall, with a mile-long, bargain-filled concourse, showcasing nine major anchor stores and 250 specialty, outlet, and discount retailers. A 28-foot animated caricature of Ben Franklin greets shoppers at the entrance of the complex. Other notable features range from a variety of restaurants and cinemas to a replica of a 19th-century train station and a family entertainment galleria, offering bowling, baseball batting cages, roller skating, miniature golf, and musical reviews. Open Monday through Saturday from 10am to 9:30pm and Sunday from 11am to 6pm.

FOOD

READING TERMINAL MARKET, 12th and Arch Streets. Tel. 922-2317.

✪ Food of every kind is on sale here. Built in 1893, this markethouse has dozens of vendors selling fresh fruits and vegetables, homemade baked goods and preserves, as well as seafood, barbecued chickens, ice cream, pastas, cheese steaks, and other ethnic specialties. Open Monday through Saturday from 8am to 6pm.

JEWELRY

JEWELER'S ROW, Sansom St. between 7th and 8th Streets.
This is one of the world's oldest and largest diamond centers, with more than 100 retailers, wholesalers, and craftspeople dealing in precious stones, gold, and silver.

8. PHILADELPHIA EVENING ENTERTAINMENT

Check the arts and entertainment pages of the local newspaper, the *Philadelphia Inquirer* for daily listings. Discount ticket booths do not exist in Philadelphia at the present time, but there are two central booking agencies for major theaters and concert halls: **Central City Ticket Office,** 1312 Sansom St. (tel. 735-1350), and **Wanamaker's Ticket Office** (tel. 568-7100). At certain times, the **Philadelphia Visitor Center,** 16th Street and John F. Kennedy Blvd. (tel. 567-0670), offers ticket-booth services for some productions; inquire at this office at the time of your visit.

The city is home to the Philadelphia Orchestra, the Opera Company of Philadelphia, Peter Nero and the Philly Pops, the Philadelphia Singers, and the Philadelphia Boys Choir.

MAJOR MULTI-PURPOSE PERFORMANCE AND CONCERT HALLS

ANNENBERG CENTER, University of Pennsylvania, 3680 Walnut St. Tel. 898-6791.
One of the city's busiest performing-arts centers is this three-theater complex. The home of the Philadelphia Drama Guild, this venue also welcomes a continuous program of guest artists, as well as touring Broadway shows. The Annenberg also hosts an international festival for children each May. The box office is open noon to 6pm weekdays and at performance times, starting 2 hours before curtain.
Prices: Tickets $15–$30.

THE ACADEMY OF MUSIC, Broad and Locust Streets. Tel. 893-1930.
This is the home of the Philadelphia Orchestra, the Philly Pops, the Opera Company of Philadelphia, the Pennsylvania Ballet, and the Concerto Soloists Chamber Orchestra of Philadelphia. Engagements by top-name stars are also featured here, and occasional touring shows. Tickets range from $5 to $45, but average between $10 and $25 for most events. The box office is open Monday through Saturday from 10am to 9pm (until 5:30pm when there is no evening performance), and at 1pm on Sunday when a performance is scheduled.
Prices: Tickets $5–$45.

SHUBERT THEATRE, 250 South Broad St. Tel. 732-5446.
Broadway shows are on tap at the Shubert Theatre, as are magic shows and performances by various opera and ballet companies. Curtain is usually at 8pm.
Prices: Tickets $20–$35.

WALNUT STREET THEATRE, 9th and Walnut Streets. Tel. 574-3550.
Established in 1809, the Walnut Street Theatre claims to be the oldest English-language theater in continuous use. A resident theatrical company performs here, but

this is also a stage for Benjamin Franklin Parkway Area–visiting opera, chamber music, dance, and Shakespearean groups. Curtain is usually at 8pm.
Prices: Tickets $15–$45.

THEATERS

FORREST THEATRE, 1114 Walnut St. Tel. 923-1513.
Shows en route to or from Broadway often stop here. Curtain is at 8pm, with Wednesday and Saturday matinees at 2pm.
Prices: Tickets $20–$40.

SOCIETY HILL PLAYHOUSE, 507 South 8th St. Tel. 923-0210.
Contemporary, experimental, and off-Broadway works are staged at the Society Hill Playhouse, offering two stages, one with 223 seats and the other with 60. It is a nonprofit institution, with performances Wednesday through Saturday at 8pm, and matinees on Sunday at 3pm.
Prices: Tickets $19–$25.

PLAYS AND PLAYERS THEATER, 1714 Delancey Place. Tel. 735-0630.
The city's top community theater for over 80 years, it presents nonprofessional and professional productions in comedy, mystery, and farce. It is also the home of the Philadelphia Theater Company and the American Music Theater Festival.
Prices: $10–$15.

WILMA THEATER, 2030 Sansom St. Tel. 732-7644.
This theater is known for producing a unique variety of regional and foreign plays. Performances are Tuesday through Saturday at 8pm and matinees on Saturday and Sunday at 2pm.
Prices: $15–$25.

RIVERFRONT DINNER THEATRE, Delaware Avenue and Poplar Street. Tel. 925-7000.
Broadway classics and contemporary productions are staged year-round at this theater. Recent shows have included "The King and I," "Annie," "Chicago," and "A Chorus Line." A buffet dinner is also served prior to each performance. Evening shows are performed Wednesday through Sunday, and matinees Wednesday through Saturday.
Prices: $26.95 Saturday nights, $22.95 other nights. Matinees $19.95.

THE CLUB AND MUSIC SCENE

Philadelphia's nightlife options are many, both in the historic area and in the main business district. For lively bars, the South Street area is a hub of ever-changing establishments that offer a wide variety of popular music, specialty music, and comedy acts. Admission or cover charges range from $5–$10 or there is no admission charge but a two-drink minimum charge; policies tend to fluctuate with the time of week or season, so always phone in advance.

For mood music and good conversation, the lounges of the major hotels and restaurants throughout the city are the venues of choice. Except for special events, these places do not charge admission, but they do require customers to buy drinks or meals.

COMEDY CLUBS If you feel like a good laugh or two, these comedy clubs are worth a visit: **The Comedy Works,** 126 Chestnut St. (tel. WACKY-97) and **The Funny Bone,** 221 South St. (tel. 440-9670).

DISCOS/DANCE CLUBS Like most major cities, Philadelphia discos and dance clubs come and go, open and close, almost as fast as our books come out, but, as we go to press, here are a few that are currently in vogue: **Aztec,** 939 Delaware Ave. (tel. 574-5730); **Katmandu,** Delaware Avenue and Poplar Street (tel. 629-1101); **Market Street Live,** 8th and Market Streets (tel. 829-2400); and **Revival,** 22 South 3rd St. (tel. 627-4825).

JAZZ The best spots to hear live jazz performed currently are the **Dock Street Brewing Company,** 18th and Cherry Streets. (tel. 668-1480); **Downey's,** Front and South Streets (tel. 629-0525); **Meiji-En,** Pier 19, North Delaware Ave. (tel. 592-7100); **Montserrat,** 623 South St (tel. 592-8393); and **Zanzibar Blue,** 301-305 South 11th St. (tel. 829-0300).

PIANO BARS Among the most popular places for easy listening in the evening are the **Ethel Barrymore Room** of the Hotel Atop the Bellevue, 115 Chancellor Court (tel. 893-1776); **Crickett Lounge** of the Latham Hotel, 135 South 17th St. (tel. 563-9444); the **Lobby Bar of the Omni Hotel,** 4th and Chestnut Streets (tel. 925-0000); 1701 **Café of the Warwick Hotel,** 17th and Locust Streets (tel. 545-4655); and the **Monte Carlo Living Room,** 2nd and South Streets (tel. 925-2220).

9. EXCURSION TO VALLEY FORGE

Situated 20 miles northwest of downtown Philadelphia, Valley Forge is a 3,600-acre expanse of woodlands and meadow. One of the best-known sites associated with the American Revolution, it was here that Gen. George Washington set up an encampment for his Continental Army during the winter of 1777–78.

A lasting symbol of bravery, courage, and endurance, Valley Forge is a unique Revolutionary landmark, because no shot was ever fired and no battle fought. Nevertheless, thousands of American soldiers died here during that winter, as they struggled to survive against hunger, disease, and the unrelenting forces of nature. On a brighter note, the Valley Forge experience also gave Gen. Washington the opportunity to reorganize and train his impromptu army, which led to ultimate victory.

The focal point of this cherished stretch of countryside is the Valley Forge National Historical Park, Route 23 and N. Gulph Road (tel. 215/783-1077). The modern Visitor Center at the entrance to the park houses displays, exhibits, and a 15-minute audiovisual program that provides background on the historic Valley Forge encampment. Free maps and brochures are also available.

You can drive or walk around the park on your own or participate in a narrated bus tour. Tours are operated from mid-May through September; charge is $5.50 for adults and $4.50 for youngsters 5 to 16. The route takes you past extensive remains and restorations of major forts and lines of earthworks, as well as the Artillery Park, Washington's Headquarters, the quarters of other officers, and the Grand Parade where Gen. von Steuben trained the army. There are also reconstructed huts, memorials, monuments, markers, walking and biking trails, and picnic areas.

Admission to the park is free, but there is $1 per person charge for entrance into the historic buildings. For more information, contact the **Valley Forge Convention and Visitors Bureau,** P.O. Box 311, Norristown, PA 19404 (tel. 215/278-3558 or toll-free 800/441-3549).

BUCKS COUNTY

With its pervasive bucolic charm, Bucks County is one of the most popular single-county destinations in the whole mid-Atlantic region. And for many good reasons. Not only did George Washington sleep here (and cross the Delaware from here), but many famous Americans have lived here over the years, from Pearl Buck and James Michener to Moss Hart, Dorothy Parker, George S. Kaufman, and legions of artists and writers. With all of Pennsylvania in his grasp, William Penn also chose Bucks County as his country retreat in the New World.

A mélange of wooded hillsides, river lowlands, sylvan towpaths, open fields, authentic historic districts, covered bridges, and welcoming country inns, Bucks County offers a blend of sightseeing, outdoor activities, and creature comforts. Bounded by the Delaware River on the east, Philadelphia to the south, bustling Montgomery County on the west, and the Lehigh Valley to the north, Bucks County is a 620-square-mile region, just 20 miles wide and 60 miles long. It is compact enough to drive around in a day, and yet so diverse that two weeks is hardly enough to see it all.

A BIT OF HISTORY

Named for Buckingham, England, the shire in which William Penn was born, Bucks County first gained prominence because of its location along the Delaware River. In the early 18th century, a number of ferries were started from the Bucks side of the river to the New Jersey shores.

The towns that sprang up around these operations were usually named after the men who ran the ferries; thus New Hope was originally called Well's Ferry, then Canby's Ferry, and Coryell's Ferry; and Reigelsville was first referred to as Shenk's Ferry. It was the McConkey Ferry in the lower part of the county that transported General Washington and his troops across the river for the historic Battle of Trenton in December of 1776. This event is still commemorated with the annual reenactment on Christmas Day of "Washington Crossing the Delaware." Washington Crossing has also been designated as a park and a place name along Rte. 32.

After the ferries, it was the Delaware Canal that spurred further development in this area during the mid-19th century. The canal, with its towpath running side-by-side along the river, provided a source of transport between Easton, Pa., and New Jersey. New Hope, in particular, became an important point along the canal, as it was the only place where four barges could pass at one time. At that time many mills were also built and operated along the river.

With the advent of the railroads and motorized transport, the ferries, canals, and mills faded into oblivion, but the historic homes and peaceful riverfront lands served to give the county a new lease on life as a colony of artists began to settle in the area. With the opening of the Bucks County Playhouse in 1939, a core of writers and performers also chose this peaceful region as a country retreat.

It didn't take long after that for a nest of country inns to spruce up their facades and for gourmet restaurants to spring up in converted mills or ferry houses throughout the county. Rustic all-purpose general stores have been joined by dozens of antique shops, art galleries, craft centers, and wineries. It's no wonder that tourists

WHAT'S SPECIAL ABOUT BUCKS COUNTY

Ace Attractions
☐ Parry Mansion, an 18th-century Georgian Colonial home in the heart of New Hope.
☐ Pearl S. Buck House, in Perkasie, furnished with the author's collection of Asian and American art and antiques.
☐ Pennsbury Manor, Morrisville, the reconstructed plantation home of William Penn.
☐ Bucks County Playhouse, in New Hope, a leading arts center for more than 50 years.

For the Kids
☐ Sesame Place, a seven-acre theme park for fans of the children's TV show *Sesame Street*.

Museums
☐ Mercer Museum, with more than 40,000 tools representing over 60 crafts and trades.

☐ James A. Michener Arts Center, Doylestown, a fine-arts museum dedicated to one of the town's favorite sons.

Parks
☐ Washington Crossing Historic Park, a 500-acre park beside the Delaware with a 19th-century village.
☐ Nockamixon State Park, the county's largest state park, with 5,400 acres and a 1,450-acre lake with 24 miles of shoreline.

Religious Shrines
☐ National Shrine of Our Lady of Czestochowa, Doylestown, commemorates a similar shrine in Poland.

flock to Bucks. If all these historic landmarks and aesthetic experiences were not enough, this is also the home of Sesame Place, the children's wonderland presided over by Big Bird.

ORIENTATION
GETTING THERE

26 miles N of Philadelphia, 54 miles NE of Wilmington, 120 miles NE of Baltimore, 158 miles NE of Washington, DC, 95 miles SW of New York, 74 miles E of Lancaster, 106 miles SE of Harrisburg.

By Air

Bucks County can be reached by air via **Philadelphia International Airport,** less than 20 miles south, where ground transport, including car rental, is readily available (see "Orientation" in Chapter 4, Philadelphia).

By Bus

The **Southeastern Pennsylvania Transportation Authority (SEPTA)** offers commuter service throughout the county, from Philadelphia (215/574-7800). In addition, **West Hunterdon Transit** buses run from the Port Authority Terminal in New York City to Doylestown, Lahaska, Buckingham, and New Hope; for information, call 212/564-8484 or 201/783-7500.

By Car

Interstate 95, the main north-south artery along the east coast, passes right through the lower part of Bucks County. The northern half of the county is just a few miles south of I-78 and Rte. 22, major east-west highways.

INFORMATION

All types of helpful brochures, a 28-page travel guide and map, accommodations lists, restaurant directories, and a calendar of events can be obtained by contacting the **Bucks County Tourist Commission,** 152 Swamp Rd., P.O. Box 912, Dept. 93, Doylestown, PA 18901 (tel. 215/345-4552). If you are visiting the office, it's located adjacent to the Moravian tile works property; Swamp Road is also known locally as Rte. 313 and is located between Rtes. 202 and 611. The office is open weekdays from 9am to 5pm, Saturdays April–October 10am–4pm. For specific data about the New Hope area, contact or visit the **New Hope Borough Information Center,** 1 West Mechanic Street, New Hope, PA 18938 (tel. 215/862-5880). Hours for this office are from 9am to 4:30pm on weekdays and from 10:30am to 5:30pm on weekends.

Area Code

Bucks County telephone numbers all have the 215 area code.

GETTING AROUND

The best way to get around Bucks County is by car, although many of the towns are easily and best explored by foot. Rte. 32 (also known as River Road) wends its way in the north-south direction along the Delaware and is the ideal route to follow to see the riverside towns including New Hope. Rte. 202 will take you from New Hope to Doylestown, and at Doylestown, a number of major roads, such as Rtes. 611 and 313, converge and branch out to other parts of the county.

TOURS

Boat Tours

For a change of pace, you can view the Bucks County riverfront from the water via the **New Hope Mule Barge,** South Main St. (tel. 862-2842). Dating back 150 years, this 1-hour, 11-mile canal excursion presents a panorama of sights ranging from riverside cottages and romantic gardens to artists' workshops. It operates daily from May 1 until October 15 at 11:30am, 1, 2, 3, 4:30, and 6pm; and on Wednesday, Saturday, and Sunday during April and October 16 to November 15, on a slightly reduced schedule. The fare is $6.95 for adults, $5.50 for students, and $4.25 for children under 12.

Another floating mode of transport is **Coryell's Ferry Boat Rides,** 22 South Main St., New Hope (tel. 862-2050). This vessel, a 40-foot pontoon, provides a half-hour cruise along the Delaware, with historic commentary. Rides are scheduled every 45 minutes from noon to 5:30pm on weekdays, and noon to 7pm on weekends. (Board the boat from the Riverside Garden dock behind the Gerenser's Exotic Ice Cream store off Main Street. The fare is $4, $2 for children under 12.

Train Tours

For a leisurely 9-mile trip around the Bucks County countryside from New Hope to Lahaska and back, it's "All aboard!" the **New Hope and Ivyland Rail Road,** 32 West Bridge St. (tel. 862-2707), a vintage 1920's coal-fired steam locomotive. Save time to explore the New Hope Station, constructed in 1891, and the rolling stock dating back to 1911, including a railway post-office mail car, caboose, and trolley cars. The 9-mile, 50-minute round-trip ride operates daily May through October, and on Saturdays and Sundays during March and April and November and December. Hours are 10am–6pm Mon–Sat and noon–6pm on Sun. The fare is $6.50 for adults and $3.25 for children (aged 3–11), and $5 for seniors.

Balloon Tours

You can see the sights from aloft via **Keystone State Balloon Tours,** Van Sant Airport, Erwinna (tel. 294-8034). This company offers hot-air balloon rides over the Bucks County countryside and sometimes across the Delaware River into Hunterdon County, N.J. A van follows the balloon and returns passengers to the boarding point

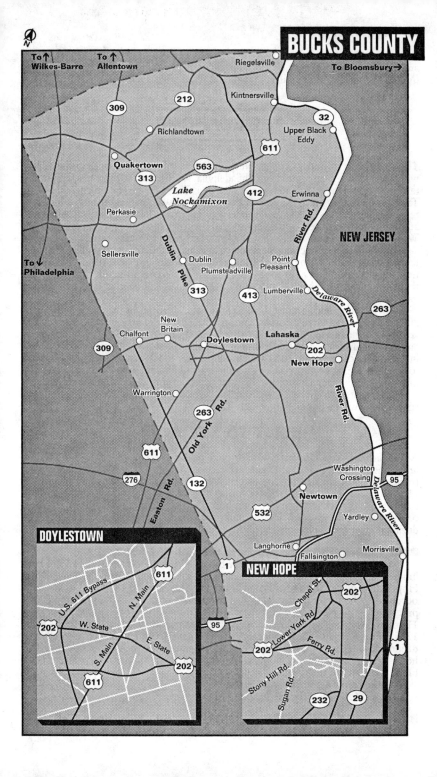

at Erwinna. Flights are offered twice a day, at sunrise and sunset, weather permitting, and reservations are necessary. Prices begin at $150 per person for a 1-hour flight. (*Note:* The mailing address is P.O. Box 162, Pipersville, PA 18947).

1. NEW HOPE

The centerpiece of Bucks County, New Hope first gained prominence in the 1720s, when John Wells, a carpenter from Philadelphia, was licensed to operate a ferry and a tavern here, and the townland became known as Well's Ferry. The original Old Ferry Tavern still exists today as the core of the building now known as the Logan Inn. The ferry operation across the Delaware was very important to the growth of this town, and as the ferry changed ownership, so also the town took on new names, and thus Well's Ferry later became known as Canby's Ferry and Coryell's Ferry.

The name New Hope was the result of another of the town's resources, grist and lumber mills. In 1790 some of the mills burned down and were rebuilt by a local resident, Benjamin Parry. To show his optimism in his new structures, he christened them as "New Hope Mills," and so the town gained still another (and permanent) name.

With its sylvan setting along the Delaware River, New Hope won fame in the early 20th century as an artist's colony, and, by the 1930s, the area became a haven for actors and writers from New York. Moss Hart and Dorothy Parker had homes here, and other luminaries came to perform at the Bucks County Playhouse, which opened in 1939. This creative ambience, which still prevails and flourishes today, has also led to the blossoming of a myriad of art galleries and antique shops. Restored country inns and gourmet restaurants also line the streets of this idyllic riverside retreat.

For all of its attractions, New Hope is a surprisingly small town (no larger than 1 square mile, with a population of only 1,500).

WHAT TO SEE & DO

A walk around New Hope is a walk through history—no fewer than 243 properties are included on the National Register of Historic Places. Parking is very limited and traffic through Main Street moves at a snail's pace on weekends. The best way to see New Hope is to park your car where you are staying or a few blocks from the heart of town and walk back in to explore it on foot. Even the sidewalks tend to be crowded on summer weekends with legions of browsers and shoppers, so consider a visit during midweek or in the off-season for your first look at New Hope.

PARRY MANSION, Main and Ferry Sts. Tel. 862-5652.
One of the loveliest old houses in the town is this residence, erected in 1784 by a lumber and gristmill owner, Benjamin Parry (the man responsible for the name "New Hope"). Parry lived in this fieldstone house until his death in 1839, and it was then occupied by his direct descendants, five generations of the Parry family, until it was purchased by the New Hope Historical Society in 1966. Now open to the public, this 11-room Georgian Colonial house is decorated in period style with furnishings from 1775 through 1900. Each room on the first and second floors is restored and decorated to represent the life-style of a short span within the 125-year period. The house is in the heart of New Hope, at the corner of South Main and Ferry Streets, one block south of the traffic light.
Admission: $4 donation per person.
Open: May–Oct, Fri–Sun 1–5pm.

BUCKS COUNTY VINEYARDS, 6123 York Rd., New Hope. Tel. 794-7449.

You can taste wine produced from Pennsylvania grapes at this winery located three miles west of New Hope, on Rte. 202, and housed in an old red barn. Begun in 1973, this winery today produces more than 20 varieties of wines. Visitors are welcome to enjoy the winery, cellars, a wine museum, and the tasting room (which includes cheese produced at the winery).
Admission: Free.
Open: Mon–Sat 10am–6pm, Sun noon–6pm.

BUCKINGHAM VALLEY VINEYARD AND WINERY, Rte. 413, Buckingham. Tel. 794-7188.
Self-guided wine tours and tastings (at no charge) are available at this winery, 2 miles south of Rte. 202. A small, family-owned enterprise, the operation was started in 1966 on 15 acres, and today produces over 100,000 bottles a year.
Admission: Free.
Open: Tues–Fri noon–6pm, Sat 10am–6pm, Sun noon–4pm (weekends only in Jan–Feb).

SAND CASTLE WINERY, River Rd. (Rte. 32), Erwinna. Tel. 294-9181.
Owned and operated by Czechoslovakian immigrants, this winery, 12 miles north of New Hope, off Rte. 32, is designed in the style of a 10th-century Bratislavian castle. Situated on a 72-acre estate that borders the Delaware River and wooded hillsides, it produces 100% vinfera wines in the European tradition, including Chardonnay, Johannisberg Reisling, Cabernet Sauvignon, and Pinot Noir. Tasting is available and tours are by appointment.
Admission: Free.
Open: Daily, Mon–Fri 10am–4pm, Sat 10am–6pm, Sun noon–6pm.

COOL FOR KIDS

QUARRY VALLEY FARM, 2302 Street Rd., Lahaska. Tel. 794-5882.
A special treat for young travelers in this area is a prototype of a 1700s farm and barnyard with animals, located off Rte. 202, between New Hope and Doylestown. Children can see demonstrations of sheep shearing and cow milking, as well as working craftspeople, including a blacksmith and weavers.
Admission: $4.50 adults, $4 children under 12.
Open: Mid-Mar–Dec, daily 10am–5pm.

SHOPPING

Step back into an 18th-century market atmosphere at **Peddler's Village,** Rtes. 202 and 263 at Lahaska (tel. 794-4000). With more than 70 craft shops, specialty boutiques, antique dealers, taverns, and restaurants, this mélange of Americana is open daily, year round, Monday through Thursday from 10am to 5:30pm; Friday until 9pm; Saturday until 6pm; and Sunday from noon to 5:30pm. Special events staged at the village include a Strawberry Festival in May, a Fine Arts Festival in early June, a Teddy Bear's Picnic in mid-July, a Country Bargain Fest in late August, a Scarecrow Festival in mid-September, an Apple Festival in early November, and a Country Christmas Festival on the first Saturday in December.

In the heart of New Hope, you'll find the **Old Franklin Print Shop,** Cannon Square, Main and Ferry Streets (tel. 862-2956). An 1860 hand press is the center of attention here, with daily demonstrations of the art of printing. Items for sale include a large selection of comic posters, book covers, citations, and newspapers, mostly in the $2-to-$5 price range. Open Monday through Saturday from 10am to 5pm, and from 1 to 5pm on Sunday.

Among the many galleries and art centers in town, a standout is the **Three Cranes Gallery,** 18–20 West Mechanic St. (tel. 862-5626). This is a treasure trove of original paintings, prints, and scrolls by more than 50 American, British, and Japanese artists, as well as jewelry, clothing, furniture, and Oriental antiques. Open daily, 11:30am to 6pm or later, but closed Tuesday in the off-season.

Bucks County is antiques territory. More than 50 dealers are located throughout the county, with the greatest concentration (more than 20) in Lahaska and New Hope; the area along Rte. 202 between New Hope and Lahaska, in fact, is commonly known as "antiques row." A guide and map outlining the antiquing centers can be obtained from the tourist office or by writing directly to the **Bucks County Antiques Dealers Association,** c/o Brenda Farmer, 406 Station Ave., P.O. Box 573, Langhorne, PA 19047 (tel. 215/752-9899).

WHERE TO STAY

The choice of places to stay in or near New Hope is mind-boggling; as you drive on River Road or along Rte. 202, you'll see many lodging signs. We've chosen a cross-section, to give you an idea of the types of accommodations available—from modern 20th-century facilities to landmark inns or bed-and-breakfast homes.

It is always wise to make a reservation before you arrive, especially in summer and on weekends at all times. You'll find that most establishments fall into the moderate-to-expensive category; many places have a 2-night minimum stay over weekends or a 3-night minimum stay during holiday periods. But don't despair if New Hope is booked up. Because Bucks County is relatively small, you can stay in Chalfont, Doylestown, or Newtown and still be within easy striking distance of all the attractions of New Hope.

EXPENSIVE

BARLEY SHEAF FARM, Rte. 202 (P.O. Box 10), Holicong, PA 18928. Tel. 215/794-5104. 10 rms (all with bath). A/C
$ Rates (including breakfast and taxes): $100–$150 double. AE. **Parking:** Free. **Closed:** Christmas week.

A 1740 stone house, this is a national historic site and one of the most popular B&B's in Bucks County, located on Rte. 202, 5 miles west of New Hope and east of Lahaska. Once the home of playwright George S. Kaufman, earlier in this century this house was a gathering spot for visitors from the performing-arts world (from the Marx Brothers to Lillian Hellman and S. J. Perelman). Set on a 30-acre working farm, this ivy-covered and mansard-roof house is the domain of Don and Ann Mills, who opened it to guests 10 years ago. Seven rooms and suites are available upstairs in the main house and three ground-level rooms in an adjoining cottage. All the rooms have queen or double beds, private bath, and antique furnishings; some rooms have fireplaces. Rates include a hearty full breakfast (eggs from the farm, fresh-baked breads, jams, and honey from the hives on the grounds), served in a lovely Colonial-style room overlooking the garden. Guests' facilities include a parlor with TV and a swimming pool in season.

GOLDEN PLOUGH INN, P.O. Box 218, Rte. 202 and Street Rd., Lahaska, PA 19831. Tel. 215/794-4004. Fax 215/794-4001. 45 rms. A/C TV TEL
$ Rates (including continental breakfast): $85–$125 double; $145–$200 suite. AE, CB, DC, DISC, MC, V. **Parking:** Free.

For a taste of Americana, try this inn located in the midst of the brick-lined paths and colorful gardens of Peddler's Village, the shopping and restaurant complex about 5 miles west of New Hope, at intersection of Rtes. 202 and 263. About half of the rooms are in the main building. The decor offers the best of country crafts and furnishings, including four-poster and canopy beds, cozy window seats, wingback chairs, hand-hooked rugs, and cherrywood armoires and cabinets. Each unit also has a private bath, sitting and dressing areas, and refrigerator; some rooms also have a working fireplace, whirlpool bath, VCR, sofa bed, or balcony.

Dining/Entertainment: The Peddler's complex includes a half-dozen restaurants ranging from self-service to gourmet cuisine and over 70 shops, as well as a pub, tavern, and dinner-theater.

MODERATE

CENTRE BRIDGE INN, P.O. Box 74, Rte. 32, New Hope, PA 18938. Tel. 215/862-2048. 9 rms. A/C TV (5 rooms)
$ Rates: $70–$115 weekday single or double; $80–$125 weekend single or double. AE, MC, V. **Parking:** Free.

⭐ Situated right beside the Delaware River, 3½ miles north of New Hope, this is a fairly new property, although there has been an inn on this spot since the early 18th century. The current building is the third (the two previous structures were destroyed by fire). The story of the previous inns (including a resident ghost) is well documented on a wall display outside the main dining room. Many of the elegant guest rooms have canopy, four-poster, or brass beds, wall-high armoires, modern private baths, air conditioning, an outside deck, and views of the river or the countryside.

HACIENDA INN, 36 W. Mechanic St., New Hope, PA 18938. Tel. 215/862-2078, or toll-free 800/272-2078. Fax 215/862-9119. 21 rms, 9 suites. A/C TV TEL
$ Rates: $75–$90 single or double, $110–$170 suite. AE, DC, MC, V. **Parking:** Free.
One of the town's most unexpected lodgings is just a block from Main Street in the center of town. Established in 1964, this unique retreat began as an extension of owner Pamela Minford's antiques business, in which she specialized in Spanish and Mexican furnishings and art. Today the inn offers modern guest rooms, ranging from standard rooms to studios and suites, decorated with original pieces selected by Pam, mirrored walls, and lots of hanging plants and fresh flowers. Many units feature kitchenettes or refrigerators, Jacuzzis, fireplaces, and terrace decks. Facilities include a restaurant, lounge, and outdoor pool.

LOGAN INN, 10 W. Ferry St., New Hope, PA 18938. Tel. 215/862-2300. 16 rms. A/C TV TEL
$ Rates (including full breakfast): $95–$125 single or double. AE, CB, DC, MC, V. **Parking:** Free.
This hotel is located in what is reputedly New Hope's oldest building (1727), at the corner of Main and Ferry Streets in the heart of town. Recently restored (it has served as an inn since George Washington's day), the hotel has had many prominent guests over the years, including Grace Kelly, Helen Hayes, and Robert Redford, who came to perform at the nearby playhouse.
The guest rooms are showcases of Colonial period pieces, canopy and four-poster beds, down quilts, lace curtains, antiques, and original art. Each room has a private bath and a view of the river or the village. Facilities include a restaurant and tavern.

BUDGET

NEW HOPE MOTEL, 400 W. Bridge St., New Hope, PA 18938. Tel. 215/862-2800. 28 rms. A/C TV
$ Rates: $45 single, $59 double. AE, CB, DC, DISC, MC, V. **Parking:** Free.

Ⓢ Just a mile west of town is this motel tucked in a peaceful woodland setting off Rte. 179. For over 30 years, this facility has offered modern ground-level rooms with private bath and one or two double beds. Open all year, it also has a swimming pool for guests' use during the summer months.

WHERE TO DINE

EXPENSIVE

JENNY'S, Rte. 202, Lahaska. Tel. 794-4020.
Cuisine: INTERNATIONAL. **Reservations:** Recommended.
$ Prices: Appetizers $2.95–$7.95; main courses $14.95–$23.95; lunch $5.95–$9.95. AE, CB, DC, DISC, MC, V.

Open: Lunch Mon–Sat 11:30am–3pm; dinner Tues–Sat 5:30–10pm, Sun 4:30–8pm.

Five miles west of New Hope, in the heart of Peddler's Village, is this modern restaurant with the decor and ambience of yesteryear. Lunch features sandwiches, salads, crêpes, quiches, omelets, pastas, and unique dishes like smoked ham and Swiss florentine. Dinner entrées include mesquite-smoked sea scallops, lobster and crab sauté, roast duckling, and veal, steak, and pasta dishes.

THE LANDING, 22 N. Main St. Tel. 862-5711.
Cuisine: INTERNATIONAL. **Reservations:** Recommended.
$ Prices: Appetizers $4.95–$7.95; main courses $17.95–$22.95; lunch $6.95–$9.95. DC, DISC, MC, V.
Open: Apr–Dec lunch daily 11am–4pm, dinner 5–10pm; Jan–Mar Thurs–Sun lunch 11am–4pm, dinner 5–10pm.

Pleasing views of the water are found at this two-story restaurant perched on its own grounds along the river. The decor reflects a bit of traditional Bucks County with vintage prints, a large open fireplace, and antique chandeliers and lamps. Salads, sandwiches, quiches, chili, and pasta dishes are the focus at lunch. Dinner entrées, which change daily, often include lobster tail, shrimp with a julienne of vegetables, coquilles St.-Jacques, and rack of lamb with eggplant and tomato chutney.

ODETTE'S, S. River Rd. and Rte. 32. Tel. 862-2432.
Cuisine: INTERNATIONAL. **Reservations:** Recommended.
$ Prices: Appetizers $4.95–$7.95; main courses $14.95–$24.95; lunch $6.95–$9.95. AE, CB, DC, MC, V.
Open: Lunch Mon–Sat 11:30am–3pm; dinner Mon–Fri 5–10pm, Sat 5–11pm, Sun 4–9pm; brunch Sun 11am–3pm.

Surrounded by the river and the canal, this restaurant is located on the southern end of town. Previously called the Riverside, it has been operating since 1794. The previous owner (1961–76) was Odette Myrtil, a Broadway and Ziegfeld Follies star; many of her photos and memorabilia fill the walls. Live entertainment (piano bar and cabaret shows) add to the theatrical atmosphere.

The menus are seasonal and change six times a year, with a cuisine that can best be described as "creative continental." Lunch features salads, sandwiches, burgers, and quiches. Dinner entrées include steaks, seafood, duck, and veal.

MODERATE

KARLA'S, 5 W. Mechanic St., New Hope. Tel. 862-2612.
Cuisine: INTERNATIONAL. **Reservations:** Required for weekends.
$ Prices: Appetizers $3.50–$8; main courses $13–$19; lunch $3.95–$7.95. AE, DC, MC, V.
Open: Sun–Thurs 11am–10pm, Fri–Sat 11am–4am.

Situated in the heart of New Hope, next door to New Hope Information Center, off Main Street, this lively and informal restaurant offers three settings—a sunlit conservatory with ceiling fans, stained glass windows, and plants; a gallery room with paintings by local artists; and a bistro-style room with tapestry chairs and marble tabletops. The eclectic menu offers choices such as grilled ribeye steak; veal francese; chicken breast with Thai-style ginger sauce; gnocchi with onions, garlic, cream, and fresh spinach; confit of duck with banana-orange glacé; and capellini with sun-dried tomato pesto. Lunch items include burgers, sandwiches, pizzas, omelets, salads, and crêpes.

MARTINE'S, 7 E. Ferry. Tel. 862-2966.
Cuisine: INTERNATIONAL. **Reservations:** Recommended.
$ Prices: Appetizers $4–$7; main courses $8–$21; lunch $5–$8. CB, D, MC, V.
Open: Lunch daily 11:30am–2:30pm; dinner daily 5:30–10pm.

Another historic site turned restaurant along the river is this 1792 building which has served this town as a salt storehouse, library, and toll house for Coryell's Ferry. A restaurant for the last 10 years, this building still has its original fireplace, along with some modern enhancements, like Tiffany lamps and tiled tables. The menus are strictly 20th century. Lunch ranges from stews, salads, and burgers to fondue with steamed vegetables, seafood pastas, and pâté and cheese plates. Dinner choices include roast game hen, shrimp florentine, brook trout with fresh spinach and crab stuffing, rack of lamb, and filet mignon with lobster cardinale sauce.

MOTHERS, 34 N. Main St. Tel. 862-9354.
  Cuisine: INTERNATIONAL. **Reservations:** Recommended.
  $ Prices: Appetizers $3.95–$7.95; main courses $7.95–$20.95; lunch $5.95–$11.95. AE, MC, V.
  Open: Breakfast daily 8am–2pm; lunch daily 11am–5pm; dinner daily 5–10:30pm.
The lines are usually outside the door for a table at this trendy, informal dining spot, two blocks north of Ferry Street. Composed of two adjoining brick houses in the middle of town, this is the place to come to if you like a decor of modern art, a background of rock music, and an imaginative cuisine. Lunch includes tofu burgers, marinated salads, omelets, and crêpes. Dinner features stir-fry foods, tasty Cajun and Mexican dishes, gourmet pizzas (such as white mushroom pizza), and Creole-stuffed trout. Desserts are so cleverly concocted here that baking classes are given regularly by the management.

BUDGET

WILDFLOWERS GARDEN CAFE, 8 W. Mechanic St. Tel. 862-2241.
  Cuisine: AMERICAN. **Reservations:** Recommended.
  $ Prices: Appetizers $3–$5; main courses $7.50–$10; lunch $4.50–$6.50. MC, V.
  Open: May–Oct Mon–Fri and Sun noon–10pm; Sat noon–11pm. Nov–Dec, Mar–Apr Fri–Sat–Sun noon–10pm; **Closed:** Jan–Feb.
  This restaurant, off Main Street, opposite New Hope Information Office, offers indoor and outdoor dining in a 250-year-old house with a screened-in patio and open terrace overlooking Ingham Creek and the Bucks County Playhouse. As its name implies, the restaurant is decorated with lots of wildflowers and plants and murals of flowers and fields. The same menu is in effect all day, with sandwiches, soups, salads, fondues, tacos, and chili. Hot entrées focus on several "back to basics" home-cooking choices, such as Yankee pot roast, old-fashioned baked chicken, and baked Virginia ham. Save room for dessert, especially the Belgian chocolate brownies or fresh fruit cobblers ($3 to $4).

EVENING ENTERTAINMENT

  Delightfully situated along the banks of the Delaware River, the **Bucks County Playhouse,** 70 S. Main St. (P.O. Box 313), New Hope, PA 18938 (tel. 862-2041), features revivals of musicals from the past and recent Broadway hits. From April through December, performances are Wednesday through Sunday plus matinees on Wednesday and Thursday (closed January through March). A former gristmill with a capacity for almost 500 people, the playhouse celebrated its 50th season in 1989. Single ticket prices range from $13 to $17. Parking is $4.
  Peddler's Village Dinner Theatre, in the Cock 'n Bull Restaurant, Routes 202 and 263, Lahaska (tel. 794-4000), features a country buffet with a varied program of entertainment ranging from solo performers to Broadway musicals. Operating from January through March, the program commences at 7pm on Friday and Saturday and at 5pm on Sunday, with a matinee at noon on Saturday. Ticket prices range from $19.50 to $28.50.
  In addition, the **Peddler's Village Murder Mystery** takes place in the Peddler's Pub at the Cock 'n Bull Restaurant, Routes 202 and 263, Lahaska (tel. 794-4000), featuring an audience-participation murder mystery show and sit-down dinner (choice of three entrées). Operating year round, on Friday and Saturday nights, at 7:30pm. Tickets are $29.50.

2. DOYLESTOWN

In the heart of Bucks County, Doylestown has been the county seat of this area since 1813. Larger than New Hope, Doylestown is a 2⅓-square-mile city, with a population of 9,000. Situated less than 15 miles north of Philadelphia, it is also at the intersection of several roads that traverse the county, including Rtes. 202, 313, and 611. It is, therefore, a central base for touring the rest of the region.

The city traces its name back to 1745, when William Doyle obtained a license for a public house. Since the pub was at the intersection of some well-traveled Colonial highways, the entire area became known variously as Doyle's Tavern, Doyle's Town, Doyletown, and finally the present Doylestown.

With a mix of Federal and Victorian architecture, Doylestown is home to the county's largest historic district on the National Register (nearly 1,200 buildings). Primarily a residential and professional community, Doylestown is the birthplace of such well-known figures as writer James Michener; anthropologist Margaret Mead; and archeologist, historian, and inventor Henry Chapman Mercer. A few miles away at Perkasie, author Pearl S. Buck also made her home.

WHAT TO SEE & DO

THE MERCER MILE

Some of Doylestown's leading sights are associated with a local entrepreneur named Henry Chapman Mercer (1856–1930), who was a master of ceramics and crafts as well as being somewhat of an archeologist and antiquarian. Because so many Mercer-built or -inspired attractions dominate a fairly small area, they are known collectively as the **Mercer Mile.** If you stroll along The Mile, here's what you will see:

FONTHILL MUSEUM, E. Court St., off Swamp Rd. (Rte. 313). Tel. 348-9461.

A National Historic Landmark, this museum, next to the Bucks County Tourist Commission office, between Rtes. 611 and 202, has the trappings of a medieval castle. Mercer built this home to exhibit his collection of tiles and prints from around the world. The inside of the house can be viewed only by guided tours from 10am to 3:30pm. Reservations are recommended.

Admission: $4 adults, $1.50 students.

Open: Mon–Sat 10am–5pm, Sun noon–5pm. **Closed:** Thanksgiving, Christmas, and New Year's Day.

MORAVIAN POTTERY AND TILE WORKS, Swamp Rd. Tel. 345-6722.

This building with tiled chimneys is adjacent to the Fonthill Museum and is where much of Mercer's work took place. Mission-shaped, it is today a living-history museum, still producing Moravian tile according to the original methods. Tours are conducted every half hour. The museum is situated next to the Bucks County Tourist Commission office, between Rtes. 611 and 202.

Admission: $2.50 adults, $1 students.

Open: Daily 10am–4pm.

MERCER MUSEUM, Pine St. at Ashland St. Tel. 345-0210.

At the other end of the Mercer Mile you'll come to this monumental building, a National Historic Landmark, with Gothic, Norman, and Spanish influences. More than 40,000 tools representing 60 different crafts and trades are on display here. The museum itself is a classic example of Mercer's own use of concrete. Inside the museum is the Spruance Library, a research collection on Bucks County genealogy and commercial history. The library is open year round on Tuesday from 1 to 9pm and Wednesday through Saturday from 10am to 5pm (except for Independence Day, Thanksgiving Day, Christmas Day, and New Year's Day).

Admission: Museum and library, $4 adults, $1.50 students.
Open: Mon–Sat 10am–5pm; Sun noon–5pm. **Closed:** Thanksgiving Day and Christmas Day.

JAMES A. MICHENER ARTS CENTER, 138 S. Pine St., Doylestown. Tel. 340-9800.

Opened in 1988, this exhibition center is a cultural tribute to one of Doylestown's favorite sons. It has been designed as a museum for fine arts and focuses on works of American artists. The site itself dates back to 1813 and once served as the Bucks County jail. The prison yard, now a courtyard, is encircled by a sculpture garden, and the former guardhouse is an exhibition gallery.
Admission: Suggested donation $3 adults, $1.50 students.
Open: Tues–Fri 10am–4:30pm, Sat–Sun 10am–5pm.

NATIONAL SHRINE OF OUR LADY OF CZESTOCHOWA, Ferry Rd. and Beacon Hill Rd., Doylestown. Tel. 345-0600.

Established in 1955, in honor of a famous religious shrine in Poland, this 240-acre estate is the site of frequent pilgrimages and gatherings of Polish cultural interest.
Admission: Free.
Open: Mon–Sat 9am–5pm.

NEARBY ATTRACTIONS

THE PEARL S. BUCK HOUSE, 520 Dublin Rd., off Rte. 313, Perkasie. Tel. 249-0100.

This is a National Historic Landmark, about 8 miles northwest of Doylestown. Known as Green Hills Farm, this 60-acre estate contains Pearl Buck's 1835 stone farmhouse, an 1827 barn, and the author's gravesite. Ten of the house's 19 rooms are on view, furnished with the author's Asian and American art and antiques, including the "*Good Earth* desk," on which she penned her famous novel. Her Nobel Prize for literature and Pulitzer Prize for fiction are also on display.
One-hour guided tours: Mar–Dec Tues–Sat 10:30am, 1:30pm, 2:30pm; Sun 1:30 and 2:30pm.
Closed: Mon, Jan–Feb, major holidays.
Admission: $5 for adults, $4 for youngsters 6–18.

QUAKERTOWN FARMERS MARKET, 201 Station Rd., Quakertown. Tel. 536-4115.

An antique and flea market, the Farmers Market has been a Bucks County institution since 1932. This huge market (equivalent to the size of two football fields) contains more than 150 individual stores, shops, factory outlets, and dealers.
Open: Fri and Sat 10am–10pm; Sun 11am–5pm.

PEACE VALLEY WINERY, 300 Old Limekiln Rd., Chalfont. Tel. 249-9058.

With 36 acres of vineyards planted with a variety of hybrid grapes imported from France, this winery produces white, blush, red, nouveau, and dessert wines. Wine-tasting is available, but no regular tours.
Admission: Free.
Open: Wed–Sun noon to 6pm.
Directions: From Doylestown, go northwest on Rte. 313 to New Galena Rd., make a left, and then go 2 miles to Old Limekiln Rd.; then make a right, and it is 1 mile to the winery.

SHOPPING

In the heart of town you'll find the **Heritage Collectors' Gallery,** 11 West Court Street, Doylestown (tel. 345-7955). This shop is so intriguing that it is often mistaken for a museum. It's filled with exhibits of original documents, letters, autographs, and manuscripts of historic figures from George Washington and Abraham Lincoln to Napoleon and Queen Victoria, as well as Elvis Presley, Marc Chagall, and many more. You'll also find books, rare prints, maps, and antique furnishings. Open Monday through Friday from 10am to 5pm, and Saturday from noon to 5pm.

WHERE TO STAY

Like New Hope, Doylestown offers many fine country inns and bed-and-breakfast homes for overnight stays. Although the rates can generally be classified as moderate, there can sometimes be surcharges on weekends and minimum-stay requirements.

EXPENSIVE

HIGHLAND FARMS, 70 East Rd., Doylestown, PA 18901. Tel. 215/340-1354. 4 rms (2 with bath). A/C

$ Rates (including breakfast): $98 double without bath, $135–$150 double with bath. MC, V. **Parking:** Free.

This stately B&B gem, directly west of intersection of Rtes. 202 and 413, was once the country retreat of Oscar Hammerstein. It's said that the view of the surrounding farmlands from the front porch inspired "Oh, What a Beautiful Morning"; innkeeper Mary Schnitzer usually has the music playing in the background as guests enter. The house is full of antiques, brass fixtures, old chiming clocks, and Hammerstein sheet music, playbills, and memorabilia. Each guest room is named after one of the great lyricist's musicals and is furnished to reflect its title: the Showboat Room, the Carousel Room, the King and I Room, and the Oklahoma Room. Guests are encouraged to relax by the fireside in the library, where Hammerstein did much of his writing; on the second-floor railed veranda; or on the sun porch, which is filled with leafy plants and wicker rockers. The 5-acre estate also offers a 60-foot swimming pool, brick patio, gardens, and tennis courts. After a day or two here, you're bound to have a song in your heart and a lot of happy memories.

MODERATE

DOYLESTOWN INN, 18 W. State St., Doylestown, PA 18901. Tel. 215/345-6610. Fax 215/345-4017. 22 rms (all with bath), 1 suite. AC TV TEL.

$ Rates: $65–$75 single, $75–$85 double, $100 suite. AE, DISC, MC, V. **Parking:** Free.

This three-story Victorian property, dating from 1871 and an inn since 1902, is situated in the heart of Doylestown, between Main Street and Hamilton Street. Listed on the National Register of Historic Places, it was completely restored and updated in 1990. The bedrooms, furnished in either Colonial or Victorian style, have a queen-size or a king-size bed, quilts, antiques, and decorative stencil trim on the walls. Facilities include a restaurant (see "Where to Dine," below) and a pub.

THE INN AT FORDHOOK FARM, 105 New Britain Rd., Doylestown, PA 18901. Tel. 215/345-1766. 5 rms (3 with bath), carriage house. A/C

$ Rates (including breakfast): $80–$100 single, $93–$126 double, $163–$227 carriage house. AE, MC, V. **Parking:** Free.

The area's top choice is this inn, an 18th-century stone house 1¼ miles west of Doylestown, off Rte. 202. Opened as a bed-and-breakfast in 1985, this gracious home is still owned by the Burpee family and contains original furnishings, fireplaces with colorful Mercer tiles, silver, china, books, and old pictures—all in a setting of a 60-acre estate with flower gardens, 200-year-old linden trees, pine forests, and walking paths.

The guest rooms are all furnished with antiques and brass, four-poster, or rope beds; they contain family heirlooms and are decorated with lots of fresh flowers and plants. Some bedrooms have working fireplaces and balconies, and all have air conditioning. A full farm breakfast is served in the dining room, and complimentary afternoon tea is provided in the living room or on the outdoor terrace. In addition, a completely renovated carriage house, with two bedrooms, private bath, and living room, can also be rented by two to four people.

OLD ARCADIA INN, 181 Park Ave., Chalfont, PA 18914. Tel. 215/822-1818. Fax 215/822-2535. 9 rms with bath. A/C TV TEL
$ Rates: (including full breakfast): $70–$125, single or double. AE, MC, V.
Parking: Free.

⭐ Surrounded by 8 acres of lawns and woods in the quiet western edge of Bucks County, this inn, 3 miles west of Doylestown, dates back to 1751 and has been masterfully restored by current owners Jack and Dee Hendrie. A huge stone fireplace is the welcoming focal point of the lobby area, but the room that draws the biggest raves is the Old Tavern, with its beamed ceiling, lantern lights, and antique oak and brass bar. Complimentary light refreshments are provided here each evening.

Most of all, the guest rooms are a delight, well equipped with air conditioning, TV, and telephone (often rare in Bucks County bed-and-breakfast inns). Each room is individually decorated with hand-stenciled walls, queen-size brass bed, designer comforter, laces and ruffles, antiques, reproductions, or wicker furniture, and fresh flowers. Some have diamond-lite windows, a working fireplace, and a whirlpool tub. A full breakfast, with gourmet menu choices, is served each morning in the plant-filled garden room, a glass-enclosed porch with fireplace. Complimentary daily newspapers are also provided.

WHERE TO DINE
VERY EXPENSIVE

SIGN OF THE SORREL HORSE, Old Bethlehem Rd., Quakertown. Tel. 536-4651.
Cuisine: FRENCH. **Reservations:** Required. **Directions:** Go north of Doylestown and Lake Nockamixon, off Rte. 313, and thence to Rte. 563 for about 2 miles; make a left turn onto Old Bethlehem Road—the restaurant is ¼ mile on the left.
$ Prices: Appetizers $4.50–$13.50; main courses $19.50–$24.95. MC, V.
Open: Dinner Wed–Sun 5:30–9pm.

⭐ Housed in an old stone building that dates back to 1749, this is the enterprise of husband-wife team Jon Atkin and Monique Gaumont, the latter of whom is a graduate of the Cordon Bleu cooking school of France. The three dining rooms present a romantic setting, complete with an aviary of nesting peace doves. The gardens outside provide herbs and flowers as flavorings and garnishes. All smoking of meats and fish is also done on the premises, and ice cream is made from scratch, using honey instead of sugar.

Given the setting, the ingredients, and the experience of the chef, it is not surprising that the menu is a gourmet's delight. Entrées include filet mignon with a mousse of foie gras and port wine sauce, lobster with a sauce of baby shrimp and Cheddar, smoked sea scallops and sweetbreads in pastry, medallions of veal with lobster and black truffles, rainbow trout stuffed with salmon mousseline and Louisiana crayfish sauce, vegetarian platter (24-hour notice required), and wild game in season. Upstairs, there are five guest rooms, each furnished individually with French period antiques.

EXPENSIVE

LAKE HOUSE INN, 1100 Old Bethlehem Rd., Perkasie. Tel. 257-5351.
Cuisine: INTERNATIONAL. **Reservations:** Recommended.
$ Prices: Appetizers $2.95–$7.95; main courses $15.95–$23.95; lunch $5.95–$12.95. AE, CB, DC, MC, V.
Open: Lunch Tues–Sat 11:30am–2:30pm; dinner Tues–Sat 5–10pm, Sun 3–8pm. Brunch Sun 11am–1:30pm. **Closed:** Early Jan.

⭐ For a lakeshore setting, drive about 10 miles north of Doylestown to this lovely establishment overlooking Lake Nockamixon from the windows of its nautical dining rooms and from its glass-enclosed deck. Sandwiches, salads, and light seafood fare are featured at lunchtime. Dinner entrées include bay crab au gratin, salmon bouquetière, tournedos with woodland mushrooms and sauce bordelaise, chicken mint julip, and duck Amaretto.

MODERATE

B. MAXWELLS, 37 N. Main St. Tel. 348-1027.
Cuisine: INTERNATIONAL. **Reservations:** Recommended for dinner.
$ Prices: Appetizers $1.95–$6.95; main courses $12.95–$17.95; lunch $2.95–$6.95. AE, MC, V.
Open: Mon–Thurs 11am–11pm; Fri–Sat 11am–midnight.
This casual two-story, Victorian-style restaurant is in the heart of downtown Doylestown. The decor is a mélange of sconce lamps, smoked-glass windows, brass fixtures, and old-fashioned booth seating. The lunch menu features sandwiches, "croissantwiches," omelets, and burgers. Dinner focuses on international cuisine, ranging from Cajun dishes, stir-fries, and pastas to steak Diane, flounder amandine, and chicken Marsala. Senior-citizen specials are available most days.

DOYLESTOWN INN, 18 W. State St., Doylestown. Tel. 345-6610.
Cuisine: AMERICAN. **Reservations:** Recommended.
$ Prices: Breakfast $3.25–$8.95; appetizers, $2.95–$6.95; main courses $9.95–$17.95; lunch $4.95–$13.95.
Open: Breakfast Mon–Sat 7–11am, Sun country breakfast buffet 8:30am–1pm; lunch Mon–Sat 11:30am–3pm; dinner Mon–Thurs 4:30–10pm, Fri–Sat 4:30–11pm, Sun 3–9pm.

A blend of Victorian and modern art-deco fixtures, this dining room overlooks Doylestown's busy Main Street. The menu offers a blend of contemporary and regional cuisine, with such entrées as broiled baby flounder, Cajun-style shrimp brochette, frogs' legs floating on biscuit rafts, char-grilled sirloin steak, Doylestown Inn chicken and vegetable pot pie, and duck à l'orange. Lunch offers salads, burgers, sandwiches, omelets, and seafoods.

WIDOW BROWN'S INN, Rte. 611 and Stump Rd., Plumsteadville. Tel. 766-7500.
Cuisine: INTERNATIONAL. **Reservations:** Recommended.
$ Prices: Appetizers $2.95–$6.95; main courses $12.95–$19.95; lunch $4.95–$8.95. AE, CB, DC, MC, V.
Open: lunch Tues–Fri 11:30am–2pm; dinner Tues–Sun 4:30–10pm.
Although the origins of this property (formerly known as the Plumsteadville Inn) can be traced to 1751, most of the present building is a lot younger, dating back to a 1968 restoration and a 1975 addition. Still, the atmosphere is rich in Colonial and Victorian trappings, with five dining rooms filled with country furnishings, plants, and a huge fireplace. But the menu is strictly 20th century, with entrées such as filet mignon béarnaise, veal scaloppine sautéed with basil butter, chicken Dijon, seafood pasta, and cioppino. Lunch includes sandwiches, burgers, omelets, salads, and pastas. In addition, upstairs there are 16 bedrooms with private bath and phone, decorated in flowery Victorian style with canopy and semicanopy beds.

BUDGET

MEYERS FAMILY RESTAURANT, 501 N. West End Blvd. (Rte. 309), Quakertown. Tel. 536-4422.
Cuisine: AMERICAN. **Reservations:** Not accepted on weekends for dinner.
$ Prices: Appetizers $.95–$4.95; main courses $7.95–$13.95; lunch $2.95–$5.95. AE, DISC, MC, V.
This restaurant is well known for its friendly atmosphere and its bakeshop full of eat-in or take-out cakes, desserts, cookies, and jams. Salads, sandwiches, and burgers are good choices at lunchtime. Dinner entrées include seafood, steaks, chicken, and turkey dishes, served with potato and vegetable. Nightly dinner specials are usually under $10 for such selections as chicken florentine, filet of whitefish, or beef turnover; breakfast is also served each day.

3. ALONG NORTH RIVER ROAD

River Road, also known as Route 32, follows the flow of the Delaware River along the eastern shoreline of Bucks County. It is an ideal path for a scenic drive at any time of the year. This 60-mile stretch is also a perfect setting for boating, canoeing, swimming, picnicking, tubing, rafting, hiking, and just plain walking. The northern section between New Hope and Riegelsville is a particular delight, with a parade of tree-lined villages, riverside inns, and clusters of country shops.

Heading north from New Hope, you'll pass **Lumberville,** a village dating back to 1785, when it was built around two sawmills, and the site of the region's only footbridge across the Delaware; **Point Pleasant,** a typical river town dating back to the mid-1700s and once the site of 28 mills; **Erwinna,** an important boat-building and repair site during the canal days of the 18th century; **Upper Black Eddy,** a village located on the longest eddy on the Delaware River and a popular fishing center; **Kintnersville,** a town bordered by 3 miles of cliff like formations; and **Riegelsville,** dating back to 1774 and the site of one of the first bridges across the river.

WHAT TO SEE & DO

Much of the outdoor joy of Bucks County is centered along the Delaware River and canal, which meander side by side along the eastern shoreline. This portion of Rte. 32, also known as River Road, which stretches between Upper Black Eddy and New Hope, is not to be missed, whether you choose to drive, walk, bicycle, or pick a favorite spot and have a picnic.

For those who prefer to be active, **Point Pleasant Canoes,** Rte. 32, Point Pleasant (tel. 215/297-TUBE), is a good place to stop. Open from mid-March to mid-November, this company can arrange for you to go tubing (rides of 3 or 4 hours from $12 a person), whitewater and leisure rafting (trips of approximately 2½ hours from $30), canoeing (2 to 4 hours from $15), and rafting (4 hours from $12) on the Delaware River. Day or evening hayrides are also available, from $6 per person for 1 hour. Operating from April to October, the firm also sets up overnight trips from 1 day to 2 weeks in duration.

Bucks County is also home to a variety of riverside and lakeland parks, including **Nockamixon State Park,** west of Rte. 412 and southeast of Quakertown. This is the county's largest state park, with 5,400 acres; it contains a 1,450-acre lake with 24 miles of shoreline. Activities include swimming, fishing, boating, picnicking, hiking, bicycling, and, in the winter months, cross-country skiing. **Tinicum Park** on River Rd., just north of Erwinna, sits on the banks of the Delaware River and canal and is an ideal spot for boating, canoeing, hiking, and winter ice-skating, while **Tyler State Park** at Newtown is a 1,700-acre inland area with over 10 miles of bike paths.

Other parks lining the river shoreline include the **Ralph Stover State Park** on Tohickon Creek at Point Pleasant (for swimming and picnicking) and the **Delaware Canal State Park** at Upper Black Eddy (for hiking and canoeing). Full information about all the parks in the region can be obtained by contacting the **Bucks County Department of Parks and Recreation,** Core Creek Park, 901 E. Bridgetown Pike, Langhorne, PA 19047 (tel. 215/757-0571 or 348-6114).

WHERE TO STAY

EXPENSIVE

ISAAC STOVER HOUSE, P.O. Box 68, River Rd., Erwinna, PA 18920. Tel. 215/294-8044. 7 rms (5 with bath). A/C
$ Rates (including breakfast): $110–$125 mid week, $150–$175 weekend, single or double. AE, MC, V. **Parking:** Free.
With a sloping mansard roof and gingerbread trim, there's great Victorian charm in

this inn owned by TV personality Sally Jessy Raphael. Dating back to 1837, this three-story brick house is located on a 13-acre estate, with the Delaware River in front and the canal behind. It is furnished (at times almost cluttered) with local antiques and assorted memorabilia gathered by owner Rafael and innkeeper Susan Tettemer. Rooms are equipped with air conditioners or ceiling fans and are decorated around a theme, such as the Secret Garden, Shakespeare Room, or Cupid's Bower. Public areas include a plant-filled sun room and a television nook with books, periodicals, and games.

MODERATE

EVERMAY-ON-THE-DELAWARE, River Rd., Erwinna, PA 18920. Tel. 215/294-9100. Fax 215/294-8249. 16 rms, 1 carriage house suite. A/C TEL

$ Rates (including continental breakfast): $50–$70 single, $75–$135 double; $185 suite. MC, V. **Parking:** Free.

Set back on its 25 acres of river shoreline, this gracious three-story hotel was a popular resort from 1870 until the 1930s, frequented by such notables as the Barrymore family. Today, restored and rejuvenated, it is a country inn with the finest Victorian traditions and trappings (from marble fireplaces to a grand piano, chiming grandfather clocks, and brocade settees). All rooms have a private bath and antique furnishings from the Victorian era. Facilities include a dining room, but dinner is served on weekends only. Two-night minimum stay required on weekends. Innkeepers are Ron Strouse and Fred Cressan.

1740 HOUSE, River Rd. (Rte. 32), Lumberville, PA 18933. Tel. 215/297-5661. Fax 215/297-5663. 24 rms. A/C

$ Rates (including breakfast): $70–$90 single or double. **Parking:** Free.

Named for the year it was built, this hotel began with 5 bedrooms, but 16 more were added in the north and south wings by owner Harry Nessler in 1967. Today there are 24 guest rooms, most with private balconies or terraces facing the river. The decor is mostly Colonial, with touches of wicker and rattan. Amenities include a restaurant, a well-stocked library, a cozy living room with a wood-burning fireplace, a card room, an outdoor heated pool, and a brick-lined patio deck for relaxing by the river.

WHERE TO DINE

EXPENSIVE

BLACK BASS INN, 3774 River Rd., Lumberville. Tel. 297-5770.
Cuisine: INTERNATIONAL. **Reservations:** Required.

$ Prices: Appetizers $4.95–$8.95; main courses $15.95–$23.95; lunch $4.95–$11.95. AE, MC, V.

Open: Lunch Mon–Sat noon–3pm, dinner Mon–Sat 5:30–10pm and Sun 4:30–8:30pm; brunch Sun 11am–3pm.

An 18th-century atmosphere is the keynote of this riverside inn, established in 1745 and in the hands of the present owner, Herb Ward, since 1949. From the moment you step inside, you can feel the ambience of yesteryear—from the antique furniture and old lanterns to the solid pewter bar. Portraits of British monarchs adorn the walls of the public rooms, reminding visitors that the early owners remained loyal to the Crown. Meals are served in three different ground-level rooms and on a romantic, screened-in veranda that overlooks the Delaware. Entrées include rainbow trout stuffed with crab and wild rice; Muscovy duck Normandie; grilled paillard of veal, and turkey pot pie. The inn also has 7 rooms and 3 suites for overnight stays, although most do not have private bath.

CUTTALOSSA INN, River Rd., Lumberville. Tel. 297-5082.
Cuisine: INTERNATIONAL. **Reservations:** Recommended.

$ Prices: Appetizers $3.95–$9.95; main courses $16.95–$30; lunch $6–$13. AE, MC, V.

Open: Lunch Mon–Sat 11am–2pm; dinner Mon–Thurs 5–9pm, Fri–Sat 5–10pm.

★ It's hard to imagine a more idyllic setting for a restaurant than this location across the road from the river and next to a rippling waterfall. Originally built around 1750, this stone inn was a stopping point for stagecoaches and then a gristmill. Listed on the National Register of Historic Places, it has been masterfully transformed into a top-caliber indoor-outdoor restaurant. The old millworks now serve as an outdoor veranda, ideal for summer evenings. The inside rooms feature open fireplaces, tables made from old sewing-machine bases, and linens of Colonial raspberry and cranberry tones.

The menus change seasonally, but you can always count on creative cuisine and fresh ingredients. Lunch usually includes omelets, quiches, eggs Benedict, and hearty dishes like beef Stroganoff or spinach lasagne. The selections at dinner range from Pekingese-style duckling and surf-and-turf to veal Oscar and the house specialty of crab imperial with a sauce made from a century-old recipe. There is a pleasant blend of live background music every night.

4. WASHINGTON CROSSING AREA

A major happening in this area is the annual Christmas reenactment of George Washington's crossing of the Delaware, the Revolutionary War event that led to victory at the Battle of Trenton. The schedule actually begins in early December and continues throughout the month, with weekend tours, musical concerts, carol singing, and the lighting of a huge community Christmas tree at the intersection of Rtes. 32 and 532. Other activities include brass ensemble music, candlelight tours, and the illumination of the historic buildings. All the festivities culminate on December 25, with a riverbank parade and the casting off of the boats for "The Crossing." A complete program, as well as more information, is available from the **Washington Crossing Historic Park,** P.O. Box 103, Washington Crossing, PA 18977 (tel. 215/493-4076).

WHAT TO SEE & DO

★ Just a few miles south of New Hope begins the famous area known as **Washington Crossing Historic Park,** Rtes. 32 and 532 (tel. 493-4076), where General Washington regrouped his forces and in a blinding snowstorm made the famous crossing of the Delaware River to Trenton on December 25, 1776. Now a 500-acre park, this historic spot contains a Visitor Center and 13 buildings, including the **McConkey Ferry Inn** (1752), the site of the final meeting between General Washington and his staff before the crossing; an 18th-century farm and industrial complex; the 19th-century village of Taylorsville; and the Durham Boat Barn, which houses four replicas of the cargo boats used for the crossing. On the grounds, you can also explore a 100-acre wildflower preserve and Bowman's Hill, the memorial hilltop "lookout" during the American Revolution. The Visitor Center, which contains a huge painting of George Washington leading his men in the crossing of the Delaware, also offers a free half-hour movie presentation at 9am, 10:30am, noon, 1:30pm, and 3pm. Walking tours of the historic buildings begin promptly after each movie showing (fee for the tours is $2.50 for adults and $1 for youths over age 6; under age 6, free). Hours are Monday through Saturday from 9am to 5pm, and Sunday from noon to 5pm. The grounds are open daily from 9am to 8pm or sunset.

For a look at 17th-century life-style, be sure to visit **Pennsbury Manor,** 400 Pennsbury Memorial Rd., Morrisville (tel. 946-0400), the reconstructed plantation country home of William Penn. Built between 1683 and 1700, this historic site is a little off the beaten track, at the southernmost tip of the county, but it is sign-posted from Washington Crossing, about a half hour away. You can tour the manor home and also wander into the adjacent smokehouse and the bake and brew houses, as well as enjoy the garden and orchard setting. Open Tuesday through Saturday from 9am to 5pm, and on Sunday from noon to 5pm (the last tour is at 3:30pm). Admission charge is $4.00 for adults, $2 for children 5 to 17 years, and children under 5, free.

The **Newtown Historic District** is also worth a stroll. Founded in 1683, it was one of the earliest place names in the county and served as county seat from 1726 until 1813, and as an important supply depot during the Revolution. No less than 230 of Newtown's structures are listed on the National Register of Historic Places. Among the 18th- and 19th-century architectural gems to be seen are Court Inn (formerly the Half Moon Inn), dating from 1733, a furnished early tavern, and the Newtown Library Company, established in 1760.

SHOPPING

One of the unique shops in this area is **The Patriot,** Rte. 532, Washington Crossing Historic Park (tel. 493-5411). Built in 1820 as a general store, across the street from the McConkey Ferry Inn, this was the focal point of the Colonial village of Taylorsville. Today it is part snackshop and part souvenir emporium, with merchandise like handmade soap, baskets, candles, cast-iron toys, handcrafted brooms, country wood carvings, rag rugs, coonskin caps, arrowheads, and penny candy. Other food items include hot dogs and sausage sandwiches, chili, ice cream, and sodas. Open Monday through Saturday from 10am to 5pm and Sunday from 1 to 5pm, with extended hours in summer.

COOL FOR KIDS

Sesame Place, Oxford Valley Road, Langhorne (tel. 757-1100), is a seven-acre wonderpark designed for Sesame Street fans, as the perfect place to climb, float, glide, bounce, or slide. Amusements include over 40 play and water activities, computer games, and live entertainment by Big Bird, Bert, Ernie, and other favorites from the TV show. Open daily from 10am to 5pm from early May through mid-June and again for the first week of September; daily from 10am to 8pm from mid-June through the first week of July; daily from 9am to 8pm from the second week of July through the end of August; and on weekends only from mid-September to mid-October, 10am to 5pm. General admission charges are from $15.95 for adults; children 3 to 15 from $17.95; and children under 2 free.

WHERE TO STAY

MODERATE

BRICK HOTEL, State St. and Washington Ave., Newtown, PA 18940. Tel. 215/860-8313. 14 rms. A/C TV TEL
$ Rates: $95–$120 single or double. AE, CB, DC, MC, V. **Parking:** Free.

This gem of a hotel was built in 1764 and has been recently restored and renovated. Listed in the National Register of Historic Places, the inn was once owned by an aide to Napoleon Bonaparte, and it is said that George Washington entertained his troops here during the Revolution. The guest rooms are beautifully updated with private baths and furnished with antiques (such modern conveniences as TVs are discreetly hidden in old armoire chests). The rooms have shutter-style windows, canopy and four-poster beds, and hand-stenciled decorations on the walls.

Meals are served in a cozy Colonial-style dining room with a large open fireplace or on a glass-enclosed veranda with a wraparound porch.

ROYCE HOTEL, 400 Oxford Valley Rd., Langhorne, PA 19047. Tel. 215/547-4100 or toll-free 800/23-ROYCE. Fax 215/547-4100 ext 297. 168 rms. A/C TV TEL

$ Rates: $125–$135 single or double. AE, CB, DC, MC, V. **Parking:** Free.
This festive, modern, 14-story hotel opened in 1987. It is situated in the lower part of Bucks County, across the street from Sesame Place. The soundproof guest rooms have oversized beds, quilted fabrics, and pastel-toned furnishings; many rooms have extra sofa beds. Other facilities include a health club, swimming pool and sauna, a full-service restaurant, and a cocktail lounge with entertainment nightly.

BUDGET

COMFORT INN, 3660 Street Rd., Bensalem, PA 19020. Tel. 215/245-0100 or toll-free 800/458-6886. Fax 215/245-0100, ext 451. 141 rms. A/C TV TEL

$ Rates: $43–$58 single, $53–$68 double. AE, CB, DC, MC, V. **Parking:** Free.

For moderate lodgings in this part of the county, one of the best choices is this hotel, off I-95 about 20 miles from the Washington Crossing area and 5 miles from Sesame Place. It is a modern, four-story property with guest rooms furnished in a bright, contemporary style. Each room has either two double beds or a queen- or king-size bed, with contemporary pastel-toned furnishings. Facilities include a café, piano lounge, gift shop, and exercise room.

WHERE TO DINE
EXPENSIVE

YARDLEY INN, Afton and Delaware Aves., Yardley. Tel. 493-3800.
Cuisine: INTERNATIONAL. **Reservations:** Recommended. **Directions:** On River Road (Rte. 32) at junction of Rte. 332.
$ Prices: Appetizers $2.95–$8.95; main courses $11.95–$22.95; lunch $5.95–$10.95. AE, DC, MC, V.
Open: Lunch Mon–Fri 11:30am–2:30pm, Sun 11am–3pm; dinner Mon–Fri 5:30–10:30pm, Sat 5:30–11pm; Sun 5:30–8pm.

This restaurant, decorated with a contemporary design, has been open since 1952. Just across the road from the Delaware River, the inn offers lovely views from its enclosed porch and from its dining room windows. The creative menu features pastas, salads, burgers, and stir-fry dishes at lunch. Dinner features smoked roast duck, veal osso buco, cioppino, stuffed rainbow trout, chicken and rock shrimp scampi, and (on Fri. and Sat. nights) prime rib.

MODERATE

WASHINGTON CROSSING INN, Rtes. 32 and 532, Washington Cross-ing. Tel. 493-3634.
Cuisine: INTERNATIONAL. **Reservations:** Recommended. **Directions:** At intersection of Rtes. 32 and 532.
$ Prices: Appetizers $2.95–$5.95; main courses $10.95–$19.95; lunch $3.95–$6.95. MC, V.
Open: Lunch Wed–Sat 11:30am–3pm; dinner Wed–Sat 5–10pm, Sun 1–8pm.
Although this restaurant has operated for over 50 years, the building dates back to 1760, when it was erected by William Taylor and the surrounding townland was known as Taylorsville. Much of the early Colonial decor survives, including the original fireplace, hand-carved mantels, crystal chandeliers, brick floors, copper pots, and a mural of Bucks County in earlier times. Salads, sandwiches, and light fare are featured at lunchtime. Dinner features chicken Cordon Bleu, prime ribs, veal Oscar, a variety of seafood, and duckling flambé. Don't be surprised when you enter the reception area—you'll probably be greeted by the resident mascot, a talking parrot named Finbar.

CHAPTER 6

PENNSYLVANIA DUTCH COUNTRY

1. LANCASTER
- **WHAT'S SPECIAL ABOUT LANCASTER**

2. READING
- **WHAT'S SPECIAL ABOUT READING**

Two English county seats gave their names to Lancaster and Reading in the 18th century, but over the years these southeastern Pennsylvania cities have evolved into the core of "Pennsylvania Dutch" country.

Contrary to popular belief, this collective name does not mean that hordes of Dutch people have settled the land. "Pennsylvania Dutch," in fact, refers to German settlers, primarily immigrants of the Amish and Mennonite sects who came here to find religious freedom. In German, *Deutsch* actually means "German," and since these people called themselves and their language Deutsch, the English-speaking settlers in the area mistakenly labeled them the Pennsylvania "Dutch."

Rather than adapting to American ways, the original Pennsylvania Dutch people clung to their traditions and style of life, and their 20th-century ancestors carry on in the same manner, using horse-drawn buggies for transport and mule-powered machinery to farm the land. Today the simple life-styles and beliefs of these people are a source of curiosity for visitors. Perhaps that is why tourism generates over $300 million in revenues annually for Lancaster County alone.

---

1. LANCASTER

64 miles W of Philadelphia, 67 miles N of Baltimore,
106 miles N of Washington, D.C., 226 miles E of Pittsburgh

GETTING THERE   By Air   Lancaster Airport, Rte. 501 (tel. 569-1221), is 8 miles north of downtown. It is served by **Allegheny Commuter Airlines** (tel. 569-0461 or toll-free 800/428-4253).

By Train   More than a dozen trains a day stop at Lancaster on **Amtrak's** corridor between Harrisburg/Pittsburgh and Philadelphia/New York. The station is at the north end of the city, 53 McGovern Ave. at North Queen Street (tel. 291-5000 or toll-free 800/USA-RAIL).

By Bus   Greyhound/Trailways provides service into Lancaster with a terminal at 22 W. Clay St. (tel. 397-4861). Local bus services within Lancaster city and county are operated by the **Red Rose Transit Authority** (tel. 397-4246); the base fare is 80¢.

By Car   The Pennsylvania Turnpike cuts right through the northern end of Lancaster County; get off at exit 21 and drive south on Rte. 222 for 15 miles to get to Lancaster City. Rte. 30 also crosses through Lancaster city and county from east to

WHAT'S SPECIAL ABOUT LANCASTER

Ace Attractions
- ☐ The People's Place, a museum focusing on the Amish and Mennonite way of life.
- ☐ Wheatland, home of 15th U.S. President, James Buchanan.

Regional Food
- ☐ Lancaster Central Market, a haven for fruits and produce direct from Amish and Mennonite farms.

- ☐ Sturgis Pretzel Factory, America's oldest pretzel bakery.
- ☐ Groff's Farm, the benchmark of Pennsylvania Dutch cuisine

Shopping
- ☐ Quilts, on sale at Amish homes throughout the countryside.
- ☐ Adamstown, the antiques capital of the United States.

---

west. In addition, Lancaster is 30 miles from York, which is traversed by I-83 in a north-south direction.

SPECIAL EVENTS   One of the leading annual gatherings in this area is the **Pennsylvania Renaissance Faire,** held on 15 successive weekends from early July through mid-October at the Mount Hope Estate and Winery, Rte. 72 at exit 20 of the Pennsylvania Turnpike, 16 miles northeast of Lancaster. This is a re-creation of a 16th-century English village festival, with costumed lords and ladies, jesters, magicians, and minstrels, not to mention craft demonstrations, medieval jousting tournaments, a human chess match, continuous street theater, and food vendors. Hours are 11am to 6pm, and the admission charge is $12.95 for adults and $4 for children 5–11. For further information, contact the **Mount Hope Estate and Winery,** P.O. Box 685, Cornwall, PA 17016 (tel. 717/665-7021).

The name **Lancaster** refers to a city and a county, both synonymous with the heartland of Pennsylvania Dutch territory. Lancaster, the city (pop. 57,000), originally known as Hickory Towne, was basically an English settlement and is laid out according to a grid plan, with Penn Square at its center. It was the largest inland city in Colonial days, serving as the nation's capital for one day in September 1777.

When most people speak of Lancaster, however, they are usually referring to all of Lancaster County, the city plus its surrounding countryside. Mention Lancaster, and distinctive images come to mind: abundant and rich foods, fertile farms, stretches of land without an electric wire, colorful hex signs, barn raisings, and horse-drawn buggies clip-clopping on peaceful country roads. Most of all, we think of a group of gentle people who live in a world set apart, the Amish.

In addition to the Amish, Lancaster County has many other claims to fame. It was the home of the 15th president of the United States, James Buchanan, and of Robert Fulton. The Conestoga wagon originated here, as did the pretzel. You'll find the Moravian influence at Lititz; a Protestant cloister at Ephrata; the Scots-Irish legacy at Donegal Springs; and railroading relics at Strasburg. You can visit wineries, breweries, and hundreds of antique dealers.

Bordered on the west by the Susquehanna River, Lancaster County is relatively small in size (averaging 30 miles from east to west and 40 miles north to south). Within minutes of Lancaster city, you can enjoy charming country villages with names like Mount Joy, Paradise, Bird-in-Hand, White Horse, Peach Bottom, Smoketown, Spring Garden, and Intercourse. This latter town, once known as Cross Keys, is said to have been named for one of two reasons: it was an entrance to a horse-racing track and became known as "Entercourse," or because two major throughways intersected here and an "Intercourse" sprang up.

THE PEOPLE

The Amish first came to Pennsylvania in the late 1720s and to Lancaster County in the 1760s. Historically, the Amish are part of the Anabaptist family, tracing their origin to Zurich, Switzerland, in 1525. Many of these people were first called Mennonites after Menno Simons, an influential leader and writer who joined the Anabaptists in 1536. In the 1600s, a man named Jacob Ammann differed with the Mennonites on some issues and formed a separate group of worshippers. These people thereafter became known as the Amish.

Both the Amish and the Mennonites suffered much persecution in their homelands of Switzerland, Germany, and France, and were happy to accept William Penn's invitation to come to a mecca of religious freedom. Lancaster County's streams and fertile soils closely resembled their native Rhineland, and these immigrants easily adapted to their new home.

Today there are several branches of Amish and Mennonite sects within the county. But the strictest group, the Old Order Amish, arouses the greatest curiosity for visitors. They drive gray horse-drawn carriages, use mules or horses to pull farm equipment in the fields, opt for diesel or gasoline for power rather than electricity, hold worship services in their homes, have their own one-room schools, and speak the Pennsylvania Dutch dialect. Amish men wear dark suits, straight-cut coats with no lapels, black footwear, and black or straw broad-brimmed hats. Adult married men let their beards grow but do not wear mustaches. Amish women wear modest dresses of solid-colored fabric, with cape and apron, full skirt, and long sleeves. They have long hair and wear a head covering or bonnet.

Lancaster County's Amish population is approximately 16,000 and ever growing. Large numbers of children are considered desirable, and the average family is 7, but 10 or more offspring are not uncommon. Most of the Amish farms are located in the eastern part of Lancaster County, and, as you drive along the country roads, you can see the farmers at work in their fields or the women displaying their quilts for sale. If you have a camera, you'll be tempted to take a photograph, but that is the one thing the Amish ask that you refrain from doing. They follow the Biblical command that exhorts against "graven images," so please bear this in mind.

ORIENTATION
AREA CODE

The majority of telephone numbers in Lancaster County belong to the 717 area code. However, a few numbers in the northern section of the county (around Adamstown) are part of the 215 area code. Assume that a 717 code is applicable, unless we indicate otherwise.

INFORMATION

For all types of information on this area, contact the **Pennsylvania Dutch Convention and Visitors Bureau,** 501 Greenfield Rd., Lancaster, PA 17601 (tel. 717/299-8901, or toll-free 800/735-2629 for free map and visitor's guide). If you are visiting in person, it is located off Rte. 30 (the Greenfield Rd. exit), 3 miles east of downtown Lancaster, and is open daily except Thanksgiving, Christmas, and New Year's Day. Hours are 9am to 5pm, with extended hours from May through October.

Staffed by helpful, knowledgeable travel advisers, this is one of the busiest tourist offices we've ever seen, with walls of informative displays and racks of brochures, and ample browsing space for all comers. This office publishes an extremely useful map and a detailed visitor's guide.

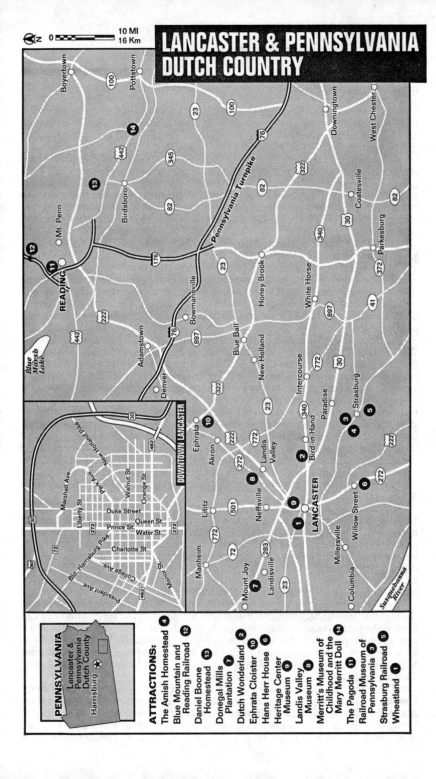

LEARNING ABOUT LANCASTER

When you arrive and look over the huge map guide produced by the tourist office, you may be overwhelmed by all there is to see and do. Where to start is a good question.

Perhaps you should drive along Rte. 30 east of Lancaster (also known locally as Lincoln Hwy. East) and be dazzled by the various interpretations of the Pennsylvania Dutch life-style; or you can head south on Rte. 896 to the railroad enclave of Strasburg or east on Rte. 340 to the farmlands of Bird-in-Hand and Intercourse, or maybe west on Rte. 283 to Mount Joy.

You could spend a month or two here and still not see everything. In many ways, seeing everything is really not as important as gaining some understanding of the gentle people who reside in this fertile farmland county along the Susquehanna. Happily, there are a number of ways in which visitors can gain an insight into the Amish and Mennonite way of life. No one source will make you an instant expert, but each of the centers described below makes a valuable contribution toward enriching your trip.

The People's Place, Main St. (Rte. 340), Intercourse (tel. 768-7171), is a people-to-people interpretation center, specializing in the story of Amish, Mennonite, and Hutterite people. The focal point is a life-style museum called Amish World, which offers insight into the aspects of the Amish culture so different from the experiences of most visitors: their modes of transportation, dress, energy, schools, sense of time, growing old, peace, and mutual aid. The admission charge is $2.50 for adults and $1.25 for children, including a magnificent display of Pennsylvania Dutch art.

For those who prefer audiovisual impact, a three-screen, 25-minute documentary, *Who Are the Amish?* illustrates the Amish way of life from birth to barn raising. This program is shown continuously from 9:30am to 5pm daily except Sundays. Admission is $2.50 for adults and $1.25 for children, and reduced-rate combination packages are available if you wish to explore the museum and see the audiovisual.

In addition, from April through October, the center also shows the full-length feature film *Hazel's People,* set in a Mennonite community and starring Geraldine Page and Pat Hingle. The movie is scheduled for each evening, Monday through Saturday, at 6 and 8pm and costs $4 for adults and $2 for children. Other facilities in this building include a courtyard gallery with art exhibits and a book and craft shop featuring Amish and Mennonite literature and work. The helpful staff will also answer individual questions. The People's Place is open daily year round except Sunday, from 9:30am to 9:30pm during April through October, and from 9:30am to 4:30pm the rest of the year.

A similar service is provided by the **Mennonite Information Center,** 2209 Millstream Rd., Lancaster (tel. 299-0954), located off Rte. 30, about 4 miles east of downtown. This simple brick building is a welcome center staffed by Mennonites who provide general brochures on the Pennsylvania Dutch country, sightseeing guidance, assistance in locating accommodations, and explanations as to the similarities and differences between the Amish and Mennonites. There are also displays on the beliefs and life-styles of the Mennonite people and a film, *A Morning Song,* shown every half hour (no charge, but a donation is welcome).

You can also tour the adjacent religious museum, which houses a reproduction of the Hebrew Tabernacle (admission charge is $3 for adults and $2 for children 7 to 12). One of the best services provided by this center is a guided tour whereby one of the staff will go in your car and guide you through the area, with relevant explanations of local life-styles. The tours require a minimum booking of two hours and cost from $20 per car. The center is open Monday through Saturday, from 9am to 4pm (except Thanksgiving Day, Christmas Day, and New Year's Day).

"There Is a Season" is a 14-minute, multi-image orientation presentation about Lancaster County, shown continuously at the information center of the **Pennsylvania Dutch Convention and Visitors Bureau,** 501 Greenfield Rd., Lancaster (tel. 299-8901). The aim of this show is to illustrate the Amish culture and life-style, as well as to give an overview of Lancaster County activities, events, and history. It will help you to decide where to go and what to see during your visit. Admission charge is $2 for adults and $1 for children 12 and under.

GETTING AROUND

Lancaster is both a city and a county. The city itself is ideal for walking tours and casual strolls. When most folks refer to touring "Lancaster Pennsylvania Dutch Country," however, they usually mean the county and the surrounding countryside with its myriad attractions and rural farmlands. The ideal way to see the county is by car; if you can't bring your own, we'll list a few rental agencies. If you prefer not to drive at all, don't despair, because there are a number of other ways to get around.

BY CAR

The following companies have autos for rent: **Avis,** 825 East Chestnut St. (tel. 397-1497); **Budget,** 1208 Manheim Pike, also known as Route 72 (tel. 392-4228); and **National,** Liberty Street and Lititz Pike (tel. 394-2158). Desks are also maintained at Lancaster Airport by Avis (tel. 569-4345) and Hertz (tel. 569-2331).

BY TAXI

If you need a taxi, call **Yellow Cab** (tel. 397-8108), or **Neff Taxi** (tel. 393-2222).

WHAT TO SEE & DO

As you drive along Lincoln Hwy. (Rte. 30) east of Lancaster, you will see a parade of billboards announcing an array of attractions. These sites are designed to show the workings of Amish life—from prototype Amish homesteads and villages to a wax-museum portrayal of Lancaster County heritage. Although each claims to be authentic and unique, you'll find that there is a lot of duplication, and one or two of these attractions will prove more than enough. Better still, get off Rte. 30 and drive along the back roads, such as Rtes. 772 and 340. Go into the towns, such as Intercourse, Bird-in-Hand, and Paradise, to see the Amish people at work and as they travel about in their distinctive buggies.

THE AMISH HOMESTEAD, 2034 Lincoln Hwy. East, Lancaster. Tel. 392-0832.

Of the attractions that purport to present a close-up look at the Amish life-style, this one is the most authentic—an occupied 71-acre Amish farm, dating back to 1744, and partially open for touring. It's situated 3 miles east of downtown Lancaster, on Rte. 462. Accompanied by a knowledgeable guide, visitors are walked through the main buildings and grounds, including the barns, and learn about various aspects of the Amish work ethic, mode of dress, customs, and traditions.

Admission: $4 adults; $2 children 6 and older; children under 6 free.
Open: Daily 9am–5pm.

HANS HERR HOUSE, 1849 Hans Herr Dr., Willow Street. Tel. 464-4438.

A good place to start a tour of the Lancaster area is this house, built by the Herr family in 1719, and now the oldest structure in Lancaster County, restored to its original medieval Germanic facade and full of authentic furnishings and farm implements. Listed in the National Register of Historic Places, it is also one of the oldest Mennonite meeting houses in America, constructed when the Lancaster area was still considered a wilderness. Other sights on the grounds include a blacksmith shop, a garden, an orchard, and a visitors' center.

Admission: $3 adults, $1 children 7–12.

Open: Apr–Dec Mon–Sat 9am–4pm. **Closed:** Thanksgiving Day and Christmas Day.

WHEATLAND, 1120 Marietta Ave., Lancaster. Tel. 392-8721.

⭐ This is the home of the only man from Pennsylvania to become president of the United States, James Buchanan. Built in 1828, it was purchased by our 15th chief executive in 1848 and used as a country estate and campaign headquarters. Federal in style, the house is listed on the National Register of Historic Places and is a showcase of American Empire and Victorian furnishings, grained woodwork, marble and slate mantels, and columned front and rear porticoes. The house, which sits on a four-acre estate, also contains many of Buchanan's personal belongings. Tours are given from 10am to 5pm, with the last tour at 4:15pm.

Admission: $4 adults, $3.25 students 12–17, $1.75 children 6–11, children under 6 free.

Open: Apr–Nov daily 10am–5pm. **Closed:** Thanksgiving Day.

LANDIS VALLEY MUSEUM, 2451 Kissel Hill Rd., Lancaster. Tel. 569-0401.

⭐ Located off Rte. 272, this museum is devoted to Pennsylvania German rural life. The complex includes a Victorian crossroads village, a steam engine building, a firehouse, a country store, a blacksmith shop, a seamstress house, a pottery shop, a print shop, a harness shop, spinning and weaving centers, and a tavern, as well as farmsteads. A Conestoga wagon, with its bonnetlike canopy, also sits on the grounds, as a tribute to Lancaster County craftspeople who originated this form of transportation. Throughout the complex, during May to October, there are demonstrations of crafts, skills, and occupations, reflecting rural life and folk culture. Guided tours are also available from November to April.

Admission: May–Oct $6 adults, $5 seniors, $4 children 6–17; Nov–Apr $5 adults, $4 seniors, $3 children 6–17; children under 6 free.

Open: Tues–Sat 9am–4:30pm, Sun noon–4:30pm.

EPHRATA CLOISTER, 632 W. Main St., Ephrata. Tel. 733-6600.

⭐ This is an 18th-century German Protestant monastic settlement, known for its original religious choral music, and for its printing and publishing achievements. It lies north of Lancaster, between Rte. 272 and Rte. 222. Visitors can tour 10 of the original buildings, which have been restored and interpreted to re-create the atmosphere of this communal village.

Admission: $4 adults, $2 youths 6–17, children under 6 free.

Open: Mon–Sat 9am–5pm, Sun noon–5pm, except major holidays.

DONEGAL MILLS PLANTATION, Trout Run Rd., Mount Joy. Tel. 653-2168.

Lancaster's Scots-Irish influence is the cornerstone of this site, an authentic historic landmark listed in the National Register and deeded by Thomas Penn in 1736. The property, southwest of Mount Joy, off Rte. 772 and Musser Rd., includes an original gristmill dating back to 1830, a working bake house, a miller's house and a stately 1870s mansion. There is also a German four-square garden and an herbal garden used for medicine and dyeing from earliest days. Tours are conducted on weekends from noon to 6pm, as baking, spinning, and weaving demonstrations are given.

Admission: $3 adults, $1.50 children 12 and under.

RAILROAD MUSEUM OF PENNSYLVANIA, Rte. 741, Strasburg. Tel. 687-8628.

The history and technology of trains is the focus of this museum. From the earliest steam engines to 20th-century innovations, you'll see a collection of locomotives, cars, artifacts, and related railroad memorabilia. This museum also provides the opportunity for visitors to enter the cab of a steam locomotive, view the stateroom of a private car, or examine the interior of a Pullman sleeper.

Admission: $5 adults, $3 youths aged 6–17, children under 6 free.
Open: Mon–Sat 9am–5pm, Sun noon–5pm. **Closed:** Mon in Nov–Apr; major holidays.

STRASBURG RAIL ROAD, Rte. 741, Strasburg. Tel. 687-7522.

★ After you've seen all the train workings at the Railroad Museum, you'll want to hop aboard this train for a scenic ride through Pennsylvania Dutch country. This is America's oldest short-line railroad, operating since 1832. This 45-minute round-trip takes you from Lancaster to Paradise via a coal-burning steam locomotive. You'll have a choice of a standard enclosed car; open-air observation deck seating, ideal for picture taking; or a first-class parlor car with beverage and food service.

Admission: Standard train car, $5.50 adults, $3 children 3–11; observation car, $6.50 adults, $4 children 3–11; parlor car $8 adults, $5 children 3–11.
Open: Daily March–Nov 10am–5pm; some weekends in winter—schedule varies, check in advance.

HERITAGE CENTER MUSEUM, 13 W. King St., Lancaster. Tel. 299-6440.

This museum is housed in the Old City Hall and the adjoining Masonic Lodge building, both dating back to the mid-1790s. Aiming to depict the art and craftsmanship of early Lancaster County, the museum offers an orderly collection of room settings, clocks, quilts, silver, pewter, copperware, prints, homemade toys, weathervanes, and other folk art.

Admission: Free.
Open: Late April through Nov, Tues–Sat 10am–4pm.

COOL FOR KIDS

Although all of Lancaster County is appealing to children, young visitors are particularly drawn to the fairy-tale-castle facade of **Dutch Wonderland,** 2249 Lincoln Hwy. East, Lancaster (tel. 291-1888), located about 4 miles east of downtown on Rte. 30. Set on 44 landscaped acres, this is a family fun park with a water slide, a miniature railroad, a riverboat, bumper cars, and shows. Open from Easter weekend through Labor Day from 10am to 6pm Monday through Saturday, and from noon to 6pm on Sunday (with slightly longer hours in June, July, and August); also open on weekends during September and October. Admission charge ranges from $10 to $14.50, depending on whether you select a package with five rides or unlimited rides. Children under 3 admitted at no charge.

TOURING AND TASTING

With its fertile farmlands and long-standing traditions of bountiful harvests, it is not surprising that Lancaster County is a great source for locally produced food and drink, from cheeses and baked goods to candy treats, as well as wine and whiskey. Here are some suggestions to whet your appetite.

Established in 1884, **Wilbur's Chocolate Company,** 46 N. Broad St., Lititz (tel. 626-0967), produces 75 million pounds of chocolate a year. Through a window, you can watch as hand-dipped chocolate candies are made, and then taste a sample in the factory outlet store. In addition, you can tour the Candy Americana Museum, a unique display of early candy-making equipment, as well as containers, tins, and chocolate pots, many of which date back to the 1700s. Hours are Monday through Saturday from 10am to 5pm, and admission is free.

Two local enterprises, specializing in making Swiss cheese, invite visitors to learn about the cheese-making process and to enjoy free samples. They are **Phillips Lancaster County Swiss Cheese,** 433 Centerville Rd., off Rte. 772, Gordonville (tel. 354-4424), and **Lengacher's Cheese House,** 5015 Lincoln Hwy. East, Kinzers (tel. 442-4388). Both are open Monday through Friday from 8am to 5pm, and Saturday from 8 or 9am to 3 or 5pm.

Lancaster County is also the home of America's oldest pretzel bakery, the **Julius**

Sturgis Pretzel House, 219 East Main St., Lititz (tel. 626-4354). This bakery dates from 1784, although the first pretzels weren't made here until 1861. Visitors can tour the 200-year-old bakery and the modern plant. Open Monday through Saturday, from 9am to 5pm. Admission is $1 per person.

For the best in Amish and Mennonite baked goods, visit the **Bird-in-Hand Bake Shop,** 542 Gibbons Rd., Bird-in-Hand (tel. 656-7947). You'll find a wide assortment of shoofly pies, breads, fruit pies, cakes, cinnamon rolls, and other treats. Open Monday through Saturday, 9am to 5pm except January through March.

WINERIES

NISSLEY WINERY, Wickersham Rd., Bainbridge. Tel. 426-3514.
Established in 1976, this family-run enterprise, off Rte. 441, is nestled on a 300-acre farm estate amid 52 acres of vineyards. Located in the western part of the county, near the banks of the Susquehanna River, the winery produces over 50,000 bottles a year. Visitors can use picnic tables on the farm grounds. Tours last a half hour.
Admission: $2 adults and children over 12 (children under 12 free).
Open: Mon–Sat noon–5pm, Sun 1–4pm. **Closed:** Easter, Thanksgiving Day, Christmas Day, and New Year's Day.

LANCASTER COUNTY WINERY, Rawlinsville Rd., Willow Street. Tel. 464-3555.
Tours and tastings are provided at this small winery, off Rte. 272, owned and operated by the Dickel family since 1972. Tastings are available at no charge to visitors over 21. Tours are conducted at 11am, noon, 1, 2, and 3pm, except Sunday.
Admission: $2.
Open: Mon–Sat 10am–4pm, Sun 1–4pm. **Closed:** Jan, Feb–Mar Wed and Sun; major holidays.

MOUNT HOPE ESTATE AND WINERY, Rte. 72, Manheim. Tel. 665-7021.
You won't actually see the workings of this winery, but if you visit you can sample the products and take a tour of the 1800 mansion of Henry Bates Grubb, one of America's wealthiest ironmasters. Listed on the National Register of Historic Places, this 32-room sandstone house (about 1 mile south of exit 20 off I-76/Pennsylvania Turnpike), resembles a feudal English manor with castle walls and turrets, but it is furnished in a Victorian theme. The interior includes a winding walnut staircase, hand-painted 18-foot ceilings, Egyptian marble fireplaces, and a greenhouse with solarium.
Admission: $4 adults, $1.50 children over 6.
Open: Mon–Sat 10am–6pm, Sun 11am–6pm (closes 5pm in the winter).

TWIN BROOK WINERY, 5697 Strasburg Rd., Rte. 2, Box 2376, Gap. Tel. 442-4915.
Producing hybrid and vinifera wines, this winery is housed in a barn on a 40-acre farm, once the centerpiece of a large tract of land granted to the religious Society of Friends nearly 300 years ago by William Penn's brother. Visitors can tour the modern wine laboratory, temperature-controlled tank storage facilities, barrel-aging cellar, and bottling rooms. The winery is located 18 miles east of Lancaster, off Rte. 30 and Swan Road.
Admission: Free.
Open: Tues–Fri 11am–7pm, Sat 10am–7pm, Sun 10am–6pm. Tours Sat–Sun or by appointment.

ORGANIZED TOURS

BUS TOURS   A good way to get your bearings is to take a guided tour. **Amish Country Tours,** Rte. 340 at North Harvest Road, Bird-in-Hand (tel. 392-8622), offers escorted 4-hour bus tours of the Amish farmland, with departures at 9am and 1pm, Monday through Saturday. The price is $17.95 for adults and $4.95 for children 4 to 14. A shorter, 2-hour itinerary is also available, departing at 10am and 2pm Monday through Saturday, and priced at $9.95 for adults and $4.95 for children 4 to 14. In addition, this company features a 3-hour "Sunday Sampler" tour, departing at noon, priced at $13.95 for adults and $4.95 for children 4 to 14. Most tours include admission to the Mill Bridge Village and an Amish buggy ride.

WALKING TOURS   If you are interested primarily in the downtown area, you can avail yourself of a 90-minute **Historic Lancaster Walking Tour.** Led by Colonially attired guides, these jaunts begin at the **Historic Lancaster office** at 100 South Queen St. (tel. 392-1776) and explore courtyards, churches, the farmers' market, and other sites. Tours depart April through October, Monday through Friday, at 10am and 1:30pm; Saturday at 10 and 11am and 1:30pm; Sunday and holidays at 1:30pm. During June through August, there is also a 6:30pm twilight tour on Monday. The cost is $4 per person.

HORSE-AND-BUGGY RIDES   If you'd like to be driven around the countryside via the local Amish mode of transport, then you'll enjoy **Ed's Buggy Rides,** Route 896, Strasburg (tel. 687-0360). Based 1½ miles south of Rte. 30, Ed and his crew will show you 3 miles of Amish farmlands from a horse-drawn open wagon or a traditional closed carriage. The cost is $6 for adults and $3 for children; rides are available all year from 9am to 5pm (in the winter months, sleighs are often substituted for wagons). If you are in the area of Rte. 340, there is also **Abe's Buggy Rides,** 2596 Old Philadelphia Pike (tel. 392-1794). Situated 1 mile west of Bird-in-Hand, Abe offers a 2-mile tour through Amish country in an Amish family carriage, priced at $10 for adults and $5 for children. This facility is also open all year, from 9am to 5pm, except Sunday. No reservations are required for either Ed's or Abe's rides.

BICYCLE TOURS   **Lancaster Bicycle Touring, Inc.,** 3 Colt Ridge Lane, Strasburg (tel. 786-4492 or 394-8475), rents bicycles by the day, starting at $15, and also organizes guided bicycle tours of the Strasburg, Lititz, and Ephrata areas. Prices range from $35 to $50 for a 1-day excursion to $180 for a 2-day or $270 for a 3-day trip. The last two options include accommodations at bed-and-breakfast inns. Advance reservations are required for all of the tours.

AIRPLANE TOURS   See the Lancaster countryside from the cockpit of a small plane via **Glick Aviation,** Smoketown Airport, Airport Dr., Smoketown (tel. 394-6476). Located off Rte. 340, between Bird-in-Hand and Lancaster, this company will fly you over 20 miles of the Pennsylvania Dutch countryside from June through October, daily from 9am to 5pm, at a cost of $15 for adults and $10 for children aged 8 and under. There is a minimum booking of two adults, and cameras are welcome. Credit cards accepted: MC and V.

WHERE TO STAY

Lancaster County has hundreds of hotels, motels, and country inns, in all price ranges. We'll describe a blend of new and old properties, starting with those easily accessible to the downtown Lancaster area. The prices quoted are summer rates, so bear in mind that you can save up to 30% to 50% by traveling at off-peak times of the year. The accommodations listed are in the moderate or budget category.

DOWNTOWN LANCASTER & ENVIRONS

BRUNSWICK HOTEL, Chestnut and Queen Sts., P.O. Box 749, Lancaster, PA 17603. Tel. 717/397-4801 or toll-free 800/233-0182. Fax 717/397-4991. 225 rms. A/C TV TEL
$ Rates: $57–$62 single, $62–$72 double. AE, CB, DC, MC, V. **Parking:** Free.
If you want to be right in the center of town, this is the best choice. Built on a site that

has been home to seven different hotels or inns since 1776, this 10-story modern contemporary structure, formerly a Hilton, is less than 20 years old. Amenities include an indoor pool and a fitness center.

Facilities include the Copper Kettle for light meals and Bernhardt's (named after Sarah Bernhardt, who performed in the Fulton Opera House in 1911) for full-service dining.

THE GARDENS OF EDEN, 1894 Eden Rd., Lancaster, PA 17601. Tel. 717/393-5179. 2 rms, 1 suite, guest cottages. A/C **Directions:** From Lancaster, take Rte. 30 to Rte. 23 east. Follow Rte. 23 to traffic light in Eden, turn right (Eden Rd.) and make another right before the bridge at yellow-brick pumping station.

$ Rates (including continental breakfast): $50–$65 room, $85 suite. MC, V. **Parking:** Free.

Although there are many bed-and-breakfast homes in Lancaster County, this brick Victorian stands out. Built in 1848 by a wealthy ironmaster, it sits on some 3 acres of residential property overlooking the Conestoga River. The grounds are full of herb gardens, 50 varieties of wildflowers, beds of perennials, woodsy trails, and scores of songbirds. Today it is the home of Marilyn and Bill Ebel, who have decorated the interior with antique furniture, including four-poster beds and sleigh beds, local artwork, homemade coverlets, and floral arrangements and wreaths made by Marilyn.

There are two guest rooms on the second floor with shared bath, and one suite with private bath. The adjoining guest cottage, once a summer kitchen, has a loft bedroom with private bath and a ground-floor kitchenette/sitting area, and is available for extended-stay rentals. Be sure to visit Marilyn's basement workshop, where she displays and sells her dried floral creations and crafts of other local artisans. Rooms are available by advance reservation only.

OLDE HICKORY INN, 2363 Oregon Pike, Lancaster, PA 17601. Tel. 717/569-0477 or toll-free 800/255-6859. Fax 717/569-6479. 65 rms, 18 suites. A/C TV TEL.

$ Rates: $75 single or double, $75–$95 suite. AE, CB, DC, MC, V. **Parking:** Free. This rambling modern inn is situated on 116 acres along Rte. 272. Surrounded by Amish farmsteads and directly across from the Landis Valley Museum, it offers rooms decorated with Amish farm prints, country-quilt bedspreads, and muted floral tones. Some rooms surround the inner courtyard, others feature front and back window doors, and many have balconies. The **Village Square,** a complex of shops, is adjacent to the hotel. Facilities include a restaurant, lounge, outdoor swimming pool, eight indoor tennis courts, four racquetball courts, exercise-weight room, sauna, and 9-hole golf course.

QUALITY INN SHERWOOD KNOLL, 500 Centerville Rd., Lancaster, PA 17601. Tel. 717/898-2431 or toll-free 800/228-5151. Fax 717/898-2431. 167 rms. A/C TV TEL

$ Rates: $49–$71 single, $49–$81 double. AE, CB, DC, MC, V. **Parking:** Free. Set on a grassy and wooded hillside, this three-story modern Colonial-style hotel, 5 miles west of downtown between Rte. 30 and Rte. 23, has a bright country decor and a choice of a king, queen, or two double beds. There is an outdoor swimming pool. A full-service restaurant, the Sherwood Knoll, features American and Pennsylvania Dutch specialties, and Quarters, the lounge, offers evening entertainment.

ACCOMMODATIONS WEST AND NORTH OF LANCASTER

CAMERON ESTATE INN, Donegal Springs Rd., R.D. 1, Box 305, Mount Joy, PA 17552. Tel. 717/653-1773. Fax 717/653-9432. 18 rms (16 with bath). A/C **Directions:** 15 miles west of Lancaster, off Route 743.

$ Rates (including continental breakfast): $60–$110 single or double. AE, D, MC, V. **Parking:** Free.

⭐ A country road through secluded farmland will lead you to this three-story Federal house listed on the National Register of Historic Places. The rural manor has been graciously transformed into an elegant inn by Abe and Betty Groff, who have also earned a reputation for their Groff's Farm Restaurant (see "Where to Dine," below). Each room is named after a historical figure and is furnished in a distinctive style, with antiques, brass beds, four-posters, Amish quilts, and plants; seven rooms have fireplaces. The grounds include a swimming pool, tennis court, 15 acres of lawns, hiking trails, and a trout-stocked stream. There is also a full-service restaurant on the premises. A golf course is slated to open in mid-1992.

GUESTHOUSE AT DONECKERS, 318–324 N. State St., Ephrata, PA 17522. Tel. 717/733-8696. Fax 717/733-4248. 15 rms, 4 suites. A/C TEL
$ Rates (including continental breakfast): $54–$140 single, $59–$115 double, $135–$145 suite. AE, CB, DC, DISC, MC, V. **Parking:** Free.
This inn is nestled in a quiet section of one of Lancaster County's most historic towns. Opened in 1984, the property is a combination of three turn-of-the-century homes, restored and connected as one inn. Each room is individually decorated with antique furnishings, folk art, and hand-cut stenciling, as well as a choice of queen-size, double, or twin beds. Some rooms also offer a private balcony, ground-floor access, private entrance, kitchenette, fireplace, or Jacuzzi bath.

Alternatively, the Doneckers enterprise recently added a fourth lodging choice two blocks away, **The 1777 House,** 301 West Main St., Ephrata, PA 17522 (tel. 717/733-8696). Dating from the 18th century, this antique-filled home offers accommodations with similar amenities and rates, with an additional 10 rooms and suites.

HISTORIC GENERAL SUTTER INN, 14 E. Main St., Lititz, PA 17543. Tel. 717/626-2115. 12 rms (all with bath). TV TEL
$ Rates: $70–$90 single or double. AE, MC, V. **Parking:** Free.
Originally known as the Sign of the Anchor, the General Sutter is located in the heart of this Moravian town. Rooms are furnished with an eclectic medley of Victorian and antique country pieces. An outdoor tree-lined brick patio overlooks the town square.

Guest facilities include a coffee shop, a lounge, and the Zum Anker Dining Room, a festive old-world enclave of cranberry walls, gas lights, and antique accessories.

ACCOMMODATIONS EAST AND SOUTH OF LANCASTER

BEST WESTERN INTERCOURSE VILLAGE MOTOR INN, Rtes. 340 and 772, Intercourse, PA 17534. Tel. 717/768-3636. or toll-free 800/528-1234. Fax 717/768-7622. 40 rms. A/C TV TEL
$ Rates: $59–$89 single or double. AE, CB, DC, MC, V. **Parking:** Free.
One of the best places to see the Amish buggies rolling by is this inn within walking distance of all the local village attractions. Designed in a country barn motif, this two-story motel offers guest rooms with a country inn decor and two double beds or one queen- or king-size bed. Facilities include a gift shop, game room, ample parking, and a small family-style restaurant serving inexpensive Amish-style meals.

FULTON STEAMBOAT INN, P.O. Box 333, Strasburg, PA 17579. Tel. 717/299-9999 or toll-free 800/922-9099. Fax 717/299-9992. 96 rooms. A/C TV TEL
$ Rates: $39–$99 single or double. AE, MC, V. **Parking:** Free.
"Sleep on a steamboat" is the motto of this unique lodging facility, located not on a river but right in the middle of Pennsylvania Dutch farm country, at the junction of Rte. 30 and Rte. 856. Named for Robert Fulton, the Lancaster County–born inventor of the steamboat, this four-story inn aims to provide a nautical experience—the exterior and interior aim to duplicate the look and feel of a steamboat.

Rooms vary according to floor, but all offer private bath, microwave oven, and refrigerator. The fourth floor or uppermost level rooms, designated as "staterooms," are the largest and most luxurious, with private outside decks, sofas or rocking chairs, choice of king- or queen-size beds, and whirlpool bath. Rooms on the third level have queen-size beds, decks, and sitting areas. The second floor offers rooms called "cabins," with the most ship-style decor (appealing particularly to youngsters), including both bunk-style and queen-size beds. The ground floor has meeting rooms and public areas, including the Clermont Café, a restaurant with a nautical theme, enclosed swimming pool, whirlpool, exercise room, gift shop, game room, and guest laundry.

GREYSTONE MANOR BED-AND-BREAKFAST, 2658 Old Philadelphia Pike, P.O. Box 270, Bird-in-Hand, PA 17505. Tel. 717/393-4233. 13 rooms, 6 suites (all with bath). A/C TV
$ Rates (including continental breakfast): $46–$62 single or double; $54–$84 suites. MC, V. **Parking:** Free.

This restored French Victorian mansion and carriage house is perched on a hill on two acres of lawns and trees. Dating from 1883, this stately old house offers rooms with an individual decor. Highlights include stained-glass windows, cut-crystal doors, and antique bath fixtures. The lobby is a showcase of Victorian leaded and beveled glass doors and plaster-cast wall and ceiling sculptures; the carriage house was originally a barn and was converted into five sleeping rooms in 1970. Ground-floor accommodations are available, and there is a quilt shop on the premises.

HERSHEY FARM MOTOR INN, Rte. 896, P.O. BOX 89, Strasburg, PA 17579. Tel. 717/687-8635. 59 rms, 3 suites. A/C TV TEL
$ Rates: $54–$84 single, $59–$89 double, $89–$109 suite. DISC, MC, V. **Parking:** Free.

This inn is not connected to the famous chocolate resort or enterprises; it's the private endeavor of local resident Ed Hershey. Set amid 17 acres of pastureland, this unique property is laid out like a farm, with a main house, a barn, and a new two-story brick addition. Thirty-two rooms in the new building are designated for nonsmokers. Each room offers a king-size bed or two double beds; some rooms also have a private patio and refrigerator. Rates include breakfast (except on Sunday).

Facilities include an outdoor swimming pool (open late May to early September), and a unique restaurant that features three types of cuisine (family-style, Pennsylvania Dutch smörgåsbord, and an à la carte menu). There is also an on-premises bake shop, where you can buy everything from 15 kinds of fudge and candies to cookbooks.

HISTORIC STRASBURG INN, Rte. 896, Strasburg, PA 17579. Tel. 717/687-7691 or toll-free 800/872-0201. Fax 717/687-6098. 103 rms. A/C TV TEL
$ Rates: $85 single or double (including breakfast). AE, CB, DC, MC, V. **Parking:** Free.

This inn on a 58-acre site surrounded by farmlands is ideal for people who like the charm of the past without sacrificing any 20th-century comforts. Laid out like an 18th-century village, the lodging offers rooms in five separate buildings clustered around a central courtyard. You might be assigned a room in the carpenter's house or the bishop's house, with the decor depending on the house's theme; all units feature Colonial print wallpaper and modern bathroom with double vanity. The complex also offers rented bicycles, quaint country shops, and a swimming pool. Dining facilities include the Washington House Restaurant and By George's Tavern.

STRASBURG VILLAGE INN, 1 W. Main St., Strasburg, PA 17579. Tel. 717/687-0900. 11 rms (all with bath). A/C TV
$ Rates (including breakfast): $69–$99 single or double. AE, MC, V. **Parking:** Free.

Originally known as the Thomas Crawford Tavern, this restored two-story brick building and adjacent warehouse date back to 1788. Situated on the main thoroughfare of Strasburg, it is now a fully renovated B&B with Colonially decorated rooms, all of varying sizes and details. The rooms feature one or two double beds or a queen-size bed; some have canopies or four-posters, private porches, or Jacuzzi. Open all year, the inn is next to the Strasburg Country Store and Creamery, where overnight guests may avail themselves of a complimentary continental breakfast in the deli/ice-cream shop.

YOUR PLACE COUNTRY INN, 2133 Lincoln Hwy. East, Lancaster, PA 17602. Tel. 717/393-3413. Fax 717/393-2889. 79 rms. A/C TV TEL.
$ Rates (including continental breakfast): $39–$89 single or double. AE, DISC, MC, V. **Parking:** Free.

Even though this new two-story inn is on the busy Rte. 30 corridor, it is set back in a relatively quiet location, and is distinguished from the other basic motels of the area because of its charming country decor—most of the furniture is handmade by local Amish craftspeople. Each guest room has an array of bright country colors, pine furniture, wood carvings, braided rugs, wreaths and dried flowers, and live plants, with two queen-size beds and a modern bathroom. Some ground-floor rooms have a veranda with rockers. Facilities include an outdoor swimming pool and an adjacent restaurant and lounge.

HARVEST DRIVE FARM MOTEL, 3370 Harvest Dr., P.O. Box 498, Intercourse, PA 17534. Tel. 717/768-7186 or toll-free 800/233-0176. 50 rms. A/C TV TEL
$ Rates: $57 single and $62 double. AE, MC, V. **Parking:** Free.

Set on a quiet country road (Clearview) off the beaten track, this motel is surrounded by Amish farmlands, yet is just a mile south of the popular village attractions. The modern two-story property offers guest rooms with 1, 2, or 3 double beds. The grounds include a craft center, gift shops, bicycle rentals, and a restaurant serving inexpensive family-style meals daily from 7am to 8pm.

RED CABOOSE MOTEL, Paradise Lane, P.O. Box 102, Strasburg, PA 17579. Tel. 717/687-6646. 39 rms (all with bath). A/C TV
$ Rates: $49.95–$69.95 single or double. AE, DISC, MC, V. **Parking:** Free.
Children of all ages love this lodging facility made entirely of converted train cabooses. This inn sits among cornfields and horse farms, by the tracks of the Old Strasburg Railroad, so you can often hear the whistles toot or watch the trains chug by in the surrounding countryside. Each unit has been refitted to include private baths, double beds, and TVs built into the pot-bellied stoves. Family units with one double bed and four bunk beds are available for $65 and up. For $15 extra a night, you can also rent an "efficiency caboose" with stove and refrigerator. The complex includes a dining car serving food all day (primarily in the budget bracket), and an old-fashioned ice-cream parlor car.

WHERE TO DINE

Nowhere in the mid-Atlantic states is there such a variety of restaurants as you will find in Lancaster County. From haute cuisine to hearty home-cooked helpings, the food here is an attraction in itself.

Pennsylvania Dutch cooking is world famous—from heaping trays of fried chicken, and hickory-smoked ham, served with garden vegetables, to shoofly pie, raspberry tarts, and homemade ice cream. One meal might keep you fueled for a whole day. Most restaurants serving this food operate on the "family-style" format, which means you sit at large tables with other guests and share huge platters of food, constantly replenished by gracious local staff.

Many of these places do not serve liquor, beer, or wine, although some allow you to bring your own. These restaurants are geared to families and often close by 8 or 9pm. Above all, they are great value—entire dinners from soup to salad to desserts for an average of $10 to $15 per person for adults and half-price for children. In this genre, you will also find some "buffet"-style restaurants that allow you to select whatever you wish—be it one, two, or 22 items—and then sit at individual tables.

Lancaster is also home to a host of very fine à la carte restaurants and country inns that can hold their own among top gourmet spots of the world. In addition, some kitchens offer a blend of Pennsylvania Dutch dishes and other all-American entrées.

You'll probably want to sample a few different types of restaurants, so we'll give you full selections.

DINING IN LANCASTER CITY & ENVIRONS
Expensive

WINDOWS ON STEINMAN PARK, 16–18 W. King St., Lancaster. Tel. 295-1316.
  Cuisine: INTERNATIONAL. **Reservations:** Recommended.
$ Prices: $6.95–$12.95; main courses $17.95–$26.95; lunch $6.95–$9.95. AE, MC, V.
  Open: Lunch Mon–Fri 11:30am–2:30pm; dinner Sun–Thurs 5:30–10pm, Fri–Sat 5:30–11pm; brunch Sun 11:30am–3pm.

Located in the heart of downtown, this gourmet enclave offers a tasteful decor of gleaming crystal chandeliers, wall mirrors, and huge bouquets of fresh flowers; a well-versed pianist adds to the genial atmosphere. The interior is laid out on three levels, and edged by three-story-tall bay windows that overlook cascading waterfalls and fountains. Complimentary parking is provided at the Central Parking Garage, West Vine Street, for patrons. Gentlemen are requested to wear jackets for dinner.

Lunch features light entrées, sandwiches, quiches, and salads, but dinner is the time to splurge and sample the expertise of chef Thomas Carter. Start with some imported Irish smoked salmon or perhaps escargot, brie in pastry, or stuffed mushrooms. Main courses include Dover sole, chicken breast stuffed with lobster and shrimp, stuffed quail, duckling with raspberry sauce, rack of lamb, and Chateaubriand.

Moderate

MARKET FARE, 25 W. King St., Lancaster. Tel. 299-7090,
  Cuisine: INTERNATIONAL. **Reservations:** Recommended.
$ Prices: Appetizers $4.25–$6.75; main courses $10.95–$23.95; lunch $4.75–$8.95. AE, CB, DC, MC, V.
  Open: Lunch Mon–Sat 11am–2:30pm; dinner Tues–Sat 5:30–10pm, Sun–Mon 5:30–9pm.

Housed in a restored 1910 building (originally a department store), it conveys the flavor of old Lancaster with its decor of exposed brick walls, 19th-century oil paintings, shelves of library books, and cushioned armchairs. There are two levels, with a café upstairs for a light breakfast or quick lunch, and the main dining room on the lower level. Dinner entrées include marinated and charbroiled sirloin of beef, surf-n-turf, roast duck, sautéed veal and chicken, and a creative variety of pastas. Soups are a special treat here and the "soup sampler" allows you to try two or three (such as chicken curry or seafood Champagne soups), served in demitasse cups.

OLDE GREENFIELD INN, 595 Greenfield Rd., Lancaster. Tel. 393-0668.
  Cuisine: INTERNATIONAL. **Reservations:** Recommended.
$ Prices: Appetizers $2.95–$6.95; main courses $10.95–$21.95; lunch $4.95–$9.95. AE, CB, DC, MC, V.
  Open: Sat–Sun breakfast 8–11:30am; lunch Tues–Fri 11:30am–2pm; dinner Tues–Sat 5:30–10pm; brunch Sun 11:30am–2pm.

You can dine in an 1820 farm atmosphere and still enjoy innovative 20th-century cuisine at this restaurant on Rte. 30, about 3 miles east of downtown. Adjacent to the visitors' information bureau, the restaurant was established in 1979 and features a decor of country-cupboard-style furnishings amid the original stone walls and beams of an authentic farmhouse.

Lunch includes seafood omelets, chicken and cashew salad, angel hair neptune salad, and savory sandwiches. Dinner features sweet-and-sour walnut shrimp, veal sesame, chicken and scallops à l'orange, roast duckling, vegetable and seafood pastas, and steaks. There is an extensive vintage wine list.

DINING AROUND THE COUNTY—WEST & NORTH
Expensive

BLACK ANGUS STEAK HOUSE, Rte. 272, Adamstown. Tel. 215/484-4385.
Cuisine: INTERNATIONAL. **Reservations:** Recommended.
$ Prices: Appetizers $2.95–$8.95; main courses $9.95–$25.95. AE, CB, DC, MC, V.
Open: Dinner Mon–Sat 5–11pm; Sun noon–9pm.

Aficionados of prime beef sing the praises of Ed Stoudt's restaurant, situated about 20 miles north of Lancaster city. Since 1962, this restaurant has concentrated on serving the best of beef in a Victorian setting, enhanced by chandeliers, antiques, fine art, and conversation pieces such as a 1928 Packard in the foyer. The menu features various cuts of steaks served with locally grown mushrooms, prime ribs cut to order, and a selection of seafood and German-Austrian dishes. There is a good raw bar, and a wine cellar featuring over 70 domestic and imported wines.

RESTAURANT AT DONECKERS, 333 N. State St., Ephrata. Tel. 738-2421.
Cuisine: FRENCH **Reservations:** Recommended.
$ Prices: Appetizers $3.75–$9.95; main courses $17.95–$24.95; lunch $6.95–$12.95. AE, CB, DC, MC, V.
Open: Thurs–Sat, Mon–Tues lunch 11am–2:30pm, dinner 5:30–10pm; brunch Sun 11:30am–3pm. Also light fare daily (except Wed and Sun) 2:30–4pm.

★ Innovative French cuisine is featured at this restaurant owned by the Donecker family and located northeast of Lancaster off Rte. 272. Part of a complex that includes a first-rate guesthouse, there is also a group of fashionable clothing shops. The six dining areas each offer a distinctive decor and ambience. The ground floor exudes a country flavor with antique furnishings, Bavarian porcelain, and an open-hearth fireplace, while the upper level is a bright and airy garden setting with skylights, plants, and patio furniture.

Lunch includes puff pastry dishes, pastas, and quiches, as well as burgers and salads. Dinner is a celebration of chef Jean-Maurice Juge's French flair with such dishes as salmon stuffed with bay scallops and herb mousse; rack of lamb roasted with mustard and rosemary; and roasted Cornish hen with Belgian endive and Virginia ham. Main courses include a spinach, green, or orange and almond salad, and assorted fresh vegetables. There is also an extensive wine cellar.

THE LOG CABIN, 11 Lehoy Forest Dr., Leola. Tel. 626-1181.
Cuisine: AMERICAN. **Reservations:** Recommended.
$ Prices: Appetizers $4–$7; main courses $15–$30. AE, CB, DC, MC, V.
Open: Dinner Mon–Sat 5–10pm, Sun 4–9pm.

★ This restaurant, off Rte. 272, is not on the beaten track, but it is certainly worth seeking out. Nestled in the secluded woodsy setting of the Lehoy Forest, beyond the Rose Hill Covered Bridge, it has been an area landmark since 1933, when it started as a speakeasy. It has expanded to seven dining rooms. The old-world decor is rich in polished logs, beamed ceilings, and fireplaces, with local memorabilia, including wagon wheels, and a unique gallery of 18th- and 19th-century paintings.

The menu is not extensive or complicated, but what is offered is hard to equal in quality of ingredients and preparation, from charbroiled sirloin steaks and double-cut lamb chops to lobster tails and roast Long Island duck.

Moderate

CATACOMBS RESTAURANT AT BUBE'S BREWERY, 102 N. Market St., Mount Joy. Tel. 653-2056.
Cuisine: AMERICAN. **Reservations:** Required.
$ Prices: Appetizers $2.95–$6.95; main courses $14.95–$19.95. AE, D, MC, V.
Open: Dinner Mon–Fri 5:30–9pm; Fri–Sat 5–10pm; Sun 5:30–9pm.

Catacombs is one of three restaurants at Bube's Brewery, a spot originally built in the

1800's to brew beer by German immigrant Alois Bube. Now a national historic landmark, it flourished in the 19th century, during Lancaster County's heyday as the "Munich of the New World" before Prohibition. Today Bube's claims to be the only surviving U.S. brewery still intact. It is a wonderland of old casks, stone walls, and brewing implements, and the catacombs area includes the aging cellars of the brewery, 43 feet underground. The staff, dressed in medieval costume, give you a minitour en route to your table in the stone-lined vaults of the catacombs. The menu includes seafood, steaks, duckling, and veal al limone. If you prefer to dine above ground, there is also a Victorian-style restaurant called **Alois** (tel. 653-2057), and a tavern with outdoor patio known as the **Bottling Works** (tel. 653-2160). The former features nouvelle American cuisine in the moderate-to-expensive range, while the latter is more of a snackery in the moderate-to-budget category; both serve dinner. The Bottling Works also offers light lunches.

GROFF'S FARM, Pinkerton Rd., Mount Joy. Tel. 653-2048.
   Cuisine: AMERICAN. **Reservations:** required for dinner only.
$ **Prices:** Appetizers $1.50–$3.50; main courses $12.75–$15.75 à la carte, or $13.50–$23.50 for a variety of main courses served family style; lunch $5–$8. DISC, MC, V.
   Open: Lunch Tues–Sat 11:30am–1:30pm; dinner Tues–Fri 5pm and 7:30pm, Sat 5pm and 8pm.

With praises from the late James Beard and Craig Claiborne, the benchmark of home-style cuisine is this restaurant, a 1756 farmhouse and the former home of Abe and Betty Groff. Surrounded by fertile fields and a new golf course (set to open in 1992), this charming setting started as an outgrowth of the Groff's Mennonite hospitality to visitors and grew with the years. Guests so loved Betty's dishes that they often flooded her with recipe requests; after answering hundreds of letters, she eventually wrote several cookbooks, among them *Country Goodness* and *Pennsylvania Dutch Cookbook*.

Dinner here is either family style or on an à la carte basis. If served family style, you select one entrée or a combination of entrées per table. Featured dishes include chicken Stolzfus, hickory-smoked ham, and seafood. The entrée price covers soup, fruit salad, vegetables, potatoes, homemade sweet and sour relishes, and dessert. The à la carte menu features individual portions of many of the family-style items or such entrées as crab-stuffed flounder, lobster tails, and steaks. Lunch features a similar à la carte menu. Wine and spirits are available.

Budget

ZINN'S DINER, Rte. 272, Denver. Tel. 215/267-2210.
   Cuisine: AMERICAN. **Reservations:** Not accepted.
$ **Prices:** Appetizers $.95–$5.50; main courses $4.95–$10.95. No credit cards.
   Open: Daily breakfast 6–11:30am; dinner 10:30am–10pm.

In the upper section of the county near the Pennsylvania Turnpike is this diner, 19 miles north of Lancaster. Operated by the Zinn family since 1950, this busy restaurant offers individualized table service. The dinner menu is with entrées, an appetizer, and two vegetables. The choices range from Pennsylvania Dutch specialties to seafood, steaks, turkey, veal, and vegetarian platters. The 32-acre Zinn complex also features an arcade, a candy outlet, a snack bar, miniature golf, and a picnic area.

DINING AROUND THE COUNTY—EAST & SOUTH

Expensive

REVERE TAVERN, 3063 Lincoln Hwy. East, Paradise. Tel. 687-8601.
   Cuisine: AMERICAN. **Reservations:** Recommended.
$ **Prices:** Appetizers $2.95–$6.95; main courses $8.95–$26.95. AE, CB, DC, DISC, MC, V.
   Open: Dinner Mon–Thurs 5–10pm, Fri–Sat 5–11pm, Sun 4–9pm.

This two-story stone building that dates back to 1740 and was once a stagecoach tavern known as the Sign of the Spread Eagle. In 1841 it was converted into a pastoral residence for the Rev. Edward Buchanan and his wife Eliza, sister of Stephen Foster, who also visited and wrote some of his music here. The house was purchased in 1854 by the pastor's brother, James Buchanan, 15th president of the United States, and, thanks to a careful restoration, it has returned to its original use as a tavern.

In the evening, the restaurant features candlelit dinners in a relaxed Colonial setting, with steaks, lobster tails, yellow-tailed flounder, Pennsylvania rainbow trout, crab au gratin, and hickory-cured ham. All main courses are accompanied by two vegetables.

Moderate

GOOD 'N PLENTY, E. Brook Rd., Rte. 896, Smoketown. Tel. 394-7111.
   Cuisine: AMERICAN. **Reservations:** Not Accepted.
   $ Prices: Fixed-price $12.90 adults, $4.95 children. No credit cards.
   Open: Feb to mid-Dec, Mon–Sat 11:30am–8pm.
A classic example of Pennsylvania Dutch–style service is this eatery, originally an Amish house built in 1871, and now a restaurant that can seat up to 650 people. As you enter, you pay the fixed price and then are seated with other guests at tables set for ten or more. It's a nice way to get to know folks from other places and to share travel experiences. The staff then starts with soup or salad and continues to bring large trays of food throughout the meal. Never worry that a platter will be empty when it gets to you, as another round will always be close behind.

You can try some of everything of just pick and choose your favorites—the assortment usually includes pork and sauerkraut, ham, roast beef, crispy fried chicken, rich creamed chicken, mashed potatoes, noodles, homemade breads, apple butter, shoofly pie, raspberry pie, ice creams, and much more, depending on what's in season.

MILLER'S SMORGASBORD, 2811 Lincoln Hwy. East, Ronks. Tel. 687-6621.
   Cuisine: AMERICAN. **Reservations:** Not required, but accepted for dinner.
   $ Prices: Fixed-price breakfast $8.50 adults, $4.25 children; dinner $16.75 adults, $5.45–$8.75 children. AE, MC, V.
   Open: Breakfast Nov–May, Sat–Sun 7am–11am; June–Oct, daily 7am–11am; dinner Mon–Sun noon–8pm. **Closed:** Christmas Eve and Christmas Day.

If you prefer to get up and select your own food, then this restaurant is designed for you. Located 7 miles east of Lancaster, this Colonial-style restaurant has an open hearth, and a tiered layout with private-table seating. The Pennsylvania dutch buffet table usually includes steamed shrimp, roast beef, honey-glazed ham, salads, vegetables, and desserts ranging from shoofly pie to almond meringue cake and cheesecakes.

Budget

STOLTZFUS FARM RESTAURANT, Rte. 772, Intercourse. Tel. 768-8156.
   Cuisine: AMERICAN. Reservations: Not required.
   $ Prices: Fixed price $11.95 adults, $5.95 children aged 4–10. MC, V.
   Open: Weekends Apr and Nov 11:30am–8pm; Mon–Sat May–Oct 11:30am–8pm.
Homemade sausage and meat from an on-premise butcher shop are the feature at this restaurant. The menu is also likely to include ham loaf, chicken, chow chow, pepper cabbage, and shoofly and cherry crumb pies.

SHADY MAPLE SMORGASBORD, Springville Rd. and Main St. (Rte. 23), East Earl. Tel. 354-8222.
   Cuisine: PENNSYLVANIA DUTCH. **Reservations:** Required only for groups.

$ Prices: Breakfast $4.99; lunch $6.99; dinner $7.99–$9.99. AE, MC, V.
Open: Mon–Sat breakfast 5–10am; lunch 10:45am–4pm; dinner 4–8pm.

Of the many all-you-can-eat style restaurants, this one is a favorite with the folks who actually live in Lancaster County—because of the quality and quantity of the food offered, and the hard-to-beat prices. Lunch or dinner buffets present Pennsylvania Dutch smörgasbords featuring a 140-foot-long food buffet of at least eight meats and 14 vegetables, 46 salad items, three soups, eight breads, four cheeses, ten cold and three hot desserts, six cakes, a sundae bar, and a variety of nonalcoholic beverages.

Dinner price depends on the featured item of the evening, which can range from steak and prime rib to seafood or grilled chicken. On the lower level, there is also a fast-food restaurant with a taco, salad, potato, and pasta bar, and a gift shop. It's a little off the beaten track, but well worth the trip, for value and variety.

SHOPPING

ARTWORKS AT DONECKERS, 100 N. State St., Ephrata. Tel. 733-7900.

Housed in a former 1920s shoe factory, this is a showplace and selling place for over 50 working artists and craftspersons. There are four floors of studios and galleries, with displays of paintings, fine art photography, wildlife art, quilts, Amish reproduction furniture, and Mennonite art, as well as demonstrations of porcelain-painting, pottery-making, wood carving, basket-weaving, jewelry-designing, glass-painting, metal sculpture work, printmaking, and much more.

Open: Mon–Tues and Thurs–Fri 11:45am–5pm, Sat 10am–5pm, Sun noon–4pm.

DOUBLE HEART GALLERY, 3449-A Old Philadelphia Pike (Main St.), Intercourse. Tel. 768-3522.

Although the works of over 20 Amish and Mennonite artists from Lancaster County are featured here, the focus is on the watercolors of self-taught artist Susie Riehl, an Old Order Amish farm wife from the nearby village of White Horse. Her paintings of colorful quilts in scenic farmyard surroundings seem to encapsulate the essence of Amish country life. Other wares on sale here include hand-braided rugs, limited edition prints, note cards, postcards, and the photographs of Shirley Wenger, who is also the proprietor of the shop.

Open: Mon–Sat 10am–5pm.

JACOB ZOOK SHOP, Rte. 30, Paradise. Tel. 687-6333.

This shop is one of the best sources for the colorful hex signs that decorate the barns and buildings of the surrounding Pennsylvania Dutch countryside. The owner of the shop, Jacob Zook, began making these signs in 1942, later authored a book on hexology, and is now recognized as one of the leading designers of this local art. Over the years, his signs have been requested by people from all 50 states, presidents, a king, a major league baseball team, and the U.S. Navy. The good-luck signs are the most popular, but Jacob stocks at least 28 original designs and other traditional symbols, as well as various local crafts.

Open: Mon–Sat 9am–6pm, Sun noon–5pm.

KITCHEN KETTLE VILLAGE, Newport Rd. (Rte. 772), Intercourse. Tel. 768-8261.

This complex of workshops was started in 1954, when Bob and Pat Burnley started making jams in their own kitchen, and it has since grown into a cluster of 30 small food and craft enterprises in a brick-lined courtyard. Today you can still see jam-in-the-making, as well as baking, fudge-making, and much more. Browse, sample, and shop in a delightful mini-village atmosphere.

Open: Mon–Sat 9am–5:30pm.

LANCASTER CENTRAL MARKET, Penn Square, Lancaster. Tel. 291-4739.

Continuously operating since the mid-1700s and fully restored in 1976, this is one of the oldest covered markets in the United States and a shopping landmark of the downtown area. It's the ideal venue to see the people and the products of this fertile county, as local Amish and Mennonite farmers bring their vegetables and fruits to this emporium. Stroll the aisles and you'll see (and smell) everything from fudge to fish, sausage to spices, preserves to pretzels, and candies to cheese. This is also a good spot to purchase handmade crafts and homemade pies and cakes.
Open: Tues and Fri 6am–4:30pm, Sat 6am–2pm.

THE OLD CANDLE BARN, Main St., Intercourse. Tel. 768-3231.

Housed in a converted Amish-style barn, this is a candle outlet store, with many irregular specimens marked at half price. Visitors are also invited to step downstairs and watch Amish craftsmen and -women at work as they hand-dip wax to make the colorful candles of all sizes, shapes, and scents. Other gift items are on sale here, from wooden crafts to bonnets and pillows, plaques, and note cards; the premises also provide a firsthand look at quilting in its quilt room.
Open: Mon–Sat 9am–5pm.

THE OLD COUNTRY STORE, Main St., Intercourse. Tel. 768-7101.

Affiliated with the People's Place educational/visitor center, this enterprise is stocked with the work of more than 450 local craftspeople, ranging from quilts, afghans, and patchwork pillows, to stuffed animals, dolls, tablecloths, potholders, sunbonnets, and wooden toys. There is also a separate Quilt Museum on the second floor.
Open: Mon–Wed and Sat 9am–5pm, Thurs and Fri 9am–9pm.

RENNIGER'S ANTIQUE MARKET, Rte. 272, Adamstown. Tel. 215/267-2177.

Antique hunters flock to this northern corner of Lancaster County, which becomes the antiques capital of the United States every weekend. Approximately 1,000 dealers display their vintage wares, both indoors and outside. And if you can't find what you want here, there are other smaller markets nearby.
Open: Daily 8am–5pm.

STRASBURG COUNTRY STORE AND CREAMERY, 1 W. Main St., Strasburg. Tel. 687-0766.

For a real 19th-century shopping experience, step into this little store, with its 1890s marble soda fountain, old-time cigar-store Indian statue, potbellied stove, and walls of antique shelves loaded with handcrafts, folk art, stenciling supplies, kitchen utensils, and herbal products. You'll find tasty treats from yesteryear, ranging from penny candy and fireballs to spice drops and cinnamon hearts. All the ice cream is made on the premises and scooped into handmade waffle cones. The adjacent Yule Shop offers a wondrous variety of Christmas ornaments and decorations.
Open: Mon–Sat 8am–6pm.

TIN BIN, 20 Valley Rd., Neffsville. Tel. 569-6210.

If you admire the electric candles in the windows of Lancaster County homes, this is a good spot to buy a few. The shelves are lined with reproductions of 18th-century candle holders, lighting devices, lanterns, and chandeliers, as well as country crafts, Amish dolls, tin figures, Amish prints, cross-stitch work, scents, pottery, fraktur work, wood carvings, toleware, and original art.
Open: Mon–Tues and Thurs–Sat 10am–5pm, Wed 10am–8pm.

WITMER QUILT SHOP, 1070 W. Main St., New Holland. Tel. 656-3411.

Although there are many signs announcing "quilts for sale" in the Lancaster County countryside, this 30-year-old home/shop is hard to match. It is run by Emma Witmer who sells her own designs and the work of more than 50 local Amish quilters.
Open: Mon–Sat 8am–6pm.

EVENING ENTERTAINMENT

True to the Pennsylvania Dutch family farming traditions, activities in this area start early and finish fairly early in the evening. You'll find that many of the restaurants, particularly the family-style places, close at 8 or 9pm. The haute cuisine restaurants, however, like Windows on Steinman Park or Doneckers, stay open later and often feature live music. The larger hotels and motor inns, such as the Quality Inn Sherwood Knoll, Olde Hickory, or Brunswick, also maintain late dining hours (until 9pm on weekdays and 10 or 11pm on weekends) and offer nightly music or entertainment.

In addition, Lancaster is home to one of our nation's oldest theaters in continuous operation (since 1852), the **Fulton Opera House,** 12 N. Prince St., Lancaster (tel. 397-7425). Named for inventor Robert Fulton, who was born in this county, over the years this theater has hosted such greats as Mark Twain, the Barrymores, Sarah Bernhardt, and George M. Cohan. Beautifully restored, it is an attraction in itself with its elaborate Victorian facade, gilt and scarlet decor, and intricately detailed baroque boxes. Today it is a showcase for drama, music, opera, dance, and special events, including the area's only professional regional theater company. The box office is open Monday through Saturday from 11am to 6pm, and on Sundays from one hour before a performance. Tickets are priced from $10 to $25, depending on the event. The curtain is usually at 8pm, Tuesday through Sunday.

The newest addition to the area's year-round entertainment scene is the **Dutch Apple Dinner Theatre,** 510 Centerville Rd., Lancaster (tel. 898-1900), 5 miles west of the city center, off Rte. 30 and next to the Quality Inn Sherwood Knoll. This is a professional company presenting musicals and comedies, ranging from "Cats" to "A Chorus Line," "Hello, Dolly," and "42nd Street." Admission charges range from $21 to $27 for adults and $14 to $16 for children under 12, including a complete buffet dinner. The meal starts at 6pm for evening performances, Tuesday through Saturday, and at 11:45am for afternoon matinees on Wednesday, Thursday, Saturday, and Sunday. Tickets to the show only can also be purchased for $15.

---

2. READING

32 miles NE of Lancaster City,
57 miles NW of Philadelphia, 57 miles E of Harrisburg

GETTING THERE By Air Two miles northwest of the downtown area on Rte. 183 is Reading Regional Airport, Bernville Road (tel. 372-4666), which handles regularly scheduled flights from Philadelphia, Pittsburgh, and Newark via **U.S./Air Express** (tel. 375-8488 or toll-free 800/428-4322), or **United Express** (tel. 372-2272 or toll-free 800/241-6522).

By Bus Bus service into Reading is operated by **Bieber Tourways,** which maintains a depot at 3rd and Court Streets (tel. 374-7700) and **Capital Trailways,** 3rd and Penn Avenues (tel. 374-3182 or toll-free 800/444-2877). Local transport within the city and county is provided by the **Berks Area Transportation Authority,** otherwise known as **BARTA** (tel. 921-0601); the base fare is 75¢.

By Car Reading is reached by many roads. It is 12 miles north of the Pennsylvania Turnpike, using exit 21 from the west and then via Rte. 222 north into Reading; or using exit 22 from the east and then north via Rte. 176. The city can also be reached via I-78 to exit 10 and then south for 15 miles via Rte. 61. Rte. 222 also traverses Reading in a north-south direction and Rte. 422 crosses through the city from east to west.

ESSENTIALS Area Code All telephone numbers in the Reading and Berks County area are part of the 215 area code.

INFORMATION For maps and travel data about Reading, outlet shopping, and other attractions of the area, contact the **Berks County Visitors Information**

WHAT'S SPECIAL ABOUT READING

Ace Attractions

- ☐ Penn Square, the focal point of the city, originally laid out in 1748 by two of William Penn's sons.
- ☐ Daniel Boone Homestead, birthplace of the famous frontiersman.
- ☐ Blue Mountain and Reading Railroad, a steam-era locomotive and sightseeing train.
- ☐ The Pagoda, a Japanese-style tower overlooking the city.
- ☐ Stokesay Castle, replica of a 13th-century English castle, with turrets and towers, now a restaurant.

Shopping

- ☐ VF Factory Outlet Complex, 40 outlet stores in eight buildings.
- ☐ Reading Outlet Center, over 70 stores in seven buildings.
- ☐ Manufacturers' Outlet Mall, a suburban complex with 70 outlets.

Association, Sheraton Berkshire, VF Factory Outlet Complex, Park Road and Hill Avenue, P.O. Box 6677, Reading, PA 19610 (tel. 215/375-4085 or toll-free 800/443-6610). The Association office is open from 9am to 5pm Monday through Friday, and also on Saturday and Sunday from June through December.

CITY LAYOUT The downtown area, which is centered at Penn Square, is easily explored on foot and some of the major outlets are within ten blocks of the main thoroughfare, Penn Avenue. Other groups of outlets are clustered north of the downtown area (around Heisters Lane) and just west of downtown and over the Schuylkill River in an area known as Wyomissing. A good number of hotels and restaurants and the tourist information office are also located on the western side of the river. To see them all, you'll need a car or taxi transport.

SPECIAL EVENTS Ever since 1950, one of the leading gatherings in this area has been the **Kutztown Folk Festival,** held in late June–early July at the Kutztown Fairgrounds, about 15 miles northeast of Reading on Rte. 222. Each year more than 100,000 people come to share in this 9-day celebration of the Pennsylvania Dutch traditions, lore, and folkways. Activities include square dancing, sheepshearing, glassblowing, hex-sign painting, coppersmithing, ox roasting, soap making, kite making, and quilting. In addition, there are demonstrations of fraktur, the Pennsylvania Dutch style of artful writing; herb and dried flower work, and portrait painting. Sights include an Amish wedding enactment, antique shows, and crafts galore. A daylight gathering, hours are 9am to 5pm, with activities until 7pm each day. Admission charge is $7 for adults and $3 for children under 12; parking is $2 per car. For further information, contact the **Kutztown Folk Festival,** 461 Vine Lane, Kutztown, PA 19530 (tel. 215/683-8707).

Much of the Pennsylvania Dutch influence that permeates Lancaster County is shared by neighboring Berks County and its chief city of Reading. But as most Reading-bound travelers will tell you, the colorful hex signs and farming traditions of yesteryear take a back seat to a strictly 20th-century lure—outlet shopping. Yes, mention Reading to almost anyone in the mid-Atlantic region and their eyes light up and say "bargains."

Reading is home to more than 250 outlet stores, from fashions to furniture, cosmetics to china, linens to leather, shoes to silver, and toys to tableware (and that's just for starters!).

The outlet method of merchandising began in the factories and mills of Reading in the 1960s when manufacturers sold overruns and seconds to employees. In time, friends and neighbors of employees wanted to be included in the rock-bottom prices.

Small stores sprang up inside the factories, and thus a new type of shopping was born and Reading became the outlet capital of the world.

There is, of course, more to Reading than outlets. Rimmed by the Blue Mountains and nestled along the banks of the Schuylkill River, Reading has a proud history, starting with the fact that Daniel Boone was born here.

A BIT OF HISTORY

Reading is directly associated with William Penn. Two of Penn's sons, Thomas and Richard, settled here in 1748 and laid out the city, naming it after their ancestral home in England. The area that they designated as the center of the town, or Market Square, is still the focal point of the city, although it is now known as Penn Square. In the 19th and early 20th centuries, Reading was a railroading and industrial center; the products manufactured here ranged from pretzels and cigars to pipe organs and bicycles.

Today, in addition to the outlets, Reading (pop. 78,300) is also synonymous with mushrooms. The surrounding Berks County countryside is a prime mushroom-growing land, so you'll find that mushroom dishes are featured prominently on restaurant menus of the region.

GETTING AROUND

BY CAR

Three companies have rental desks at the airport: **Avis** (tel. 372-6636); **Hertz** (tel. 374-1448); and **National** (tel. 376-3235). In addition, **Budget** offers three rental bases in the area, at 815 Lancaster Ave. (tel. 775-4888); 3728 Pottsville Pike (tel. 921-1444); and 601 Penn Square Center (tel. 372-2888). **Dollar** is located at 2526 Centre Ave. (tel. 921-9121).

BY TAXI

If you need a cab, call **Reading Metro Taxi** (tel. 374-5111 or 374-3113).

WHAT TO SEE & DO

The downtown core of Reading is **Penn Square,** originally named Market Square, the area laid out by William Penn's sons in 1748. Reading's first courthouse was located here, as were the city's original farmers' markets and commercial buildings. It was later a setting for Victorian storefronts, many of which remain today. The square is now the center of Reading's historic district, which extends along 5th Street (originally named "Callowhill" after Penn's second wife) from Buttonwood Street south to Laurel Street. A self-guided walking-tour folder of this entire district is available free from the Berks County Visitors Information Association.

THE PAGODA, Duryea Dr. and Skyline Blvd. Tel. 372-0553.
Panoramic views of Reading and the entire Schuylkill Valley can be seen from this seven-story Japanese-style tower located on top of Mt. Penn. Listed in the National Register of Historic Places, the 610-foot pagoda was built of red brick and tile in 1908 by local businessman William Witman and is reputed to be the only Japanese pagoda east of California. The interior includes a 1739 temple bell from Obama, Japan, and an observation deck, while the grounds boast a collection of Japanese cherry trees, a bonsai island, an Oriental bridge, and a gazebo.
   Admission: 25¢.
   Open: Daily summer 11am–9pm; off-season noon–9pm.

BLUE MOUNTAIN AND READING RAILROAD, Rte. 61, South Hamburg. Tel. 562-4083.

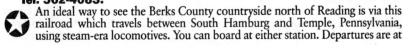

   An ideal way to see the Berks County countryside north of Reading is via this railroad which travels between South Hamburg and Temple, Pennsylvania, using steam-era locomotives. You can board at either station. Departures are at noon, 2pm, and 4pm from South Hamburg, which is located on Rte. 61, one mile south of exit 9A off I-78; or at 1 and 3pm from Temple Station on Tuckerton Road, 2½ miles north of Reading Bypass, off Rte. 61. Each trip, which is 26 miles long and lasts an hour and a half, has a live narration en route.

Admission: $7 adults, $6 seniors, $5 children 3–12.
Open: May–June and Sept–Oct weekends; June–Aug daily.

DANIEL BOONE HOMESTEAD, Daniel Boone Rd., Birdsboro. Tel. 582-4900.

✪ In this two-story stone house, dating back to 1730, the famous frontiersman was born on November 2, 1734, and lived for 16 years. A collection of 18th-century farm furniture is displayed in the building, as are many items and memorabilia relating to Daniel Boone. The well-signposted grounds also include a blacksmith shop, a sawmill, barn, picnic areas, nature trails, and a lake on 579 acres.

Admission: To grounds, free. Guided tours of house, $1.50 adults, $1 seniors (over 65), 50¢ children 6–17.
Open: Tues–Sat 9am–5pm; Sun noon–5pm.

MERRITT'S MUSEUM OF CHILDHOOD AND THE MARY MERRITT DOLL MUSEUM, Rte. 422, Douglassville. Tel. 385-3408.

Step back to Colonial times at this museum where you will find an extensive collection of antique dolls, dollhouses, and toys, as well as early baby carriages and children's wagons and carts. There are also Colonial lighting devices, pottery, pewter, china, cookie cutters, and crafts, as well as Pennsylvania Dutch fraktur (a local style of calligraphy) and American Indian implements.

Admission: $2 adults, $1 children aged 5–12.
Open: Mon–Sat, 10am–5pm; Sun 1–5pm. **Closed:** Major holidays.

WHERE TO STAY

Most of Reading's lodgings are either downtown or in the factory outlet areas, particularly the Wyomissing area, west of the city center on the other side of the Schuylkill River, along Rte. 422. This is because Wyomissing is home to the VF Factory outlet, the Berkshire Mall, and other shopping outlets.

DOWNTOWN

Expensive

THE INN AT CENTRE PARK, 730 Centre Ave., Reading, PA 19601. Tel. 215/374-8557. Fax 215/374-8725. 3 rms, 1 suite. A/C MINIBAR TV TEL.

$ Rates (including breakfast): $130 single or double, $150 suite. AE, MC, V. **Parking:** Free.

Located in a quiet residential neighborhood facing the park from which it derives its name, this imposing 19th-century Gothic Victorian mansion recalls Reading's heydays. It is rich in Victorian elegance, from its gabled roof and stone facade, to its original leaded glass windows, elaborate fireplaces, and ornate plasterwork. Each room is a gem, with antique furnishings and hand-carved woodwork. There are two front porches for relaxing and private parking in the rear. Innkeepers are Andrea and Michael Smith.

Moderate

HUNTER HOUSE, 118 S. Fifth St., Reading, PA 19602. Tel. 215/374-6608. 2 rms, with shared bath; 2 suites, private bath. A/C TV.

$ Rates (including breakfast): $50 single, $60 double, $60–$70 suite. MC, V. **Parking:** Free.

Describing itself as a blend of English bed-and-breakfast, French hostellerie, and Italian pensione, this three-story restored 1840 town house offers a homey lodging option in downtown Reading. Each guest room is individually decorated with antique furnishings; two rooms are on the ground level and two are on the third floor, and all either have kitchenettes or access to kitchenettes. Although phones are not a fixture in guest rooms, there are phone jacks, so you can request a phone if you wish. There is a private courtyard on the side of the house and private parking in the rear. Innkeepers are Norma and Ray Staron.

OUTLET AREAS & OTHER SUBURBS

Moderate

INN AT READING, 1040 Park Rd., Wyomissing, PA 19610. Tel. 215/ 372-7811 or toll-free 800/383-9713. Fax 215/372-4545. 250 rms. A/C TV TEL
$ **Rates:** $73–$83 single, $83–$93 double. AE, CB, DC, DISC, MC, V. **Parking:** Free.

This two-story hotel is located in a grassy setting just off Rte. 422, 1½ miles from the downtown area. Rooms have a homey Early American decor, with reproduction furnishings, king-size or two double beds, separate vanity area, and built-in luggage storage area; some units have whirlpool baths. There is also an outdoor swimming pool, gift shop, guest launderette, and a very popular restaurant/lounge with a Colonial atmosphere, The Publick House.

SHERATON BERKSHIRE, Rte. 422 and Paper Mill Rd., Reading, PA 19610. Tel. 215/376-3811 or toll-free 800/325-3535. Fax 215/375-7562. 260 rms. A/C TV TEL
$ **Rates:** $95–$115 for single or double. AE, CB, DC, MC, V. **Parking:** Free.
Set on a hillside with mountain views in the distance, this modern five-story property sports an art-deco look, from its marble-tiled lobby to its rounded furniture and brass rails. The rooms have a contemporary pastel decor with a choice of bed sizes, and full-length mirrors. Some guest rooms are available on the ground floor.
Dining/Entertainment: The Green Parrot serves moderately priced food all day. There is also an art deco–themed dining room, City Limits, open in the evening, and a lively lounge called GoodNites.
Facilities: Indoor heated pool, saunas, exercise room.

Budget

DUTCH COLONY MOTOR INN, 4635 Perkiomen Ave., Reading, PA 19606. Tel. 215/779-2345. 77 rms. A/C TV TEL
$ **Rates:** $47 single, $52 double. AE, DC, DISC, MC, V. **Parking:** Free.

Nestled in a wooded country setting, this lodging is attentively run by the Breithaupt and Wagner families. The two- and three-story motel with a Colonial motif offers guestrooms with contemporary furnishings and two double beds. Amenities include an outdoor swimming pool, picnic area, and aeronautically themed lounge bar and restaurant, decorated with antique airplanes.

WHERE TO DINE

DOWNTOWN

Very Expensive

JOE'S RESTAURANT, 450 S. 7th St. Tel. 373-6794.
Cuisine: AMERICAN. **Reservations:** Required.

$ Prices: Appetizers $6–$14; main courses $26.50–$35. AE, CB, DC, MC, V.
Open: Tues–Fri 5:30–9pm; Sat 4:30–9:30pm.

⭐ Mushrooms are the magic ingredient at this restaurant, originally started as a tavern in 1916 by Polish-born Jozef and Magdalena Czarnecki; it is now in the hands of the third generation of the same family, chefs Jack and Heidi Czarnecki.

Open just for dinner, the award-winning menu offers a variety of beef, veal, fowl, and seafood choices, but the hand-picked local mushroom enhancements are the pièce de résistance. Specialties include a velvety wild mushroom soup; mushroom seafood strudel; filet mignon with peppercorn sauce and wild mushrooms; and rack of veal or lamb with mushrooms; as well as seasonal dishes such as ragoût of Dakota black bear or breast of goose. There is a service charge of 18%, but the cuisine and staff are well worth it.

Expensive

WIDOW FINNEY'S, 30 S. 4th St. Tel. 378-1776.
 Cuisine: AMERICAN. **Reservations:** Recommended.
 $ Prices: Appetizers $2–$8; main courses $15–$20. AE, CB, DC, MC, V.
 Open: Dinner Tues–Sat 5:30–8pm.
This midcity landmark exudes a Colonial atmosphere. Listed in the National Register of Historic Places, it is named for one of Reading's first residents. The four dining rooms are a showcase of brass hurricane lamps, beam ceilings, all-wood floors, and brick walls. Guests can also dine in an enclosed brick courtyard behind the log house. Dinner entrées feature Colonial cuisine; the menu changes often, but might include such favorites as mahi mahi in parchment, salmon in leek sauce, chicken breast stuffed with crab, veal sautéed with cream, cognac, and walnuts, and the "Finney Duo" (seasoned shrimp and steak cooked over charcoal). Service charge is 18%. A strolling guitarist often enhances the mood on Saturday nights.

Moderate

JIMMIE KRAMER'S PEANUT BAR, 332 Penn St. Tel. 376-8500.
 Cuisine: INTERNATIONAL. **Reservations:** Recommended.
 $ Prices: Appetizers $1.95–$5.95; main courses $8.95–$18.95; lunch $2.95–$8.95. AE, DISC, MC, V.
 Open: Lunch Mon–Thurs 11am–2pm, Fri–Sat 11am–5pm; dinner Mon–Thurs 5–11pm, Fri–Sat 5pm–midnight. **Closed:** First two weeks of September.

🅂 Ever since 1924, this homey restaurant has been a tradition in downtown Reading—this tavern has been in the same family for three generations. The decor is reminiscent of the 1930s with an old-time long bar, globe wall lights, and wood walls. Complimentary dishes of unshelled peanuts are on every table and patrons are encouraged to discard the shells like sawdust on the floor. Luncheon fare includes salads, burgers, and hot dishes. Dinner entrées feature seafood platters, mesquite-grilled chicken, steaks, racks of ribs, Maryland crab cakes, and other regional specialties.

OUTLET AREAS & OTHER SUBURBS
Moderate

MOSELEM SPRINGS INN, Rtes. 222 and 662, Fleetwood. Tel. 215/944-8213.
 Cuisine: AMERICAN/PENNSYLVANIA DUTCH. **Reservations:** Recommended.
 $ Prices: Appetizers $2.95–$5.95; main courses $9–$18; lunch $4.95–$9.95. AE, CB, DC, MC, V.

Open: Mon–Sat lunch 11:30am–3pm, dinner 3–9pm.

⭐ For Colonial atmosphere and good Pennsylvania Dutch cooking, it's hard to match this local landmark. Established in 1852, it was named after the springs and streams nearby—Moselem (Ma-*sil*-em) means "trout stream" in the language of Lenni-Lenape Indians. In addition to the main building, the property includes an original smokehouse that is still used today to smoke meats served at the restaurant.

Entrées include smokehouse sausage with apple fritters; country-smoked ham with raisin sauce; traditional Berks County turkey with all the trimmings; barbecued chicken breast with steamed shrimp; charbroiled swordfish; crabcakes; sea scallops with Cheddar sauce; short ribs of beef; and various cuts of steaks.

STOKESAY CASTLE, Hill Rd. and Spook Lane. Tel. 375-4588.

Cuisine: INTERNATIONAL. **Reservations:** Recommended. **Directions:** From downtown, take Franklin Street east to Hill Road; follow Hill to Spook Lane and turn right.

$ Prices: Appetizers $2.95–$7.95; main courses $14.95–$19.95; lunch $4.95–$9.95. AE, DC, DISC, MC, V.

Open: Lunch Mon–Sat noon–3:30pm; dinner Mon–Thurs 4–9:30pm; Fri–Sat 4–10pm, and Sun noon–8pm.

A replica of a 13th-century English castle, this restaurant is perched high on Penn Hill, overlooking Reading. The building is a blend of Norman stucco turrets, Tudor wings, and stone archways; the interior decoration sets the mood with suits of armor, crossed swords, massive oak doors, hand-carved beams, and electric candle chandeliers. Dining rooms range from the splendor of the Great Hall to the charm of the Library or Keep Tavern. In summer, you can dine on a tree-shaded and canopied flagstone patio with a 20-mile view of the Reading horizon.

Signature dishes at dinner include shrimp Sebastian (stuffed with crab imperial); frogs' legs sautéed in white wine and garlic; steak Diane; boneless breast of capon; beef Stroganoff; and kingly or queenly portions of prime ribs. The restaurant is located in a posh residential section east of downtown on a well-signposted route.

Budget

HITCHING POST, 3337 Penn Ave., West Lawn. Tel. 678-2495.

Cuisine: GREEK/AMERICAN. **Reservations:** Only for parties of 4 or more.

$ Rates: Appetizers $1.95–$4.95; main courses $5.95–$12.95; lunch $1.95–$3.95. MC, V.

Open: Daily 11am–10pm.

Ⓢ This restaurant, about 2 miles west of downtown, is a favorite with families. The restaurant/cocktail lounge features authentic Greek dishes—lunch, for example, features moussaka along with the standard sandwiches and salads. Dinner entrées include Colorado brook trout amandine, roast turkey, Yankee pot roast, Greek lamb stew in casserole, and steaks.

SHOPPING

Reading's outlet shopping centers are located throughout the city, in the Wyomissing area, and in other more suburban points. The merchandise can range from irregulars to first quality, with discounts of up to 80%. Brand names run rampant across the walls, windows, and doors of every shop.

To sweeten your savings, there is no tax on clothing in Pennsylvania. The shopping season is at its frantic height from mid-July to Thanksgiving weekend, although busy buying times really run from April right through December.

All of the major city outlet complexes are well signposted with color-coded directional signs; they also have ample parking lots and many offer shuttle transport from your car to the outlet doors. In addition, there are a number of individual outlets and two suburban outlet complexes: the 70-unit **Manufacturers' Outlet Mall (MOM)** at Morgantown, 12 miles south of Reading on Rte. 176; and the new **Robesonia Outlet Center,** 10 miles west of the city, on Rte. 422. The Berks

County Information Center publishes a handy (and free) map guide to all of the major outlets.

READING OUTLET CENTER, 801 N. 9th St. Tel. 373-5495.

This is the largest downtown outlet, with over 70 individual stores housed in seven buildings within two city blocks. You'll find such brand names as Jaeger, Liz Claiborne, London Fog, J. G. Hook, Polo/Ralph Lauren, Carter's, Manhattan, Levi Strauss, Ship-n-Shore, Van Heusen, Fisher-Price Toys, Corning Designs, and Proctor-Silex.

Open: Mon–Wed from 9:30am–6pm; Thurs–Sat from 9:30am–8pm; and Sun noon–5pm.

Closed: Major holidays and early, 3pm, closings on Christmas Eve and New Year's Eve.

BIG MILL, 730 N. 8th St., at Oley St. Tel. 378-9100.

This former shoe-factory building, with three levels and two open courtyards in its center, houses 20 outlets. Featured products include Adolfo Sport Collectibles, Gitano sportswear, Delta hosiery, Deerskin shoes, Maidenform, Warners, Playtex, Toy Warehouse (Mattel, Kenner, Ideal, Coleco, Milton Bradley, Hasbro, and others), candy, and cookies.

Open: Mon–Wed 9:30am–6pm, Thurs–Sat 9:30am–8pm, Sun 11am–5pm; some late evenings.

THE OUTLETS ON HEISTERS LANE, 755 Heisters Lane at Kutztown Rd. Tel. 921-9394.

Located on the northern edge of the city, this 10-outlet, three-building complex combines the Flemington Fashion Outlet, David Crystal, Mikasa, Burlington Coat, and All-in-One Linen (Fieldcrest, Cannon, Wamsutta, Martex, Springmaid, Bill Blass, Laura Ashley, and others).

Open: Mon–Sat 9:30am–5:30pm, Sun noon–5pm; some units also open weekdays until 9pm and on Sat until 8pm in fall season and other selected times, some (e.g., Burlington Coat), open late every night except Sun.

Closed: Easter, Thanksgiving Day, and Christmas Day.

VF FACTORY OUTLET COMPLEX, Hill Ave. and Park Rd. Tel. 378-0408.

Among the oldest of this genre is this outlet, which opened in 1970 to sell surplus hosiery, sleepwear, and Vanity Fair lingerie. There are now 40 outlet stores housed in eight buildings. Vanity Fair is still one of the leading manufacturers whose products are sold, along with Lee Jeans and L. L. Bean. These three accept cash or personal checks only. Other companies featured in this complex include Laura Ashley, Windsor shirts, Freeman shoes, Jonathan Logan, Totes, Oneida stainless flatware, Reading China and Glass, Black & Decker, and an assortment of electronic, candy, pretzel, and toy companies.

Open: Mon–Fri 9am–9pm, Sat 9am–6pm, Sun 11am–5pm; extended hours in fall months.

THE POCONOS

Eight million people a year vacation in the Pocono Mountains, making it the number-one resort destination in Pennsylvania. Situated in the northeast corner of the state, the Poconos are composed of four neighboring counties (Monroe, Pike, Carbon, and Wayne), with an aggregate area of 2,400 square miles, spread over a panorama of mountainous peaks, rolling hills, glistening lakes, rushing rivers, and gentle valleys. The area is about 100 miles north of Philadelphia, 90 miles west of New York, 150 miles northeast of Baltimore, and 300 miles southwest of Boston.

Although champagne baths and heart-shaped swimming pools have earned the Poconos the title of "honeymoon capital of the world," this multifaceted corner of Pennsylvania is equally popular with families. And best of all, it is a full-fledged resort for all seasons, thriving equally well in the winter ski months, spring blossom time, and fall foliage period, as well as at the height of summer.

A BIT OF BACKGROUND

Part of the Appalachian chain, the Pocono Mountains derive their name from the Indian world *pocohonne,* which means "stream between the mountains." Of course, to this day, there are hundreds of streams between the Pocono Mountains, as well as lakes, ponds, and creeks. To top off this idyllic landscape, both the Delaware and Lehigh Rivers add to the scene. The Delaware provides the eastern boundary for the region and the Lehigh flows along part of the western edge.

It is therefore quite natural that water, in all its forms, plays an important part in the Pocono attractions, from swimming at lakeshore beaches to boating, fishing, whitewater rafting, and tubing in the warmer months to skiing, ice skating, snowmobiling, and tobogganing in the winter. Hand-in-hand with watersports, this natural paradise welcomes visitors to enjoy walking and hiking trails, picnicking, horseback riding, golfing, and myriad other outdoor activities.

Although the Poconos have been attracting vacationers since the 1700s, it is only in the last 40 years that the honeymoon industry has taken a firm hold. Resorts of all sizes and shapes have sprung up in the most idyllic and romantic locations, many with a "couples-only" format. This is where the heart-shaped swimming pool originated, not to mention the heart-shaped Jacuzzi and the champagne-glass-shaped whirlpool bath for two. Road signs that say CAUTION: DEARS CROSSING are not unusual, nor are red-velvet furnishings, mirrored ceilings, and "his and her" breakfasts in bed.

Although there are 12 enclaves that cater exclusively to a "couples clientele," hundreds of other resorts, hotels, motels, and country inns welcome couples, families, singles, or groups of all sizes. In this single chapter, it is impossible to give a complete review of all the properties, but we'll give a cross-section of all categories, and in various parts of the region.

For ease of reading (and getting around), we are breaking this chapter down into four areas. The first section, "Stroudsburg," describes what is often considered the gateway to the region, especially for traffic from the east. The main visitor information office and the Delaware Water Gap are also part of this area. Next, we'll take you to the central Poconos, primarily Monroe County, where the greatest concentration of resorts and inns are located, from Mt. Airy Lodge and Pocono Manor to Skytop. The third part will describe highlights around Lake Wallenpaupack, and the fourth will

THE POCONOS

PENNSYLVANIA

Harrisburg ★
Poconos

1 Stroudsburg Area
2 Central Poconos
3 Lake Wallenpaupack
4 Western Poconos

Skiing

WHAT'S SPECIAL ABOUT THE POCONOS

Ace Attractions

☐ Lake Wallenpaupack, a 13-mile-long artificial lake and water-sports playground in the heart of the Poconos.

☐ Jim Thorpe, a Switzerland-style mountain village with a Victorian historic district, named for the famous 1912 Olympic athlete.

☐ Bushkill Falls, eight dramatic waterfalls of various levels, known as the Niagara Falls of Pennsylvania.

Activities

☐ Ride the rapids along the Lehigh River of the western Poconos.

☐ Golf at more than 20 Pocono Mountain public courses.

☐ Ski at more than a dozen mountain slopes and resorts.

☐ Go horseback riding and "mule-teering."

For the Kids

☐ Quiet Valley Living Historical Farm, in Stroudsburg, a prototype of an early Pennsylvania Dutch farm.

☐ Claws 'n' Paws Wild Animal Park, home to more than 70 species of animals.

---

lead you over to the western Poconos, where attractions range from whitewater rafting and mule riding to the historic district of Jim Thorpe.

GETTING THERE

BY AIR

The Poconos are served by two nearby airports, **Wilkes-Barre/Scranton** to the west and **Allentown-Bethlehem-Easton** in the Lehigh Valley. Both are a maximum of 45 minutes away from major Pocono attractions. In addition, **Newark Airport** in New Jersey is only one hour and 15 minutes away from the heart of the Poconos. **Pocono Limousine Service** (tel. 717/839-2111) operates direct transfers to the Poconos from major airports, including Kennedy and LaGuardia in New York, Philadelphia, and Newark, as well as Wilkes-Barre/Scranton and Allentown-Bethlehem-Easton.

BY BUS

Bus service to the Poconos is operated into Stroudsburg by **Greyhound/Martz,** which maintains a depot at 231 Park Ave. (tel. 717/421-3040). Local taxis are available at this terminal. Greyhound/Martz makes an additional stop in Mt. Pocono at 26 Pocono Blvd. (tel. 717/839-7443). Many leading resorts, if advised in advance, will provide a shuttle service from Mt. Pocono to their front doors. At certain times of the year, additional stops may be made at Delaware Water Gap and Jim Thorpe. Check with the bus company in advance.

BY CAR

The majority of visitors to the Poconos arrive by car, and a car is really an asset if you want to get around. Of course, many of the large resorts are geared to keeping you housed and happy for your entire stay, so you don't have to bring a car. Assuming that you are driving, however, it is useful to know that major and interstate highways criss-cross throughout the 2,400-square-mile area. Both I-80 and I-84 traverse the county in an east-west direction, and I-81 and Rte. 9 (the Pennsylvania Turnpike

Northeast extension) go from north to south. A network of smaller roads also weaves in all directions throughout the four counties.

ORIENTATION

TOURIST INFORMATION

Comprehensive brochures and directories on all of the Poconos are available by contacting the **Pocono Mountain Vacation Bureau,** 1004 Main St., Stroudsburg, PA 18360 (tel. 717/424-6050 or toll-free east of the Mississippi 800/POCONOS).

AREA CODE

All telephone numbers in the Pocono Mountain region are part of the 717 area code, unless otherwise indicated.

GETTING AROUND

BY CAR

The Poconos area is fairly compact and easy to negotiate by car. From Stroudsburg, it is only an hour's drive to Lake Wallenpaupack or White Haven. For east-west travel, I-80 crosses the region's lower half, while I-84 runs across the northern spread. In addition, many local roads run parallel to the interstates and extend in other directions as well. You can easily base yourself in one location and explore all other parts of the Poconos by taking day trips. Or you may choose to get a feel for different sections by spending a night or two in each of the areas that are outlined on the following pages.

TOURS

SIGHTSEEING BY PLANE

For an overview of the entire area, you can take an air tour with **Moyer Aviation,** Pocono Mt. Municipal Airport, Rte. 611, Mt. Pocono (tel. 717/839-7161 or 839-6080), located 1½ miles north of Mt. Pocono. Open daily year round, this service offers a variety of small aircraft tours of the area, ranging from 25 to 80 miles in scope and priced from $12 to $30 per person, based on a minimum of two passengers. The planes operate from 8am to sunset, and reservations are suggested.

1. STROUDSBURG AREA

Stroudsburg (pop. 5,100) is the chief town in the Poconos. The main visitor information center is located here and many of the prime roads, such as I-80 and Rtes. 611, 209, 447, and 191, converge here and branch out to other parts of the region. With a wide main street, Stroudsburg has an assortment of shops and stores. It is named for Col. Jacob Stroud, who settled the area in 1761. There are actually two towns—Stroudsburg and East Stroudsburg, the latter of which is the location of a state university. Both towns are connected by Rte. 209.

The two Stroudsburgs lie beside the Delaware Water Gap, considered the natural gateway to the Poconos. An attraction in itself, the Gap was formed over the years by slow erosion, allowing the Delaware River to chisel a deep crevice through the mountains, leaving walls that tower up to 700 feet above the waterway. It is said that the rock tells a geological story over 400 million years, and the river itself is 150 million years old.

WHAT TO SEE & DO
HIKING & TRAIL WALKING

⭐ National Park rangers conduct a number of programs along the 35-mile **Delaware Water Gap,** maintaining visitor centers from April through October at Kittatinny, off I-80 (tel. 908/496-4458), and at Dingman's Falls, off Rte. 209 (tel. 717/828-7802). Among the activities are beach walks, river walks, nature walks, and discovery hikes. Picnicking facilities are also available. For advance information, contact the **Delaware Water Gap NRA,** Bushkill, PA 18324 (tel. 717/588-2435).

SWIMMING

There is a lovely secluded strand at **Smithfield Beach,** just north of Shawnee on River Road; there are also boat and canoe ramps, picnic tables, and restrooms here. Another good spot is at Milford Beach, just north of the toll bridge that crosses the Delaware on Rte. 209.

WHITEWATER RAFTING

Kittatinny Canoes Inc., Dingmans Ferry (tel. 828-2338 or toll-free 800/FLOAT-KC), offers canoe and raft trips that cover the most popular 10-mile section of the Delaware River. These excursions range from 5 to 17 miles in length with varying degrees of difficulty; longer trips are also available. Rates range from $19 per person on weekdays to $22 on weekends. This company can also arrange daily tubing trips from $10 per person, kayaking from $28, and camping from $8 per day. Hours are, mid-April through October, 8am to 6pm. Other outfitters in the area that also arrange canoeing and rafting trips include **Adventure Tours,** Marshalls Creek (tel. 223-0505); and **Shawnee Canoe Trips,** P.O. Box 93, Shawnee-on-Delaware (tel. 424-1139).

GOLF

The **Cherry Valley Golf Course,** Cherry Valley Road, Stroudsburg (tel. 421-1350) features an 18-hole course, 2 miles west of the Delaware Water Gap. Greens fees are $12 per person midweek and $18 on weekends; cart fees are $22. The **Shawnee Inn and Country Club,** Shawnee-on-Delaware (tel. 421-1500), has three 9-hole courses; greens fees are $33 weekdays and $53 weekends (prices include cart). Other nearby facilities include 27 holes at **Fernwood Golf Club,** Bushkill (tel. 588-6661) and 18 holes at **Tamiment Resort,** Tamiment (tel. 588-6652).

SKIING

With an elevation of 1,350 feet and a vertical drop of 700 feet, **Shawnee Mountain,** Shawnee-on-Delaware (tel. 421-7231), is a leading ski center. There are 23 slopes and trails, one triple and eight double chair lifts, a ski-rental shop, and ski school. Midweek lift tickets are priced from $30 and weekend from $33; night-skiing from $21. Other resorts in this area include **Fernwood,** Rte. 209, Bushkill (tel. 588-6661); **Saw Creek,** off Rte. 209, Bushkill (tel. 588-9266); and **Tamiment Resort,** Tamiment (tel. 588-6652). These facilities have average vertical drops between 200 and 300 feet and offer lift tickets between $15 to $25.

NEARBY ATTRACTIONS

⭐ Fifteen miles northwest of Stroudsburg (on Rte. 209) is one of the most famous of the Poconos' sightseeing attractions, **Bushkill Falls,** Bushkill Falls Road, Bushkill (tel. 588-6682). Often called the "Niagara Falls of Pennsylvania," this site dates back to 1904 and includes eight falls of various levels, signposted walking trails, a wildlife gallery, shops, fishing pond, picnicking sites, and paddleboats. Open April through November, 9am to dusk, the admission charge is $4.50 for adults, $1 for children aged 6 to 12. There is a supplementary charge for the paddleboats of $3 per each 15 minutes for two people. Fishing is $1.50 for adults and 50¢ for children.

QUIET VALLEY LIVING HISTORICAL FARM, Quiet Valley Rd., off Rte. 209, Stroudsburg. Tel. 992-6161
Listed on the National Register of Historic Places and maintained by the Department of the Interior, this prototype of an early Pennsylvania Dutch farm, 3½ miles south of Stroudsburg, re-creates the daily routine of a family who lived at this location from 1765 to 1913. The complex includes 14 buildings; some are original, such as a log house built in 1765, and others are reconstructions. Costumed guides demonstrate the skills of farming, meat-smoking, spinning, weaving, baking, as well as tending to animals and gardening.
Admission: $5 adults, $3 children aged 3–12.
Open: End of June–Labor Day, Mon–Sat 9:30am–5:30pm, and Sun 1–5:30pm.

WHERE TO STAY

Rates for Poconos accommodations are at their highest in summer and during the ski season. In some cases, a two-night minimum also applies for weekend stays. However, you can often save money by traveling here midweek, rather than on weekends. Many properties also offer package deals throughout the year, with especially good savings during the spring and fall months. Be sure to inquire what special prices may be in effect at the time you plan to visit.

EXPENSIVE

THE SHAWNEE INN, River Rd., Shawnee-on-Delaware, PA 18356. Tel. 717/421-1500 or toll-free 800-SHAWNEE. Fax 717/424-9168. 84 rms. A/C MINIBAR TV TEL **Directions:** Take I-80 to exit 52 and follow Rte. 209 north to Shawnee.
$ Rates (including breakfast and dinner): $63–$100 single, $105–$180 double. AE, DISC, MC, V. **Parking:** Free.
This grand, turn-of-the-century lodge was made famous by its previous owner, bandleader Fred Waring. Idyllically set on the banks of the Delaware River in the shadow of nearby mountains, the four-story hotel with Spanish-tile roof is surrounded by a 27-hole golf course. The inn's rooms have private baths, vintage decor, and many have panoramic views. Rates include full breakfast and dinner. Free activities include indoor and outdoor swimming pools, outdoor tennis, putting greens, historical walks, ice skating, shuffleboard, bocci, horseshoe games, and jogging trails. Guests also enjoy a free round of golf for each night of stay and free ski lift tickets for midweek bookings. Reductions on other activities, including the racquet club, horseback riding, and canoe trips, are available. Meals are served in a wide-windowed dining room that has views of the river. A summer theater is also on the grounds.

MODERATE

SHERATON POCONO INN, 1220 W. Main St., Stroudsburg, PA 18360. Tel. 717/424-1930 or toll-free 800/325-3535. Fax 717/424-5909. 134 rms. A/C TV TEL
$ Rates: $90–$109 single or double. AE, CB, DC, MC, V. **Parking:** Free.
A convenient, convivial place to stay is this modern hotel, a mile south of the town center in a quiet wooded setting with a winding stream. The guest rooms are furnished with contemporary furnishings, mountain colors, and offer a choice of two double beds or king- or queen-size beds; many have balconies overlooking an indoor tropical courtyard, and others offer wide picture-window views of the surrounding mountain scenery.
Facilities: Restaurant, lounge, indoor and outdoor swimming pools, saunas, game room, and gift shop.

BUDGET

BLACK WALNUT COUNTRY INN, 509 Fire Tower Road, R.D. 2, Box 9285, Milford, PA 18337. Tel. 717/296-6322 or toll-free 800/866-9870. 12 rms (8 with bath).

$ Rates (including breakfast): $50–$85 single or double. AE, MC, V. **Parking:** Free.

Thirty-five miles northeast of Stroudsburg, along the Delaware, is the Black Walnut Country Inn. A good base for touring the northern Poconos, the B&B is just south of I-84 (exit 10); the other side of the Delaware River marks the New York/New Jersey border. As you drive into this 150-acre estate, you'll be charmed by the Tudor stone facade, with its adjacent lake and well-landscaped grounds.

A country-style decor prevails inside with a marble fireplace and homey furnishings. The guest rooms each have an individual personality, many with antiques and brass beds. The rates include a "welcome" glass of sherry, afternoon tea, and breakfast served in the dining room overlooking the lake or outside on the patio deck. Guest amenities include paddleboating, fishing, and swimming in the lake; lawn games; and the use of a common parlor with TV and VCR. There are also stables for horseback riding (from $20 per hour), and the estate is ideal for watching wildlife.

BEST WESTERN POCONO INN, 700 Main St., Stroudsburg, PA 18360. Tel. 717/421-2200 or toll-free 800/528-1234. Fax 717/421-5561. 90 rms. A/C TV TEL

$ Rates: $52–$68 single, $58–$74 double. AE, CB, DC, MC, V. **Parking:** Free.

In the heart of town is this modern four-story motor hotel. Recently updated and refurbished, this facility served as the Pocono Hilton and the Penn-Stroud Town and Country Inn in previous years. The modern guest rooms are equipped with contemporary furnishings and a choice of two double beds or a king-size bed. There is also an indoor heated swimming pool, a fitness center, a video-game room, a coffee shop, a lounge, and a steakhouse.

WHERE TO DINE

Top-notch restaurants are a keystone of the Poconos, and in the Stroudsburg area, you'll find an international mix of cuisines.

EXPENSIVE

BEAVER HOUSE, 1001 N. Ninth St., Stroudsburg. Tel. 424-1020.
   Cuisine: SEAFOOD/INTERNATIONAL. **Reservations:** Recommended.
$ Prices: Appetizers $1.95–$5.95; main courses $10.95–$26.95; lunch $4.95–$8.95. AE, CB, DC, MC, V.
   Open: Lunch Mon–Fri 11:30am–2pm; dinner Mon–Sat 5–10:30pm, Sun 1–8pm, or 9pm (in summer); à la carte menu also available Mon–Sat 2–5pm.

A landmark of the area is this 40-year-old rustic inn, where lobster and fresh seafood predominate on the menu. As you enter, the lobster tanks by the door offer a preview of what is to follow. The rest of the decor is nautical and Bavarian, with an eclectic collection of porcelain figurines, mugs, jugs, and mounted birds and wildlife; etched glass and curtained booths add to the old-world atmosphere. Lunch focuses mainly on light platters, omelets, salads, and sandwiches. The main event of the day is dinner, when a selection of one to four lobster dishes is offered, either baked, broiled, steamed, or stuffed. The menu also includes sirloin steaks served ceremoniously on wooden dishes, prime rib, king crab in the shell, rainbow trout amandine, and duckling. Chances are you'll be greeted by the congenial host and head chef, both of whom have put in more than 30 years of pleasing customers here.

PEPPE'S RISTORANTE, Eagle Valley Mall, East Stroudsburg. Tel. 421-4460.
   Cuisine: ITALIAN. **Reservations:** Recommended.

$ Prices: Appetizers $2.95–$8.95; main courses $9.95–$23.95; lunch $4.95–$11.95. AE, CB, DC, MC, V.
Open: Lunch Mon–Fri 11:30am–2:30pm; dinner Mon–Fri 5:30–10pm, Sat 4–11pm, Sun 3–9pm.

A Roman villa atmosphere awaits you at this restaurant. Although you would ordinarily expect to find only fast-food eateries in a shopping center, this is one case when appearances are deceiving. Opera plays in the background as you are seated amidst a romantic decor of flowers, brick arches, wrought-iron ceiling lanterns, candelabras, and fine linens. The dinner menu features Italian specialties such as scampi; calamari; lobster tail fra diavolo; rack of veal stuffed with prosciutto, cheese, and mushrooms; saltimbocca alla Romana; Italian pepper steak; and fresh pastas. The entrées, many prepared tableside, are accompanied by an intermezzo sorbet, vegetable, and potato or spaghetti.

MODERATE

DANSBURY DEPOT, 50 Crystal St., East Stroudsburg. Tel. 476-0500.
Cuisine: AMERICAN. **Reservations:** Accepted only for parties of eight or more.
$ Prices: Appetizers $2.95–$5.95; main courses $9.95–$16.95; lunch $3.95–$7.95. AE, D, MC, V.
Open: Lunch Mon–Sat 11:30–5:30pm, Sun noon–4pm; dinner Mon–Thurs 5:30–10pm, Fri–Sat 5:30–11pm, Sun 4–9pm.

Built in 1864 as a train station and freight house when the town was called Dansbury, this historic building was converted into a restaurant 5 years ago. The decor is full of vintage railroad memorabilia. The cuisine is typically American, with salads, sandwiches, light entrées, and burgers for lunch. The entrées at dinner include pastas, prime ribs of beef, seafood, barbecued chicken, veal dishes, and steaks.

2. CENTRAL POCONOS

We're identifying the central Poconos as the area west of Stroudsburg, east of White Haven, just south of I-80, and as far north as Skytop. This is primarily Monroe County, although, to be technical, Stroudsburg and the Delaware Water Gap are also part of Monroe. The majority of resorts and honeymoon destinations are clustered in this area, as are a wide selection of hotels, motels, and country inns.

This stretch of Pocono country is also the home of several great ski resorts including Camelback and Alpine Mountain, a variety of fine golf courses, and some of the region's most charming towns, such as Canadensis, Mt. Pocono, Mountainhome, Cresco, and Paradise Valley.

WHAT TO SEE & DO

HORSEBACK RIDING

More than 60 acres of trails are available at **Carsons Riding Stables,** Rte. 611, Cresco (tel. 839-9841), 1 mile south of Mt. Pocono. This 30-year-old establishment offers 3-mile guided rides, every hour on the hour from 10am to 4pm, year round (reservations are recommended; and you should arrive 15 minutes before the ride you wish to take). The rate is $15 per person.

GOLF

Pocono Manor Inn and Golf Club, Rtes. 314 and 940, Pocono Manor (tel. 839-7111), has two championship courses, with greens fees ranging from $18 per course on weekdays to $27 on weekends. Carts are $13 per person for 18 holes. There is also an 18-hole course at **Mt. Airy Lodge,** off Rte. 611, Mt. Pocono (tel.

839-8811), with midweek (Monday to Thursday) greens fees set at $25 for lodge guests (and $30 on Friday, Saturday, and Sunday). For nonguests the fee is $35 midweek (Monday to Thursday) and $45 weekends (Friday, Saturday, and Sunday). Cart rentals are $15.90 per person.

A 9-hole course is also available at **Evergreen Park Golf Course,** Rte. 314, Analomink (tel. 421-7721), with midweek greens fees starting at $11 and weekend rates from $12 to $15. Cart rentals are $14 to $15 for nine holes and $19 to $20 for 18 holes.

SKIING

The largest of the Pocono ski resorts is **Camelback,** Rtes. 611 and 715, **Tannersville** (tel. 629-1661; snow reports toll-free 800/233-8100), at exit 45 on I-80. There is an 800-foot vertical drop, 25 slopes and trails, 11 lifts including eight double chairs, two triple chairs and a quad chair, a rental shop, a ski school, and a child-care program. Lift tickets range from $30 on weekdays to $35 on weekends, and night skiing from $22.

Nearby is **Alpine Mountain,** Rte. 447, Analomink (tel. 595-2150 or toll-free 800/233-8240) located 9 miles north of I-80. With a 500-foot vertical drop and 14 slopes and trails, this facility also offers a poma lift, two quad chairs, two T-bars; a rental shop; and a school. Lift tickets cost $22 at midweek and $27 on weekends.

This area is also the home of **Mt. Airy Lodge,** off Rte. 611, Mt. Pocono (tel. 839-8811), with a 240-foot vertical drop; and the **Pocono Manor Inn,** Rtes. 314 and 940, Pocono Manor (tel. 839-7111), with a 250-foot vertical drop.

FOOD-SAMPLING TOURS

For a change of pace, this region invites you to indulge in some unique food-sampling tours. At **Callie's Candy Kitchen,** Rte. 390, Mountainhome (tel. 595-2280), you can see candy in the making and enjoy free samples. Started in 1952, this small enterprise turns out over 30 varieties of sweets, from chocolate-covered fresh strawberries and raspberry fudge to two local favorites, Pocono Mountain Bark and Pocono Mountain Crunch. Four miles south is **Callie's Pretzel Factory,** on Rtes. 390 and 191, Cresco (tel. 595-3257), a similar operation that produces soft pretzels, with choices ranging from pizza pretzels to garlic, cinnamon, or hot-dog pretzels. There are also 37 varieties of flavored gourmet popcorn. Open from 10am to 8:30pm in summer and from 10am to 5pm other times. Tours and samplings are free; all major credit cards are accepted.

WHERE TO STAY

Many places in this region are "total resorts," meaning that guests can stay put and enjoy all sorts of sporting activities, entertainment, and two or three meals a day, as part of the daily rate. Rates at most properties will average over $100 per person a day, but that can be classified as a moderate price when you consider all you are getting for your money. Actually, comparing rates can be a bit confusing because some places charge more, but give more. After glancing through these descriptions, contact the **Pocono Mountain Vacation Bureau** and ask to receive a variety of accommodation brochures, so that you can compare for yourself.

INNS & RESORTS
Expensive

MT. AIRY LODGE, Mt. Pocono, PA 18344. Tel. 717/839-8811 or toll-free 800/441-4410. Fax 717/839-8811, ext. 7000. 475 rms, 126 suites. A/C TV TEL
$ Rates (including 2 meals): $86 single, $120 double, $215 suite. AE, CB, DC, DISC, MC, V. **Parking:** Free.
This lodge is probably the most famous of the Poconos resorts because of the big-name stars it draws to entertain its guests and because of its catchy advertising

jingles. Started over 50 years ago as a boardinghouse with 16 rooms, Mt. Airy has grown enormously, and is now one of the largest and most complete resorts in the east, in a secluded setting surrounded by a private lake and an 18-hole golf course. The bedrooms have custom interiors, and many have balconies. In addition, there is a variety of suites designed just for couples, with heart-shaped whirlpool baths for two, monarch-size or round beds, in-suite indoor-outdoor pools, private sun and lounge patios, and saunas. Horseback riding is also available at a supplementary charge. Evening entertainment includes top-name stars, dancing to three bands, and two discos.

Facilities: Olympic indoor and outdoor pools, private lake with sandy beach, marina with sailboats and paddleboats, 21 indoor and outdoor tennis courts, 18-hole golf course, team sports, health club, and winter sports—skiing, sleighing, ice skating, and snowmobiling.

POCONO MANOR, Rte. 314, Pocono Manor, PA 18349. Tel. 717/839-7111 or toll free 800/233-8150. Fax 717/830-0708. 255 rms, 6 suites. A/C TV TEL. **Directions:** Take I-80 to I-380 west to exit 8, turn right and follow signs to Manor.

$ Rates (including breakfast and dinner): $96–$101 single, $162–$172 double, suites $50 extra. AE, DC, MC, V.

Located high in the Poconos, this is one of the grand old resorts of the region, dating back to 1902 when it opened as a small, 65-room country inn by a group of Quakers from Philadelphia. Over the years, it has grown and expanded to its present size (3,000 acres) and layout, and evolved to private ownership, but the original stone facade and much of the turn-of-the-century charm remains.

Guest rooms are spread out among the four-story main building, a seven-story tower wing, and three adjacent lodges. Each unit is decorated in traditional style with dark woods and floral fabrics; most rooms have panoramic views. In addition to two meals daily, the overnight rates include complimentary golf greens fees, and the use of tennis courts, swimming pools, sauna, ice skating rink, and cross-country skiing trails.

Dining/Entertainment: Choices include the candlelit Main Dining Room and the Lamplighter Lounge.

Facilities: Two 18-hole championship golf courses, driving range, indoor and outdoor tennis courts, indoor and outdoor swimming pools, sauna, exercise room, trap shooting range, bicycle rentals, ski and skate rentals, equestrian stables, skiing, snowmobiles, ice skating, and horse-drawn sleigh rides.

SKYTOP LODGE, Skytop, PA 18357. Tel. 717/595-7401 or toll-free 800/345-7759. Fax 717/595-9618. 180 rms, 3 suites. A/C TV TEL

$ Rates (including 3 meals daily for 2 people): $123 single, $258 double, $298 suite. AE, DC, MC, V. **Parking:** Free.

This gracious property, erected in 1928, sits on a lake amid 5,500 acres in the heights of the mountains, as its name implies. The rambling gray-stone building began as a private club, and indeed still operates on a membership basis, although it opened to the public for lodging about 20 years ago. Most rooms are furnished with antique reproductions, including a small writing desk, butterfly Windsors, traditional iron lamps, and pine beds, either twin or queen-size. Guests enjoy free movies, concerts, and art exhibits. (There are modest supplementary charges for some activities).

Facilities: Indoor and outdoor pool, health club, exercise room, sauna, whirlpool, hiking and fitness trails, shuffleboard, horseshoe pitching, table tennis, archery, miniature golf, downhill and cross-country skiing, ice skating, tobogganing, sledding, supervised play area for children, card room, library, and TV room with 5-foot screen.

Moderate

OVERLOOK INN, Dutch Hill Road, Canadensis, PA 18325. Tel. 717/595-7519 or toll-free 800/441-0177. Fax 717/588-9679. 20 rms. A/C TV TEL

$ Rates (including breakfast and dinner): $75–$95 per person single or double. AE, MC, V. **Parking:** Free.

Down a country road, deep in the mountains, off Rte. 447, you'll find this three-story turn-of-the-century structure that started out as a boardinghouse. Managed by Jeanne Pomager, the inn actually incorporates an older (1860s) farmhouse plus a carriage house and small lodge. Twelve guest rooms are located in the main house, with eight in the other two buildings. Country prints and crafts decorate the rooms, which are eclectically furnished with iron bedsteads, pine chests, quilts, oak dressers, and a plant or two. You'll also find a complimentary carafe of wine in your room. The inn's facilities include a restaurant, 15 acres of woods and meadows, an outdoor pool, a library, and a color TV.

PINE KNOB INN, Rte. 447, P.O. Box 275, Canadensis, PA 18325. Tel. 717/595-2532. 18 rms, 2 suites with bath.

$ Rates (including breakfast and dinner): $74 single, $69 double per person, $74 suites per person. MC, V. **Parking:** Free.

★ This two-story, pre–Civil War home tucked in a forest setting beside the Brodhead Creek has been welcoming guests since the 1880s. Now in the hands of congenial hosts Annie and Scott Frankel, this charming house offers a cheery blend of antiques, a piano, and paintings by local artists, including the lady of the house. Each bedroom is furnished differently, with country curtains, hobnail spreads, and antique quilts, as well as brass, Victorian carved-oak, or mahogany four-poster beds and needlepoint chairs. Guest facilities include a restaurant, bar, outdoor swimming pool, tennis, badminton, shuffleboard, and lawn games. At certain times of the year, creative workshops are offered, featuring leading painters and photographers as lecturers.

LODGES & MOTOR INNS
Expensive

COMFORT INN, Rte. 611, P.O. Box 184, Bartonsville, PA 18321. Tel. 717/476-1500 or toll-free 800/228-5150. 120 rms. A/C TV TEL.

$ Rates (including continental breakfast): $52.95–$161.95 single; $58.95–$161.95 double. AE, CB, DC, MC, V. **Parking:** Free.

This two-story property is located on shady grounds 3 miles west of Stroudsburg and 6 miles east of Camelback. Each room has a contemporary decor, a choice of double or queen- or king-size beds, and a room safe. Some rooms also feature a Jacuzzi or a waterbed. There is an outdoor swimming pool with a hot tub, a cocktail lounge with entertainment on the premises (Thurs to Sat), and a coin-operated laundry.

Moderate

CRESCENT LODGE, Rtes. 191 and 940, Paradise Valley, Cresco, PA 18326. Tel. 717/595-7486 or toll-free 800/392-9400. 30 rms, suites, cottages. A/C TV TEL

Directions: Take exit 52 off I-80; go north on Rte. 447 to Rte. 191 N. The hotel is at the intersection.

$ Rates: $65–$115 single or double; $95–$130 suite; $95–$250 cottage. AE, CB, DC, DISC, MC, V. **Parking:** Free.

★ This small, friendly inn is nestled in a quiet forest setting near the junction of two main roads. A favorite with skiers, it's located 8 miles from Camelback. Developed by the Dunlop family over the last 40 years, the accommodations consist of 12 rooms and suites in the main lodge and 18 units in motel-style cottages, each with wall-to-wall carpeting, a tiled bath, and early-American furnishings. Many cottages feature a kitchenette, private Jacuzzi, fireplace, or garden patio/sun deck. Amenities include an outdoor heated pool, tennis courts, and an Alpine-style restaurant.

POCONO LODGE, Rte. 715 and I-80, P.O. Box 131, Tannersville, PA 18372. Tel. 717/629-4100 or toll-free 800/441-2193. 88 rms. A/C TV TEL

$ Rates: $39.95–$95.95 weekday, single or double; $49.95–$139.95 weekends. AE, CB, DC, DISC, MC, V. **Parking:** Free.

Located 2 miles from Camelback at exit 45 off I-80, this chalet-style inn is perched on a hillside amid well-landscaped grounds. The guest rooms are equipped with two double beds or a king-size bed, dark wood furnishings, and bright-colored fabrics; about half have individual fireplaces. Most rooms have lovely mountain views, and some also offer a private Jacuzzi or waterbed. Guest facilities include an outdoor swimming pool, a hot tub, and a game room.

WHERE TO DINE

EXPENSIVE

PUMP HOUSE INN, Skytop Rd., Canadensis, PA 18325. Tel. 717/595-7501.
   Cuisine: AMERICAN. **Reservations:** Recommended.
$ **Prices:** Appetizers $2.95–$6.95; main courses $12.95–$23.95. AE, CB, DC, MC, V.
   Open: Dinner Tues–Sat 5–10pm, Sun 2:30–8:30pm.

Set high in the mountains, 2 miles north of Canadensis, this delightful country restaurant is known for its inviting tavern with a fireplace, as well as its conversation-piece furnishings, books, and antiques from around the world, and an oil-painting collection of sailing ships. But most of all, people flock here for the food—a gourmet's delight. Although the menu changes seasonally, dishes usually featured are apple pecan-stuffed chicken breast; poached Norwegian salmon filet in dill lemon butter sauce; lobster tails with crab stuffing; or rack of lamb. The entrées include salad, potato, vegetable, and hot-fruit compote.

In addition, the Pump House also has 10 rooms and 3 suites upstairs and in an adjoining cottage, which are available on a bed-and-breakfast basis.

HOMESTEAD INN, Sandspring Dr., Cresco. Tel. 595-3171.
   Cuisine: INTERNATIONAL. **Reservations:** Recommended.
$ **Prices:** Appetizers $2.95–$6.95; main courses $10.95–$21.95. AE, CB, DC, MC, V.
   Open: Dinner Mon–Sat 5–10pm, Sun 4–9pm. **Closed:** Tues in winter.
Nestled amid giant old pines, this small restaurant is situated in a wooded residential area. It has a striking barn-siding exterior and a giant boulder resting in its front garden. The interior features an Early American decor with Wyeth prints on the walls, but the cuisine has an international flair. Entrées include steaks and filet au poivre, roast duckling in Chambord sauce, red snapper in tomato basil sauce, baked ham in brown-sugar cinnamon sauce, and fettuccine Alfredo.

WINE PRESS INN, Star Rte., Bartonsville Avenue, off Rte. 611. Tel. 629-4302.
   Cuisine: ITALIAN. **Reservations:** Recommended.
$ **Prices:** Appetizers $2.95–$5.95; main courses $9.95–$21.95. AE, CB, DC, MC, V.
   Open: Dinner Mon, Wed–Thurs 5–9pm, Fri–Sat 5–10:30pm, Sun 4–9pm.
For a taste of Italy, try this restaurant, where chef-owner Joe Vesce encourages special requests. The decor includes an indoor grape garden, wine casks, and a lobster tank, which foretell a fine wine list and good seafood. Entrées include scrod oreganata, zuppa di pesce, lobster Guiseppe (served in the shell, Newburg-style, with shrimp and mushrooms), chicken parmigiana, and pork scaloppine lemon.

MODERATE

INN AT TANNERSVILLE, Rte. 611, Tannersville. Tel. 629-3131.
   Cuisine: AMERICAN. **Reservations:** Recommended on weekends.
$ **Prices:** Appetizers $2.95–$5.95; main courses $8.95–$19.95. AE, MC, V.

Open: Mon–Sat 11:30am–11pm.
A favorite spot for a casual drink or a fine meal is this Pocono landmark enthusiastically run by the Jakubowitz family. The layout includes an old-world "saloon," lined with memorabilia reflecting the inn's 155 years of existence. In contrast, there is a modern solarium filled with white wrought-iron furniture and hanging plants. Dinner entrées, served by candlelight, include rainbow trout with wine butter and almonds, bluefish, whole coho salmon, and honey-dipped fried chicken.

3. LAKE WALLENPAUPACK

Lake Wallenpaupack is a 13-mile long, 5,700-acre body of water that dominates the Pocono's northern region. With a 52-mile uninterrupted shoreline and a maximum depth of 60 feet, it is a paradise for watersports enthusiasts, honeymooners, campers, photographers, painters, and just plain folks who appreciate a new scenic vista at every turn.

Although it looks like a natural wonder, the lake is actually artificial, created for hydroelectric power by the Pennsylvania Power and Light Company in 1926. It was formed from an old Indian Creek of the same name. To the Indians, Wallenpaupack meant "stream of swift and slow water."

The chief towns by Lake Wallenpaupack are Lakeville, Hawley, Greentown, and South Sterling. Rtes. 590 and 507 circle the main lake shoreline, and I-84 runs directly south in an east-west direction, for easy access.

WHAT TO SEE & DO
WATER SPORTS

On the south shore of the lake is **Pine Crest Boat Rentals,** Rte. 507, Greentown (717/857-1136), a leading water sports center. Located on the south shore of Lake Wallenpaupack, this is a complete boating facility with a marina, 500 feet of lakefront grounds, and a sailing school on the premises. You can rent all types of ski and family boats, cruising boats, motorboats, catamarans, fishing boats, and sailboats from 13 to 22 feet in length. A 2-hour minimum applies for all rentals on weekends and holidays, with rates ranging from $25 for a sunfish to $45 for a 22-foot Catalina sailboat, for 2 hours. Open mid-April to September/October.

Boats can also be rented from **Pocono Action Sports,** at the Lakeview Hotel, Rte. 507, Greentown (tel. 857-1976).

HORSEBACK RIDING

There are two horseback-riding facilities near the north shore of the lake. **Triple W Ranch and Stables,** off Rte. 6, Honesdale (tel. 226-2620), is 4 miles north of Hawley, on a 170-acre horse farm. Visitors can go trail riding with a guide, from $19 to $24 per hour, depending on the day of the week and the number of people in the riding group. There are four trails, meandering through woods, lakelands, meadows, or mountains. Overnight trail rides and hayrides are also organized, by reservation. Open all year, from 9am to 5pm.

You can also arrange to ride at the **Happy Trails Stables,** off Rte. 590, Hamlin Corners (tel. 698-6996), on the northwest side of the lake. This center offers 1-hour trail rides, daily on the hour, from 9am to 5pm, at a cost of $15 per person per hour; 2-hour trails for experienced riders can also be arranged, from $30 and up.

CAMPING

The Pennsylvania Power and Light Company maintains four areas around Lake Wallenpaupack for camping and recreation, each with its own resident director. Two of the sites are near Greentown on the southern shore, and there is one each near Lakeville and Hawley on the north and east shores, respectively. Campers have access to electricity, coin-operated washing machines and clothes dryers, and hot showers. Open between the last Saturday in April and the third Sunday in October, each area has a small general store, boat rental, docks, launching ramps, and picnic areas.

In the winter, the sites remain open, but only with the restrooms and a frost-free water supply for visitors.

Reservations are advised, but you may also camp on a first-come basis for 1 to 21 nights. The fees are $12 per night for one to four persons, $1 per night for each additional person; electricity is included in the fee during the summer months. For further information and a brochure describing all four camp sites, contact Sherwood J. Krum, **Pennsylvania Power and Light Co.,** Lake Wallenpaupack Superinten-dent, Box 122, Hawley, PA 18428-0122 (tel. 717/226-3702).

SKIING

On the south side of the lake is **Tanglewood,** off Rte. 390, Tafton (tel. 226-9500), a major resort overlooking Lake Wallenpaupack, with a 415-foot vertical drop and nine slopes and trails. There are two double-chair lifts, two T-bars, and one beginner's lift. Midweek rates start at $16 and on weekends from $25; there is also night skiing from $12 on weekdays and $15 on weekends. Other facilities include a cross-country center, rentals, lessons, and a ski school.

COOL FOR KIDS

More than 70 species of animals from all over the world are displayed in natural settings at **Claws 'n' Paws Wild Animal Park,** Rte. 590, Lake Ariel (tel. 698-6154). Children are enchanted by the live animal shows and large petting area with tame deer, goats, and lambs. Other attractions include a wildlife trail, a gift shop, and a picnic area. Open daily May through late October from 10am to 6pm. Admission charges are $6.50 for adults and $4 for children 3 to 11.

WHERE TO STAY
EXPENSIVE

COVE HAVEN, Lakeville, PA 18438. Tel. 717/226-2101 or toll-free 800/ 233-4141. Fax 717/226-4697. 282 rms. A/C TV TEL
$ Rates (including 2 meals): $198–$289 double. AE, CB, DC, MC, V. **Parking:** Free.
Situated directly on the northern shore of Lake Wallenpaupack is this quintessential honeymoon resort, where the heart-shaped pool was introduced (1963). Designed for couples, this resort attracts a fair share of honeymooners, although 70% of the twosomes who come here are general vacationers of all ages. In addition to the heart-shaped pools, baths, and Jacuzzis, you can also frolic in whirlpools-for-two, designed in the shape of champagne glasses, and Roman-style sunken baths. The decors of most rooms feature red carpet on the floors and walls, gold-louvered windows, mirrored headboards and ceilings, and huge round beds. There are eight types of accommodations, ranging from romantic, dimly lit rooms with no windows to harbor-front rooms with picture windows and private balconies. Most rooms have refrigerators and log-burning fireplaces. The rates include two meals a day; most people avail themselves of 2- or 3-night packages.

Cove Haven is one of four Caesar's resorts in the Poconos. The others are **Brookdale-on-the-Lake,** Rte. 611, P.O. Box 400, Scotrun, PA 18355 (tel. 717/839-8843), for couples and families in the central Poconos; **Paradise Stream,** Rte. 940, Mt. Pocono, PA 18344 (tel. 717/226-2101), a couples-only resort in the central Poconos; and **Pocono Palace,** Rte. 209, Marshalls Creeks, PA 18335 (tel. 717/226-2127), 5 miles north of Stroudsburg; also for couples only.

Facilities: Nightclub with entertainment and dancing; roller-skating rink, gym, heated indoor and outdoor pools, health club, spa, marina; and use of the tennis courts, paddleboats, speedboats, sailboats, water skis, and bicycles. In the winter, you can enjoy skiing, tobogganing, and snowmobiling. There is also horseback riding, at a supplementary charge.

INN AT WOODLOCH PINES, R.D. 1, Box 280, Hawley, PA 18428. Tel. 717/685-7121. Fax 717/685-2644. 138 rms. A/C TV TEL
$ Rates (including 3 meals): $95–$200 double per person. Package rates available. MC, V. **Parking:** Free. **Closed:** Last two weeks of December.

A secluded tree-shaded spot on Lake Teedyuskung is the setting for this family inn, about 10 miles northeast of Lake Wallenpaupack, off Rte. 590. Long a popular site for time-sharing apartments, this 200-acre property offers four types of accommodations, ranging from cottages with motel-style rooms to two- and three-story lakefront buildings with oversized rooms and suites, many with private balconies. The price includes 3 meals per day and use of a wide variety of facilities, including evening entertainment. At certain times of the year, Woodloch is totally booked up to a year in advance, so it is wise to reserve early.

Facilities: Tennis, waterskiing, outdoor pool, cookouts, paddleboats, and an indoor sports complex with pool, sauna, and exercise room.

MODERATE

STERLING INN, Rte. 191, S. Sterling, PA 18460. Tel. 717/676-3311 or toll-free 800/523-8200. Fax 717/676-9786. 39 rms, 16 suites. A/C TV
Directions: On Route 191, 25 miles north of Stroudsburg, and 8 miles south of I-84.
$ Rates (including breakfast and dinner): $75–$90 single; $65–$75 per person double; $90–$95 cottage; $80–$90 suite. AE, MC, V. **Parking:** Free.

Situated on 103 acres of wooded countryside high in the mountains and beside Wallenpaupack Creek, this inn is laid out almost like a village unto itself. You can stay in the main hotel building, which offers 25 rooms and suites, as well as spacious lounges and a charming dining room with a huge fireplace. If you prefer an ambience more akin to a private home, select a room or suite in the 7-unit guesthouse or 12-unit lodge across the street, or perhaps in one of the 2- or 3-unit cottages. There is even a rustic log cabin hidden high in the woods overlooking the creek and the rest of the complex. The accommodations will allow you to be as convivial or secluded as you wish, and innkeepers Ron and Mary Kay Logan are adept at matching guests up with their hearts' desires. Rooms are furnished with local antiques; some units have balconies and/or wood-burning stoves, and all have private bath. At Christmas, stockings are hung (and filled with surprises) on every guest door, and there's a gift for every guest under the tree. The Logans also offer a number of special packages, such as jazz, golf, or mystery weekends, and seminars for aficionados of wildflowers/nature.

Dining/Entertainment: A candlelit restaurant and poolside lounge.

Facilities: Year-round indoor swimming pool, private lake with beach, paddleboats, tennis courts, 9-hole putting course, shuffleboard, 2 hiking trails, and a trout stream. In the winter, there is ice skating, cross-country skiing, tobogganing, and horse-drawn sleigh rides.

SILVER BIRCHES, Star Rte. 2, Box 105, Hawley, PA 18428. Tel. 717/226-4388. 21 rms. A/C TV
$ Rates: $45–$68 per room; $35–$48 per person, with breakfast and dinner; $45–$85 for cottages, no meals. MC, V. **Parking:** Free.

⑤ This hotel is situated on the southern shore of Lake Wallenpaupack, on Rte. 507 and 1 mile south of Rte. 6. Operated by the Ehrhardt family since 1943, these accommodations consist of lakeside rooms in the main lodge, and several individual motel units. All rooms have two double beds, wall-to-wall carpeting, and private bath. Some two-bedroom family units and housekeeping cottages are also available, accommodating from two to four persons. The prices include use of two swimming pools, a shuffleboard, waterskiing, boating, and badminton. (There is an extra charge for rowboats with motors and for sailboats.)

Meals are served at the adjacent Ehrhardt's Lakeside restaurant (see "Where to Dine," below).

WHERE TO DINE

MODERATE

ERHARDT'S LAKESIDE, Rte. 507, Hawley. Tel. 226-2124.
   Cuisine: AMERICAN/SEAFOOD. **Reservations:** Recommended.
$ Prices: Appetizers $2.95–$5.95; main courses $8.95–$17.95; lunch $1.95–$5.95. MC, V.
   Open: July–Aug Mon–Thurs and Sun 11am–11pm, Fri–Sat 11am–midnight; Sept–June Sun–Mon and Wed–Thurs 11am–9pm, Fri–Sat 11am–midnight.

Perched on the southern shore of Lake Wallenpaupack, 1 mile south of Rte. 6, this restaurant offers not only great waterside views but also fine food. It is under the same management as the Silver Birches resort (see "Where to Stay," above). Dinner entrées range from steaks and southern fried chicken to seafood samplers, lobster tails, snow crab legs, stuffed red snapper, scallops mornay, and shrimp marinara, to bouillabaisse. Lunch includes sandwiches, burgers, salads, and Mexican snacks such as tacos, burritos, and nachos.

SETTLERS INN, 4 Main Ave., Hawley. Tel. 717/226-2993 or 226-2448.
   Cuisine: AMERICAN. **Reservations:** Recommended.
$ Prices: Appetizers $2.25–$6.50; main courses $11.95–$19.95; lunch $4.95–$7.95. AE, MC, V.
   Open: Lunch Mon–Sat 11:30am–2pm; dinner daily 5–9pm; brunch Sun 10:30am–2pm.

Dating from 1927, this three-story Tudor-style inn sits on the eastern edge of the lumbering town of Hawley, opposite the town park. Restored and refurbished in 1980 by Jeanne and Grant Genzlinger, it offers a high-ceilinged dining room with a candlelit Colonial atmosphere. The menu is designed to reflect regional food traditions and emphasizes locally produced ingredients, including herbs and spices, organic fruits and vegetables, and farm cheeses. Meats are smoked and cured in-house, and all breads and desserts are made on the premises. Pennsylvania wines and beers are also featured. Entrées include roast chicken breast stuffed with cornbread and country ham; boneless pheasant breast, with sage sausage stuffing and braised cabbage; wine-braised Pennsylvania trout filled with leeks, carrots, and celery; and broiled strip loin beef filet with wild mushrooms, radish salad, and savory bread pudding. Lunch offers equally innovative fare with dishes such as black-bean chili accented by sour cream and farmer's cheese, ham and smoked gouda cheese on four grain bread, and smoked chicken and potato salad. The inn also offers 18 guest rooms, all with private bath.

4. WESTERN POCONOS

Really rural territory awaits you in the western Poconos. As you head west on I-80 or Rte. 940, you'll find fewer resorts and more natural parklands and open spaces.

Besides the mountains, this section is dominated by the Lehigh River. Most people come here, in fact, to enjoy whitewater rafting, although skiing, golfing, and hiking are also popular. In addition, this is ideal territory for mule-riding and all-terrain biking. The chief center for most of these sports is **White Haven,** an outpost of 2,000 residents, named for Josiah White, an 18th-century navigator of the Lehigh.

This remote part of the Poconos is also the home of Jim Thorpe, a charming mountain village (pop. 5,300), named in 1954 to honor the famous 1912 Olympic athlete. The real Jim Thorpe never visited here, but his remains were transferred to a 20-ton granite mausoleum at the entrance to the town when the local citizens decided to perpetuate his memory.

Originally called Coalville, then Mauch Chunk (an Indian name meaning "Bear Mountain"), this settlement was once known as the "Switzerland of America" because of its 19th-century architecture, narrow streets, and European layout, but most of all for its idyllic location on the Lehigh River, surrounded by broad mountain vistas.

A prominent rail transfer point in the coal era of the 1850s, Jim Thorpe was the home of Asa Packer, a local entrepreneur and philanthropist who started the Lehigh Valley Railroad and Lehigh University (in Bethlehem). Today visitors delight in touring Asa Packer's Italianate mansion as well as other prominent, well-preserved buildings of the town.

WHAT TO SEE & DO
WHITEWATER RAFTING

Without a doubt, this sport is king in these parts. Anyone can participate, novice or experienced, although most companies have a minimum age requirement of 10 years. In general, they operate from March through June and from September through November. Here are some of the services available.

White Water Challengers, I-80, exit 40, White Haven (tel. 443-9532), offers half-day trips from $19, full-day treks from $40, or overnight packages from $79 per person. This firm offers trips for a variety of age and experience levels, including "first-timers." Other firms offering similar services are **Jim Thorpe River Adventures Inc.,** 1 Adventure Lane, Jim Thorpe (tel. 325-2570 or toll-free 800/424-RAFT), offers similar services; **Pocono Whitewater/Adventures,** Rte. 903, Jim Thorpe (tel. 325-3655); and **Whitewater Rafting Rentals,** White Haven (tel. 443-4441).

Adjacent to Hickory Run Park, you'll find **Whitewater Rafting Adventures Inc.,** Rte. 534, Albrightsville (tel. 722-0285). This firm operates raft trips at $33–$42 per person.

GOLF

The **Mountain Laurel Resort,** Rte. 940, White Haven (tel. 443-8411), offers an 18-hole PGA course, with greens fees and cart for $40.

MULE RIDES

"Mu-le-teer-ing" rides are conducted by **Pocono Adventures,** Star Route, off Rte. 903, Jim Thorpe (tel. 325-2036). Open daily year round, this company will lead you through 45,000 acres of backwood trails, various guided treks, including a 1-day adventurer's ride, up and down mountains in the scenic wilderness, priced from $80, including breakfast, lunch, and dinner. In addition, there are overnight treks, as well as horse-riding, hayrides, fishing, and hunting packages.

MOUNTAIN BIKING

Described as "all-terrain" vehicles of the bike world, these two-wheelers have fat knobby tires and heavy frames to enable a biker to travel over rock, through mud and sand, and across grassy areas with ease. The bikes have up to 15 speeds for climbing hills and rocky terrain. Guided treks with these bikes are offered by **Whitewater Challengers Inc.,** off I-80, exit 40, White Haven (tel. 443-9532). The cost is $26 to $29 for a 4-hour trip.

OUTDOOR ADULT GAMES

Capture the Flag, off I-80, exit 40, White Haven (tel. 443-9371), organizes "friendly American combat games" in the wilderness of the western Poconos. These games pit teams of two to 20 players in combative sport. The games are set up from March through mid-December, at a cost of $26 to $29 per person. Reservations are required at least 2 weeks in advance. Another firm offering a similar service is **Skirmish,** Rte. 903, Jim Thorpe (tel. 325-3654), charging $27 for a full game or $18 for a shorter version.

SKIING

There are two major ski resorts in the western Poconos. The oldest is **Big Boulder,** Rte. 903, Lake Harmony (tel. 722-0100), started in the 1950s. This facility has a 475-foot vertical drop, 11 slopes and trails, six double chair lifts, and one beginner's triple chair. Lift tickets cost $25 midweek, $32 on weekends, and $20-$25 at night. Nearby is **Jack Frost Mountain,** Rte. 940, White Haven (tel. 443-8425), with a 600-foot vertical drop, 20 slopes and trails, and five double and two triple chair lifts. Lift tickets cost $25 midweek and $32 on weekends. Both resorts offer interchangeable lift tickets, allowing you to ski Jack Frost during the day and Big Boulder at night.

RAIL TOURS

The **Victorian railroad station** in the heart of town, which is today the local visitor information center, is the home base for tours of the western Poconos via restored vintage trains. Operating on weekends from mid-May through October, the trains follow a 8-mile round-trip route through the surrounding countryside for a 40-minute ride, with 34-mile, 2½ hour trips during fall foliage season. Departure times vary, and the price ranges from $4 to $11 for adults and $2 to $6 for children 3 to 11. Reservations are recommended, especially for the popular fall foliage trips. For more information, contact **Rail Tours,** P.O. Box 285, Jim Thorpe, PA 18229 (tel. 717/325-4606) or the **Carbon County Tourist Promotion Agency,** Railroad Station, P.O. Box 90, Jim Thorpe, PA 18229 (tel. 717/325-3673).

WHERE TO STAY

Unlike other parts of the Poconos, the western region does not have a huge choice of accommodations, but the places here are top-notch and each one is distinctive in its own way.

EXPENSIVE

SPLIT ROCK RESORT, Moseywood Road, Lake Harmony, PA 18624. Tel. 717/722-9111 or toll-free 800/255-7625. Fax 717/722-8608. 402 rms and suites. A/C TV TEL.
$ Rates (including breakfast and dinner): $100–$200 single, $130–$230 double. AE, CB, DC, MC, V. **Parking:** Free.

Nestled in a secluded wooded setting beside Lake Harmony, this resort is a community unto itself. It is signposted off Rte. 940, 4 miles east of Rte. 9/Pennsylvania Turnpike extension; there's a 25¢ toll to enter the property. The guest units are spread out over a variety of different lake, forest, garden, or golf course settings—lodges, villas, cottages, and a contemporary three-story hotel known as the Galleria. This building offers the most luxurious accommodations, including suites with full kitchenette, separate sitting room, and Jacuzzi bath. Furnishings range from rustic and Alpine themes to modern art-deco styles, but all units have private bath and other up-to-date amenities; most have either a kitchenette, wet bar, or refrigerator, and some offer a private sauna or log-burning fireplace. A shuttle service operates every 30 minutes, connecting the various buildings and sports facilities.

Dining/Entertainment: Three restaurants, three lounges, two coffee shops, deli, first-run movie theater.

Facilities: 18-hole championship golf course, indoor and outdoor swimming pools, indoor and outdoor tennis courts, racquetball courts, fitness center, sauna-steam room, billiards room, game room, indoor and outdoor basketball courts, softball field, archery range, soccer field, bocci court, bowling lanes, canoes, rowboats, sailboats, motorboats, paddleboats, water volleyball, ski rentals, bike rentals, two gift shops, beauty salon.

MODERATE

MOUNTAIN LAUREL RESORT, Rte. 940, P.O. Box 126, White Haven, PA 18661. Tel. 717/443-8411 or toll-free 800/458-5921. Fax 717/443-9741. 250 rms. A/C TV TEL
$ Rates (including breakfast and dinner): $87–$122 single, $67–$92 double per person. Package rates available. AE, CB, DC, MC, V. **Parking:** Free.

Panoramic mountain and woodland views prevail at this modern three-story resort, nestled in a setting of 300 acres. Each room is furnished in bright, contemporary style; many units have balconies or private patios. Most guests avail themselves of a weekend or midweek package plan, particularly in the spring, fall, and winter months.

Dining/Entertainment: Dining facilities include two restaurants, Treetops and Touch of Vanilla. In addition, there is an ice-cream parlor, a lounge with nightly music, and a tavern.

Services: Free shuttle service to nearby downhill resorts of Jack Frost or Big Boulder; full-time activities for youngsters.

Facilities: Olympic-size indoor and outdoor pools, sauna, exercise room, tennis courts, archery, shuffleboard, miniature golf, horseshoe pits, ice skating, sledding, tobogganing, cross-country skiing, and barnyard petting zoo. (There's a supplementary fee for playing on the hotel's 18-hole golf course.)

HARRY PACKER MANSION, Packer Hill, P.O. Box 4581, Jim Thorpe, PA 18229. Tel. 717/325-8566. 13 rms, 1 suite. A/C
$ Rates (including breakfast): $75–$85 single or double, $95–$110 suite. MC, V. **Parking:** Free.
Built in 1874, this hilltop Second Empire mansion's interior reflects high Victorian grandeur, with walnut woodwork, parquet floors, marble mantels, bronze and polished brass chandeliers, Tiffany windows, and Oriental rugs. On the second and third floors there are seven bedrooms delightfully filled with antiques, which are available to overnight guests; six additional rooms, all with private bath, are also available in the adjacent carriage house.

All guests can enjoy the front veranda, which overlooks the town of Jim Thorpe, and the distinctive ladies' and gentlemen's parlors. For those who can't stay here, there are tours available (Sun–Mon and Thurs–Fri, noon–5pm, on the hour, last tour at 4pm; the cost is $2.50 for adults and $1.50 for children).

INN AT JIM THORPE, 24 Broadway, Jim Thorpe, PA 18229. Tel. 717/325-2599. 21 rms, all with private bath. A/C TV TEL.
$ Rates (including continental breakfast): $65–$95 single or double. AE, MC, V. **Parking:** Free.

Dating back to 1850, this four-story, Victorian-style building stands out because of its historic facade of ornamental iron porches, which adds a touch of New Orleans to the Poconos. Built during the heyday of the coal industry, the inn hosted U.S. presidents and generals, as well as personalities like Buffalo Bill and Thomas Edison. Although it eventually fell into disuse, it was restored and refurbished in 1990. The bedrooms are furnished in a Victorian theme, with ornate headboards, oversized armoires, brass fixtures, and quilted floral bedspreads. Some ground-floor rooms are available. Facilities at the inn include a restaurant and lounge.

WHERE TO DINE

MODERATE

HOTEL SWITZERLAND, 5 Hazard Square. Tel. 325-4563.
Cuisine: INTERNATIONAL. **Reservations:** Recommended for dinner.

$ Prices: Appetizers $1.95–$4.95; main courses $9.95–$16.95; lunch $2.95–$4.95. AE, MC, V.

Open: Lunch daily 11:30am–3:30pm; dinner Fri–Sat 5–9pm.

If you're looking for a good spot to eat after walking the historic streets of Jim Thorpe, this is a fitting choice. Reputedly the oldest remaining structure of the town, dating from the 1830s, this small restaurant will impart a sense of yesteryear from the moment you step inside. To the right is a beautifully restored cherry-and-mahogany bar with marble columns and brass fixtures. In the rear is the Victorian Dining Room, a small restaurant furnished with a carved buffet piece, an antique cupboard, ornate wallpaper in cranberry and ivory shades, and a tin ceiling. Dinner entrées include chicken burgundy, sole amandine, and steaks.

RICHIE'S, Rte. 940, White Haven. Tel. 443-9528.

Cuisine: AMERICAN. **Reservations:** Recommended.

$ Prices: Appetizers $1.95–$5.95; main courses $10.95–$17.95. AE, MC, V.

Open: Dinner daily 4–9pm.

If you long for a good steak, this is the place to go. For over 30 years, Richie (now with son Eric) has catered to skiers, rafters, or vacationers who seek a simple and straightforward meal and a relaxing atmosphere. Besides steaks, the menu offers prime ribs, seafoods, and chicken dishes.

CHAPTER 8

THE LEHIGH VALLEY

- **WHAT'S SPECIAL ABOUT THE LEHIGH VALLEY**
1. **ALLENTOWN**
2. **BETHLEHEM**
3. **EASTON**

Two counties, Northampton and Lehigh, make up the area known as the Lehigh Valley. The region takes its name from the Lehigh River, which meanders in a fertile valley between Philadelphia and the Poconos. Although much of Northampton and the Lehigh counties are farmland, three cities dominate the region: Allentown, Bethlehem, and Easton, an urban trio rich in historical and natural attractions. Over the centuries, the Lehigh Valley was also influenced by strong Biblical traditions, and that is why you'll find that many roads lead to Nazareth, Egypt, and Emmaus.

GETTING THERE

BY AIR

The Lehigh Valley has its own airport, named for its three major metropolitan areas, **Allentown-Bethlehem-Easton International Airport** (tel. 266-6000), known as A-B-E for short. It is located between Allentown and Bethlehem, north of both cities at the juncture of Rtes. 22 and 987 (locally, Airport Road). The following airlines fly scheduled services into **A-B-E: United** (tel. 821-7870 or toll-free 800/241-6522); **USAir** (tel. 437-9801 or toll-free 800/428-4322); **Continental Express** (tel. 433-6255 or toll-free 800/525-0280). Almost all hotels and motels operate complimentary shuttle services to and from the airport for their guests. Transfer time from the airport is 6 minutes to Bethlehem, 10 minutes to Allentown, and 15 minutes to Easton.

BY TRAIN

The nearest train service is into Philadelphia, some 60 to 70 miles south of this area.

BY BUS

Service into Allentown is operated by **Greyhound/Trailways,** which maintains a depot at 27 S. 6th St. (tel. 434-6188). Bethlehem is served by **Greyhound,** into 3rd St. and Brodhead Ave. (tel. 867-3988). Easton is also reached by Greyhound, stopping at 154 Northampton St. (tel. 253-4126). Local bus service within and among the three cities is operated by **Lehigh and Northampton Transportation Authority,** otherwise known as **LANTA-METRO** (tel. 776-7433 or 258-0479); the fare is $1 in exact change.

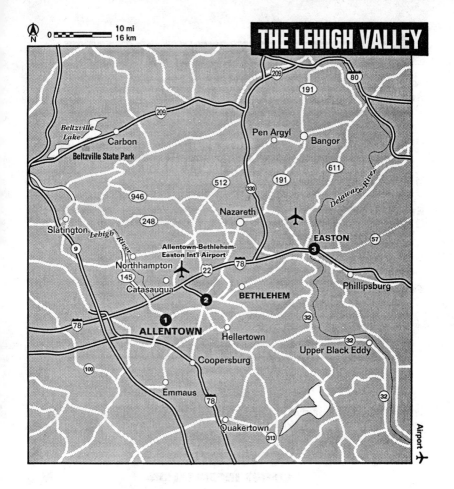

THE LEHIGH VALLEY

0 | 10 mi
0 | 16 km

Beltzville Lake
Carbon
Beltzville State Park

Pen Argyl
Bangor

209

191

80

611

Delaware River

512
330
191

946

Nazareth

248

Slatington
Lehigh River
Northhampton

Allentown-Bethlehem-
Easton Int'l Airport

EASTON

57

9

145
Catasauqua

22
78

BETHLEHEM

Phillipsburg

78

ALLENTOWN

Hellertown

32

Coopersburg

32
Upper Black Eddy

100

Emmaus

78

Quakertown
313

32

Airport

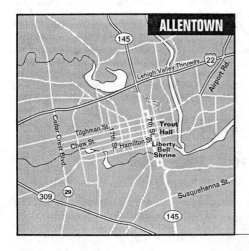

ALLENTOWN

145
Lehigh Valley Thruway
22
Airport Rd.

Cedar Crest Blvd.
Tilghman St.
Chew St.
5th St.
7th St.
Hamilton St.
Trout Hall
Liberty Bell Shrine

309
29

Susquehanna St.

145

Allentown ❶
Bethlehem ❷
Easton ❸

WHAT'S SPECIAL ABOUT THE LEHIGH VALLEY

Ace Attractions
☐ Liberty Bell Shrine, in Allentown, displaying a full-size replica of the famous symbol of freedom.
☐ Lehigh County Velodrome, in Allentown, the "bicycle-racing capital of America."
☐ 18th-Century Industrial Area, a restoration of a Moravian settlement.

Events/Festivals
☐ Bethlehem's Musikfest, 9 days of world-class music from Bach to bluegrass.
☐ Christmas at Bethlehem, a monthlong yuletide celebration.

For the Kids
☐ Dorney Park and Wildwater Kingdom, in Allentown, home of one of the world's tallest wooden roller coasters.

Museums
☐ Allentown Art Museum, exhibiting six centuries of American and European art.
☐ Canal Museum, in Easton, with canal-era memorabilia, a park, and boat rides.

Shopping
☐ Christmas Barn, in Bethlehem, for holiday shopping year round.
☐ Bixler's, in Bethlehem and Easton, America's oldest jeweler and silversmith.

BY CAR

From the east and west, the cities of Allentown, Bethlehem, and Easton are traversed by I-78 and Rte. 22. The Pennsylvania Turnpike's northeast extension, Rte. 9, also passes west of Allentown in a north-south direction.

ORIENTATION
TOURIST INFORMATION

The entire area that includes the cities of Allentown, Bethlehem, and Easton is served by the **Lehigh Valley Convention and Visitors Bureau Inc.,** located at Allentown-Bethlehem-Easton (A-B-E) Airport, International Airport Terminal Building, P.O. Box 2605, Lehigh Valley, PA 18001 (tel. 215/266-0560 or toll-free 800/747-0561). In the summer months, this office also operates **information booths** at two points along Rte. 22 (at North 7th Street, Allentown, and at I-78 and Rte. 100, Fogelsville). Both of these visitor centers are open daily from 9am to 6pm. In addition, as you will see on the following pages, all three major cities, Allentown, Bethlehem, and Easton, maintain an individual information center in their respective downtown districts.

Area Code   All telephone numbers in the Lehigh Valley region belong to the 215 area code.

GETTING AROUND
BY CAR

If you wish to rent a car, depots are maintained at the airport by **Avis** (tel. 264-4571), **Budget** (tel. 266-0666), **Hertz** (tel. 264-4571), and **National** (tel. 264-5535). In addition, **Hertz** has a rental station at 121 Northampton Rd. in Easton (tel. 258-9969); **Budget** has one at the Sheraton Hotel, Easton (tel. 250-8899); and

National has one at 15th and Tilghman Streets, Allentown (tel. 820-6907). If you need a cab, call **Quick Taxi** (tel. 434-8132) or **Yellow Cab** (tel. 258-9141).

---

1. ALLENTOWN

62 miles N of Philadelphia, 162 miles N of Baltimore, 300 miles E of Pittsburgh, 75 miles NE of Lancaster, 40 miles S of Poconos.

GETTING THERE   By Air   There are frequent flights on most major airlines into Allentown-Bethlehem-Easton International Airport, about a 10-minute drive from town.

By Train   The nearest service via **Amtrak** is into Philadelphia, 45 miles south of here.

By Bus   Service into Allentown is operated by **Greyhound,** which maintains a depot at 27 S. 6th Street (tel. 434-6188).

By Car   From the east and west, use I-78 or Rte. 22. From the north and south, use Rte. 9, the Pennsylvania Turnpike NE extension.

ESSENTIALS   Information   Specific data about Allentown can be obtained from the **Allentown-Lehigh Chamber of Commerce,** 462 Walnut St., P.O. Box 1229, Allentown, PA 18105 (tel. 215/437-9661). Open Monday through Friday from 8:30am to 5pm.

City Layout   Bounded on the east by the Lehigh River, Allentown is laid out for the most part on a grid system, with its focus on Hamilton St., which runs east-west, and 7th St., which runs north-south. Although the city is currently in the midst of restoring much of its historic residential area, the downtown skyline is dominated by the modern 23-story tower of the Pennsylvania Power and Light Company.

Special Events   Allentown's parks and gardens provide the setting for **May-fair,** usually slated for five days over the Memorial Day weekend. The program offers over 200 free events including jazz, folk, and big-band music; dancing and fiddling competitions; and concerts, as well as arts-and-crafts exhibitions, jugglers, clowns, and puppeteers. For more information, contact Mayfair, 2020 Hamilton St., Allentown, PA 18104 (tel. 215/437-6900).

The treasured **Liberty Bell** of Philadelphia considers Allentown its second home. Originally a rural village known as Northamptontowne, this area was chosen by George Washington during Revolutionary War times as a place to hide the Liberty Bell while the British occupied Philadelphia. Fearing that the bell would be melted down for British bullets, a contingent of Washington's men brought it by covered wagon to the basement of a local church in Northamptontowne in 1777. The bell remained here for a year until the colonists retook the City of Brotherly Love and it was safe for the symbol of freedom to return.

It was not until a few years later that the name Allentown was adopted in honor of William Allen, one-time chief justice of Pennsylvania and the official founder of this pleasant Lehigh Valley city.

Located 45 miles north of Philadelphia and surrounded by rich farming territory, Allentown today (pop. 103,000) is the hub of industry and manufacturing; such well-known product names as Kraft, Keebler, Alpo, and Stroh's are all here. Allentown is also the home of Muhlenberg College, founded in 1848 to honor the patriarch of Lutheranism in the United States.

WHAT TO SEE & DO

If you tire of walking in the downtown Allentown area, you can always hop on board the **Trolley,** a gasoline-powered version of the original trolleys of yesteryear. It circles the heart of the city every 10 minutes and, best of all, it's free. The route runs up Hamilton Street, from 12th Street to Penn Street, over to Linden, and back down Linden to 12th Street. The Trolley operates Monday through Saturday from 11am to 4pm, with extended evening hours on Thursday until 8pm.

TROUT HALL, 414 Walnut St. Tel. 435-4664.

A good place to start a tour of this city is at Allentown's oldest home, built in 1770 as a summer residence of James Allen, son of William, the city's founder. The property on which the house stands was obtained by William Allen, former mayor of Philadelphia and chief justice of Pennsylvania. Listed in the National Register of Historic Places, this fully restored Georgian Colonial stone house is administered by the Lehigh County Historical Society. Tour guides will take you throughout the house, telling the story of Allentown through the pictures on the walls and the furnishings on display. You'll see portraits of the city founder and his family. Some of the memorabilia are a trundle and rope bed, an old-fashioned bed warmer, a rare music box, needlepoint work, books, and toys.
Admission: Free.
Open: Apr–Nov Tues–Sat noon–3pm, Sun 1–4pm.

LIBERTY BELL SHRINE, 622 Hamilton Mall. Tel. 435-4232.

This is probably Allentown's most celebrated sight. Housed in the Zion Reformed Church, this is where the Liberty Bell was brought when Philadelphia fell to the British in September of 1777. The present church, constructed in 1886, is the fourth to occupy this site. The basement shrine includes a full-size replica of the bell, designed in 1962 as part of Allentown's Bicentennial celebration, and a 46-foot wall mural depicting the Liberty Bell's trek to Allentown; there are also Colonial artifacts and displays of our nation's earliest flags.
Admission: Free.
Open: Mid–Apr to mid–Oct Mon–Sat noon–4pm, Sun 2–4pm; off season Mon–Sat noon–4pm.

LEHIGH COUNTY MUSEUM, Fifth and Hamilton Sts. Tel. 435-4664.

This museum will give you a glimpse of the economic, social, and cultural history of the Lehigh Valley. Housed in Allentown's Old Courthouse building, this is a permanent exhibit spotlighting the region's Native American artifacts, mineral and geological findings, the silk industry of the early 1900s, trucking and agricultural traditions, and leading industries of the 20th century.
Admission: Free, but donation requested.
Open: Mon–Fri 9am–4pm, Sat–Sun 1–4pm.

ALLENTOWN ART MUSEUM, 31 N. Fifth St. Tel. 432-4333.

This complex of eight galleries on three floors includes exhibits on European and American paintings and graphic arts from the 14th to the 20th century, representing everything from classical Greek and French impressionist works to Pennsylvania Dutch folk art. Other highlights include the Frank Lloyd Wright Library, a children's participation and puppet area, and a museum shop well stocked with local handcrafts.
Admission: Free, but a $1 contribution welcomed.
Open: Tues–Sat 10am–5pm, Sun 1–5pm.

TROXELL-STECKEL HOUSE AND FARM MUSEUM, 4229 Reliance St., Egypt. Tel. 435-4664.

This museum is housed in a Colonial stone farmhouse. Built in 1755–56 by John Peter Troxell and now owned by the Lehigh County Historical Society, it is an example of German medieval-style architecture brought to eastern Pennsylvania by early settlers. The adjacent Swiss-style bank barn contains an exhibit of farming implements and carpenter tools on the ground floor; upstairs there are all kinds of carriages, ploughs, sleighs, surrey wagons, and an early omnibus.
Admission: Free.
Open: June–Oct Sat–Sun 1–4pm.

COOL FOR KIDS

One of the best-known attractions in the Lehigh Valley is **Dorney Park and Wildwater Kingdom,** 3830 Dorney Park Rd. (tel. 395-3724), 2 miles west of downtown, off Rte. 222. Over a million people a year flock to this theme-and-water park, which offers three roller coasters, including one of the world's tallest wooden roller coasters, a wave pool, and dozens of rides, shows, and shops. Open on weekends in April and early May and in September; daily in June, July, and August. The hours are from 11am to 8 or 10pm on most days, with slight variations. Admission to Dorney Park and Wildwater Kingdom is $19.95 for adults and $11 for children 3 to 6; reduced-rate admission is also possible to one or the other of these attractions. Parking is $1.50 per car.

Eight miles north of Allentown is the **Trexler-Lehigh County Game Preserve,** off Rte. 309, Schnecksville (tel. 799-4171). Founded in 1909 by Harry Trexler, who also endowed the city's park system, this 1,500-acre natural expanse is home to camels, bison, deer, elk, and palomino ponies, as well as rare birds and exotic animals. There is also a children's zoo and facilities for picnicking, hiking, and bird-watching.

Open daily, Memorial Day through Labor Day from 10am to 5pm; and Sunday only from 10am to 5pm in April and May and September through October. Admission charge is $2 for adults and $1 for children 2 to 12.

SPORTS & ACTIVITIES

Located just west of Allentown, the **Lehigh County Velodrome,** Rtes. 222 and 100, Trexlertown (tel. 965-6930), is often referred to as the "bicycle racing capital of North America." Built in 1975, this high-speed facility is the home of world-class championships and a regular season of pro-am racing from May through September. Most events take place on Tuesday or Friday nights; tickets range from $3 for general admission to $5 for finish-line seating. If you are a speed cycler yourself, the Velodrome is open for public use in the off-season; the grounds also include free parking, a playground, and a picnic pavilion.

JOGGING & WALKING

Special circuits for walkers and joggers are part of the layout in **Trexler Memorial Park,** Cedar Crest and Memorial Boulevards (tel. 437-7628), on the city's western edge. Named for Harry Trexler (1854–1933) who established Allentown's park system, a local game preserve, and a national trust for the maintenance of parks, this complex also includes rose gardens, a trout nursery, and picnicking areas. No admission charge.

SKIING

Allentown is just 17 miles from the **Blue Mountain Ski Area,** Rte. 145, Palmerton, PA (tel. 215/826-7700). Although technically a part of the Poconos, Blue Mountain is often considered Lehigh Valley turf. Open from December through March, this resort sports a vertical drop of 923 feet and offers 14 slopes, five lifts, snow-making facilities, night skiing, and a ski school. Lifts operate from 8:30am to 10pm on weekdays and from 7:30am to 10pm on Saturday, Sunday, and holidays. Lift rates range from $18 to $35 for adults and $16 to $33 for children (aged 12 and under); ski rentals are $17 for adults and $10 to $12 for children.

SHOPPING

Bring home a taste of the Lehigh Valley by stopping at **Josh Early Candies,** 4574 Tilghman Blvd. (tel. 395-4321), a local landmark for more than 50 years. Sold by the piece or the pound, there are 84 varieties of confections ranging from toasted coconut marshmallow fluffs, molasses honey comb, pecan patties, and mint meltaways to chocolate butter creams. Samples are always on the counter to help you decide. Open weekdays from 9am to 9pm and Sunday from 1 to 6pm, Josh Early also maintains a location at 3620 Nazareth Pike, Bethlehem (tel. 865-0580).

Another local enterprise worth a visit is the **Early American Candle Shop,** 5573 Hamilton Blvd., Wescosville (tel. 395-3995), situated 3 miles west of Allentown on Rte. 222. You'll see displays of wax creations in all shapes, sizes, and scents, and you can watch demonstrations of candle making. Open Monday through Friday from 10am to 9pm, Saturday from 10am to 5pm, and Sunday from noon to 5pm.

WHERE TO STAY

The center of commerce for the Lehigh Valley, Allentown is a hub of business traffic during the week. To encourage weekend visitors, many hotels have developed reduced-rate packages. You can therefore enjoy considerable savings if you travel here on a Friday or Saturday night. Be sure to check with the lodging of your choice to see what special deal may apply at the time of your visit.

DOWNTOWN

Expensive/Moderate

ALLENTOWN HILTON, 904 Hamilton Mall, Allentown, PA 18101. Tel. 215/433-2221. Fax 215/433-6455. 219 rms, 8 suites. A/C TV TEL
$ Rates: $82–$92 for single or double; $165–$195 suite. AE, CB, DC, MC, V. **Parking:** Off premises.
In the heart of the downtown shopping district is this modern 10-story property. All guest rooms are decorated in bright pastel contemporary tones and are equipped with one or two double beds. Suites are bilevel with spiral staircases. Guest facilities include a restaurant, a lounge, an indoor swimming pool, a health club, an exercise room and sauna, and parking. Services include room service, laundry, and valet services.

HAMILTON PLAZA, 4th and Hamilton Sts., P.O. Box 273, Allentown, PA 18105. Tel. 215/437-9876. Fax 215/437-9853. 99 rms, 4 suites. A/C TV TEL
$ Rates: $59 single; $69 double; $120 suite. AE, CB, DC, MC, V. **Parking:** Free.
The top choice in the downtown area is this deluxe seven-story property. The guest rooms are decorated with pastels and period furniture, and most rooms have wraparound bay windows and city views; there are also four theme suites (featuring decors reflecting Bali, an Arabian caravan, Victoriana, and a Stardust motif). Facilities include a restaurant and lounge. Services include room service, laundry, and valet services.

RADISSON HOTEL AMERICUS CENTRE, 6th and Hamilton Sts., Allentown, PA. Tel. 215/434-6101 or toll-free 800/333-3333. Fax 215/434-0159. 85 rms, 4 suites. A/C TV TEL
$ Rates: $89 single or double; $118 suite. AE, CB, DC, MC, V. **Parking:** Valet parking $5 per day.
This hotel is located in the heart of downtown, next to Symphony Hall and the city bus terminal. The landmark 11-story building, which dates back to the 1920s, offers a warm old-world atmosphere in its public rooms, while the guest rooms have been renovated and refurbished. All bedrooms and suites are decorated with light colors and dark woods, and some units have Jacuzzis or kitchenettes. Guest facilities include a concierge desk, a gift shop, and a hair salon for men and women.

Dining/Entertainment: Lobby lounge with piano entertainment on most evenings, and a full-service restaurant, the Rose Garden.

SUBURBS
Moderate

COMFORT SUITES, 3712 Hamilton Blvd., Allentown, PA 18103. Tel. 215/437-9100 or toll-free 800/228-5150. Fax 215/437-0221. 122 suites. A/C TV TEL
$ Rates (including continental breakfast): $49–$75 single; $59–$85 double. AE, CB, DC, DISC, MC, V. **Parking:** Free.

One of the newest hotels in the Lehigh Valley, this four-story, all-suite property opened in late 1990. It is ideal for families, business travelers, or anyone who craves more than just a standard bedroom. Each guest unit has a sleeping area, with choice of two double or a king-size bed, large modern bathroom with separate vanity cabinet, and a sitting area with sofa, table and chairs, plus microwave oven, and refrigerator; some king-bedded suites also have a whirlpool bath. The furnishings are contemporary, with designer fabrics and deep pastel tones; access to rooms is via computer-card key.

Facilities: An informal restaurant/pub, O'Hara's; an exercise room; a game room; and VCR and video-tape rentals.

Services: Complimentary limousine service to airport, valet-laundry service.

SHERATON JETPORT, 3400 Airport Rd., Allentown, PA 18103. Tel. 215/266-1000 or toll-free 800/325-3535. Fax 215/266-1888. 130 rms, 20 suites. A/C TV TEL
$ Rates: $91–$101 single; $95 double; $125 suite. AE, CB, DC, MC, V. **Parking:** Free.

Just across the street from the A-B-E airfield is this modern three-story T-shaped hotel. Each room has either two double beds or one king-size bed, with floor-to-ceiling mirrored closets, and a radio/alarm clock. Guest amenities include a heated indoor pool, a Jacuzzi, a sauna, a courtyard, ample parking, a nightclub that features top-40 hits, and a full-service restaurant called Teddy's.

Budget

DAYS INN, 1151 Bulldog Dr., Allentown, PA 18104. Tel. 215/395-3731 or toll-free 800/325-2525. Fax 215/395-9899. 284 rms. A/C TV TEL
Directions: At Rtes. 22 and 309, ½ mile east of exit 33 of Pennsylvania Turnpike Extension.
$ Rates: $40–$65 single, $45–$70 double. AE, DC, DISC, MC, V. **Parking:** Free.

This hotel is conveniently situated in a westerly direction, 5 miles from downtown. Formerly a Holiday Inn, this rambling, mostly one-story property has an alpine style and decor. Facilities include an all-day café, lounge, gift shop, and an outdoor pool. It offers room service.

WHERE TO DINE
DOWNTOWN
Moderate

B & G STATION, 318 Hamilton St. Tel. 439-4900.
Cuisine: INTERNATIONAL. **Reservations:** Recommended.
$ Prices: Appetizers $3.95–$7.95; main courses $9.95–$19.95; lunch $3.95–$9.95. MC V. **Open:** Lunch Mon–Sat 11am–2:30pm; dinner Mon–Thurs 4–10pm, Fri–Sat 4–11pm, Sun 4–9pm; brunch Sun 11am–2:30pm.

Comprised of a restored vintage train station and an adjacent railroad car, this restaurant will make you want to say "All aboard!" as you sit down to dine. Besides a lot of railroad memorabilia, the decor is rich in dark mahogany woodwork, brass and wrought-iron fixtures, and stained-glass windows. The eclectic menu offers such entrées as sesame shrimp, Norwegian salmon, charbroiled sword-fish, and lobster from the tank, as well as prime ribs, steaks, veal Oscar or florentine, chicken teriyaki, and stir-fry dishes. Lunch focuses on sandwiches, salads, burgers, burritos, fajitas, pastas, and light seafood and meat selections.

PATIO RESTAURANT, 9th and Hamilton Sts. Tel. 821-4377.
　Cuisine: INTERNATIONAL. **Reservations:** Recommended.
$ **Prices:** Appetizers $2.95–$6.95; main courses $6.95–$24.95; lunch, same menu. AE, MC, V.
　Open: Mon, Thurs–Fri 11am–8pm; Tues–Wed and Sat 11am–5pm; Sun noon–5pm.

One of the dining surprises downtown is this restaurant on the lower level of Hess's, a shopping emporium founded in 1897 and an Allentown institution in its own right. Here we have a real star. Lunch choices include a creative array of salads and sandwiches. The extensive international dinner menu, available all day, includes lobster tail Newburg in a patty shell, stuffed shrimp, salmon steak, stir-fry dishes, seafood tempura, prime ribs, steaks, and vegetable platters. The Patio is also known for its display of irresistible desserts, such as strawberry tart, lemon sponge pie, and southern pecan pie ($1.95 to $2.95).

SUBURBS
Expensive

BLAIR CREEK INN, R.R. 2, P.O. Box 20, off Rte. 222, Mertztown, PA 19539. Tel. 215/682-6700.
　Cuisine: INTERNATIONAL. **Reservations:** Recommended.
$ **Prices:** Appetizers $6–$10; main courses $16–$28; lunch $5.95–$10.95. MC, V.
　Open: Lunch Wed–Fri 11am–2pm; dinner Wed–Sat 5:30–9pm; Sun brunch 10:30am–1:30pm. **Closed:** July 4th weekend.

For a gourmet treat in a country setting, venture 10 miles southwest of Allentown to this restaurant built in 1847 as a Quaker meetinghouse. Later used as a farmhouse and eventually a hotel in the late 19th century, the inn was purchased and opened as a restaurant in 1988 by the Miller family. There are four dining rooms, each meticulously restored and furnished with local antiques, oil paintings, and quilted hangings. The windows look out onto the farmland country-side and the inn's well-tended flower gardens.

Entrées at dinner include roast quail, pheasant en croute, wild boar, rack of lamb, chateaubriand, and a unique "phantom of black pasta" (seafood medley of shrimp, lobster, scallops, and crab in a garlic chablis sauce with black fettuccine). The inn also offers an impressive Sunday brunch with more than 15 entrées, from eggs Benedict to Welsh rarebit and finnan haddie to chicken in the pot.

Moderate

KING GEORGE INN, 3141 Hamilton Blvd. Tel. 435-1723.
　Cuisine: INTERNATIONAL/SEAFOOD. **Reservations:** Recommended.
$ **Prices:** Appetizers $5.95–$7.95; main courses $11.95–$21.95; lunch $3.95–$8.95. AE, CB, DC, MC, V.
　Open: Lunch Mon–Sat 11:30am–4:30pm; dinner Mon–Thurs 4:30–10pm, Fri–Sat 4:30pm–midnight; Sun dinner 4–9pm or 10pm.

The aura of Colonial Allentown is alive and well at this two-story stone structure, established as a stagecoach hotel in 1756 and listed in the National Register. There are four dining rooms, including the original ground-level Hearth Room with exposed brick walls and an open fireplace. Upstairs is featured a glass-enclosed porch setting and the Prince of Wales Tavern, with various coats of arms on the walls. Dinner entrées include steaks, chicken Cajun, lobster, imported Irish salmon, Maryland crab cakes, and shrimp Newburg.

WALP'S, 911 Union Blvd. Tel. 437-4841.
   Cuisine: AMERICAN/PENNSYLVANIA DUTCH. **Reservations:** Recommended.
$ Prices: Appetizers $1.95–$4.95; main courses $6.95–$14.95. AE, DISC, MC, V.
   Open: Mon 6:30am–9pm, Tues–Sun 6:30am–10pm. **Closed:** July 4th, Christmas.

Ⓢ Pennsylvania Dutch cooking and American cuisine are featured at this family-oriented restaurant with four separate dining rooms. Founded over 50 years ago, it's decorated in a country cupboard theme, with pewter dishes and tankards, stained-glass windows, and curio sideboards. The extensive menu features Schnitz un Knepp, Yankee pot roast, smoked sausage, and chicken and dumplings, as well as seafood and steaks. Desserts, made fresh daily in the on-premises bake shop, include puddings, cakes, and a variety of pies (the shoofly pie is irresistible). Breakfast and lunch are also served, but the greatest values are at dinnertime. "Early bird" specials are available Mon–Fri 11am–5:30pm.

WIDOW BROWN'S INN, 4939 Hamilton Blvd., Wescosville. Tel. 398-1300.
   Cuisine: INTERNATIONAL. **Reservations:** Recommended.
$ Prices: Appetizers $2.95–$6.95; main courses $10.95–$18.95; lunch $4.95–$7.95. AE, CB, DC, MC, V.
   Open: Lunch Mon–Fri 11:30am–2pm; dinner Mon–Sat 4:30–10pm, Sun 1–9pm.

★ Great value is offered at this restaurant, where an old-fashioned schoolhouse theme pervades, with copybook menu covers, shelves of timeworn textbooks, wall maps, and globes—all that's missing is the teachers and homework! Dinner
Ⓢ entrées include broiled seafood dishes, veal Cordon Bleu, shrimp scampi, and prime ribs. All main courses entitle you to unlimited trips to the unique revolving salad bar. A second Widow Brown's Inn is located 10 miles north of Easton at Main and Bushkill Streets, Stockertown (tel. 759-7404).

EVENING ENTERTAINMENT

Top Broadway plays are presented by the **Pennsylvania Stage Company,** at the **J. I. Rodale Theatre,** 837 Linden St. (tel. 433-3394). Once a church, this 274-seat facility opened as a theater in 1977, and is a year-round showcase for professionally produced musicals and dramas. Tickets range from $15 to $20; the curtain is at 8pm on Tuesday through Saturday, and at 7pm on Sunday, with matinees on Thursday at noon and Sunday at 2pm.

   Allentown Symphony Hall, 23 North 6th St. (tel. 432-7961), presents frequent performances by the Allentown Symphony Orchestra as well as Broadway plays and other works by visiting companies. Schedules vary, but tickets usually range from $15 to $25. The box office is open Monday through Friday from 10am to 5pm and Saturday from 10am to 1pm.

2. BETHLEHEM

9 miles E of Allentown, 59 miles N of Philadelphia,
12 miles W of Easton, 40 miles S of the Poconos

GETTING THERE   By Air   There are frequent flights on most major airlines into Allentown-Bethlehem-Easton International Airport, about a 6-minute drive from town.

By Train   The nearest train service is **Amtrak** into Philadelphia, 59 miles south of here.

By Bus   Greyhound provides service into nearby Allentown and Easton.

By Car From the east or west, use I-78 or Rte. 22. From the north or south, use Rte. 9.

ESSENTIALS Brochures on the attractions of the area are available from the **Bethlehem of Pennsylvania Visitor Center,** 509 Main St., Bethlehem, PA 18018 (tel. 215/868-1513). This office publishes a handy tourist brochure called *The Bethlehem Star.* In the centerfold, you'll find a self-guided walking tour and a map of the historic district. There is also a half-hour orientation film shown here at 11am and 2pm. Open Monday through Friday from 9am to 5pm and on Saturday from 10am to 4pm. There is a charge for the film of $1.50 for adults and 50¢ for children.

SPECIAL EVENTS Over 600 free musical events are part of the program of Bethlehem's annual **Musikfest,** held in mid-August. Drawing performers from throughout the United States and Europe, this 9-day program features everything from Bach to bluegrass, big bands to brass choirs, and vesper concerts, chamber music, ethnic folk dancing, and street balladeers. Concerts generally take place outdoors at various sites throughout the city, such as the Sun Inn courtyard, the fairgrounds, Main Street, and Broad Street. Admission is free to most daytime attractions, although evening indoor candlelight concerts cost $7 to $12. A complete schedule and more information are available from the **Bethlehem Musikfest Association,** 556 Main St., Bethlehem, PA 18018 (tel. 215/861-0678).

⭐ **Christmas at Bethlehem** is a month-long celebration of more than 60 events, including tree-lighting ceremonies, lantern walking tours, and Bach choir concerts. Many events are free, although the popular **Night-Light Tours,** which are offered seven nights a week, at 6:15, 7:30, and 8:45pm, cost $5 for adults and $1.50 for children (reservations are required, tel. 215/868-1513). The mid-December **Bach choir concerts** also require reservations and cost from $10 a person. Order tickets from the Bach Choir, 423 Heckwelder Pl., Bethlehem, PA 18018 (tel. 215/866-4382). Further information and a complete program can be obtained from the **Bethlehem Area Chamber of Commerce,** 459 Old York Rd., Bethlehem, PA 18018 (tel. 215/868-1513).

─────────────────

In the heart of the Lehigh Valley between Allentown and Easton is **Bethlehem,** an area first settled by Moravian missionaries from Europe. Shortly after they arrived, a small group gathered to sing hymns on Christmas Eve of 1741. As they raised their voices to praise Christ's little town of Bethlehem, they also came upon a name for their new community.

Ever since then, America's Bethlehem has prospered. The Moravians built a thriving industrial center along the banks of the Lehigh River and this was followed by the steel mills of the 19th and 20th centuries. Today Bethlehem Steel is still the area's largest employer, with its corporate headquarters dominating a four-mile stretch of the town. Modern Bethlehem is also distinguished by its institutions of higher learning, such as Lehigh University and Moravian College.

But, most of all, this little patch of Pennsylvania is "America's Christmas City." As you enter the downtown area, a series of brown signs, each with a shining white star, will lead you to the historic district of America's Bethlehem, still a city of Moravian influence and traditions. Most of all, this is a place where Christmas lives year round in the songs and hearts of the people.

WHAT TO SEE & DO

18TH-CENTURY INDUSTRIAL AREA, 459 Old York Rd., access via Union Boulevard. Tel. 691-5300.

⭐ This is the best place to start a tour of this historic city. Here you will see Bethlehem as it looked in the mid-1700s as a prosperous Moravian settlement along the banks of the Monocacy Creek. You'll see a tannery, a gristmill, a springhouse, a miller's house, and the waterworks, considered the first municipal water-pumping system in the United States; and in every building, interpretive guides demonstrate the crafts and trades of yesteryear. Totally restored, this 10-acre site is listed in the National Register of Historic Places. Guided tours are also conducted April through December, on Saturday from 10am to 4pm and on Sunday from 1pm to 4pm; and from late-June through Labor Day, also on Tuesday through Friday from 10am to 4pm.

Admission: $3 adults, $2 students.

Open: Apr–June and Sept–Dec Sat 10am–4pm, Sun noon–4pm; July–Aug Tues–Sat 10am–4pm, Sun 1–4.

GEMEIN HAUS, 66 W. Church St. Tel. 867-0173.

 The oldest building in Bethlehem, otherwise known as the "community house" or the Moravian Museum, is located on the hillside overlooking the industrial area. Built in 1741, this five-story white-oak log house is staffed by women in traditional Moravian dress who will guide you through the 15 rooms and tell the story of early Bethlehem. You'll see artifacts reflecting the life and interests of the early settlers, such as Moravian furniture, clocks, musical instruments, art, and needlework. The guides will answer questions about the history of the Moravian church back to the 1400s.

Admission: $3 adults, $1 children.

Open: Tues–Sat 1–4pm. **Closed:** Jan and holidays.

GOUNDIE HOUSE, 501 Main St. Tel. 691-5300.

Built in 1810, this is the first Federal-style brick town house erected in Bethlehem. It was the home of John Sebastian Goundie, a prominent Moravian brewer. The ground-floor rooms (dining room, hallway, and kitchen) have been restored and are furnished to reflect the 19th century.

Admission: Free.

Open: Daily Mon–Fri 11am–4pm, Sat 10am–4pm, Sun 1–4pm.

KEMERER MUSEUM OF DECORATIVE ARTS, 427 North New Street. Tel. 868-6868.

This museum features a collection of American furniture, regional paintings, and local textiles, glass, toys, and dolls, as well as Pennsylvania German art and artifacts. Established in 1954 through the will of a local collector, Annie Kemerer, the museum aims to tell the story of the Lehigh Valley from the 18th through the 20th centuries.

Admission: Free, but donations are accepted.

Open: Tues–Fri 1–4pm; Sat 10am–4pm, Sun noon–4pm. **Closed:** Jan.

SHOPPING

Bethlehem is an ideal place to buy Christmas wares—any time of the year. A fitting place to start a holiday spree is the **Christmas Barn,** 4186 Easton Ave. (tel. 861-0477), housed in a gem of an old barn on the northeast edge of town. It's a one-stop source for holiday cards, wrappings, ornaments, and nutcrackers, as well as over 1,000 music boxes from around the world. Open Monday through Thursday and Saturday from 10am to 5pm; Friday from 10am to 9pm, and Sunday from noon to 5pm, with extended hours from October 1 through December 24.

For holiday decorations, wreaths, and candles of all kinds, don't miss the **Early American Candle Shop,** Rtes. 22 and 512, Park Plaza (tel. 865-4700), housed in a restored Colonial mansion. Open Monday through Friday from 10am to 9pm, Saturday from 10am to 5pm, and Sunday from noon to 5pm.

For stocking stuffers or yummy gifts, visit **Josh Early Candies,** 3620 Nazareth Pike (tel. 865-0580), an area landmark for over 50 years. You'll find more than 80 varieties of confections ranging from toasted coconut marshmallow fluffs, molasses honeycomb, pecan patties, and mint meltaways to chocolate butter creams, and, of course, candy canes. Open weekdays from 9am to 9pm and Sunday from 1 to 6pm. No credit cards.

Dating from the 18th century, the **Moravian Book Shop,** 428–434 Main St. (tel. 866-5481), is a tradition in the heart of the historic district. It's a great place not only for books, but also for cards, gifts, gourmet foods, and local crafts.

There is also a café/deli section that sells freshly made soups, salads, quiches, sandwiches, and pastries. Open Monday through Wednesday and Friday from 10am to 6pm; Thursday from 10am to 8pm; and Saturday from 10am to 5pm.

WHERE TO STAY
DOWNTOWN

HOTEL BETHLEHEM, 437 Main St., Bethlehem, PA 18018. Tel. 215/ 867-3711. Fax 215/867-0598. 130 rms. A/C TV TEL
$ Rates: $79–$85 single or double. AE, CB, DC, MC, V. **Parking:** Free.
The only choice downtown is this gracious old-world property dating from the 1920s and recently refurbished. Situated in the midst of the historic area, this hotel offers individually decorated rooms with traditional reproduction furnishings and a choice of bed size; some rooms also have Jacuzzi-type baths. Guest facilities include a beauty salon, a boutique, and a gift shop. The restaurant has a Colonial-style motif, including old lanterns and a mural of old Bethlehem highlights.

SUBURBS
Moderate

HOLIDAY INN, Rtes. 22 and 512 off Center Street, Bethlehem, PA 18017. Tel. 215/866-5800 or toll-free 800/HOL-IDAY. Fax 215/867-9120. 195 rms. A/C TV TEL
$ Rates: $73 single, $81 double. AE, CB, DC, MC, V. **Parking:** Free.
This modern two-story property features a blend of rich burgundy tones and mirrors in its public rooms. The contemporary bedrooms have two double beds or a king-size bed, light woods, and pastel-toned fabrics. Amenities include an outdoor swimming pool; a nightclub, Encore; and a restaurant, Krista's, featuring nouvelle American cuisine.

Budget

COMFORT INN, 3191 Highfield Dr., Bethlehem, PA 18017. Tel. 215/ 865-6300 or toll-free 800/228-5150. Fax 215/865-6300, ext. 333. 116 rms. A/C TV TEL
$ Rates: (including continental breakfast): $43–$53 single, $58–$68 double. AE, DC, DISC, MC, V. **Parking:** Free.
Set back from the main road in a grassy hilltop setting, this three-story modern property has rooms with king- or queen-size or two double beds, contemporary pastel furnishings, and VCRs. Some units have a Jacuzzi bath. Guest facilities include a lounge, Cheers, and a game room.

WHERE TO DINE
DOWNTOWN
Moderate

SUN INN, 564 Main St. Tel. 974-9451.
Cuisine: AMERICAN. **Reservations:** Recommended.
$ Prices: Appetizers $4.50–$7.95; main courses $15.50–$21; lunch $5.95–$7.95. MC, V.
Open: Lunch Tues–Sat 11:30am–2pm; dinner Tues–Sat 5–9pm.
In the heart of the historic downtown area is Bethlehem's top restaurant, which is also a major sightseeing attraction. First opened as an inn in 1760, records show that early guests included George Washington, John Hancock, Ethan Allen, John Adams, and the Marquis de Lafayette. Authentically restored in 1982, this Moravian building is furnished with many unique pieces from its early days, such as a

10-leg bench and antique glass from Lititz. There are three candlelit dining rooms upstairs, and a Colonial courtyard in back for all fresco dining in the summer. Dinner entrées include 18th-century recipes, ranging from chicken baked in plum-and-walnut sauce to stuffed Cornish hen.

THE CAFE, 221 W. Broad St. Tel. 866-1686.
  Cuisine: INTERNATIONAL. **Reservations:** Recommended.
  $ Prices: Appetizers $4–$6; main courses $14–$19; lunch $5–$7. AE, DC, MC, V.
  Open: Lunch Tues–Fri 11am–2pm; dinner Tues–Sat 5–9pm. Sat brunch 9am–2pm.

A Victorian atmosphere prevails in this lovely pink house with a sloping mansard roof and gingerbread trim. Eclectically furnished with dark woods and tapestries, it has a lounge bar in the main parlor and a small dining room downstairs and four more distinctive dining rooms upstairs. Dinner entrées include chicken with cashews, Thai shrimp curry, pasta with seasonal vegetables, and ever-changing beef and veal dishes. A tempting array of homemade cheesecakes and fruit tarts is offered for dessert; there is also a small bakery shop on the main level, if you prefer to have your sweets to go.

3. EASTON

70 miles N of Philadelphia, 12 miles E of Bethlehem,
18 miles E of Allentown, 40 miles S of the Poconos

GETTING THERE   By Air   There are frequent flights on most major airlines into Allentown-Bethlehem-Easton International Airport, about a 15-minute drive from town.

By Train   The nearest service is via **Amtrak** into Philadelphia, 70 miles south of here.

By Bus   Greyhound provides service to Easton, stopping at 154 Northampton St. (tel. 253-4126).

By Car   From the east or west, use I-78 or Rte. 22. From the north, use Rte. 33 or 611. From the south, use Rte. 611.

ESSENTIALS   For specific data on Easton, contact the **Two Rivers Area Commerce Council,** 157 S. 4th St., Easton, PA 18042 (tel. 215/253-4211). A visitor center is maintained at this address from 8am to 5pm Monday through Friday. Self-guided walking tour folders of the city are also available here, free of charge.

The smallest of the Lehigh Valley cities, Easton (pop. 26,000) was founded in 1752 by Thomas Penn, son of William. The name Easton was chosen in honor of the English homestead of the younger Penn's wife, Juliana.

From the beginning, the streets were laid out in a grid pattern, surrounding a central plaza called Centre Square. The scene of early Indian treaties, the square had its greatest moment when the Declaration of Independence was proclaimed aloud for the first time on July 8, 1776, making Easton one of three cities to share the honor (Philadelphia and Trenton were the other two).

In the 19th century, Easton became one of America's key commercial and transport centers, owing to its location at the junction of the Lehigh and Delaware Rivers; three canals and five major railroads also came together here. In its prime, Easton served as a valuable conduit between the booming anthracite coal regions of northeastern Pennsylvania and the major east coast cities of Philadelphia and New York.

A college town, like Allentown and Bethlehem, Easton is the setting of the 110-acre campus of Lafayette College, a landmark in the northern hills overlooking the city. Currently in the process of restoring many of its great 18th- and 19th-century buildings, Easton is also the home of a unique museum that pays tribute to America's canal history.

WHAT TO SEE & DO

The historic and geographic heart of Easton is its central plaza or **Centre Square,** at the intersection of Northampton Street (which runs east to west) and Third Street (which runs north to south). This large square was the site of pre-Revolutionary Native American peace treaties held between 1756 and 1762. Then the Northampton County Courthouse was built here and stood from 1765 until 1862. Most significant of all, this is the spot where the Declaration of Independence was proclaimed verbally on July 8, 1776, along with simultaneous readings in Philadelphia and Trenton, following its formal adoption on July 4. Markers commemorate all of these moments in history, and, in addition, a granite Civil War memorial dedicated to local veterans has stood here since 1900. The square is also used for public gatherings and for outdoor farmers' markets.

✪ The heyday of America's inland waterways is celebrated at the **Canal Museum,** 200 S. Delaware Dr. (tel. 250-6700), south of the city at the juncture of the Lehigh and Delaware Rivers on Rte. 611. This fascinating exhibit invites visitors to step back into the 18th and 19th centuries, when 1,200 miles of canals stretched across Pennsylvania, more than any other state, linking cities, villages, mines, factories, and farms. A 6-minute video presentation describes the history of canals and locks in the United States, and particularly the Lehigh and Delaware Canal, the last of the great canals. Exhibits also focus on the people who made their living from the canals and what life was like for them. Open year round, Monday through Saturday from 10am to 4pm and Sunday from 1 to 5pm. Admission charge is $1.50 for adults and 75¢ for children aged 5 to 12.

If you're between 3 and 103 years old and want to stay healthy, then plan a visit to Easton's **Weller Center for Health Education,** 2009 Lehigh St. (tel. 258-8500), a preventive health education complex, with ongoing instructional programs for students and adults. Established in 1982, this was one of the first trend-setting centers of its kind in the United States. Basic health concerns are discussed in small groups with the aid of sophisticated visual aids, three-dimensional exhibits and models, and colorful electronic devices. There are 14 student and seven adult programs, discussing general health, family life, nutrition, and drug education. Although many programs are designed for groups, the center is also open for walk-ins, from 9am to 2:30pm in the summer; participation in a 1½-hour adult program costs $3.50; students $1.75.

SPORTS & ACTIVITIES

The **Hugh Moore Park,** 200 S. Delaware Drive (tel. 250-6700), is next to the Canal Museum and runs for 6 miles along the Lehigh River. It includes the Lehigh Canal, locks, a cable suspension bridge, a locktender's house, and other canal structures, many of which have been included in the National Registery of Historic Places. Named for a local resident and supporter who founded the Dixie Cup company, the 260-acre park includes picnic sites, a 4-mile bike path, two hiking trails, and facilities for boating. Paddleboats, canoes, and bikes can be rented (from $5 an hour). The picnic and park areas are open year round from dawn to dusk. Sports equipment rental is available from Memorial Day weekend through Labor Day, Wednesday through Friday from 11am to 5pm; Saturday from 11am to 7:30pm, Sunday from 12:30pm to 7:30pm; and in September on weekends only.

Nearby is the starting point for **Canal Boat Rides,** at 25th Street on the Canal (tel. 250-6700). This company offers one-hour rides on a restored section of the Lehigh Canal via an authentic mule-drawn canal boat called *Josiah White.* The craft operates from Memorial Day weekend through Labor Day, Wednesday through Saturday at 11am, 1, 2:30, and 4pm; on Sunday at 1, 2:30, and 4pm; and in September on weekends only at 1, 2:30, and 4pm. Tickets are $4 for adults and $2 for children 5 to 12.

More active sportspeople flock to the **Point Pleasant Canoe Outfitters,**

Martins Creek, Rte. 611 (tel. 258-2606), 5 miles north of Easton. This is a branch location of the company that maintains a large rafting, tubing, and canoeing operation at Point Pleasant in Bucks County, about 20 miles south of here. This depot primarily provides for multiple-day canoe and rafting trips, and the rental of camping equipment, from Memorial Day to Labor Day only. A 40-mile, 2-day trip is priced from $30 per person; a 3-day, 60-mile trip costs from $40 per person; and rafting can be organized from $40 a day for a two-person raft. For a brochure describing all possibilities and prices, contact **Point Pleasant Canoe,** P.O. Box 6, Point Pleasant, PA 18950 (215/297-8181).

SHOPPING

Easton is the home of **Bixler's,** 24 Centre Square (tel. 253-3589), an enterprise that is reputed to be America's oldest jeweler and silversmith, founded by Christian Bixler in 1785. The original Bixler was a clockmaker and silversmith, who made over 465 clocks and dozens of silver spoons, many of which are still on display today in the store, as well as 18th-century ledgers and other historical memorabilia. Currently operated by the sixth generation of the same family, Bixler's is still known for its silver and clocks. Open Monday through Saturday from 9:30am to 5pm, and until 8pm on Friday. Bixler's also operates a branch in Bethlehem at 514 Main St. (tel. 866-8711).

WHERE TO STAY

Like the rest of the city, the hotels of Easton have been undergoing restoration or refurbishment in recent years. You won't find a great choice of accommodations, but the properties listed below offer a warm and eager welcome.

MODERATE

SHERATON-EASTON INN, S. Third St. and Larry Holmes Dr., Easton, PA 18042. Tel. 215/253-9131 or toll-free 800/325-3535. **Fax** 215/252-5145. 84 rms. A/C TV TEL
$ Rates: $65–$73 single, $73–$86 double. AE, CB, DC, MC, V. **Parking:** Free.
This modern four-story property is near the banks of the Lehigh River and next to a six-film movie theater. It offers rooms of varying pastel tones and contemporary furnishings, some with city views and others overlooking the outdoor swimming pool and courtyard.
   Hary's Canal Restaurant, on the ground floor, conveys an old-Easton atmosphere with a waterfall, stone walls, and Colonial-style furniture.

BUDGET

DAYS INN, Rte. 22 at the 25th St. Shopping Center, Easton, PA 18042. Tel. 215/253-0546 or toll-free 800/325-2525. Fax 215/252-8952. 84 rms. A/C TV TEL
$ Rates: $40–$55 single, $48–$65 double. AE, DC, DISC, MC, V. **Parking:** Free.
This modern four-story hotel offers contemporary rooms with a choice of double- or king-size beds. Some nonsmoking rooms are available, and there are several ground-floor rooms.

WHERE TO DINE
MODERATE

WIDOW BROWN'S INN, Main and Bushkill Sts., Stockertown. Tel. 759-7404.
   Cuisine: INTERNATIONAL. **Reservations:** Recommended.
$ Prices: Appetizers $2.95–$6.95; main courses $10.95–$18.95; lunch $4.95–$7.95. AE, CB, DC, MC, V.
   Open: Lunch Mon–Fri 11:30am–2pm; dinner Mon–Fri 4:30–10pm, Sat 5–10pm, Sun 1–9pm.

Like its other branch in Allentown, this spot is a real find for great food at moderate prices. A vintage schoolhouse theme dominates the decor, with old books and local memorabilia on the shelves. Broiled seafood dishes, steaks, veal or chicken Cordon Bleu, and shrimp scampi, as well as generous cuts of prime ribs (the house specialty), are the features at dinner. All main courses entitle you to unlimited trips to the rotating salad bar.

EVENING ENTERTAINMENT

Easton's main hotel, the **Sheraton Inn** (tel. 253-9131), provides evening music in its lounge, particularly on weekends. In addition, you can enjoy a wide range of entertainment at the **State Theatre,** 453 Northampton St. (tel. 252-3132). This renovated Beaux-Arts building, a former vaudeville palace built in 1926, is a regional center for the performing arts, with operas, jazz concerts, ballets, and top-class plays. Tickets average $16 to $20, depending on the event; the curtain is usually at 8pm. The box office is open from 10am to 5pm, and on performance days from 5pm to curtain time.

CHAPTER 9

HARRISBURG & HERSHEY

1. HARRISBURG
- **WHAT'S SPECIAL ABOUT HARRISBURG**

2. HERSHEY
- **WHAT'S SPECIAL ABOUT HERSHEY**

In the heart of south central Pennsylvania, Harrisburg and Hershey are known as capitals for different reasons. Harrisburg is, of course, the state capital, but, in many ways, Hershey is better known because it is the world capital of chocolate making. Just 10 miles apart, Harrisburg and Hershey can easily be visited together.

---

1. HARRISBURG

105 miles W of Philadelphia, 208 miles E of Pittsburgh, 75 miles N of Baltimore

GETTING THERE   By Air   Harrisburg International Airport (tel. 948-3913) is located at Middletown, about 15 minutes from downtown Harrisburg. It now has a new $14 million terminal with all-weather jetways and expanded parking facilities. Airlines serving this facility include **American** (tel. 233-5700 and toll-free 800/433-7300); **Delta** (tel. 948-2921 or toll-free 800/221-1212); and **USAir** (tel. 948-3611 or toll-free 800/428-4322).

By Train   Amtrak operates regular daily service to Harrisburg from Philadelphia and the Northeast Corridor and via the New York–Chicago route. All trains come into the **Pennsylvania Railroad Station,** 4th and Chestnut Streets (tel. 232-3916), two blocks from the State Capitol buildings, where there's a taxi stand.

By Bus   Harrisburg is served by **Greyhound/Capitol Trailways,** 411 Market St. (232-4251).

By Car   From east and west, Harrisburg can be reached via the Pennsylvania Turnpike; from the north and south, via I-81. An approach from the south can also be made via I-83. In addition, Rte. 15 also runs from north to south through Harrisburg.

ESSENTIALS   Area Code   The Harrisburg area code is 717.

INFORMATION   Brochures, maps, and other helpful data can be obtained from the **Capital Region Chamber of Commerce,** 114 Walnut St., P.O. Box 969, Harrisburg, PA 17108-0969 (tel. 717/232-1377), midway between 2nd Street and Front Street. In addition, the headquarters for the tourism authority for the whole state of Pennsylvania is located here; it's the **Bureau of Travel Marketing,** Pennsylvania Department of Commerce, 453 Forum Building, Harrisburg, PA 17120 (tel. 717/787-5453 or toll-free 800/VISIT-PA).

The capital of Pennsylvania since 1810, Harrisburg (pop. 53,000) is situated in the middle of the state, almost equidistant between the two major metropolitan areas of Philadelphia and Pittsburgh.

Nestled on the shores of the Susquehanna, this area was originally known as Louisborg, for Louis XVI. Credit for the first settlement goes to John Harris, who

WHAT'S SPECIAL ABOUT HARRISBURG

Ace Attractions
- ☐ State Capitol Complex, a 65-acre site with archives, museum, library, concert hall, and government buildings.
- ☐ Governor's Residence.
- ☐ Three Mile Island, the "famous" nuclear power plant, now open for touring.

Architectural Highlights
- ☐ Capitol Building, with dome styled after St. Peter's in Rome.

Museums
- ☐ State Museum of Pennsylvania, six stories of exhibits and a planetarium.
- ☐ Museum of Scientific Discovery, offering 65 hands-on exhibits.

Parks
- ☐ City Island, 64 acres of parkland on an island in the Susquehanna River.

established a trading post here in 1710; in 1733 he obtained a grant of 800 acres of land. Twenty years later, his son, John Jr., began operating a ferry across the river; he eventually laid out the town in 1785 and asked for the name change to Harrisburg. Visitors to this city today not only enjoy the results of John Harris Jr.'s efforts as a city planner, but they can also visit his house on Front St.

Although the main attraction of this city is understandably the State Capitol Complex, there are many other historic buildings of interest to visitors. From the brick-lined district of Shipoke to the original Market Square, you'll see an 18th-, 19th-, and early 20th-century blend of residential neighborhoods, town house streetscapes, and riverfront mansions. In addition, four historic bridges, built between 1890 and 1926, span the Susquehanna River with both pedestrian and motorway crossings.

GETTING AROUND

BY CAR

Since so many hotels are located on the outskirts of the city, you will probably want to drive to the center of the city and park. There are four large parking garages (on Chestnut, Locust, Walnut, and Market), all within walking distance to the State Capitol and other major sights. Parking averages $2 an hour or $6 a day.

Rental agencies with local desks at Harrisburg International include **Avis** (tel. 944-4401); **Budget** (tel. 944-4019); **Hertz** (tel. 944-4088); **National** (tel. 948-3710); and **Thrifty** (tel. 944-4000).

BY TAXI

If you prefer to get around by taxi, call **Yellow Cab** (tel. 238-7252); **Penn-Harris Taxi** (tel. 238-7377); or **West Shore Taxi** (tel. 795-8294). Taxi service from the airport to Harrisburg and Hershey is provided by **Airport Limo** (tel. 944-4019); **Diamonds S. Cab** (tel. 944-2516); **Penn-Harris Taxi; West Shore;** and **Yellow Cab.**

WHAT TO SEE & DO

As the capital of Pennsylvania, Harrisburg naturally revolves around the State Capitol Complex, a 65-acre area in the heart of the city, including executive, legislative, and judicial government buildings, as well as archives, a museum, a library, and a concert hall.

MAIN CAPITOL BUILDING, 3rd and State Sts. Tel. 787-6810.

✪ This is the focal point of the State Capitol Complex. Constructed in 1906, this is a grand Italian Renaissance edifice with a dome styled after St. Peter's Basilica in Rome and a staircase inspired by the Paris Grand Opera House. It is open to the public for tours on a hourly basis (except noon).

Admission: Free.
Open: Mon–Sat 9am–4pm.

STATE MUSEUM OF PENNSYLVANIA, 3rd and North Sts. Tel. 787-4978.

✪ Established in 1905, this is the official museum of the Commonwealth of Pennsylvania. Moved to its present location in 1965, this six-story circular building is the home of exhibits on the state's archeology, decorative arts, fine arts, geology, military history, natural science, science, industry, and technology. There is also a planetarium, a café, and two intriguing museum shops. The planetarium shows are on Saturday and Sunday at 1:30pm and 3pm.

Admission: Free for museum, but there's a charge for movies and shows of $1 for adults, 50¢ for seniors or children 12 and under.
Open: Tues–Sat 9am–5pm, Sun noon–5pm.

GOVERNOR'S RESIDENCE, 2035 N. Front St. Tel. 787-1192.

Completed in 1968, this Georgian Revival residence is the third official executive mansion to have been located in Harrisburg. Exhibits include displays of Pennsylvania crafts, local art, and an outside garden planted with trees and shrubs native to the state. Tours are given to the public.

Admission: Free.
Open: Apr–Oct, Tues and Thurs 10am–2pm.

JOHN HARRIS AND SIMON CAMERON MANSION, 219 S. Front St. Tel. 233-3462.

Listed in the National Register of Historic Places, this riverfront building contains a museum that reflects Harrisburg's early days, plus a reference library and the offices of the local county historical society. Tours are given Monday through Friday from 11am to 3pm and the second and fourth Sundays of the month, 1–4pm. The library is open Monday through Thursday from 1 to 4pm.

Admission: $2.50 adults, $2 seniors, $1 children 8 and over.
Open: Mon–Fri 11am–3pm, and 2nd and 4th Sun of each month 1–4pm.

MUSEUM OF SCIENTIFIC DISCOVERY, 3rd and Walnut Streets. Tel. 233-7969.

✪ Harrisburg is also home to this unique "hands-on" museum designed for the scientifically curious of all ages. There are more than 65 exhibits that encourage visitors to send a whisper, freeze a shadow, feel a calorie, and many other feats.

Admission: $3 adults, $2 students 3 to 17.
Open: Tues–Sat 10am–6pm, Sun noon–5pm.

FORT HUNTER MANSION, 5300 N. Front St. Tel. 599-5751 or 255-1369.

Rich with history, this mansion overlooks the Susquehanna River. The spot was originally settled in 1725 and, through the years, served variously as a prosperous milling center, military fort, dairy farm, frontier village, and distillery to a private estate. The central house, listed in the National Register of Historic Places, is a testament to two centuries of Pennsylvania living, with furnishings of Early American, Empire, and Victorian styles. The grounds, dotted with buttonwood trees dating back to William Penn's time and herb gardens, also include two historic barns, an icehouse, a tavern, a springhouse, and a blacksmith shop. Admission fees include tours by trained guides.

Admission: $3 adults, $1 children over 6.

Open: May–Dec Tues–Sat 10am–4:30pm, Sun noon–4:30pm.

THREE MILE ISLAND, T.M.I. Visitor Center, P.O. Box 480, Middletown, PA 17057. Tel. 717/948-8588 or 948-8829 (for tours only).

Even since the accident at this nuclear plant on March 28, 1979, Three Mile Island has drawn worldwide attention. Visitors can tour the facility via 25-passenger buses on regularly scheduled tours, either 1½ hours or 2½ hours in duration. Both tours are prefaced by an explanation of nuclear power operations, with ample time for questions. The tours are appropriate for all ages. Tours must be reserved at least 2 weeks in advance.

Admission: Free.

Open: Tues–Fri 10am–4:30pm, Sat noon–4:30pm.

SPORTS & ACTIVITIES

If you're looking for a good place to jog or bike, try **Riverfront Park,** which runs along the city's eastern edge at Front Street. Developed from 1902 to 1930, this open park is the focus of Harrisburg's "City Beautiful" movement. It contains trails and pathways extending for 5 miles along the Susquehanna River, from the historic district of Shipoke on the south side to the city line in the north.

From Riverfront Park it is just a walk (via Walnut St. Bridge) or a drive (via Market Street Bridge) over the Susquehanna to **City Island.** This floating midriver island contains 64 acres of parkland with a sports complex, public beach, picnic sites, and an excellent view of the Harrisburg skyline.

City Island is also the home base for the ***Pride of the Susquehanna*** (tel. 234-6500). This handsome, 150-passenger paddlewheel riverboat offers continuous 40-minute narrated sightseeing excursions, daily from June through Labor Day, with more limited service in May and September to October. The cost is $4.75 for adults and $3 for children.

From May to September, the **Harrisburg Harbor Ferry** also crosses between City Island and the downtown area. The 12-passenger ferries operate 7 days a week, from 9am to 9pm, offering a water-taxi shuttle service for a $1 per person fare. The boats also provide half-hour sightseeing tours at $2 per person. For more information, call 761-2630.

Six miles north of downtown is **Fort Hunter Park,** 5300 N. Front St. (tel. 599-5751), a 37-acre grassy knoll along the Susquehanna River with picnic tables, riverside walking trails, a comfort station, and lighted walkways. All facilities are available free of charge, on a first-come basis.

Fifteen miles northeast of Harrisburg is the **Penn National Race Course,** exit 28 off I-81, Grantville (tel. 469-2211). A setting for thoroughbred horse racing, this track is about 5 miles from Hershey. Racing is scheduled year round, daily from March to November (except Tuesday and Thursday), and once or twice a week at other times. Post time is 7:30pm on weekdays and 1:30pm on Sundays and holidays. Admission is $1.50 to the grandstand and $3 for the clubhouse reserved seating. Parking is $1.

SHOPPING

Much of Harrisburg's shopping activity is now focused on **Strawberry Square,** 3rd and Walnut Streets, a block of renovated buildings transformed into a three-story midtown mall. Housing more than 50 specialty shops and ethnic food nooks, this trendy enclave was built in 1977, and was the first phase of a major downtown revitalization project. Currently being enlarged to include an adjacent block of 11 more historic structures (and more new shops and restaurants), this complex is located across the street from the State Capitol. Open Monday through Friday from 10am to 6pm, and on Saturday from 10am to 5pm.

Harrisburg also boasts one of the oldest continuously operating (since 1860) farmers' market houses in Pennsylvania, the **Broad Street Market,** at 3rd and Verbeke Streets. Restored in 1976 with new landscaping and a central brick plaza, this market is a great source for fresh farm produce, snacks, home-baked goods, gifts, and local crafts. Open Thursday and Friday from 7am to 6pm and on Saturday from 7am to 4pm.

WHERE TO STAY

Although many hotels and motor inns claim a Harrisburg address, most properties lie outside the downtown area. Harrisburg is well served by a network of roads, however, so that no distance is really very far.

In general, Harrisburg hotels are heavily booked with business traffic during weekdays, so most of the normal rates quoted below are expensive. But if you visit on a Friday or Saturday night, you'll probably be eligible for weekend packages that could mean savings of 35% to 40%. Be sure to check when you book a room.

DOWNTOWN
Expensive

HARRISBURG HILTON & TOWERS, One North Second Street, Harrisburg, PA 17101. Tel. 717/233-6000 or toll-free 800/HILTONS. Fax 717/233-6271. 326 rms, 15 suites. A/C MINIBAR TV TEL.

$ Rates: $116–$145 single, $126–$175 double, $275 suite. AE, CB, DC, DISC, MC, V. **Parking:** Free.

Opened in late 1990, this $40-million, 15-story development has given Pennsylvania's capital a world-class hotel at last. The welcoming decor of the lobby and other public areas is enhanced by the artwork of 10 Harrisburg-area artists, including a 200-foot-square impressionist mural depicting the city's riverfront skyline during a spring sunrise.

The guest rooms are equally impressive, with dark woods and bright rich-toned fabrics, tile and marble bathrooms, and many extras, such as at least two phones, and computer card key access. The 14th and 15th floors, known as The Towers, are geared to executive travelers, with upgraded furnishings and amenities, limited elevator access, separate check-in, private lounge, complimentary continental breakfast, and concierge service.

Dining/Entertainment: Options include the Golden Sheaf (see "Where to Dine," below) for a formal setting, as well as the more casual Raspberries, Market Square Café, and The Bar, a piano lounge.

Services: Room service, valet and shoe-shine service, complimentary transport to airport.

Facilities: Indoor swimming pool, health club, 16 meeting rooms, gift shop, travel agency, enclosed parking garage.

Moderate

HOLIDAY INN CENTER CITY, 23 S. 2nd St., Harrisburg, PA 17101. Tel. 717/234-5021 or toll-free 800/238-8000. Fax 717/234-5021, ext. 125. 261 rms. A/C TV TEL.

$ Rates: $69–$109 single or double. AE, CB, DC, MC, V. **Parking:** Free.

This hotel is in the heart of the city, two blocks from the rail/bus terminal and three blocks from the State Capitol Complex. The 10-story modern tower was recently (1980) renovated and offers contemporary rooms with king- or queen-size or double beds, as well as smoking or nonsmoking units. Each room has a radio. Other facilities include an indoor pool, valet parking, game room, and gift shop.

Dining/Entertainment: Located just off the lobby is Syd's, a combination of restaurant and lounge, with a bright and brassy decor.

SUBURBS
Moderate

SHERATON HARRISBURG EAST, 800 E. Park Dr., Harrisburg, PA

17111. Tel. 717/561-2800 or toll-free 800/325-3535. Fax 717/561-8398. 160 rms, 12 suites. A/C TV TEL
$ Rates: $75 single; $85 double; $135–$150 suite. AE, CB, DC, MC, V. **Parking:** Free.

This is an ideal place to stay if you're dividing your time between Harrisburg and Hershey (9 miles east). In a country garden setting, the Sheraton is designed around a spacious, brick-lined courtyard with a skylit atrium. The modern bedrooms are furnished with dark woods and contemporary colors, with a choice of double or queen- or king-size beds. Amenities include courtesy shuttle service to and from the airport, indoor swimming pool, and a health club with sauna, whirlpool, and exercise program. In addition, there is a lounge, Bourbon Street, with weekend entertainment; and a full-service restaurant, Mr. Smith's.

DAYS INN AIRPORT—HARRISBURG, 815 Eisenhower Blvd., Middle-town, PA 17057. Tel. 717/939-1600 or toll-free 800/325-2525. Fax 717/939-8763. 135 rms, 50 suites. A/C TV TEL
$ Rates (including complimentary hot breakfast): $64–$69 single, $74–$79 double, $89–$119 suite. AE, CB, DC, DISC, MC, V. **Parking:** Free.

Almost midway between the airport and downtown, this six-story hotel offers particularly good value along this busy strip. The standard guest rooms are furnished with dark woods, contemporary fabrics, two double beds, desk, and chairs, and have a bathroom with separate vanity area. The suites have a queen-size bed and a pull-out sofa, plus microwave oven, refrigerator, and coffee maker. Facilities include an indoor swimming pool, exercise room, sauna, piano lounge, meeting rooms, and complimentary shuttle to airport.

Budget

COMFORT INN—HARRISBURG EAST, 4021 Union Deposit Rd., Harrisburg, PA 17109. Tel. 717/561-8100 or toll-free 800/228-5150. Fax 717/561-1357. 117 rms. A/C TV TEL
$ Rates (including continental breakfast): $59–$62 single, $66–$69 double. AE, CB, DC, DISC, MC, V. **Parking:** Free.

The attractive, five-story brick exterior of this hotel and the inviting Williamsburg-style decor of its lobby set the tone throughout. The guest rooms are handsomely furnished with dark woods, gilt-framed prints, bright pastel and floral fabrics, work desk, reclining chair and ottoman, well-lit bathroom with large vanity area, and choice of two double beds or a king-size bed. There are more than a dozen ground-floor rooms, and two floors (3 and 5) are set aside for nonsmokers. Guest facilities include an outdoor heated swimming pool, fitness center, guest laundry, complimentary shuttle to airport, 24-hour coffee service, and three meeting rooms.

FAIRFIELD INN—HARRISBURG WEST, 175 Beacon Hill Blvd., New Cumberland, PA 17070. Tel. 717/774-6200 or toll-free 800/228-2800. Fax 717/774-6200. 105 rooms. A/C TV TEL
$ Prices: $39.95–$42.95 single, $45.95–$48.95 double. AE, CB, DC, MC, V. **Parking:** Free.

The first of its chain to open in Pennsylvania, this three-story property debuted in late 1990, offering comfortable and attractively furnished accommodations at low prices, in an accessible location. There are three types of bedrooms—a compact one-bedded room ideal for a single traveler, standard double, and a larger room with a king-size bed. All units have homey touches such as full-length mirror, alarm clock, lounge chair, work desk, and oversized towels.

Complimentary coffee and newspapers are offered in the lobby. Facilities include an outdoor swimming pool, laundry service, computer-card keys, elevator, and a meeting room.

WHERE TO DINE
DOWNTOWN
Expensive

AU JOUR LE JOUR, 540 Race St. Tel. 236-2048.
Cuisine: FRENCH. **Reservations:** Required.
$ Prices: Appetizers $3.95–$8.95; main courses $13.95–$22.95; lunch $7–$12.
AE, CB, DC, MC, V.
Open: Lunch Mon–Fri 11:45am–1:30pm; dinner Mon–Sat 5–9pm.

A French menu and decor prevails at this little restaurant housed in a small brick town house in Shipoke, near the river. This is an old section of the city that is currently undergoing extensive restoration and renovation. Brick walls, burgundy tones, and pictures of Paris dominate the inside decor of this intimate bistro. Lunch concentrates on light French dishes like coq au vin, legumes au gratin, and seafood pasta salad. Dinner features such creations as center-cut pork loin filled with sausage, prunes, and herbs; filet of fish poached in white wine; beef au poivre; and lump crab in puff pastry.

GOLDEN SHEAF, One North Second St. Tel. 233-6000.
Cuisine: INTERNATIONAL. **Reservations:** Required.
$ Prices: Appetizers $3.95–$9.95; main courses $14.95–$25.95; lunch $6.95–$12.95. AE, CB, DC, DISC, MC, V.
Open: Lunch Mon–Fri 11:30am–2pm; dinner Mon–Fri 6–10pm, Sat 6–11pm.

Small and intimate, this is one of the few Harrisburg hotel restaurants that can stand on its own. The decor is a blend of plush banquettes and floral-design sofas, and striking paintings by local artists depicting still-life subjects with bold primary colors. The tables are set with marble plates, fine silver, and fresh flowers.

The menu is equally impressive, with such entrées as poached sole with lobster stuffing, grilled chicken breast Dijon, roast duck with Bordelaise sauce, pork with peppercorn mustard crust and cider gravy, salmon stuffed with sole mousseline, and dry-aged strip steak with blue-cheese butter. Lunch offers a selection of creative meat or seafood salads and hot entrées.

Moderate

HOPE STATION, 606 N. Second St. Tel. 257-4480.
Cuisine: INTERNATIONAL. **Reservations:** Recommended.
$ Prices: Appetizers $3.95–$7.95; main courses $12.95–$25.95; lunch $4.95–$8.95. AE, CB, DC, DISC, MC, V.
Open: Lunch Mon–Fri 11am–3pm; dinner Mon–Fri 5–10pm, Sat 5–11pm.

In the heart of Harrisburg, opposite the capitol, is Hope Station, tucked in a converted landmark firehouse dating back to 1871. The restaurant itself is quite new (1985) but the old building's architectural charms remain, plus the added touches of crisp linens, fresh flowers, and a very personable staff.

An innovative menu is featured at dinner, with such dishes as filet mignon topped with shiitake mushroom and port sauce, shrimp Amaretto, chicken stuffed with veal mousse, fresh-cut Australian venison of the day, and a variety of pasta dishes. Lunch items range from salads and sandwiches to burgers, stir-fry dishes, and pizzas. There is mellow jazz piano music on many nights.

Budget

HARRIS HOUSE TAVERN, 14–16 N. 3rd St. Tel. 236-0861.
Cuisine: AMERICAN. **Reservations:** Not required.
$ Prices: Appetizers $1.95–$4.95; main courses $5.95–$17.95; lunch $2–$5. AE, CB, DC, DISC, MC, V.
Open: Mon–Sat 11am–10:30pm.

Located one block from the capitol complex, the Harris House Tavern has been a favorite with government employees for the last 30 years. The decor conveys the ambience of Old Harrisburg with city memorabilia mounted on the walls, plus an eclectic blend of old lampposts, stained glass, theatrical lights, and oil paintings by local artists. Dinner primarily features charcoal- and rotisserie-cooked steaks, chicken, and seafood.

SUBURBS
Expensive

ALFRED'S VICTORIAN, 38 N. Union St., Middletown. Tel. 944-5373.
   Cuisine: INTERNATIONAL. **Reservations:** Recommended.
   $ Prices: Appetizers $4.95–$6.95; main courses $14.95–$27.95; lunch $4.99–$12.99. AE, CB, DC, DISC, MC, V.
   Open: Lunch Mon–Fri 11:30am–2pm; dinner Mon–Sat 5–10pm; Sun dinner 3–9pm.

As the name implies, this restaurant is housed in a turn-of-the-century Victorian home built in 1888, and the current owner/chef, Alfred Pellegrini, has restored and revived all the fanciful trappings. The facade is a feast of gables, peaks, and gingerbread trim, while the ornate interior is rich in stained glass, beveled mirrors, intricate woodwork, chandeliers, and window seats.

And best of all, the food is worthy of the setting! Dinner entrées have an international slant, with veal saltimbocca, steak Diane, crêpes fruits de mer, crab and shrimp imperial, and lobster tail Wellington, as well as a dozen northern Italian pasta dishes.

Moderate

CASA RILLO, 451 N. 21st St., Camp Hill. Tel. 761-8617.
   Cuisine: ITALIAN. **Reservations:** Recommended.
   $ Prices: Appetizers $2.95–$6.95; main courses $9.95–$23.95; lunch $4.95–$11.95. AE, CB, DC, MC, V.
   Open: Lunch Mon–Fri 11:30am–4:30pm; dinner Sun–Thurs 5–10pm, Fri–Sat 5–11pm.
This domain of the Rillo brothers is surrounded by colorful gardens and is located in a mostly residential neighborhood, on the western side of the river. The interior decor features rose-colored walls, tapestries, and knotty-pine trim. Try the huge "tuna godfather" at lunch. Dinner offers an array of Italian specialties—veal with artichokes and prosciutto in cream sauce, crab and pasta, eggplant parmigiana, and "grandma's favorite" (linguine with shrimp and marinara sauce).

CATALANO'S, 461 S. Front St., Wormleysburg. Tel. 763-7905.
   Cuisine: ITALIAN. **Reservations:** Recommended.
   $ Prices: Appetizers $5.25–$9.95; main courses $12.95–$19.95; lunch $3.95–$10.95. AE, DC, DISC, MC, V.
   Open: Mon–Fri 11:30am–10pm, Sat noon–10pm.
For the best view of the Susquehanna River and the Harrisburg skyline, take the Market Street Bridge across the river to this restaurant. Situated right on the water, Catalano's presents wide vistas from its screened-in Venetian terrace and wide-windowed dining room. Dinner includes fresh seafood and steaks, plus such Italian dishes as veal saltimbocca, chicken cacciatore, shrimp scampi, and fettuccine Alfredo. Prime rib is also featured on Thursday, Friday, and Saturday nights.

EVENING ENTERTAINMENT

Harrisburg's performing arts are centered at **The Forum,** 5th and Walnut Streets (tel. 787-3197), part of the capitol complex. This 1,800-seat theater is an attraction in itself, with marble walls and columns, maps of nations, and a remarkable astrological ceiling. It is the home of the Harrisburg Symphony Orchestra and the venue for a varied year-round program of concerts, opera, ballet, jazz, and other musical recitals. Most tickets average $12 to $20, and performances are usually at 8pm.

Tickets to the Forum and to all types of other cultural and sporting events in the

Harrisburg–Hershey region can be purchased at **Ticket Place,** on the first floor of Strawberry Square, 3rd and Walnut Streets (tel. 236-0483), a one-stop central box office. Open Monday through Friday from 10am to 4pm, and Saturday from 11am to 4pm.

Information about current and upcoming events can also be obtained by calling the **Arts Hotline** (tel. 232-ARTS).

About 20 miles southwest of Harrisburg is the highly acclaimed **Allenberry Playhouse,** Rte. 174, Boiling Springs (tel. 717/258-6120), an entertainment complex owned by the Heinze family since 1944. Located in a wooded country setting on the Yellow Breeches Creek, it offers musicals, comedies, dramas, and Broadway classics. Performances are scheduled from April through November, on Wednesday through Saturday at 8:30pm, with matinees on Wednesday through Sunday at 2 or 3pm. Tickets average $11 to $18; show/buffet meal combinations are also available from $21.95 to $31.95.

The complex also includes two lodges and three cottages with a total of 57 rooms with bath, available year round, plus an Olympic-size swimming pool, four tennis courts, a fly-fishing school, and a full-service restaurant serving lunch and dinner to the public in the moderate price bracket. Rates for a double room start at $85. For more information about overnighting, dining, or fishing, contact the **Allenberry Resort Inn,** P.O. Box 7, Boiling Springs, PA 17007 (tel. 717/258-3211).

2. HERSHEY

12 miles E of Harrisburg, 80 miles N of Baltimore, 95 miles NW of Philadelphia, 180 miles E of Pittsburgh, 10 miles E of Harrisburg

GETTING THERE   By Air   Hershey is served by the **Harrisburg International Airport** (tel. 948-3913), in Middletown, 20 minutes southwest of Hershey. Flights are available from **American** (tel. 233-5500 and toll-free 800/433-7300); **TWA** (tel. 238-0861 and toll-free 800/221-2000); and **USAir** (tel. 948-3611 and toll-free 800/428-4322).

By Train   **Amtrak** operates regular daily service to Harrisburg from Philadelphia and the Northeast Corridor and via the New York–Chicago route. All trains come into the **Pennsylvania Railroad Station,** 4th and Chestnut Streets (tel. 232-3916),

WHAT'S SPECIAL ABOUT HERSHEY

Ace Attractions
- ☐ Hersheypark, a "Candyland" of amusements and recreation spread over 87 acres.
- ☐ Hershey's Chocolate World, tracing the story of the candy bar.

Events/Festivals
- ☐ Great American Chocolate Festival, a weekend feast for chocolate enthusiasts.
- ☐ Hershey Arts, a spring feast of arts and crafts amid the Hershey Gardens.

- ☐ Christmas at Hershey, a month of winter wonderland and holiday hoopla.

Gardens
- ☐ Hershey Gardens, a 23-acre botanical wonderland.

Museums
- ☐ Hershey Museum, an entertaining and educational look at American life.

Zoo
- ☐ ZooAmerica, 11 acres of animals in natural settings.

and there's a taxi stand outside for the 10-mile transfer to Hershey. If you are staying at the Hershey Hotel or Lodge, complimentary transport will be provided to and from the airport or train station.

By Bus   Greyhound/Trailways serves the Harrisburg depot, 411 Market St., 10 miles west of Hershey.

By Car   Hershey is 10 miles east of Harrisburg via Rtes. 322 and 422 (see "Getting There, By Car" in the Harrisburg section above). If you are traveling from the east, get off the Pennsylvania Turnpike at exit 20 and then take Rte. 72 north to Rte. 322, which will bring you into Hershey.

Special Events   Hershey is the ideal venue for the annual **Great American Chocolate Festival.** This "one sweet weekend" is held in mid-February, a delight to chocolate enthusiasts of all ages. Events include the ultimate chocolate meal, a chocolate "blast from the past" 1950s hop, and a chocolate fashion show. Both the Hotel Hershey and the Hershey Lodge have special packages for this festival; for further information write to the hotels or call toll-free 800/533-3311.

Hershey Arts is a fine arts-and-crafts festival that takes place at the end of June in the Hershey Gardens. The program, which runs from 9am to dusk on Saturday and until 5pm on Sunday, includes instrumentalists, wandering street entertainers, puppeteers, folk and jazz performers, and exhibits of arts and crafts. Admission is $3 for adults and $1 for children 4 to 18. For more information and a complete program, call 717/534-3492.

◐ Christmas at Hershey, which extends from late November through December, is a winter wonderland setting of madrigal dinners, choral concerts, breakfasts with Santa Claus, magic shows, traditional carriage rides, caroling, ice-carving demonstrations, Christmas light tours, puppet shows, flute music, animated holiday characters performing in village shop windows, old-time toy trains chugging through winter scenes, candlelight ceremonies, and all the usual Hersheypark attractions, many opened with extended hours. For a brochure and more information call toll-free 800/533-3131.

▌t is not hard to tell you've arrived in Hershey—the sweet aroma of chocolate is in the air, street lights are in the shape of candy kisses, and thoroughfares are named "Chocolate Avenue" and "Cocoa Avenue." At every turn, you are welcomed to the "Chocolate Crossroads of the World"; even huge bayberry bushes are meticulously shaped to spell out the words "Hershey Cocoa."

Although this area was originally settled in the early 1700s, Hershey today owes its name and success as a chocolate capital to Milton S. Hershey. He not only started a chocolate factory here in 1903, but also planned and built the surrounding community and resort.

Hershey (pop. 18,000) is still widely recognized for the production of chocolate (the huge silos at the chocolate factory in the center of town hold more than 90 million pounds of cocoa beans), but thanks to Milton Hershey, it's also a major complex of visitor attractions—from Hersheypark and Hershey Gardens to the Hershey Theatre, the Hershey Arena, and the Hershey Museum of American Life. You can even learn how candy is made at Chocolate World, a see-and-smell museum that illustrates the whole process, in various stages, from the cocoa bean to the chocolate bar.

ORIENTATION
AREA CODE

Hershey's area code is 717.

INFORMATION

The **Hershey Information Center,** 300 Park Blvd., Hershey, PA 17033 (tel. toll-free 800/HERSHEY) is staffed by helpful Hershey representatives. This office is located at the main entrance to the amusement park and is well stocked with brochures, maps, and lists of events.

CITY LAYOUT

Hershey is spread out over several miles, with the grand old Hotel Hershey and the Hershey Gardens high on a hilltop overlooking the rest of the town, and the Hershey Lodge on lower ground at the west edge of town. Most other motels are concentrated on Chocolate Avenue (Rte. 422), east or west of the downtown area. The Hersheypark attractions, however, are all grouped together and are adjacent to the Information Center, the arena, the stadium, and Chocolate World. Founders Hall, the Hershey Theatre, the Country Club and Parkview golf courses, and the main downtown area are all a short drive away from the hotels or the main entrance to Hersheypark.

GETTING AROUND

BY SHUTTLE BUS

In the summer months, a free **Hershey Shuttle** bus stops at the following locations: Hotel Hershey, the Hershey Lodge, Hershey Highmeadow Camp, ZooAmerica, Hershey Gardens, and Tram Circle at Hersheypark. The bus runs on the hour between 9am and 10pm.

GUIDED TOUR BUS

In addition, there is the **Hershey Trolley Works** (tel. 533-3000), a guided tour service via an air-conditioned trolley-type bus designed in a turn-of-the-century motif. Trolley staff, dressed in period costumes, take visitors on a 45-minute trip around the town, with a narration that imparts a sampling of both historical tidbits and barbershop quartet singing.

The trolleys leave on the hour from the Tram Circle area of Hersheypark. The schedule is daily from 11am to 3pm, early June to early September. The cost is $4.95 for adults, $3.95 for young visitors 5 to 14, and free for children 4 and under. Reservations are not required. From mid-September to December, there are weekend guided tours without performers; from 11am to 3pm, priced at $4 for adults and $2 for young visitors 5 to 14; children under 4 free.

BY MONORAIL

During the off-season months, the **Hersheypark monorail** serves as a swift and scenic link between the park and downtown (the fare is $2 round-trip or $1 one way). The monorail runs every 15 minutes.

BY TAXI

If you prefer a taxi, local service is provided by **Diamond S. Cabs** (tel. 939-7805) and **Penn Harris Cabs** (tel. 238-7377).

WHAT TO SEE & DO

HERSHEYPARK, 100 W. Hersheypark Dr. Tel. 534-3900.

The center of attention is this amusement and theme park on 87 landscaped and tree-filled acres in the heart of Hershey. Originally established in 1907, it started as a picnic and pleasure ground for Hershey employees and gradually evolved into a giant wonderland for people from all parts of the world.

Often called America's "cleanest and greenest" theme park, Hersheypark has more than three dozen rides, four roller coasters, a monorail, a water-slide ride, five theaters, eight theme areas, six restaurants, and more than 50 fast-food and snack locations. Visitors can get a sky-high overview of the park by entering a 330-foot tower with candy-kiss-shaped windows that serves as an observation-style ride. Admission fee entitles you to all attractions and rides (except paddleboats and miniature golf), live performances, and ZooAmerica.

Admission: $20.95 adults, $17.95 children 4 to 8, $13.75 seniors 62 and over.

Open: Late May–Aug daily 10:30am–10pm, Sept–early Oct Sat–Sun 10:30am–10pm (except certain evenings, when park closes at 6 or 8pm).

HERSHEY MUSEUM, 170 W. Hersheypark Dr. Tel. 534-3439.

This museum offers an entertaining and educational look at America and her people, including exhibits on Pennsylvania German life in the early 1800s, Native American and Eskimo galleries, and the story of Milton Hershey, the "man behind the chocolate bar." You'll also see a unique animated Apostolic clock, and collections of early photographs, musical instruments, and music boxes.

Admission: $3.50 adults, $1.25 children 4 to 18, children 3 and under free.

Open: Memorial Day–Labor Day daily 10am–6pm, off-season daily 10am–5pm.

Closed: Thanksgiving Day, Christmas Day, and New Year's Day.

HERSHEY GARDENS, Hotel Rd. Tel. 534-3492.

Established in 1936 as a three-acre rose garden, the Hershey Gardens have grown into a 23-acre botanical oasis including 15,000 roses, 50,000 tulips, 12,000 annuals, and hundreds of rare trees, vines, and shrubs. To help you appreciate what you're seeing, all the trees and plants are identified with small plaques. The award-winning roses are particularly fascinating because many species are named after famous people or places (from John F. Kennedy and Dolly Parton to the Blue Nile and Las Vegas). Musical concerts are featured during summer evenings.

Admission: $3.50 adults, $1 young visitors 4 to 18, children 3 and under free, seniors $3.

Open: Apr–Dec daily 9am–5pm; Memorial Day–Labor Day daily 9am–7pm.

ZOOAMERICA, North American Wildlife Park, 100 W. Hersheypark Dr. Tel. 534-3860.

This 11-acre zoo opened in 1978 and is home to more than 200 animals, ranging from bison and bears to elk and eagles. The animals thrive in natural settings, created to duplicate their own habitat from all parts of North America.

Admission: $3.50 adults, $2.25 children 3 to 12, children 3 and under free.

Open: Daily 10am–dusk. **Closed:** Thanksgiving Day, Christmas Day, and New Year's Day.

HERSHEY'S CHOCOLATE WORLD, 800 Park Blvd. Tel. 534-4900.

Since visitors are no longer permitted at the Hershey Chocolate factory, the next best thing is this Disney-style visitors' center of the Hershey Food Corporation. The story of chocolate is told via an automated ride. You'll board seven-passenger gliding cars, each with its own video monitor, for an enactment of the candy-making process from cocoa bean to chocolate bar. After the tour, you can browse in the adjacent complex of shops that offer chocolates and chocolate-related souvenirs, as well as the 300-seat food court and skylit tropical conservatory.

Admission: Free.

Open: Jan–Mar Mon–Sat 9am–4:45pm, Sun noon–4:45pm; Apr to mid–June, daily 9am–4:45pm; mid–June to Labor Day, daily 9am–6:45pm; early Sept–Dec 31, daily 9am–4:45pm. **Closed:** Thanksgiving Day, Christmas Day, Easter, and New Year's Day.

FOUNDERS HALL, Homestead Lane. Tel. 534-3500.

This is the visitors' center and hub of the Milton Hershey School, founded by the entrepreneur of the chocolate world to provide a home and tuition-free education for 1,200 children. The impressive dome atop the edifice is the largest unsupported dome in the western hemisphere, and second in the world only to St. Peter's in Rome. A short film and walk-through displays tell the story of the legendary school that had its beginnings in its founder's home.

Admission: Free.

Open: Mon–Fri 10am–4pm, Sat–Sun 10am–3pm. **Closed:** Major holidays.

COOL FOR KIDS

In addition to the many attractions for all ages at Hershey, this area is also the home of **Indian Echo Caverns,** off U.S. Rte. 322 at Hummelstown (tel. 566-8131). Just 3 miles west of Hersheypark, this underground wonder is full of massive pillars, pipes, and cascades of stone. Once the preserve of the Susquehannock Indians, these caves have been opened to early explorers since the 1600s, but it is only since 1929 that the natural paths have been enhanced with electric lights and walkways for visitor safety. Facilities include a Trading Post shop, playgrounds, and picnic areas. Open from April through October, the hours are daily from 10am to 4pm (except from Memorial Day to Labor Day, when the schedule is 9am to 6pm); also on weekends, March and November, 10am to 4pm. Admission price is $6 for visitors over 12 years of age, $3 for children 5 to 11, and free for younger children.

SPORTS & ACTIVITIES

Hershey is known as the "golf capital" of Pennsylvania, with 72 holes of golf, all in a small radius. Below is a rundown of the facilities and applicable charges.

Hershey Country Club (tel. 533-2464), two nationally acclaimed 18-hole courses, with greens fees ranging from $35 to $50 on weekdays and on weekends; electric cart fees are $13.50 per person at both courses and club rental is $15.

The **Hotel Hershey's** nine-hole course (tel. 533-2171, ext. 4082) charges $14 for greens fees on weekdays and $16 on weekends, with a cart fee of $10 per nine holes; club rental is $4.

The 18-hole **Parkview Course** (tel. 534-3450) has a greens fee price of $16 on weekdays and $22 on weekends; cart fees are $10.60 per person for 18 holes; clubs are $15 per day.

Spring Creek is a nine-hole course (tel. 533-2847) that charges $11 for greens fees on weekdays and $13 on weekends all day; cart fees are $7.50 for nine holes.

The **Hotel Hershey Riding Stables** (tel. 534-1928) provide public horseback-riding facilities amid miles of wooded trails surrounding the Hotel Hershey. Riding fees are $16 per half hour and $20 per hour. Horse-drawn carriage rides can also be arranged around the Hotel Hershey grounds, at $5 to $15 per person, depending on duration. Open from 8am to noon and from 2 to 6pm (and some evenings, on demand) from Memorial Day through Labor Day; and from 11am to 4pm weekends in the fall, winter, and spring months.

WHERE TO STAY

A Hershey chocolate bar to greet you at check-in or chocolate candy kisses on your pillow at night—these are just two of the special touches that sweeten an overnight visit in Hershey.

Of course, most visitors want to stay at either the old-world Hotel Hershey or the modern Hershey Lodge. The hotel is a traditional resort in the grandest style, suitable for couples or families with older children. The sprawling lodge, with its movie theater and trio of restaurants, is ideal for families with younger children (room service will even deliver pizza). In addition, Hershey also has a number of good motor inns and motels, located mostly along Rte. 422 (also known locally as Chocolate Avenue), on the east and west sides of the town of Hershey.

The rates quoted below are for the peak summer months. If you travel in the spring, fall, or winter, prices are lower and at many times of the year special reduced-rate packages are also in effect. Be sure to check for available packages and discounts—you could save yourself up to 50%.

VERY EXPENSIVE

HOTEL HERSHEY, P.O. Box BB, Hershey, PA 17033. Tel. 717/533-2171 or toll-free 800/533-3131. Fax 717/534-8887. 250 rms. A/C TV TEL

$ Rates (including breakfast and dinner): $99–$120 per person. AE, CB, DC, MC, V. **Parking:** Free.

Ever since 1933, the place to stay at in Hershey has been this hotel, a complete year-round resort set on a 90-acre hilltop wooded estate. Styled after the 19th-century grand villas of the Mediterranean, this palatial property is a showcase of splendid fountains and chandeliers, lavish interiors, exotic sculpture, and magnificent greenery; plus an award-winning dining room. The guest rooms have either double, twin, or queen-size beds and decors that range from old-world elegance to contemporary designer styles, depending on whether you are in the old section or the new wings. Nonsmoking rooms are available. Bathrooms are finished in marble and brass and many have a whirlpool bath.

Dining/Entertainment: Meals are served in the award-winning Circular Dining Room (see "Where to Dine," below), and there is also a coffee shop, Cocoa Bean Alley, and the Iberian Lounge.

Services: Express check-out, room service, valet service, turn-down service.

Facilities: Indoor and outdoor pools, saunas, whirlpools, shuffleboard, table tennis, croquet, tennis courts, golf, horseback riding, lawn bowling, hiking, and bicycling.

EXPENSIVE

HERSHEY LODGE AND CONVENTION CENTER, W. Chocolate Ave. and University Dr., P.O. Box V, Hershey, PA 17033. Tel. 717/533-3311 or toll-free 800/533-3131. Fax 717/533-9642. 460 rms. A/C TV TEL
$ Rates: $106 single, $120 double. AE, CB, DC, MC, V. **Parking:** Free.

In contrast to its sister property, the Hotel Hershey, this facility is a modern complex, spread over 30 well-landscaped acres and almost a mini-village unto itself. It is designed in a mostly one- and two-story ranch-style format, with a facade of brick, paned windows, arches, and window shutters, reflecting a Colonial motif. The guest rooms are warmly furnished with dark woods and designer fabrics, and most have two doors, one leading to an interior connecting corridor and the other opening out to the parking area. There is a choice of configurations and bed sizes, and many nonsmoking units are available.

Dining/Entertainment: An ideal choice for families is the Copper Kettle, an informal and inexpensive eatery, open from 7am to 10pm daily. There is a homey fireside atmosphere at the Hearth Restaurant, with moderately priced meals. For those with gourmet appetites, there is the posh Tack Room (see "Where to Dine," below). Bars include J. P. Mallards Lounge, with music and dancing nightly, and the rustic Forebay lounge.

Services: Room service, valet laundry service, baby-sitting service.

Facilities: Indoor and outdoor swimming pools, sauna, whirlpool, exercise room, lighted tennis and platform tennis courts, 9-hole pitch-and-putt golf course, bicycles, and a 350-seat, first-run movie theater.

MODERATE

COMFORT INN—HERSHEY, 1200 Mae St., Hummelstown, PA 17036. Tel. 717/566-2050 or toll-free 800/221-2222. Fax 717/566-8656. 125 rms.
$ Rates (including hot breakfast): $45–$125 single, $55–$135 double. AE, CB, DC, DISC, MC, V. **Parking:** Free.

Although this hotel's mailing address is Hummelstown, it is located on the western edge of the Hershey area, at the interchange of Rtes. 39, 422, and 322. Opened in 1990, it has an attractive seven-story brick exterior of modern Victorian/Georgian design, including a mansard-style roof. The lobby offers a homey ambience with an Old Williamsburg–style decor and a ceiling mural of painted clouds.

The guest rooms, which offer a choice of one queen-size or two double beds, are furnished with dark woods, brass fixtures, gilt-framed pictures, rich pastel fabrics, desk, and easy chairs; 24 units are efficiencies and executive suites, with kitchenettes, refrigerator, coffee maker, and microwave oven. Guest facilities include an indoor swimming pool, exercise room, cocktail lounge serving light meals, and two meeting rooms.

DAYS INN—HERSHEY, 350 W. Chocolate Ave., Hershey, PA 17033. Tel. 717/534-2162 or toll-free 800/325-2525. Fax 717/533-6409. 61 rms, 14 suites. A/C TV TEL

$ Rates (including continental breakfast): $58–$84 single, $68–$88 double, $105–$150 suite. AE, CB, DC, DISC, MC, V. **Parking:** Free.

⑤ Opened in 1989, this four-story property has a handy location, within walking distance to the town of Hershey and most of the major attractions. It also has an attractive Colonial-style brick facade that blends in well with the adjacent buildings and houses. The guest rooms are contemporary in style, with pastel colors and light wood furnishings, and a choice of king- or queen-size beds. The suites also have a wet bar and a sofa bed. The third floor is set aside for nonsmokers, and there is a 24-hour coffee service in the lobby.

BUDGET

FAIRWAY, 1043 E. Chocolate Ave., Hershey, PA 17033. Tel. 717/533-5179. 26 rms. A/C TV TEL

$ Rates: $48–$86, single or double. AE, MC, V. **Parking:** Free. **Closed:** Dec 15–Jan 15.

⑤ This modern two-story motel overlooks the greens of the Hershey Country Club. It offers rooms with balconies, contemporary furnishings, and two double beds; nonsmoking rooms are available. Other guest facilities are heated indoor swimming pool, patio, and well-landscaped gardens.

MILTON MOTEL, 1733 E. Chocolate Ave., Hershey, PA 17033. Tel. 717/533-4533. Fax 717/533-0369. 30 rms. A/C TV TEL

$ Rates: $35–$60 single, $48–$78 double. AE, DC, DISC, MC, V. **Parking:** Free. This modern two-story motel offers rooms with contemporary furnishings and a choice of one or two double beds; upper-level units have balconies. There are some nonsmoking rooms and some units with refrigerators. Guest amenities include a heated swimming pool, a picnic and play area, and a game room.

SPINNER'S INN, 845 E. Chocolate Ave., Hershey, PA 17033. Tel. 717/533-9157. Fax 717/534-1189. 52 rms. A/C TV TEL

$ Rates (including continental breakfast): $40–$80 single, $50–$95 double. AE, CB, DC, MC, V. **Parking:** Free.
Adjacent to the restaurant of the same name (see "Where to Dine," below), this motel is designed in a modernized Georgian/Victorian motif, with rooms surrounding a central courtyard. The units are tastefully furnished with standard appointments, and offer a choice of one or two double beds. In addition to the restaurant, there is a cocktail lounge, outdoor swimming pool in the central courtyard, and game room.

WHITE ROSE MOTEL, 1060 E. Chocolate Ave., Hershey, PA 17033. Tel. 717/533-9876. 24 rms. A/C TV TEL

$ Rates: $37–$85, single or double. AE, DC, MC, V. **Parking:** Free.
Surrounded by flower gardens, this is an extremely well-kept, family-run facility, with a Colonial decor and stencil designs on the walls. The rooms all have two double beds and coffee- and tea-making equipment. Upper-level rooms have balconies. Guest facilities include an outdoor heated pool, a patio, and an American country gift store.

CAMPING

Hershey Highmeadow Camp, 300 Park Blvd., P.O. Box 860, Hershey, PA 17033 (tel. 566-0902), welcomes year-round campers to 260 sites on 55 acres of open and shaded rolling terrain, 2 miles from Hersheypark. Facilities are provided for tents, campers, trailers, and motor homes, plus cabin rentals, two swimming pools, a game room, a laundromat, a grocery and supply store, and a free shuttle to Hershey attractions. Rates with hookup, electric, water, and sewer start at about $25 a day or $150 per week. Cabin rentals are available from $26 a day (for four people).

WHERE TO DINE
EXPENSIVE

CIRCULAR DINING ROOM, Hotel Hershey, Hotel Rd. Tel. 533-2171.
    Cuisine: INTERNATIONAL. **Reservations:** Required.
$ Prices: Appetizers (included in set dinner rate); dinner rate $32–$40 per person; breakfast and lunch buffets $10–$15 per person.
    Open: Daily lunch noon–2pm; dinner (two seatings) 6pm and 8:30pm. AE, CB, DC, MC, V.

Exuding the aura of yesteryear, this is the Hotel Hershey's award-winning main restaurant—grandiose and bustling, dominated by original stained-glass windows overlooking well-manicured formal gardens. It caters primarily to overnight guests, who usually purchase meal plans as part of their lodging rate. If there is space, however, nonhotel guests can secure a reservation and pay for a meal only. Although the room is huge and hundreds of people are dining at once, the experience is extremely personalized, thanks to a very attentive and experienced team of waiting staff.

The dinner menu changes nightly, but usually includes such items as shrimp, scallop, and lobster sauté, steamed breast of chicken nouvelle cuisine, sirloin of beef, and leg of lamb. Breakfast and lunch consist of extensive buffets of hot and cold foods. Men are required to wear jackets for dinner.

THE TACK ROOM, W. Chocolate Ave. and University Dr. Tel. 533-3311.
    Cuisine: INTERNATIONAL. **Reservations:** Recommended.
$ Prices: Appetizers $3.95–$7.95; main courses $15.50–$24.75; lunch $5.95–$12.95. AE, CB, DC, MC, V.
    Open: Lunch Mon–Sat 11:30am–2pm; dinner Sun–Thurs 5:30–10pm, Fri–Sat 5:30–11pm; brunch Sun 11am–3pm.

Designed to reflect an equestrian theme, this restaurant is the centerpiece of fine dining at the Hershey Lodge, appropriately decorated with racing silks, saddles, and harnesses. Dinner entrées focus primarily on steaks and seafood, with such dishes as flounder florentine en croute, medallions of lobster, rack of lamb, and chateaubriand. This is also the ideal place to try desserts made with Hershey chocolate products.

MODERATE

SPINNER'S, 845 E. Chocolate Ave. Tel. 533-9050.
    Cuisine: FRENCH/CONTINENTAL. **Reservations:** Recommended.
$ Prices: Appetizers $2.95–$7.95; main courses $10.95–$19.95. AE, CB, DC, MC, V.
    Open: Tues–Sat 5–10pm.
A tradition in the area for 45 years, this restaurant was started by Zurich-born William Spinner, once the personal chef to Milton Hershey and former head chef of the Hotel Hershey, and it is now continued by his son Joseph and wife Pat. The menu specializes in fresh seafood and certified Angus beef, with such items as baked stuffed lobster tail with Maryland crabmeat and filet mignon with mushroom caps, as well as breast of chicken in champagne sauce, roast spring lamb, and *la cuisine à la bon vie* (a daily selection of foods prepared with consideration for the health-conscious patrons).

BUDGET

TUDOR ROSE TAVERN, Hersheypark Ave. Tel. 534-3868.
    Cuisine: INTERNATIONAL. **Reservations:** Not required.

$ Prices: Appetizers $1.95–$4.95; main courses $5.95–$12.95; lunch $2.95–$4.95. AE, CB, DC, MC, V.

Open: Mid–May to mid–Sept, and Christmas season, lunch daily 11am–4:30pm; dinner daily 4:30–9pm. **Closed:** Oct–Nov and Jan–April.

This restaurant is a great favorite for families. Entrées at dinner range from refreshing pasta salads to steaks, crab cakes, stuffed flounder, center-cut pork chops, and boneless turkey breast. All main courses entitle you to unlimited trips to the soup, salad, and hot vegetable bar. Throughout the day, there is a reduced-price menu for youngsters under 12. Breakfast is served in summer.

EVENING ENTERTAINMENT

Top-name entertainers like Kenny Rogers and Randy Travis and attractions such as the Ice Capades appear regularly at the **Hersheypark Arena,** a 10,000-seat facility adjacent to Hersheypark. Opened in 1936, this hall is also home to the Hershey Bears hockey team. The nearby **Hersheypark Stadium,** with a capacity for 25,000 spectators, is the setting for high school, college, and all-star football, drum and bugle competitions, and outdoor concerts. Tickets to all events are available at **The Hersheypark Arena Box Office,** 100 West Hersheypark Drive (tel. 534-3911). Box office hours: Monday through Saturday from 9am to 5pm. Shows and games are usually at 7:30pm and tickets are priced from $8 to $18, depending on the event.

The **Hershey Theatre,** East Caracas Avenue (tel. 534-3405), is a magnificent old-world theater of arched ceilings and gilded trim, located downtown. The program features a wide range of entertainment from classic films to Broadway shows, and classical and popular music concerts. The *Nutcracker* is a tradition in mid-December. The box office is open Monday through Friday from 10am to 5pm and immediately before showtimes. Film prices are $4 for adults and $2 for children; tickets to live performances average from $15 to $40, depending on the event.

The **Hershey Lodge Cinema** (tel. 533-5610) features an ever-changing program of current family-oriented movies, with shows each evening at 7 and 9pm and matinees on many Sunday afternoons at 2pm. The charge is $3.50 for adults and $2.50 for children 12 and under.

CENTRAL PENNSYLVANIA

A collage of historic towns, fertile farms, and verdant valleys, central Pennsylvania is an expansive area covering over 200 miles. Much of this land, from north to south, is also influenced by the gentle waters of the Susquehanna River.

Some of the more well-known parts of this region, such as Harrisburg, Hershey, and Lancaster, are already covered in other chapters of this book. This chapter focuses on the other highlights of central Pennsylvania—from the hallowed battlegrounds of Gettysburg and the historic streets of York to the covered bridges of Columbia and Montour counties and the riverfront lumbering traditions of Williamsport.

1. GETTYSBURG

118 miles W of Philadelphia, 36 miles S of Harrisburg,
54 miles NW of Baltimore, 53 miles SW of Lancaster

GETTING THERE **By Air** The nearest airport is **Harrisburg International,** about 45 miles northwest of Gettysburg.

By Train The nearest **Amtrak** train station is in Harrisburg.

By Bus Bus service into the town is provided by **Greyhound,** which pulls into the town's bus stop on Carlisle Street, next to Gettysburg College.

By Car Situated in the central part of the state, Gettysburg is on the southern edge, fewer than 10 miles from the Maryland border. From the east or west, Rte. 30 will lead you into the heart of Gettysburg; from the north or south, Rte. 15 crosses the town.

ESSENTIALS **Area Code** The area code for Gettysburg is 717.

Information Brochures, hotel and restaurant guides, schedules of festivals, walking tour leaflets, and other information are available from the **Gettysburg Travel Council,** 35 Carlisle St., Gettysburg, PA 17325 (tel. 717/334-6274). This office is housed in the former Western Maryland Railway Station, the depot where President Lincoln arrived in town prior to his historic Gettysburg address.

The ideal starting point for most Gettysburg sightseeing activities is either this office or the visitor center of the **Gettysburg National Military Park,** on Rte. 134, just south of the downtown area.

SPECIAL EVENTS One of the best times to visit is late June and early July, when the ○ **Civil War Heritage Days** are scheduled. This observance commemorates

WHAT'S SPECIAL ABOUT GETTYSBURG

Ace Attractions

☐ Gettysburg National Military Park, the 3,500-acre battle site that was the turning point of the Civil War.

☐ Eisenhower National Historic Site, the farm home of the 34th U.S. president.

☐ Cyclorama Center, a revolving circular painting that tells the story of the Civil War.

☐ Lincoln Room Museum, where President Lincoln prepared his Gettysburg Address.

☐ Gettysburg Railroad, a scenic ride in the Civil War countryside.

Events

☐ Civil War Heritage Days, a reenactment of the famous battle.

For the Kids

☐ Land of Little Horses, the world's smallest equine specimens

Shopping

☐ Old Gettysburg Village, a cluster of a dozen shops with an 1863 atmosphere.

☐ Centennial General Store, for Union and Confederate uniforms.

☐ Irish Brigade, focusing on the Civil War's Irish connections.

---

the Battle of Gettysburg with a "living history" encampment, battle reenactments, concerts, lectures by some of America's foremost historians, and a fireman's festival. In addition, a Civil War collectors' show features rare collections of antique arms, uniforms, accoutrements, documents, books, photographs, and personal effects. Admission to the show is $3 for anyone over 16. For information, contact the Gettysburg Travel Council, 35 Carlisle St., Gettysburg, PA 17325 (tel. 717/334-6274).

A highlight every fall is the **Apple Harvest Festival,** traditionally held on the first two weekends of October at the South Mountain Fairgrounds on Rte. 234, Arendtsville, 10 miles northwest of downtown. The program includes continuous free entertainment, tours of the orchards, peanut roastings, arts-and-crafts shows, antique gas-engine displays, apple bobbing, and pie-eating contests. Among the foods on sale are apple jellies and syrups, hot-spiced cider, apple butter boil, and apple pancakes. Admission is $3 for adults; children under 12 are free. Parking is $2 per car. Festival hours are from 9am to 6pm. For a complete schedule of events, contact the Gettysburg Travel Council, 35 Carlisle St., Gettysburg, PA 17325 (tel. 717/334-6274).

Everyone who has ever recited "Four score and seven years ago . . ." knows of Gettysburg. Each year hundreds of thousands of Americans flock here to see the spot where President Lincoln stood as he delivered his history-making Gettysburg Address on November 19, 1863. Thanks to a well-organized tourist industry, they can also see a draft of the speech in the president's own handwriting, visit the room where he stayed as he penned the final words, and hear "his" voice reciting the words.

But Abraham Lincoln's speech is only half the Gettysburg story. Lincoln delivered his Address 4 months after the major Civil War encounter that took place here in July 1863. He arrived to dedicate the cemetery and to offer the nation words of consolation and hope.

Today's visitors can tour the historic battlefield and walk the hallowed ground. They can also see the battle reenacted through a variety of media, from wax figures and dioramas to films, revolving artwork, and sound-and-light shows. No one will walk away without a better understanding of what happened here.

A small town (pop. 7,000), surrounded by apple orchards on the Pennsylvania–Maryland border, Gettysburg has indeed been thrust into the tourism industry by history's events. Although the late 1800s are the focus of much of Gettysburg's lore, the town itself dates back to the early 1700s, when Samuel Gettys acquired 381 acres of land from the descendants of William Penn and opened a tavern. It was his son, James, who eventually had the town lots drawn up and named the area Gettysburg.

In this century, the town's most famous resident has been former President Dwight D. Eisenhower, who chose a peaceful corner of Gettysburg farmland as his retirement home.

WHAT TO SEE & DO

GETTYSBURG NATIONAL MILITARY PARK, Rte. 134. Tel. 334-1124.

Plan to devote at least a day to seeing the historic 3,500-acre site commemorating the July 1863 Battle of Gettysburg. The bloodiest battle of the Civil War, with 51,000 casualties, this event was a turning point in the action as Union forces drove back the Confederate troops of Gen. Robert E. Lee.

Start your tour at the Visitor Center, where you'll find orientation displays, Civil War exhibits, and a schedule of ranger-conducted programs, talks, walks, and tours. You can also obtain a free pamphlet detailing a self-conducted auto tour of the battlefield (2 to 3 hours in duration). Various trails have been marked off for walking tours of the area. Students will find walks particularly educational, as all sites are marked with plaques. The Visitor Center is open from 8am to 6pm in the summer and from 8am to 5pm during the rest of the year.

Admission: Free.
Open: Daily 6am–10pm.

ATTRACTIONS WITHIN GETTYSBURG PARK

ELECTRIC MAP, Gettysburg National Park Visitors Center, Rte. 134. Tel. 334-1124.

This is an orientation program within the Visitor Center that explains the movements of the Battle of Gettysburg by means of a large relief map with colored lights and narration, in a theater setting. The 30-minute program is shown every 45 minutes.

Admission: $2 adults; children under 15 free.
Open: Daily 8am–5pm.

CYCLORAMA CENTER, Gettysburg National Park, Rte. 134. Tel. 334-1124.

Housed in a specially built structure adjacent to the Visitor Center, this is a giant circular oil painting of the Battle of Gettysburg. The work of artist Paul Philippoteaux, it is 356 feet wide and 26 feet high. You feel as if you're right in the midst of the battlefield as you step onto a platform in the center of the painting. A 20-minute sound-and-light narration helps you to focus on the various scenes of the painting as you are moved in a circular direction. The Cyclorama building also contains other exhibits of interest including a copy of the second draft of the Gettysburg Address (courtesy of the Library of Congress), on display in summer months only.

Admission: $2 adults; children under 16 free.
Open: Daily 9am–5pm.

OTHER GETTYSBURG ATTRACTIONS

NATIONAL TOWER, Rte. 134. Tel. 334-6754.

This attraction provides the best overall views of the battlefield and the surrounding Gettysburg countryside. Elevators whisk you to the 300-foot-high observation decks, including a glass-enclosed level that provides a 12-minute audio program and an upper open-air platform with telescopes, ideal for picture taking.

Admission: $3.75 adults, $1.75 children 6–14, children under 6 free.
Open: Summer 9am–7:30pm; spring and fall 9am–5pm.

NATIONAL CIVIL WAR WAX MUSEUM, 297 Steinwehr Ave. Tel. 334-6245.

This popular attraction, just outside the battlefield, tells the story of the Civil War

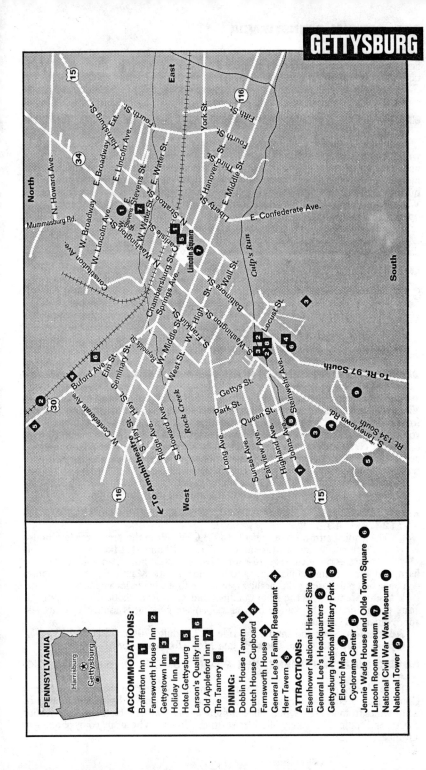

GETTYSBURG

PENNSYLVANIA

Harrisburg
Gettysburg ★

ACCOMMODATIONS:

Brafferton Inn **1**
Farnsworth House Inn **2**
Gettystown Inn **3**
Holiday Inn **4**
Hotel Gettysburg **5**
Larson's Quality Inn **6**
Old Appleford Inn **7**
The Tannery **8**

DINING:

Dobbin House Tavern **1**
Dutch House Cupboard **2**
Farnsworth House **3**
General Lee's Family Restaurant **4**
Herr Tavern **5**

ATTRACTIONS:

Eisenhower National Historic Site **1**
General Lee's Headquarters **2**
Gettysburg National Military Park **3**
Electric Map **4**
Cyclorama Center **5**
Jennie Wade House and Olde Town Square **6**
Lincoln Room Museum **7**
National Civil War Wax Museum **8**
National Tower **9**

in 30 different scenes with lifelike wax figures, backed by narration. An animated figure of President Lincoln delivering his Gettysburg Address is also on view. Auto tape tours of the entire Gettysburg area are also on sale at this facility.

Admission: $4.25 adults, $2.50 young visitors 13–17, $1.75 children 6–12.
Open: Daily 9am–9pm.

GENERAL LEE'S HEADQUARTERS, Bulford Ave. and Rte 30. Tel. 334-3141.

A fine collection of Civil War memorabilia is on display at this house, complete with 20-inch stone walls, built in the 1700s. General Lee established his personal headquarters here on July 1, 1863, and planned his battle-line strategy. Exhibits include Union and Confederate military equipment, rifles and sabers, uniforms, buttons, belt buckles, saddles, and cavalry equipment, plus original kitchen and Civil War–period furnishings. The house is one of the few original Gettysburg homes now open to the public.

Admission: Free.
Open: Mid-Mar–mid-Apr, mid-Oct–Nov daily 9am–5pm; mid-Apr–mid-Oct daily 9am–9pm.

LINCOLN ROOM MUSEUM, 12 Lincoln Square. Tel. 334-8188.

This is a showcase of the room where the 16th U.S. President prepared the final draft of his Gettysburg Address. Located on the second floor of the David I. Wills House, the room has been preserved with many original furnishings. Visitors can also view a tableau with a lifelike figure of Lincoln reciting the speech.

Admission: $3 adults, $1.50 youngsters 8–18.
Open: Summer Sun–Thurs 9am–7pm, Fri–Sat 9am–9pm; spring and fall daily 9am–5pm.

JENNIE WADE HOUSE AND OLDE TOWN SQUARE, Baltimore St. Tel. 334-4100.

This attraction commemorates the story of the battle's only civilian casualty, Mary Virginia (Jennie) Wade. As this young girl was standing in the kitchen, a stray shot from a sharpshooter's gun pierced through the wall and killed her instantly. Today you can tour the house, see the bullet holes, and hear the saga. Behind the house is an old village courtyard, re-created as it was in Jennie's time. You'll see a barbershop, a general store, a blacksmith, and a printer, all part of a self-guided walking tour with recorded narration.

Admission: $3.85 adults, $2.20 children 6–11.
Open: Summer daily 9am–10pm, spring and fall daily 9am–5pm.

EISENHOWER NATIONAL HISTORIC SITE, Business Rte. 15. Tel. 334-1124, ext. 432.

The leading attraction not related to the Civil War in this area is the farmhouse of President Dwight D. Eisenhower. The only home that Ike ever owned, this 495-acre estate includes a 15-room Georgian-style house, an 1887 bank-style barn, and lots of memorabilia relating to Ike and his wife, Mamie. To tour the house, you must first purchase a ticket at the Eisenhower Tour Center, located in the National Park Visitor Center (Electric Map building) and open from 8:30am to 4:15pm. All visits to the site are by shuttle bus, as no on-site parking is available. Tours last approximately 1½ hours.

Admission: Tour and shuttle bus ride $2.25 adults, 70¢ children 6–12.
Open: Daily 9am–4pm. **Closed:** Jan; Mon–Tues early spring–late autumn.

ADAMS COUNTY WINERY, 251 Peach Tree Rd., Orrtanna. Tel. 334-4631.

For a change of pace, visit this winery, which is situated in the midst of Adams County fruit orchards. Originally planted in 1974, this vineyard produces a range of white wines from its grapes, plus a line of more unusual wines such as strawberry, sour cherry, and apple. The winery offers free tastings. Tours can be arranged by phoning in advance.

Admission: Free.
Open: Thurs–Mon 12:30pm–6pm.

ESCORTED TOURS
By Train

⭐ The steam passenger trains of the **Gettysburg Railroad,** 106 North Washington St. (tel. 334-6932), provide a way of seeing the sights of the surrounding countryside. These trains offer a 16-mile round-trip between Gettysburg and Biglerville, operating Monday through Friday during July and August (11am and 1pm) and on weekends from May through October (1 and 3pm). The fare is $6 for adults and $3 for children. In addition, a 50-mile round-trip itinerary is also available between Gettysburg and Mount Holly Springs on some weekends at 10am (by reservation only). That fare is $15 for adults and $8 for children 3 to 12.

By Bus

Two-hour narrated sightseeing trips around the area are conducted by **Battlefield Bus Tours,** from the Gettysburg Tour Center, 778 Baltimore St. (tel. 334-6296), open every day except Christmas Day. Using open-air double-decker buses or conventional equipment, these tours depart every half hour and take in all the major battlefield areas and town sights, with a choice of a recorded narration by Raymond Massey with a cast of Hollywood actors or a commentary by a registered guide. The prices are $9.75 for adults and $6.55 for children 6 to 11. A free trolleylike shuttle service is operated from most major hotels to the tour depot.

This company also operates several package plans involving a bus tour, plus admission to many of the town's attractions at a reduced cost. If you purchase a package, you can use free trolley shuttle transport between the attractions.

By Car

The best way to see the Gettysburg National Military Park in your own car is to engage the services of a licensed battlefield guide ($17 for two hours). You can arrange for such a tour at the **National Park Visitor Center,** Rte. 15 (tel. 334-1124, ext. 31), or at the guide station on Rte. 30 (tel. 334-9876), 1 mile west of Gettysburg. If you wish to drive around yourself, you can also rent a 90-minute auto tape and player ($10.50) from the **National Civil War Wax Museum,** Rte. 297, Steinwehr Ave. (tel. 334-6245).

By Foot

Self-guided strolls are easy, thanks to an eight-page walking-tour folder of the downtown area including a very detailed map, available free from the Gettysburg Travel Council. The walk covers 14 blocks and is 1½ miles long, taking about 2 hours at a leisurely pace. You'll notice small plaques on certain buildings, indicating that they were constructed prior to the Civil War; a total of 118 buildings have these bronze plaques.

By Horse-Drawn Carriage

See the sights of the town or the battlefield the old-fashioned way, via a horse-drawn carriage, operated by **Dayhoff's Carriages,** 523 Baltimore St. (tel. 337-2276). Tours operate on weekends during April, May, and October, from 1pm until dusk; and daily June through September, 4pm until dusk. The price ranges from $5 to $15 for adults and $3 to $6 for children 8 to 12, depending on the length of the trip (from a minimum of 1 mile to 3 miles or more). Tours begin from the parking area of the Dutch Cupboard Restaurant, across from the Jennie Wade House.

SHOPPING

OLD GETTYSBURG VILLAGE, 777 Baltimore St.
An 1863 atmosphere is re-created at this complex of a dozen old-world shops.

Amid cobblestone streets you can shop for all sorts of wares ranging from fudge and ice cream to Civil War relics, dolls, hand-carvings, and moccasins. Most stores are open daily from 10am to 9pm.

CENTENNIAL GENERAL STORE, 237 Steinwehr Ave. Tel. 334-9712.
This general store is housed in a gray-stone dwelling that served as a hospital during the Civil War. Appropriately enough, it specializes in Union and Confederate war uniforms and officers' hats and other Civil War accoutrements.
Open: Daily from 9am to 9pm during summer; shorter hours in off-season.

AMERICAN PRINT GALLERY—FINE MILITARY ART, 404 Baltimore St. Tel. 337-2898.
Limited-edition military prints, oil paintings, and bronze sculptures are featured at this gallery.
Open: Mon–Sat 9am–4pm, Sunday 10am–4pm.

CODORI'S BAVARIAN GIFT SHOP, 19 Barlow St. Tel. 334-5019.
One of the most fascinating shops is this one in a residential setting off North Stratton Street on the north side of town. The chalet-style store sells German and Scandinavian gifts, Black Forest cuckoo clocks, toy soldiers, hand puppets, teddy bears from around the world, collector dolls from Europe and the United States, hundreds of types of music boxes, and Victorian Christmas ornaments. Hours are Monday through Saturday from 9:30am to 8pm and on Sunday from noon to 5pm.

HISTORIC COUNTRY STORE AND MUSEUM, Rte. 34 at Biglerville. Tel. 677-7447.
Seven miles north of Gettysburg is this landmark building consisting of three floors and more than 50,000 products—from china and calicoes to lamps, long johns, penny candy, handmade quilts, top hats, and wedding gowns. Open year round, Monday through Wednesday from 9:30 to 5pm; Thursday and Friday until 8:30pm; and Saturday from 9:30am to 5pm.

QUILT PATCH, 1897 Hanover Pike. Tel. 359-4121.
In the countryside south of Gettysburg, there are many interesting shops in scenic locations, and this is one of the best for country crafts. It's housed in a 5,000-square-foot barn in a rural setting on Rte. 194, 3 miles east of Littlestown. The ground floor is devoted to locally made quilts, fine-art prints, oak furniture, pottery, and pewter. The second floor is geared to quilters and craftspersons, with over 1,200 bolts of fabrics, patterns, stencils, and quilting supplies. You'll also find country ruffled curtains, as well as Victorian window lace and table lace. Open year round, Monday through Saturday, from 9:30am to 5pm; and also on Sunday, from 1 to 5pm, April through December.

KOONY'S BARN, 1295 Frederick Pike, Littlestown. Tel. 359-7411.
One mile west of Littlestown Square, on Rte. 194, is this 100-year-old Pennsylvania bank barn full of country antiques—pottery, salt-glazed stoneware, candles, apothecary jars, primitive dolls, and trunk hardware. There's also a Christmas shop and seasonal items like corn-husk flowers, scarecrows, wreaths, and potpourri. Open April through December, Monday through Saturday from 10am to 5pm, and Sunday from noon to 5pm; and January through March, Wednesday through Saturday from 10am to 5pm, and Sunday from noon to 5pm.

SMOKEHOUSE CRAFTS, 3830 Baltimore Pike (Rte. 97), Littlestown. Tel. 359-4514.
A pre–Civil War stone building is the setting for this shop 6 miles south of Gettysburg. It offers local folk art, pottery, country furniture, and jewelry; there's also a Christmas Room. Open April through December, Sunday through Wednesday from 10am to 6pm, and Thursday through Saturday from 10am to 9pm; and January through March, Wednesday through Saturday, from 10am to 6pm.

IRISH BRIGADE, 504 Baltimore St. Tel. 337-2519.
Taking its name and theme from one of the best-known brigades of the Civil War,

this shop sells books and scholarly memorabilia about the Irish Brigade and other Civil War–related items, as well as jewelry, knitwear, linens, china, crystal, note cards, musical tapes, and other gift items from Ireland. Open Monday through Thursday 10am to 6pm, Friday 10am to 7pm, Saturday 10am to 8pm, and Sunday 1 to 6pm.

SPORTS & ACTIVITIES

Gettysburg is ideal territory for bikers, so bring your own if you have one. If not, you can rent a six- or three-speed model from **Artillery Ridge Bicycle Shop,** 610 Taneytown Rd. (tel. 334-1288). Open April through October, Monday through Friday from 9am to 5pm and Saturday from 9am to 4pm. The charge is $4 to $6 an hour, or $12 to $15 a day.

You can rent a horse at the **National Riding Stable,** 610 Taneytown Rd. (tel. 334-1288), situated on the grounds of the Artillery Ridge Campground. All rides follow trails in the Gettysburg National Park and are accompanied by a trail master. Hourly rates are $15 per person, and reservations are required. Open April through October, daily from 9am to 5pm.

Visitors are welcome at the **Piney Apple Golf Course,** 165 Slattersville Rd., Biglerville (tel. 677-9264). Greens fees for nine holes are $5.50 on weekends and $4.50 on weekdays; for 18 holes, fees are $9 on weekends and $7.50 on weekdays. Motorized carts can be rented at $7 for nine holes and $12.50 for 18 holes. Clubs are also available from $2.50 and up a set.

COOL FOR KIDS

Some of the world's smallest horses are on view at the **Land of Little Horses,** located at 125 Glenwood Drive, Gettysburg, off Rte. 30 (tel. 334-7259). Children of all ages are fascinated by the miniature pintos, appaloosas, draft horses, and thoroughbreds. Open daily from Memorial Day through Labor Day from 10am to 6pm, with indoor arena shows scheduled at 11am, 1, 3, and 5pm; also open from April 1 to Memorial Day and from Labor Day to November from 10am to 5pm and with slightly different times for shows. Other attractions include rides, a picnic area, a gift shop, and a snack bar. Admission for adults is $5.95 and $3 for children 3 to 12.

WHERE TO STAY

There are dozens of hotels, motels, and motor inns lining the streets in and around Gettysburg. In general, you'll find that rates are at their highest from June to September, although, even then, they are mostly moderate.

If you can travel in the spring or fall, expect to save up to 35% or 40% off summer room rates. On the other hand, you'll also find that room prices can be subject to surcharges on holiday weekends or at festival times, so check in advance.

For something in keeping with the 1800s aura of the town, consider staying in one of Gettysburg's very fine bed-and-breakfast inns.

MODERATE

BRAFFERTON INN, 44-46 York St., Gettysburg, PA 17325 Tel. 717/ 337-3423. 8 rms (4 with private bath). A/C TV TEL
$ Rates (including breakfast): $50–$80 single, $75–$95 double. MC, V. **Parking:** Free.

This inn, in the heart of town on the main street, is actually two houses, a two-story 1786 stone Federal home and a pre–Civil War clapboard addition. The larger structure is the earliest deeded house in the town plan designed by James Gettys and is listed in the National Register of Historic Places. Opened as a B&B in 1986, the guest rooms of this beautifully restored building are decorated in Colonial style, from canopy, four-poster, or brass beds to antiques, samplers, and oil paintings. Guests can also enjoy a sunlit glass-covered atrium filled with plants and flowers from the garden.

The dining room, where a sumptuous breakfast (including such specialties as peaches and cream French toast) is served each morning, has a fascinating hand-painted primitive wall mural depicting 18 of Gettysburg's most famous buildings. Innkeepers are Mimi and Jim Agard.

FARNSWORTH HOUSE INN, 401 Baltimore St., Gettysburg, PA 17325. Tel. 717/334-8838. 4 rms, all with bath. A/C
$ Rates (including breakfast): $65–$80, single or double. AE, DISC, MC, V. **Parking:** Free.
Dating back to 1810, this two-story brick house was originally a private home and then served as a Union headquarters during the Civil War. In 1972 it was restored to its 1863 appearance and opened as a restaurant/tavern (see "Where to Dine," below), and in 1989 as a lodging facility.

Guest rooms, all on the second floor and all with queen-size beds, are decorated individually with 19th-century antiques, colorful carpets, fine draperies, and assorted Victorian memorabilia. Breakfast is served in the dining room or outdoors in the garden. Guests can relax, read, or watch television in the bright and airy sunroom, filled with plants and wicker furnishings. On the third floor, there is a unique garret museum where three Confederate sharpshooters held a position and fired on Union troops during the Civil War, leaving the south wall with over 100 bullet holes. Tours are given daily at 3pm.

HOTEL GETTYSBURG, One Lincoln Square, Gettysburg, PA 17325. Tel. 717/337-6200. Fax 717/337-6891. 80 rms, 3 suites. A/C TV TEL
$ Rates (including breakfast): $48–$107 single or double; $65–$127 suite. AE, CB, DC, DISC, MC, V. **Parking:** Free.
For many years, the historic Gettysburg Hotel (established in 1797) played host to prominent national figures, from Daniel Webster and Ulysses S. Grant to Dwight Eisenhower, before it fell into disrepair. It is set to reopen as a six-story full-service hotel, after an extensive reconstruction and refurbishment. Rooms offer every modern amenity, with double or king-size beds; suites have a fireplace and a Jacuzzi bath.

GETTYSTOWN INN, 89 Steinwehr Ave., Gettysburg, PA 17325. Tel. 717/334-4930. Fax 717/334-6905. 5 rms (all with bath). A/C
$ Rates: $69–$75 single, $75–$95 double. AE, MC, V. **Parking:** Free.
Fully renovated and restored to convey an 1863 atmosphere, this Civil War–era stone house overlooks the spot where Lincoln gave his Gettysburg Address. It's furnished with brass, trundle, and canopy beds, hooked and braided rugs, and antique chests and nightstands. This inn is the guesthouse for the Dobbin House restaurant next door, and overnight guests enjoy a hearty country breakfast in the sun parlor of the restaurant. No smoking is permitted in the inn.

HOLIDAY INN, 516 Baltimore Street, Gettysburg, PA 17325. Tel. 717/334-6211 or toll-free 800/HOLIDAY. Fax 717/334-7183. 100 rms. A/C MINIBAR TV TEL
$ Rates: $85–$90 single, $95–$110 double. AE, CB, DC, MC, V. **Parking:** Free.
You can't get a better location than this hotel, right in the heart of all the attractions, between the downtown area and the Gettysburg Battlefield. Just park your car and you can walk to just about everything during your stay. Recently renovated, the hotel has a Colonial facade and decor, with a fountain and rock garden in its lobby. Many rooms have balconies that overlook the outdoor pool or the town.

The Plantation Room restaurant usually offers buffet-style meals, although individual service is also available. Other facilities include a lounge and outdoor swimming pool.

OLD APPLEFORD INN, 218 Carlisle St., Gettysburg, PA 17325. Tel. 717/337-1711. 12 rms (all with bath). A/C
$ Rates (including breakfast): $83–$103 single or double. AE, MC, V. **Parking:** Free.
Dating back to 1867, this Federal-style mansion opened as a B&B in 1984 and is

currently owned by Frank and Maribeth Skradski. The bedrooms feature hand-stenciled artwork and furnishings dating back to the 1850–90 period, including brass and canopy beds; two have working fireplaces. Guests can enjoy the parlor with a 1912 baby grand piano, an upstairs sun room with a balcony, and the well-stocked library that displays menus from local restaurants. Rates include afternoon sherry, tea, and cookies.

RAMADA INN, 2634 Emmitsburg Rd., Gettysburg, PA 17325. Tel. 717/334-8121 or toll-free 800/228-2828. Fax 717/334-6066. 203 rms. A/C **$ Rates:** $79 single or double. AE, CB, DC, MC, V. **Parking:** Free.

Formerly a Sheraton, this hotel, the largest in the area, is in a quiet country setting near the Eisenhower farm. The modern property is designed in a Tudor motif, and many rooms have private patios or balconies.

Dining/Entertainment: The Deli is open for light snacks; nautical-style restaurant, the Old Wharf and the Mayflower Lounge are open for regular meals.

Facilities: Outdoor and indoor swimming pool, sauna, tropical courtyard, tennis and racquetball courts, and jogging trail.

THE TANNERY, 449 Baltimore St., P.O. Box 4565, Gettysburg, PA 17325. Tel. 717/334-2454. 5 rms, all with bath. A/C **$ Rates** (including continental breakfast): $65–$85 single or double. MC, V. **Parking:** Free.

One of the newest bed-and-breakfast homes in the area, this Gothic-style house is within walking distance of all major Gettysburg attractions. It was built in 1868 by John Rupp, and his family occupied the home for many years and operated a tannery at the rear of the property. All guest rooms are individually decorated with traditional furnishings and Civil War memorabilia. Guests have use of a large wraparound porch with rocking chairs, and parlor and activity/game room. Innkeepers are Charlotte and Jule Swope. Open April to October.

BUDGET

COMFORT INN OF GETTYSBURG, 871 York Rd., Gettysburg, PA 17325. Tel. 717/337-2400 or toll-free 800/221-2222. Fax 717/337-2400, ext. 301. 52 rms. A/C TV TEL **$ Rates** (including continental breakfast): $35–$60 single, $40–$70 double. AE, CB, DC, DISC, MC, V. **Parking:** Free.

One of the newest properties in the Gettysburg area, this two-story inn sits back from the main road in a well-maintained setting. Guest rooms are spacious and bright, offering a choice of two double beds or a king-size bed, and are decorated with pastel fabrics, light-wood furniture, brass lamps, and a large marble bath with a separate vanity area. Guest facilities include an indoor pool, a fitness center, a meeting room, and an elevator.

DAYS INN GETTYSBURG, 865 York Rd., Gettysburg, PA 17325. Tel. 717/334-0030 or toll-free 800/325-2525. Fax 717/337-1002. 113 rms. **$ Rates:** $42–$65 single, $47–$75 double. AE, DC, DISC, MC, V. **Parking:** Free.

With a modern art-deco facade, this five-story hotel is set back from the main road outside the eastern edge of town. Guest rooms have two queen beds, large full bathrooms, and computer card-key access, with a decor of Civil War prints, floral fabrics, and dark woods. Facilities include an outdoor swimming pool, exercise room, miniature golf, sun patio, guest laundry, four meeting rooms, and adjacent restaurant.

LARSON'S QUALITY INN, 401 Buford Ave., Gettysburg, PA 17325. Tel. 717/334-3141 or toll-free 800/228-5151. 41 rms. A/C TV TEL **$ Rates:** $32–$88 single, $42–$98 double. AE, CB, DC, MC, V. **Parking:** Free.

This inn is situated in a well-landscaped area next to General Lee's headquarters, on Rte. 30. Rooms have one or two double beds and a Colonial-style motif. Guest amenities include an outdoor pool and a putting green; the General Lee Family Restaurant is adjacent to it.

BLUE SKY MOTEL, 2585 Biglerville Rd., Gettysburg, PA 17325. Tel. 717/677-7736. 16 rms. A/C TV TEL
$ Rates: $38 single, $44–$50 double. MC, V. **Parking:** Free.

This modern one-story motel is adjacent to farm lands on Rte. 34. Rooms have standard furnishings. Guest facilities include an outdoor swimming pool and a picnic area.

PERFECT REST MOTEL, 2450 Emmitsburg Rd., Gettysburg, PA 17325. Tel. 717/334-1345. 20 rms, 5 suites. A/C TV
$ Rates: $34–$50 single, $38–$58 double. MC, V. **Parking:** Free.

This motel is in a quiet garden setting on Business Rte. 15, south of the battlefield. Some rooms have king-size beds. Two-room family suites are also available. All rooms are clustered around a well-landscaped outdoor pool and patio area.

WHERE TO DINE

Tourist attractions in themselves, many of Gettysburg's restaurants are historic landmarks or sites that featured in the town's history. Because Gettysburg is a great favorite with young visitors and students, many dining spots are also geared to families. You'll find most prices to be in the moderate range or even lower.

EXPENSIVE

DOBBIN HOUSE TAVERN, 89 Steinwehr Ave. Tel. 334-2100.
Cuisine: AMERICAN. **Reservations:** Recommended. **Directions:** Head south of downtown, at juncture of Business Rte. 15 and Rte. 97.
$ Prices: Appetizers $3.95–$7.95, main courses $14.95–$22.95; lunch $3.95–$11.95. AE, MC, V.
Open: Lunch daily 11:30–10pm; dinner daily 5–10pm.

This top choice in Gettysburg is listed in the National Register of Historic Places. Built in 1776 by Rev. Alexander Dobbin, this structure started as his family home and a classical school and was then used as a Civil War hospital. Today it still has its original two-foot thick stone walls, walk-in hearth, hand-carved woodwork, and seven fireplaces. Three natural springs, which were a source of water and a refrigerating facility, are still in the basement, now the Springhouse Tavern, where lunch items and light entrées are served all day.

The upstairs Alexander Dobbin Dining Rooms offer six different settings for dinner, including a library, a parlor, a study, a spinning room, and a bedroom (yes, you can even dine in bed!). All are furnished in early-American style with hurricane lamps and Colonial crockery and background music from the 1800s. Entrées include Cumberland chicken with mushroom and blue-cheese sauce, prime ribs, roast duck with cider sauce and citrus herbs, rainbow trout with crabmeat, and a seafarer's feast (flounder, shrimp, scallops, crab, and lobster tail). Save room for the homemade desserts ($2), such as warm gingerbread with lemon sauce.

MODERATE

FARNSWORTH HOUSE, 401 Baltimore St. Tel. 334-8838.
Cuisine: AMERICAN. **Reservations:** Recommended.
$ Prices: Appetizers $1.75–$3.95; main courses $9.95–$18.95. AE, DISC, MC, V.
Open: Daily dinner 5–9:30pm.

More than 100 bullet holes are visible in the walls of this restaurant, an 1810 brick-and-wood structure in the center of town named after Union Brigadier General Elon John Farnsworth, who was killed on the third day of the battle of

Gettysburg. The original walls, flooring, and rafters of the building have stood the test of time, and today a Civil War decor sets the tone for lunch and dinner as 19th-century music plays in the background. In summer, you can also dine al fresco under ancient trees on a garden deck beside a freshwater stream.

At dinner the Civil War–period costumed staff starts your meal off with hot spoon bread, corn relish, and apple butter. The menu features early-American cuisine— peanut butter soup, game pie (pheasant, duck, and turkey blended with mushrooms, bacon, red currant jelly, and long-grained and wild rice), and Virginia chipped ham with grape sauce, as well as a variety of seafood, from crab imperial to surf-n-turf. Desserts average $3 for such old-time treats as rum cream pie or walnut apple cake.

HERR TAVERN, 900 Chambersburg Rd. Tel. 334-4332.
Cuisine: INTERNATIONAL. **Reservations:** Recommended.
$ Prices: Appetizers $2.99–$5.99; main courses $10.99–$14.99; lunch $2.95–$4.95. AE, DISC, MC, V.
Open: Lunch daily 11am–5pm; dinner Mon–Thurs 5–9pm, Fri–Sat 5–10pm, Sun 5–8pm.

Dating back to 1828, this stone building has led a varied life: as a stagecoach stop, a tavern, a counterfeiter's den, a Civil War hospital, and a private residence. Now modernized and expanded, but still retaining its original stone walls, fireplaces, and beamed ceilings, this restaurant offers an extensive lunch menu of hearty tavern sandwiches, vegetable plates, cheese steaks, quiches, and homemade soups with cornbread muffins. Dinner includes shrimp Creole, crab cakes, rainbow trout, prime ribs, chicken Kiev, veal parmesan, and duck with cherry sauce.

BUDGET

BALI INN, 65 West Middle St. Tel. 337-3891.
Cuisine: INTERNATIONAL. **Reservations:** Recommended.
$ Prices: Appetizers $1.50–$3.50; main courses $5.99–$12.99; lunch $2.95–$6.95. AE, CB, DC, MC, V.
Open: Lunch Tues–Fri 11am–2:30pm; dinner Tues–Thurs 5–8pm, Fri–Sat 5–9pm, Sun 4–8pm.

For a change of pace and an international atmosphere, try this restaurant with a European, Chinese, and Indonesian menu. Choices at lunch include curries, pan-fried noodles, and stir-fried vegetables and meats. The entrées at dinner range from authentic rijstaffel, sate (Indonesian kebab), chicken pancakes, pepper steak, and sweet-and-sour shrimp, to sauerbraten, wienerschnitzel, and bratwurst with sauerkraut. No liquor is sold, but you are welcome to bring your own.

GENERAL LEE'S FAMILY RESTAURANT, 401 Buford Ave. Tel. 334-2200.
Cuisine: AMERICAN. **Reservations:** Not required.
$ Prices: Appetizers $1.95–$4.95; main courses $6.95–$13.95; lunch $1.95–$6.95; breakfast $2.95–$4.95. AE, CB, DC, DISC, MC, V.
Open: Daily breakfast 7am–11am, lunch 11am–4pm, dinner 4–9pm.

Another favorite with all ages is this restaurant next to General Lee's historic headquarters. There are three dining rooms, with authentic beamed ceilings, whitewashed walls, old stone fireplaces, and pictures of early Gettysburg. Breakfast features country omelets, corned-beef hash, scrapple, creamed chipped beef, and apple fritters, while lunch offers sandwiches and burgers. Down-home country cuisine means meatloaf, cabbage rolls, chicken pot pie, ham steak, and roast turkey, as well as steaks and seafood. Cocktails are available.

DUTCH CUPBOARD, 523 Baltimore St. Tel. 334-6227.
Cuisine: AMERICAN. **Reservations:** Not required.
$ Prices: Appetizers $1.50–$2; main courses $6.95–$8.95; lunch $2.95–$6.95; breakfast $2–$5. MC, V.

Open: Daily lunch 11am–3pm; dinner 4–9pm.
Pennsylvania Dutch cooking is on the menu at this family restaurant conveniently located between downtown and the battlefield. The decor conveys a farmhouse atmosphere, with walls displaying Pennsylvania Dutch sayings as well as an array of kitchen implements, ladles, and dinner bells. Entrées range from chicken and dumplings to beef and noodles, fried country ham, pan-fried chicken, roast turkey, and meatloaf. Beer and wine are available.

EXCURSION TO CHAMBERSBURG

No visit to Gettysburg is complete without an excursion to neighboring Chambersburg, about 25 miles west in the heart of the Cumberland Valley. Founded in 1730 by Benjamin Chambers, this town was settled by Scots-Irish and German emigrants and figured prominently in Colonial times.

In the Civil War era, Chambersburg was the only town north of the Mason-Dixon Line burned by the Confederates. More than 500 buildings were destroyed, but the town never gave up, and it eventually rose from the ashes.

Today Chambersburg and its surrounding communities offer many historical and contemporary attractions. Mercersburg, listed on the National Register of Historic Places, is the birthplace of President James Buchanan, and the home of one of Pennsylvania's grandest inns. Other towns, such as Greencastle and Waynesborough, are also known for their museums and historic landmarks.

INFORMATION

For full particulars about the area, contact the **Cumberland Valley Visitors Station,** 1235 Lincoln Way East (Rte. 30), Chambersburg, PA 17201 Tel. 717/261-1200. Located at exit 6 of I-81, this tourism office is a welcoming destination in itself, with visitor information videos, a picnic area, a nature walk, restrooms, a souvenir shop, a restored 1943 Pennsylvania Railroad caboose, and ample parking.

WHAT TO SEE & DO

OLD JAILHOUSE, 175 E. King St. (Rte. 11), Chambersburg. Tel. 264-1667.

One of the leading attractions in downtown Chambersburg is this site dating back to 1818. Restored and renovated for use as the Kittochtinny Historical Society's Museum and Library, it houses an extensive display of historical and genealogical data, local artifacts, silver, guns, and costumes.
Admission: Free, but donations are accepted.
Open: April–Dec Thurs–Sat 9:30am–4pm, with shorter hours off-season.

RENFREW MUSEUM AND PARK, 1010 E. Main St., Waynesborough. Tel. 762-4723.

This museum on a 107-acre park along Antietam Creek houses a collection of the Bell family pottery pieces, American decorative arts (1790–1830), ceramics, quilts, and metalware.
Admission: $1.50 adults, $1 children over 6.
Open: Apr–Oct Thurs, Sat–Sun 1–4pm.

BINGHAM'S FRUIT MARKET AND ORCHARDS, 9823 Lincoln Way West, St. Thomas. Tel. 369-2218.

A rich agricultural and fruit-growing land, the Chambersburg area is home to dozens of farm stands. One of the largest and oldest (dating from 1927), is this one located 10 miles west of Chambersburg on Rte. 30. Here you can literally have your pick of the best apples, peaches, cherries, pears, and plums, as well as cider, apple butter, fudge, candy, and local crafts. You can also tour the 300-acre orchard and cider-making operations; there is no charge for a tour, but advance reservations are required. Call Bob or Betty Kriner for an appointment.

Admission: Free.

Open: Daily year round, hours vary with seasons.

WHERE TO STAY

MERCERSBURG INN, 405 S. Main St., Mercersburg, PA 17236. Tel. 717/328-5231 or toll-free 800/533-INNS. 15 rms (with bath) A/C TV TEL.

$ Rates (including breakfast): $105–$175 single or double. AE, MC, V. **Parking:** Free.

⭐ The top choice for lodging is this inn set on six acres of land with views of the Tuscarora range of the Blue Ridge Mountains. Dating from 1910, it was the private residence of local business magnate Harry Bryon, who believed that no expense should be spared. Consequently, this stately Greek Revival mansion is rich in mahogany and black-walnut paneling, leaded-glass chandeliers, tile and oak flooring, wrought-iron balustrades, and marble columns. Opened as an inn in 1987, the building offers rooms furnished with restored antiques or locally made pieces; some have private balconies, fireplaces, or king-size four-poster beds with hand-knotted canopies. Innkeeper is Fran Wolfe.

Guest facilities include a game room with working fireplace, an antique billiards table, library, lounge, sun room with antique wicker furniture, an elevator, and a fine dining room, *The Morel,* which serves dinner Wednesday through Sunday.

WHERE TO DINE

ANTRIM HOUSE, 104 E. Baltimore St., Greencastle. Tel. 597-8111.

Cuisine: INTERNATIONAL. **Reservations:** Not required.

$ Prices: Appetizers $.95–$2.95; main courses $5.95–$12.95; lunch $1.95–$3.95. Lunch buffet $5.95, dinner buffet $7.95–$9.95. AE, MC, V.

Open: Mon–Sat lunch 11am–2pm; dinner 6–9pm.

⭐ⓈFor more than 125 years, a favorite for good food and good value has been this historic spot. Besides steaks, prime ribs, and seafood, Pennsylvania Dutch cooking is featured, with items such as creamed chipped beef, chicken pot pie, stuffed cabbage, and pan-fried chicken. Lunch choices include sandwiches, salads, hoagies, and burgers. One-price buffets are often served for lunch and dinner. No liquor or wine is served.

---

2. YORK

25 miles S of Harrisburg, 50 miles N of Baltimore, 90 miles W of Philadelphia, 30 miles E of Gettysburg

GETTING THERE   By Air   The closest full-service airports to York are **Harrisburg International** (a half-hour drive), and **Baltimore International Airport** (95 minutes away).

By Train   The closest train stations are either Harrisburg or Baltimore for **Amtrak.**

By Bus   Service into York is operated by **Capitol Trailways/Greyhound,** 315 North George St. (tel. 843-0095). Local bus transport within the city (except Sunday) is provided by **YATA (York Area Transportation Authority),** 401 Yale St. (tel. 846-9282); an exact fare of 85¢ is required.

By Car   30 miles east of Gettysburg, York is traversed in a north-south direction by I-83, and Rte. 30 cuts through York from east to west. There is also good access to York via I-81 (30 miles north) and the Pennsylvania Turnpike (17 miles north).

ESSENTIALS   Information   For self-guided walking tour brochures and

WHAT'S SPECIAL ABOUT YORK

Ace Attractions
- [ ] York County Courthouse, commemorating York's brief tenure as the national capital.
- [ ] Golden Plough Tavern, Colonial landmark and York's oldest structure.
- [ ] Historical Society of York, a wellspring of York crafts, history, and folk art.
- [ ] Harley Davidson Motorcycle Museum, headquarters of America's only motorcycle manufacturer.
- [ ] Bob Hoffman's Weightlifting and Softball Hall of Fame, a must for fitness buffs.

Events/Festivals
- [ ] Olde York Street Fair, outdoor festival of crafts, music, and food.

Shopping
- [ ] Village at Meadowbrook, two dozen shops and outlets in a Colonial setting.
- [ ] Central Market House, one of three year-round farmer's markets.

complete information about York, contact the **York County Convention and Visitors Bureau,** One Marketway East, P.O. Box 1229, York, PA 17405 (tel. 717/848-4000). In York, there is also a walk-in **Visitors Information Center** at 2811 Whiteford Road (tel. 717/755-9638), located at The Village at Meadowbrook, off the Rte. 30/Mt. Zion Interchange.

Getting Around If you need a cab, call **York Cab,** 53 East King St. (tel. 843-8811). The only car-rental company in York is **Avis,** 1439 Mt. Rose Ave. (tel. 843-1147).

Special Events Since 1973, the **Olde York Street Fair** has been a highlight among the yearly festivals in southern Pennsylvania. Held on Mother's Day, this outdoor gathering is centered in a five-block stretch of Market Street in the historic district. The attractions include more than 35 performing groups and ethnic folk dancers, plus 300 craftspeople displaying their handmade jewelry, weavings, artwork, and homemade foods. There is no admission charge; hours are 1 to 7pm. Complete details are available from the York County Tourist Convention and Visitors Bureau.

Thirty miles east of Gettysburg is York, an area first settled in 1736. Named for York, England, this city had its moments of glory between September 30, 1777, and June 28, 1778, when the Colonial capital was moved here from Philadelphia. The Continental Congress met at the York Courthouse during that period and adopted the Articles of Confederation. Since this was the first document to describe the colonies as the United States of America, York lays claim to being our nation's first legal capital.

In addition, while serving as capital, York was the site of the first proclamation establishing Thanksgiving as a national holiday.

Today York (pop. 50,000) has preserved or restored much of its original architecture. The midtown historic district is the largest in Pennsylvania outside of Philadelphia. With landmark Continental Square at its heart, this city retains many Colonial street names like King, Queen, Princess, and Duke. The restored York County Colonial Courthouse stands across from a 1741 tavern and near a parade of Federal and Victorian buildings, many with brick walkways, carved doors, stained-glass windows, or cast-iron trim.

But York's charm is not all from the past. A prosperous industrial city situated on the banks of the Codorus Creek, modern York is famous as a candy-making center and for its nearby orchards and wineries. York is home to a trio of farmers' markets and a variety of other attractions ranging from the Harley-Davidson Motorcycle Museum to the Bob Hoffman Weightlifting Hall of Fame.

WHAT TO SEE & DO

YORK COUNTY COLONIAL COURTHOUSE, 205 West Market St. Tel. 846-1977.

A good place to start a tour of York is at this authentic reconstruction of the building where the Continental Congress adopted the Articles of Confederation in 1777. This landmark houses 200-year-old artifacts and memorabilia as well as a multimedia presentation on York's epic year as our nation's capital.

Admission: $1 adults, 50¢ children 12 and under.
Open: Mon–Fri 10am–4pm; Sat 10am–4pm; Sun 1–4pm.

GOLDEN PLOUGH TAVERN, 157 W. Market St. Tel. 845-2951.

Across the street from the courthouse is a Germanic half-timber building dating from 1741. Thought to be the oldest surviving structure in York, this tavern contains a fine collection of early-18th-century furnishings. It is also the centerpiece in a cluster of three historic buildings on this corner. Adjacent to it is the **General Gates House,** once the Colonial residence of Horatio Gates and the place where Lafayette gave a historic toast to General Washington that ensured his continued command of the continental forces. The third building is the **Bobb Log House,** an 1811 dwelling typifying life in York in the early 19th century. One price covers admission to all three attractions.

Admission: $3.50 adults, $1.75 children 6–13.
Open: Mon–Sat 10am–4pm, Sun 1–4pm.

THE HISTORICAL SOCIETY OF YORK COUNTY, at 250 East Market St. Tel. 848-1587.

Another highlight of the historic district is this restored brick town house. Exhibits include the crafts and customs of early settlers, models of local architecture and industry, early automobiles, and a life-size village square. You'll also see drawings by Lewis Miller, York's folk artist of the 1800s; old newspapers on display; and as a restored 1804 organ.

Admission: $2 adults, $1 children 6–13.
Open: Mon–Sat 9am–5pm, Sun 1–4pm.

HARLEY-DAVIDSON MOTORCYCLE MUSEUM, 1425 Eden Road. Tel. 848-1177.

This museum is the headquarters of the only American motorcycle manufacturer and includes exhibits of vintage models of motorcycles from 1903 to the present. Half-hour guided museum tours are conducted Monday through Saturday at 10am, 12:30pm, and 2pm. On weekdays, you can tour the plant and see motorcycles in the making; the hours of these tours vary, so it is best to check in advance (children under 12 are not permitted in the plant).

Admission: Free.

BOB HOFFMAN WEIGHTLIFTING AND SOFTBALL HALL OF FAME, 3300 Board Rd. Tel. 767-6481.

This attraction honors Olympic weightlifters, power lifters, bodybuilders, and strongmen. There is also a display spotlighting the history of softball.

Admission: Free.
Open: Mon–Sat 10am–4pm. **Closed:** Holidays.

SHOPPING

One of the city's best shopping areas is located east of downtown at **The Village at Meadowbrook,** 2900 Whiteford Rd., York (tel. 755-0899). This is the home of the highly acclaimed Meadowbrook Inn restaurant (see "Where to Dine," below), as well as more than two dozen fine shops including outlets for

Pfaltzgraff, the oldest and largest manufacturer of tableware in the United States; Jonathan Logan; Van Heusen; Izod; Harvé Benard; Delta Hosiery; Hamilton Watch and Clock; Pewtarex; Manhattan Sportwear; and Bass Shoes. The shops are laid out in a Colonial village setting, with landscaped grounds, including a covered bridge, duck pond, and gazebo. Open Monday through Saturday from 10am to 9pm, and on Sunday from noon to 5pm.

FARMERS' MARKETS

As a rich agricultural area, York is well known for its farmers' markets, which started years ago when local farmers gathered in the square on market days to sell produce from their wagons. Today, however, York's markets are housed in all-weather buildings. Their wares include homemade cakes and pies, soups, fruits and vegetables, candy, flowers, meat and poultry, jellies, and hand-crafted items.

York's three main markets, which operate year round, are **Central Market House,** 34 West Philadelphia Street (tel. 848-2243), open Tuesday, Thursday, and Saturday (6am to 3pm); **Farmers' Market West,** 380 West Market Street (tel. 848-1402), open Tuesday, Friday, and Saturday (7am to 3:30pm); and **New Eastern Market,** 201 Memory Lane (tel. 755-5811), open Friday noon to 8pm.

NEARBY ATTRACTIONS

About 15 miles southeast of downtown York is the home of **Naylor Wines,** R.D. 3, Ebaugh Road, Stewartstown (tel. 993-2431), an area that was one of the original grape-growing and wine-making regions in America. This particular winery dates from 1975, with its first wine production in 1978. Visitors can tour the 27-acre vineyards as well as the extensive, award-winning indoor winery operations. There is no charge for touring or sampling. Open daily 11am to 6pm and Sunday from noon to 5pm.

WHERE TO STAY

Although you'll find one of York's best hotels, the Yorktowne, in the heart of downtown, most other lodging choices are on major access routes outside the city. In general, rates are moderate and some properties also offer cost-saving weekend packages. Be sure to check for the best rate when you reserve a room.

MODERATE

DAYS INN, 1415 Kenneth Rd., P.O. Box 1348, York, PA 17404. Tel. 717/767-6931 or toll-free 800/325-2525. Fax 717/767-6938. 105 rms, 4 suites. A/C TV TEL
$ Rates: $50–$56 single, $60–$66 double. AE, CB, DC, DISC, MC, V. **Parking:** Free.
This modern three-story hotel is located in a rural setting just off Rte. 30. Rooms are equipped with two queen-size beds plus two vanities and a clock radio. The decor includes contemporary furnishings with light woods and pastel tones. Guest amenities include a lounge and a game room; three restaurants are nearby. Kitchenette suites are also available.

HOLIDAY INN, Rtes. 30 and 74, York, PA 17404. Tel. 717/846-9500 or toll-free 800/HOLIDAY. Fax 717/846-9500. 181 rms. A/C TV TEL
$ Rates: $59–$89 single, $74–$89 double. AE, CB, DC, MC, V. **Parking:** Free.
This hotel is adjacent to the West Manchester Mall, a 100-unit shopping complex. A cheery blend of art deco and contemporary design, it offers rooms, all newly renovated in 1990, with two double beds or a king-size bed. Facilities include indoor and outdoor swimming pools, saunas and fitness equipment, a game room, and a miniature golf course.

There is also a multi-level restaurant and lounge, Harrigan's.

YORKTOWNE HOTEL, 48 E. Market St., P.O. Box 1106, York, PA 17405. Tel. 717/848-1111 toll-free 800/233-9323. Fax 717/854-7678. 160 rms. A/C TV TEL

$ Rates: $82 single, $89 double. AE, CB, DC, MC, V. **Parking:** Free.

The grande dame of lodgings in this area is this hotel located in the center of the historic district. Originally opened in 1925, this National Register Landmark was completely and graciously renovated in 1983. An old-world aura still prevails in the public rooms with dark paneled walls, crystal chandeliers, and high ceilings of ornate plasterwork. The bedrooms have been handsomely refurbished with Colonial-style dark-wood furniture, floral fabrics, and live plants; each has two double beds or a queen- or king-size bed, plus tiled marble bathrooms.

There's a clubby café-lounge called Autographs (for breakfast, lunch, snacks, or contemporary dance music), and a full-service restaurant, the Wedgwood Room. Services include VCR and video rentals, complimentary valet parking, turn-down and shoe-shine services, and valet/laundry service.

BUDGET

BARNHART'S MOTEL, 3021 E. Market St., York, PA 17402. Tel. 717/ 755-2806. 40 rms. A/C TV TEL

$ Rates: $30–$45 double. AE, DC, MC, V. **Parking:** Free.

This one-story motel near the Eastern Farmers' Market has a garden setting surrounded by blue spruce trees. Each room has one or two double beds, an AM-FM radio, contemporary furnishings, and a tiled bathroom.

WHERE TO DINE

EXPENSIVE

ACCOMAC INN, S. River Dr. at Accomac Road, Wrightsville. Tel. 252-1521.

Cuisine: INTERNATIONAL. **Reservations:** Recommended.

$ Prices: Appetizers $3.95–$9.95; main courses $15.95–$24.95; lunch $6.95–$9.95. AE, CB, DC, MC, V.

Open: Lunch Mon–Sat 11:30am–2:30pm, dinner 5:30–9:30pm; brunch Sun 11am–2:30pm, dinner 4:30–8:30pm.

Sylvan views of the Susquehanna River are part of the charm of this restaurant, dating from 1775. The inn today is favored by guests who seek gourmet cuisine and old-world ambience. The lunch menu features pot au feu en croute, skewered beef with mushrooms, and bay scallops sautéed with artichoke hearts. Dinner offers such tableside choices as steak Diane, duck flambé, pheasant, rack of lamb, medallions of veal, and mako shark.

MEADOWBROOK INN, 2819 Whiteford Rd., York. Tel. 757-3500.

Cuisine: INTERNATIONAL. **Reservations:** Recommended.

$ Prices: Appetizers $2.95–$7.95; main courses $12.95–$24.95; lunch $5.95–$9.95. AE, MC, V.

Open: Lunch Mon–Sat 11am–3pm; dinner 5–10pm; brunch Sun 11am–3pm, dinner Sun 4–8pm.

Country-mansion elegance and top-class cuisine await you at the Meadowbrook Inn, a few miles east of downtown at the Village in the Meadowbrook shopping complex. Dating from the early 19th century, this three-story Georgian Revival building was originally a private home. Restored with authentic furnishings and fixtures, today it offers seven different dining areas, including a den, a billiard room, and a coach room, as well as more formal dining rooms. Dinner includes roast duckling framboise, Norwegian salmon in puff pastry, filet mignon with shrimp and scallops, and prime ribs.

MODERATE

GINGERBREAD MAN, Foundry Plaza, 200 W. Philadelphia St. Tel. 854-1555.
Cuisine: INTERNATIONAL. **Reservations:** Not required.
$ **Prices:** Appetizers $1.95–$5.95; main courses $6.95–$15.95; lunch $4–$7. AE, CB, DC, MC, V.
Open: Daily 11–2am.

York's century-old Foundry Building, listed on the National Register of Historic Places, houses the Gingerbread Man, with two indoor dining areas plus an outdoor deck overlooking the water. Brick walls, brass rails, colored tiles, and ceiling fans dominate the décor. Lunch features sandwiches, burgers, omelets, pizzas, and Mexican tacos. Dinner entrées include steaks, fried shrimp, honey-dipped chicken, and veal parmigiana. There is also a sports-theme bar upstairs.

BUDGET

RUTTER'S, 1440 Mt. Zion Rd., York. Tel. 755-6616.
Cuisine: AMERICAN. **Reservations:** Not accepted.
$ **Prices:** Appetizers $1.50–$3.50; main courses $4.95–$9.95; lunch $2.95–$5.95. DISC, MC, V.
Open: Sun–Thurs lunch and dinner 11am–11pm, Fri–Sat lunch and dinner 11am–midnight.

Geared for families, this restaurant offers straightforward meals at affordable prices, featuring the same menu of sandwiches, burgers, salads, and platters throughout the day. Favorite entrées include chicken stir-fried, roast turkey, broiled salmon steak, crab cakes, sliced top round of beef, and pasta primavera. There is also a large soup and salad bar, available for a flat price as a meal or for a supplementary charge to the price of a regular entrée. The menu includes a "light and healthy" section, with nutritional information about 20 different entrées.

EVENING ENTERTAINMENT

Plan an evening at the **Strand-Capitol Performing Arts Center,** 50 North George St. (tel. 846-1111). A former vaudeville hall and a 1920s movie palace, this 1,214-seat theater, restored in 1980, is the venue for a varied program of Broadway shows, symphony concerts, ballet, opera, and big bands; on weekends, there is also a selection of classical movies. The box office is open Monday through Friday from 11:30am to 5pm and on Saturday from 10am to 1pm. Tickets to most live performances range from $10 to $25, and films are $4 to $6 for adults and $1 to $3 for children under 12.

In contrast, the **York Little Theatre,** 27 South Belmont St. (tel. 854-3894), is a community playhouse showcasing amateur actors with professional directors. The repertoire includes six main stage productions a year (musical, drama, and comedy), plus four children's productions and five innovative "Studio Five" dramas. Box-office hours are weekdays from 9am to 5pm; tickets are priced from $9 to $12.

3. COLUMBIA & MONTOUR COUNTIES

50 miles W of the Poconos, 140 miles NW of Philadelphia,
70 miles NE of Harrisburg, 90 miles NW of Allentown

GETTING THERE   By Air   The nearest airports are at Williamsport (45 miles), Wilkes-Barre (65 miles), and Harrisburg (80 miles).

By Bus   Greyhound/Trailways buses stop in both Danville and Bloomsburg.

By Car   The best way to get to Columbia and Montour counties is by car, whether

WHAT'S SPECIAL ABOUT COLUMBIA & MONTOUR COUNTIES

Ace Attractions
☐ "Covered Bridge Capital" of the United States, with two dozen covered bridges.
☐ Bloomsburg Historic District, with 650 buildings of architectural interest.

Events/Festivals
☐ Bloomsburg Fair, the largest 6-day fair in the United States.

For the Kids
☐ Knoebels Amusement Park, in Elysburg, offering fun in a forest setting.

Parks
☐ Bloomsburg Town Park, outdoor haven on the Susquehanna River.

☐ P. P. and L. Montour Preserve, in Washingtonville, for nature trails and picnicking.

Shopping
☐ Christmas Shop, in Danville, offering holiday items in an 18th-century barn.
☐ Red Mill Antiques, in Bloomsburg, comprising one-of-a-kind treasures.
☐ Farmer's Curb Market, in Bloomsburg, for just-picked fruits and vegetables and baked goods.
☐ Roadside Stands at Catawissa, for fresh local produce.

---

your own or rented. I-80 runs through the county from east to west, with exits 34 and 35 at Bloomsburg and exit 33 at Danville. The counties can also be approached from the north or south via Rtes. 15 and 11 or, slightly to the east, via I-81.

ESSENTIALS Information Information on all visitor attractions, activities, accommodations, and events can be obtained from the **Columbia-Montour Tourist Promotion Agency,** R.D. 2, 121 Paper Mill Rd., at exit 35 of I-80, Bloomsburg, PA 17815 (tel. 717/784-8279).

Area Code All telephone numbers in the Columbia and Montour counties are part of the 717 area code.

SPECIAL EVENTS Ever since 1854, the ✪ **Bloomsburg Fair** has drawn people to Columbia County. Always scheduled to start on the third Monday after Labor Day, this event has become the largest 6-day fair in the United States, spread over permanent fairgrounds of 236 acres and 50 spacious buildings. Highlights of the fair include big-name entertainment, an all-weather racetrack, a demolition derby, marching bands, arts and crafts, and all types of agricultural exhibits. General admission is $2. For full information, contact the **Columbia-Montour Tourist Promotion Agency** or call the festival committee (tel. 784-4949).

A major highlight of the fall foliage season is the annual **Covered Bridge Festival,** usually slated for mid-October. As its name implies, this 3-day, two-county event offers a program of guided tours of the area's many covered bridges, plus a variety of other activities, ranging from arts-and-crafts exhibits to square dancing and country music, horse and carriage rides, and apple butter boiling. For full details, contact the Columbia-Montour Tourist Promotion Agency.

Located about 50 miles west of the Poconos, Columbia and Montour counties are best known as "the nation's covered-bridge capital." This area is home to more than 24 such structures, including a twin covered bridge, believed to be the only one of its kind left in the United States.

Bisected in the middle by I-80, Columbia and Montour comprise a relatively small destination, approximately 30 miles wide and 35 miles from the most northerly to southerly points. The region's two principal towns, **Bloomsburg** and **Danville,** are both well known for different reasons. Bloomsburg (pop. 11,700) is the home of a top university, and Danville (pop. 5,200), just 10 miles west, is the headquarters of the internationally acclaimed Geisinger Medical Center.

Historically, Columbia County, which was part of Northumberland County until March 1813, is often associated with the origin of the song "Hail, Columbia." Montour County, in turn, was formed from Columbia County in 1850 and named in honor of Madame Montour, a woman of considerable education, who was conversant in English, French, and a variety of Native American tongues. It is said that she was frequently present at Native American conferences and treaties in the early formation days of the county.

In addition to the covered bridges and other landmarks of days gone by, some of Pennsylvania's most productive and scenic farmlands are located in Columbia and Montour counties. Happily for visitors, these natural attributes are supplemented by a blend of top-notch culinary experiences, classic country inns, and craft shops.

WHAT TO SEE & DO

It is not surprising that a covered bridge is the joint emblem of Columbia and Montour counties. Within a small radius, you can tour 24 **covered bridges,** including the only twin covered bridges in the United States, named East and West Paden at Forks (on Rte. 487). With the earliest specimen dating back to 1844, almost all of the bridges are well over 100 years old. To help you plot a route to take in as many bridges as possible, obtain a free guide-map of all the bridges from the Columbia-Montour Tourism Agency.

BLOOMSBURG HISTORIC DISTRICT

Pennsylvania's only incorporated town, Bloomsburg has more than 650 homes that are designated as part of a National Historic District. Mostly private dwellings or commercial enterprises, these buildings span a 150-year period and include a diversity of styles—from Georgian, Federal, and Italianate to Gothic Revival, Victorian, Colonial Revival, Queen Anne, and art deco. The historic district encompasses all of Main Street, and East Market Street to Fifth Street. A good starting point is the **Columbia County Court House** (1891) in the center of town. Largely Romanesque, this building is admired for its flowing arches, columns, and chiming clock. Other contrasting structures include the **Greek Revival post office** and the **art-deco fire station.** Self-guided walking tour pamphlets are available from the Columbia-Montour Tourist Office or at the various hotels and restaurants in the town. During the months of June through October, Bloomsburg's Market Square is also the scene of a colorful **farmers' curb market,** every Tuesday, Thursday, and Saturday from 7am to 1pm. Local farmers pull in their vans along the tree-shaded curb to sell a variety of fresh-picked vegetables and fruits as well as flowers and baked goods.

No matter where you wander around downtown Bloomsburg, one sight dominates the horizon—**Carver Hall** (1867), at the entrance to Bloomsburg University, College Hill (tel. 389-3900). With an ornately carved dome-shaped Colonial tower, this landmark has become a symbol of the town and the nucleus of the school's sprawling 173-acre campus. Visitors are welcome to walk around the grounds and visit the library and other public exhibits.

In addition to Bloomsburg, other towns in this dual-county area (especially Danville, Lightstreet, and Orangeville) are also worth a walk or a drive to see the neat rows of Federal-style buildings and the gaily painted Victorian houses with turrets, gazebos, and gingerbread trim. Plan to spend a few hours a day driving the back roads, particularly Rte. 487, both north and south of I-80. This meandering country route provides ever-changing vistas of tree-lined mountains and expansive valleys with horse, dairy, and vegetable farms. If you're looking to take fresh produce home, the Catawissa area, 8 miles south of Bloomsburg, is home to a variety of roadside stands along Rte. 487, such as Rohrbach's and Krum's.

The **Susquehanna Valley Winery,** R.R. 5, Danville (tel. 275-2364), is situated on a hilltop farm overlooking the Susquehanna River. It isn't the easiest place to find, but it is well signposted off Rte. 11, about midway between Bloomsburg and Danville. It's worth the drive on this rural country road just to see this sylvan spot. Both white and red wines are produced here, from grape to bottle, and visitors are welcome to tour the winery and taste a few samples. Hours are Wednesday through Sunday, from 10am to 6pm. There's no admission charge.

Although technically in neighboring Schuylkill County, the **Pioneer Tunnel,** Rte. 61, Ashland (tel. 875-3850), is so close to Columbia that you shouldn't miss it. Located in the heart of Pennsylvania's anthracite coal region, this is a genuine horizontal drift mine, running 1,800 feet straight into the side of Mahanoy Mountain. Visitors can tour the mine (adults $4.50 and children 4 to 11 $2.50) and take a steam-locomotive (lokie) ride around mine country (adults $2 and children 4 to 11 $1). Open weekends only in May, September, and October, and daily from May 30 through Labor Day weekend from 10am to 6pm. Picnic and playground facilities are available in the park adjoining Pioneer Tunnel, and 200 yards away is the state-sponsored **Museum of Anthracite Mining** (tel. 875-4708), an exhibit devoted to mining technology and geology. Maintaining the same opening hours as the Pioneer Tunnel (except only from noon to 6pm on Sunday), the museum charges $2 for adults and $1 for children 4 to 11.

SPORTS & ACTIVITIES

With facilities that include a fitness track, tennis courts, a municipal swimming pool with a sunbathing area, picnic tables, and outdoor grills, **Bloomsburg Town Park** (tel. 387-0443) is a playground for residents and visitors alike. In a sylvan setting along the banks of the Susquehanna River, the park is located at the juncture of Market Street and Fort McClure Boulevard on the southern edge of the town. There's no admission charge.

A variety of nature trails (including a multi-sensory Braille Trail) draws many visitors to the **P. P. & L. Montour Preserve,** Rte. 54, Washingtonville (tel. 437-3131), north of exit 33 on I-80. Open year round, the preserve includes areas for picnicking (with tables, benches, and outdoor grills) and a lake for fishing and bird watching. Admission is free; opening times for the grounds vary seasonally, but a **Visitors Center** is open Monday through Friday from 9am until 4pm all year and from 2 until 5pm on Saturday and Sunday, from the second weekend of April to the second weekend of September. For more information, write to P. P. & L. Montour Preserve, R.R. 1, Box 292, Turbotville, PA 17772.

Although just about any spot along a country road is ideal for a picnic, one special venue is the park at the **Twin Bridges** at Forks, Rte. 487, north of exit 35 off I-80. Picnic tables are provided both under and beside the bridges in a sheltered brookside setting. There's no admission charge.

Visiting golfers are warmly received at the **Mill Race Golf Resort,** Rte. 487, Benton (tel. 925-2040), an 18-hole complex 16 miles north of I-80. Greens fees average $12 for 18 holes on weekdays and $16 on weekends. Motorized carts are available for rent from $9 and up per person per cart.

COOL FOR KIDS

Described as Pennsylvania's number-one family fun park, **Knoebels Amusement Park,** Rte. 487, Elysburg (tel. 672-2572), is in a secluded forest setting, just south of Columbia County. This complex is a children's haven with outdoor games and rides such as bumper boats and cars, water slides, and a classic wooden roller coaster (most rides average 50¢ to $1 in price). Parking, general admission, and picnic facilities are free. The park also offers 400 campsites as well as swimming pools, gift shops, restaurants, and cafeterias. Open daily, mid-June to Labor Day, from 11am to 10pm; and weekends only from late April to mid-June and early September from 10am to 8pm.

SHOPPING

With so many Victorian- and Federal-style homes lining the streets of Bloomsburg, Danville, Berwick, Lightstreet, and Orangeville, you'll find frequent yard, barn, and porch sales along the major and minor roads. Among the permanent shops worth a stop is **Red Mill Antiques,** 44 Red Mill Rd., Bloomsburg (tel. 784-7146). This is a three-story converted gristmill loaded with antique and country furniture, brass fixtures, baskets, candlesticks, lamps, and the like. Open Monday through Saturday from 9am to 5pm, and on Sundays from 1 to 4pm.

Another shop worth a visit for its sightseeing value as well as its wares is **The Village Sampler,** Rte. 54, Riverside (tel. 275-0690), just across the river from Danville. Actually a pair of shops, this dual enterprise is housed in buildings that served as the local railroad depot and Susquehanna Hotel. The former is chock-full of gift items from folk art to cross-stitch supplies, and the latter is an emporium of country and traditional furnishings. Open Monday through Saturday from 9:30am to 5:30pm (Friday until 9pm).

For country crafts, quilt hangings, soaps and scents, and unusual gifts, browse in the **Country Charm,** 36 W. Main St., Bloomsburg (tel. 784-6039). Open Monday through Wednesday, 10am–5pm, Thursday and Friday 10am–9pm, Saturday 10am–5pm, Sunday 1–5pm.

✪ There is always a holiday spirit at **The Christmas Shoppe,** Rte. 642 West, Danville (tel. 275-7785), just south of I-80 exit 33. A restored 18th-century bank barn, this is a yuletide treasure trove any time of year. Ornaments are arranged in aisles—from angels, bears, and baubles to Santas, sports cars, and farm animals. *Nutcracker* figurines, music boxes, puppets, and heirloom dolls also line the walls. Open from March through December, this festive emporium operates daily from 10am to 5pm. Monday and Tuesday and Thursday through Saturday, and from 1 to 5pm on Sunday.

WHERE TO STAY

Country inns and classic old-world hotels dominate the scene in Columbia and Montour, although there are also modern motels. With the exception of suites, most accommodations are in the moderate price range.

BLOOMSBURG AREA
Moderate

INN AT TURKEY HILL, 991 Central Rd., Bloomsburg, PA 17815. Tel. 717/387-1500. 18 rms, 2 suites (all with bath). A/C TV TEL
$ Rates (including continental breakfast): $60–$80 single, $68–$90 double, $120–$140 suite. AE, MC, V. **Parking:** Free.

✪ This hotel, owned and managed by the Pruden family, imparts the history and ambience of a family home dating back to 1839. Although it's just south of the major highway, the inn is secluded in peaceful rolling farmlands with a beautifully landscaped courtyard, a lily pond, and a sturdy old barn. With an enthusiastic and well-trained young staff, the inn offers two rooms in the original house and the rest in new cottage-style buildings. The rooms are individually furnished and decorated with country crafts; there are two suites, each with a working fireplace and Jacuzzi bath. Facilities include a fine restaurant (see "Where to Dine," below).

MAGEE'S MAIN STREET INN, 20 W. Main St., Bloomsburg, PA 17815. Tel. 717/784-3200 or toll-free 800/331-9815. Fax 717/784-3200, ext. 115. 45 rms, 5 suites. A/C TV TEL

$ Rates (including full breakfast): $47–$57 single, $52–$57 double, $62 suite. AE, CB, DC, DISC, MC, V. **Parking:** Free.

Dating back to 1855 and formerly known as the Hotel Magee, this landmark three-story hostelry was totally revamped and refurbished in 1988–90 and turned into a bed-and-breakfast inn. All guest rooms have private bathrooms and every modern amenity, yet preserve an aura of yesteryear with reproduction furnishings, designer fabrics, plush carpeting, and little extras such as complimentary coffee service, sparkling waters, and fruit juices. Suites have separate bedroom and living room areas. Facilities include an adjacent restaurant/lounge, Harry's Grille (see "Where to Dine," below).

DANVILLE AREA
Moderate

DAYS INN, R.D. 2, Box 100, Danville, PA 17821. Tel. 717/275-5510 or toll-free 800/325-2525. 146 rms. A/C TV TEL

$ Rates: $35–$55 single or double. AE, CB, DC, MC, V. **Parking:** Free.

Formerly a Sheraton, this modern property surrounds a central courtyard with a heated indoor pool, an open-air café, and rows of hanging plants and palms. The bedrooms are spacious, with two double beds and country-style furnishings including rocking chairs, autumn-toned bedspreads and drapes, and pictures of farm scenes.

Facilities: Whirlpool, miniature golf, and gift shop, restaurant, and a lounge with evening entertainment.

PINE BARN INN, 1 Pine Barn Place, Danville, PA 17821. Tel. 717/275-2071. 73 rms. A/C MINIBAR TV TEL

$ Rates: $34–$64 single, $38–$68 double. AE, CB, DC, DISC, MC, V. **Parking:** Free.

A 19th-century barn has formed the cornerstone of this lodging and restaurant complex. With various additions over the last 40 years, the inn now has 69 bedrooms of varying sizes and shapes, with one or two double beds or a king-size bed. All rooms have private bath and are furnished with Colonial-style furniture. Located off Bloom Street in a quiet corner of Danville, away from all the highways, the Pine Barn is adjacent to the famous Geisinger Medical Center.

Budget

PINE BARN GUEST HOUSE, 641 Bloom St., Danville, PA 17821. Tel. 717/275-2071. 6 rms (none with bath).

$ Rates: $20 single or double. AE, CB, DC, DISC, MC, V. **Parking:** Free.

Established in 1983, this lodging is a three-story residence adjacent to the 40-year-old inn of the same name. With cheery bedrooms and two shared bathrooms, this Colonial-style house offers simple lodgings.

WHERE TO DINE

In addition to the fine dining rooms of the above inns, the Columbia/Montour area has a variety of good restaurants of both contemporary and country inn types, all mostly in the moderate price category.

BLOOMSBURG AREA
Expensive

INN AT TURKEY HILL, 991 Central Rd., Bloomsburg. Tel. 717/387-1500.

Cuisine: AMERICAN. **Reservations:** Recommended.

$ Prices: Appetizers $4–$9; lunch $3–$8; main courses $12–$20. AE, MC, V.

Open: Lunch Mon–Sat 11am–2pm; dinner Mon–Thurs 5–9pm, Fri–Sat 5–10pm, Sun 4–8pm; brunch Sun 11am–2pm.

★ This country inn restaurant offers two settings—the Greenhouse, a glass-enclosed and plant-filled conservatory overlooking the gardens and lily pond, or two cozy Early American–themed dining rooms in the main house, with wall murals depicting Turkey Hill as it was 150 years ago. The menu, which is the same in all rooms, offers a creative and ever-changing array of dishes, such as rolled duck in wild cherry sauce, fresh salmon in puff pastry, orange roughy and shrimp in champagne sauce, and chicken florentine in sherry sauce. The service, usually rendered by students from nearby Bloomsburg University, is very enthusiastic and competent.

Moderate

HARRY'S GRILLE, 20 W. Main St., Bloomsburg. Tel. 784-3200.
   Cuisine: AMERICAN. **Reservations:** Recommended.
$ **Prices:** Appetizers $2.95–$5.95; main courses $7.95–$16.95; light fare $3.95–$6.95. AE, CB, DC, DISC, MC, V.
   Open: Mon–Tues lunch 11am–4pm, dinner 4–10pm; Wed–Sat lunch 11am–4pm, dinner 4pm–midnight; Sun brunch 10am–2pm, dinner 2–10pm.
Located in the heart of town next to Magee's Main Street Inn (See "Where to Stay," above), this is a lively and casual brasserie-style restaurant and lounge, serving light and quick items or full dinner selections. Entrées include chicken in lemon butter sauce, barbecued baby back ribs, grilled salmon, and sea scallops tossed in light garlic bread crumbs, as well as a selection of steaks and pastas. Lighter dishes range from burgers, salads, and sandwiches to fajitas, nachos, wings, and stuffed potatoes.

LIGHTSTREET HOTEL, Main St. Tel. 784-1070.
   Cuisine: AMERICAN. **Reservations:** Recommended.
$ **Prices:** Appetizers $1.95–$4.95; main courses $9.95–$19.95; lunch $4–$8. AE, DISC, MC, V.
   Open: Mon–Sat 11am–10pm; Sun 11am–7pm.
★ Although it's worth a visit to this little town just to see the rows of immaculate Federal-style houses, most people head here to feast at the Lightstreet Hotel. Founded in 1856, the inn is now exclusively a restaurant, with three dining rooms and a convivial lounge bar, all done in Early American decor. Light snacks are featured at lunch, but the restaurant is busiest at dinnertime when the menu features steaks from Montfort of Colorado, chicken breast with mushrooms, and various seafood dishes such as boneless rainbow trout and crab au gratin.

RIDGWAY'S, 801 Central Road, Bloomsburg. Tel. 784-8354.
   Cuisine: INTERNATIONAL. **Reservations:** Recommended. **Directions:** Head south from exit 35 off I-80 and the Inn at Turkey Hill.
$ **Prices:** Appetizers $2.95–$7.95; main courses $11.95–$19.95; lunch $2.95–$10.95. AE, DISC, MC, V.
   Open: Mon–Sat 11:30am–midnight; Sun 4–10pm.
A country setting surrounds this restaurant. The building is rustic inside and out with old sidebarn decor and fixtures. In addition to a cozy bar and a main dining room, there is a shaded deck outside for cocktails or snacks. Dinner entrées include chicken Kiev, charbroiled filet mignon, crab legs, and combination dishes (pairing steak with chicken or seafood).

RUSSELL'S, 117 W. Main St. Tel. 387-1332.
   Cuisine: INTERNATIONAL. **Reservations:** Recommended for dinner.
$ **Prices:** Appetizers $3.95–$7.95; main courses $9.95–$18.95; lunch $3.95–$9.95. MC, V.
   Open: Mon–Sat 10am–2am; Sun noon–10pm.
★ Established in 1981, this trendy restaurant is housed in one of Bloomsburg's oldest buildings. Lemon, peach, olive, and cream tones dominate the decor, which is also enhanced by watercolor and oil paintings and a wealth of hanging plants and flowers. Creations such as chicken with champagne and cashews, prime ribs of beef, beef Wellington, paella Valenciana, and a dozen seafood choices, such as

flounder stuffed with crab, Cajun shrimp, and scallops florentine, are the draw. The service is extremely attentive and eager.

Budget

HERITAGE HOUSE, Rte. 487, Orangeville Tel. 387-5272.
   Cuisine: AMERICAN. **Reservations:** Not required.
$ **Prices:** Appetizers $1.25–$1.95; main courses $6.95–$14.95; lunch $2.95–$4.95. MC, V.
   Open: Mon–Sun 7am–10pm.

(S) North of Bloomsburg and Lightstreet, you'll find good value and a country-inn atmosphere at the Heritage House. Breakfast, lunch, snacks, and dinner are served, with evening entrées ranging from roast beef and seafood to turkey and smoked ham. Freshly baked pies and homemade ice creams are also featured. A 115-year-old reconstructed covered bridge adds a welcoming touch to the outside of the restaurant and the interior decor, which changes seasonally, features Columbia County antiques.

DANVILLE AREA

Moderate

PINE BARN INN, 1 Pine Barn Place, Danville. Tel. 275-2071.
   Cuisine: AMERICAN. **Reservations:** Recommended for dinner.
$ **Prices:** Appetizers $1.95–$6.95; main courses $11.95–$21.95; lunch $3.95–$9.95. AE, CB, DC, DISC, MC, V.
   Open: Mon–Sat 7am–10pm, Sun 7am–8pm.

(★) As the heart of the inn, this restaurant occupies a 19th-century barn, with an appropriate Americana-style decor of rustic trim, country crafts, and local art. It serves light fare continuously throughout the day, and then goes gourmet in the evenings. Entrées range from whole lobsters, prime ribs of beef, French-cut lamb chops, and filet mignon, to more traditional dishes, such as Yankee pot roast, Virginia ham, and stuffed turkey. After dinner, you may wish to browse in the Pine Barn's adjacent Swallow Gift Shop.

Budget

OLD HARDWARE STORE, 336 Mill St. Tel. 275-6615.
   Cuisine: AMERICAN. **Reservations:** Not required.
$ **Prices:** Appetizers $1.95–$4.95; main courses $5.95–$12.95; lunch $2.95–$5.95. MC, V.
   Open: Mon–Thurs 11am–8pm; Fri–Sat 11am–9pm; Sun 11:30am–2pm.

(★) Appropriately called the Old Hardware Store, this spacious, high-ceilinged structure consists of several dining sections, all with a bright, airy atmosphere enhanced by potted and hanging plants and a collection of seasoned hardware
(S) implements hung along the spotlessly white walls. As you munch on burgers, sandwiches, or pasta dishes, you can glance up at the classic old farm tools, rug-beaters, and washboards. There is no liquor license, but there's a wide choice of sodas, fruit juices, coffees, and teas.

EVENING ENTERTAINMENT

The region's only resident professional company, the **Bloomsburg Theatre Ensemble** performs throughout the year at the refurbished art-deco **Alvina Krause Theatre,** 226 Center St., Bloomsburg (tel. 784-8181), about a block away from the Hotel Magee. Recent plays have ranged from classics like *The School for Scandal* to contemporary Neil Simon Broadway hits. Performances are staged on Thursdays,

Fridays, and Saturdays at 8pm (tickets are $12 to $15, with half-price rates for seniors and children). The box office is open from 10am to 5pm Monday through Friday; from noon to 4pm on Saturday; and one hour before each performance.

4. WILLIAMSPORT

167 miles NW of Philadelphia, 197 NE of Pittsburgh, 125 miles NW of Lancaster, 135 miles NW of Allentown, 81 miles N of Harrisburg

GETTING THERE By Air USAir Commuter (tel. toll-free 800/428-4322) operates regular small-craft air service into Williamsport/Lycoming County Airport, at Montoursville (tel. 368-2444), 4 miles east of downtown Williamsport.

By Bus A daily schedule of services from other cities in Pennsylvania, New York, and beyond is operated by **Susquehanna Trailways,** 56 East Third St. (tel. 326-1511 or toll-free 800/692-6314). Local transport is provided by **City Bus,** 1500 West Third St. (tel. 326-2500).

By Car The best way to reach Williamsport is by car; the city is 15 miles north of exit 30 (Rte. 15) on the east-west I-80. From a north-south direction, Rte. 15 passes through the city.

ESSENTIALS Information Brochures and maps about Williamsport and the surrounding county can be obtained by contacting the **Lycoming County Tourist Promotion Agency,** 848 West Fourth St., Williamsport, PA 17701 (tel. 717/326-1974 and toll-free 800/358-9900).

Area Code The area code for Williamsport and the surrounding region is 717.

Getting Around Three car-rental agencies have desks at the airport, **Avis** (tel. 368-2683), **National** (tel. 368-8151), and **Hertz** (tel. 368-1961). Local taxi service is provided by **Billtown Cabs** (tel. 322-2222).

Special Events The **Susquehanna Boom Festival,** in June, is named for the lumber era that spurred Williamsport from a small village into the "lumber capital of the world." This 9-day celebration includes a parade, a hot-air-balloon rally, a professional horse show, a professional woodsman's rally, and top-name entertainment nightly. Tickets to various events range from $2 to $10. For more information and a program, contact the tourist bureau or the Susquehanna Boom Festival, 848 West Fourth St., Williamsport, PA 17701 (tel. 717/321-1203 or toll-free 800/358-9900).

The most famous event is the **Little League World Series.** Held in late August, this is an international celebration, with top Little League players from around the world competing in an elimination tournament before thousands of fans, proud families, stars from the major leagues, and leading sports broadcasters. There is no admission charge for the games; all tickets for the 9,000-seat Lamade Stadium are complimentary. For further information, contact the Little League Baseball Series, P.O. Box 3485, Williamsport, PA 17701 (tel. 717/326-1921).

T he largest city in north-central Pennsylvania, Williamsport (pop. 33,000) is bisected by the Susquehanna River in a sylvan setting of woodland and mountain vistas.

In the late 19th century, this well-forested area boomed as one of the largest lumbering centers in the world. Local timber tycoons prospered and built grand homes in the town. It is said that Williamsport had more millionaires per capita than any other city in the United States. To this day, West Fourth Street, lined with Gothic and Victorian mansions, is still called "Millionaires' Row." Small wonder that other

WHAT'S SPECIAL ABOUT WILLIAMSPORT

Ace Attractions
☐ Peter J. McGovern Little League Baseball Museum, showcase for Little League fans of all ages.
☐ Millionaire's Row, posh "lumbering era" historic district.
☐ Lycoming County Historical Museum, exhibiting local memorabilia and a unique toy train collection.
☐ Fin, Fur, and Feather Museum, in Lock Haven, an outpost of wildlife exhibits and a gallery of sporting art.

Events
☐ Little League World Series.

Offbeat
☐ Clyde Peeling's Reptiland, in Allenwood, a natural-history safari focusing on crawling creatures.

Parks
☐ Susquehanna State Park, riverside recreation area.
☐ Little Pine State Park, Waterville, with year-round outdoor activity in the heart of Pennsylvania's "Grand Canyon Country."

Shopping
☐ Dixie Baseball Card Shop, offering everything for the collector.
☐ Lambert House, selling country crafts in a Federal town house.

---

streets in midtown still bear appropriate names like Spruce, Walnut, Birch, Locust, Laurel, Cherry, Willow, Maple, Pine, and Lumber.

In this century, Williamsport also became the birthplace of Little League baseball (1939). Ever since then, thousands of young fans come here each year to see the Little League Museum and the annual World Series.

The forests that surround Williamsport today are primarily used for recreation, offering an abundance of hiking and hunting trails, fishing and boating sports. Williamsport is also the home base for the Hiawatha paddleboat cruises along the Susquehanna River.

WHAT TO SEE & DO

PETER J. MCGOVERN LITTLE LEAGUE BASEBALL MUSEUM, Rte. 15. Tel. 326-3607.

Nearly 3 million youngsters in 28 countries will be quick to tell you that 1989 was the 50th anniversary of Little League. You're sure to relish a trip to Williamsport, the home of this museum. The "hands-on" baseball showcase for all ages invites visitors to participate in the batting and pitching cages, relive the highlights of past World Series, and see films and exhibits that tell the story of Little League's growth to over 7,000 leagues.

Admission: $4 adults; $2 seniors; $1 children 5–13; or inclusive family charge of $8 for parents and dependent children.

Open: Memorial Day to Labor Day Mon–Sat 9am–7pm, Sun noon–7pm; off-season Mon–Sat 9am–5pm; Sun noon–5pm. **Closed:** Thanksgiving Day, Christmas Day, and New Year's Day.

HIAWATHA RIVERBOAT CRUISE, Susquehanna State Park Dock, off Reach Rd. Tel. 717/321-1200 or toll-free 800/358-9900.

Many travelers come to Williamsport just to take a 1-hour narrated cruise along the Susquehanna River on board the *Hiawatha*, an authentic paddlewheel riverboat. Dinner and brunch cruises are also available, by advance reservation (call for details). For reservations and full information, contact the **Williamsport Chamber of Commerce,** 454 Pine St., Williamsport, PA 17701 (tel. 717/326-1971) or toll-free 800/358-9900.

Fare: $5 adults, $3 children 13 and under.
Open: Mid-May–end May, Tues–Fri 11:30am and 1pm, Sat and Sun 2 and 3:30pm; June–Oct Tues–Fri 11:30am, 1, 2:30, 4pm, Sat–Sun 12:30, 2, 3:30pm; June–Aug extra departure at 6pm. Ticket sales begin at 10am on day of cruise.

LYCOMING COUNTY HISTORICAL MUSEUM, 858 West Fourth St. Tel. 326-3326.
This modern structure contains a host of local memorabilia, including the components of a Colonial kitchen, a one-room school, an 1870 Millionaires' Row Victorian parlor, and an 1896 bedroom. In addition, there are dioramas of a Native American village and an early lumbering community, as well as the $400,000 Shempp Toy Train Collection, with 337 complete trains and 100 individual locomotives, of which 12 are one-of-a-kind. There is also an operate-it-yourself train set that delights visitors of all ages.
Admission: $3 adults, $1 children 12 and under.
Open: Tues–Sat 9:30am–4pm, Sun 1:30–4pm.

OLD JAIL CENTER, 154 W. 3rd St. Tel. 323-2770.
This unique attraction, a 125-year-old prison, is listed on the National Register of Historic Places and was recently converted into an arts center. The original cells have been masterfully transformed into nooks and crannies for artisans and craftspeople to demonstrate and sell their wares. You'll see painters, jewelers, bakers, weavers, potters, leathercrafters. The walls of this two-story landmark also serve as a gallery for frequent art exhibitions.
Admission: Free.
Open: Mon–Fri 10am–5:30pm, Sat 10am–5pm.

FIN, FUR, AND FEATHER WILDLIFE MUSEUM, Rte. 44, Lock Haven. Tel. 769-6620.
This rural outpost, located about 20 miles northwest of Williamsport, offers a panorama of life-size wildlife exhibits and explores the roles of the hunter, trapper, fisherman, and conservationist. A gallery of sporting art is also located here, as is a "trading post," featuring clothing, books, and gifts designed for the outdoor life. The shop is open daily year round.
Admission: $5 adults, $3 children 3–12.
Open: Mid-April to mid-December daily 9am–5pm; late Dec to mid-Apr Sat–Sun 9am–5pm.

THE HERDIC TROLLEY, 1500 W. Third St., Williamsport. Tel. 326-2500.
This motorized trolley takes visitors on a 75-minute circuit covering the sightseeing highlights of Williamsport, including the legendary Millionaire's Row, the Lycoming County Historical Museum, the Little League field, and the *Hiawatha* paddlewheeler. One fare allows passengers to get on and off once at a downtown stop and at two outlying stops on a single day.
Fare: $1.50 adults, 75¢ children 6–12.
Schedule: May–Oct Thurs 8:30am–4:30pm, Sat 9:30am–4:30pm.

SPORTS & ACTIVITIES

Susquehanna State Park, on the western edge of the city, is an ideal spot for walking, jogging, picnicking, and water sports. From May through October, **Deliverance Lifetime Sports** maintains a stand near the *Hiawatha* dock, offering canoes for $4 an hour or $20 per day.

About a half hour north and west of Williamsport is **Pine Creek Valley,** a haven for canoeing, fishing, hiking, hunting, camping, skiing, and snowmobiling. Named for Little Pine Creek, one of the main streams used to raft logs during the great lumber years, this area is known locally as Pennsylvania's Grand Canyon country. It is a natural woodland expanse of twisting mountain roads, rambling brooks and creeks, giant pines, mountain trails, and free-roaming wildlife. The focal point for sports enthusiasts is **Little Pine State Park,** off Rte. 44, HC 63 Box 100, Waterville, PA 17776 (tel. 717/753-8209). Open year round, this park is the best overall source for rowboat rentals ($5 an hour or $25 a day); paddleboats ($5 an hour); camping ($5 a night); and fishing (7-day licenses from $15 and up).

About 5 miles south of Williamsport is the **White Deer Golf Course,** Rte. 15, Montgomery (tel. 547-2186). This 18-hole public course welcomes visitors; greens fees are $12 on weekdays and $15 on weekends; electric carts can be rented for $10 per person. Facilities include a pro shop and a cafeteria-style restaurant.

COOL FOR KIDS

From the Little League Museum to the *Hiawatha,* almost all of this area holds fascination for youngsters. Another nearby attraction is **Clyde Peeling's Reptiland** on Rte. 15, Allenwood (tel. 538-1869), about 10 miles south of Williamsport. Described as a natural-history safari, this unique zoo is home to cobras, giant pythons, boa constrictors, rattlesnakes, crocodiles, alligators, lizards, tortoises, and 50 other species. Open daily May 15 through September 15 from 9am to 7pm, plus weekends in spring and fall from 10am to 5pm (closed January, February, and March). Admission charges are $6 for adults, $3 for children 4 to 11, and free for youngsters under 4.

SHOPPING

Baseball card collectors flock to the **Dixie Baseball Card Shop,** Rte. 15, South Williamsport (tel. 326-1297). More than 4 million baseball cards and posters from 1900 to the present are stocked here. Open 7 days a week from noon to 5pm.

For country crafts of top quality, the **Lambert House,** 1429 West Southern Ave., (Rte. 654 W.), South Williamsport (tel. 322-7939), is in a class by itself. A two-story Federal town house, this 13-room shop is so cleverly decorated that all of the items for sale combine to reflect the aura of a Colonial home. The crafts, which represent the efforts of more than 100 local artisans, include home furnishings, candles, crockery, wreaths, wood carvings, baskets, homespun fabrics, stencils, dried flowers, and pewter. Open Monday through Saturday from 10am to 5pm and Sunday noon to 5pm.

THE WOOLRICH STORE, Park Avenue, Woolrich. Tel. 769-7401.

For over 150 years, this has been known as a leading store for outdoor people, with an extensive selection of wool coats, jackets, blankets, huntwear, and classic European down comforters, and with a fabric center offering the largest selection of fine woolens in Pennsylvania. The best bargains are in the Backroom, with marked-down prices on racks of men's and women's slightly irregular and substandard garments as well as selected first-grade garments.

Open: Mon–Thurs and Sat 8:30am–5:30pm, Fri 8:30am–9pm.

WHERE TO STAY

MODERATE

GENETTI HOTEL AND CONVENTION CENTER, W. Fourth and William Sts., Williamsport, PA 17701. Tel. 717/326-6600 or toll-free 800/321-1388. 186 rms. 14 suites. A/C TV TEL

$ Rates: $29–$59 single, $35–$65 double, $59–$139 suite. AE, CB, DC, DISC, MC, V. **Parking:** Free.

Located in the heart of the business district, this hotel dates back to 1922, but it provides every modern comfort, thanks to a total renovation and refurbishment in 1990. The guest rooms offer a blend of old-world and contemporary decors, some with brass beds, armoires, and Queen Anne chairs and others with modern light-wood furnishings. Guest facilities include a restaurant/lounge with a theatrical theme, Legends, as well as an outdoor swimming pool, beauty salon, exercise room, sauna, and 10 meeting rooms.

QUALITY INN, 234 Montgomery Pike (Rte. 15), South Williamsport, PA 17701. Tel. 717/323-9801 or toll-free 800/221-2222. Fax 717/322-5231. 115 rms, 3 suites. A/C MINIBAR TV TEL
$ **Rates:** $45–$71 single, $51–$71 double, $75 suite. AE, CB, DC, DISC, MC, V. **Parking:** Free.
On the south side of the Susquehanna near the Little League Museum is this modern property nestled in a forest setting with views of both mountains and the city. Bedrooms have been recently refurbished and offer a choice of double, twin, or king-size beds. Facilities include an outdoor pool, a sauna, a restaurant, and an adjoining lounge with nightly musical entertainment.

REIGHARD HOUSE, 1323 E. Third St., Williamsport, PA 17701. Tel. 717/326-3593. 6 rms. A/C TV TEL
$ **Rates** (including breakfast): $48–$68 single, $58–$78 double. AE, CB, DC, MC, V. **Parking:** Free.

If you'd like to experience the glamour and style of the city's lumbering era, the top choice is this hotel. Located 1 mile east of midtown, this grand old Victorian mansion was built in 1905 on a hillside near the Susquehanna. It was lovingly restored and turned into a B&B in 1986. The bedrooms are all decorated individually with four-posters, canopy, or brass beds, and now have spacious private bathrooms.

Guests can also enjoy a front porch overlooking the river, a music room with a grand piano, a library, a TV room, and an oak-paneled dining room. The rates include not only a country breakfast but afternoon refreshments, off-street parking, and airport pickup and delivery. The personable and obliging Reighards will also suggest local sightseeing itineraries and go to great lengths to make sure your stay in Williamsport is a happy one. No smoking is permitted in the bedrooms or eating areas.

SHERATON INN, 100 Pine St., Williamsport, PA 17701. Tel. 717/327-8231 or toll-free 800/325-3535. Fax 717/322-2957. 148 rms. A/C TV TEL
$ **Rates:** $65 single, $75 double. AE, CB, DC, MC, V. **Parking:** Free.
In the city center, near the main Market Street Bridge, is this modern hotel, which affords distant mountain views. Fairly new to the area (1983), this brick structure enjoys an ideal location two blocks from the banks of the Susquehanna. The rooms have contemporary decor, and double or oversized beds. Amenities include an indoor heated pool, a lounge with entertainment nightly, and a full-service restaurant called Seasons.

BUDGET

CITY VIEW, Rte. 15, R.D. 4, Box 550, South Williamsport, PA 17701. Tel. 717/326-2601. 36 rms. A/C TV TEL
$ **Rates:** $40–$50, single or double. AE, DISC, MC, V. **Parking:** Free.

A favorite with families is this motel overlooking the downtown area and the Little League Park. Each room is equipped with two double beds; some rooms also have balconies. Facilities include a country-style restaurant and lounge.

WHERE TO DINE
EXPENSIVE

PETER HERDIC HOUSE, 407 W. Fourth St. Tel. 322-0165.
Cuisine: INTERNATIONAL. **Reservations:** Recommended.
$ **Prices:** Appetizers $2.95–$7.95; main courses $10.95–$21.95; lunch $3.95–$8.95. AE, MC, V.
Open: Lunch Mon–Fri 11am–2pm; dinner Mon–Sat 5–10pm.

The best restaurant in the city is this restored Italian-style villa on Millionaires' Row. Built by the city's most famous lumbering baron in 1854–55, this beautifully restored home was opened as a restaurant in 1984 by two local sisters, Marcia and Gloria Miele. The decor is a mix of furnishings from Williamsport's earlier days, including a bar that was once a witness stand in the courthouse, a double crystal chandelier, floral frescoes, hurricane candle lamps, lace table coverings, plush velour Victorian chairs, and spotlit paintings of the Herdic House during its heyday.

Lunch features light entrées (such as tenderloin tips, barbecued seafood, or parmesan chicken). The gourmet choices at dinner might be chicken with champagne cream sauce, flounder Macadamia, veal with chanterelles, or scallops with Irish Mist.

MODERATE

HILLSIDE RESTAURANT, 2725 Four Mile Dr., Montoursville. Tel. 326-6779.
   Cuisine: INTERNATIONAL. **Reservations:** Recommended.
$ Prices: Appetizers $3.75–$4.95; main courses $8.95–$17.95; lunch $3.95–$6.95. AE, CB, DC, MC, V.
   Open: Lunch Mon–Fri 11am–4:30pm; dinner Mon–Sat 4:30–10pm.
Panoramic views of Williamsport are part of the dining experience at this restaurant, in a residential area. Dinner entrées are a creative blend of American cuisine (such as blackened filet of fish with Cajun-spiced shrimp), international dishes (cashew chicken, veal Romano, and duck à l'orange), steaks, and seafood (king crab, red snapper, salmon, and halibut).

BUDGET

COURT AND WILLOW CAFE, 326 Court St. Tel. 322-0135.
   Cuisine: INTERNATIONAL. **Reservations:** Not required.
$ Prices: Appetizers $1.95–$3.95; main courses $6.95–$9.95; lunch $1.95–$4.95. No credit cards.
   Open: Lunch Mon–Fri 11am–3:30pm; dinner Mon–Fri 4–8pm.
The Miele sisters, the same capable duo who have transformed the Peter Herdic House into a gourmet gem, are the proprietors of this restaurant and are ably assisted by two other generations of their family. This bistro-style restaurant offers light menus with fresh ingredients and lots of home-baked breads and desserts. Dinner entrées include quiches, pastas, pan-fried seafood, chicken Diane, and freshly roasted turkey. There is no bar, but soft drinks, juices, and beer are available.

CHAPTER 11

WESTERN PENNSYLVANIA

1. PITTSBURGH
• WHAT'S SPECIAL
  ABOUT PITTSBURGH
2. ERIE
• WHAT'S SPECIAL
  ABOUT ERIE

Reaching all the way to the Ohio border is the western edge of this vast state of Pennsylvania. Encompassing the major cities of Pittsburgh and Erie, the 180-mile stretch of land takes in the Allegheny Mountains, various rivers, and the southern shores of Lake Erie.

To the south, western Pennsylvania is also bordered by West Virginia and Maryland, and to the north it is edged by New York State.

We acknowledge that this is a huge chunk of territory and we are only scratching the surface by highlighting the attractions of Pittsburgh and Erie, Pennsylvania's second- and third-largest cities. But we hope this survey will whet your appetite and encourage you to explore the area more fully for yourself.

1. PITTSBURGH

288 miles W of Philadelphia, 129 miles SE of Cleveland,
208 miles W of Harrisburg, 180 miles NW of Gettysburg

GETTING THERE   By Air   Greater Pittsburgh International Airport, Airport Parkway, Rte. 60 (tel. 412/778-2504), is 16 miles west of downtown Pittsburgh, near Coraopolis. With up to 1,000 flights a day, this airport is planning to add a new air terminal, with an increased capacity of 90 to 100 gates, by 1992.

Leading airlines that currently fly into Pittsburgh International include **American** (tel. 771-4437 or toll-free 800/433-7300); **Continental** (tel. 391-6910); **Delta** (tel. 566-2100 or toll-free 800/336-4940); **Pan Am** (tel. toll-free 800/221-1111); **Northwest** (tel. toll-free 800/225-2525); **Trans World** (tel. 391-3600 or toll-free 800/438-2929); **United** (tel. toll-free 800/631-1500); **USAir** (tel. 922-7500 or toll-free 800/438-4322); **British Airways** (tel. toll-free 800/247-9297); and **Midway** (tel. toll-free 800/621-5700).

The following **car rental** firms maintain desks at the airport: **Avis** (tel. 262-5160); **Budget** (tel. 262-1500); **Dollar** (tel. 262-1300); **Hertz** (tel. 262-1705); and **National** (tel. 642-7400). Motorcoach and mini-bus service between the airport and downtown is operated by **Airlines Transportation Co.** (tel. 471-8900). The fare is $9 each way. Taxi service is $27 each way.

By Train   Amtrak provides regular daily service between Pittsburgh and Philadelphia/New York, Chicago, and other onward and intermediate points. All trains arrive and depart from the Amtrak station, Liberty and Grant Streets (tel. 471/621-4850 or toll-free 800/USA-RAIL). The station is downtown, one block from the David Lawrence Convention Center and close to all major hotels and attractions.

WHAT'S SPECIAL ABOUT PITTSBURGH

Ace Attractions
☐ Station Square, a riverside complex of shops and restaurants.
☐ Cathedral of Learning, a Gothic revival showplace of world culture.
☐ Pittsburgh Aviary, the only indoor facility in the United States devoted totally to birds.

Activities
☐ Gateway Clipper, for cruises of the three rivers.
☐ Monongahela and Duquesne Inclines, scenic rides to the top of Mount Washington.

Architectural Highlights
☐ USX Tower, tallest skyscraper between New York and Chicago.

☐ PPG Tower, a 40-story Gothic "cathedral" of glass.
☐ Alcoa Building, 30 stories of aluminum.

Festivals
☐ Three Rivers Regatta, a festival of air, land, and water shows.

For the Kids
☐ Pittsburgh Children's Museum, three floors of hands-on exhibits.

Museums
☐ The Carnegie, the city's greatest complex of art and natural history museums.
☐ Frick Art Museum, a treasury of European art.

By Bus   **Greyhound** operates regular services into Pittsburgh. The terminal is located at 11th St. and Liberty Ave. (tel. 391-2300), within a block of the Convention Center and close to major hotels.

By Car   Pittsburgh is surrounded by major highways, with easy access from any direction. From the north or south, I-79 is the best route, and then onto I-279, taking the Fort Pitt tunnel into downtown. The best approach from east or west is via the Pennsylvania Turnpike (I-76), and then via I-376 to the Grant Street exit for the center of the city.

SPECIAL EVENTS   The **Three Rivers Arts Festival** is a 17-day gala of visual arts, music, and food, held annually in mid-June. This open-air event happens on the grounds of the Gateway Center, Point State Park, PPG Place, and several Grant Street locations. Exhibits include painting and craft demonstrations, children's activities, and live music and dance performances, plus films, videos, and an artists' market. The schedule goes from noon to 10pm and is free. For a complete program, contact the Greater Pittsburgh Visitors Bureau.

The major summer event is the **Three Rivers Regatta,** Point State Park, held in late July to early August. This is a free, family-oriented weekend of water, land, and air exhibitions highlighting the city's three rivers. The activities include a water festival featuring ski shows, turn-of-the-century sternwheeler and "anything that floats" races, and a Formula One Grand Prix, plus parades of decorated boats, and hot-air-balloon competitions. The hours are 8am to dusk. Full details can be obtained from the **Greater Pittsburgh Visitors Bureau.**

Pittsburgh's past and present have been shaped by its unique location embracing the confluence of three rivers, at the point where the Allegheny and Monongahela rivers form the Ohio. A natural fortress, the area was first surveyed by George Washington when he was a 21-year-old major in the Virginia militia, and it was quickly recognized as a strategic gateway to the west. In 1758 it was named Fort Pitt and then Pittsburgh, in honor of the elder British statesman William Pitt.

Pittsburgh's early years after the Revolution were marked by great prosperity. Coal, glass, iron, and steel made Pittsburgh an industrial giant, but they also covered the metropolis with billows of polluted air, earning it the image of "Smoky City."

By the end of World War II, however, things began to change and the smoke has been cleared in more ways than one. Thanks to enlightened urban planning, a $5 billion renewal program, and spirited community efforts, Pittsburgh has been refashioned into a smoke-free urban center. The horizon is now a vista of aesthetically impressive skyscrapers in an open milieu of parklets, pedestrian walkways, trees, fountains, waterfalls, and flowers.

Still a leader in commerce, this "Renaissance city" has attracted many top Fortune 500 companies, and is the fifth-largest corporate headquarters city in the nation. Westinghouse, Rockwell, Heinz, and USX are just some of the names you'll find here. Pittsburgh is also the site of more than 700 firms involved in advanced technology, and home to 31 colleges and universities, including Carnegie Mellon, Duquesne, and the University of Pittsburgh.

The city skyline has changed dramatically in recent years, with the construction of such skyscrapers as the $200 million Gothic glass "palace" called PPG Place, and with Oxford Centre, a fashionable office, shopping, and restaurant complex. There is a swift and clean new subway system and a trendy riverside complex called Station Square—a delightful blend of shops, restaurants, and sightseeing in a restored railroad depot.

As a mark of its ecological achievements, Pittsburgh also claims to have more trees within its limits than any other city in America. Clusters of greenery abound here, including the 36-acre Point State Park, the downtown tip of the city at the meeting of the three rivers.

Truly the metropolitan hub of western Pennsylvania, Pittsburgh has a city population of 375,230 in its compact downtown area (1½ square miles), with more than 1.3 million more people residing in the sprawling greater metropolitan area.

ORIENTATION
INFORMATION

For maps, brochures, and helpful data, contact the **Greater Pittsburgh Convention and Visitors Bureau,** Four Gateway Center, Pittsburgh, PA 15222 (tel. 412/281-7711 or toll-free 800/366-0093). Once you get to town, stop by the **Visitor Information Center** on Liberty Avenue, adjacent to the Equitable Plaza. The hours are March through December Monday through Friday from 9:30am to 5pm; Saturday and Sunday from 9:30am to 3pm. It's closed January through February. For daily information about what's going on in Pittsburgh, call 391-6840 for a recorded message. Visitor information centers are also located atop Mount Washington in Carnegie Library's branch (tel. 381-5131) and in Oakland on the campus of the University of Pittsburgh (tel. 624-4660).

AREA CODE

Unless otherwise specified, all telephone numbers in the Pittsburgh area are part of the 412 area code.

CITY LAYOUT

The heart of Pittsburgh's downtown area is concentrated in a 1½-square-mile tip of land known as the **Golden Triangle,** named for the triangular shape of the area formed by the three rivers (Allegheny, Monongahela, and Ohio) that surround it. In this section, you will find **Point State Park,** where the city had its early beginnings, and the major buildings that have signaled the "renaissance" of the Pittsburgh skyline. The Golden Triangle is also the location of the city's major downtown hotels, restaurants, theaters, and shops. In addition, the town's original **Market Square,** now a modern plaza, is here, as are the rail and bus stations.

The streets and avenues are a hodgepodge of diagonal and perpendicular shapes.

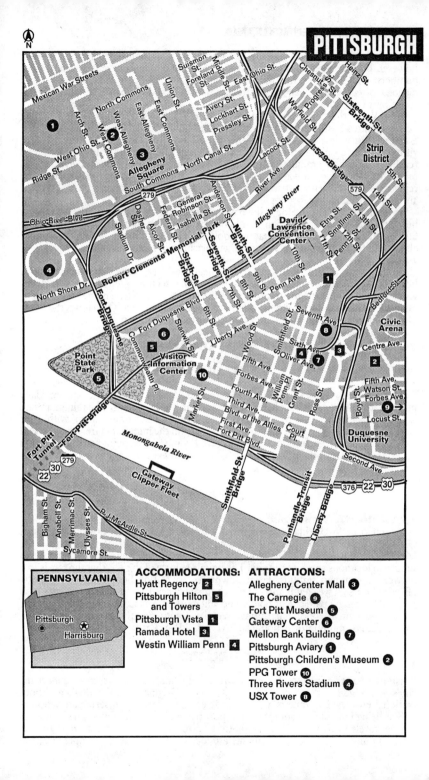

PITTSBURGH

Mexican War Streets

North Commons

Suismon St.
Foreland St.
Middle St.
East Ohio St.

Chestnut St.
Progress St.
Heinz St.

Sixteenth St. Bridge

Union St.
East St.
Avery St.
Lockhart St.
Pressley St.

Warfield St.

Strip District

West Allegheny
West Commons
Arch St.
West Ohio St.
West Commons

East Allegheny
East Commons

I-579 Bridge

579

15th St.
4th St.

Ridge St.

Allegheny Square

South Commons · North Canal St.

Lacock Ave.

River Ave.

Allegheny River

Etna St.
Smallman St.
13th St.
12th St.
11th St.
Penn St.

Ohio River Blvd.

279

General Robinson St.
Isabella St.

Anderson St.

David Lawrence Convention Center

Stadium Dr.
Dosher St.
Federal St.
Alcot St.

10th St.
Penn Ave.

Bedford St.

North Shore Dr.

Robert Clemente Memorial Park

Sixth St. Bridge
Seventh St. Bridge
Ninth St. Bridge

9th St.
8th St.
7th St.

Seventh Ave.

Civic Arena

1

Centre Ave.

Fort Duquesne Bridge

Fort Duquesne Blvd.

Stanwix St.
6th St.

Liberty Ave.
Wood St.
Smithfield St.

Sixth Ave.
Oliver Ave.

8

4

3

2

Point State Park

Commonwealth Pl.

6
5 Visitor Information Center

Fifth Ave.

7

Fifth Ave.
Watson St.
Forbes Ave.

Boyd St.
Ross St.

9 →
Locust St.

5

10

Forbes Ave.

William Penn Pl.
Grant St.

Fourth Ave.

Duquesne University

Market St.

Third Ave.
Blvd. of the Allies
First Ave.
Fort Pitt Blvd.

Court Pl.

Second Ave.

Fort Pitt Tunnel

Fort Pitt Bridge

22 30 279

Monongabela River

Gateway Clipper Fleet

Smithfield St. Bridge

Panhandle Transit Bridge

Liberty Bridge

376 22 30

Bigham St.
Anabell St.
Merrimac St.
Ulysses St.

P.J. McArdle St.

Sycamore St.

Most of the avenues, which go in an east-west pattern, are numbered (Second Avenue, however, is also called Boulevard of the Allies); other avenues have names instead of numbers. Some avenues, like the main thoroughfares of Penn and Liberty, go in a diagonal direction. Likewise, some streets have names and some have numbers, so it is really best to follow a good street map.

Thanks to the development of the former Pittsburgh and Lake Erie Railroad Terminal into a bustling mecca of shops and restaurants called **Station Square,** the **South Side** is fast becoming the alter ego of the Golden Triangle, especially for visitors. Located on the other side of the Monongahela River, the South Side can be reached in less than 5 minutes by car (over the Smithfield, Fort Pitt, or Liberty bridges) or via the sleek new subway. The Station Square development has also spurred the rejuvenation of this entire strip (Carson Street) and has encouraged a flock of artists, antique dealers, and craftspeople to set up shop.

In addition, the South Side is the base of Pittsburgh's two inclines, the Monongahela and the Duquesne, which climb the steep hill to **Mount Washington,** a fashionable residential enclave that overlooks the Golden Triangle. This hilltop area is also home to a dozen fine restaurants that specialize in haute cuisine and "haut pas" views.

In the opposite direction, beyond the Allegheny River, is the city's **North Side,** home of the Three Rivers Stadium. The other prime section of Pittsburgh that draws visitors is the **Oakland district,** east of the Golden Triangle. The headquarters of many of the city's cultural, educational, and medical landmarks, Oakland is the home of the University of Pittsburgh and Carnegie Mellon University.

GETTING AROUND

BY BUS

Port Authority Transit (PAT), 534 Smithfield St. (tel. 231-5707), operates daily bus and trolley service throughout the city and surrounding areas. The minimum fare is $1 and exact change is required. Fares are based on the zone system, with most destinations used by visitors, such as Oakland, within the minimum fare. If you should be traveling farther, each additional zone costs 25¢ more. One point worth noting: On buses heading out of the downtown area, pay as you exit; and pay as you enter when coming into town.

BY SUBWAY

Port Authority Transit also operates a light rail transit service called the "T." Inaugurated in 1985, this system currently travels between four downtown points, Gateway Center, Wood Street, Penn Station, and Steel Plaza. It then crosses the Monongahela River by bridge, stopping at Station Square, before continuing on to suburban locations south of the city. The unique feature of the T is that the fare is free between downtown stations. From downtown to Station Square, the fare is 60¢ off-peak hours on weekends and nonrush hours on weekdays, $1 during weekday rush hours. All fares are paid at exit points, and you must have exact change. Trains operate daily from 6am to midnight during weekdays, with slightly curtailed service on weekends. For more information, call PAT (tel. 231-5705).

BY INCLINE

Pittsburgh has two inclines, better known as hill-climbing trolleys, that connect the city's South Side to the Mount Washington area. Originated in the 1870s and both National Historic Landmarks, these hillside cable cars are a sightseeing attraction as well as being the quickest source of transport between the two points. The Duquesne incline travels from 1197 W. Carson Street up to the section of Grandview Avenue where a number of leading restaurants are located (tel. 381-1665). It operates from

5:30am to 12:45am Monday through Saturday, and from 7am to 12:45am on Sunday and holidays. The one-way fare is $1. The Monongahela incline climbs from Station Square to a residential section of Grandview Avenue, where there is a scenic overlook. It operates from 6am to 12:45am Monday through Saturday, and from 7:30am to midnight on Sunday and holidays. The one-way fare is $1 for adults and 50¢ for children 6 to 12. There is ample parking on ground levels. For further information, call 231-5707.

BY TAXI

Cabs line up at the city's downtown hotels and outside of midtown attractions, theaters, and hospitals. Taxis can be hailed as they cruise the streets or, to be sure, phone in advance to **People's Cabs** (tel. 681-3131) or **Yellow Cabs** (tel. 665-8100).

BY RENTED CAR

If you haven't brought your own car to Pittsburgh, you won't need one to see the major downtown sights. If you need a car to get out to the suburban areas or for onward travel, however, you can rent one at these downtown locations: **Avis,** 625 Stanwix St. (tel. 261-0540); **Budget,** 700 Fifth Ave. (tel. 261-3320); **Dollar,** 412 Stanwix St. (tel. 261-4500); **Hertz,** Nine Parkway Ctr. (tel. 922-6470); and **National,** 436 Blvd. of the Allies (tel. 642-7400). Downtown parking is extremely limited, but public parking garages and lots are plentiful. Rates can range from 50¢ an hour in open lots to $7 to $8 a day in underground or covered facilities.

WHAT TO SEE & DO

Pittsburgh's skyline is an impressive tableau of multistory **skyscrapers** of modern concrete and glass. Most of these buildings are surrounded by grassy plazas with fountains, trees, plants, and benches that beckon the pedestrian to sit down and be a part of the scene. You'll get a good feel for the city if you start at Point State Park and stroll eastward into the heart of the city. Take special note of such hallmarks as the **Gateway Center,** a cluster of skyscrapers with a two-acre pedestrian garden walkway; the **PPG Tower,** a 40-story Gothic-style "cathedral" of glass between Third and Fourth Avenues; the **Alcoa Building,** 425 Sixth Ave., 30 stories of aluminum; the **Mellon Bank Building,** Fifth Avenue and William Penn Place, finished in stainless steel panels; and the **USX Tower,** 600 Grant St., the tallest skyscraper (64 stories) between New York and Chicago.

FORT PITT MUSEUM, Point State Park. Tel. 281-9284.
Pittsburgh's earliest years are depicted at this fort museum located at the point of the Golden Triangle, where the Allegheny and Monongahela Rivers meet to form the Ohio. The city first began here, as French and British forces fought for control of this gateway to the west. At one time, this was the most elaborate British fortress in the Colonies, and it also served as a place for trade and negotiation with the Indians.
After the British left in 1772, Fort Pitt remained a key spot in the development of early Pittsburgh, as the city literally grew up around it. The present fort museum is a reconstruction, built to duplicate the look of the original bastions. Displays include dioramas, exhibits of original objects, models, and reconstructed rooms. While you are here, take time to enjoy the surrounding park, riverwalks, and the sights across the waters, such as the Three Rivers Stadium to the north and the hills of Mount Washington to the south.
Admission: $3 adults, $1 children 6–17.
Open: Wed–Sat 10am–4:30pm, Sun noon–4:30pm.

CATHEDRAL OF LEARNING, Fifth Ave. at Bigelow Blvd. Tel. 624-6000.

This is the focal point of the University of Pittsburgh campus in the Oakland section of the city. Designed as a meeting of modern skyscraper and medieval cathedral, this 42-story building was begun in 1926, and the first classes were held in 1935. A National Historic Landmark, it is considered the last great monument of Gothic revival in the United States, with 165,000 blocks of Indiana limestone on its exterior walls. Among the highlights are 23 different exhibit rooms displaying the cultures of many lands. Guided tours are scheduled daily; reservations are required.

Admission: To the rooms free; tours $2 adults, 50¢ children 8–18.
Open: Mon–Fri 9am–5pm; Sat 9:30am–3pm; Sun 11am–3pm.

THE CARNEGIE, 4400 Forbes Ave. Tel. 622-3313.

This museum complex is located in the Oakland section of the city, a 10-minute cab or bus ride from downtown. The Carnegie consists of the Museum of Art, with a permanent collection of European painting, sculpture, and graphic arts from the Renaissance to the 20th century; and the Museum of Natural History, with a much-heralded Dinosaur Hall, as well as a Botany Hall, Polar World, Benedum Hall of Geology, and the Hillman Hall of Minerals and Gems. The last is a display of 2,500 dazzling specimens, including a 197-carat opal, a 500-pound section of amethyst geode, and a "touchable" meteorite.

Admission: $5 adults, $3 youngsters 3–18.
Open: Tues–Thurs and Sat 10am–5pm; Sun 1–5pm; Fri 1–9pm; also Mon 10am–5pm July–Labor Day.

FRICK ART MUSEUM, 7227 Reynolds St. Tel. 371-0600.

Located in a grassy setting across from Frick Park and established in 1970, this Italian Renaissance–style building houses a permanent collection of Italian, Flemish, and French paintings and tapestries from the 15th through the 18th century. Other treasured objects on display include an 18th-century marble urn from the gardens at Versailles, a 15th-century Florentine stone fireplace, two chairs made for Marie Antoinette and the palace at St. Cloud, imperial Russian parcel-gilt silver pieces, and ancient Chinese porcelains.

Admission: Free.
Open: Tues–Sat 10am–5:30pm; Sun noon–6pm.

PITTSBURGH AVIARY, Ridge Ave. and Arch St. Tel. 323-7236.

Claiming to be the only indoor facility in the country totally devoted to birds, this walk-through zoo displays over 250 species in free flight. With exhibits and rooms planted with tropical foliage and trees, this unique feathered zoo illustrates the color and song of birds from around the world.

Admission: $2.50 adults, 50¢ children 2–12.
Open: Daily 9am–4:30pm.

THREE RIVERS STADIUM, 400 Stadium Circle. Tel. 321-0650.

Also on the North Side is this stadium, home of the Pittsburgh Pirates baseball team and the Pittsburgh Steelers football team. During days when no events are scheduled, the staff conducts 1-hour walking tours of the stadium. For those who want to spend another hour here, there is also a 1-hour tour of the Hall of Fame Museum and Theatre, featuring sports highlights and blooper films.

Admission: Tour, $2.75 adults, $2.25 youngsters 18 and under; tour begins at Hall of Fame Theatre.
Open: Daily 8am–5pm.

ORGANIZED TOURS

By Bus

Gray Line of Pittsburgh operates several escorted bus tours during the period from mid-April through October, all departing from downtown hotels. The choice includes a 2-hour basic tour, priced at $14 for adults and $7 for children 6 to 11; and a 5-hour trip that includes all the basic sightseeing of the previous tour, plus a river cruise and a visit to Station Square, priced at $21 for adults and $11 for children 6 to

11. Both tours depart at 9am daily. For complete information, check at hotels or call 761-7000.

By Riverboat

✪ The **Gateway Clipper Fleet,** Station Square Dock, (tel. 355-7980), operates a variety of different paddlewheel riverboat cruises, scheduled throughout the year, including the following:

Good Ship Lollipop Cruises: 1-hour narrated cruises of the harbor, departing hourly from 11am through 4pm Monday through Friday, plus hourly departures noon through 7pm on weekends. The charge is $5.25 for adults and $3.25 for children 12 and under.

Three Rivers Cruises: 2-hour narrated riverboat tours of the city, on Monday through Saturday at noon, and Sunday at 1:30 and 2:30pm. The fare is $7.50 for adults and $4.25 for children 12 and under. In addition, there are 2½-hour twilight fountain cruises on Tuesday and Thursday at 7:30pm, for the same price as the basic 2-hour tours.

Captain's Dinner Dance Cruises: 3-hour cruises, including a buffet dinner, live music, and dancing. Operates daily, from Memorial Day through Labor Day, and on a more limited basis in the spring and fall. Boarding is at 6pm and cruising from 7 to 10pm. Cocktail and beverage service is available. The price is $21.95 on Monday through Thursday, $23.95 on Friday, $26.95 on Saturday, and $22.95 on Sunday.

COOL FOR KIDS

The **Pittsburgh Children's Museum,** One Landmarks Square, Allegheny Center (tel. 322-5058), is a unique, youth-oriented complex housed in the city's Old Post Office Building on the North Side. There are three floors of exhibit areas designed just for children, including an international puppet collection, an audio and video communication center where children can "appear" on TV, and a summertime circus. Open Monday through Saturday from 11am to 5pm and Sunday from 1 to 5pm. Admission is $3 per person.

SHOPPING

In downtown Pittsburgh, **Kaufmann's,** 400 Fifth Ave. (tel. 232-2000), is a tradition. In business since 1898, this is a grand emporium, with 12 fashion shops, a budget store, beauty salons, a dental clinic, and a post office. Open Monday and Thursday from 10am to 9pm; and every other day (except Sunday) from 10am to 5:45pm. Another longtime favorite is **Horne's,** Penn Ave. and Stanwix St. (tel. 553-8000), with similar shopping hours.

Just two blocks away, you'll find one of the newest midcity shopping complexes, **One Oxford Centre,** Grant St. and Fourth Ave. (tel. 391-5300). This is a 46-story office tower with a glass atrium filled with such shops as Ann Taylor, Ralph Lauren, and Gucci. It's open weekdays from 10am to 5:30pm, with late opening until 9pm on Monday and Thursday; and Saturday from 10am to 5:30pm.

✪ Sunday shopping is never a problem at the **Shops at Station Square,** Smithfield Street Bridge and W. Carson St. (tel. 261-9911), open daily from 10am to 9pm and Sunday from noon to 5pm. A tourist attraction as well as a shopping complex, this is a restored turn-of-the-century railroad center with 70 shops and restaurants, much like San Francisco's Ghirardelli Square or New York's South Street Seaport. The merchandise here ranges from imported fashions and vintage Pennsylvania wines to Laura Ashley and Crabtree and Evelyn products, as well as candies and crafts, teddy bears, and tobaccos.

Don't miss Oakland's **South Craig Street,** a four-block treasure trove for shoppers in search of distinctive quality crafts. The shops here include **Made by Hand** (tel. 681-8346) and the **Irish Design Center** (tel. 682-6125), both at 303 S. Craig St.; the **Marcus/Gordon Poster Gallery,** 418 S. Craig St. (tel. 682-2841); **Watermelon Blues,** 311 S. Craig St. (tel. 681-8451); and **Papyrus Designs,** 319 S. Craig St. (tel. 682-3237).

WHERE TO STAY

Downtown Pittsburgh doesn't offer a great choice of hotels; in fact, only 3,000 rooms are available. Most are expensive and all are affiliated with national chains.

An additional 5,000 hotel rooms are available in the outlying regions. These suburban hotels, located primarily near hospitals, universities, shopping malls, and major industries, are ideal for business traffic, although a bit remote for the average tourist.

If you bring your own car to Pittsburgh, however, you'll find that areas like Green Tree and Monroeville can provide convenient, economical bases, especially if you're traveling with children. On the other hand, if you fly or train into town with only a couple of days to explore Pittsburgh, then it's worth the big splurge to check into a city center luxury property. Like those in most major cities, Pittsburgh hotels are at their busiest Monday through Thursday nights, and usually offer greatly reduced rates on weekends. Many properties also have weekend packages that can save you up to 50% off regular rates, with lots of other goodies thrown in. Be sure to ask if special rates or packages apply at the time you're planning to be there.

DOWNTOWN
Expensive

HYATT REGENCY, 112 Washington Place, Pittsburgh, PA 15219. Tel. 412/471-1234 or toll-free 800/233-1234. Fax 412/281-4797. 400 rms. A/C TV TEL

$ Rates: $130 single, $150 double. AE, CB, DC, DISC, MC, V. **Parking:** $6–$12.
Renovated and refurbished in 1990, this is a sleek 21-story brick-and-glass structure. The guest rooms offer contemporary furnishings and wide-windowed views of the city and its rivers, and each unit features either two double beds or a king-sized bed.

Dining/Entertainment: Pietro's Bistro offers northern Italian cuisine and Pietro's Bar features light fare, specialty drinks, and entertainment on a big-screen TV.

Services: In-room video checkout.

Facilities: Indoor heated swimming pool, sauna, health club privileges, and pay garage.

PITTSBURGH HILTON AND TOWERS, 600 Commonwealth Place, at Gateway Center, Pittsburgh, PA 15222. Tel. 412/391-4600 or toll-free 800/445-8667. Fax 412/594-5161. 714 rms. A/C MINIBAR TV TEL

$ Rates: $125–$155 single, $145–$175 double. AE, CB, DC, MC, V. **Parking:** $12.
This modern 24-story tower has been recently refurbished and renovated. Guest rooms are outfitted with contemporary furnishings and two double or queen- or king-size beds; many rooms have views of the three rivers or Three Rivers Stadium.

Dining/Entertainment: Choices include the clubby main restaurant, Sterling's, the informal Promenade Café, and the Pub Sports Bar.

Facilities: Health club, barber and beauty salons, and valet parking garage.

PITTSBURGH VISTA, 1000 Penn Ave., Pittsburgh, PA 15222-3873. Tel. 412/281-3700 or toll-free 800/HILTONS. Fax 412/281-2652. 616 rms, 45 suites. A/C MINIBAR TV TEL

$ Rates: $135–$155 single, $155–$175 double, $225 suite. AE, CB, DC, MC, V. **Parking:** $3–$8.

The centerpiece of Liberty Center, a commercial complex, is this hotel. A $69.8 million property, it is connected by a pedestrian bridge walkway to the David L. Lawrence Convention Center. The dramatic facade consists of a four-story glass atrium lobby with a 21-story guest-room tower. The expansive lobby, with its transparent glass roof, is a panorama of imported marble, cherry wood paneling, bronze fixtures, and original pottery, paintings, and ceramics created by local artisans.

Guest rooms offer contemporary decor with mahogany furniture, pastel-tone fabrics, and prints by local artists. Each unit has a sitting area, a work desk, an armchair, and a sofa, all decorated with contemporary furnishings. The entire 14th floor is reserved for nonsmokers, as is part of the 24th-floor executive wing.

Dining/Entertainment: The top choice is The Harvest (see "Where to Dine," below); other options are the Orchard Café, for moderately priced meals and the Motions lounge for nightlife.

Services: Concierge, valet, 24-hour room service, express checkout.

Facilities: Fitness center with indoor swimming pool, exercise equipment, whirlpool, sauna, aerobics room.

RAMADA HOTEL, One Bigelow Square, Pittsburgh, PA 15219. Tel. 412/281-5800 or toll-free 800/225-5858. Fax 412/281-8467. 321 suites. A/C TV TEL

$ Rates: $95 single, $105 double. AE, CB, DC, MC, V. **Parking:** $5.

An all-suite property, this hotel has a homey, residential feeling, with room furnishings that include comfortable reclining chairs. Most units have a separate sitting or dining area and a fully equipped kitchen or kitchenette. Facilities include an indoor pool, full-service health club, valet parking, a gift shop, a travel agency, and a coin-operated laundry. There is also an informal restaurant, the Ruddy Duck, and a cocktail lounge.

WESTIN WILLIAM PENN, 530 William Penn Way, Mellon Square, Pittsburgh, PA 15219. Tel. 412/281-7100 or toll-free 800/228-3000. Fax 412/281-3498. 595 rms. A/C TV TEL

$ Rates: $130–$160 single, $150–$180 double. AE, CB, DC, MC, V. **Parking:** $4–$8.

★ Originally built in 1916 by industrialist William Clay Frick, the Westin has three 23-story towers. A recent $30 million renovation has returned this National Historic Landmark to its former splendor. The Georgian lobby, with crystal chandeliers and a palm court, serves as an old-world setting for afternoon tea or cocktails. The bedrooms are decorated in a Colonial Williamsburg, French Provincial, or Italianate style, all with mahogany furnishings, plush carpeting, marble baths, and a choice of king- or queen-size or two double beds.

Dining/Entertainment: The Terrace Room is the hotel's formal dining room, with rich walnut paneling, crystal chandeliers, and a mural depicting George Washington at Fort Pitt. Lighter fare is served in the Coffee Garden Deli and the La Plume lounge. The Palm Court lounge offers cocktails and live piano music most evenings.

Services: 24-hour room service, laundry/valet service, shoe-shine service.

Facilities: Fitness center, newsstand, gift shop, airline ticket counter, barber shop.

IN THE SUBURBS

Expensive

HOLIDAY INN—AT UNIVERSITY CENTER, 100 Lytton Ave. at Bigelow Blvd., Pittsburgh, PA 15213. Tel. 412/682-6200 or toll-free 800/ HOLIDAY. Fax 412/681-4749. 253 rms. A/C TV TEL

$ Rates: $102–$155 single, $115–$155 double. AE, CB, DC, MC, V. **Parking:** $7.

There are no fewer than 10 Holiday Inns in the greater Pittsburgh area. One of the newest of the group is this hotel, situated 2 miles from downtown. It's a modern 10-story property, with an indoor swimming pool, sauna, exercise room, and parking garage. In addition, there is a lobby lounge, and a trendy multi-level restaurant, Foster's Bar and Grill. Guest rooms are contemporary in style, with bold, dark tones and art-deco influences.

PITTSBURGH GREEN TREE MARRIOTT, 101 Marriott Dr., Pittsburgh,

PA 15205. Tel. 412/922-8400 or toll-free 800/525-5902. Fax 412/922-7854. 467 rms. A/C TV TEL
$ Rates: $117–$125 single, $120–$130 double. AE, CB, DC, DISC, MC, V. **Parking:** Free.

In a wooded setting, this seven-story property offers rooms with a contemporary decor, dark woods, and designer fabrics.

Dining/Entertainment: There are two restaurants, Prime House, featuring fine American cuisine, and the Market Snack Shoppe for moderate all-day meals. The hotel also has a piano bar lounge and a disco with live entertainment and video dancing. In the summer months, a giant tent on the grounds becomes a dinner theater, featuring a top-notch show and buffet for $35 on Thursday, Friday, and Saturday nights.

Facilities: Two outdoor pools, indoor pool, tennis courts, sauna, Jacuzzi, exercise room, gift shop, and hair salon.

SHERATON HOTEL, 7 Station Square Dr., Pittsburgh, PA 15219. Tel. 412/261-2000 or toll-free 800/325-3535. Fax 412/261-2932. 293 rms. A/C TV TEL
$ Rates: $125 single, $140 double. AE, CB, DC, DISC, MC, V. **Parking:** Free.

⭐ On the city's South Side overlooking downtown, the Sheraton is right on the banks of the Monongahela River. The modern 15-story hotel is adjacent to the Station Square shopping and restaurant complex, and across the street from the Monongahela Incline. The skylit lobby features a seven-story atrium, with fountains, plants, and a waterfall. Many guest rooms face this indoor courtyard and others look onto the river and the cityscape.

Dining/Entertainment: Restaurants include the Waterfall Terrace in the center of the atrium, an outdoor Fountainview Patio, and Reflections, a dining room featuring American and continental cuisine, with views of the Pittsburgh skyline.

Facilities: Heated indoor pool, whirlpool, sauna, health center, beauty salon, and barber shop.

Moderate/Budget

HAMPTON INN, 3315 Hamlet St., Pittsburgh, PA 15213. Tel. 412/681-1000 or toll-free 800/HAMPTON. Fax 412/681-1000. 133 rms. A/C TV TEL
$ Rates (including free continental breakfast): $69–$79 single; $77–$87 double. AE, CB, DC, DISC, MC, V. **Parking:** Free.

Ⓢ With an ideal location at the entrance to the Oakland area, this hotel is within walking distance to all of the major universities, museums, and hospitals of the area. Opened in spring of 1991, it is designed in the usual format of this chain. Guest rooms are decorated in a bright contemporary style with comfortable furniture including lounge chairs and ottomans. Services and facilities are limited, but it's a good choice for location and value.

WHERE TO DINE

In addition to those downtown spots near the major hotels, Pittsburgh's restaurants are spread throughout the surrounding areas, with major clusters in Station Square and the South Side; Mount Washington, overlooking the city; and Oakland, near the university and medical centers.

DOWNTOWN
Expensive

COMMON PLEA, 308 Ross St. Tel. 281-5140.
Cuisine: INTERNATIONAL. **Reservations:** Recommended.
$ Prices: Appetizers $3.95–$7.95; main courses $17.95–$25.95; lunch $6.95–$12.95. AE, CB, DC, MC, V.
Open: Lunch Mon–Fri 11:30am–2:30pm; dinner Mon–Sat 5–10:30pm, Sept–mid-May Sun 4–9pm.

⭐ With its impressive stone facade and arched front entrance, this restaurant, a block from the City-County Building and the Courthouse, fits right into the neighborhood. It's become a beacon of fine cuisine in this judicial row. The plush furnishings, dark-paneled walls, and antique prints set the tone, and the menus, which are printed in the format of a "summons," add to the courthouse atmosphere. The dinner menu features pan-fried trout, crab-stuffed sole, and bouillabaisse, as well as steaks and a half-dozen veal choices. The fine food and ambience are always enhanced by extremely attentive service.

THE HARVEST, 1000 Penn Ave. Tel. 281-3700.
   Cuisine: AMERICAN REGIONAL. **Reservations:** Recommended.
$ Prices: Appetizers $3.50–$7.50; main courses $14.50–$23.50; lunch $8.50–$15. AE, CB, DC, DISC, MC, V.
   Open: Lunch Mon–Fri 11:45am–2:30pm; dinner Mon–Fri 6–10:30pm, Sat 5:30–10:30pm.

⭐ Of all the hotel restaurants in Pittsburgh, this one stands out on its own. The decor reflects an Edwardian era ambience, with decorative beveled mirrors, walls paneled with American cherry wood, brass wall sconces, gaslight-style chandeliers, and specially commissioned impressionist paintings depicting the harvest bounty.

A different American regional cuisine is featured each season, and ingredients come from all parts of the United States. Choices often include prime ribs, rack of lamb, veal loin steak, Atlantic salmon, lobster, blackened redfish, and brace of quail.

JAKE'S ABOVE THE SQUARE, 430 Market St. Tel. 338-0900.
   Cuisine: REGIONAL AMERICAN/NORTHERN ITALIAN.
   Reservations: Recommended.
$ Prices: Appetizers $3.95–$11.95; main courses $17.50–$29.50; lunch $6.50–$16.50. AE, CB, DC, MC, V.
   Open: Lunch Mon–Fri 11:30am–5pm; dinner Mon–Thurs 5–11pm, Fri–Sat 5pm–midnight, Sun 4–10pm.

Praised by local critics for its food, ambience, and the enthusiasm of host Jake Hickton and chef David McKinney, this is a bright contemporary second-floor dining spot, with a modern art-deco look framed by huge windows overlooking Market Square. Featured dishes include veal osso bucco or saltimbocca, blackened steaks, jumbo lump crabmeat amandine, Norwegian salmon over black pepper fettuccine, lamb chops grilled over a wood fire, and a variety of pasta and risotto dishes. Lunch choices are similar, plus a variety of salads and egg dishes.

KLEIN'S, 330 Fourth Ave. Tel. 232-3311.
   Cuisine: SEAFOOD. **Reservations:** Recommended.
$ Prices: Appetizers $5.95–$8.95; main courses $14.95–$25; lunch $4.95–$12.95. AE, CB, DC, MC, V.
   Open: Mon–Fri 11am–9:30pm; Sat 4:30–10pm.

⭐ Established in 1900, this is one of the city's best seafood houses. Fish tanks, ships' lanterns, captain's chairs, steering wheels, and pictures of Pittsburgh's waterfront dominate the decor. The seasonal menu often includes bouillabaisse, shrimp jambalaya, mahi-mahi, red snapper, Florida stone crabs, boned mountain trout, mesquite-smoked tuna, mako shark, breaded catfish, and lobster, as well as prime ribs and other limited meat selections. Klein's is also noted for its Caesar salad ($6.50).

TOP OF THE TRIANGLE, 600 Grant St. Tel. 471-4100.
   Cuisine: AMERICAN. **Reservations:** Recommended.
$ Prices: Appetizers $2.95–$6.95; main courses $12–$22; lunch $6–$12. AE, CB, DC, MC, V.
   Open: Lunch Mon–Fri 11:30am–3pm, Sat noon–3pm; dinner Mon–Fri 5–10pm, Sat 5:30pm–midnight.

Sixty-two stories above the city's hustle and bustle is this skyscraper rooftop restaurant. If you choose to view the city in the noonday sun, you'll have a choice of

Maryland crab cakes, shrimp stir-fry, prime-rib sandwich, and more. Watching the sunset brings a more elaborate menu, with seafood brochette, steak Diane, or roast duckling. Cocktails are available until 2am each evening (except Sunday) in the Triangle Lounge, which also offers great city views for the price of a drink (from $3).

Moderate

BRAVO FRANCO, 613 Penn Ave. Tel. 642-6677.
   Cuisine: ITALIAN. **Reservations:** Recommended.
$ Prices: Appetizers $2.95–$7.95; main courses $12.95–$21.95; lunch $4.95–$9.95. AE, DC, MC, V.
   Open: Lunch Mon–Fri 11:30am–4pm; dinner Mon–Sat 4–10pm.

Located in the heart of the theater district, this is a good spot if you are going to a show. The decor is bright and brassy, with lots of mirrors and plants, and the atmosphere is lively. The menu focuses on such dishes as veal osso bucco, steak siciliano, broiled lobster fra Diavolo, and stuffed lemon sole, as well as a variety of pastas and sauces. The lunch menu offers smaller portions of many of the same choices that are offered at dinner, plus salads and sandwiches. A sister restaurant, **Bravo Trattoria,** is located at 134 6th St. (tel. 642-7600), also in the theater district.

1902 TAVERN, 24 Market Square. Tel. 471-1902.
   Cuisine: INTERNATIONAL. **Reservations:** Recommended.
$ Prices: Appetizers $3.95–$9.95; main courses $9.95–$21.95; lunch $6.95–$9.95. AE, CB, DC, MC, V.
   Open: Mon–Sat 11:30am–2am.

This restaurant is as authentic as its name implies. Just look at the vintage map of Pittsburgh, the brass beer pumps, and the old crank-handle phone to experience the turn-of-the-century ambience. If you come for lunch, don't miss the oyster bar entrées or the hearty 1902-style sandwiches. Dinner choices include beef, veal, chicken, and pasta dishes, as well as an array of fresh fish. Most regulars select the house specialty, seafood Nicole ($25.95 for two people), a bounty of shrimp, clams, scallops, mussels, oysters, and baby whitefish served in marinara sauce over imported linguine.

F. TAMBELLINI, 139 Seventh St. Tel. 391-1091.
   Cuisine: ITALIAN. **Reservations:** Recommended for parties of 8 or more.
$ Prices: Appetizers $4.95–$8.95; main courses $10.95–$21.95; lunch $6.95–$8.95. AE, DC, MC, V.
   Open: Lunch Mon–Sat 11:30am–4pm; dinner 4–11pm.
The Convention Center area is known for its excellent Italian restaurants, such as this one, which has been around for over 20 years. At lunchtime, the menu focuses on seafood, steaks, and salads, with daily pasta specials. In the evening, all entrées are cooked to order, with emphasis on northern Italian veal dishes such as osso bucco and veal parmesan, and homemade pastas. Fried zucchini is a house specialty throughout the day.

DINGBATS, 301 Grant St. Tel. 392-0350.
   Cuisine: AMERICAN. **Reservations:** Usually not accepted.
$ Prices: Appetizers $2.95–$5.95; main courses $5.95–$14.95; lunch $3.95–$10.95. AE, MC, V.
   Open: Mon–Fri 7am–midnight; Sat 11:30am–1am.
This is an informal, contemporary oyster bar–style restaurant, with multi-level seating, tiled floors, and lots of oversized plants and greenery, plus outdoor-café seating in summer. The emphasis is on "fun" foods—nachos, peel-'n'-eat shrimp, potato skins, chicken fingers, burgers, pizza, and exotic salads. Dinner entrées feature charbroiled seafoods, pastas, and meats. On Friday evenings there is classic rock and dancing.

GALLAGHER'S PUB, 2 S. Market Place, Market Square. Tel. 261-5554.
   Cuisine: AMERICAN. **Reservations:** Not required.
$ Prices: Lunch $3.95–$6.95. AE, CB, DC, MC, V.
   Open: Lunch Mon–Fri 11am–2:30pm; Sat noon–3pm.

For a hearty Irish beef stew at lunch, try this pub. A variety of sandwiches, salads, burgers, and hoagies are also on the menu. Gallagher's also has a sing-along piano bar at night, from 9pm to 1:30am on Monday and Saturday, and from 5 to 7pm Wednesday through Friday. You might want to wet your whistle with some Irish coffee or a Harp beer.

Budget

RICHEST, 140 Sixth St. Tel. 471-7799.
  Cuisine: KOSHER. **Reservations:** Not required.
  Directions: In the theater district, opposite Heinz Hall.
$ **Prices:** $2.95–$9.95. AE, CB, DC, MC, V.
  Open: Mon–Wed 9am–9pm; Thurs–Sat 9am–midnight.

If you are looking for a tasty meal before a show, don't miss the oldest kosher deli in western Pennsylvania, established in 1936. All the usual deli goodies are featured, plus a full bar and a low-cost dinner menu as well as early-bird (4 to 8pm) specials, in a casual and relaxed atmosphere.

SUBURBS
Expensive

CHRISTOPHER'S, 1411 Grandview Ave., Mount Washington. Tel. 381-4500.
  Cuisine: INTERNATIONAL. **Reservations:** Required.
$ **Prices:** Appetizers $5–$12; main courses $15–$29. AE, CB, DC, MC, V.
  Open: Dinner Mon–Thurs 5–11pm, Fri–Sat 5pm–midnight.

For 15 years, Christopher's has towered over all in Pittsburgh's Mount Washington district. An exterior glass elevator brings you up to the 12th floor and this panoramic trilevel restaurant. Three walls of windows, said to be the tallest glass walls in the country, emphasize the view. The setting also includes a 60-foot-long wall made entirely of coal; four central columns and platforms signifying Pittsburgh's four major industries of coal, steel, iron, and glass; and a collection of original rod sculptures. Strolling violinists add a touch of romance. There is also a mini-museum of artifacts and mementos of the city's past, from old telephones and presidential campaign buttons to baseball equipment.

The emphasis here is on tableside entrées such as steak Diane and lobster ravioli, as well as a wide selection of seafood dishes, including Idaho rainbow trout, lemon sole, and a combination platter of petit lobster, sole, crab imperial, oysters Rockefeller, and shrimp. Jackets are required for men.

GRAND CONCOURSE, One Station Square. Tel. 261-1717.
  Cuisine: INTERNATIONAL. **Reservations:** Recommended.
$ **Prices:** Appetizers $3.95–$8.95; main courses $13–$20; lunch $7.95–$12.95.
  Open: Lunch Mon–Fri 11:30am–2:30pm; dinner Mon–Fri 4:30–10pm, Fri–Sat 5–11pm, Sun 5–9pm; brunch Sun 10am–2:30pm.

It's worth the trip to Station Square just to see this palatial beaux-arts landmark, built in 1901 as the terminal of the Pittsburgh and Lake Erie Railroad. Recently restored at a cost of over $2 million, the Grand Concourse is set on the banks of the Monongahela River. The decor abounds in stained glass, decorative marble, and mosaics.

Seafood is featured here, although meat and chicken dishes are also excellent. The lunch menu ranges from shrimp pastas and salads to baby halibut, red snapper, burgers, and crêpes. Dinner entrées feature scallops primavera, paella, Norwegian salmon in parchment paper, and Louisiana redfish, as well as chicken parmesan and rack of lamb.

LeMONT, 1114 Grandview Ave., Mount Washington. Tel. 431-3100.
  Cuisine: INTERNATIONAL. **Reservations:** Recommended.
$ **Prices:** Appetizers $3.95–$9.95; main courses $12.95–$24.95. AE, CB, DC, MC, V.

Open: Mon–Fri 5–10:30pm, Sat 5–11:30pm, Sun 4–9:30pm.

⭐ This restaurant is open for dinner only. Decorated in a classic contemporary style, it stresses Italian and French cuisine. Some of the specialty dishes include tournedos of veal and lobster, roast duck in raspberry sauce, medallions of beef topped with lump crabmeat in béarnaise sauce, and seafood au gratin in an eggplant boat. In summer, light dishes such as veal scaloppine, trout francese, and chicken romano are featured every night but Saturday, priced from $7.95 to $9.95. Desserts include tempting fresh pastries and white-chocolate mousse pie. Jackets required for men.

LE POMMIER, 2104 E. Carson St., South Side. Tel. 431-1901.
Cuisine: FRENCH. **Reservations:** Required.
$ Prices: Appetizers $4–$12; main courses $15–$25; lunch $5–$12. AE, CB, DC, MC, V.
Open: Lunch Tues–Sat 11:30am–2:30pm; dinner Mon–Sat 5:30–10pm, Sun 4:30–8:30pm.

⭐ The apple-tree-shaped sign over the door of this three-story building beckons you to enjoy dinner in the rustic atmosphere of a French country inn in the midst of the city's South Side. The one-page menu, which changes daily, offers anything from quail and venison to salmon en papillote and Roquefort-glazed sirloin. The 14-page wine list begins at $17 and goes to $150 a bottle.

SHILOH INN, 123 Shiloh St., Mount Washington. Tel. 431-4000.
Cuisine: ITALIAN. **Reservations:** Recommended.
$ Prices: Appetizers $5–$10; main courses $15–$24. AE, CB, DC, MC, V.
Open: Mon–Sat 5:30–11:30pm.
You'll be charmed by the old-world atmosphere here, from the open fireplace to the stained-glass windows and pictures that reflect another era. The menu showcases Italian cuisine with at least six veal dishes, including picatta, romano, and marsala. Beef and seafood choices are basically American in style.

Moderate

ANGEL'S CORNER, 405 Atwood St. at Bates St., Oakland. Tel. 682-1879.
Cuisine: INTERNATIONAL. **Reservations:** Recommended.
$ Prices: Appetizers $3.95–$7.95; main courses $11.95–$19.95. AE, MC, V.
Open: Dinner Mon–Sat 5–10pm.
Housed in a converted church, Angel's Corner is complete with stained-glass windows and a classical guitarist playing in the choir loft. The "divine" dishes include coho salmon jardiniere, sole St.-Jacques stuffed with scallop mousse and garnished with king crab and caviar, casmaron chicken (with jumbo crabmeat served over fettuccine), and medallions of pork with a creamy Dijon sauce.

BRADY STREET BRIDGE CAFE, 2228 E. Carson St., near Birmingham Bridge. Tel. 488-1818.
Cuisine: AMERICAN. **Reservations:** Recommended for dinner.
$ Prices: Appetizers $3.25–$7.50; main courses $11.95–$18.95; lunch $3.95–$7.95. AE, DC, DISC, MC, V.
Open: Lunch Mon–Fri 11:30am–2:30pm; dinner Mon–Thurs 5–10pm, Fri–Sat 5–11:30pm.

Ⓢ Situated in the South Side area, this restored riverside tavern offers two dining areas: a homey Victorian dining parlor with textured wallpaper and old oak fireplace, and a bright, leafy conservatory-style room. In summer, there is also an outdoor garden patio. The menu emphasizes American regional cuisine. Try the chicken and fruit salad with peanuts or the turkey or crab Devonshire sandwich at lunch. Dinner entrées include pastas, steaks, and seafoods, as well as veal picatta, chicken provençal with a three-cheese and spinach stuffing, and grilled tenderloin of lamb. There's live entertainment on Saturday nights and an adjacent parking lot for customers.

GEORGETOWNE INN, 1230 Grandview Ave., Mount Washington. Tel. 481-4424.
    Cuisine: AMERICAN. **Reservations:** Recommended.
$ Prices: Appetizers $4–$8; main courses $11–$22; lunch $5.50–$8.95. AE, CB, DC, MC, V.
    Open: Lunch Mon–Sat 11am–3pm; dinner Mon–Thurs 5pm–midnight, Fri–Sat 5pm–1am, Sun 4–10pm.

S One of the few restaurants in this area that serve lunch, this spot blends a rustic decor with 20th-century wraparound windows. Ideal for families, the emphasis here is on good value. Most choices are below $15, and that includes cheeseboard, soup or juice, salad, potatoes or pasta, vegetable, coffee, and dessert. The typically American menu offers everything from steak or prime ribs to sole or crab legs. At lunchtime, there is a wide variety of salads and overstuffed sandwiches.

GREAT SCOT, 413 S. Craig St., Oakland. Tel. 683-1450.
    Cuisine: AMERICAN. **Reservations:** Recommended for dinner.
$ Prices: Appetizers $4.25–$6.75; main courses $11.95–$14.95; lunch $4–$6. AE, D, MC, V.
    Open: Lunch daily 11am–3pm; dinner daily 5–10pm.
If you're visiting the Carnegie Museum and would like a change of pace, try this pub-style restaurant. The menu, which changes biweekly to reflect regional American recipes, offers burgers, salads, and vegetable quiches for lunch. Dinner entrées include apple-stuffed pork chops, lamb chops with apricot-ginger sauce, and filet mignon. Soups (try the chilled blueberry or pumpkin, at $2.95) are tasty and creative.

Budget

CHEESE CELLAR, Station Square. Tel. 471-3355.
    Cuisine: AMERICAN. **Reservations:** Not required.
$ Prices: Appetizers $2.95–$6.95; main courses $8.95–$12.95; lunch $4.95–$7.95. AE, CB, DC, MC, V.
    Open: Mon–Sat 11am–1am; Sun 10:30am–2pm and 2:30–11pm.
The ambience and decor of a European wine cellar prevail at this spot. The eclectic menu ranges from cheese fondues to chili, pizza, croissant sandwiches, and burgers. Dinners feature stir-fry dishes, chargrilled seafood and meats, and a half-dozen pastas.

MUSEUM CAFE, The Carnegie Institute, 4400 Forbes Ave., Oakland. Tel. 622-3144.
    Cuisine: AMERICAN. **Reservations:** Not required.
$ Prices: Lunch $4.95–$8.95. AE, MC, V.
    Open: Lunch Tues–Fri 11:30am–3:30pm.

S For a lunch with an artsy ambience, don't miss this café, featuring a decor of contemporary prints, fine linen, and fresh flowers. Salads and hot entrées prevail, and there is full-bar service. In the lower level of the Museum of Natural History, you can also enjoy budget-stretching, cafeteria-style meals (entrées from $3 to $5) from 9am to 4pm Tuesday through Friday. No credit cards in the cafeteria.

EVENING ENTERTAINMENT

Pittsburgh offers many opportunities to enjoy the performing arts. Like many major cities, it also has a convenient center for half-price, same-day ticket sales for shows, concerts, and major events. It's the **TIX Booth,** located at the USX Plaza, 600 Grant Ave. (tel. 642-ARTS). Advance sale tickets are also available, at full price. Hours are 11am to 6pm Monday through Saturday.

THEATERS & CONCERT HALLS

✪ Pittsburgh's premier stage is the **Heinz Hall for the Performing Arts,** 600 Penn Ave. (tel. 392-4800), a restored 1926 movie theater, situated downtown, between Sixth and Seventh Streets. A variety of concerts and Broadway shows are featured throughout the year, as are regular performances by the Pittsburgh Symphony Orchestra. Times and dates vary, so it is best to check in advance. Ticket prices vary from $12 to $35, depending on the event. (*Note:* This splendid theater itself can be toured by appointment; call 392-4844).

The **Benedum Center for the Performing Arts,** 719 Liberty Ave. (tel. 456-6666), is the home of the **Pittsburgh Opera** (tel. 281-0912), the **Civic Light Opera** (tel. (281-3973), the **Pittsburgh Ballet** (tel. 281-0360), and the **Pittsburgh Dance Council** (tel. 355-0330). Broadway shows are also performed here. Originally built in 1928 as the Stanley Theatre, this facility was recently restored, from its hand-loomed carpets and gilded plasterwork to the chandeliered ceiling. Ticket prices range from $15 to $35, depending on the event.

Pittsburgh's modern **Civic Arena,** Auditorium Place (tel. 624-1800), is a frequent setting for major concerts, circuses, and ice shows, as well as professional hockey and soccer. This $22-million structure is an attraction in itself, with a stainless-steel retractable dome roof, three times the size of the dome of St. Peter's in Rome. Ticket prices range from $10 to $30, depending on the attraction.

Syria Mosque, 4423 Bigelow Blvd., Oakland (tel. 333-9550), is a unique theater adjacent to the University of Pittsburgh. Known for its great acoustics, it is also an attraction in itself, with a facade and decor that represent Hollywood's interpretation of an Islamic structure. Concerts are featured here year round, with ticket prices from $16 to $20.

✪ From September through May, you can enjoy the **River City Brass Band** (tel. 322-7222). Often called the "Boston Pops of Brass," this is a group of 27 virtuoso musicians, with a repertoire ranging from Bach to the Beatles. Performances are held on Thursday through Sunday, at various locations throughout the city, with most tickets pegged between $8 and $18. Phone in advance for exact times and venues, or check with the Greater Pittsburgh Convention and Visitors Bureau.

DINNER THEATER

During summer, you can enjoy an outdoor stage show under a tent at the **Marriott Green Tree Theatre-on-the-Green,** 101 Marriott Dr. (tel. 922-8400), 3 miles west of downtown. Scheduled on Thursday, Friday, and Saturday evenings, buffet dinner starts at 7pm, with showtime at 9pm. Cost for dinner and show is $35.

MUSIC/COMEDY LOUNGES

For nightly contemporary music and dancing, try **Chauncy's,** Station Square (tel. 232-0601) and the **Gandy Dancer,** at the Grand Concourse, One Station Square (tel. 261-1717). For a laugh or two, stop in at the Funny Bone at Station Square (tel. 281-3130).

THE LAUREL HIGHLANDS

Just a few miles from the heart of Pittsburgh you'll come to an exuberant area known as the Laurel Highlands. Often overlooked as an adjunct to Pittsburgh, the Laurel Highlands are indeed a full-fledged destination in their own right, with fresh country air and outdoor living.

Encompassing a region that begins at New Kensington north of Pittsburgh and stretches 60 miles eastward to Johnstown, and 45 miles as far south as the Maryland and West Virginia borders, the Laurel Highlands take in the counties of Westmoreland, Fayette, Somerset, Greene, and Cambria. This area embraces Pennsylvania's tallest mountain range, the Alleghenies, and Mount Davis, the highest point in the state. As its name implies, the land is also rich in mountain laurel, the official flower of Pennsylvania.

Historically, this was the western frontier, the wilderness on the edge of the Revolutionary War battlefields, and today's visitor will find old forts and military strongholds, a frontier courthouse site, restored stagecoach inns, and log taverns. Most of all, the Laurel Highlands draw people to lush forest and mountain scenery and a wealth of year-round outdoor sports. The major city on the eastern rim of the area, Johnstown, is nestled in a deep valley, surrounded by mountain and river landscapes. Unfortunately, this idyllic setting has also led to the city's tragic history as America's "Flood City."

Since 1808 Johnstown has been flooded 22 times, but the one most remembered was in 1889 as a result of the collapse of the South Fork Dam, about 10 miles east of the city. This tragic flood claimed over 2,200 lives in fewer than 10 minutes. Other floods in this century, most notably in 1936 and 1977, also took their toll on the city. Today you can see the high-water marks etched on many buildings, including the sturdy, stone-faced City Hall.

But Johnstown today (pop. 35,500) is a city of great spunk and spirit and has managed to recover and prosper. Some leading sites, like the inclined plane and the museum, were built as the result of flood waters, but have become tourist attractions.

VISITOR INFORMATION

For a helpful packet of brochures, advice, and up-to-date data, contact the **Laurel Highlands, Inc.,** Town Hall, 120 E. Main St., Ligonier, PA 15658 (tel. 412/238-5661 or toll-free 800/333-5661).

WHAT TO SEE & DO

FALLINGWATER, Rte. 381, Mill Run. Tel. 329-8501.

Among the most heralded spots of this area is this unusual house designed by Frank Lloyd Wright in 1936. Perched over a waterfall, the house was created as a mountain retreat for a Pittsburgh department store owner, Edgar J. Kaufmann. It was opened to the public in 1964. Tours are available on weekends in the winter months. Reservations are recommended; the drive from Pittsburgh takes approximately 2 hours.

Admission: $6 weekdays, $8 weekends.

Open: Apr through mid-Nov Tues–Sun 10am–4pm; off-season Sat–Sun 10am–4pm.

LINDEN HALL, off Rte. 51, Dawson. Tel. 529-7543.

This opulent turn-of-the-century mountaintop mansion dates back to 1913. The estate originally belonged to Phillip J. Cochran, who amassed a fortune by operating the first profitable beehive coke ovens in this part of the state. Sixty stonemasons were brought from Italy to complete the mansion, which is fueled by three natural-gas wells and also displays glass from the Tiffany studios, an Aeolian pipe organ, and Chippendale furniture. It is currently operated as the Walter J. Burke Labor Education Center by the United Steelworkers of America. Tours are conducted every hour.

Admission: $6 adults, $1 children 13 and under.

Open: Mar–Oct daily 1–5pm; Nov–mid-Dec Sat–Sun 1–5pm.

COMPASS INN MUSEUM, Rte. 30, Laughlintown. Tel. 238-4983.

Built in 1799, this log house was originally a drovers' and traders' tavern. A fine stone addition was added in 1820. Completely restored today, it is furnished with documented pieces and implements, and includes a cookhouse, a blacksmith shop, a barn, and an authentic Conestoga wagon. Costumed guides lead the 90-minute tours. Candlelight tours are scheduled in November and December.

Admission: $3 adults, $1.50 youngsters 6–16.

Open: May, June, Sept, Oct Tues–Sun noon–4pm; July–Aug Tues–Sat 10am–4pm, Sun noon–4pm; Nov–Dec Sat–Sun 2–5pm; hours extended during summer.

LAUREL CAVERNS, off Rt. 40, Farmington, PA 15437. Tel. 329-5968.

This is the largest natural cave in Pennsylvania and north of the Mason-Dixon line.

This natural wonder has 4½ acres of floor space and 2⅓ miles of passages. Qualified guides lead hourly explorations, with narrations on the cave's history and geology. Because of its size, Laurel Caverns is the only cave in the northeastern United States that features self-guided spelunking (exploring part of the cave in its natural state).

Admission: $7 adults, $5 children 6–12 for a guided tour.

Open: May–Oct daily 9am–5pm, Mar, Apr, Nov Sat–Sun 9am–5pm.

INCLINED PLANE RAILWAY, Vine St. and Roosevelt Blvd., Johnstown. Tel. 536-1816.

This attraction is to Johnstown what the cable car is to San Francisco: No visit to this city is complete without a ride on this unique conveyance. It's located on the west edge of town and connects the downtown area with Westmont, a residential section 500 feet above.

Constructed after the 1889 flood, the inclined plane was built as a "lifesaver" to prevent people from becoming stranded on low ground if more floods followed. Today it serves as a commuter run for people who live on the hill, and it is also the city's prime tourist attraction. The original cars, motorworks, and gear drives are still used, although the steam has been replaced by 400 horsepower electric current.

Listed in the National Register of Historic Places, this inclined plane has carried more than 40 million people and is the world's steepest passenger funicular railway, often described as a "trip to the stars." Reaching the top also rewards passengers with a panoramic view of Johnstown and the surrounding mountain valleys.

Admission: $1.25 one way, $2 round-trip adults; 75¢ one way, $1.25 round-trip children 5–12.

Open: Mon–Fri 6:30–9pm; Sat 7:30–9pm; Sun 9am–9pm. Hours slightly shorter in winter.

JOHNSTOWN FLOOD MUSEUM, 304 Washington St., Johnstown. Tel. 539-1889.

The best place to learn about the city's dramatic history is this grand French Gothic building built in 1891, after the disastrous flood of 1889, as a library and a gift to the city from Andrew Carnegie. It was totally renovated and expanded in 1989 in conjunction with the flood centennial. The displays, which chronicle almost 200 years of life in Johnstown, pay particular attention to the momentous flood. Special exhibits include a large-scale, light-animated map of the flood's path and a sculptural wall depicting the flood wreckage, as well as photographs and newspaper stories. There is also a new 77-seat theater where you can view a 25-minute narrated film that dramatically re-creates the destruction and rehabilitation of the city.

Admission: $3 adults, $1.50 students 6–18.

Open: Mon–Thurs 10am–5pm; Fri–Sat 10am–8pm; Sun 10am–5pm.

THE GREAT OUTDOORS

Of all the reasons to go to the Laurel Highlands, **whitewater rafting** tops many a list. Ohiopyle and Confluence, two towns about 70 miles southeast of Pittsburgh, are leading center for whitewater rafting and canoeing. Rates vary from about $25 to $60 a person, depending on the day (highest rates on weekends) and the length of the raft trip. The season runs from March through October on some rivers and March through June on others; 2-day packages are also available. For reservations and further information, contact any of the following: **Laurel Highlands River Tours,** Box 107, Ohiopyle, PA 15470 (tel. 329-8531 or toll-free 800/4-RAFTIN); **Mountain Streams and Trails Outfitters,** Box 106, Ohiopyle, PA 15470 (tel. 329-8810 or toll-free 800/245-4090); **Youghiogheny Outfitters,** P.O. Box 21, Ohiopyle, PA 15470 (tel. 329-4549); **Riversport, Inc.,** 213 Yough St., Confluence, PA 15424 (tel. 814/395-5744); **White Water Adventures,** Box 31, Ohiopyle, PA 15470 (tel. 329-8850 or toll-free 800/WWA-RAFT); and **Wilderness Voyageurs Inc.,** Box 97, Ohiopyle, PA 15470 (tel. 329-4752 or toll-free 800/272-4141).

The Laurel Highlands are equally popular in the winter with facilities for both downhill and cross-country skiing in several locations. There are 30 miles of trails with a dual/triple chairlift at the **Hidden Valley Resort,** R.D. 6, Box 322, Somerset, PA 15501 (tel. 814/443-6454 or toll-free 800/458-0175). Two other large and challenging complexes are the **Blue Knob Resort,** Rte. 869W, Claysburg, PA 15531 (tel. 814/239-5111), and the **Seven Springs Resort** at Champion, PA 15622 (tel. 814/352-7777).

WHERE TO STAY
Moderate

HOLIDAY INN, 250 Market St., Johnstown, PA 15907. Tel. 814/535-7777 or toll-free 800/HOLIDAY. Fax 814/535-7777. 164 rms. A/C TV TEL
$ Rates: $66–$90 single, $76–$95 double. AE, CB, DC, MC, V. **Parking:** Free.
Located right in the heart of downtown Johnstown, this modern six-story hotel is the social and meeting hub of the city, and is within easy walking distance of the Flood Museum and the Inclined Plane. Rooms are furnished in contemporary style, with rich pastel tones, dark wood furniture, table and chairs or sitting areas, and a choice of two double beds or a king-size bed.
   Facilities include an indoor heated pool, sauna, whirlpool and fitness equipment, meeting rooms, and a greenhouse-style restaurant/lounge.

LIGONIER COUNTRY INN, Rt. 30, Laughlintown, PA 15655. Tel. 412/238-3651. Fax 412/238-7862. 16 rms (all with bath). A/C TV TEL
$ Rates (including continental breakfast): $60–$75 single or double. AE, DC, DISC, MC, V. **Parking:** Free.
Located at the base of Laurel Mountain and dating back to 1927, the three-story inn has been handsomely restored and furnished in a Colonial motif by innkeeper Maggie Steitz. The bedrooms are individually decorated in soft pastels, many with brass beds and stenciled walls. Amenities include a restaurant (see "Where to Dine," below), an activity/sitting room, a fireside lounge, a patio, and an outdoor pool.

MOUNTAIN VIEW INN, 1001 Village Drive, Greensburg, PA 15601. Tel. 412/834-5300. Fax 412/834-5304. 36 rms, 20 suites (all with bath). A/C TV TEL **Directions:** Head 30 miles east of Pittsburgh, off Rte. 30, between Greensburg and Latrobe.
$ Rates: $44–$55 single, $49–$65 double, $66–$85 suite. AE, CB, DC, MC, V. **Parking:** Free.
   One of the best places to savor the surroundings is at this inn, where you'll enjoy panoramic views of Chestnut Ridge and the foothills of the Alleghenies. An early-American atmosphere prevails in the public rooms, with a prototype Colonial parlor re-created near the lobby. The corridors and halls are lined with cherrywood benches, rolltop desks, kerosene lanterns, and cupboards full of china and porcelain. In addition, there are timeworn prints of early Greensburg and the first days at the hotel in 1925. The bedrooms are also furnished with antiques and touches of Americana; you might even find a spinning wheel in your room.
   Guest facilities include the 1776 Tavern for cocktails and light fare and a Colonial-style restaurant, the Candlelight Room (see "Where to Dine," below).

NOON–COLLINS INN, 114 E. High St., Ebensburg, PA 15931. Tel. 814/472-4311. 7 rms (all with bath). A/C TV TEL
$ Rates (including breakfast): $55 single or double. AE, CB, DC, MC, V. **Parking:** Free.
   A 19th-century ambience prevails at this charming lodging, the pride and joy of enthusiastic innkeepers Lewis and Jeannette Ripley. Listed on the National Register of Historic Places, this Federal-style stone mansion was built in 1934 as a private residence for a Cambria County judge. Located fewer than 20 miles from downtown Johnstown, it is a delightful and affordable alternative to the more modern hotels and motels of the area. The Ripleys have taken great care to preserve the original atmosphere of the house, with antique furnishings, family heirlooms, and

many original fixtures. Facilities include a parlor with a fireplace, and a first-rate dining room.

WHERE TO DINE

Moderate

THE CANDLELIGHT ROOM, 1001 Village Dr., Greensburg. Tel. 834-5300.
   Cuisine: REGIONAL AMERICAN. **Reservations:** Recommended.
$ Prices: Appetizers $2.95–$6.95; main courses $9.95–$19.95; lunch $3.95–$9.95. AE, CB, DC, MC, V.
   Open: Daily lunch 11:30–2:30pm, dinner 5–9pm.

⭐ Housed in the Mountain View Inn (see "Where to Stay," above), this restaurant is an attraction in itself, with Colonial-style furnishings, dark woods, and brass and pewter fixtures. The menu blends traditional and modern dishes, with choices ranging from grilled Cornish game hen and baked ham, to fresh seafood, prime ribs, and beef Wellington. The adjacent 1776 Tavern serves light fare, sandwiches, and burgers, as well as drinks.

INCLINE STATION, 713 Edgehill Dr., Johnstown. Tel. 536-7550.
   Cuisine: AMERICAN. **Reservations:** Recommended.
$ Prices: Appetizers $3.95–$7.95; main courses $11.95–$19.95; lunch $3.95–$7.95. AE, DISC, MC, V.
   Open: Mon–Sat lunch 11:30am–4:30pm, dinner 4:30–9:30pm.

Set on a hillside at the top of the Johnstown Inclined Plane, this informal restaurant-pub provides spectacular wide-windowed views of the city and the surrounding valleys. The menu includes roast duckling, chicken Dijon, lamb and veal chops, steaks, and a selection of seafood, from coho salmon to lobster in pastry. Lunch items focus on sandwiches, salads, create-your-own-omelets, burgers, and light entrées.

LIGONIER COUNTRY INN, Rte. 30, Laughlintown. Tel. 238-3651.
   Cuisine: AMERICAN. **Reservations:** Recommended.
$ Prices: Appetizers $1.95–$5.95; main courses $9.95–$19.95; lunch $4.95–$8.95. AE, DISC, MC, V.
   Hours: Lunch Sat–Sun 11:30–2:30pm; dinner Mon–Thurs 5–8pm, Fri–Sat 5–10pm, Sun 3:30–8pm; Sun brunch 10am–2pm.

⭐ Situated in the heart of the Laurel Highlands, this cozy 70-year-old country inn exudes an old-world charm, with an open fireplace and dark wood furnishings. The menu offers such dishes as pan-fried mountain trout with almonds and Amaretto, fettuccine with shrimp, roast raspberry duck, and brochette of beef with garden vegetables. Be sure to sample the house specialty, "flower pot bread."

2. ERIE

127 miles N of Pittsburgh, 421 miles NW of Philadelphia,
305 miles NW of Harrisburg, 188 miles NW of Johnstown,
257 miles NW of Williamsport

GETTING THERE   By Air   Erie International Airport, W. 12th St. at Asbury Rd. (Rte. 5) (tel. 833-4258), 4 miles west of downtown, is served by **USAir** (tel. 455-4569 or toll-free 800/428-4322); **Northwest** (tel. 833-3030 or toll-free 800/225-2525); and **Continental** (tel. 833-7246 or toll-free 800/525-0280).

By Train   Daily service into Erie is provided by **Amtrak** via the corridor between

WHAT'S SPECIAL ABOUT ERIE

Ace Attractions

☐ Flagship *Niagara*, history-making ship from the War of 1812.
☐ Old Customs House (circa 1839), home of Erie Art Museum.
☐ Erie Historical Museum and Planetarium.
☐ Firefighters Historical Museum.

Activities

☐ Narrated boat cruises of Lake Erie.
☐ Wine-tasting at the four wineries of nearby Northeast.

Festivals

☐ Erie Summer Festival of the Arts, a week of great music.

For the Kids

☐ Waldameer Park and Water World, 33 different rides and amusements.

Park

☐ Presque Isle State Park, natural expanse of beaches and parklands on the shores of Lake Erie.

Zoo

☐ Erie Zoo, 15 acres devoted to over 300 animals.

Boston/New York and Cleveland/Chicago. For further information and schedules, contact Amtrak, Union Station, 14th and Peach Streets (tel. 452-2177 or toll-free 800/USA-RAIL).

By Bus   Erie is also served by **Greyhound Bus Lines,** which pulls into the bus depot at 5759 Peach St. (tel. 454-2421).

By Car   Situated directly north of Pittsburgh, Erie is a 2½-hour drive via I-79. The northern leg of this highway terminates in downtown Erie. From an east-west direction, Erie is best approached by I-90, or Rte. 20 or 5. Rte. 5 runs through the city and becomes 12th Street, and Rte. 20 also crosses through the heart of Erie as 26th Street.

ESSENTIALS   Information   Brochures on accommodations, restaurants, attractions, and activities can be obtained from the **Greater Erie Area Chamber of Commerce,** 1006 State Street, Erie, PA 16501 (tel. 814/454-7191).

Area Code   All numbers in the Erie area belong to the 814 area code.

SPECIAL EVENTS   Scheduled for the third week of June, the **Erie Summer Festival of the Arts** is an annual week-long music fest that features big bands, local rock groups, the Erie Philharmonic, the Erie Chamber Orchestra, and the Pennsylvania Dance Theatre. Admission is free and it is held on the campus of Villa Maria College. For further information, contact the SummerFestival of the Arts Committee, Room 106, Villa Maria College, 2551 W. Lake Rd. (tel. 452-3427).
   We Love Erie Days is an annual event held on the lakefront in mid-August. The program includes a 10-kilometer race, stage performances, sailboat races, waterskiing shows, parachute shows, food fests, and fireworks. Admission is free to most events. For full details, contact the Chamber of Commerce (tel. 454-7191).

A little over 125 miles north of the Pittsburgh area is Erie, Pennsylvania's only port on the Great Lakes and the state's third-largest city.
   Named for the Eriez Indians who first inhabited this area, Erie was subsequently

ruled by the French and the British in the 17th century. Erie's great moment in history came during the War of 1812 when Commodore Oliver Hazard Perry, commanding the flagship *Niagara,* forced the British squadron to surrender. It was Perry who proclaimed the famous words, "We have met the enemy, and they are ours."

Today's Erie (pop. 118,000), known officially as the Flagship City, is a major industrial area and inland port, midway between New York and Chicago. The downtown area, laid out in a grid with State Street as its central thoroughfare dividing east and west, is currently undergoing a significant revitalization.

The recreational focus of Erie is Presque Isle State Park, 3 miles from midtown. This thin peninsula stretches like an arm out into the lake and then curves back toward the city. It is said that the Indians used the word *presque,* meaning "arm of God," to describe this beautiful natural expanse of beach and parkland.

GETTING AROUND

BY BUS

The **Erie Metropolitan Transit Authority (EMTA),** 127 E. 14th St. provides local bus services throughout the city (tel. 452-3515); the exact fare (75¢) is required.

BY CAR

If you need to rent a car, the following firms maintain stations at the airport: **Avis** (tel. 833-9879), **Hertz** (tel. 838-9691), **National** (tel. 838-7739), and **Budget** (tel. 838-4502).

BY TAXI

For local taxi service, call **Area Taxi** (tel. 725-3677), **Yellow Cab** (tel. 455-4441), or **Erie Independent Cab** (tel. 899-4566).

BY FERRY

In the summer months, May through September, **daily ferry service** is operated between the Erie Public Dock, at the foot of State Street, and Presque Isle State Park. The service is scheduled continuously, from 10:30am to 6:30pm, and the fare is $1.50 each way. No reservations required; for more information, call 455-5892.

WHAT TO SEE & DO

A locally based company, **Erie Tours and Convention Services (ETCS),** 707 Aline Dr. (tel. 866-0900), also conducts escorted individual and group tours. Itineraries include a "heritage trail" within the city or sightseeing in the surrounding countryside. Operating throughout the year, ETCS trips require advance reservation and will depart according to request. A flat rate of $35 per day (or $25 per half day) is charged for one or two individuals or an entire family.

✪ Synonymous with Lake Erie, the **Niagara** is docked at Litton Pier, at the foot of Holland Street (tel. 871-4596) on the lakefront. Originally constructed in Erie, this famous brig served as Commodore Oliver Hazard Perry's flagship in the victorious battle of Lake Erie against the British fleet on September 10, 1813. Listed on the National Register of Historic Places, this vessel is one of only three American warships surviving from the War of 1812. It was restored in 1913 and later opened to the public. More recently, the Pennsylvania Historical and Museum Commission began a total refurbishment and overhaul to make the vessel seaworthy again. In September of 1988, the hull was unveiled, in conjunction with the 175th anniversary of the ship's history-making victory, and work on the entire ship was complete by the end of 1990. Open Mon–Sat 9am–5pm and Sun noon–5pm. Admission is $3 adults and $1 youngsters 6–17.

OLD CUSTOMS HOUSE, 411 State St. Tel. 459-5477.
In the heart of downtown is this impressive Greek Revival edifice built in 1839 as a

branch of the U.S. Bank of Pennsylvania. The front steps and columns of the building are made from Vermont marble, brought from the quarry to the Erie Canal by oxcart, thence to Buffalo, and via Lake Erie to the city. Listed in the National Register of Historic Places, this was one of the first major buildings in the country to use native marble. Today it serves as a home for the permanent and ever-changing collections of the Erie Art Museum.

Admission: $1.50 adults, 50¢ children 12 and under; free on Wed.
Open: Tues–Sat 11am–5pm; Sun 1–5pm.

CASHIER'S HOUSE, 417 State St. Tel. 454-1813.

Also in the National Register is this Greek Revival town house built in 1839 as a residence for the cashier from the adjacent United States Bank. Notable features include the keyhole door and window frames with scroll decoration and coffer ceilings, along with furnishings that reflect both the American Empire and Victorian periods. Housing an excellent library, this three-story structure is the headquarters of the Erie County Historical Society and the Erie Society for Genealogical Research.

Admission: $1.
Open: Tues–Fri 9am–4pm, Sat 1–4pm.

ERIE HISTORICAL MUSEUM AND PLANETARIUM, 356 W. 6th St. Tel. 453-5811.

In the residential area west of downtown is this Victorian mansion built in 1889–91. The interior is a showcase of elaborate woodwork, paneled walls, marble and tile fireplaces, glass and marble mosaics, wall and ceiling friezes, and restored Tiffany windows. The house also offers a number of exhibits including a multimedia presentation on the Battle of Lake Erie and a regional history. Admission is free on Tuesday. In addition, the adjacent 19th-century carriage house is a planetarium under a 20-foot dome, with weekend shows scheduled throughout the year. There is an additional admission charge of $1 for adults and 50¢ for children.

Admission: $1 adults, children over 16.
Open: Sept–May Sun 1–5pm; June–Aug Tues–Fri 10am–5pm, Sat–Sun 1–5pm.

FIREFIGHTERS HISTORICAL MUSEUM, 428 Chestnut St. Tel. 456-5969.

Also on the western side of the city is this museum housed in the Old Station House Number Four. More than 1,000 articles are gathered here, including a large collection of antique fire-extinguishing equipment, as well as an 1830 hand-pumper, an 1886 hand-pulled hose cart, and a 1927 American LaFrance fire truck.

Admission: $1.50 adults; 50¢ children 10–18.
Open: May–Aug, Sat 10am–5pm, Sun 1–5pm; Sept–Oct, Sat–Sun 1–5pm and by appointment.

WINERY TOURS

Erie is the third-largest grape-growing area in the United States. Four wineries are situated about 10 miles northeast of downtown Erie, at a town appropriately named North East. Located within a few miles of each other and all open daily, these four wineries make a pleasant afternoon's tour. Here are the particulars: **Heritage Wine Cellars,** 12162 E. Main Rd. (tel. 725-8015), offers free tours and tastings, and is located on Rte. 20; also on Rte. 20 is **Presque Isle Wine Cellars,** 9440 Buffalo Rd. (tel. 725-1314), which gives tastings but no formal tours; **Mazza Vineyards and Winery,** 11815 East Lake Rd. (tel. 725-8695), offers wine tastings and conducted tours for a $1 charge, and is located on Rte. 5; and **Penn Shore Vineyards,** 10225 East Lake Rd., also on Rte. 5, which has free self-guided tours and tastings (tel. 725-8688).

COOL FOR KIDS

Erie Zoo, 423 W. 38th St. (tel. 864-6272), is a 15-acre park with over 300 animals, but the highlight is Pixieland, a section where children can see and feed baby animals.

Open year round from 10am to 5pm, and until 7pm on Sunday and holidays during the summer. Admission is $3.50 for adults and $2 for children 3 to 11; children under 2 enter free. In addition, there is a 75¢ charge for a train ride to Safariland, where wild deer and bison wander.

Waldameer Park and Water World, Rte. 832 (tel. 838-3591), located near the entrance of Presque Isle, offers 33 amusement rides, slides, and picnic facilities. Individual ride tickets are 55¢ or you can purchase all-day ride-a-rama tickets for $8.95 per person. Open mid-May through Labor Day except Mondays.

SPORTS & RECREATION

✪ A host of outdoor sporting activities is available year round at the 3,200-acre **Presque Isle State Park,** off Rte. 832 and Rte. 5. (tel. 871-4251). Situated on the shores of Lake Erie, this facility includes 18 sandy beaches, waterways, hiking trails, bike paths, picnicking areas, and a nature center. In addition, there are lagoons, a bird-watching sanctuary, and an ecological preserve for ferns and marshes. Admission is free, and the park is open from dawn to sunset all year.

BIKE RENTAL

Presque Isle is ideal for cycling. If you haven't brought your own, you can rent from **Sara's Bike Rental,** Sara Coyne Plaza, 50 Peninsula Dr., Presque Isle State Park entrance, off Rte. 832 (tel. 833-3442). Rates start at $2.50 an hour and $12 a day; tandems from $4.50 an hour and up or $15 a day. Open daily 8am to dusk, from April through October.

BOAT CRUISES

Narrated sightseeing cruises around the Lake Erie harbor are operated daily, from May through September, by **Rugare's Sightseeing and Ferry Service,** Dobbins Landing, Public Dock (tel. 455-5892), at the foot of State Street. Departures begin at 10:30am and continue until 9pm. The fare is $5 for adults and $3 for children 12 and under. **Dinner, lunch, and cocktail cruises** are also available. Reservations are required.

FISHING

From May through October, fishing boats leave the Public Dock, according to demand and advance reservations. Species caught include coho salmon, bass, perch, and walleyed pike. Half-day charters cost $275 for six people and full-day excursions are $400. For full information, contact **Rugare's Fishing Boats,** Public Dock (tel. 455-5892).

ICE SKATING

Erie has an expansive indoor ice-skating facility, the **John M. Cochran Ice-Arena,** 38th and Cherry Streets (tel. 868-3652), adjacent to the Erie Zoo. Open from October through March, admission is $3 for adults and $2 for children under 12; skates are also available for rent for $1.50 a pair and up.

WHERE TO STAY

MODERATE

BEL AIRE HOTEL, 2800 W. 8th St., Erie, PA 16505-4084. Tel. 814/833-1116 or toll-free 800/888-8781. Fax 814/838-3242. 135 rms, 2 suites. A/C TV TEL

$ Rates: $79–$95 single, $89–$95 double, $155–$200 suite. AE, CB, DC, MC, V. **Parking:** Free.

Set on its own tree-lined grounds, this modern one- and two-story resort offers guest rooms of varied sizes and styles, with contemporary furnishings and a choice of double or queen- or king-size bed configurations. Guest amenities include a California garden–style indoor swimming pool, an outdoor pool, saunas, Jacuzzi, and exercise room. For meals, there is Maxi's, a casual café, as well as Victor's, a formal dining room.

COMFORT INN, 8051 Peach St., Erie, PA 16509. Tel. 814/866-6666 or toll-free 800/221-2222. Fax 814/866-6666. 60 rms, 50 suites. A/C TV TEL
$ Rates: (including continental breakfast): $59–$75 single, $69–$99 double. AE, CB, DC, DISC, MC, V. **Parking:** Free.

One of the newest choices in the area (opened in 1989), this two-story contemporary property is set back from the road, but with easy access to the interstate highway. The welcoming lodge-style lobby sets the tone, with an informal wide-windowed sitting area and a huge brick fireplace. Half of the guest rooms overlook a central brick courtyard and the others face the grounds.

Most standard units are decorated with light-wood furnishings, floral fabrics, desk, reclining chair, sofa, and a choice of two double beds or a queen-size bed. The suites have darker woods, mirrored closets, king-size bed, whirlpool, refrigerator, microwave oven, wet bar, and two telephones; many have private balconies. Facilities include an outdoor swimming pool, indoor hot tub, whirlpool, fitness center, VCR equipment, and tape rentals.

ERIE PLAZA, 16 W. 10th St., Erie, PA 16501. Tel. 814/459-2220. Fax 814/459-2322. 191 rms. A/C TV TEL
$ Rates: $55–$85 single or double. AE, CB, DC, MC, V. **Parking:** Free.
This modern eight-story hotel sits in the heart of the revitalized downtown area, near major theaters and historic sights and a 10-block walk from the lakefront. Formerly operated under the Hilton and Quality Inn banners, this now-independent property offers rooms of contemporary style, all of which were slated for refurbishment as we go to press. Reduced-rate weekend packages are often available.

Dining/Entertainment: Options include the Garden Room for breakfast, the Hunt Room for lunch and dinner, and Billy's Saloon, a lounge with music on most evenings.

Facilities: Indoor heated swimming pool, saunas, exercise room, meeting rooms, covered parking.

BUDGET

DAYS INN, 7400 Schultz Rd., Erie, PA 16509. Tel. 814/868-8521 or toll-free 800/325-2525. Fax 814/868-8521, ext. 151. 112 rms. A/C TV TEL
$ Rates (including continental breakfast): $43–$51 single, $46–$65 double. AE, DC, DISC, MC, V. **Parking:** Free.

Of the main chain hotels clustered around the busy intersection of I-90 and Rte. 97, this four-story contemporary property is one of the most reliable choices. The guest rooms, accessible via computer card keys, are furnished in contemporary style with two double beds or a queen-size bed, light woods, floral fabrics, pastel tones, desk, sofa, and two phones. Facilities include an outdoor heated swimming pool, sun deck, and four meeting rooms.

LAKEVIEW ON THE LAKE, 8696 East Lake Rd., Erie, PA 16511. Tel. 814/899-6948. 8 rms, 3 cottages. A/C TV
$ Rates: $40–$50, single or double in rooms, $40–$60 cottages. MC, V. **Parking:** Free.

If you'd like a room with a view of the water, the ideal choice is this lovely motel, perched on high ground overlooking Lake Erie. It is set on a 10-acre site in a residential area, with dozens of shady trees and well-tended lawns. Accommodations include a choice of motel units or modern cottages, each with one or two double beds, tiled baths, knotty pine decor, and refrigerator.

Motel units also have microwave ovens and the cottages have decks. Facilities include an outdoor swimming pool, playground, picnic tables, barbecue grills, and bicycles for guest use. Continental breakfast is included in the rates during July–August.

WHERE TO DINE

Erie's restaurants are located both downtown and by the water along the public dock.

MODERATE

BUOY, 4 State St. Tel. 459-0617.
  Cuisine: AMERICAN/SEAFOOD. **Reservations:** Recommended.
$ Prices: Appetizers $2.50–$6.95; main courses $9.95–$23.95. AE, CB, DC, DISC, MC, V.
  Open: Mon–Thurs 5–10pm; Fri–Sat 5–11pm; Sun 4–9pm. **Closed:** Oct–Apr Sun.

The best of the city's lakefront restaurants is this spot with wide windows and a nautical decor of authentic harpoons, anchors, solid brass buoy lamps, captain's chairs, and spotlit oil paintings of historic sea scenes. Seating is tiered on two levels, allowing most of the tables to enjoy views of Lake Erie, including splendid sunsets. Open only for dinner, the selection ranges from Lake Erie perch and Great Lakes yellow pike to bouillabaisse, rock shrimp, and lobster, as well as steaks and poultry.

HIBACHI STEAK HOUSE, 3000 W. 12th St. Tel. 838-2495.
  Cuisine: JAPANESE. **Reservations:** Required.
$ Prices: Appetizers $2.50–$4.50; main courses $7.95–$23.95. AE, MC, V.
  Open: Sun–Thurs 4:30–10pm, Fri–Sat 4:30–11pm.

Located near Presque Isle, this restaurant is decorated with painted screens and wall hangings to convey the aura of Japan. Meals are served at teppanyaki-style tables, shared by up to eight people at a time and with the chef cooking the food before your eyes. Entrée choices focus on steak, lobster, chicken, crab legs, and scallops. For true connoisseurs of Japanese cuisine, there are also sushi and tempura choices, as well as all-seafood dinners.

PUFFERBELLY RESTAURANT, 414 French St. Tel. 454-1557.
  Cuisine: AMERICAN. **Reservations:** Accepted for dinner only.
$ Prices: Appetizers $2.50–$4.95; main courses $8.95–$15.95; lunch $3.95–$6.95. AE, MC, V.
  Open: Mon–Thurs 11am–10pm; Fri–Sat 11am–midnight; Sun 11am–7pm.

This restaurant is named after the steam pumpers used to fight fires in the 19th century. Housed in a restored 1907 firehouse in the downtown area, the eatery is decorated with artifacts and memorabilia of the Erie Fire Department dating back to 1816. As you dine on eclectic American cuisine, you'll be surrounded with vintage fire hats, fire hoses, ladders, and photographs. Lunch features salads, chili, quiches, pizzas, omelets, vegetable stir-fry, burgers, and sandwiches. The menu at dinner includes shrimp sautéed with sherry and pea pods; steaks; seafood pastas; barbecued ribs; and veal marsala.

WATERFALL, 5735 East Lake Rd. Tel. 899-8173.
  Cuisine: AMERICAN. **Reservations:** Recommended. **Directions:** Three miles east of downtown, off Rte. 5.
$ Prices: Appetizers $1.95–$5.95; main courses $7.95–$22.95; lunch $3.95–$6.95. AE, CB, DC, MC, V.
  Open: Lunch Mon–Fri 11:30am–1:30pm; dinner Mon–Sat 4–9pm or 10pm; Sun noon–8pm.

For over 50 years, this has been a favorite dining spot along Erie's lakeshore. As its name implies, it is set beside a waterfall in a tree-shaded setting, and lovely views are part of the ambience. Lunch items include sandwiches, salads, and

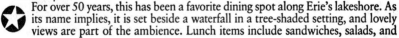

burgers. The emphasis at dinner is on fresh seafood, from Lake Erie perch to lobster, as well as prime ribs, veal, and pastas, and many daily specials. There is also an excellent choice of local wines.

EVENING ENTERTAINMENT

Concerts and national touring shows are featured at the **Warner Theatre,** 811 State St. (tel. 452-4857), a 2,500-seat art-deco landmark dating back to 1931. Originally commissioned by Warner Brothers as a movie theater, this building has recently been restored as part of the Erie Civic Center complex. Now the home of the Erie Philharmonic, it is considered the city's chief performing-arts center. Tickets are usually priced from $10 to $20, depending on the event. Check with the box office or the Chamber of Commerce for an up-to-date schedule. If you visit during the summer months, there is an annual film classic series, at 7:30pm on Tuesday, Wednesday, and Thursday evenings, and a Wednesday matinee at 1:30pm. All seats are $3. Tickets are also available at the Civic Center Box Office, 809 French St. (tel. 452-4857).

One of the oldest community theaters in the United States is the **Erie Playhouse,** 13 W. 10th St. (tel. 454-2851), founded over 70 years ago. This local troupe performs in a 550-seat building that was the old Strand movie theater, subsequently renovated by local volunteer efforts in 1983. The ever-changing repertoire, averaging 20 productions a year, ranges from *Flower Drum Song* and *Can Can* to *The Odd Couple* and other Broadway favorites. Shows are scheduled for Thursday, Friday, and Saturday nights at 8pm, with some Sunday matinees at 3pm. The Playhouse Box Office is open weekdays from 10am to 4:30pm and on Saturday from 10am to 2pm or prior to shows. Ticket prices average $10.

CHAPTER 12

WILMINGTON & ENVIRONS

Tucked under the Pennsylvania border, Wilmington and its environs dominate northern Delaware. An area less than 15 miles at its widest or longest, this corridor of Delaware is the busiest part of the state. With the Delaware Memorial Bridge at its eastern shore and I-95 cutting through its middle, Wilmington is the hub of the state's industrial, cultural, and social activity.

For such a compact area, it is amazing how much there is to see and do. On the next few pages, we'll describe the highlights of this cosmopolitan, charming city, and we'll also explore two of Wilmington's best-known suburbs, New Castle and the Brandywine Valley, both of which can stand on their own merits as outstanding travel destinations as well as being vital parts of the overall Wilmington experience.

---

1. WILMINGTON

31 miles SW of Philadelphia, 45 miles N of Dover,
88 miles NW of Rehoboth Beach, 116 miles NW of Ocean City,
87 miles NW of Atlantic City, 68 miles NE of Baltimore

GETTING THERE   By Air   Most people flying into the northern Delaware area use the **Philadelphia International Airport** as a gateway. It is within a half hour's ride of downtown Wilmington, and many Wilmington hotels operate courtesy transfer services to or from the Philadelphia Airport.

In addition, **Airport Shuttle Service Inc.** operates a 24-hour transfer system between Philadelphia International Airport and any address in Delaware. The company has telephones located on courtesy phone boards at the airport and a downtown location at the Radisson Hotel, 700 King St. at Customs House Plaza (tel. 302/655-8878). Rates per person range from approximately $15.50 to $24.50, depending on pick-up point. Departures are scheduled from Philadelphia Airport every 5 to 20 minutes between 6:30am and 11:30pm and every 10 to 40 minutes between 11:30pm and 6:30am.

By Train   Wilmington is a stop on the main east coast corridor of **Amtrak**, between Philadelphia and Baltimore. The Wilmington Amtrak station is located at Martin Luther King Blvd. and French Street (tel. 658-1515), on the city's southern edge, adjacent to the Christina River. This imposing structure, originally designed and built in 1907, is an attraction in itself, with terra-cotta window arches, red-clay tile roofing, and marble steps. Recently restored to its former glory, it is now on the National Register of Historic Places. There's a taxi stand outside the station.

By Bus   Daily service is provided into the Wilmington Transportation Center at 318 N. Market St. (tel. 652-7391), by **Greyhound/Trailways** (tel. 655-6111).

By Car   The best way to drive to Wilmington is via I-95, which cuts across the city

WHAT'S SPECIAL ABOUT WILMINGTON, THE BRANDYWINE VALLEY & NEW CASTLE

Ace Attractions
- ☐ Winterthur Museum and Gardens, the world's premier collection of American antiques and decorative arts.
- ☐ Nemours Mansion and Gardens, a 102-room French-style château.
- ☐ Wilmington Old Town Hall, depicting life in Delaware over the centuries.
- ☐ Old Swedes Church, one of the oldest churches in the United States.

Activities
- ☐ Sightsee in the countryside aboard the Wilmington & Western Railroad.
- ☐ Sample the oak-aged vintages at the Chadds Ford Winery.

Architectural Highlights
- ☐ Grand Opera House, one of the finest examples of cast-iron architecture in America.
- ☐ Welsh Tract Church, in Newark, the oldest Baptist church in the United States.

Gardens
- ☐ Longwood Gardens, the world's most celebrated horticultural display.

Museums
- ☐ Brandywine River Museum, in Chadds Ford, showcase for Brandywine River School and other American artists.
- ☐ Delaware Museum of Natural History, housing one of the largest shell collections in this hemisphere.

Parks
- ☐ Fort Delaware State Park, an offshore island with wildlife preserves, nature trails, and a Civil War fortress.

Zoos
- ☐ Brandywine Zoo, with animals from North and South America.

at its center. The Delaware Memorial Bridge also connects Wilmington to the New Jersey Turnpike and points north. From the south, Rte. 13 will bring you into the city via Virginia and southern Delaware.

ESSENTIALS Information A complete selection of literature about Wilmington, the Brandywine Valley, and historic New Castle is available from the **Greater Wilmington Convention and Visitors Bureau,** 1300 Market St., Suite 504, Wilmington, DE 19801 (tel. 302/652-4088 or toll-free 800/422-1181). One publication, the *Visitors Guide,* lists accommodations, restaurants, attractions, shopping, and activities for the entire northern Delaware area.

In addition, for motorists passing through the area, the bureau maintains a **Visitors Information Center** on I-95 (tel. 737-4059). It is located just south of the city, between Rtes. 272 and 896, and operates from 8am to 8pm, with an automatic hotel reservation system provided at other times.

Wilmington, Delaware's largest city, is located in the northeast corner of the state, in New Castle County, at the confluence of the Christina, Brandywine, and Delaware Rivers.

First settled 350 years ago by the Swedes, who planted a permanent settlement at the mouth of the Christina River, this area was initially known as New Sweden until the Dutch conquered the colony and it became part of New Netherland. The English eventually claimed the land and thus it evolved into prominence during Revolutionary times as Wilmington.

The city's ability to generate water power spurred its growth in the 18th century. By 1802, Wilmington also attracted a Frenchman named Éleuthère Irénée du Pont de Nemours, who established a black-powder mill on the banks of the Brandywine. This mill, of course, was the foundation of a family empire that was to become the largest chemical company in America and a powerful influence, to this day, on the city and the whole state of Delaware.

Today Wilmington is an industrial, financial, and banking hub with an ever-changing skyline of sleek new buildings. It is also the gateway to the scenic and historic Brandywine Valley, home to some of America's greatest living history museums and art treasures.

GETTING AROUND
BY BUS

Wilmington has no subway, but it does have an efficient bus system known as **DART (Delaware Administration for Regional Transit).** Blue-and-white signs indicating DART stops are located throughout the city, and regular routes can take you to museums, theaters, parks, hotels, and the Greater Wilmington Airport, as well as such popular sights as Winterthur and New Castle. Exact fares, based on a zone system, are required; the minimum fare for one zone is $1.15. Complete information on schedules and applicable fares is available at most banks or by calling the DARTLINE (tel. 655-3381).

BY TAXI

Taxi stands are located at the du Pont Hotel, the Radisson Hotel, and the train station. If you wish to order a cab, call **Diamond Cab** (tel. 658-4321) or **Yellow Cab** (tel. 656-8151).

BY RENTED CAR

Major car-rental firms represented in the Wilmington area include **Avis,** 903 Washington St. (tel. 654-0379); **Budget,** 35th and Market Sts. (tel. 764-3300); **Dollar,** 2100 Gov. Printz Blvd. (tel. 655-7117); **Hertz,** Front and French Sts. (tel. 658-6400); and at the Christiana Hilton (tel. 328-5163); and **National,** Sheraton Brandywine Hotel, 4727 Concord Pike (tel. 478-4778).

WHAT TO SEE & DO

Thanks to the restoration of the Wilmington Railroad Station, much of the city's waterfront is taking on a new vitality. An "Avenue of the Arts" has sprung up along the banks of the Christina River and many people see this as a forerunner to a new "inner harbor" development much like Baltimore's. The central downtown area has also been restored into a five-block pedestrian area of shops and restaurants known as **Market Street Mall.**

Although many of Wilmington's historic and cultural attractions are still to be found on the outskirts of the city in New Castle or the Brandywine Valley, the downtown area has much to offer in its own right.

OLD TOWN HALL, 512 Market Street Mall. Tel. 655-7161.

Now a museum operated by the Historical Society of Delaware, this landmark building in the heart of the city features permanent and rotating exhibits that depict life in Delaware over the centuries. Antique silver, furniture, and related objects of Americana are on display. In addition, restored jail cells in the basement are also open to the public. This building also contains a museum store with a variety of gifts reflecting early Delaware.

Admission: Free, but donations are welcome.

Open: Tues–Fri noon–4pm; Sat 10am–4pm.

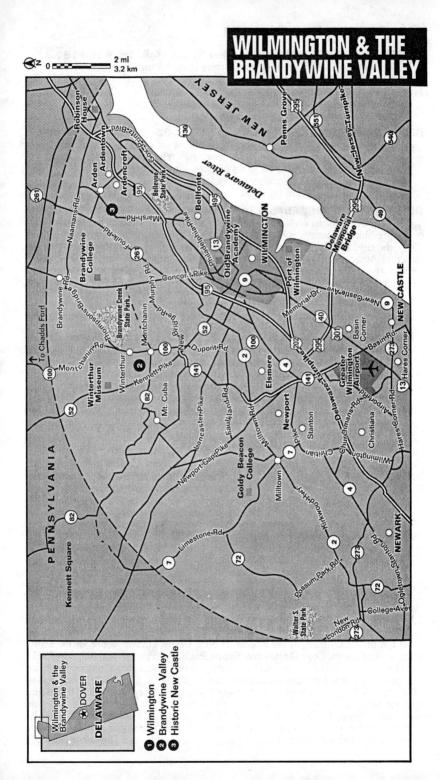

WILLINGTOWN SQUARE, 506 Market Street Mall. Tel. 655-7161.

These four stately 18th-century houses were moved from other parts of the city to this site in 1975–76; they now enclose a beautiful brick courtyard. Owned by the Historical Society, the houses are not open to the public.

Admission: To square, free.
Open: All hours.

OLD SWEDES CHURCH, 606 Church St. Tel. 652-5629.

Located near the Christina River, this is one of the oldest houses of worship in the United States. Erected in 1698, the church remains in its original form, and is still regularly used for religious services. Guide service is available.

Admission: Free, but donations are welcome.
Tours: Mon, Wed, Fri noon–4pm.

DELAWARE ART MUSEUM, 2301 Kentmere Pkwy. Tel. 571-9590.

Renowned for its collections of American art (from 1840 to the present), this prestigious museum is located just north of downtown in a residential area of the city. This is the home of the largest holding of works by Howard Pyle, the father of American illustration and founder of the Brandywine school of painting. Other outstanding examples of American sculpture, photography and crafts, traditional and contemporary, are also on view here, as is the largest display of English pre-Raphaelite art in the United States.

Admission: Free.
Open: Tues 10am–9pm, Wed–Sat 10am–5pm, Sun noon–5pm.

DELAWARE MUSEUM OF NATURAL HISTORY, Rte. 52 between Greenville and Centreville. Tel. 658-9111.

One of the largest shell collections in this hemisphere (over 1.7 million) is housed at this museum. Other highlights include an African water-hole diorama, a walk over the Great Barrier Reef, the largest bird egg in the world, and a 500-pound clam.

Admission: $3.50 adults; $2.50 seniors, students; $2 youngsters 3–18; children under 3 free.
Open: Mon–Sat 9:30am–4:30pm, Sun noon–5pm.

NEARBY SIGHTS

Fourteen miles southwest of Wilmington is Newark, New Castle County's second-largest city (pop. 24,000). It is a thriving center in its own right, although sometimes considered part of the greater Wilmington metropolitan area. Many of Wilmington's hotels have a Newark postal address.

Not to be confused with the metropolis of the same name in New Jersey, this Newark is pronounced "New Ark" and is first and foremost a college town, home of the University of Delaware. A leading center of higher learning in the state, the university traces its origin as far back as 1743, with the Newark campus established in 1765.

Local sights in the area include the **Welsh Tract Baptist Church,** the oldest primitive Baptist church in the United States, dating back to 1703 (located west of Rte. 896), and **Cooch's Bridge,** the scene of the Battle of Cooch's Bridge, the only Revolutionary War engagement fought on Delaware soil. Tradition holds that the new 13-star flag, the Stars and Stripes, was unfurled during this encounter. It is located on Rte. 4, east of Rte. 896.

South of Wilmington, in the middle of New Castle County, is one of the state's most unusual parks, **Fort Delaware State Park,** Pea Patch Island (tel. 834-7941). Located a mile offshore in the Delaware River, the park surrounds a massive five-sided granite fortress that served as a detention center during the Civil War. In addition to 19th-century cells, dungeons, and armaments, the current layout includes a museum and an audiovisual presentation about the history of the site. There is also an observation tower for bird-watchers, since the island has since become a popular nesting spot for egrets, herons, and other marsh fowl. Visitors can also enjoy nature trails and facilities for fishing and picnicking. It is accessible via a 10-minute boat ride from Delaware City (cost: $3.50 adults, $1.50 for children under 15). Once you cross over on the boat, there is no fee for admission to Pea Patch Island. Open: April–Sept 11am–6pm.

SIGHTSEEING TOURS

The **Wilmington and Western Railroad** offers sightseeing excursions in the neighboring countryside south of the city via vintage steam trains. This tourist railroad is located at Greenbank Station on Rte. 41, near the junction of Rte. 2 (tel. 998-1930). The basic itinerary is a one-hour, 10-mile ride through the Red Clay Valley to the Mount Cuba picnic grove or Hockhessin. The fare for adults is $5 to $10; for children 2 to 12, $3 to $5; free for children under 2. Trains operate from May to October on Sunday at 12:30pm, 2 and 3:30pm, to Mount Cuba; and from June to August on Saturday at noon and 2:30pm to Hockhessin. Reservations are not required.

SPORTS & RECREATION

Wilmington's playground is **Bellevue State Park,** 800 Carr Rd. (tel. 577-3390). Located on the northern perimeter of the city, this 270-acre park was once the home of the William du Pont family. Facilities include picnic areas, garden paths for walking, and fitness trails for jogging. Admission is free, but a $4 parking fee is charged between Memorial Day and Labor Day.

HORSE RACING

From mid-March to November, racing fans flock to **Delaware Park Race Course,** Rte. 7, off I-95 exit 4N, Stanton (tel. 994-2521), about 5 miles south of Wilmington. Daytime thoroughbred racing is scheduled on various days of the week in a picturesque setting with a tree-lined picnic grove. Post time is 1pm, and admission is $2 for adults; children under 12 free. Parking is $1.

COOL FOR KIDS

Children of all ages take delight in looking at the many exotic species of animals from North and South America on view at the **Brandywine Zoo,** 1001 N. Park Dr., Brandywine Park (tel. 571-7747). Open daily from 10am to 4pm, admission is free from November to March; from April to October, there is a $2 charge for adults and $1 for children aged 3 to 12.

WHERE TO STAY

No matter where you go in Delaware, when the natives refer to the "hotel," you can be sure they mean the du Pont in Wilmington. For the last 75 years, this hotel has dominated the Delaware lodging scene. Consequently, there are relatively few other full-service hotels in downtown Wilmington. In recent years, however, as the Wilmington suburbs have grown, a number of new hotels and motels have sprung up in the surrounding areas.

Wilmington hotels, like other city hotels, charge top dollar during the Sunday-through-Thursday period. The best way to save money is to reserve a 1- or 2-night (Friday and Saturday) weekend package, which, in most cases, can represent a 50% reduction off normal midweek room rates.

DOWNTOWN

Expensive

HOTEL DU PONT, 11th and Market Sts., Wilmington, DE 19801. Tel. 302/594-3100 or toll-free 800/441-9019. Fax 302/656-2145. 217 rms, several suites. A/C TV TEL

$ Rates: $120–$180, single or double; $155–$200 executive room; $270–$350

suite; $80–$125 weekend. AE, CB, DC, MC, V. **Parking:** $8 weekdays, free on weekends.

⭐ Opened in 1913 and owned by E. I. du Pont de Nemours and Company, this is the benchmark for all other Delaware hotels. Located in the heart of the city, this palatial structure is a showcase of polished marble, elegant coffered ceilings, richly carved walnut, oak paneling, original artwork, and genteel services. *Note:* The hotel's bedrooms have been closed for renovation, with reopening slated for early 1993. (When it reopens, the hotel will have 217 rooms and a number of suites not yet determined.) All other parts of the hotel, however, remain open.

Dining/Entertainment: The hotel has two fine restaurants, the highly ranked Green Room (see "Where to Dine," below) and the smaller Brandywine Room (see "Where to Dine," below). In addition, the imposing old-world Lobby Lounge is a popular spot for cocktails, weekend jazz sessions, afternoon tea, or people watching.

Services: Room service, concierge desk, turn-down service, valet/laundry service, complimentary morning newspapers.

Facilities: Bank, brokerage, barbershop, beauty salon, gift shops, and theater on premises.

MARRIOTT SUITES, 422 Delaware Ave., Wilmington, DE 19801. Tel. 302/654-8300 or toll-free 800/228-9290. Fax 302/654-6036. 230 suites. A/C TV TEL

$ Rates: $139 single; $154 double; $79 weekend. **Parking:** $6.

⭐ In the heart of Wilmington's corporate and financial section, this contemporary 16-story hotel has brought an extra dose of class to the city. Decorated with subdued art-deco tones, the lobby is rich in columns, mirrors, and marble flooring. Each unit has a full bedroom and a separate living room, large well-lit bathroom, and dressing area. Amenities include two telephones with call-waiting services and computer access lines, dining/work table, desk, wet bar, and refrigerator with complimentary soft drinks.

Dining/Entertainment: The conservatory-style Windows restaurant and lounge offers moderately priced food and drink on the lobby level.

Services: Bell staff, morning and evening room service, dry cleaning/valet services, baby-sitting.

Facilities: Indoor swimming pool, sauna, and exercise room, express video check-out, gift shop, meeting rooms, self-service launderette on 16th floor, underground parking.

Moderate

CHRISTINA HOUSE, 707 King St., Wilmington, DE 19801. Tel. 302/656-9300 or toll-free 800/543-9106. Fax 302/656-2459. 39 suites. A/C MINIBAR TV TEL

$ Rates (including continental breakfast): $95–$125 midweek suite; $75 weekend suite. AE, CB, DC, MC, V. **Parking:** $5.

Ⓢ If you prefer a homey lodging in the heart of town, the best choice is this unusual hotel adjacent to the historic Market Street Mall. Opened in 1987, it was created from a cluster of vintage three- and four-story brick buildings that were thoroughly renovated and then linked together with a central atrium and two elevators.

The result is a small but unique all-suite hotel with a nouveau European decor. Each guest unit has a parlor, bedroom, and well-equipped bathroom, as well as a refrigerator, two TVs, and three phones. On the ground floor, there is a small lobby with an open fireplace and a skylit sitting area.

Dining/Entertainment: The restaurant/bar, Bistro, on the ground floor, features American cuisine.

Services: Room service, laundry service, valet parking.

Facilities: Fitness center.

RADISSON HOTEL, 700 King St. at Customs House Plaza, Wilmington,

DE 19801. Tel. 302/655-0400 or toll-free 800/333-3333. Fax 302/655-5488. 217 rms. A/C TV TEL

$ Rates: $109–$119 Mon–Thurs, single or double; $65–$75 weekend, single or double. AE, CB, DC, DISC, MC, V. **Parking:** $5.

A modern glass-and-concrete facade fronts this nine-story structure just three blocks from the grandiose Hotel du Pont. Conveniently located in the heart of Wilmington's business and financial district, this hotel is also a half-block from the Opera House and the Market Street Mall. The rooms are decorated in a contemporary style, with double or queen-size beds and colorful wall hangings; many units also overlook a tropical indoor garden and patio with swimming pool.

Dining/Entertainment: The American Bar & Grill restaurant provides a delightful setting for meals, snacks, or a drink, with its wall-length Brandywine Valley murals.

Services: Room service, laundry service.

Facilities: Whirlpool, swimming pool, exercise room, indoor parking, gift shop, and airport shuttle service.

SUBURBS
Expensive

CHRISTIANA HILTON INN, 100 Continental Dr., Newark, DE 19713. Tel. 302/454-1500 or toll-free 800/HIL-TONS. Fax 302/454-0233. 266 rms, A/C TV TEL

$ Rates: $95–$125 single, $110–$140 double weekday; $65 weekend, single or double. AE, CB, DC, MC, V. **Parking:** Free.

For a suburban location, the top choice is this hotel nestled amid a grassy setting. Located in a burgeoning area near Delaware's major university at Newark and a variety of mega-shopping malls, it boasts a modernized four-story, Victorian-style brick exterior and is topped by a mansard-style roof.

The bedrooms are decorated in the Old Williamsburg tradition, with dark-wood furniture and Colonial prints and colors, combined with modern mirrored closets and tiled baths. The exterior includes a brick-lined courtyard, gazebo, pond, and English-style topiary gardens.

Dining/Entertainment: The European-style café, the Brasserie, serves moderate fare for breakfast, lunch, and dinner. For more formal dining and Sunday brunch, Ashleys restaurant offers regional American cuisine in a setting of banquette seating and arched Palladian windows overlooking an outdoor pond with swans. The conservatory-style lounge offers a relaxed setting for cocktails, a snack, or high tea.

Services: Room service, concierge desk, same-day valet service, turndown service, free shuttle service to downtown Wilmington, and express checkout.

Facilities: Outdoor swimming pool, health and fitness room, gift shop, computer-card access system, and nine meeting rooms.

SHERATON BRANDYWINE INN, 4727 Concord Pike, Wilmington, DE 19803. Tel. 302/478-6000 or toll-free 800/325-3535. Fax 302/478-6000. 149 rms. A/C TV TEL

$ Rates: $114 single or double. AE, CB, DC, DISC, MC, V. **Parking:** Free.

Just north of downtown Wilmington, a few miles from the major historic museums and gardens, is this modern seven-story structure. Bedrooms have designer furnishings, double or king-size beds, and easy chair/recliner. Dining facilities include the Copperfield Grille, an all-day eatery with emphasis on American/Southwest cuisine. Guest facilities include an outdoor swimming pool, a lounge with evening entertainment, and a courtesy limousine service to downtown.

WILMINGTON HILTON, I-95 and Naamans Rd., Wilmington, DE 19703. Tel. 302/792-2700. Fax 302/798-6182. 193 rms. A/C TV TEL

$ Rates: $80–$118 single, $90–$128 double, $300 suite. AE, CB, DC, MC, V. **Parking:** Free.

Business travelers often choose this hotel because of its handy location, close to the

Tri-State industrial complex and the Northtowne Plaza shopping mall; it's also just 12 miles from Philadelphia Airport. The contemporary rooms are designed in various configurations as bedroom/sitting rooms, queen studios, king rooms, and suites.

Amenities include room service, valet/laundry, an outdoor swimming pool, a complimentary shuttle to and from the airport, and a lounge called Whispers, with DJ entertainment on most evenings. The main restaurant, Evergreens, is a trilevel dining room with a garden atmosphere.

SUBURBS
Moderate

BEST WESTERN EL CAPITAN, 1807 Concord Pike, Wilmington, DE 19803. Tel. 302/656-9436 or toll-free 800/528-1234. Fax 302/656-8564. 102 rms. A/C TV TEL

$ Rates: $72.50 single, $82.50 double. AE, CB, DC, DISC, MC, V. Weekend packages available. **Parking:** Free.

Another hotel on the rim of the Brandywine Valley is this villa-style hostelry designed in a Spanish motif with white walls and black and red trim. The units have double or queen- or king-size beds, modern Georgian-style furniture and wall-to-wall carpeting; some have kitchenettes. Many rooms face the pool and gardens, which are spotlit at night. Other advantages of this hotel include a full-time valet/concierge service, room service, and laundry service.

COURTYARD, 48 Geoffrey Dr., Newark, DE 19713. Tel. 302/456-3800 or toll-free 800/321-2211. Fax 302/456-3824. 152 rms, 12 suites. A/C TV TEL

$ Rates: $56–$74 single, $56–$84 double, $76–$100 suite. AE, CB, DC, DISC, MC, V. **Parking:** Free.

Opened in 1991, this four-story property is not only one of Delaware's newest lodgings but also the first of its chain to open in the state. The layout follows the usual Courtyard plan, with sliding glass windows and balconies or patios facing a central landscaped terrace. Guest units—decorated in contemporary style, with dark woods and pastel-toned fabrics—are spacious with a separate sitting area, desk, and coffee-making fixtures. Hotel facilities include a restaurant, lounge, elevator, indoor swimming pool, and whirlpool.

DAYS INN, 900 Churchman's Rd., Newark, DE 19713. Tel. 302/368-2400 or toll-free 800/325-2525. Fax 302/731-8620. 150 rms. A/C TV TEL

$ Rates: $50–$70 single, $60–$75 double. AE, DISC, MC, V. **Parking:** Free.

This modern three-story motel-style facility offers standard rooms with extra amenities, such as in-room coffee-makers and hairdryers. Facilities include an outdoor swimming pool and a restaurant called Gatwicks Inn, which is decorated in a country theme and serves moderately priced meals.

Budget

FAIRFIELD INN, 65 Geoffrey Dr., Newark, DE 19713. Tel. 302/292-1500 or toll-free 800/228-2800. Fax 302/292-1500. 105 rms. A/C TV TEL

$ Rates: $43.95–$46.95 single, $49.95–$52.95 double. AE, CB, DC, MC, V. **Parking:** Free.

The first of its chain to open in Delaware, this three-story property offers comfortable and attractively furnished accommodations at low prices, in a very accessible location. There are three types of bedrooms: a compact one-bedded room ideal for a single traveler, a standard double, and a larger room with a king-size bed. All units have full-length mirror, alarm clock, lounge chair and reading light, work desk, and oversized towels.

Complimentary coffee and newspapers are offered in the lobby. Facilities include an outdoor swimming pool, computer-card keys, and a meeting room.

TALLY HO MOTOR LODGE, 5209 Concord Pike, Wilmington, DE 19803. Tel. 302/478-0300. 100 rms. A/C TV TEL

$ Rates: $42–$48 single or double. AE, CB, DC, DISC, MC, V. **Parking:** Free.
Located on the busy Rte. 202 strip, this modern two-story motel has rooms equipped
with one or two double beds or king-size bed; some have kitchenettes. Other facilities
include an outdoor swimming pool and a guest laundromat.

WHERE TO DINE

With so many fine hotel dining rooms, it is not surprising that Wilmington's
restaurants are also of a very high standard. As our selections show, many of the best
restaurants are not located in the downtown business and financial sections of the city,
but are clustered in residential areas. The dining spots listed in the Brandywine and
New Castle sections of this chapter are also considered part of the Wilmington
gastronomic experience.

DOWNTOWN
Very Expensive

THE GREEN ROOM, Hotel du Pont, 11th and Market Sts. Tel. 594-3155.
  Cuisine: FRENCH. **Reservations:** Required.
$ Prices: Appetizers $4.95–$15.95; main courses $19.50–$29.50; lunch $8.95–
  $16.95. AE, CB, DC, MC, V.
  Open: Lunch Mon–Sat 11:30am–2pm; dinner Fri–Sat 6–9:30pm.

⭐ Even if you can't overnight at the Hotel du Pont, treat yourself to a meal in this
posh restaurant, known for its impressive decor of tall arching windows, walls
of quartered oak paneling, and handcrafted golden chandeliers from Spain. To
complete the tableau, tuxedoed waiters provide impeccable service and a classical
harpist plays in the background.

Entrées range from poached Maine lobster and sautéed Norwegian salmon to
roast loin of lamb and filet of veal in pastry. The menu is pricey, but Delawareans
consider this to be the state's top spot for a memorable evening. Jackets are required
for men.

Expensive

**THE BRANDYWINE ROOM, Hotel du Pont, 11th and Market Sts. Tel.
594-3155.**
  Cuisine: AMERICAN/CONTINENTAL. **Reservations:** Recommended.
$ Prices: Appetizers $4.95–$9.95; main courses $15.50–$27. AE, CB, DC,
  MC, V.
  Open: Sat–Thurs 6–11pm

⭐ This is the Hotel du Pont's smaller and more clubby restaurant, open only for
dinner. It is decorated with original art featuring works by three generations of
the Wyeth family. Entrées include lobster and crab imperial, veal Oscar, crab
cakes, and filet mignon. Jackets are required for men.

COLUMBUS INN, 2216 Pennsylvania Ave. Tel. 571-1492.
  Cuisine: AMERICAN/CONTINENTAL. **Reservations:** Recommended.
$ Prices: Appetizers $4.95–$9.95; main courses $15.95–$23.95; lunch $6.95–
  $10.95. AE, CB, DC, MC, V.
  Open: Lunch Mon–Sat 11:30am–2:30pm; dinner Mon–Sat 5pm–midnight, Sun
  4–9pm.

⭐ One of the city's oldest buildings, this stone house dates from 1798 and is set
on a hill overlooking the main route (Rte. 52) to the Brandywine Valley. The
decor is a clubby Colonial blend of old brick walls, brass fixtures, and original
oil paintings of the area. It's a popular lunch spot for Wilmington businesspeople who
enjoy the choice of hot beef and seafood entrées, salads, sandwich board, or burgers.

The dinner menu includes a shore dinner (lobster tail, oysters Rockefeller, jumbo shrimp, clams casino, scallops, and flounder), veal francese, roast duck, and breast of capon. Jackets are required for men after 6pm, and there is a piano player on Friday and Saturday evenings.

CONSTANTINOU'S HOUSE OF BEEF, 1616 Delaware Ave. Tel. 652-0653.
   Cuisine: INTERNATIONAL. **Reservations:** Recommended.
$ Prices: Appetizers $2.95–$8.95; main courses $15–$30; lunch $5.95–$12.95. AE, CB, DC, DISC, MC, V.
   Open: Lunch Mon–Fri 11:15–4pm; dinner Sun–Thurs 4–10pm, Fri–Sat 4:30–11pm.

For the best steak in town, head here. You'll also enjoy the Victorian decor filled with original tankards, prints, and bric-a-brac from around the world. Flags of all nations, American eagles and gold-framed mirrors, and tuxedoed waiters add to the charm. Lunch includes prime rib and steak teriyaki, as well as seafood platters, salads, and hearty sandwiches. Aged tender beef takes center stage at night with a variety of cuts of prime Kansas steaks as well as cut-to-order prime rib. Other favorites include rack of lamb, surf-and-turf, lobster tails, shrimp scampi, and jumbo crab imperial. Prices are slightly higher on Sunday, Monday, and Thursday, when all entrées include unlimited raw bar selections.

SILK PURSE, 1307 North Scott St., Tel. 654-7666.
   Cuisine: INTERNATIONAL. **Reservations:** Recommended.
$ Prices: Appetizers $6.50–$12.50; main courses $18.50–$28.50. MC, V.
   Open: Dinner Mon–Sat 6–9:30pm.

One of the most heralded of the city's restaurants, this spot is tucked in the middle of a quiet residential block in a private house. It has a contemporary interior decorated with fresh flowers, graceful glass lamps, framed gallery prints, and rattan furniture. The menu and service are all very personalized here, reflecting the private-home ambience.

Dinner entrées include such creations as salmon with red wine sauce and French lentils, zinfandel-marinated roast duck, roast grouper with ginger and citrus, lamb with rosemary cream sauce, and tenderloin of beef with caramelized shallots and bordelaise sauce. The Silk Purse is also known for its inventive greens, such as salmon salad with bacon dressing, and crispy quail salad with sesame dressing.

Moderate

SOW'S EAR, 1307 North Scott St. Tel. 654-7666.
   Cuisine: MEDITERRANEAN. **Reservations:** Recommended.
$ Prices: Appetizers $2.75–$5.75; main courses $9.75–$14.75; lunch $5.75–$9.75. MC, V.
   Open: Lunch Mon–Fri 11:30am–1:30pm; dinner Mon–Sat 5:30–10pm.

Operated by the same management as the highly acclaimed Silk Purse, this is a more informal and moderately priced alternative, located on the second floor in the same building. The decor is bright and fun with stenciled walls, Persian carpet, upholstered banquettes, and red-wood floor. The menu here is more exotic than at its sister restaurant, but the same characteristic quality is in evidence. Featured items range from chili-marinated shrimp and Moroccan chicken en brochette to marinated lamb steak and mozzarella basil pizza.

WATERWORKS CAFE, 16th and French Sts. Tel. 652-6022.
   Cuisine: INTERNATIONAL. **Reservations:** Recommended.
$ Prices: Appetizers $3.95–$6.95; main courses $12.95–$20.95; lunch $4.95–$11.95. MC, V.
   Open: Lunch Tues–Fri 11:30am–2:30pm; dinner Tues–Sat 5:30–10pm.

Overlooking the Brandywine, this trendy midcity restaurant is housed in the former water-station buildings on the banks of the river. The decor is colorful and contemporary; there is also an outdoor deck and patio seating in good weather. Lunch includes a variety of fish and meat entrées, omelets, and cold platters (try the Great Oceans salad). At dinnertime the selections include roast duckling Brandywine, chicken Oscar, and Oriental sautéed filet mignon and scallops.

KID SHELLEEN'S, 14th and Scott Sts. Tel. 658-4600.
Cuisine: AMERICAN. **Reservations:** Not required.
$ Prices: Appetizers $1.95–$5.95; main courses $8.95–$14.95; lunch $2.95–$6.95. AE, MC, V.
Open: Daily 11am–midnight.

Tucked in a residential area on the city's north side, this lively restaurant is known for its casual atmosphere and open charcoal kitchen. The decor is highlighted by oil paintings of old Wilmington and New Castle on brick and wood walls. Dinner entrées include blackened grouper, barbecued chicken, baby back ribs, center-cut swordfish, sirloin steak, and seafood or beef brochettes. The bar here is known for its "kreamie" drinks (made with ice cream and liqueurs)—ideal for dessert and priced from $3.25 to $3.95.

Budget

TEMPTATIONS, 11A Trolley Square, Delaware Ave. Tel. 429-9162.
Cuisine: AMERICAN. **Reservations:** Not accepted.
$ Prices: All items $2.95–$6.95. AE, CB, DC, MC, V.
Open: Mon 10am–5pm; Tues–Thurs 10am–9pm; Fri–Sat 10am–10pm.

If you have a sweet tooth, you'll succumb to this ice-cream parlor and restaurant. It serves an all-day selection of sandwiches, salads, and burgers, as well as an extensive selection of ice creams. The menu includes more than a dozen sundaes, such as the appropriately named "Original Sin" (a huge banana split, with fig leaves in season), priced at $3.95. For four to six people, there is a family-size "Demolition Derby," a monster dish of 10 flavors of ice cream and every topping in the house ($10.95).

SUBURBS
Expensive

BELLEVUE IN THE PARK, 911 Philadelphia Pike. Tel. 798-7666.
Cuisine: INTERNATIONAL. **Reservations:** Recommended.
$ Prices: Appetizers $2.95–$6.95; main courses $12.95–$23.95; lunch $6.95–$12.95. AE, CB, DC, DISC, MC, V.
Open: Lunch Mon–Fri 11am–2pm; dinner Mon–Sat 5–10pm; brunch Sun 10:30am–2:30pm.

No restaurant conveys Delaware's southern charm better than this one. The former home of William du Pont, this mansion is right in the heart of the city's Bellevue State Park. You'll feel as pampered as a du Pont in this idyllic setting of Greek Revival architecture with crystal chandeliers, fine linens, and tuxedoed waiters.

The dinner menu features lobster, blackened redfish, breast of chicken framboise, bouillabaisse, veal piccante, roast duckling, and chateaubriand. A sumptuous Sunday brunch buffet is also popular with Wilmington families; it includes soups, salads, specialty omelets, hot casseroles, and pastries, as well as main courses like fresh salmon and roast beef cut to order. The price for adults is $17.95 and $10 for children 3 to 10. Be sure to save time for a stroll in the gardens. Jackets are required for men.

PICCIOTTI'S, 3001 Lancaster Ave. Tel. 652-3563.
Cuisine: INTERNATIONAL. **Reservations:** Recommended.
$ Prices: Appetizers $2.95–$8.95; main courses $10.95–$25.95. AE, CB, DC, MC, V.
Open: Mon–Sat 5–10pm; Sun 5–9pm.

This restaurant, known for outstanding beef, has a tradition that goes back over 55 years. It was first established at 4th St. and du Pont St. but moved to its present location over 5 years ago. The exterior is unpretentious, but inside great culinary things happen. Most people come here for the filet mignon, touted as the best in Delaware and beyond; we heartily concur—Picciotti's filets are as tender and flavorful as you will find anywhere. Try to come on Thursday, when all filet mignon dinners are served at a specially reduced price. If beef is not your dish, you'll also find fresh seafood, from crab cakes and lobster tails to shrimp scampi, as well as a variety of pastas.

SAL'S PETITE MARMITE, 603 North Lincoln St. Tel. 652-1200.
   Cuisine: ITALIAN/FRENCH. **Reservations:** Recommended.
$ **Prices:** Appetizers $4.95–$10.95; main courses $13.95–$25.95; lunch $8.95–$16.95. AE, CB, DC, MC, V.
   Open: Lunch Mon–Fri 11:30am–2pm; dinner Mon–Sat 5:30–10pm.

Tucked away in the heart of Little Italy, you'll find the award-winning restaurant of master-chef Sal Buono. With rich leather furnishings and a country-club atmosphere, this restaurant is a blend of French and Italian cuisines. Great care is taken to obtain the freshest and best ingredients daily; all the tomatoes and herbs, for example, are grown in the owner's private garden.

Lunch focuses on salads and light entrées such as shrimp scampi, veal piccata, coquilles St-Jacques, and fettuccine Alfredo. Dinner, more of an event, depends on what is in season, but can often include salmon filet, whole Dover sole, frogs' legs, duckling flambé, beef Wellington, rack of lamb, or game dishes. The restaurant has a nonsmoking section and a private parking lot. Jackets for men are required.

Moderate

DINARDO'S, 405 North Lincoln St. Tel. 656-3685.
   Cuisine: SEAFOOD. **Reservations:** Not accepted.
$ **Prices:** Appetizers $2.95–$6.95; main courses $8.95–$17.95; lunch $3.95–$7.95. AE, CB, DC, MC, V.
   Open: Mon–Sat 11am–10pm; Sun 3–10pm.

Crabs are the pièce de résistance at this small, casual, family-run Little Italy restaurant, a tradition in Delaware since 1938—just the place to go if you enjoy cracking your own crustaceans. Crabs are flown in daily year round from Louisiana and are served steamed or sautéed. Lunchtime choices include crab and shellfish platters, salads, and pastas. Dinner entrées, in addition to crabs in the shell, range from crab cakes, crab claws, crab legs, and crab imperial to shrimp, lobster, flounder, scallops, oysters, and steaks as well as combination platters ($7.95 to $16.95). Crabs are also available to go, singly (from $2) or by the bushel ($90).

SCHOONOVER'S, 3858 Kennett Pike (Rte. 52), Greenville. Tel. 571-0561.
   Cuisine: AMERICAN. **Reservations:** Recommended.
$ **Prices:** Appetizers $3.95–$5.95; main courses $12.95–$19.95; lunch $3.95–$13.95. AE, CB, DC, MC, V.
   Open: Lunch Mon–Fri 11am–3:30pm, Sat 12:15–2:30pm; dinner Mon–Sat 5–9pm.

Named for the Brandywine Valley artist Frank Schoonover, whose paintings decorate the premises, this Colonial-style brick building is full of arches and alcoves, cozy booths and shelves of timeworn books. Lunch features burgers, salads, and creative sandwiches (try Brie, bacon, and onion or turkey julienne on a croissant). Dinner choices include low-cholesterol and diet dishes, as well as roast duckling, fresh seafood, filet mignon, and pasta.

EVENING ENTERTAINMENT

Much of Wilmington's nightlife is centered around the **Grand Opera House,** 818 N. Market St. (tel. 658-7897 for information; box office tel. 652-5577). Built in 1871 as part of a Masonic Temple, this 1,100-seat showplace is one of the finest examples of cast-iron architecture in America and is listed on the National Register of Historic Places. This splendidly restored Victorian theater serves as Delaware's Center for the Performing Arts; it is home to OperaDelaware and serves as one of the many venues for performances of the Delaware Symphony Orchestra. It also offers an ever-changing program of guest artists in ballet, jazz, chamber music, pop concerts, and theatrical productions. Tickets average $20 to $35. Box office hours are 11am to 4pm Monday to Friday, and from 11am to showtime on days of performances.

The **Delaware Theatre Company,** 200 Water St., at the foot of Orange Street, next to Avenue of the Arts (tel. 594-1104; box office tel. 594-1100), is the state's only resident professional company. This is a modern 300-seat state-of-the-art facility, with no seat more than 12 rows from the stage. An ever-changing program of classic and contemporary plays is produced throughout the year. Performances are Tuesday through Saturday at 8pm, with matinees on Wednesday at 12:30pm, Saturday at 2 and 4pm, and Sunday at 2pm. Prices vary with the production and with the day of the week, but are usually between $15 and $25 a ticket.

For more than 80 years, big-name Broadway companies have brought their hits to the **Playhouse,** 10th and Market Sts. (tel. 656-4401), the 1,250-seat theater housed in the du Pont Building. Over the years, audiences here have applauded stars from Sarah Bernhardt to Kathleen Turner and hits like *Cats* and *Les Misérables*. Performances are usually scheduled for Tuesday through Saturday nights, curtain at 8pm and matinees on Wednesday and Saturday at 2pm and Sunday at 3pm; and ticket prices from $16 to $49.

Delaware's first and longest running dinner theater is the **Candlelight Music Dinner-Theatre,** 2208 Miller Rd. (tel. 475-2313). For over 20 years, this resident company has staged such productions as *Camelot, Gigi, My Fair Lady, Man of La Mancha,* and *Fiddler on the Roof* in a restored red barn. Each performance begins with cocktails at 6pm, followed by a buffet dinner at 6:30pm and showtime at 8:15pm. Members of the cast and crew double as costumed waiters and waitresses. Performances are scheduled year round, on Thursday, Friday, Saturday, and Sunday; prices range from $19.50 to $23, plus gratuity. Box office hours are 10am to 5pm daily, and until 11pm on show nights. The theater, which is located in the Wilmington suburb of Arden near the Hilton Hotel, is signposted off Harvey Road.

The Wilmington dancing-and-disco scene is centered largely on the big hotel lounges such as **Copperfields** at the Sheraton Brandywine (tel. 478-6000) and **Whispers** at the Hilton (tel. 972-2701). In addition, there's nightly piano music at the **Lobby Lounge** of the Hotel du Pont and the **Conservatory Lounge** of the Christiana Hilton. Other popular spots for live or DJ music include **Klecko's,** 1616 Delaware Ave. (tel. 652-1120); **Kelly's Logan House,** 1701 Delaware Ave. (tel. 652-9493); **Cavanaugh's,** 703 Market St. (tel. 656-4067); **Apples Café and Jazz Club,** 1313 Market St. in the Hercules Building (tel. 655-3380); and **O'Friel's Irish Pub,** 706 Delaware Ave. (tel. 654-9952).

Note: For most Wilmington performing-arts events, tickets are available at **B & B Tickettown,** 322 West 9th St. (tel. 656-9797), at the corner of West Street, behind the Marriott Suites Hotel.

2. THE BRANDYWINE VALLEY

10 miles N of Wilmington, 35 miles W of Philadelphia,
80 miles E of Harrisburg, 90 miles N of Baltimore,
120 miles N of Washington, DC, 45 miles E of Lancaster

GETTING THERE **By Car** Accessible via I-95, I-276, I-76, U.S. Rte. 1, Rte. 202, and the Pennsylvania and New Jersey turnpikes.

ESSENTIALS **Information** Since the Brandywine Valley includes parts of northern Delaware and southeastern Pennsylvania, there are three sources of information that are well worth tapping: the **Greater Wilmington Convention and Visitors Bureau,** 1300 Market St., Wilmington, DE 19801 (tel. 302/652-4088); the **Brandywine Valley Tourist Information Center,** Rte. 1 at the entrance to Longwood Gardens, P.O. Box 910, Kennett Square, PA 19348 (tel. 215/388-2900 or toll-free 800/228-9933); and the **Delaware County Conven-**

tion and Visitors Bureau, 202 East State St., Suite 100, Media, PA 19063 (tel. 215/565-3679 or toll-free 800/343-3983).

Area Code Like the rest of Delaware, the Brandywine Valley attractions located in the Wilmington area belong to the 302 area code. Many neighboring sights, inns, and restaurants of the Brandywine Valley are located on the Pennsylvania side of the border, however, and they belong to the 215 area code. To avoid confusion, we'll specify the area code for every listing.

The scenic and historic Brandywine Valley is in a unique geographic position, embracing part of Delaware and part of Pennsylvania. Technically, the Brandywine starts as a creek in Philadelphia's western suburbs and ends 35 miles south, a full-scale tributary emptying into the Delaware River at Wilmington. The entire 15-mile-wide valley can be traversed by a number of routes, often crisscrossing and paralleling each other, and intertwining the attractions across state lines.

We chose to put the Brandywine Valley section in this part of the book because the most outstanding attractions and museums are in Delaware. At the same time, we are quick to point out that the majority of country inns and restaurants are scattered on the Pennsylvania side of the border.

So rich in history is this lovely valley that it might draw you here for a visit on its own merits, not just because you happen to be visiting Wilmington or Philadelphia. If you are coming to either one of these two cities, however, be sure to save some time for the Brandywine Valley—you'll find an incomparable blend of historical museums, art galleries, idyllic gardens, and a parade of welcoming inns and gourmet restaurants.

WHAT TO SEE & DO

WINTERTHUR MUSEUM AND GARDENS, Rte. 52, Winterthur, DE 19735. Tel. 302/888-4600 or toll-free 800/448-3883.

This nine-story mansion, once the country home of Henry Francis du Pont, is the most famous of all the attractions in the area and is named for a town in Switzerland. A collector of furniture, du Pont himself made the initial acquisitions that laid the foundation for perhaps the world's premier collection of American antiques and decorative arts. All objects, displayed in 196 different period room settings, were used in this country between 1640 and 1860, including Chippendale furniture, silver tankards by Paul Revere, and a dinner service made for George Washington. Adding to the splendid aura of the house, the 980-acre grounds are meticulously landscaped in the naturalistic tradition of an 18th-century English garden.

The museum staff conducts several types of guided tours (in small groups of 4 to 10 persons), 1 or 2 hours in length; most require advance reservations. The gardens can be explored separately, April to mid-November, or in conjunction with a house tour. The reserved tours cost $12.50 for adults and $6 for young adults 12 to 16. The knowledgeable staff also conducts a variety of seasonal tours, such as "Yuletide at Winterthur," from mid-November through December; the cost is $9 for adults, $4.50 for youngsters under age 17. The estate also serves as a venue for amateur steeplechase racing each May, a Point-to-Point event. There is also a cafeteria and a variety of gift shops on site.

Admission: $9 adults, $6.50 students 12 or over; children under 12 free.
Open: Tues–Sat 9:30am–5pm; Sun noon–5pm.

HAGLEY MUSEUM, Rte. 141, Wilmington, DE 19807. Tel. 302/658-2400.

Another du Pont family undertaking is in this peaceful woodland setting directly on the Brandywine River. This is the spot that drew French émigré Eleuthère Irénée du Pont de Nemours to establish a black-powder mill here in 1802. The first of the du Pont family developments in America, the mill was the forerunner of the large chemical companies developed by subsequent generations.

Today this 230-acre outdoor museum site re-creates the life-style and atmosphere of the original 19th-century mill village through a series of restored buildings, displays, replicas, demonstrations, working machines, and gardens. The highlight of this museum, however, is a building called Eleutherian Mills, the first (1803) du Pont home in America, a Georgian-style residence furnished to reflect five generations of the du Ponts.

Admission: $8 adults, $6.50 students and seniors, $3 children 6–14, children under 6 free.

Open: Apr–Dec daily 9:30am–4:30pm; Jan–Mar Sat–Sun 9:30am–4:30pm.

Closed: New Year's Day, Christmas Day.

NEMOURS MANSION AND GARDENS, Rockland Rd., P.O. Box 109, Wilmington, DE 19899. Tel. 302/651-6912.

Yet another du Pont home is this 300-acre estate of Alfred I. du Pont, a 102-room Louis XVI-style château with landscaped gardens. Built in 1909–10, Nemours was named after the du Pont ancestral home in north central France. The house contains antique furnishings, Oriental rugs, tapestries, and paintings dating from the 15th century, as well as personal items—vintage automobiles, billiards equipment, and bowling alleys.

The gardens, which stretch almost a third of a mile along the main vista from the mansion, represent one of the finest examples of formal French-style gardens in America. As at Winterthur, tours of the rooms and gardens are conducted by qualified guides and take a minimum of 2 hours. Reservations are usually required for these tours; visitors must be over 16 years of age.

Admission: $8 adults.

Open: May–Nov Tues–Sat tours at 9am, 11am, 1pm, and 3pm; Sun tours at 11am, 1pm, and 3pm.

LONGWOOD GARDENS, Rte. 1, Kennett Square, PA 19348. Tel. 215/388-6741.

This is one of the world's most celebrated horticultural displays. More than 11,000 different types of plants and flowers thrive here amid 1,050 acres of outdoor gardens and woodlands, and indoor conservatories. Longwood's attractions include not only ever-changing seasonal plant displays, but also illumi-nated fountains and open-air theater programs. Admittance to the conservatories is from 10am to 5pm. Fountain shows are held mid-June through August at 9:15pm on Tuesday, Thursday, and Saturday.

Admission: $10 adults, $2 children 6–14; children under 6 free.

Open: Apr–Oct daily 9am–6pm; Nov–Mar daily 9am–5pm.

ROCKWOOD MUSEUM, 610 Shipley Rd., Tel. 571-7776.

A Victorian theme prevails at this rural Gothic mansion, situated on 72 tree-filled acres. Inspired by an English country house, it was designed in 1851 for Joseph Shipley, one of the city's early merchant bankers. The house itself is furnished with a lavish mélange of 17th-, 18th-, and 19th-century decorative arts from the United States, Britain, and continental Europe, while the elaborate conservatory features a brilliant array of Victorian flora. Outbuildings include a porter's lodge, gardener's cottage, carriage house, and barn. Six acres of exotic foliage and landscaped grounds complete the tableau. Seasonal programs include a Victorian Ice Cream Festival in July and Christmas Candlelight tours in December.

Admission: $3 adults, $1 students 5–16, seniors $2.50; slightly higher for special events.

Open: Tues–Sat, 11am–3pm.

BRANDYWINE RIVER MUSEUM, Rtes. 1 and 100, P.O. Box 141, Chadds Ford, PA 19317. Tel. 215/459-1900.

Housed in a Civil War-era restored gristmill, this museum is surrounded by nature trails and wildflower gardens. The paintings on display here reflect the best of Brandywine area artists including Howard Pyle, Frank Schoonover, and three generations of Wyeths, as well as 100 other American artists and illustrators.

Admission: $4 adults, $2 children.
Open: Daily 9:30am–4:30pm.

MUSHROOM MUSEUM AT PHILLIPS PLACE, Rte. 1, Kennett Square, PA 19348. Tel. 215/388-6082.

Just as great artistry is synonymous with this region, so too is mushroom farming. A good place to learn about this activity is at this museum where displays illustrate the history, lore, and development of mushrooms, from the ordinary to the exotic. There is also a shop, selling freshly picked mushrooms, gourmet products, and gift items with mushroom motifs.

Admission: $1.25 adults, 50¢ children 7–12.
Open: Daily 10am–6pm, except holidays.

CHADDSFORD WINERY, Rte. 1, Chadds Ford, PA 19317. Tel. 215/388-6221.

Housed in a restored barn, this small winery produces some lovely oak-aged Chardonnays, Seyval Blancs, and Cabernet Sauvignons, as well as table wines. Visitors are encouraged to tour, free of charge. Tours are usually conducted on weekends, between 1 and 4pm.

Admission: Free. *Note:* There is a $5-per-glass fee to participate in a full tasting session on weekends.
Open: Tues–Sat 10am–5:30pm, Sun noon–5pm.

WHERE TO STAY

Most Wilmington area hotels are convenient bases from which to tour the Brandywine Valley. In addition, there are a few nearby inns that are on the Pennsylvania side of the border.

MODERATE

BRANDYWINE RIVER HOTEL, Rtes. 1 and 100, P.O. Box 1058, Chadds Ford, PA 19317-1058. Tel. 215/388-1200. Fax 215/388-1200, ext. 301. 40 rms, 4 suites. A/C TV TEL

$ Rates (including "European Plus" continental breakfast): $119 single or double; $125 suite. AE, CB, DC, MC, V. **Parking:** Free.

✪ Built to meld perfectly with this scenic and historic region, this hotel is perched on a hillside in the heart of the valley. Two stories high, with a facade of brick and cedar shingle, it is set beside a cluster of rustic shops, art galleries, and an artisans' cooperative; and the historic Chadd's Ford Inn restaurant is just a few steps away via a brick-lined path.

The guest rooms, half of which are on ground-floor level, are decorated with Colonial-style cherrywood furnishings, brass fixtures, chintz fabrics, and paintings in the Brandywine tradition. Each unit has a queen-size bed or two double beds and a private bath; some suites have an individual fireplace and a Jacuzzi. Breakfast is served in an attractive "hospitality room" with a fireplace and old-world furnishings. The lobby/reception area also offers a huge stone open fireplace and a homey ambience.

LONGWOOD INN, 815 East Baltimore Pike (Rte. 1), Kennett Square, PA 19348. Tel. 215/444-3515. 28 rms. A/C TV TEL

$ Rates: $60–$80 double, including complimentary buffet breakfast. AE, MC, V. **Parking:** Free.

This inn is surrounded by beautifully landscaped flower beds and gardens. The accommodations are modern, almost motel-style, with a Colonial motif; the bedrooms all have garden views, a private bath, and one or two double beds. Facilities include a lounge and restaurant (see "Where to Dine," below).

MENDENHALL HOTEL, Rte. 52, P.O. Box 208, Mendenhall, PA 19357. Tel. 215/388-1181. Fax 215/388-1184. 70 rms, 4 suites. A/C TV TEL

$ Rates (including continental breakfast): $79–$89, single or double; $125–$150 suite with jacuzzi. AE, CB, DC, DISC, MC, V. **Parking:** Free.

Deep in the heart of the Brandywine Valley, this property is part of an original Penn Land Grant purchased by Benjamin Mendenhall in 1703. The current complex is a blend of old and new—the Mendenhall's 1796 lumber mill that is now part of the restaurant structure and an adjacent three-story complex of modern bedrooms with conference center.

The guest rooms have country-style furnishings, with pine headboards or four-posters, desks, armoires, and cabinets, and modern touches such as hairdryers, clock-radios, bathroom phones, and computer-card keys.

Dining/Entertainment: The restaurant, traditionally known as the Mendenhall Inn, offers country French and American cuisine in five different rooms, and a tavern setting for a more informal atmosphere.

Facilities: An exercise room, gardens and brick courtyard, and five meeting rooms.

BUDGET

ABBEY GREEN MOTOR LODGE, 1036 Wilmington Pike (Rte. 202), West Chester, PA 19382. Tel. 215/692-3310. 18 rms. A/C TV TEL
$ Rates: $42–$55 single or double. AE, DC, DISC, MC, V. **Parking:** Free.

An excellent budget choice in the Brandywine region is this lodging near the Brandywine Battlefield Park close to scenic Rtes. 52 and 100. The family-run motel is designed in a courtyard-style and is set back from the road on its own grounds with picnic tables, gazebo, and an outdoor fireplace. All rooms have double beds and a refrigerator, and six units have individual fireplaces. The owners also operate a quality gift shop on the premises.

WHERE TO DINE

EXPENSIVE/MODERATE

CHADDS FORD INN, Rtes. 1 and 100, Chadds Ford, PA. Tel. 215/388-7361.
Cuisine: INTERNATIONAL. **Reservations:** Recommended.
$ Prices: Appetizers $2.95–$6.95; main courses $13.95–$20.95; lunch $5.95–$8.95. AE, MC, V.
Open: Lunch Mon–Sat 11:30am–2pm; dinner Mon–Thurs 5:30–10pm, Fri–Sat 5–10:30pm, Sun 5–9pm; brunch Sun 11:30am–2pm.

Dating back to the early 1700s, this sturdy stone building was first the home of the Chadsey family, and then a tavern and a hotel. Recently renovated and with a completely new kitchen, the inn still retains much of its Colonial charm with antique furnishings and century-old memorabilia. The walls proudly display paintings by local artists like Andrew and Jamie Wyeth. Lunch choices reflect 20th-century tastes (shrimp salad croissants, tortellini Alfredo, and sole and spinach roulade). Dinner entrées include dishes to please many palates—from grilled duck steak with port, Cornish game hen and braised quail, to veal Oscar, shrimp and lobster pasta, and stuffed baby salmon en croute.

CUISINES RESTAURANT, 200 Wilmington–West Chester Pike (Rte. 202), Chadds Ford, PA. Tel. 215/459-3390.
Cuisine: INTERNATIONAL. **Reservations:** Recommended.
$ Prices: Appetizers $3.95–$8.95; main courses $11.95–$22.95; lunch $3.95–$9.95. AE, MC, V.
Open: Lunch Mon–Fri 11am–2pm; dinner daily 5:30–9pm or 10pm.

International dining is the theme of this contemporary restaurant furnished with a relaxing blend of earth-toned fabrics, plush chairs, light wood trim, and plenty of glass and brass. Dinner entrées include recipes from many lands—paella, sole buerre blanc, curry chicken, sirloin steak Creole, shepherd's pie, and veal saltimbocca. Classical guitar or piano is featured in the evenings and on weekends.

DILWORTHTOWN INN, Old Wilmington Pike and Brinton Bridge Rd., Dilworthtown, PA. Tel. 215/399-1390.
  Cuisine: INTERNATIONAL. **Reservations:** Recommended.
$ **Prices:** Appetizers $4.95–$9.95; main courses $11.95–$24.95. AE, CB, DC, MC, V.
  Open: Mon–Sat dinner 5:30–10:30pm; Sun 3–9pm.

Located on the road that was once the principal connection between Wilmington and West Chester, this establishment was built as a house by James Dilworth in 1758, and thanks to its strategic position, it became a tavern within 10 years. Restored in 1972, the restaurant now has 12 dining rooms, on two levels, including the house's original kitchen. The decor consists of Early American furniture, hand-stenciled walls, 11 fireplaces, gas and candlelight lamps, and Andrew Wyeth paintings.

The menu features a gourmet medley of entrées such as filet mignon Beaujolais, breast of capon, shrimp scampi, crab en casserole, and a variety of lobster dishes. The extensive wine cellar offers 900 different labels.

LENAPE INN, Rtes. 52 and 100, West Chester, PA. Tel. 215/793-2005.
  Cuisine: AMERICAN/CONTINENTAL. **Reservations:** Recommended.
$ **Prices:** Appetizers $4.95–$8.95; main courses $10.95–$25.95; lunch $4.95–$10.95. AE, D, MC, V.
  Open: Mon–Sat lunch 11:30am–3pm; dinner Mon–Sat 4:30–10:30pm, Sun 3–9pm.

Expansive views of the Brandywine River and a modern decor are the keynotes of this multi-level brick-facade restaurant. Evening selections range from salmon in puff pastry, Dover sole, rainbow trout, and lobster medallions in champagne sauce to duckling with cider and apples, breast of capon with ginger, rack of lamb, and prime western sirloin steaks.

LONGWOOD INN, 815 East Baltimore Pike (Rte. 1), Kennett Square, PA 19348. Tel. 215/444-3515.
  Cuisine: AMERICAN. **Reservations:** Recommended.
$ **Prices:** Appetizers $2.95–$6.95; main courses $13.95–$23.95; lunch $4.95–$9.95. AE, MC, V.
  Open: Lunch daily 11:30am–3:30pm; dinner daily 4–9pm.

Mushrooms are the specialty here and it's not surprising since this is the heart of Pennsylvania's "mushroom-growing country." Specialties include mushrooms stuffed with crab imperial, mushroom strudel, mushroom omelets, mushroom burgers, and cream of mushroom soup, as well as mushroom-laden salads. Other dishes range from prime rib of beef and rack of lamb to shrimp tempura and shrimp Newburg. The decor is country style. The management also operates a gift shop and an adjacent 28-room motel.

LA GRANDE RESTAURANT, 451 Wilmington–West Chester Pike, Glens Mills, PA. Tel. 215/459-9915.
  Cuisine: INTERNATIONAL. **Reservations:** Recommended.
$ **Prices:** Appetizers $2.95–$4.95; main courses are all $11.95–$12.95 and include salad and dessert bar; lunch $3.95–$6.95. AE, CB, DC, MC, V.
  Open: Lunch Mon–Sat 11am–3:30pm; dinner Mon–Sat 4–10pm, Sun 4–9pm; brunch Sun 10:30am–2pm.

A 30-foot soup, salad, and dessert bar is the secret of success for this restaurant owned and operated by the Mangan family. Brass chandeliers, skylights, mirrored walls, captain's chairs, and paintings by a local artist decorate the interior. Gourmet sandwiches, hot salads, burgers, and pastas, as well as hot/cold salad bar selections, are featured at lunch. The dinner menu offers such dishes as fettuccine Alfredo, crab imperial, London broil, shrimp tempura, veal fontina, and turkey piccata. The soup, salad, and dessert (make your own sundae) bar is part of all dinner selections. An early-bird menu is available 4 to 6pm Tuesday through Saturday.

3. HISTORIC NEW CASTLE

**7 miles S of Wilmington, 40 miles SW of Philadelphia,
66 miles NE of Baltimore, 111 miles NW of Ocean City, MD**

GETTING THERE **By Car** From Wilmington take Rte. 13 south to Rte. 273 and then east to New Castle; or from Wilmington, take Rte. 9 south to New Castle.

ESSENTIALS For information, contact the Wilmington Convention and Visitors Bureau.

SPECIAL EVENTS For more than 60 years, on the third Saturday of May, the residents of this historic district have opened their doors and staged **A Day in Old New Castle,** a grand open-house tour of the whole town. On this one day, New Castle's private homes, public buildings, gardens, churches, and museums are all simultaneously open to the public from 10am to 5pm. In addition, special events, such as a maypole dance, carriage rides, musical programs, and bell-ringing are scheduled throughout the day. Tickets, $10 for adults and $8.50 for students, can be purchased at the Old Court House on the day of the tour; advance reservations are not necessary. Proceeds are used for the preservation and continued restoration of the town's historic buildings. For further information, contact A Day in Old New Castle, P.O. Box 166, New Castle, DE 19720 (tel. 302/328-2413).

Located 7 miles south of Wilmington, New Castle was Delaware's original capital and a major Colonial seaport. First known as Fort Casimir, this area was purchased from the Indians as a Dutch settlement by Peter Stuyvesant in 1651. It is said, in fact, that Stuyvesant designed the town's central Green by "pegging it off" with his wooden leg.

Later conquered by the Swedes and then the English, who named it New Castle, this stretch of land along the west bank of the Delaware River is today much the way it was in the 17th and 18th centuries. Original houses and public buildings have been restored and preserved, the sidewalks are made of brick and the streets of cobblestones, and the people subscribe to the "commons" system of government— every property owner is part owner of the city.

WHAT TO SEE & DO

✪ Chief among the sights in this historic district is the **Old Courthouse,** Delaware St. (tel. 323-4453), the hub of the town, and one of the oldest known surviving courthouses in the United States. Originally built in 1732, with modifications and remodeling throughout its history, this landmark was Delaware's Colonial capital and meeting place of the State Assembly until 1777.

One of the courthouse's other claims to fame is its cupola, the center of the "12-mile circle," which creates the northern boundary between Delaware and Pennsylvania. Among the contents on view are portraits of men important to Delaware's early history, the original Speaker's chair, and excavated artifacts pertaining to the various periods during which the building was in official use. Tours are conducted free of charge, Tuesday through Saturday from 10am to 4:30pm, and on Sunday from 1:30 to 4:30pm (donations are welcome).

Among the restored residences open to the public is the ✪ **George Read II House,** 42 The Strand (tel. 322-8411), on the banks of the Delaware River. This house was built between 1797 and 1804, a fine example of Federal architecture in a garden setting. The man for whom it is named was a prominent lawyer and the son of a signer of the Declaration of Independence. Interior features include elaborately carved woodwork, relief plasterwork, gilded fanlights, and silver door hardware, all reflecting the height of Federal fashion. The house is open year round, Tuesday through Saturday from 10am to 4pm, and Sunday from noon to 4pm (weekends only in January and February). Admission charge is $4 for adults and $2 for children.

These are just two of the more than 50 buildings and sites that can be seen throughout the New Castle district. The ideal way to explore the area is to take a self-guided walking tour called the **New Castle Heritage Trail.** This route is described in a leaflet proudly produced by the mayor and council of New Castle and the trustees of New Castle Common. To obtain a copy, contact the Mayor and Council, 220 Delaware St., New Castle, DE 19720 (tel. 302/322-9802).

WHERE TO STAY

Even though New Castle is fewer than 10 miles from Wilmington, many visitors choose to stay overnight or longer in this charming corner of Delaware. If you have a car, New Castle can even be a convenient base for touring all of the northern part of the state, including the Brandywine Valley.

EXPENSIVE/MODERATE

DAVID FINNEY INN, 216 Delaware St., New Castle, DE 19720. Tel. 302/322-6367 or 800/334-6640. Fax 302/324-4319. 13 rms, 4 suites. A/C
$ Rates (including continental breakfast): $60–$85 double; $110–$125 suite. AE, D, MC, V. **Parking:** Free.

The best way to enjoy the ambience of this old-world town is to check into this historic lodging. Dating back to the 17th century and originally two separate structures, this building has had a varied life as an inn and private home. With its brick walls, original fireplaces, and antique furnishings, the inn is much the way it used to be. The guest rooms, some of which overlook the river and some the Town Green, all have private bath; and for those who wish a color television or phone, portables are available.

Meals are served in the gracious Colonial-style dining room or in the outdoor courtyard, which is surrounded by well-tended rose gardens.

RAMADA INN—NEW CASTLE, I-295 and Rte. 13, P.O. Box 647, Manor Branch, New Castle, DE 19720. Tel. 302/658-8511 or toll-free 800/228-2828. Fax 302/658-3071. 130 rms. A/C TV TEL
$ Rates: $69–$85 single or double; $55 weekends. AE, CB, DC, MC, V. **Parking:** Free.

Close to the Delaware Memorial Bridge, this modern two-story property is designed in a modernized Colonial motif; the rooms, which are decorated with watercolors of local attractions, have two double beds or a king-size bed. Guest facilities include an outdoor swimming pool, a cozy lounge, and a full-service restaurant.

DUTCH VILLAGE MOTOR INN, 111 South du Pont Hwy., New Castle, DE 19720. Tel. 302/328-6246 or toll-free 800/321-6246. Fax 302/328-9493. 41 rms. A/C TV TEL
$ Rates: $35–$45 single; $40–$55 double. AE, DISC, MC, V. **Parking:** Free.
As its name implies, this distinctive motel is laid out like a little village of individual cottage units with Amsterdam-style tile roofs and facades and front gardens. Set back from the main road, with shady trees and an outdoor swimming pool, the motel offers large modern rooms with king beds or two double beds; all rooms are ground-floor level and many are nonsmoking.

WHERE TO DINE

In addition to being the home of a very historic district, the New Castle area is also the location of the Greater Wilmington Airport and a growing number of commercial industries. Consequently, restaurants conveniently line the du Pont Highway, otherwise known as Rte. 13.

EXPENSIVE/MODERATE

AIR TRANSPORT COMMAND, 143 North du Pont Hwy., New Castle. Tel. 328-3527.

Cuisine: INTERNATIONAL. **Reservations:** Recommended.

$ **Prices:** Appetizers $3.95–$8.95; main courses $12.95–$22.95; lunch $6.95–$14.95. AE, CB, DC, MC, V.

Open: Lunch Mon–Fri 11am–4pm, Sat 11am–3:30pm; dinner Mon–Thurs 5–11pm, Fri 5pm–midnight, Sat 4:30–midnight, Sun 4:30–10pm; brunch Sun 11am–3pm.

Authentic Air Force memorabilia sets the tone at this restaurant appropriately located close to the runways of New Castle County Airport. The restaurant commemorates the flying heroes and heroines of World War II with a decor of aviation memorabilia including old uniforms, newspaper clippings, pictures, and flying equipment. You can even pick up a set of headphones and listen to the ground-to-air instructions at the nearby control tower. The layout of the restaurant lends itself to browsing with lots of nooks and alcoves; 1940s music adds to the vintage atmosphere.

Dinner entrées include veal saltimbocca, rack of lamb, prime rib, shrimp and lobster stir-fry, farmhouse chicken, and roast duckling. There is also a bountiful Sunday brunch priced at $14.95 for adults, $7.95 for children 10 to 12, and $3.50 for children 9 and under.

LYNNHAVEN INN, 154 North du Pont Hwy., New Castle. Tel. 328-2041.

Cuisine: AMERICAN/SEAFOOD. **Reservations:** Recommended.

$ **Prices:** Appetizers $3.95–$7.95; main courses $11.95–$25.95; lunch $3.95–$11.95. AE, CB, DC, MC, V.

Open: Mon–Fri 11:30am–9pm, Sat 4–10pm, Sun 1–9pm.

This reliable, 30-year-old restaurant opposite the airport has an early-American decor of honey-colored brick walls, Colonial-style furniture and lots of brass fixtures, including a huge American eagle over the open fireplace. Lunchtime selections range from sandwiches, omelets, and salads, to hot seafood, beef, and chicken dishes. Dinner entrées include prime beef and steaks, veal dishes, and eastern shore seafoods.

NEW CASTLE INN, Market St. Tel. 328-1798.

Cuisine: INTERNATIONAL. **Reservations:** Recommended.

$ **Prices:** Appetizers $2.95–$6.95; main courses $12.95–$21.95; lunch $3.95–$8.95. AE, MC, V.

Open: Lunch Mon–Sat 11:30am–2:30pm; dinner Mon–Sat 5–9pm, Sun 3:30–8pm; brunch Sun 11:30am–2:30pm.

A standout in the historic district is this restaurant housed in a restored building erected by the federal government in 1809. The site was originally an office building and a school before becoming a restaurant in 1955. There are two dining rooms, one with a fireplace and both decorated with Colonial-style furnishings, artifacts, and memorabilia. Colonial or classical music plays in the background as the costumed staff serve a variety of regional dishes. Lunch items include hot and cold sandwiches, salads, soups, and quiches.

Entrées range from traditional chicken and oyster pie and roast stuffed quail to lobster-and-spinach fettuccine, sole with wild mushrooms, and steaks. Favorite appetizers are sherried five-onion soup and seafood chowders.

CHAPTER 13

DOVER & CENTRAL DELAWARE

Dover is the capital of Delaware, the hub of local government and home to many historic sites. Located literally at Delaware's geographic center, Dover is equally accessible from all parts of the state.

Plotted in 1717 according to a charter rendered in 1683 by William Penn, Dover was originally designed as the courthouse seat for Kent County, which was then, as it has continued to be, a rich grain farming area.

In 1777, however, this agrarian city's importance was greatly increased. The legislature of Delaware, seeking a safe inland location as an alternative to the old capital of New Castle on Delaware Bay, moved to Dover.

Dover subsequently became the state's permanent capital in 1792. One of the city's greatest claims to fame lies in the fact that the Dover Green was the site of the Delaware convention that ratified the Federal Constitution on December 7, 1787. Since it was the first state to ratify, Delaware has ceremonial precedence as "First State" in all national occasions.

Today's Dover, a city of 30,000 people, is also the home for a cross-section of American industry. At least 20 major companies, from International Playtex and Scott Paper to General Foods, are located here. So don't be surprised, as you drive into Dover, if you suddenly find the aroma of chocolate pudding in the air!

1. ORIENTATION

The area of Dover and central Delaware lies 45 miles south of Wilmington, 86 miles southeast of Baltimore, and 77 miles south of Philadelphia. It is easily accessible by air (from nearby Philadelphia) as well as by train and bus.

GETTING THERE   By Air   The closest major gateway for regularly scheduled flights from all parts of the United States is **Philadelphia International Airport,** 55 miles north of Dover. In addition, **Airport Shuttle Service Inc.** operates a 24-hour transfer system between Philadelphia International Airport and any address in Delaware (for full details, see Wilmington, Chapter 12).

By Train   There is daily service from all parts of the United States via Amtrak into Wilmington (see "Wilmington," Chapter 12).

By Bus   **Carolina Trailways** provides regular service into Dover, arriving at 650 Bay Court Plaza (tel. 302/734-1417 or toll-free 800/334-1590).

✓ WHAT'S SPECIAL ABOUT DOVER & CENTRAL DELAWARE

Ace Attractions
☐ Dover Air Force Base, home of the world's largest operational aircraft.
☐ Historic Houses of Odessa, a well-preserved 18th-century town.
☐ Bombay Hook National Wildlife Refuge, a 15,000-acre preserve.

Activities
☐ Dover Downs International Speedway, home of "Budweiser 500" and "Delaware 500" auto races.

Events
☐ Old Dover Days, "open house" at the finest historic homes.

Museums
☐ Delaware Agricultural Museum, 200 years of farming heritage.
☐ Barratt's Chapel and Museum, the "cradle of Methodism" in America.

Parks
☐ Killens Pond State Park, a 580-acre state park.

Shopping
☐ Spence's Bazaar, historic indoor-outdoor marketplace.
☐ Rose Valley Quilt Shop, craft shop operated by the Amish.

By Car   The best way to reach Dover from points north and west is to take I-95 or I-295 to Wilmington and then proceed southward via Rte. 13 to Dover. Rte. 13, which runs the entire length of Delaware, is also the best way to approach Dover from the south, via Virginia.

ESSENTIALS   Information   Contact the **Margaret O'Neill Visitor Center,** Federal St. and Court St., Dover, DE 19901 (tel. 302/736-4266). Centrally located near Dover's historic Green, this office provides a wide range of literature on city and state attractions, as well as a free 8-minute audiovisual profiling the major landmarks and historic buildings. Hours are Monday through Saturday from 8:30am to 4:30pm, and Sunday from 1:30 to 4:30pm.

City Layout   The downtown area is concentrated in a relatively small radius around The Green, a historic area where you'll find brick sidewalks and most of the government buildings and sightseeing attractions. You can park your car and easily explore on foot. Dover's hotels, however, are concentrated east of the historic district, primarily along Rte. 13, otherwise known as du Pont Highway. This strip, also home to the Dover Downs Raceway, the Delaware Agricultural Museum, Delaware State College, the Dover Shopping Mall, and Dover Air Force Base, extends for several miles and requires a car to get from place to place.

SPECIAL EVENTS   Old Dover Days is held each year on the first weekend in May. On these two days, Dover's leading Colonial, Federal, and Victorian homes, mostly private residences, are all opened to the public. These 18th- and 19th-century homes, many clustered around The Green, include the Ridgely House, the Hughes-Jackson House, and the Carey House, as well as the governor's house. Hostesses in period costumes greet visitors and answer questions. The buildings are open from 10am to 4:30pm, and there are parades, music, maypole dancing, refreshments, and traditional crafts on sale on The Green. The admission fee is $8 per person for the house and garden tour. For advance information, contact the **Visitor Center** or **Friends of Old Dover,** P.O. Box 44, Dover, DE 19903 (tel. 734-7034).

2. GETTING AROUND

BY PUBLIC TRANSPORT

Central Delaware Transit (CDT), P.O. Box 1347, Dover, DE 19903-1347 (tel. 739-3282), a public bus system operating in the greater Dover area, provides service between posted stops within downtown and major residential/shopping/college areas, Monday through Friday, from 7am to 6pm. The fare is 75¢ adults, 50¢ students, and 30¢ seniors. Exact change is required.

BY RENTED CAR

If you haven't brought your own car to this area, some of the major car-rental agencies that have offices in Dover include **Avis,** 1620 South du Pont Highway (tel. 734-5550); **Budget,** Rte. 13 and Roosevelt Ave. (tel. 734-5688); **Hertz,** 41 South Bay Rd. (tel. 678-1722); and **National,** Rtes. 13 and 113 (tel. 734-5774).

BY TAXI

City Cab of Dover (tel. 734-5968) operates a reliable taxi service, with 24-hour radio-dispatched vehicles.

3. ACCOMMODATIONS

Dover does not boast grand or historic hotels. It does, however, have many fine modern motels and motor inns, open year round and set on their own grounds, with ample parking facilities. The major properties are on Rte. 13 (du Pont Hwy.), a commercial strip full of shopping and fast-food establishments.

In general, the rates for accommodations are moderate. On some weekends, however, slightly higher prices are in effect, and surcharges as high as $30 a night can be levied during the May and September races at Dover Downs. It is best to check in advance, in case your planned visit coincides with a peak period.

MODERATE

SHERATON INN—DOVER, 1570 N. du Pont Hwy., Dover, DE 19901. Tel. 302/678-8500 or toll-free 800/325-3535. Fax 302/678-8500. 145 rms. A/C TV TEL

$ Rates: $67–$75 double. AE, CB, DC, DISC, MC, V. **Parking:** Free.

The most complete facility along the main north-south corridor, just east of town, is this seven-story hotel. Guest rooms are furnished in a bright contemporary motif. Amenities include a full-service restaurant, the Carlisle Room, and a rooftop lounge, as well as a swimming pool, two tennis courts, and a putting green. It offers baby-sitting services, room service, and valet/laundry service.

BUDGET

COMFORT INN OF DOVER, 222 S. du Pont Hwy., Dover, DE 19901. Tel. 302/674-3300 or toll-free 800/228-5151. 94 rms. A/C TV TEL

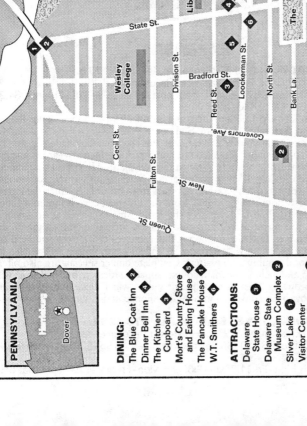

DOVER

PENNSYLVANIA

Harrisburg

Dover

DINING:
The Blue Coat Inn ②
Dinner Bell Inn ④
The Kitchen
Cupboard ③
Mort's Country Store
and Eating House ⑤
The Pancake House ①
W.T. Smithers ⑥

ATTRACTIONS:
Delaware
State House ③
Delaware State
Museum Complex ②
Silver Lake ①
Visitor Center
(Margaret O'Neill) ④

U.S. 13 (du Pont Highway)

Park

Park

Silver Lake ①

State Capitol Mall

Post Office

Federal St.

City Hall

Delaware Ave.

Kings Highway

The Plaza

④

③

Library

④

State St.

⑥

The Green

State St.

State St.

⑤

Wesley College

Division St.

Bradford St.

③

Loockerman St.

North St.

Bank La.

Water St.

Reed St.

Governors Ave.

Cecil St.

Fulton St.

New St.

②

Queen St.

N

$ Rates: $39–$46 single, $44–$51 double. AE, CB, DC, DISC, MC, V. **Parking:** Free.

The closest motel to the city's historic district, this facility is laid out in two adjoining bilevel wings; some nonsmoking rooms are available. Facilities include an outdoor swimming pool. There's complimentary morning coffee for guests.

DOVER BUDGET INN, 1426 N. du Pont Hwy., Dover, DE 19901. Tel. 302/734-4433. 68 rms. A/C TV TEL

$ Rates: $38–$45 single, $43–$50 double. AE, DISC, DC, MC, V. **Parking:** Free.
This two-story brick facility offers rooms—some of them nonsmoking—with one or two double beds or a king-size bed; many rooms have balconies. There is an outdoor swimming pool for guests.

DOVER DAYS INN, Rte. 113 at Rte. 10, Dover, DE. 19901. Tel. 302/735-4700 or toll-free 800/325-2525. 64 rms. A/C TV TEL

$ Rates: $40–$44 single, $45–$55 double. AE, DC, DISC, MC, V. **Parking:** Free.

Although it is situated at the junction of busy Rte. 113, this two-story motel is set back from the road on a small hillside. It is one of the newest lodgings in the area, with rooms nicely decorated in dark woods and pastel-toned fabrics. Units have either two double beds or a king-size bed, along with the standard Days Inn furnishings. Facilities are limited to a Jacuzzi and a meeting room. A choice of restaurants is nearby.

4. DINING

EXPENSIVE

THE BLUE COAT INN, 800 N. State St. Tel. 674-1776.
  Cuisine: AMERICAN. **Reservations:** Recommended.
$ Prices: Appetizers $1.75–$5.95; main courses $12.95–$26.95; lunch $4.95–$10.95. AE, CB, DC, DISC, MC, V.
  Open: Lunch Tues–Fri 11:30am–4pm and Sat 11:30am–2:30pm; dinner Tues–Fri 4:30–10:00pm, Sat 4:30–10:30pm, Sun noon–9pm.

Opened as a restaurant over 25 years ago, this lakefront Colonial-style structure was once a private home. Located just north of downtown in a garden setting, it takes its name from the uniform worn by the Delaware Regiment that marched from Dover Green in July 1776 to join General Washington's army. Four original stone fireplaces, weathered timbers, and antiques from the area enhance the interior. The names of the various dining rooms, from the Independence Room and Liberty Room to the George Tavern, also reflect the Early American theme. At lunchtime there is an extensive menu of hot and cold entrées, including crab au gratin, crab cakes, stuffed flounder, and filet mignon. Dinner entrées range from southern crab couplet (Maryland blue crab with Virginia Smithfield ham), shrimp Rockefeller, and prime rib to seafood combination platters. Complete dinner specials are also offered starting at $15.95 and include the main course, appetizer, dessert, and a glass of wine. For after-meal browsing, there is an adjacent stable, which once housed thoroughbreds and has now been converted into a Gift Shoppe and Countrie Store.

DINNER BELL INN, 121 S. State St. Tel. 678-1234.
  Cuisine: INTERNATIONAL. **Reservations:** Recommended.
$ Prices: Appetizers $1.50–$5.95; main courses $8.95–$20.95; lunch $3.95–$9.95. AE, MC, V.
  Open: Lunch Mon–Fri 11:30am–2:30pm; Mon–Fri dinner 5–10pm, Sat 5:30–10:30pm.

In the heart of Dover's downtown district, you'll find this Colonial-style restaurant, a favorite with Dover-area businesspeople. Especially busy at lunch, this restaurant features a menu of hot and cold sandwiches, omelets, salads, and entrées ranging from chicken parmesan to veal à la Gruyère, crab cakes, and stuffed shrimp. Dinner choices focus on an extensive seafood list (crab imperial, stuffed flounder, and shrimp scampi), as well as a variety of beef, veal, and chicken dishes.

MODERATE

CAFE CALYPSO, 65 N. du Pont Hwy. Tel. 734-1020.
Cuisine: AMERICAN. **Reservations:** Recommended.
$ Prices: Appetizers: $2.50–$7.95; main courses $12.95–$18.95; lunch $3.95–$7.95. MC, V.
Open: Lunch Mon–Sat 11am–2pm, dinner Mon–Thurs 5–9:30pm, Fri–Sat 5–10pm.

Located right on the busy main highway with a nondescript exterior, this restaurant is a real surprise inside, with a lovely decor of brick walls, orchids and candlelight on each table, an old chiming clock, and paintings by members of the Dover Art League. In spite of its name, it offers a background of classical music and a relaxed atmosphere.

The menu is best described as "nouvelle Delaware," with lots of local produce and ingredients. Specialties include chicken sap sago (with sap sago cheese and lime butter), tenderloin of pork with apples and schnapps, calves' liver with red onion marmalade and bacon, oven-poached salmon with almonds and cream, sea scallops with bananas and cream, and grilled tuna steak with Madeira butter sauce, as well as crab imperial, rack of lamb, and steak au poivre.

CAPTAIN JOHN'S, 518 Bay Rd. at Rte. 113. Tel. 678-8166.
Cuisine: AMERICAN/SEAFOOD. **Reservations:** Recommended.
$ Prices: Appetizers $1.95–$4.95; main courses $7.95–$15.95; lunch $2.95–$5.95; breakfast $2.95–$5.95. MC, V.
Open: Fri–Sat 24 hrs; Sun–Thurs 6am–10pm.

A favorite stop at any time of day for travelers along the Delaware coast is this nautical-style restaurant. Breakfast, served at all hours, includes an omelet bar, country platters, pancakes, and the "best waffles in Delaware." Lunch features sandwiches and burgers. Dinner entrées, which include a 60-item salad bar, feature fried chicken, seafood platter (shrimp, scallops, and flounder), crab imperial, steaks, and prime rib. Captain John's is also famous for its all-you-can-eat buffets on weekends.

SAMBO'S TAVERN, Front St., Leipsic. Tel. 674-9724.
Cuisine: SEAFOOD. **Reservations:** Recommended for dinner.
$ Prices: Appetizers $1.50–$2.95; main courses $5.95–$14.95; lunch $1.95–$5.95. No credit cards.
Open: Mon–Sat 11am–10:30pm.

Overlooking the Leipsic River, this informal restaurant/tavern is a local favorite for heaping plates of steamed crabs and shrimp, served "in the rough." Other entrées include steaks, burgers, crab cakes, crab imperial, honey-dipped chicken, and seafood samplers (flounder, clams, shrimp, oysters, and scallops). Lunch items include burgers, sandwiches, and chowders.

VILLAGE INN, Rte. 9, Little Creek. Tel. 734-3245.
Cuisine: SEAFOOD. **Reservations:** Required.
$ Prices: Appetizers $1.95–$5.95; main courses $11.95–$19.95; lunch $5.95–$9.95. MC, V.
Open: Lunch Tues–Fri 11am–2pm; dinner Tues–Fri 4:30–10pm; Sat 11am–10pm, Sun noon–9pm.

About 4 miles east of Dover, past several cornfields, is this restaurant, in the town of Little Creek, on the Mahon and Little rivers off Delaware Bay. Founded 20 years ago and still run by a local family named Roe, the restaurant has built its reputation on an ever-fresh seafood menu. The interior is a cheery blend of nautical and floral decor, with local handcrafts and grapevine wreaths. Lunch consists mainly of sandwiches, salads, chowders, and seafood platters. The house specialty on the dinner menu is fresh flounder, served stuffed with crab, breaded, poached, or however you wish. Other seafood entrées include oyster pot pie, lobster thermidor, stuffed butterflied gulf shrimp, and a steamed seafood pot (king crab legs, clams, scallops, and shrimp). Steaks, chicken, veal, duck, and prime ribs are also featured.

W. T. SMITHERS, 140 S. State St. Tel. 674-8875.

Cuisine: INTERNATIONAL. **Reservations:** Recommended.

$ Prices: Appetizers $3.50–$6.50; main courses $11.95–$19.95; lunch $4.95–$8.95. AE, DC, MC, V.

Open: Lunch Mon–Fri 11am–2pm, Sat noon–2pm; dinner Mon–Sat 5–9pm.

One of Dover's newest restaurants, W. T. Smithers is named in honor of a local hero who was, at various times, a baseball player, a lawyer, a member of the state's 1897 constitutional convention, and one of Teddy Roosevelt's Rough Riders. Handsomely redecorated and renovated, the Victorian-style restaurant offers a choice of eight different dining rooms, including a library, a parlor, a tavern, a trophy room, and an "anniversary" room, ideal for special dinners for two to four persons. The menu at lunch features double-decker sandwiches, burgers, pasta, and vegetarian platters. Dinner entrées include steaks, chicken Cordon Bleu, lobster fettuccine, and a creatively presented seafood mosaic (lobster, shrimp, crab, and scallops).

BUDGET

THE KITCHEN CUPBOARD, 150 S. Bradford St. Tel. 674-3433.

Cuisine: AMERICAN/HEALTH. **Reservations:** Usually not required, but accepted.

$ Prices: Breakfast $1.25–$4.95; lunch $3.75–$6.95. AE, MC, V.

Open: Mon–Fri 8:30am–7pm, Sat 8:30am–5pm.

As its name implies, this delightful little restaurant has a homey atmosphere. The selection changes daily, but always includes a variety of salads, sandwiches, pâtés, and cheeses, as well as many all-vegetable and meatless choices. Breakfast offers fruit plates, omelets, and freshly baked croissants and muffins. Seating is available downstairs beside a shop full of gourmet foods, spices, cookware, cookbooks, and gadgetry; upstairs in small individualized dining rooms; or outdoors on the front porch.

MORT'S COUNTRY STORE AND EATING HOUSE, 25 Loockerman St. Tel. 734-9701.

Cuisine: ISRAELI/ITALIAN. **Reservations:** Not required.

$ Prices: Appetizers $1–$3; lunch $2–$5; breakfast $1–$4. No credit cards.

Open: Mon–Fri 6am–4pm.

A Dover fixture for over 25 years, this restaurant is run by Mort, a friendly and obliging chef/host. The menu includes cheese steaks, salads, hot and cold sandwiches, subs, and Mort's Special, corned beef with coleslaw and Russian dressing. Breakfast items are also available until 11am each day (try the eggs and salami for a fast start).

THE PANCAKE HOUSE, 950 N. State St. Tel. 674-8310.

Cuisine: AMERICAN. **Reservations:** Not accepted.

$ Prices: Lunch $1.95–$5.95; breakfast $1.95–$5.95; dinner $4.95–$7.95. No credit cards accepted.

Open: Mon–Sat 5:30am–8pm, Sun 5:30am–3pm.

A good choice for a hearty meal in a lovely setting at a low price is this restaurant, a sister operation to the more pricey Blue Coat Inn. It is an ideal spot for pancakes, served traditional style or with fruit and nut fillings, as well as for waffles and crêpes. It also serves omelets and sandwiches, as well as dinner entrées. Take-out is available.

5. ATTRACTIONS

Dover is centered around a parklike square, called simply The Green, laid out in 1722 in accordance with William Penn's order of 1683. From the beginning, it was the site of public meetings, farmers' markets, and fairs. Today it is also the focus of activity for both the county seat and the state capital. Most of Dover's landmark buildings surround The Green, and the Visitor Center is just a few steps away.

DELAWARE STATE HOUSE, S. State St. Tel. 739-4266.

This is the second-oldest state house in continuous use in America. Built in 1792, the building was restored in 1976 as part of Delaware's Bicentennial celebration. It contains a courtroom, a ceremonial governor's office, legislative chambers, and county offices. Although the Delaware General Assembly moved to the nearby Legislative Hall in 1934, the State House still remains Delaware's symbolic capitol.

Admission: Free.
Open: Tues–Sat 10am–4:30pm, Sun 1:30–4:30pm.

DELAWARE STATE MUSEUM COMPLEX, 316 S. Governors Ave. Tel. 739-3260.

Three important museums are clustered here: the Meetinghouse Gallery, formerly a Presbyterian church, built in 1790, and now the home of rotating exhibits highlighting life in Delaware; the 1880 Gallery, a showcase for turn-of-the-century crafts; and the Johnson Memorial Building, a tribute to Dover-born Eldridge Reeves Johnson, inventor and founder of the Victor Talking Machine Company, known today as RCA. The third museum, actually located one block west of the other two buildings at Bank Lane and New Street, is designed as a 1920s Victrola dealer's store, with an extensive collection of talking machines, early recordings, and an oil painting of Nipper, the dog that made the RCA trademark, "His Master's Voice," a household name in the early 20th century.

Admission: Free.
Open: Tues–Sat 10am–4:30pm, Sun 1:30–4:30pm.

DELAWARE AGRICULTURAL MUSEUM, 866 N. du Pont Hwy. Tel. 734-1618.

This museum is devoted to the preservation of 200 years of Delaware's agricultural heritage. The large main museum building houses permanent and temporary exhibitions on the poultry, dairy, and produce industries, harvesting and farm machinery, and a gift shop. Other smaller buildings include a one-room schoolhouse, gristmill and sawmill, blacksmith shop, and farmhouse, all depicting farm life of yesteryear. In addition, special events are often held on the grounds.

Admission: $3 adults, $2 children 10–16, children under 10 free.
Open: Apr–Dec Tues–Sat 10am–4pm, Sun 1–4pm.

DOVER AIR FORCE BASE, Rte. 113. Tel. 677-3373.

Five miles south of Dover is the home of the giant C-5 Galaxy airplanes, one of the world's largest operational aircraft; it is the equivalent of an eight-lane bowling alley. The base is Dover's second-largest industry and the biggest airport facility on the east coast, with a 6,000-plus workforce. Normally closed to the public, you can enter the base if you go on one of the "mini-open-house" days on the third Saturday in May, June, July, or August; then you can get a look at the C-5's, with crew members on board to answer questions. On these days you can enter the base at the North Gate on U.S. 113. There is also an Airbase Museum displaying flight jackets, World War II memorabilia, and other flight materials.

Admission: Free.
Open: Third Sat in May, June, July, and Aug 10am–2pm.

JOHN DICKINSON PLANTATION, Kitts-Hummock Rd. Tel. 739-3277.

This is the former home of John Dickinson, one of Delaware's foremost statesman of the Revolutionary and Federal periods. It is a fine example of Delaware plantation architecture, built around 1740 and furnished with antiques of the period.

Admission: Free.

Open: Tues–Sat 10am–4:30pm, Sun 1:30–4:30pm.

BARRATT'S CHAPEL AND MUSEUM, Rte. 113, R.D. 2, Box 25, Frederica. Tel. 335-5544.

This simple brick chapel is one of Delaware's most significant religious sites. Considered to be the "cradle of Methodism in America," it was erected in 1780, due largely to the efforts of a local landowner, Philip Barratt. It was here, in 1784, that evangelist Francis Asbury met with a representative of John Wesley and established the New World chapter of their religion.

Admission: Free, but donations are welcome.

Open: Sat–Sun 1:30–4:30pm and by appointment.

HISTORIC HOUSES OF ODESSA, Main St., Odessa. Tel. 378-4069.

⭐ Dating back to the 17th century, Odessa, north of Dover, was settled by the Dutch and first named Appoquinimink, after the creek on which it lies. In 1731 it became known as Cantwell's Bridge, and in 1855 the name Odessa was adopted in honor of the Ukrainian seaport. Over the years, the town prospered as a grain-shipping port and peach grower. Today Odessa is a good example of a rural American adaptation of urban Georgian architecture; its historic houses are the centerpiece of the town. Administered by the Winterthur Museum, the structures include the Corbit-Sharp House, a three-story brick home, dating back to 1774; the Wilson-Warner House, built in 1769; and the Brick Hotel Gallery, a Federal-style building from 1822.

Admission: One house, $3 adults, $2.25 seniors; two houses, $5 adults, $4 seniors; three houses, $6 adults, $5 seniors. Free admission to all houses for children under 12.

Open: Mar–Dec Tues–Sat 10am–4pm, Sun 1–4pm.

BOMBAY HOOK NATIONAL WILDLIFE REFUGE, off Rte. 9, RFD 1, Box 147, Smyrna. Tel. 653-9345 or 653-6872.

⭐ Eight miles northeast of Dover is the Bombay Hook Wildlife Refuge, a 15,000-acre haven for over 300 species of migrating and resident waterfowl and animals. Created in 1937, it is one of the state's most important environmental resources and an essential link in the Great Atlantic Flyway, the chain of refuges that extend from the Gulf of Mexico to Canada. The site includes acres of marsh, swamp, freshwater pools, croplands, and woods, attracting such species as Canadian and snow geese, great egrets, black-crowned night heron, and the bald eagle, which nests here from early December to mid-May, as well as white-tailed deer, foxes, otters, opossums, woodchucks, and muskrats. For human visitors, there are auto-tour routes, walking paths, nature trails, and 30-foot observation towers.

To get there, take Rte. 13 north of Dover to Rte. 42; travel east to Rte. 9 and then north on Rte. 9 for 2 miles to Rte. 85, which leads to the refuge's entrance.

Admission: $3 per vehicle.

Open: Mon–Fri 8am–4pm, Sat–Sun 9am–5pm.

GUIDED WALKING TOURS

An ideal way to get your bearings in Dover is to take a 2-hour walking tour conducted by the knowledgeable guides of **Dover Heritage Trail**, P.O. Box 1628, Dover, DE 19903 (tel. 678-2040). Two different itineraries are available: the Old Dover historic district, commencing from the Visitor Center; and the streets of Victorian Dover, departing from the Delaware Department of Natural Resources and Environmental Control, 89 Kings Hwy. Both walks are scheduled for Thursday at 10am, May through October; no advance reservation is required. Tours can also be arranged for other days and times by appointment, year round. Rates are $5 for adults and $2 for youngsters 5 to 17.

6. SPORTS & RECREATION

PARKS

Dover's beautiful **Silver Lake** is the core of a parkside recreation area in the heart of the city. Biking, swimming, and picnicking are among the activities available. The park is open each day from sunrise to sundown, with entrances on State Street and Kings Highway. Complete information is available from the **City of Dover Parks and Recreation Division,** P.O. Box 475, Dover, DE 19901 (tel. 736-7050).

About 10 miles south of Dover is Kent County's only state park, **Killens Pond State Park,** Rte. 13, R.D. 1, Box 198, Felton (tel. 284-4526). With a mill pond at its core, it is a 580-acre natural inland haven. Facilities include picnic areas, guarded swimming pool and wading pool, shuffleboard and horseshoe courts, and hiking trails.

RACING

For horse racing, it's the **Harrington Raceway,** Rte. 13, P.O. Box 28, Harrington (tel. 398-3269). The oldest pari-mutuel racing track in the United States, it is situated on the state fair grounds, about 15 miles south of Dover. Racing is scheduled September through November, daily 7 to 11pm. Admission is $2 per person.

Car-racing fans flock to the **Dover Downs International Speedway,** Rte. 13, P.O. Box 843, Dover, DE 19903 (tel. 302/674-4600 or toll-free 800/441-RACE; or, in Delaware only, 302/734-RACE), described as the world's most challenging high-banked super-speedway and the home of the "Budweiser 500" and the "Delaware 500" auto races. Traditionally held during the first weekend of June and third weekend in September, the 500 races draw 40 of the world's top stock-car drivers. Ticket prices for adults range from $20 for general admission on Saturday to $28 to $100 for reserved seat tickets on Sunday. Mail orders are accepted. In addition, from November through March, this track is open for a full program of harness racing. Post time is 7:30pm Tuesday through Saturday and at 1pm on Sunday.

7. SAVVY SHOPPING

Since the state of Delaware charges no sales tax, many people travel here to shop. Like many capital cities, Dover has its share of shopping clusters, including the sprawling Dover Mall on Rte. 13. It offers four major department stores and more than 100 smaller boutiques and shops, selling everything from clothes and carpets to appliances and artworks. Among Dover's smaller, more personalized shopping experiences are the following:

DELAWARE MADE, 214 S. State St. Tel. 736-1419.
Housed in a restored 18th-century house in the heart of Dover's historic district, this shop presents a wonderful array of arts, crafts, and gifts made in the state. It's well worth a visit to browse from room to room and to see an overview of Delaware's best paintings, pottery, textiles, woodwork, dolls, and toys.
Open: Mon–Sat 9:30am–6pm.

SPENCE'S BAZAAR, 550 S. New St. Tel. 734-3441.
Started over 50 years ago, Spence's is a combination of farm stand, flea market, and

auction house—all ensconced in a big red building, formerly a tomato cannery. Local craftspeople and entrepreneurs gather here to sell, as do the Amish, who bring homemade breads, pies, cheese, and sausages.

Open: Tues and Fri 8am–9pm

ROSE VALLEY QUILT SHOP, Rose Valley Rd. (Rte. 198).

This fine craft shop is operated by a member of Dover's Amish community, in the heart of the farming countryside. Local Amish and Mennonite women handcraft the items on sale—from a dazzling array of colorful quilts in all sizes and patterns to place mats and baby booties. Special orders are taken and a mail-order service is also operated. It's hard to find better prices or a better selection of Amish quilts anywhere—even in Pennsylvania's Lancaster County.

To get there, drive west on Loockerman Street and follow Rte. 8 west for 4½ miles to Rte. 198 (also known as Rose Valley Road); turn left and continue for about 1 mile—the shop is on the left, opposite an Amish school.

Open: Mon–Wed and Fri 9am–6pm, Sat 9am–5pm.

CHAPTER 14

THE DELAWARE BEACHES

1. LEWES
- **WHAT'S SPECIAL ABOUT THE DELAWARE BEACHES**
2. REHOBOTH BEACH & DEWEY BEACH
3. BETHANY BEACH & FENWICK ISLAND

Nestled along Delaware's Atlantic coast, the beach communities of Lewes, Rehoboth, Dewey, Bethany, and Fenwick Island are in a class by themselves—28 miles of sandy and serene shoreline, clean and well kept, dune filled, and uncommercialized. Swimming, boating, fishing, and crabbing play a large part in the "good life" along the Delaware beaches. And each of the beaches is distinctive, with its own personality and ambience.

Taken collectively, these five beach areas easily comprise the busiest segment of Sussex County, Delaware's most southerly county, a region ranked largest in size, but normally smallest in population. During the summer season, however, the beaches quadruple in population as they draw visitors from all over Delaware and many surrounding states.

Unmistakably the most rural of Delaware's three counties, Sussex is not only rich in miles of uninterrupted and unspoiled Atlantic coast beaches, but also in interior farmlands and orchards, nature preserves and wildlife areas, state parks and forests, bays and rivers.

This lower part of Delaware is an important agricultural area, yielding bountiful supplies of grains, soy beans, corn, tomatoes, asparagus, strawberries, peaches, canteloupe, and watermelon. It also produces more broiler chickens than any other county in the nation—more than 180 million a year.

With all of this, it is still the beaches that attract the most unbridled enthusiasm and glowing praise. So if you hear the beaches described as "delmarvelous," don't be surprised. Because Delaware's beaches share the same peninsula with Ocean City, Md., and Virginia's eastern shore, the whole tristate area is usually referred to as "Del-Mar-Va" or "Delmarva."

---

1. LEWES

40 miles SE of Dover, 86 miles SE of Wilmington,
7 miles N of Rehoboth Beach, 34 miles N of Ocean City,
121 miles from Washington, D.C., 107 miles SE of Baltimore,
117 miles S of Philadelphia

GETTING THERE   By Air   The closest gateways for regularly scheduled flights from all parts of the United States are **Philadelphia International Airport** (see Chapter 4, "Philadelphia") and **Baltimore International Airport** (see Chapter 15, "Baltimore"). For commuter flights, the nearest gateways are Ocean City and Salisbury, Md. (see Chapter 17, "Maryland's Eastern Shore").

By Train   There is daily service from all parts of the United States via **Amtrak** into Wilmington (see "Wilmington & Environs," Chapter 12).

By Bus   Carolina Trailways provides regular service into the Rehoboth Bus Center, 1104 Hwy. 1, Rehoboth Beach (tel. 302/645-7044), about 5 miles south of Lewes.

WHAT'S SPECIAL ABOUT THE DELAWARE BEACHES

Ace Attractions

☐ Zwaanendael Museum, in Lewes, replica of a Dutch town hall.

☐ Fenwick Island Lighthouse, one of Delaware shore's oldest landmarks, with beams that project 15 miles.

☐ Nanticoke Indian Museum, Millsboro, with exhibits on the area's first residents.

☐ Treasures of the Sea Exhibit, in Georgetown, containing gold, silver, and other artifacts from a 1622 shipwreck.

Activities

☐ Boat cruises on Delaware Bay from Lewes Harbor.

☐ Windsurfing or sailing at Dewey Beach.

Events

☐ Fishing Tournaments at Lewes in late May to August and in October.

☐ Annual Rehoboth Beach Sandcastle Contest, for the best in sandcastle and whale sculptures.

For the Kids

☐ Funland, Playland, and Sports Complex at Rehoboth Beach.

Parks

☐ Cape Henlopen State Park, 2,500-acre playground bordered by the Atlantic Ocean and Delaware Bay.

☐ Fenwick Island State Park, 3 miles of beaches and dunes and over 300 acres of parklands, bayfront, and wildlife areas.

Shopping

☐ Ocean Outlets, at Rehoboth Beach, a cluster of 40 factory outlets.

By Car   From points north or south, take Rtes. 113 and 13 to Rte. 1 and thence to Rte. 9 into town. From the west, take Rte. 50 to Rte. 1 or 9.

By Ferry   Many visitors come to Lewes via the **Cape May–Lewes Ferry,** a convenient 70-minute Delaware Bay mini-cruise that connects southern New Jersey to mid-Delaware and saves considerable driving mileage for north- or south-bound passengers along the Atlantic coast.

In operation since 1964, this ferry service maintains a fleet of five vessels, each holding up to 800 passengers and 100 cars. Departures are operated daily year round, from early morning until evening, with almost hourly service in the summer months from 7am to midnight.

Passenger rates begin at $4 per trip; vehicle fares, calculated by car length, range from $16 for most cars to $50 for large trucks, with reduced prices for motorcycle and bicycle passengers. A drive-on, drive-off service is operated, so reservations are not necessary. The Lewes Terminal is next to the Cape Henlopen State Park entrance, about a mile from the center of town. Further information can be obtained by calling 609/886-2718, in Cape May, or 302/645-6313, in Lewes.

ESSENTIALS   Contact the **Lewes Chamber of Commerce,** P.O. Box 1, Lewes, DE 19958 (tel. 302/645-8073). The chamber's offices are in the charming Fisher-Martin House at Kings Hwy., next to the Zwaanendael Museum. Moved from its original location at Coolspring, this structure was once owned by Joshua Fisher, who is credited with charting Delaware Bay and River. This is one of almost 50 houses in Lewes, many transported from surrounding areas, that are now fully restored and in present-day use in the town. Summer hours are from 10am to 3pm on Monday through Saturday, with a reduced schedule during the rest of the year.

SPECIAL EVENTS   Throughout the summer, Lewes is the setting for a number of **fishing tournaments,** including competitions for trout (late May), shark (late June), tuna (mid-July), marlin (early August), and blackfish (October). Whether you want to

THE DELAWARE BEACHES

Atlantic Ocean

Breakwater Harbor

Cape Henlopen State Park

Lewes & Rehoboth Canal

LEWES

REHOBOTH BEACH

DEWEY BEACH

Rehoboth Bay

Delaware Seashore State Park

Indian River Bay

Ocean View

Millville

BETHANY BEACH

South Bethany

Fenwick Island State Park →

Indian River

Milton

Georgetown

Dagsboro

Frankford

Selbyville

Millsboro

Trap Pond State Park

Bridgeville

Seaford

Blades

Bethel

Laurel

Nanticoke Wildlife Area

Delmar

MARYLAND

DELAWARE

★ DOVER

The Delaware Beaches

Lewes ❶
Rehoboth Beach & Dewey Beach ❷
Bethany Beach & Fenwick Island ❸

cast a line or just watch the action, you can obtain complete details from the **Lewes Chamber of Commerce,** P.O. Box 1, Lewes, DE 19958 (tel. 302/645-8073). You can always get an update on the tournaments by calling the **Lewes Harbor Marina** (tel. 645-6227).

Situated at the tip of Cape Henlopen, between the Atlantic Ocean, Delaware Bay, and the Lewes-Rehoboth Canal, Lewes (pronounced "*Loo*-is") is the northernmost of the beach communities. In many ways, history plays a large part in the character of the town, touted as Delaware's oldest community.

Lewes was settled in 1631 by the Dutch, who sought to establish a whaling center called Zwaanendael (meaning "Valley of the Swans"). Although the settlement lasted only a year, the Lewes area has since been recognized as Delaware's first European colony.

In later years, Lewes was known by various names (from "Whorekill" to "Port Lewes," after a namesake in England) and was ruled alternately by the Dutch and the English, until it finally rested under William Penn's control in 1682. It evolved into a prosperous maritime town and seaport, occasional county seat, and leading fish-processing center.

During the War of 1812, the British formed a blockade on Delaware Bay and began to bombard Lewes. The local militia, under Col. Samuel Boyer Davis, returned fire with a small group of cannons. No lives were lost and no homes were destroyed, but one house was hit with a cannon ball that lodged in its foundation. It is still referred to as the Cannon Ball House.

Today's Lewes (pop. 2,600) is still inseparably involved with the sea—as a beach resort, as a boating marina, and as a port for dozens of fishing fleets. Also located here is the College of Marine Studies of the University of Delaware, with its own shoreline park and harbor and with two research vessels. In 1984 the waters off Lewes were the site of the discovery of the fabled HMS *DeBraak,* a British brig that was sunk off the coast of Cape Henlopen in 1798.

GETTING AROUND
BY MINIBUS

The **Jolley Trolley Seaport Shuttle of Lewes,** 306 Savannah Rd. (tel. 645-6800), operates a regular 12- to 14-passenger sightseeing service, from the ferry terminal to the downtown area. The motorized trolleys meet each arriving ferry and transport passengers to the historic district, with guided commentary en route. Each tour takes about ½ hour and you are free to remain in Lewes as long as you wish, returning to the terminal on a later shuttle. The trolleys operate weekends only May to June and September to October 9am to 9pm and daily during July and August 9am to 9pm. The fare is $1 per person.

BY TAXI

Local services are operated by **Webb Transport,** 217 Monroe Ave. (tel. 645-0600).

BY RENTED CAR

Cars can be rented from **Hertz,** 1101 Hwy. 1 (tel. 645-7044) and **National,** 788 Kings Hwy. (tel. 645-2622).

WHAT TO SEE & DO

Most visitors are drawn to Lewes by the beaches and marina, but you will find many other intriguing attractions well worth a visit once you come to this friendly, historic town.

Throughout the streets of Lewes, you'll see beautifully restored 17th-, 18th-, and 19th-century structures functioning as private homes, shops, churches, and public buildings, such as the **visitor information center** at the **Fisher-Martin House** (circa 1730). To guide you around, the Lewes Chamber of Commerce has designed a free pocket-size brochure detailing a self-guided walking tour of the town. Some of the highlights include:

✪ **Zwaanendael Museum,** Kings Hwy. and Savannah Rd. (tel. 645-9418). Designed in memory of Lewes's first Dutch settlers, this museum was built in 1931 to duplicate the architectural style of the town hall of Hoorn, Holland. The exhibits inside the Zwaanendael explore the rich and varied history of the area from the original colony to the present. Open Tuesday through Saturday from 10am to 4:30pm, and on Sunday from 1:30pm to 4:30pm. Free admission, but donations are welcome.

✪ The **Lewes Historical Complex** is a cluster of buildings administered by the Lewes Historical Society, 3rd St. and Shipcarpenter St. (tel. 645-0458). The buildings include an early plank house, a country store, and the Burton-Ingram House (circa 1789). This home, known for its fine collection of Early American furniture, is constructed of hand-hewn timbers and cypress shingles and also has cellar walls made of stones and bricks once used as a ship's ballast. The entire complex is open on weekends from 1 to 3pm in April, May, and June, and from Tuesday through Friday from 10am to 3pm, Saturday from 10 to 12:30; admission is $4. In addition, guided tours, priced at $5 per person, are conducted on Thursday, Friday, and Saturday at 10:30am during July, August, and September.

A recent focus of visitor attention has been the *DeBraak*—the 18th-century, treasure-laden British ship that was discovered off the coast of Lewes in 1984. A Nevada-based company called Sub-Sal used side-scan sonar to track the craft under the seas and raised the hull in August of 1986. If you are interested in having a look at some of the well-preserved artifacts and solid gold coins, inquire at the Lewes Chamber of Commerce to arrange an appointment.

INLAND EXCURSION

If you tire of the waterfront activities, head west about 15 miles, via Rte. 9/404 to Georgetown, the county seat of Sussex since 1791, chosen simply by virtue of its location in the middle of the county. It is a delightful 18th-century town, with a center designated as the Circle, dominated by a red brick Greek Revival courthouse (1839).

Every two years, Georgetown is the focus of statewide attention with the traditional celebration of **"Return Day,"** two days after Election Day. All candidates for office, victorious and otherwise, gather at Georgetown. The highlight is a reading of the election results, but the festivities include a parade that pairs winners and losers of all statewide and county races in horse-drawn carriages and antique autos, followed by speeches and revelry.

The newest attraction in the area is the **Treasures of the Sea Exhibit,** Rte. 18, Georgetown (tel. 856-5700). Located just west of the town and west of Rte. 113 at the Delaware Technical and Community College, this display presents a collection of gold, silver, and other artifacts recovered from the 1622 shipwreck of the Spanish galleon *Nuestra Senora de Atocha.* It is open April to December, Saturday and Monday to Tuesday, from 10am to 4pm, and Sunday from 1 to 5pm. Admission charge is $2 for adults and $1 for children 4 to 12.

FISHING

With easy access to both Delaware Bay and the Atlantic, Lewes offers a wide variety of sportfishing opportunities. The fishing season starts when the ocean fills with huge schools of mackerel in late March through April; large sea trout (weakfish) invade the waters in early May and June; and flounder arrive in May and remain throughout the summer, as do bluefish and shark. As the ocean warms up in June, it is also time for offshore species such as tuna and marlin. Bottom fishing in the bay for trout, flounder, sea bass, and blues continues all summer, with late August through September often providing the largest catches. October and November also bring porgies, shad, and blackfish.

From April through November, head boats leave every morning at 7am from the docks at Lewes harbor. A full day's fishing (8 hours) costs $28 to $35 per person. From May 30 to October 1, additional boats go out for half-day trips, either from 8am to 1pm or from 1:30 to 6pm ($16 per person). From May through Labor Day, night trips also operate from Wednesday through Sunday, leaving at 7pm and returning at 3am ($33). Half-price rates apply in most cases for children under 12. No license is required for most deep-sea fishing; rod rental is $5 to $7, depending on the length of the trip, and free bait is supplied. Arrangements can be made through **Fisherman's Wharf** at the Drawbridge (tel. 645-8862 or 645-8541) or the **Angler's Fishing Center** at the end of Anglers Road (tel. 645-8212 or 645-5775).

BOAT CRUISES

A good way to see the Delaware Bay and the Lewes Canal harbor is to take a boat cruise. Two-hour narrated sightseeing excursions are operated by the **Angler's Fishing Center** at the end of Anglers Road (tel. 645-8212 or 645-5775) daily at 7pm. In addition, another 7pm cruise leaves from Fisherman's Wharf at the Drawbridge (tel. 645-8862) each evening. Prices are $6 for adults and $4 for children under 12, from June 30 to Labor Day.

A selection of 15-foot fiberglass boats with a small outboard are available from **U-Drive-Em Rod & Reel Boat Rentals,** Fisherman's Wharf (tel. 645-8862). Rates, which range from $20 for the first hour, $6 for each additional hour, to $55 for an 8-hour day, include oars, one tank of gas and oil, life jackets and/or safety flotation cushions, and a map of the bay. Pontoon boats are also available from $70 for 2 hours.

BICYCLING

Lewes's historic streets and shoreline paths are also ideal for cycling. If you haven't brought your own, hire a bike from the **Lewes Cycle Shop,** in Beacon Motel, Savannah Road (tel. 645-4544). This shop also rents bicycles and tandems from 9am to 5pm 7 days a week, June through Labor Day, and on weekends during the rest of the year. Charges average $9 to $14 for a day or $23 to $39 for a week.

☉ **Cape Henlopen State Park,** 1 mile east of Lewes, is a 2,500-acre outdoor playground bordered on one side by the Atlantic and on another by Delaware Bay—just the spot for beach swimming, tennis, picnicking, nature trails, bayshore crabbing, and pier fishing. This is also the home of the famous "walking dunes," most notably the 80-foot Great Dune, the highest sand dune between Cape Hatteras and Cape Cod. For those who enjoy a good climb, a refurbished World War II observation tower (115 steps) offers some of the best coastal views for miles. In addition, there are 155 campsites, available from April 1 through October 31, on a first-come, first-served basis, costing $10 per night for up to six people. Admission charges to the park are $2 for Delaware cars and $4 for all out-of-state cars, plus 50¢ for each person in addition to a car's driver. For further information on the park's attractions, contact the **Cape Henlopen State Park,** 42 Cape Henlopen Drive, Lewes, DE 19958 (tel. 302/645-8983).

WHERE TO STAY

Lewes's choice of accommodations has expanded in recent years and now includes handsome downtown inns as well as traditional motels. In general, the prices are in the moderate-to-expensive range in the summer months and in the moderate-to-inexpensive range at other times of the year. Check what rate is in effect at the time you plan to visit, and whether any minimum-night stays are required. Reservations are required in the summer months and recommended at other times, since the total room capacity barely exceeds 300. All properties described here are clustered in the town near the canal and wharf areas, but not directly on the beach.

EXPENSIVE

THE INN AT CANAL SQUARE, 122 Market St., Lewes, DE 19958. Tel. 302/645-8499. 17 rms, 2 suites, 1 houseboat. A/C TV TEL

$ Rates (including continental breakfast): $75–$120 single or double, $100–$150 suites, in main building; adjacent houseboat that sleeps four, $175–$250. AE, MC, V. **Parking:** Free.

⭐ Located in an ideal setting overlooking the marina, this four-story bed-and-breakfast hotel has a country-inn atmosphere with luxurious touches. The guest rooms are extra large, almost mini-suites, each with a queen- or king-size bed, and most with a balcony or porch overlooking the water. The decor includes designer fabrics, waterfowl art prints, live plants, and 18th-century reproductions of headboards, nightstands, armoires, brass lamps, and comfortable arm chairs. The modern bathrooms offer a contrast of sleek black-and-white marble and tile appointments, each with separate vanity area and hairdryer.

Facilities include a sitting room/parlor and a conference center. If you are looking for something a little different, the inn also rents a custom-designed, two-bedroom houseboat, permanently moored on the marina. It has a full galley and sleeps four adults.

THE NEW DEVON INN, Second and Market Sts., P.O. Box 516, Lewes, DE 19958. Tel. 302/645-6466. 24 rms, 2 suites. A/C TEL

$ Rates (including continental breakfast): $70–$105 single or double, $85–$140 suite. AE, MC, V. **Parking:** Free.

⭐ Dating back to the 1920s, this recently restored three-story brick hotel sits right in the heart of Lewes. The lobby includes a modern sitting area with art-deco tones, a small music room, a wicker-filled breakfast/TV room, and six attractive shops; the lower level has an art gallery. On the second and third floors are the guest rooms, each individually furnished with local antiques, crystal or brass lamps, and fine comforters and linens. The bathrooms are modern and have hairdryers. Facilities include four meeting rooms.

MODERATE

ANGLER'S MOTEL, Anglers Rd. and Market St., P.O. Box 511, Lewes, DE 19958. Tel. 302/645-2831 or toll-free 800/523-3312, (DC, MD, NJ, NY, PA, and VA only). 25 rms. A/C TV TEL

$ Rates: $55–$75 single or double. AE, CB, DC, MC, V. **Parking:** Free.

⑤ One of the oldest lodgings in the area, this very well kept motel is a favorite with fishing guests. Most of the rooms enjoy views of the wharf and marina, and there is a very pleasant sun deck. All rooms have one or two double beds. A 3-day minimum stay applies on weekends; reduced rates are in effect from mid-September to mid-May.

Note: This is one of several properties in town using the name Angler. There is also a restaurant, not associated with the motel, using the name, as well as a marina and a road. For a community so involved with fishing, the frequent use of the word "angler" is understandable, although it can be a bit confusing for visitors.

THE BEACON MOTEL, 514 Savannah Rd., P.O. Box 609, Lewes, DE 19958. Tel. 302/645-4888 or toll-free 800/735-4888. 66 rms. A/C TV TEL

$ Rates: $40–$85 single or double. AE, MC, V. **Parking:** Free.

Closed: Late Dec–Mar.

⑤ This new (1989) motel occupies the top two floors of a three-story property, with the ground level devoted to shops and a reception area. Rooms are bright and cheery, furnished with pastel tones and seashell art. Each unit has two double beds and standard furnishings, plus a refrigerator and a small balcony with sliding glass doors. Facilities include a swimming pool and sun deck.

CAPE HENLOPEN MOTEL, Savannah and Anglers Rds., P.O. Box 243, Lewes, DE 19958. Tel. 302/645-2828 or toll-free 800/447-3158. 28 rms. A/C TV TEL

$ Rates: $30–$70 single, $35–$75 double. AE, MC, V. **Parking:** Free.

This modern two-story, Gothic L-shaped structure has fully carpeted, wood-paneled rooms. All second-floor rooms have balconies. There is a 2-night minimum on weekends and a 3-night minimum during holiday weekends in the summer. Open all year.

BUDGET

SAVANNAH INN, 330 Savannah Rd. (Rte. 9), Lewes, DE 19958. Tel. 302/645-5592. 7 rms (none with private bath).

$ Rates (including breakfast): $38 single, $38–54 double. No credit cards. **Parking:** Free. **Closed:** Oct–late May.

The ambience of a bygone era is what Dick and Susan Stafursky offer guests. A gracious old brick semi-Victorian house with wraparound enclosed porch, this bed-and-breakfast facility is conveniently situated in the heart of midtown Lewes. The bedrooms are of varying size and decor, all with shared baths. Some rooms can accommodate three or four persons, at a rate of $48 to $60. The inn accepts reservations only for a 2-night minimum on weekends and a 3-night minimum on holidays. The rates include breakfast, consisting of local fruits, juices, homemade breads or muffins, jams, granola, and a choice of hot beverages. (*Note:* Rooms are available at reduced rates without breakfast during the off-season.)

WHERE TO DINE

EXPENSIVE

KUPCHICK'S, 3 East Bay Ave. Tel. 645-0420.
  Cuisine: INTERNATIONAL. **Reservations:** Recommended.
$ Prices: Appetizers $3.50–$7.50; main courses $14–$24; lunch $5–$14. CB, DC, MC, V.
  Open: Lunch Mon–Sun 11am–4pm; dinner Sun–Thurs 5–10pm, Fri–Sat 5–11pm.

★ This beachfront restaurant, opened in 1985, carries on a tradition of fine food started in 1913 when the present owners' grandparents, immigrants from Romania, began the first Kupchick's in Toronto and later added a second restaurant of the same name in Montreal. There are two dining rooms on the ground floor, each with a European ambience and decor, and a more casual upper-level open deck for sea-view meals on warm summer days.

Dinner entrées include crab imperial, shrimp scampi, chicken piccata, stuffed quail, lobster, fresh swordfish, chateaubriand and certified Angus steaks. Kupchick's is also known for its "delmarvelous" chowder and desserts—key lime cheesecake, chocolate walnut pie, and raspberry soufflé. Light jazz is featured on weekends. Hours are slightly shorter in winter.

MODERATE

GILLIGAN'S, 134 Market St., Canal Square. Tel. 645-7866.
  Cuisine: SEAFOOD. **Reservations:** Not accepted.
$ Prices: Appetizers $3–$7; main courses $13.95–$19.95. AE, MC, V.
  Open: Apr–Oct, daily 11am–11pm, continuous menu.

One of the unique dining spots in Lewes is Gilligan's, next to the Inn at Canal Square and right on the water. The restaurant consists of a refurbished diving boat anchored on the marina, attached to a renovated chicken coop on the dock. Although it sounds outlandish, the result is a charming harborfront structure with a trendy deck bar and several small glass-walled dining rooms.

Seafood dominates the dinner menu, with such choices as crab cakes, tuna steak, lemon-pepper shrimp, and lobster tail. For landlubbers, there's also a variety of chicken, veal, pork, and steak dishes. Live entertainment is offered on summer weekend evenings. In the off-season months (mid-Oct to mid-Apr), the restaurant is closed.

LA ROSA NEGRA, 128 Second St. Tel. 645-1980

Cuisine: ITALIAN. **Reservations:** Recommended.
$ **Prices:** Appetizers $2.50–$5.95; main courses $6.95–$15.95. MC, V.
Open: Dinner Sun–Thurs 5–9:30pm, Fri–Sat 5–10pm.

In a town known for seafood, this small shopfront restaurant is a piquant change of pace. The decor is highlighted by a black rose (*rosa negra*) etched on stained glass in the front window; the table settings carry on the same theme with black-and-white linens and pottery. The white walls are enlivened by local art. Specialties include veal and shrimp marsala, chicken florentine gorganzola, mussels marinara, scampi alla ceci (with chickpeas, black olives, and white wine over linguine), and sole puttonesca (with chopped olives, garlic, and tomatoes, over linguine pesto), as well as vegetarian dishes such as mushroom pasta primavera.

THE LIGHTHOUSE RESTAURANT, Savannah and Anglers Rds. Tel. 645-6271.
Cuisine: SEAFOOD. **Reservations:** Accepted only for parties of 8 or more.
$ **Prices:** Appetizers $2.95–$9.95; main courses $11.95–$24.95; lunch $3.95–$12.95. MC, V.
Open: Lunch Mon–Fri 11:30am–5pm; dinner Mon–Thurs 5–9pm, Fri–Sat 5–10pm.

Pleasant views of the marina and a nautical decor are featured at this restaurant. An all-day menu features soups, salads, sandwiches, and platters; especially worth trying are the seaside salads (greens topped with sautéed shrimp, scallops, and crab). The dinner menu also emphasizes a selection of fish dishes, such as crab cakes, combination platters, and lobster.

LINGO'S ROSE AND CROWN RESTAURANT AND PUB, 108 Second St. Tel. 645-2373.
Cuisine: INTERNATIONAL. **Reservations:** Recommended.
$ **Prices:** Appetizers $2.95–$7.95; main courses $10.95–$16.95; lunch $5–$7. AE, MC, V.
Open: Lunch daily 11:30am–4pm; dinner daily 5–11pm.

Housed in the historic 1930s Walsh Building, this restaurant offers three separate eating areas: a bright and plant-filled front room with large windows overlooking busy Second Street; a clubby bar area with brass fixtures, skylit ceiling, and wall hangings from England and Ireland; and a cozy back room with dark wood trim, exposed-brick walls, and a tin ceiling.

Lunch fare includes pub salads, homemade soups, quiches, shepherd's pie, Welsh rabbit, and fish and chips. Dinner features such entrées as London broil, English cottage beef pie, pork stew in cider, and crab imperial.

---

2. REHOBOTH BEACH & DEWEY BEACH

43 miles SE of Dover, 88 miles SE of Wilmington, 7 miles from Lewes, 27 miles N of Ocean City, 124 miles SE of Washington, D.C., 110 miles SE of Baltimore, 120 miles S of Philadelphia

GETTING THERE   By Air   The closest gateways for regularly scheduled flights from all parts of the United States are **Philadelphia International Airport** (see Chapter 4, "Philadelphia") and **Baltimore International Airport** (see Chapter 15, "Baltimore"). For commuter flights, the nearest gateways are Ocean City and Salisbury, Md. (see Chapter 17, "Maryland's Eastern Shore").

By Train   There is daily service from all parts of the United States via **Amtrak** into Wilmington (see Chapter 12, "Wilmington & Environs").

By Bus   **Carolina Trailways** provides regular service into the Rehoboth Bus Center, 1104 Hwy. 1, Rehoboth Beach (tel. 302/645-7044). During the summer months, **Delaware Resort Transit (DRT)** operates a shuttle bus service between the Cape May/Lewes ferry dock to Rehoboth and Dewey beaches. Shuttles run from

7am to midnight daily; the fare is 75¢ for adults and 50¢ for students. For more information, call toll-free in Delaware 800/892-7000.

By Car   From points north or south, take Rtes. 113 and 13 to Rte. 1.

By Ferry   See "Lewes," above.

ESSENTIALS   Sightseeing brochures, maps, descriptions of accommodations, and restaurant listings are available from the **Rehoboth Beach–Dewey Beach Chamber of Commerce,** 501 Rehoboth Ave., P.O. Box 216, Rehoboth Beach, DE 19971 (tel. 302/227-2233 or toll-free 800/441-1329). The office is open year round Monday through Friday, from 9am to 4:30pm; in addition, from Memorial Day through Labor Day there are Saturday and Sunday hours from 10am to 2pm.

SPECIAL EVENTS   Highlight of the summer calendar is the **Annual Rehoboth Beach Sandcastle Contest,** on the first Saturday of August. Held at Fishermen's Beach, just north of the Henlopen Hotel, this competition is open to all, free of charge; divisions include sand castle, whale sculpture, and free form, all in children's and adult categories. If outdoor fairs and antique shows interest you, plan a visit to Rehoboth in the spring or fall. **Sidewalk sales,** held along Rehoboth Avenue during the third weekend of May and the third weekend of September, draw enthusiastic followers. The Chamber of Commerce is the best source for information on all of these gatherings.

Of all the Delaware beaches, the most popular is Rehoboth, a small year-round coastal community that swells from its normal population of 4,000 in winter to over 50,000 in the summer months. Although considered small by some standards, it is Delaware's largest Atlantic shore town.

Founded on strong religious traditions, Rehoboth traces its origin back to 1873, when it was selected by the Methodist Church as a site for summer camp meetings. It was an inspirational spot—with the ocean waves meeting the sandy shores, amid groves of holly and pine. Even the name, Rehoboth, is biblical in origin, meaning "room enough."

Rehoboth's popularity owes much to its idyllic location—a pleasant tree-shaded strip of land, bordered on the east by the Atlantic, on the west by the Rehoboth-Lewes Canal, and on the south by a natural waterfowl refuge called Silver Lake. The town is immaculately maintained, with many Victorian homes and turn-of-the-century cottages, tree-lined streets, up-to-date motels, fine restaurants, and all kinds of intriguing shops.

Neighboring Dewey Beach, named for Spanish American War hero Admiral George Dewey, is a relatively new community. Nestled just south of Rehoboth Beach on the lower shore of Silver Lake, Dewey is a unique stretch of real estate—only two blocks wide, divided in the center by Rte. 1, with the Atlantic Ocean on the east and Rehoboth Bay to the west.

No matter where people go at Dewey Beach, views of the water are always in sight, providing mesmerizing natural spectacles, from the amber sunrise on splashing ocean waves in early morning to the golden sunset over the calm ripples of Rehoboth Bay each evening.

In contrast to Rehoboth Beach, Dewey is the shore's youngest town, with no boardwalk and no one central thoroughfare, other than Rte. 1, also known as Hwy. 1 and Ocean Hwy. The entire strip is lined with motels, beach houses, apartments, restaurants, and fast-food establishments, all designed to cater to a beach-going clientele. It is also a lively night-time spot, making it a great favorite with young vacationers.

GETTING AROUND

There is more to Rehoboth than its beach and boardwalk, and the best way to see the town's highlights is to take a ride on the **Jolly Trolley,** a 10-mile narrated sightseeing tour. Operating on weekends in May and September, and daily from June through August, the trolley departs regularly, from 9:30am through 8:30pm, from the Boardwalk at Rehoboth Avenue. The fare is $3; free for children under 5 (tel. 302/227-1197).

For people interested in visiting the Rusty Rudder Restaurant and its affiliated attractions at Dewey Beach, **Ruddertowne Transit Trolley Service** (tel. 227-3888) operates a complimentary daily shuttle from the Boardwalk at Rehoboth Avenue to Dewey and back, from noon to 1am, Memorial Day to Labor Day, and on weekends in May and September.

Parking in Rehoboth Beach can be difficult. Metered parking is in effect (30 minutes, hourly, and up to 12 hours, with the majority of machines programmed for the first two time limits). This system operates from 10am to midnight on weekends during May and 7 days a week from June 1 to 1 week after Labor Day; head-in or parallel parking only is permitted. The number of spaces can rarely accommodate the demand; to ease the situation, most lodging places offer free parking to their guests and many people choose to park their car and leave it at the hotel or motel until departure for home. Rehoboth is small enough that walking usually proves to be the best way to get around.

For those who are not staying at downtown hotels, **Delaware Resort Transit (DRT)** operates a Park-N-Ride service. The parking lot is located on Rte. 1 at Country Club Road, directly north of the intersection of Rtes. 1 and 1A. Buses are in operation at least 20 hours a day from Memorial Day to Labor Day, with intermittent stops between the lot and the Rehoboth Beach Boardwalk at Rehoboth Avenue and Dewey Beach. Roundtrip fare is $2 per day per car for driver and all passengers; riders only (with no car in lot) pay 50¢ per person. For additional information, call toll-free in Delaware 800/892-7000.

WHAT TO SEE & DO

Most of Rehoboth's activity centers around the 1-mile-long boardwalk and Rehoboth Avenue, the main street that runs perpendicular to the boardwalk at its center point. The **Boardwalk** itself is just right for strolling and sampling the variety of amusements, games, fast-food concessions, and shops. When the mood strikes, don't miss two unique Rehoboth experiences: **Dolle's Taffy** (established 1927) and **Grotto's Pizza** (operating since 1960). On weekend evenings in summer, concerts and other musical events are held (usually at 8pm) at the Bandstand on Rehoboth Avenue, adjacent to the Boardwalk. Check with the Chamber of Commerce for an up-to-date schedule for the time of your visit.

A good place to gain a perspective on Rehoboth and its early days is the **Anna Hazzard Museum** at Martin's Lawn between Rehoboth Avenue and Christian Street (tel. 227-3859 or 227-3297). A camp-meeting-era building, named for a former owner and civic leader, this house now serves as a museum for the area. It's open to the public free of charge on weekend afternoons, Memorial Day through Labor Day, from 2 to 5pm, and by appointment at other times.

SPORTS & ACTIVITIES

Swimming and sunning on Rehoboth's wide sandy beaches are the top activities. All the beaches have public access and offer a wide range of daily rental services: umbrellas $5, chairs $2.50, and rafts $5.

Bay Sports, 11 Dickinson St., Dewey Beach (tel. 227-7590) rents windsurfers, sunfish, and jet skis by the half hour or hour or by the day. Rates for a windsurfer or sunfish are $20 first hour, $7 for every hour after that; and jet skis are $35–$50 for a half hour. Sailing and windsurfing lessons are also arranged.

✪ For a selection of water sports, plan to visit the **Delaware Seashore State Park,** Rte. 1 (tel. 227-2800), located 2 miles south of Rehoboth Beach. This 10-mile-long beachland paradise offers both the crashing surf of the Atlantic and the gentle waters of Rehoboth Bay. Facilities include lifeguard-supervised swimming, surfing, and fishing. In addition, there is a full-service boating marina and a bayshore campground with over 300 sites for RVs and trailers. Admission to the park is $2 for Delaware cars and $4 for out-of-state vehicles.

The flat Rehoboth terrain and cool sea breezes also make bicycling popular here. Bikes are allowed on the boardwalk during the hours of 5am to 10am from May 15 to September 15. You can rent all types of equipment from **Boardwalk Bikes,** on the Boardwalk at 1 Virginia Ave., Rehoboth Beach (tel. 227-8520), open daily from 7am to 5pm; rates range from $3 to $5 an hour and $7 to $15 a day. Also try **Bob's Rentals,** N. 1st St., at Maryland Avenue, Rehoboth Beach (tel. 227-7966), for two- and three-wheelers by the hour, day, or week.

COOL FOR KIDS

A Summer Children's Theatre is operated at the Epworth United Methodist Church, 20 Baltimore Ave. (tel. 227-6766). Curtain time is at 7:30pm on Tuesday, Wednesday, and Thursday, and 8pm on Friday and Saturday. Prices range from $3.50 to $9, depending on the event. The repertoire includes *Snow White, The Magic Flute,* and *Peter Pan.*

Rehoboth Beach has two summertime Boardwalk family amusement areas: **Funland,** situated off Delaware Avenue, with rides and games (opens at 1pm daily); and **Playland,** off Wilmington Avenue, which features video games for all ages (open from 10am to midnight). About 1½ miles north of town there is also **Sports Complex,** Rte. 1 and Country Club Road (tel. 227-8121). This is a family fun park with go-kart tracks, miniature golf, a water slide, bumper boats, kiddie canoes, and other outdoor rides. Open weekends April through May and September, and daily from Memorial Day to Labor Day.

Just in case it rains, you can take the children to **Bad Beach Day Matinees** at the Midway Palace Multi-Theatre, Midway Shopping Centre, Rte. 1 (tel. 645-0200). On wet days, this complex offers family-oriented movies at 1pm.

WHERE TO STAY

Most of the accommodations in Rehoboth and Dewey are moderate, although in July and August it is hard to find any room (single or double occupancy) near the beach for under $100 a night. If you must be by the water, be ready to pay top dollar, or better yet, try traveling here in May, June, September, or October. And if you must come in the summer, be prepared to accept lodgings on side streets without views of the water and with compulsory minimum stays. In any case, reservations are always necessary in the summer and strongly recommended at other times.

REHOBOTH BEACH

Expensive

ATLANTIC SANDS HOTEL, Boardwalk at Baltimore Ave., Rehoboth Beach, DE 19971. Tel. 302/227-2511 or toll-free 800/422-0600. Fax 302/227-9476. 114 rms. A/C TV TEL
$ Rates: $55–$200 single or double. AE, CB, DC, MC, V. **Parking:** Free.
Rehoboth's largest lodging facility is this recently expanded five-story inn, the only oceanfront property in town with an outdoor pool. The doubles rate depends on the time of year and whether a room is "oceanfront" or "ocean view." At certain periods, a 4-night minimum applies. Facilities include a restaurant, rooftop sun deck, lounge, and parking. Open year round.

BRIGHTON SUITES HOTEL, 34 Wilmington Ave., Rehoboth Beach, DE 19971. Tel. 302/227-5780 or toll-free 800/227-5788. Fax 302/227-6815. 66 suites. A/C TV TEL
$ Rates: $59–$169 suite. AE, DISC, MC, V. **Parking:** Free.
For families or two couples traveling together, the best bet is this hotel, a short walk from the beach in a mostly residential area. The sandy pink four-story property is an all-suite hotel; each unit has a bedroom with a king-size bed,

large bathroom, and a separate living room with sleep-sofa. The equipment includes a wet bar, refrigerator, a safe, and a hairdryer. The decor is bright, with lots of light woods and pastel tones. There is a 3-night minimum for holidays and summer weekends. Rooms for nonsmokers and the disabled are available, and there is a heated indoor pool.

HENLOPEN HOTEL, Lake Ave. and the Boardwalk, P.O. Box 16, Rehoboth Beach, DE 19971. Tel. 302/227-2551 and toll-free 800/441-8450. Fax 302/227-8147. 92 rms. A/C TV TEL
$ Rates: Summer $130–$170 single or double; off-season $55–$100 single or double. AE, CB, DC, MC, V. **Parking:** Free.

At the north end of the boardwalk is this top-rated beachfront hotel with a tradition dating back to 1879 when the first Henlopen Hotel was built on this site. The present modern structure has 12 oceanfront rooms and 80 with ocean views, each with its own balcony. There are 2-night minimums for all weekend bookings and 3-night minimums for holiday weekend reservations.

Dining and entertainment facilities include a rooftop restaurant and lounge, the Horizon Room.

Moderate

ADMIRAL MOTEL, 2 Baltimore Ave., Rehoboth Beach, DE 19971. Tel. 302/227-2103 or toll-free 800/428-2424. 66 rms. A/C TV TEL
$ Rates: $45–$110 single or double. AE, MC, V. **Parking:** Free.
In the heart of the beach district, this modern five-story motel has its own outdoor rooftop swimming pool. All rooms have double or king-size beds, partial ocean views, and in-room coffee equipment; most rooms have a private balcony. There are 3-night minimums in the summer and supplementary charges for some peak or holiday weekends.

OCEANUS MOTEL, 6 Second St., P.O. Box 324, Rehoboth Beach, DE 19971. Tel. 302/227-9436 or toll-free 800/852-5011. 38 rms. A/C TV TEL
$ Rates (including continental breakfast): $36–$96 double. AE, MC, V. **Parking:** Free. **Closed:** Mid-Oct to late Mar.
Located 2 blocks from the beach and just off Rehoboth Avenue, in a quiet neighborhood, is this L-shaped, three-story motel. Each room is outfitted with rattan furniture and a refrigerator; some rooms have balconies. Guest facilities include an outdoor swimming pool and free morning coffee. At certain times weekend supplements of $10 to $20 a night prevail.

SANDCASTLE MOTEL, 61 Rehoboth Ave., Rehoboth Beach, DE 19971. Tel. 302/227-0400 or toll-free 800/372-2112. 60 rms. A/C TV TEL
$ Rates: $40–$105 single or double. AE, MC, V. **Parking:** Free.
Two blocks from the beach and right off the main thoroughfare is this handsome five-story motel. Each of the fully carpeted and designer-furnished rooms has a private balcony and a refrigerator. Facilities include an enclosed parking garage, an elevated sun deck, and an indoor/outdoor swimming pool with lifeguard. Minimum stays apply during peak season. Open all year.

DEWEY BEACH

Expensive/Moderate

ATLANTIC OCEANSIDE, 1700 Hwy. 1, Dewey Beach, DE 19971. Tel. 302/227-8811. 60 rms. A/C TV TEL
$ Rates: $35–$95 single or double. AE, MC, V. **Parking:** Free. **Closed:** Nov–Apr
This modern three-story structure is set on the main north-south beach highway and enjoys equal distance from the bay and the ocean (both about 1 block away). There is a weekend surcharge in effect at certain periods and a 3-night minimum required for

summer weekends. Complimentary coffee is provided to guests. Facilities include an outdoor heated pool and sun deck. Rooms have coffeemakers, microwaves, and refrigerators.

BAY RESORT, Bellevue St., P.O. Box 461, Dewey Beach, DE 19971. Tel. 302/227-6400 or toll-free 800/922-9240. 68 rms. A/C TV TEL
$ **Rates** (including continental breakfast): $40–$115 single or double. AE, MC, V. **Parking:** Free. **Closed:** Mid-Oct–Apr.

The ideal place from which to watch the sun go down on Rehoboth Bay is at this motel and efficiency complex, located on a strip of land between the bay and the ocean. Each room has designer-decorated furnishings, a balcony, and extra-length double or king-size beds. All guest rooms face either the pool or the bay, with slightly higher charges for the latter and for efficiency units with kitchenettes. Facilities include an outdoor pool, a water sports center, a private beach, and a 250-foot pier on the bay. Depending on the time of year, there can also be a weekend surcharge of $15 to $25 per night and a 3-night minimum on holidays.

BEST WESTERN GOLD LEAF RESORT, 1400 Rte. 1, Dewey Beach, DE 19971. Tel. 302/226-1100 or toll-free 800/422-8566 or 800/528-1234. Fax 302/226-9785. 76 rms. A/C TV TEL
$ **Rates:** $45–$124 single or double. AE, CB, DC, DISC, MC, V. **Parking:** Free.

One of the newest properties in the area is this cleverly constructed hotel, located 1 block from both the beach and the bay. The property offers bright contemporary rooms with balconies and a view of the bay or ocean or both. Rooms are also equipped with a refrigerator and a safe. The complex includes an elevator and four levels of enclosed parking, topped by a rooftop swimming pool and sun deck. There is a weekend surcharge and 2- and 3-night minimums in the summer. Rooms for nonsmokers and the disabled are also available. Complimentary coffee is provided for guests in the lobby. Open year round, with reduced-rate packages November through March.

WHERE TO DINE

Since many motels do not have restaurants, here are some of the leading venues for a morning meal: **Dinner Bell Inn** (8am to 11am); **Royal Treat** (8am to 11:30am); **Café on the Green** (8am to noon or 2pm); the **Lamp Post** (8am to 11am). For addresses and telephone numbers, see below.

REHOBOTH BEACH
Expensive

BACK PORCH CAFE, 59 Rehoboth Ave. Tel. 227-3674.
Cuisine: INTERNATIONAL. **Reservations:** Recommended on weekends.
$ **Prices:** Appetizers $4–$7; main courses $17–$25; lunch $5–$10. MC, V.
Open: Apr–Oct daily lunch 11am–3pm; dinner 6–11pm.
A Key West atmosphere prevails at this restaurant. The decor is a mix of indoor alcoves with three outdoor decks, all furnished with an eclectic collection of plants, stained glass, and handmade tables. Lunch items include various omelets, basil ratatouille, and sampler plates. Dinner entrées range from tenderloin of beef with gorgonzola butter and filet mignon of veal to roast swordfish.

CHEZ LA MER, 210 Second St. Tel. 227-6494.
Cuisine: FRENCH. **Reservations:** Required.
$ **Prices:** Appetizers $5–$10; main courses $15–$25. AE, CB, DC, MC, V.
Closed: Jan to mid-Apr.
Open: Apr–Oct dinner Mon–Thurs 5:30–10pm, Fri–Sat 5:30–10:30pm; and Nov–Dec weekends only, 5–10pm.

Although this area is full of good restaurants, Chez la Mer is the only one with French country-inn decor, cuisine, and service; it's no wonder that the three intimate little dining rooms fill up quickly. Specialties include veal sweetbreads, soft-shell crabs, and a spicy bouillabaisse (available every night for a minimum of two persons). All dishes are cooked to order, and special diets, such as low sodium, can be accommodated. Proper attire is a must.

CLUB POTPOURRI, 316 Rehoboth Ave. Tel. 227-4227.
   Cuisine: INTERNATIONAL. **Reservations:** Recommended.
   $ Prices: Appetizers $3.50–$7.50; main courses $12–$22. AE, DC, MC, V.
   Open: Dinner Mon–Thurs 5–11pm, Fri–Sat 5pm–midnight.
A classy café ambience prevails at this restaurant, a mecca for fans of live jazz as well as good food. The decor blends brass, globe lanterns, skylights, mirrored walls, and lots of garden plants. The dinner menu ranges from coquilles St-Jacques and lobster francese and cioppino to steak Diane. Early-bird specials are featured from 5 to 7pm in the summer.

SEA HORSE, Rehoboth Ave. and State Rd. Tel. 227-7451.
   Cuisine: INTERNATIONAL. **Reservations:** Recommended.
   $ Prices: Appetizers $3.95–$7.95; main courses $9.95–$23.95; lunch $4.95–$12.95. AE, CB, DC, MC, V.
   Open: Mon–Thurs 11:30am–10pm, Fri–Sat 11:30am–11pm.
For straightforward quality food and hefty portions, it's hard to beat the Sea Horse. The plush and welcoming dining room is filled with sturdy captain's chairs, copper lanterns, a huge stone fireplace, mirrored panels and historical prints. Lunch ranges from burgers to crab imperial. Dinner offers a wide selection of beef (from prime ribs to chateaubriand) and seafood (monkfish, salmon, flounder, rock lobster tails). There is a huge guest parking lot.

Moderate

CAFE ON THE GREEN, 247 Rehoboth Ave. Tel. 227-0789.
   Cuisine: INTERNATIONAL. **Reservations:** Recommended.
   $ Prices: Appetizers $2.75–$7.50; main courses $11.95–$20.95; lunch $2.95–$8.95. AE, MC, V.
   Open: Daily noon–5pm for lunch and 5–10pm for dinner. **Closed:** Tues–Wed in winter.
For more than 20 years, visitors have enjoyed the garden ambience at this cottage-style restaurant. Lunch fare ranges from seafood platters to croissant sandwiches, quiche, burgers, and salads. Specialties for dinner range from prime rib and chicken Oscar to crab cakes, seafood au gratin, and surf-n-turf.

DINNER BELL INN, 2 Christian St. Tel. 227-2561.
   Cuisine: SEAFOOD. **Reservations:** Recommended.
   $ Prices: Appetizers $3–$5; main courses $7.95–$18.95; lunch $2.95–$7.95. AE, CB, DC, DISC, MC, V.
   Open: Lunch Mon–Fri noon–2pm; dinner Mon–Fri 5:30–9:30pm, Fri–Sat 5–10pm. **Closed:** Oct–Mar, weekdays in Apr.
It's hard to find a restaurant offering better value than this one, an area landmark that celebrated its 50th anniversary in 1988. Surrounded by flowering gardens, the restaurant is furnished in a patio-style theme, with white latticework, wrought iron, rattan, and Polynesian-style chairs. The star value here is dinner—each evening brings a wide choice of meat dishes, including Delaware panned chicken, Virginia baked ham, and prime rib cut to order, as well as a dozen fresh seafood selections, from scallops to swordfish. For the indecisive, you can't beat the Captain's Plate (shrimp and crab au gratin, crab imperial, and seafood Newburg) or the Neptune Platter (broiled fish, lobster tail, clams, steamed shrimp, and king crab legs).

LAMP POST, Rtes. 1 and 24. Tel. 645-9132.
   Cuisine: INTERNATIONAL. **Reservations:** Not accepted.
   $ Prices: Appetizers $3.50–$8.50; main courses $10–$19.95; lunch $3.95–$8.95. MC, V.
   Open: Sun–Thurs noon–9pm, Fri–Sat noon–10pm.

Ⓢ   Three miles north of town is the Lamp Post, a convenient restaurant if you are in transit along the beach coast or staying in one of the motels on the highway. Founded in 1953 by award-winning restaurateur Ruth Steele, this friendly spot has been expanded by three generations of the Steele family. Tables are handcrafted from authentic hatch-cover tops from the Liberty ships of World War II. Entrées include such dishes as broiled flounder, mussels marinara, grilled beef liver, steak en sauce, and "delmarvelous" fried chicken. Other choices include prime rib, surf-n-turf, veal and crab, and scallops au gratin. There is live entertainment on weekends.

OBIE'S BY THE SEA, on the boardwalk at Olive Ave. Tel. 227-6261.
> **Cuisine:** AMERICAN. **Reservations:** Not required.
> **$ Prices:** Dinner and lunch $3.95–$14.95. AE, MC, V.
> **Open:** Daily 11:30am–1am. **Closed:** Oct–Apr.

You can't dine any closer to the ocean than at this restaurant. A casual seaside atmosphere prevails here, with an all-day menu of sandwiches, burgers, ribs, salads, and clam bakes (steamed clams, spiced shrimp, barbecued chicken, corn on the cob, and muffins). There is DJ music and dancing on weekends.

THE DELI, 50 Wilmington Ave. Tel. 226-2088.
> **Cuisine:** AMERICAN/SNACK. **Reservations:** Not required.
> **$ Prices:** Breakfast $1.50–$4.95; lunch $2.95–$9.95. No credit cards.
> **Open:** 8am–4pm, with extended hours in summer.

For something fast and light (a beach picnic perhaps), this New York–style delicatessen offers take-out and delivery services, as well as eat-in seating. Breakfast items range from pastries and muffins, and biscuits and bagels, to blintzes and knishes. All types of sandwiches, subs, salads, and cold platters are available throughout the day, with lots of fresh ingredients and gourmet touches.

Budget

ROYAL TREAT, 4 Wilmington Ave. Tel. 227-6277.
> **Cuisine:** AMERICAN. **Reservations:** Not accepted.
> **$ Prices:** Dinner and lunch $2–$5. No credit cards.
> **Open:** Lunch daily 8–11:30am, dinner daily 1–11:30pm.

For breakfast and refreshing snacks, try this little restaurant, a restored Rehoboth landmark, next to the Boardwalk, with an ice-cream-parlor ambience.

DEWEY BEACH

RUSTY RUDDER, Dickinson St. on the Bay. Tel. 227-3888.
> **Cuisine:** AMERICAN. **Reservations:** Not accepted.
> **$ Prices:** Appetizers $2.95–$7.95; main courses $9.95–$22.95; lunch $3.95–$7.95. MC, V.
> **Open:** Lunch 11:30am–5pm, dinner 4–11pm.

★   The gathering place for the young (and young at heart) at Dewey Beach is this trendy restaurant and entertainment spot right on the bay. Opened in 1979, the Rusty Rudder is a modern California-style eatery of indoor and outdoor dining rooms, open decks, and terraces. Success has also brought the recent development of the adjacent Ruddertowne, a beachside complex of galleries, shops, seafood carryouts, snackeries, and bars. Lunches range from salads and sandwiches to Cajun catfish and other fish specials. Dinner entrées, which allow for unlimited trips to the bountiful salad bar, include chicken parmesan, pan-fried backfin crab cakes, and prime rib. There is nightly entertainment with frequent big-name concerts on weekends. Early-bird dinners are served between 4 and 5pm.

WATERFRONT, McKinley St. on the Bay. Tel. 227-9292.
> **Cuisine:** AMERICAN. **Reservations:** Not accepted.

$ Prices: Appetizers $2.95–$6.95; main courses $10.95–$21.95; lunch $2.95–$6.95. AE, MC, V.
Open: Daily noon–9pm. **Closed:** Oct–Apr.

Bayside sunsets and charcoal-grilled meats and seafood are the main draws at this restaurant, which boasts an open deck, a gazebo, and wide-windowed dining rooms overlooking the water. The restaurant is known for its outdoor open-pit barbecue cooking, and at lunch the menu offers barbecue shrimp and burgers, plus soups, salads, and sandwiches. Dinner entrées include barbecued ribs, chicken, swordfish, steaks, and shish kebabs, as well as 1-pound lobsters and a variety of other steamed, baked, and broiled seafood.

SHOPPING

Rehoboth Beach is the home of **Ocean Outlets,** Rte. 1 (tel. 227-6860), a 40-unit factory outlet complex. Manufacturers represented include Aileen, American Tourister, Bass Shoe, Corning Revere, Fanny Farmer, Hanes, Harve Benard, Izod/Lacoste, Money, Oneida, Ship 'n Shore, Totes, and Van Heusen. There is also a food court and miniature golf range. Hours are Monday through Saturday, 10am to 9pm and Sunday 11am to 6pm.

---

3. BETHANY BEACH & FENWICK ISLAND

60 miles SE of Dover, 100 miles SE of Wilmington,
23 miles S of Lewes, 130 miles SE of Washington, D.C.,
120 miles SE of Baltimore, 135 miles S of Philadelphia

GETTING THERE   By Air   The closest gateways for regularly scheduled flights from all parts of the United States are **Philadelphia International Airport** (see Chapter 4, "Philadelphia") and **Baltimore International Airport** (see Chapter 15, "Baltimore"). For commuter flights, the nearest gateways are Ocean City and Salisbury, Md. (see Chapter 17, "Maryland's Eastern Shore").

By Train   There is daily service from all parts of the United States via **Amtrak** into Wilmington (see Chapter 12, "Wilmington & Environs").

By Bus   **Carolina Trailways** provides regular pickup and drop-off service during the summer season at Harry's Bait and Tackle Shop, 201 Central Blvd., Bethany Beach (tel. 302/539-6244 or 539-7455).

By Car   From points north or south, take Rtes. 113 and 13 to Rte 1. From the west, take Rte. 50 to Ocean City and north on Ocean Hwy. to Fenwick Island.

By Ferry   See "Lewes," above.

ESSENTIALS   The **Bethany-Fenwick Area Chamber of Commerce,** P.O. Box 1450, Bethany Beach, DE 19930 (tel. 302/539-2100 or toll-free 800/962-7873), is situated on Rte. 1, otherwise known as Ocean Hwy., adjacent to the Fenwick Island State Park at the Fenwick line. The office is designed like a beach house, with wide windows overlooking the ocean and snow-white sands. The Chamber publishes a very helpful booklet called *The Quiet Resorts,* and also stocks brochures from leading motels, restaurants, and other visitor services. Hours are June through September from 9am to 5pm Monday through Friday, and from 10am to 2pm on Saturday, Sunday, and holidays; October through May from 10am to 4pm Monday through Friday.

Getting Around   Since Bethany Beach and Fenwick Island are within 5 miles of each other, the predominant mode of transport is car. Most visitors bring their own vehicles or rent cars from nearby Ocean City, in Maryland, or Dover and Wilmington. Like Rehoboth, many Bethany and Fenwick streets are subject to meter or permit parking and the rules are strictly enforced. Fortunately, all the motels provide free parking for guests and most of the restaurants also have access to plentiful parking for customers.

SPECIAL EVENTS   The Bethany area's major happening is the **Boardwalk Arts Festival.** Held on the third or fourth Saturday in August, this show attracts craftspeople, artisans, and spectators from near and far, taking up the entire length of the boardwalk. This is a juried show of original creations in wood carving, photography, handmade jewelry, batik, metal sculpture, calligraphy, oil and watercolor painting, toys, dolls, and painted porcelain. Hours are 9am to 5pm; a full program is available in advance from the Bethany-Fenwick Area Chamber of Commerce.

Bethany Beach and Fenwick Island form a thin and mostly fingerlike stretch of land between the Delaware Seashore State Park and the Maryland border. This southernmost tip of Delaware is fittingly referred to as the "land of the quiet resorts."

With the Atlantic Ocean on its eastern shore and various stretches of inland waters (from the Indian River Bay to the Little Assawoman Bay) to the west, these quiet resorts are relatively undeveloped, compared with the side-by-side condos, towering hotels, and bustling nightclubs of nearby Ocean City, Md.

Like Rehoboth, Bethany was named after a biblical place (Bethany was the home of Lazarus). Also like Rehoboth, Bethany Beach got its start when it was chosen as a site for 19th-century gatherings of a religious group (the Christian Church Conference).

Of more recent origin, Fenwick, 1 mile north of the Maryland-Delaware border, is actually divided into two distinct areas. The southern section is unincorporated and county-zoned (multifamily dwellings, such as motels, are allowed) and the northern section is an incorporated town with building codes that call primarily for single-family residences.

Both Bethany and Fenwick pride themselves on being quiet family-style resorts. These communities are still very residential, with strict control on the height and size of any new buildings. You won't find any large resort hotels, sophisticated tourist attractions, or entertainment complexes here. With almost everything geared to a tranquil atmosphere and a low-key pace, Bethany and Fenwick are unique finds, almost undiscovered by the average east coast beach traveler.

WHAT TO SEE & DO

✪ The 1-mile-long **Bethany Beach Boardwalk,** relatively free of commercial enterprises, is an attraction in itself for those who enjoy a quiet beachside walk and unobstructed views of the wide-open strand. The locals also claim that this is the only boardwalk where you can actually sit safely beneath it. The boardwalk is the focal point of the town and most of the shops and fast-food eateries are located on Garfield Parkway, the street that runs perpendicular to the center of the boardwalk.

Fenwick, while lacking a boardwalk, has a wide-open beach with gentle dunes. There are no concessions or fast-food outlets along the shoreline, only private homes and rental properties. Most of the shops and business enterprises are concentrated 1 block inland along Rte. 1, also known as the Coastal Hwy.

✪ Chief among the sights here is the **Fenwick Island Lighthouse** on the Transpeninsular Line, Rte. 54, about ¼ mile west of Rte. 1. Built in 1859, this is one of the Delaware shore's oldest landmarks still in operation today, with beams that can be seen for 15 miles.

On the south side of the lighthouse you'll see the **First Stone of the Transpeninsular Line,** between Rte. 1 and Rte. 54, literally on the Delaware-Maryland border. This stone monument, erected on April 26, 1751, marks the eastern end of the Transpeninsular Line surveyed in 1750–51 by John Watson and William

Parsons of Pennsylvania and John Emory and Thomas Jones of Maryland. This line established the east-west boundary between Pennsylvania's "Three Lower Counties" (now Delaware) and the Colony of Maryland. The Transpeninsular Line served as the earliest foundation upon which the Mason-Dixon line of 1764–67 was based.

INLAND EXCURSIONS

The end of the Delaware shoreline at Fenwick Island is by no means the end of the attractions in the region. There is much to explore inland.

Millsboro, 13 miles from the Atlantic coast and at the headwaters of the Indian River, is the home of **Carey's Camp Meeting Ground,** Rte. 24, one of the state's original camp meeting grounds, established by the Methodists in 1888. Listed on the National Register of Historic Places, it is still an active meeting site for families who return each summer. The open-frame tabernacle is surrounded by 47 open-front cottages called "tents."

This area also has great links with the Nanticoke Indian tribe, whose ancestors were among the first residents of Delaware. Five miles east of Millsboro, on the banks of the Indian River, is the Nanticoke Indian Museum (Oak Orchard, at the intersection of Rte. 24 and Rte. 5, tel. 945-7022). Ensconced in a former Indian schoolhouse, it contains artifacts and various historical displays. In addition, the life-style of the Nanticokes is celebrated each September when a Pow Wow is held. Remaining members of the tribe, about 500 in number, convene for two days of ceremonial dancing, story telling, crafts, and food. The public is also welcome.

The largest city in Sussex County is Seaford, about 20 miles west of Millsboro. Established in 1726 on land settled by Thomas Hooper and his family, it was primarily a farming community until the arrival of the Delaware Railroad in 1856, an extension of service from Wilmington. Seaford soon became the main railhead for the entire eastern shore and the shipping point for seafood and produce bound for Philadelphia and New York. Seaford's role as the commercial hub was further enhanced in 1939 when the local du Pont company produced the first strands of the synthetic fiber nylon. In the years since, Seaford has become the "nylon capital of the world," as well as the county's largest business and commercial district.

SPORTS & ACTIVITIES

Ideal for swimming and sunning, **Bethany Beach** is a free public facility for all to enjoy. **Bethany Beach Rentals,** 201 Central Ave. (tel. 539-6244 or 539-2224), operates a rental concession on the beach, offering 8-foot umbrellas, surf mats, and boogie boards for $5 a day and highback or lounge chairs for $2 a day.

In addition, **Resort Rentals,** 5th St. and Pennsylvania Ave., Bethany Beach (tel. 537-1522) and at York Beach Mall (tel. 539-6679), 1 mile south of Sea Colony, specializes in combination rentals (such as a large umbrella and two sand chairs for $20 a week).

Harry's Bait and Tackle Shop, 201 Central Blvd. and Pennsylvania Ave., Bethany Beach (tel. 539-6244), also has a full line of beach accessories, as well as fishing and crabbing supplies, plus a fleet of bicycles, from $2.50 an hour and up or $7 per day. (This shop is also the **Carolina Trailways Bus Depot** for the area.)

✪ A paradise for water-sports enthusiasts is **Fenwick Island State Park,** Rte. 1. (tel. 539-9060), just south of Bethany Beach. With the Atlantic on one side and Little Assawoman Bay on the other, this park has 3 miles of seacoast beaches and dunes as well as 344 acres of parkland and open bayfront, ideal for fishing, crabbing, and boating. The facilities include a boardwalk with picnic tables, gift shop, and refreshments; shower and changing rooms; a first-aid room; and lifeguards. Surfing is permitted and access is allowed for four-wheel-drive vehicles. In addition, bird-watchers will find rare seabirds, such as tern, piping plover, and black skimmer, nesting in protected areas. Admission is $4 for out-of-state cars and $2 for Delaware cars.

Adjacent to the park on the bayside is **Sailing Inc.,** Rte. 1, Fenwick Island (tel.

539-7999), a source for rental of sailboards and sunfish from $35 and up an hour; and catamarans in three sizes, from $35 to $40 an hour. Sailing lessons are also available from $20 and up for an hour. Jet skis and wave runners are also available.

COOL FOR KIDS

The **Fenwick Island Boardwalk,** Rtes. 1 and 54, Fenwick Island (tel. 539-8129), is an inland amusement park across the street from the Fenwick Island Lighthouse. This summertime attraction features a water slide, miniature golf, and go-cart rides.

WHERE TO STAY

Like other Delaware coastal resorts, Bethany Beach and Fenwick Island depend on the summer season when the beaches are at their best. Rooms are not only booked out months in advance for July and August, but they are also more expensive, often with weekend surcharges and 2- or 3-night minimums. Motels that would otherwise be in a moderate or budget category at other times will run between $70 and $100 for a double. If you'd like to keep the costs reasonable, come during midweek or consider a visit in May, June, September, or October when the weather can be almost as warm.

BETHANY BEACH

Expensive

SEA COLONY, Middlesex, Drawer L, Bethany Beach, DE 19930. Tel. 302/539-6961 or toll-free 800/732-2656. 500 apartments. A/C TV TEL
$ Rates: $140–$250 for a weekend; $575–$1,250 per week, per apartment. No credit cards. **Parking:** Free.
This condominium resort comprises 10 different buildings, many as high as 14 stories. It is the only high-rise residential property in the area, built before current restrictions were put into effect. Although most of the units are for sale, a limited number are available for short-term rentals. Accommodations (with a choice of one to four bedrooms) range from oceanfront apartments to secluded town house villas in garden, seaside, or tennis community settings. Each unit is equipped with a dishwasher, washer/dryer, self-cleaning oven, refrigerator, disposal, and modern furnishings; some also have a private deck or patio and a hot tub. Guest amenities include a half mile of beachfront, 37 acres of gardens and greenery, seven swimming pools, a sauna and health club, and 21 tennis courts.

Moderate

BETHANY ARMS MOTEL AND APTS., Atlantic Ave. and Hollywood St., P.O. Box 1600, Bethany Beach, DE 19930. Tel. 302/539-9603. 52 rms. A/C TV TEL
$ Rates: $45–$85 double; $60–$130 apartment. MC, V. **Parking:** Free. **Closed:** Late Oct to early Mar.
This modern five-building complex offers a choice of basic motel units with two double beds and a refrigerator, or efficiencies (many with oceanfront views) with fully equipped kitchens, and double or queen-size beds. Two buildings are right on the boardwalk and the other three are situated just behind the first two, between the boardwalk and Atlantic Avenue; all are two or three stories high. A 2-night minimum is in effect on summer weekends; holiday periods (such as Memorial Day and Labor Day weekends) often have 3-night minimums and some surcharges.

HARBOR VIEW MOTEL, Rte. 1, R.D. 1, Box 102, Bethany Beach, DE 19930. Tel. 302/539-0500. Fax 302/539-5170. 60 rms. A/C TV TEL
$ Rates (including continental breakfast): $40–$90 single or double; $50–$110 efficiencies. AE, DC, DISC, MC, V. **Parking:** Free. **Closed:** Jan–Feb.

Located 2 miles north of Bethany Beach, this motel is on the bay side, but has views of both the bay and ocean. The modern two-story building offers both rooms and efficiencies; some are equipped with an individual Jacuzzi, and all have balconies. There are weekend surcharges and 3-day minimums in season. Guest facilities include an outdoor swimming pool, a sun deck on the bay, and a launderette.

FENWICK ISLAND
Moderate

FENWICK ISLANDER, Rte. 1 and South Carolina Ave., Fenwick Island, DE 19944. Tel. 302/539-2333 and toll-free 800/346-4520. 63 rms. A/C TV TEL
$ Rates: $30–$105 single or double. AE, DISC, MC, V. **Parking:** Free. **Closed:** Nov–Mar.

On the bay side of the highway is this bright and modern three-story efficiency motel. The fully carpeted rooms are pleasantly furnished in pastels and are equipped with a refrigerator and kitchenette facilities; second- and third-floor rooms have balconies. Guest amenities include an outdoor swimming pool and a launderette. Weekend and holiday rates are subject to surcharges.

SEA CHARM, Oceanfront and Lighthouse Rd., Fenwick Island, DE 19944. Tel. 302/539-9613. 19 rms. A/C TV
$ Rates: $50–$80 double; $60–$130 apartment. MC, V. **Parking:** Free. **Closed:** Nov–mid-May.

The only accommodations you'll find right on the beach in Fenwick are at this vintage three-story house with wraparound porches on two levels. Fully renovated and converted, this family-run inn offers a choice of motel rooms, oceanfront efficiencies, and one- to three-bedroom oceanview apartments. A 3-night minimum reservation is required throughout the season, and some surcharges apply on weekends. Facilities for guests include balconies with some rooms and the use of an outdoor swimming pool and a ground-level patio/deck with picnic furniture and outdoor grills.

SEASIDE SAILS DAYS INN, Ocean Hwy. (Rte. 1), Fenwick Island, DE 19944. Tel. 302/537-1900 or toll-free 800/542-4444. 58 rms. A/C TV TEL
$ Rates: $59–$139 single or double. AE, CB, DC, MC, V. **Parking:** Free. **Closed:** Early Sept–Mar.

The newest property on this strip is located on the ocean side of the main road. The three-story exterior is beach white and boxy, but each of the bedrooms offers a restful decor of contemporary blue sea tones, along with a balcony (third-floor rooms have ocean views); most units have extra sleeper sofas, and 40 have small kitchenettes. Guest facilities include a small courtyard swimming pool and parking.

SANDS MOTEL, Rte. 1. (Ocean Hwy.), Fenwick Island, DE 19944. Tel. 302/539-7745 or 302/539-8200; from Dec–Mar 301/289-2152. 18 rms. A/C TV TEL
$ Rates: $30–$70 single or double; $40–$95 apartment and efficiency. AE, CB, DC, DISC, MC, V. **Parking:** Free. **Closed:** Nov–Mar.

Situated on the ocean side of the highway but not directly on the oceanfront is this modern building offering a choice of doubles, efficiencies, and apartments. Some rooms on the second floor have views of the bay or ocean. Facilities include a large kidney-shaped pool and easy access to the beach. Rates are subject to a 3-day minimum stay in season, holidays, and weekends; surcharges also apply for certain weekend bookings.

WHERE TO DINE

The restaurants of the Bethany Beach and Fenwick Island area provide a pleasant blend of waterside and inland dining, all at fairly moderate prices. Because these two resorts are popular with families, there are also some fine lower-priced restaurants that offer a high level of quality, ambience, and creative cooking. Most restaurants serve liquor, unless otherwise noted. (*Note:* In Bethany, alcoholic beverages are available only in restaurants—there are no bars.)

Since most motels in Bethany and Fenwick do not serve breakfast, you can try some of the places below either for breakfast—for example, Libby's and Warren Station—or for early lunch.

HOLIDAY HOUSE SEAFOOD RESTAURANT, Garfield Pkwy. and the Boardwalk, Bethany Beach. Tel. 539-7298.
   Cuisine: SEAFOOD. **Reservations:** Recommended.
$ Prices: Appetizers $2.95–$6.95; main courses $8.95–$21.95; lunch $5–$10. AE, MC, V.
   Open: Lunch 11:30am–2pm; dinner 5–9pm.
For oceanfront dining, don't miss this pleasant restaurant. Light fare, sandwiches, and salads are available for lunch. The menu at dinner includes prime rib, Delaware fried chicken, and veal and pork dishes. But the emphasis is on seafood—from sautéed shrimp scampi and broiled scallops to local soft-shell crabs and broiled crab-stuffed flounder. On summer nights, a seafood smörgåsbord is featured.

MAGNOLIA'S RESTAURANT, Cedar Neck Rd., Ocean View. Tel. 539-5671.
   Cuisine: SOUTHERN. **Reservations:** Recommended for dinner.
$ Prices: Appetizers $3.95–$6.95; main courses $11.95–$21.95, lunch $2.95–$10.95. AE, MC, V.
   Open: Daily 11am–11pm.
A Carolina-style cuisine and decor is the main feature of this restaurant. There are no great sea views or wide windows here, but there is an elegant decor of lace curtains and tablecloths, light woods, colored glass, and lots of leafy plants and flowers. The dinner menu is a medley of dishes influenced by the old South—from baked Dixie chicken and scallops Savannah to Cajun-style stuffed flounder and seafood Norfolk. A light menu of "fun foods" is also available from 11am to midnight for lunch or snacks in an adjacent pub room, priced from $2.75 to $5.95.

PEPPERMILL RESTAURANT, Rte. 1, Bethany Beach. Tel. 539-4722.
   Cuisine: CONTINENTAL. **Reservations:** Recommended.
$ Prices: Appetizers $2.95–$6.95; main courses $10.95–$19.95; lunch $2.95–$8.95. AE, MC, V.
   Open: Lunch Mon–Sat 11am–3pm; dinner Mon–Thurs 5–10pm, Fri–Sat 5–11pm; Sun brunch 10am–2pm.
South of Bethany is this small cottage-style restaurant. The cheery decor includes a fireplace, lantern lights, etched-glass globes, framed prints, and a giant working peppermill. Dinner entrées range from beef Wellington and French pepper steak to duckling in raspberry sauce and scallops in champagne. Featured is Seafood Peppermill, consisting of scallops, shrimp, crab, and flounder, sautéed in a light garlic and lemon sauce.

BETHANY BEACH
Moderate

HARBOR LIGHTS RESTAURANT, Rte. 1, Bethany Beach. Tel. 539-3061.
   Cuisine: SEAFOOD. **Reservations:** Not required.
$ Prices: Appetizers $1.95–$5.95; main courses $9.95–$19.95; lunch $2.95–$6.95. MC, V.
   Open: Mon–Fri 11am–9pm, Sat–Sun 11am–10pm. **Closed:** Nov–Mar.
North of central Bethany is this restaurant with ideal views of the bay, the ocean, and the adjacent sand dunes. There is a lively lounge on the lower level with entertainment most evenings from 10pm to 1am, and an upstairs restaurant with a contemporary and open decor featuring colorful kites and windsocks. Lunch features salads, sandwiches, and burgers. At dinner there is a wide choice of bay and seafood entrées,

including soft-shell crabs, swordfish, and flounder florentine. Meat dishes range from veal Oscar to steaks.

Budget

LIBBY'S, Ocean Hwy., Fenwick Island. Tel. 539-7379.
   Cuisine: AMERICAN. **Reservations:** Not accepted.
$ **Prices:** Appetizers $1.95–$3.95; main courses $6.95–$18.95; lunch $2.95–$7.95; breakfast $2.65–$5.95. MC, V.
   Open: Breakfast daily 7am–3pm; lunch daily 11:30am–3pm; dinner daily 3–10pm. **Closed:** Nov–Easter.

A favorite for all ages is this restaurant, known far and wide for its polka-dot facade and huge breakfasts. Choices include pancakes "with personality" (royal cherry, Georgia pecan, chocolate chip), old-fashioned buckwheat cakes, waffles, French toast, omelets, as well as low-calorie breakfasts. Lunch features a wide variety of overstuffed sandwiches, burgers, and salads. Dinner entrées come with trips to the salad bar and range from soft-shell crabs and shrimp to steaks and chicken "in the basket." Cocktails are served with meals. Since 1985, Libby's also operates a branch in the heart of Bethany Beach at 116 Garfield Pkwy. (tel. 539-4500).

WARREN STATION, Ocean Hwy. (Rte. 1), Fenwick Island. Tel. 539-7156.
   Cuisine: AMERICAN. **Reservations:** Not accepted.
$ **Prices:** Breakfast $2–$5; lunch $2–$6; appetizers $1.95–$3.95; main courses $5.95–$15.95. MC, V.
   Open: Mid May–early Sept lunch Sun–Thurs 11am–4pm; dinner Sun–Thurs 4–9pm, Fri–Sat 4–10pm. **Closed:** Oct–Apr.

For more than 20 years, wholesome cooking at reasonable prices has been the trademark of this homey and casual restaurant. Recently renovated to duplicate the look of the old Indian River Coast Guard Station, the decor features light woods, lots of windows, and bright blue canvas dividers. Sandwiches, burgers, soups, and salads are available for lunch. At dinner, turkey is the specialty of the house, roasted fresh daily and hand carved to order, priced from $9.50 and up for a complete dinner. Other entrées include "delmarvelous fried chicken," sugar-cured ham with raisin sauce, charbroiled T-bone steaks, crab cutlets, and flounder stuffed with crab imperial. Complete dinners—with appetizer or soup, salad, two vegetables, and beverage—range from $8 to $14. No alcohol is served.

FENWICK ISLAND

Expensive

HARPOON HANNA'S, Rte. 54 on the Bay, Fenwick Island. Tel. 539-3095.
   Cuisine: SEAFOOD. **Reservations:** Not accepted.
$ **Prices:** Appetizers $3.95–$8.95; main courses $9.95–$21.95; lunch $3.95–$7.95. AE, MC, V.
   Open: Lunch daily 11am–4pm; dinner 4–11pm.

Dining in Delaware with views of Maryland is all part of the experience at this restaurant located on Assawoman Bay near the border. The half dozen large and lively dining rooms have a nautical decor, with window tables offering views of the water, and live music, with dancing, nightly. Lunch ranges from salads to sandwiches and omelets (try the Harpoon Seafood Omelet, overflowing with shrimp, crab, mild Cheddar, tomatoes, and sautéed mushrooms). In the evening fresh fish lead the menu—from swordfish and sea trout to tuna and tilefish.

Moderate

COUNTRY CRAB, Rte. 54. Tel. 436-5022.
   Cuisine: SEAFOOD. **Reservations:** Not accepted.

$ Prices: Appetizers $1.95–$4.95; main courses $9.95–$15.95; lunch $2.95–$7.95. AE, CB, DC, MC, V.

Open: Daily 10am–1am.

For a relaxed atmosphere, try this restaurant situated about 1 mile west of Rte 1. (Ocean Hwy.). Located in a rustic old building, the restaurant is on the bay, but don't come here for the views, as most tables don't face the water. The big draw is the freshly caught and simply prepared seafood.

Lunch items include crab cake or flounder sandwiches, steamed shrimp, and chowders. The dinner entrées focus on Chesapeake Bay and eastern shore seafoods, including Maryland soft- and hard-shell crabs, local flounder, clams, and oysters. Steaks, chops, calves' liver, and chicken are also available. All items on the main menus are also available for take-out orders. In the summer there is live country-music entertainment on weekend nights.

BALTIMORE

Midway between north and south, Baltimore, named after Lord Baltimore of Britain (1580?–1632), is a city proud of its heritage. Founded in 1729 and incorporated in 1797, this key port in the mid-Atlantic region of the United States has many claims to fame.

Birthplace of "The Star-Spangled Banner" and the famous Baltimore clipper ships, Baltimore was briefly the nation's capital; it was also the starting point for the first U.S. railroad and the site of the first railroad passenger and freight station. The first telegraph communication ("What hath God wrought") was beamed to Baltimore in 1844, and the nation's oldest cathedral is also here. Over the years, Baltimore has been home to a parade of personalities from Edgar Allan Poe and H. L. Mencken to Babe Ruth and the duchess of Windsor.

As a travel destination, Baltimore has been called the "Cinderella City" because of its rags-to-riches renewal. In the last 20 years, it has been artfully transformed from a scruffy city into a spiffy urban blend of futuristic skyscrapers, overhead walkways, cascading fountains, open-air plazas, and a bustling harborside recreational area. Best of all, this renaissance has paid proper homage to the gracious Federal homes and row houses, amiably blending the city's old-world charm with the new cosmopolitan ambience. So successful has Baltimore been in rejuvenating itself that tourism is now the city's third-largest industry, attracting more than 5 million visitors a year.

1. ORIENTATION

Situated on the Patapsco River off Chesapeake Bay, Baltimore today is a world-class seaport with 45 miles of waterfront, the third-largest in the United States, located 37 miles north of Washington and 96 miles south of Philadelphia. With a 79-mile square area, it is also Maryland's major urban center and a prime economic and manufacturing center, with a city population of 745,000 and a metropolitan-area population of 2,357,700.

ARRIVING

BY AIR

The **Baltimore–Washington International Airport**, Rte. 46 (tel. 859-7100), is 10 miles south of downtown Baltimore, off I-695 and the Baltimore-Washington Parkway (I-295). Each day, hundreds of flights from both domestic and international points land at this airport. Some useful local airline telephone numbers are:

WHAT'S SPECIAL ABOUT BALTIMORE

Ace Attractions
- ☐ Harborplace, the focal point of the Inner Harbor, with shops, boutiques, food markets, restaurants, music, and more.
- ☐ National Aquarium, a "must see" complex of sea creatures.
- ☐ U.S. frigate *Constellation*, dating back to 1787.
- ☐ Fort McHenry National Monument and Historic Shrine, birthplace of the "Star-Spangled Banner," now a national park.

Activities
- ☐ Sightseeing cruises around the waters of the Inner Harbor aboard the "patriot" boats *Lady Baltimore* and *Bay Lady*.
- ☐ Sailing on board *Clipper City*, the tallest ship licensed to carry passengers in the United States.

Events/Festivals
- ☐ Harbor Lights Music Festival, featuring top-name stars in concert beside the Inner Harbor.

- ☐ Preakness Celebration, the second jewel in thoroughbred racing's Triple Crown.

Museums/Galleries
- ☐ Maryland Science Center, with a hands-on exhibit of Baltimore and the Chesapeake Bay, plus a planetarium and IMAX theater.
- ☐ Walters Art Gallery, world-class repository of art spanning 5,000 years.
- ☐ Star-Spangled Banner Flag House and 1812 Museum.
- ☐ Babe Ruth Birthplace and Museum, also housing Maryland's Baseball Hall of Fame.

Shopping
- ☐ Harborplace, with over 135 shops.

American, tel. toll-free 800/433-7300; **Delta,** tel. 768-9000; **Continental,** tel. 337-2061; **Northwest Orient,** tel. toll-free 800/225-2525; **Pan Am,** tel. 685-2115; **TWA** tel. toll-free 800/221-2000; **United,** tel. 850-4557; and **USAir,** tel. 727-0825 or tel. toll-free 800/428-4322.

BY TRAIN

Baltimore is a stop on the main east coast corridor of Amtrak, between Wilmington and Washington, D.C. All trains arrive at and depart from Baltimore's **Pennsylvania Station,** 1525 N. Charles St. (tel. 539-2112), on the north side of the city. Recently restored to the tune of $3.5 million, this building is a beaux-arts gem and the sixth-busiest station in the Amtrak system.

BY BUS

Regular bus service is provided to and from Baltimore via **Greyhound/Trailways,** 210 W. Fayette St. (tel. 744-9311).

BY CAR

From the northeast and south, I-95 has access to downtown areas via I-695 and the **Baltimore-Washington Parkway** (I-295). From the north, exit 53 off I-95 South will lead straight into the center of town. Traffic from the west approaches downtown from I-70, I-695, and Rte. 40. Southbound access is via I-83. The newly completed Fort McHenry Tunnel (I-895) is the final connection of I-95 through Baltimore, running under the Patapsco River and providing easy access from the north to downtown Baltimore. Opened in November of 1985, this eight-lane structure is the widest tunnel in the world and one of the largest public works developments in history; the toll per car is $1.

Once you arrive, you'll find that many hotels provide indoor parking; otherwise, public metered lots and street parking are available throughout the city. Rates at the numerous commercial lots and garages average about $2 an hour. Most maps produced by the tourism office clearly indicate public parking places.

TOURIST INFORMATION

Once you are in town, there are several **visitor centers** open daily for on-the-spot inquiries. These locations include a ground-floor walk-in office at 300 W. Pratt St. (tel. 837-4636); a booth next to the Light Street Pavilion, Harborplace; a kiosk in the main lobby of the Pennsylvania Railroad Station, 1525 N. Charles St.; and booths at the Baltimore-Washington International Airport at Pier C (main entrance) and Pier D (international terminal). In addition to general sightseeing brochures, all offices distribute copies of the *Quick City Guide,* a comprehensive, magazine-style guide to what's happening in and around the city.

CITY LAYOUT

You'll hardly be in Baltimore an hour before you will be drawn to see the **Inner Harbor** at the city's southern edge. With its dazzling pavilions of boutiques, markets, and restaurants, and its modern museums, open-air concert decks, state-of-the-art convention center, and boats of all sizes, the Inner Harbor is a showplace of Baltimore at its best. Once a row of abandoned warehouses and factories, this vibrant waterfront is the epitome of successful urban restoration.

MAIN ARTERIES & STREETS

Although much emphasis is justifiably put on the Inner Harbor, there is a lot more to the city beyond this recreational development. The main downtown area radiates around the **Charles Center,** a 33-acre complex incorporating apartments, office buildings, hotels, shops, landscaped plazas, and a theater, all connected by an overhead walkway. Begun in 1956, this center is the cornerstone of Baltimore's downtown renaissance, and a model for urban-renewal projects. It is bounded by **Liberty, Saratoga, Lombard, and Charles Streets,** the latter of which divides Baltimore from east to west.

Also within this perimeter is **Baltimore Street,** which divides the city from north to south. Almost all downtown streets run only one way, although the important exceptions are **Howard and Eutaw Streets.** All of Baltimore's numbered streets run east and west.

NEIGHBORHOODS IN BRIEF

Toward the northern end of Charles Street is an area known as **Mount Vernon,** dominated by a 178-foot monument dedicated to George Washington. Laid out in 1827, Mount Vernon was once the city's most fashionable residential district, and it is still a delight, with its elegant town houses and four parklike squares. This is also the location of many of the city's oldest churches and cultural institutions including the **Peabody Conservatory of Music,** one of the leading music schools in the world, and the **Walters Art Gallery.**

To the east of the Inner Harbor is **Little Italy,** one of Baltimore's most colorful and self-contained ethnic neighborhoods and the location of about two dozen fine

Italian restaurants. Here you will also see some fine examples of neighborhood row houses, with their gleaming white marble front stoops, which the residents still scrub daily. In this section, as in many of the Baltimore ethnic neighborhoods, the practice of window-screen painting is still carried on by craftspeople. Passersby can't see in, but window sitters can see out.

Moving still more to the east is the **Fells Point** section, the old seaport where Baltimore originally started. Fells Point today is an old-world area with brick-lined streets and more than 350 original residential structures reflecting the architecture of the American Federal period.

MAPS

For maps, brochures, and useful pamphlets to help you plan and enjoy your trip, contact the **Baltimore Area Convention and Visitors Association,** One E. Pratt Street, Plaza Level, Baltimore, MD 21202 (tel. 301/659-7300 or toll-free 800/282-6632 in Maryland).

2. GETTING AROUND

BY PUBLIC TRANSPORTATION
SUBWAY

Baltimore's **Mass Transit Administration (MTA)** operates a subway system that connects the downtown area with many of the local suburbs. However, as we go to press, 27 miles of new above-ground rail lines are being laid. The extended rail service, known as the Central Light–Line Corridor, will connect the Baltimore-Washington International Airport to Baltimore's Pennsylvania Railroad Station, and it will also have stops near the new baseball stadium and within walking distance of the Inner Harbor. The new lines are a modern version of the old trolley cars, attached to overhead wires, with a total of 35 stops available. The minimum subway fare is $1.10; for more information, call 539-5000.

BUS

The MTA also operates a network of buses that connect all sections of the city. The base fare is $1.10 and exact change is necessary. For information and schedules, call 539-5000.

TROLLEY

One of the best ways to tour Baltimore is via the Baltimore Trolley, a motorized trolley-style bus that is a replica of Baltimore's original cabled vehicles. These colorful trolleys operate continuously in the heart of the city (north on Charles Street, south on Maryland/Cathedral/Howard Streets) and in an east-west direction along the Inner Harbor to Fells Point and Little Italy. The trolley ride, which is fully narrated, operates continuously, stopping at all major hotels and attractions. You can board at any point along the route, ride the complete circuit, board and reboard as many times as you wish for an inclusive 1-day price. The cost is $9 for adults and $4.50 for children 5–12; children under 5 free. Trolleys operate daily, year round, from 10am to 5:30pm. For full information, call 837-1234.

WATER TAXIS

For sightseeing in the Inner Harbor area, the ideal way to get around is via water taxi boats. This service provides a water link between Harborplace and to other area attractions, such as the National Aquarium, the Maryland Science Center, Pier 6 Concert Pavilion, Little Italy, and Fells Point. Taxis operate continuously from 11am to 11pm from May through August and from 11am to 9pm in April and September to October. The fare, $3.25 for adults and $2.25 for children under age 10, allows unlimited on/off use of the taxis for a 1-day period. Reservations are not necessary and you can board at any of the well-signposted stops along the Inner Harbor. For more information, contact **Harbor Boating,** Constellation Dock, Pier One (tel. 547-0090).

BY TAXI

All taxis in the city are metered; the three largest fleets are **Yellow Cab** (tel. 685-1212); **Sun Cab** (tel. 235-0300); and **Diamond Cab** (tel. 947-3333). For airport trips, call **BWI Airport Cab** (tel. 859-1100).

BY CAR

There are many car-rental firms with offices in downtown Baltimore and at Baltimore-Washington International Airport, including: **Avis,** 315 W. Baltimore St. (toll-free 800/331-1212) and at the airport (toll-free 800/331-1212); **Budget,** 10 S. Howard St. (tel. 659-0106) and at the airport (tel. 859-1224); **Dollar,** at the airport (tel. 859-8950); **Hertz,** 501 W. Lombard St. (tel. 332-0015) and at the airport (tel. 850-7400); and **National,** 300 W. Lombard St. (tel. 752-1127).

BY FOOT

Although Baltimore is an easy city to walk, the trek from downtown Charles Center to the Inner Harbor is made even easier by a new elevated pedestrian walkway called **Skywalk.** Following an indoor-outdoor path, the well-signposted route begins at Charles and Saratoga Streets and ends at Harborplace, connecting commercial buildings, shops, theaters, pedestrian plazas, the Baltimore Convention Center, restaurants, and hotels along its safe and traffic-free route.

 BALTIMORE

Area Code Baltimore's area code is 301.

Car Rentals See "Getting Around" in Chapter 2.

Climate See "When to Go" in the previous chapter.

Drugstores Look under "Pharmacies" in the *Yellow Pages.* Downtown branches of major chains include **Rite Aid** at Howard and Lexington Sts. (tel. 685-9682) and **Valu-Rite,** 816 Cathedral St. (tel. 837-2696).

Emergencies Dial 911 for fire, police, or ambulance.

Eyeglasses: Many national optical chains operate in the Baltimore area, including **Lens Crafters** and **Pearle Vision Center.** For exact locations, consult the *Yellow Pages.*

Hairdressers/Barbers Two downtown shops that welcome "walk-ins" are the **Hair Cuttery,** 1017 Light St. (tel. 539-9704) and **Hair Extraordinaire,** 225 E. Redwood St. (tel. 685-4782).

Hospitals The **Johns Hopkins Hospital,** 600 N. Wolfe St. (tel. 955-5000), and **Mercy Medical Center,** 301 St. Paul Place (tel. 332-9000).

Information See "Tourist Information" in this chapter.

Laundry/Dry Cleaning Most hotels provide same-day laundry services. Convenient local firms include **Apex 1-Hr. Cleaners,** 5 E. Redwood St. (tel. 752-5066), and **Martone Cleaners,** 415 N. Howard St. (tel. 752-0417).

Libraries Enoch Pratt Free Library is at 400 Cathedral St. (tel. 396-5500). There are more than 30 branches throughout the city.

Liquor Laws Restaurants, bars, hotels, and other places serving alcoholic beverages may be open from 6 to 2am except on Sunday and election days, when some opt to close. The minimum age for buying or consuming alcohol is 21.

Newspapers/Magazines   The major daily newspaper is the *Baltimore Sun*; the *Washington Post* is also widely read. The leading monthly local magazine is *Baltimore Magazine*.

Photographic Needs   Reliable downtown shops include Baltimore Photo Supply Co., 320 N. Charles St. (tel. 752-4475) for repairs; and Ritz Camera, 200 E. Pratt St. (tel. 685-0077) for 1-hour processing.

Police   See "Emergencies" above.

Post Office   The main post office is at 900 East Fayette St. (tel. 347-4425). Hours are 8:30am to 5pm.

Safety   As large cities go, Baltimore is generally safe. But there are precautions you should take whenever you are traveling in an unfamiliar city or country. Stay alert and be aware of your immediate surroundings. Wear a moneybelt and keep a close eye on your possessions. Be particularly careful with cameras, purses, and wallets—all favorite targets of thieves and pickpockets. Be especially careful when walking on dark streets and in parks after dark. Every society has its criminals. It's your responsibility to be aware and alert even in the most heavily touristed areas.

Taxes   The local sales tax is 5%. The local hotel tax is 7%.

Taxis   See "Getting Around" in this chapter.

Telegrams/Telex   **Western Union,** 17 Commerce St. (tel. 685-6020 or toll-free 800/227-5899).

Transit Information   Call Baltimore's Mass Transit Administration **(MTA)** at 539-5000.

3. BALTIMORE ACCOMMODATIONS

Ten years ago, Baltimore had only 1,500 low- to medium-grade hotel rooms. Thanks to the city's overall urban renewal, however, the current hotel picture has changed dramatically.

Modern new hotels have sprung up, especially around the Inner Harbor, and the grand older properties have been restored and renovated. There are now more than 5,300 hotel rooms, most of them first-class and deluxe. This means that it can be hard to find a double for under $100 during the week; happily, most hotels offer special weekend rates that represent savings of 35% to 50% off normal Sunday-through-Thursday tariffs. So don't be scared off by your first look at the room prices—try to time your visit for a weekend.

INNER HARBOR AREA

VERY EXPENSIVE

HARBOR COURT HOTEL, 550 Light St., Baltimore, MD 21202. Tel. 301/234-0550 or toll-free 800/824-0076. Fax 301/659-5925. 203 rms, 25 suites. A/C MINIBAR TV TEL

$ Rates: $175–$205 single, $190–$220 double; $145–$175 weekends, single or double; weekend suites $325–$1,750 and up. AE, CB, DC, MC, V. **Parking:** $9.50 self, $10.50 valet.

⭐ For the best location overlooking the water, treat yourself to a stay at this lovely, intimate property with old-world charm. Under the same management as the prestigious Hay-Adams in Washington, D.C., it was built for $80 million and it shows in the marble floors, crystal chandeliers, paneled walls, masterful artworks, and fine reproduction furniture. Over half the spacious guest rooms face the harbor and each is outfitted with period-style furnishings and designer fabrics.

Dining/Entertainment: The choices include the Café Brighton; a gourmet restaurant, Hampton's, for French/American cuisine; and Explorer's Club Lounge, a cozy enclave with piano music nightly.

Services: Full-time concierge, valet parking.

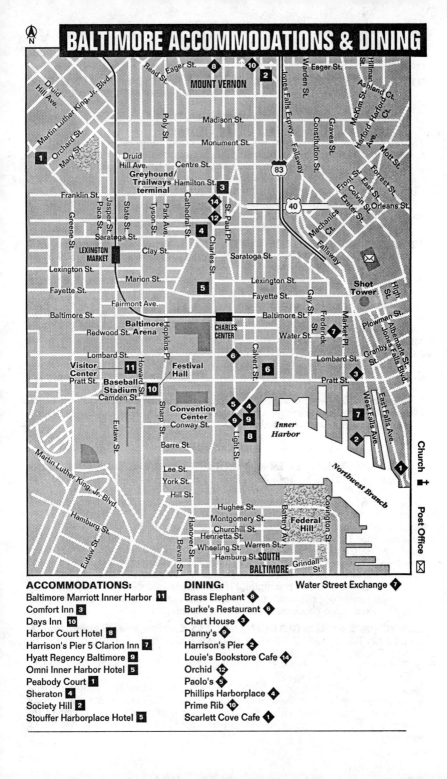

BALTIMORE ACCOMMODATIONS & DINING

ACCOMMODATIONS:
Baltimore Marriott Inner Harbor **11**
Comfort Inn **3**
Days Inn **10**
Harbor Court Hotel **8**
Harrison's Pier 5 Clarion Inn **7**
Hyatt Regency Baltimore **9**
Omni Inner Harbor Hotel **5**
Peabody Court **1**
Sheraton **4**
Society Hill **2**
Stouffer Harborplace Hotel **5**

DINING:
Brass Elephant **8**
Burke's Restaurant **6**
Chart House **3**
Danny's **9**
Harrison's Pier **2**
Louie's Bookstore Cafe **14**
Orchid **12**
Paolo's **5**
Phillips Harborplace **4**
Prime Rib **10**
Scarlett Cove Cafe **1**

Water Street Exchange **7**

Church **✝**

Post Office **⊠**

Facilities: Health club, swimming pool, whirlpool, saunas, exercise room, racquetball, squash, tennis, and croquet.

HYATT REGENCY BALTIMORE, 300 Light St., Baltimore, MD 21202. Tel. 301/528-1234 or toll-free 800/233-1234. Fax 301/685-3362. 490 rms. AC MINIBAR TV TEL

$ Rates: $160–$200 single, $180–$220 double; $119 weekend, single or double. AE, CB, DC, MC, V. **Parking:** $7 self, $10 valet.

This ultramodern hotel is right on the Inner Harbor, adjacent to the convention center. The mirrored glass exterior reflects the passing boats and the myriad activities of Harborplace. The bedrooms are contemporary, with light woods and pastel tones, and with emphasis on wide windows and dramatic views of the water or the city. Guests have direct access to the Convention Center.

Dining/Entertainment: Choices include the rooftop (15th-floor) restaurant/lounge, Berry and Elliot's; the Lobbibar; and Bistro 300.

Facilities: Outdoor pool, tennis courts, jogging track, health club.

STOUFFER HARBORPLACE HOTEL, 202 E. Pratt St., Baltimore, MD 21202. Tel. 301/547-1200 or toll-free 800/468-3571. Fax 301/539-5780. 622 rms. A/C MINIBAR TV TEL

$ Rates: $165–$215 single, $185–$235 double; $109–$129 weekend, single or double. AE, CB, DC, MC, V. **Parking:** $8 self, $11 valet.

With Harborplace at its doorstep, fine views are a draw at this hotel, one of the largest in the waterfront area. Opened in 1988, this $75-million property is part of the Gallery at Harborplace, a complex that includes an office tower, underground parking garage, and a glass-enclosed atrium of 75 shops and restaurants. Each guest room has a contemporary decor and king-size or two queen-size beds.

Dining/Entertainment: Windows, an all-day restaurant/lounge, offers expansive views of the Inner Harbor and fine food and beverages; there is also a Lobby Bar for cocktails.

Services: Concierge desk, valet service, complimentary coffee and newspaper, 24-hour room service, evening turn-down service.

Facilities: Indoor pool, health club, sauna, and whirlpool.

EXPENSIVE

BALTIMORE MARRIOTT INNER HARBOR, Pratt and Eutaw Sts., Baltimore, MD 21201. Tel. 301/962-0202 or toll-free 800/228-9290. Fax 301/962-8585. 525 rms, 26 suites. AC MINIBAR TV TEL

$ Rates: $175 single, $190 double, $250–$550 suites. $119–$195, single or double, $109 weekend, single or double. AE, CB, DC, MC, V. **Parking:** $7.

Equally convenient to the Charles Center and the Convention Center is this 10-story crescent-shaped tower that overlooks the city's historic Bromo-Seltzer Clock. The hotel was started as the Baltimore Plaza, a deluxe Howard Johnson, but was taken over by Marriott in 1986. The appealing lobby has a cascading waterfall and a serene decor of teal and cherry tones. The bedrooms are designed in restful shades.

Other facilities include a restaurant, Promenade, and a cocktail lounge, Illusions; a game room; an indoor swimming pool and a fitness center with saunas and whirlpool. There is also a video check-out and message system.

HARRISON'S PIER 5 CLARION INN, 711 Eastern Ave., Baltimore, MD 21202. Tel. 301/783-5553 or toll-free 800/CLARION. Fax 301/783-1787. 66 rms, 5 suites. A/C MINIBAR TV TEL

$ Rates: $89–$165 single, $117–$183 double, $250–$350 suite. AE, CB, DC, DISC, MC, V. **Parking:** $7.

With a facade reflecting the charm of a Chesapeake Bay lighthouse, this three-story hotel sits right on the water of the Inner Harbor. A nautical decor prevails inside also, with a 40-foot skipjack sailing ship in the center of the atrium-style lobby, and guest rooms named after historic Chesapeake Bay sailing vessels.

Each room has traditional Georgian mahogany furniture, designer fabrics, framed seafaring and wildfowl prints, and a spacious well-lit bathroom with phone and hairdryer. Some rooms have balconies and others have cathedral ceilings; suites have a Jacuzzi bath. Facilities include the Eastern Shore Restaurant (see "Baltimore Dining," below), Skipjack Bar, a patio deck, ice-cream parlor, shops, room service, and turndown service.

SHERATON, 300 S. Charles St., Baltimore, MD 21201. Tel. 301/962-8300 or toll-free 800/325-3535. Fax 301/962-8211. 339 rms. AC MINIBAR TV TEL

$ Rates: $147–$182 single, $162–$197 double; $109–$129 weekend, single or double. AE, CB, DC, MC, V. **Parking:** $9.

This hotel is close to Harborplace, the Convention Center, and the Skywalk route. Although the harbor views are an attraction, American art, with emphasis on works by Maryland artists, is the main focus of this hotel's decor. The modern rooms offer a choice of styles, with computer card access, light wood furnishings, and mirrored closets.

Dining/Entertainment: The main restaurant, McHenry's, is known for its Maryland seafood. There is also a lobby-level piano bar, and a nightclub called Impulse.

Facilities: Indoor pool, health club, sauna.

MODERATE

DAYS INN, 100 Hopkins Place, Baltimore, MD 21202. Tel. 301/576-1000 or toll-free 800/325-2525. Fax 301/576-1000, ext. 7124. 251 rms. A/C TV TEL

$ Rates: $64–$90 single, $74–$100 double. AE, CB, DC, MC, V. **Parking:** $4.50.

One of the best downtown bargains is this hotel, conveniently situated between the Arena and Convention Center. The nine-story hotel is built with a brick facade that conveys an old-world Baltimore charm. Amenities include an outdoor heated pool, a patio courtyard, and a full-service restaurant, Ashley's.

CHARLES STREET/MT. VERNON AREA

EXPENSIVE

OMNI INNER HARBOR HOTEL, 101 W. Fayette St., Baltimore, MD 21201. Tel. 301/752-1100 or toll-free 800/THE-OMNI. Fax 301/752-6832. 702 rms. A/C MINIBAR TV TEL

$ Rates: $119–$139 single, $135–$155 double. AE, CB, DC, MC, V. **Parking:** $7 self, $9 valet.

The largest hotel in Maryland, the Omni Inner Harbor Hotel has recently undergone a major renovation. Two beige towers—27 and 23 floors in height, respectively—are situated opposite the Charles Center and the Baltimore Arena. Most bedrooms are L-shaped, with mirrored closets, traditional dark-wood furnishings, and designer fabrics.

Dining/Entertainment: Choices include the Baltimore Grille, Jackie's Café, and the Corner Bar.

Facilities: Outdoor swimming pool, fitness center, gift shop.

PEABODY COURT, 612 Cathedral St., Baltimore, MD 21201. Tel. 301/727-7101 or toll-free 800/732-5301. Fax 301/789-3312. 105 rms. A/C MINIBAR TV TEL

$ Rates: $132–$152 single, $167–$187 double. Weekend discounts available. AE, CB, DC, MC, V. **Parking:** $10.

★ Dating back to 1930, this Mount Vernon–area hotel first opened in 1930; it was later converted into an apartment building, and re-emerged in 1985 as a hotel. The building has undergone a total renovation and rejuvenation, earning it a place on the roster of Grand Heritage Hotels. As you step inside the lobby, dominated by a 6-foot, 500-pound Baccarat crystal chandelier, a sense of grandeur greets you. The public rooms feature period furniture, hand-loomed carpeting, and original art. Each of the guest rooms has period furniture, imported lamps, and a marble bathroom.

Dining/Entertainment: The choices are Peabody's American Grill and Outdoor Café for moderate meals and the glass-enclosed rooftop Conservatory restaurant for gourmet French cuisine.

MODERATE

SOCIETY HILL, 58 W. Biddle St., Baltimore, MD 21201. Tel. 301/837-3630. Fax 301/837-4654. 15 rms. AC TV TEL
$ Rates (including continental breakfast): $80–$120 single, $110–$120 single or double. Summer discounts available. AE, MC, V. **Parking:** Free.
For a homey atmosphere, try this 1906 bed-and-breakfast in fashionable Mount Vernon. Opened in 1984, this gracious town house is within walking distance of leading cultural attractions. The bedrooms, each individually furnished, feature beds with canopies or brass headboards, as well as antique furnishings, Victorian-era wallpaper patterns and borders, local artwork, and books. Amenities include a restaurant and lounge.

BUDGET

COMFORT INN, 24 W. Franklin St., Baltimore, MD 21201. Tel. 301/727-2000 or toll-free 800/245-5256. Fax 301/576-9300. 149 rms, 10 suites. AC TV TEL
$ Rates: $65–$115 single, $72–$115 double, $115 suite. AE, CB, DC, MC, V. **Parking:** $5.
⑤ At one time a YMCA, this seven-story historic landmark dates back to 1907. Renovated, it has rooms furnished in contemporary style, with dark woods and print fabrics. Some units have unique loft layouts and a Jacuzzi bath. Other amenities include a guest launderette, Michael's restaurant, valet service, and complimentary shuttle service to Inner Harbor.

FELLS POINT/LITTLE ITALY

MODERATE

ADMIRAL FELL INN, 888 S. Broadway, Baltimore, MD 21231. Tel. 301/522-7377 or toll-free 800/292-INNS. Fax 301/522-0707. 34 rms, 4 suites. AC TV TEL
$ Rates (including continental breakfast): $89–$120 single or double. AE, MC, V. **Parking:** Free.
★ In the Fells Point neighborhood is this charming inn composed of four buildings; the buildings date from 1850–1910 and blend Victorian and Georgian architectures. Originally a boardinghouse for sailors, later a YMCA, and then a vinegar bottling plant, this delightful facility was completely renovated in 1985 to include an antique-filled lobby, an atrium, a restaurant/pub, a library, and a courtyard.

The guest rooms are individually decorated, with modern bathrooms; many have four-poster beds and are named after historical characters (for example, Carroll Room and Calvert Room). The inn also offers little extras—a free shoe-shine service, complimentary van transport to the downtown area, and daily newspapers. Suites are equipped with a Jacuzzi.

4. BALTIMORE DINING

"Crabtown" has always been well known for its excellent seafood restaurants, and the recent development of the Inner Harbor has provided an impetus and an ideal setting for even more eateries emphasizing the sea's bounty.

Baltimore is also home to a wide array of restaurants featuring regional and ethnic cuisines, and traditional steak houses. In addition to the waterfront, you'll find clusters of restaurants downtown along Charles Street (known locally as "restaurant row") and in the older neighborhoods such as Little Italy and Fells Point.

INNER HARBOR AREA

EXPENSIVE

CHART HOUSE, 601 E. Pratt St. Tel. 539-6616.
Cuisine: INTERNATIONAL. **Reservations:** Recommended.
$ **Prices:** Appetizers $3.95–$11.95; main courses $16.95–$22.95; lunch $6.95–$8.95. AE, CB, DC, DISC, MC, V.
Open: Lunch daily 11:30am–3pm; dinner Mon–Thurs 5–10:30pm, Fri 5pm–11:30pm, Sat 4–11:30pm, Sun 3–10pm.

Just east of Harborplace is this restaurant right on the water's edge. Originally a warehouse for the nearby power plant, this building has been tastefully converted into a bilevel restaurant with an outside deck. The decor is appropriately nautical, with ship replicas and carvings, and photos of the sea and the old Baltimore waterfront. Lunch features super-deli sandwiches (from crab salad to smoked turkey) and raw-bar selections, such as cream of crab soup, oysters, shrimp, clams, and other shellfish treats. Dinner entrées include exotic fish such as mahi mahi, mako, and yellow fin tuna, as well as baked stuffed flounder, lobster tails; steaks are also served. For dessert, don't miss the mud pie.

PHILLIPS HARBORPLACE, lower level, Light Street Pavilion, Harborplace. Tel. 685-6600.
Cuisine: SEAFOOD. **Reservations:** Not accepted.
$ **Prices:** Appetizers $3.95–$6.95; main courses $9.95–$25.95; lunch $6.95–$10.95. AE, DISC, MC, V.
Open: Daily 11am–11pm.

Of the more than a dozen restaurants and sidewalk cafés in the festive Harborplace development, this is a standout. It's a branch of the very successful establishment of the same name that has been an Ocean City, Md., landmark since 1956. Dinner is a feast of fresh seafood, featuring crab in many forms—soft-shell crabs stuffed with a tasty mixture of lump crab and ham, crab and lobster sauté, crab cakes, crab leg, crab claws, crab imperial, and all-you-can-eat portions of steamed crab. Steaks and other meats are also available.

This is a fun restaurant with a lively sing-along piano bar and entertainment at night. Even though reservations are not taken, there rarely is too long a wait, except at peak times. Once you are seated, however, service is swift and attentive and the food is great.

SCARLETT COVE CAFE, 200 S. President St. Tel. 783-8760.
Cuisine: INTERNATIONAL. **Reservations:** Recommended.
$ **Prices:** Appetizers: $4.95–$7.95; entrées $15.95–$22.95; lunch $3.95–$11.95. AE, CB, DC, MC, V.
Open: Lunch Mon–Fri 11am–2:30pm; dinner Mon–Fri 5–11pm, Sat 4–11:30pm; Sun 1–10pm.

Located on the eastern edge of the Inner Harbor, this is an art deco–style eatery with a serene decor of pinks and grays, subdued lighting, mirrors, and large windows that look out on the bustle of Pier 6 activity. The menu ranges from veal Oscar and chicken Scarlett (stuffed with crab imperial) to paella, pastas and vegetarian dishes, and a dish known as the "Three Amigos" (filet mignon, lump crab cake, and jumbo shrimp). Lunch items include salad, hot and cold sandwiches, pastas, salads, and omelets.

WATER STREET EXCHANGE, Water Street Exchange, 110 Water St. Tel. 332-4060.
   Cuisine: AMERICAN. **Reservations:** Recommended.
$ **Prices:** Appetizers $2.95–$11.95; main courses $14.95–$22.95; lunch $5.95–$11.95. AE, MC, V.
   Open: Mon–Sat 11:30am–11pm.

Just a block north of Pratt Street and Harborplace is this restaurant offering an authentic Victorian setting on a brick-lined courtyard. Resting on the site of an old wharf, this building has been beautifully restored into a multilevel restaurant with original brick walls, local artwork, brass fixtures, and a huge mahogany bar.

American cuisine is the focus at lunch, with salads and crêpes to pastas and omelets. Dinner has a more international flair, with such dishes as veal saltimbocca, seafood Alfredo, sole bonne femme, veal Cordon Bleu, shrimp niçoise, and steak au poivre.

MODERATE

BURKE'S RESTAURANT, 36 Light St. at Lombard St. Tel. 752-4189.
   Cuisine: INTERNATIONAL. **Reservations:** Recommended for dinner.
$ **Prices:** Appetizers $2–$6; main courses $7.95–$16.95; lunch $3–$7. MC, V.
   Open: Lunch daily 11:30am–3pm; dinner 5:30pm–1:30am.

For more than 50 years, Burke's has been a downtown fixture. Located opposite Harborplace, this tavern eatery is known for its pub atmosphere and exotic cocktails (there's a separate drink menu with over 80 listings from melon-ball sours to Kahlua coladas, mostly priced from $2 to $3). A long bar dominates the decor, which also features lots of dark wood, ceiling fans, old barrels, pewter tankards, and booth and stool seating. The food is particularly good here; the menu is surprisingly extensive, and the crab cakes are a perennial standout. Dinner entrées include steaks, beef ribs, barbecued chicken, and a delicious soft-crab imperial (sautéed soft-shell crabs covered in lump crab meat and topped with mornay sauce).

HARRISON'S PIER 5, 711 Eastern Ave. Tel. 783-5533.
   Cuisine: SEAFOOD/REGIONAL. **Reservations:** Recommended.
$ **Prices:** Appetizers $2.95–$7.95; main courses $12.95–$19.95; lunch $5.95–$8.95. AE, CB, DC, DISC, MC, V.
   Open: Lunch daily 11:30am–4pm; dinner Sun–Thurs 4–10pm, Fri–Sat 4–11:30pm.

Owned and operated by the same family who are renowned for Chesapeake Bay seafood on Tilghman Island, this restaurant understandably puts emphasis on a nautical decor, great views of the Inner Harbor, and the best of the local catch. Entrées include fresh crab and other fish choices, depending on the season, as well as eastern shore favorites, such as pan-fried chicken and veal Tilghman (topped with Smithfield ham, crabmeat, and melted Swiss cheese). In the summer months, you can also opt to dine informally on board one of two restored 19th-century crab boats docked beside the restaurant. Each evening all-you-can-eat crab feasts are held, priced at $30 per head for a complete meal of steamed crabs, beer, raw bar, and accompaniments.

PAOLO'S, 301 Light St., Harborplace. Tel. 539-7060.
   Cuisine: ITALIAN/AMERICAN. **Reservations:** Not accepted.
$ **Prices:** Appetizers $3.95–$6.95; main courses $7.95–$16.95; lunch $4.95–$8.95. AE, CB, DC, MC, V.
   Open: Mon–Fri lunch and dinner 11am–midnight; Sat–Sun brunch 10:30am–3pm, dinner 3pm–midnight.

S One of the newest restaurants at Harborplace, this informal wide-windowed spot with indoor/outdoor dining and an open kitchen is fast earning a reputation for its creative food at reasonable prices. Entrées include veal a la mozzarella, oak-grilled rack of lamb, and grilled jumbo shrimp with fresh herbs, pesto, and plum tomatoes; plus a variety of pastas, such as duck sausage lasagne and fettuccine with smoked salmon, as well as pizzas made in a wood-burning oven with a variety of traditional and exotic toppings. Same menu all day.

CHARLES STREET/MOUNT VERNON

VERY EXPENSIVE

DANNY'S, 1201 N. Charles St. Tel. 539-1393.
   Cuisine: INTERNATIONAL. **Reservations:** Recommended.
$ Prices: Appetizers $5–$12; main courses $16–$35; lunch $6.50–$13.50. AE, CB, DC, MC, V.
   Open: Mon–Fri 11:30am–11pm, Sat 5pm–midnight.

★ Ever since 1961, this restaurant has been known for serving "cuisine for the gourmet." This is a family-run restaurant, the pride and joy of Danny and Beatrice Dickman, located in fashionable Mount Vernon. There are four dining rooms, with a plush contemporary decor with lots of mirrors, leather seating, and wood paneling. Lunch includes petit steaks, seafood, omelets, salads, and sandwiches. But at dinner you can get just about anything your heart desires. Entrées range from lobster thermidor and Dover sole to chateaubriand, steak Diane flambé, beef Wellington, and prime ribs (all prime Black Angus beef). On Monday through Saturday, there is a five-course prix-fixe dinner for under $20 (including courtesy bus to the theater).

PRIME RIB, 1101 N. Calvert St. Tel. 539-1804.
   Cuisine: AMERICAN. **Reservations:** Required.
$ Prices: Appetizers $4.50–$9.75; main courses $14–$30. AE, CB, DC, MC, V.
   Open: Dinner Mon–Sat 5pm–midnight, Sun 5–11pm.

★ Between Biddle and Chase Streets is another standout for beef. Prime Rib, a fixture since 1965, is open only for dinner. In addition to aged midwestern beef, fresh Chesapeake Bay seafood is a specialty of the chef, who has won accolades from the prestigious Chaine des Rotisseurs. Most people start with the house trademark, Greenberg potato skins, named after a regular customer. Entrées include prime ribs, steaks, rack of lamb, veal chops, and such seafood dishes as blackened swordfish, crab cakes, and lobster tails.

EXPENSIVE

BRASS ELEPHANT, 924 N. Charles St. Tel. 547-8480.
   Cuisine: AMERICAN/ITALIAN. **Reservations:** Required.
$ Prices: Appetizers $3–$7; main courses $15–$22; lunch $5.95–$9.95. AE, DC, MC, V.
   Open: Lunch Mon–Fri 11:30am–2pm; dinner Mon–Thurs 5:30–9:30pm, Fri–Sat 5:30–10:30pm, Sun 5–9pm.
Mount Vernon is also home to this restaurant in a restored 1861 town house, originally the home of businessman Charles Stuart. The decor carries on the 19th-century tradition with an open fireplace, gold-leaf trim, chandeliers, and, as its name implies, lots of brass fixtures. Gentle shades of blue and classical background music add to the serene atmosphere. Lunch ranges from open-faced sandwiches and omelets to pastas and light entrées. Dinner choices include grilled salmon al pesto, yellow fin, seafood cioppino, veal, shrimp and scallops marinara, medallions of beef marsala, and rack of lamb. Early-bird diners can take advantage of a fixed-price theater-supper that offers a complete dinner including appetizer for under $20.

LA PROVENCE, 9 Hopkins Plaza. Tel. 837-6600.

Cuisine: FRENCH. **Reservations:** Recommended.

$ Prices: Appetizers $3.95–$7.95; main courses $16.95–$22.95; lunch $7.95–$12.95. AE, MC, V.

Open: Mon–Sat lunch 11:30am–2:30pm, dinner 5–9pm.

A French wine-cellar atmosphere prevails at this restaurant, with beamed ceilings, brick walls, and wood pillars. Featured dishes include steak au poivre, veal francese, swordfish béarnaise, salmon Hollandaise, shrimp Dijon, swordfish thermidor, and a local favorite, "New York Chesapeake" (steak covered with lump crabmeat and coated with béarnaise sauce). Lunch choices range from light entrées to salads, omelets, sandwiches, and quiches. Pretheater complete dinners are also available at fixed prices under $20.

ORCHID, 419 N. Charles St. Tel. 837-0080.

Cuisine: INTERNATIONAL. **Reservations:** Recommended.

$ Prices: Appetizers $3–$8; main courses $11.95–$21.95; lunch $3.95–$9.95. AE, MC, V.

Open: Lunch Mon–Fri 11:30am–2:30pm; dinner Mon–Thurs 5:30–10:30pm, Fri 5:30–11pm, Sat 5:30–11pm, Sun 4pm–9:30pm. **Closed:** Mon in July–Sept.

For a mixed menu of French, Szechuan, and hybrid dishes, try this restaurant in a converted row house near Franklin Street. The decor is lovely, with a fireplace, crisp linens, brass chandeliers, and, of course, orchids on each table. The dinner menu is eclectic, with Peking shrimp and Mongolian beef, as well as duck au poivre vert, and the house special, flounder with crispy almonds, ginger, and pineapple in a lemon butter sauce. The lunch menu offers a variety of pastas, omelets, seafood, and salads.

MODERATE

LE BISTRO AT LA PROVENCE, 9 Hopkins Plaza. Tel. 837-6600.

Cuisine: INTERNATIONAL. **Reservations:** Not required.

$ Prices: Appetizers $2.95–$6.95; main courses $6.95–$14.95; lunch $3.95–$6.95. AE, MC, V.

Open: Mon–Sat lunch 11:30am–5pm, dinner 5–9pm.

As its name implies, this is the informal café-style eatery attached to the upscale French restaurant La Provence. With wide windows overlooking Hopkins Plaza, this informal eatery is bright and airy, with a modern art-deco atmosphere. Entrées range from blackened salmon and shrimp Dijon to veal francese, steaks, burgers, sandwiches, quiches, pastas, and salads. After 9pm, light fare is available, with a live jazz program.

LOUIE'S BOOKSTORE CAFE, 518 N. Charles St. Tel. 962-1224.

Cuisine: INTERNATIONAL. **Reservations:** Not accepted.

$ Prices: Appetizers $2.95–$7.95; main courses $8.95–$12.95; lunch $3.95–$8.95. MC, V.

Open: Tues–Sat 11:30am–2am, Sun 10:30am–midnight, Mon 11:30am–midnight.

As its name implies, this café, on "restaurant row," is a blend of bookstore and bistro. Staffed by artists and musicians, this unusual eatery is decorated with paintings by local talent and an eclectic blend of furniture, with chamber music emanating from the background. Lunch features creative salads (such as artichoke and feta with spinach), as well as filet of fish, steak sandwiches, and charbroiled chicken marinated in a curry. Dinner entrées include steaks, vegetable stir-fry, crab and shrimp casserole, and chicken marinated in a curry, garlic, and lemon sauce. There is live solo or duo music every night.

FELLS POINT/LITTLE ITALY
EXPENSIVE

DA MIMMO, 217 S. High St. Tel. 727-6876.

Cuisine: ITALIAN. **Reservations:** Recommended.

$ Prices: Appetizers $5–$13; main courses $15–$35; lunch $8–$12. AE, CB, DC, MC, V.
Open: Mon–Thurs 11:30am–11:30pm, Fri 11:30am–1am, Sat 5pm–1am, Sun 2pm–11:30pm.

If you like music with your meal, head to this small candlelit Little Italy restaurant with piano entertainment (Wednesday through Sunday) in the Roman-style lounge. Lunch is also available here, with sandwiches, pastas, and seafood dishes. The varied menu features everything from chicken cacciatore, lobster pizzaiola, and filet mignon to an award-winning butterflied veal chops and the Mimmo seafood special for two (shrimp, clams, calamari, and mussels in marinara sauce and on a bed of linguine).

CHIAPPARELLI'S, 237 S. High St. Tel. 837-0309.

Cuisine: ITALIAN. **Reservations:** Recommended.
$ Prices: Appetizers $3–$10; main courses $9.95–$24; lunch $5–$12. AE, CB, DC, MC, V.
Open: Sun–Thurs 11am–11pm, Fri 11am–1am, Sat 11am–2am.

In the heart of Little Italy, this is a longtime favorite. Southern Italian dishes are the trademark here, with special plaudits for Mom Chiapparelli's raviolis (stuffed with spinach and ricotta). Dinner is the main event, and veal is the star of the menu, cooked at least a dozen different ways, along with tasty chicken dishes and such classics as lobster fra diavolo and steak Italiana.

HAUSSNER'S, 3244 Eastern Ave. Tel. 327-8365.

Cuisine: INTERNATIONAL. **Reservations:** Accepted only for lunch.
$ Prices: Appetizers $2.95–$6.95; main courses $6.95–$23.95; lunch $3.95–$13.95. AE, D, DISC, MC, V.
Open: Lunch Tues–Fri 11am–4pm, Sat 11am–2pm; dinner Tues–Fri 4–10pm, Sat 4–11pm.

In the German section of east Baltimore known as Highland Town, you'll find this restaurant, established in 1926 by Bavarian-born William Henry Haussner. Moved to its present location in 1936, the restaurant is still carried on by the founder's widow, Frances, and family. A Baltimore institution that you have to see to believe, this is not only a great place to go to for good value and good food (the main dining room seats 500), it is also an art and antique gallery, with paintings, porcelains, sculptures, clocks, figurines, and old plates. Everywhere you look there is art, collected over the years by the Haussners; even the menu features sample paintings.

Lunch choices include seafood salads, omelets, and hot dishes, but dinner is the pièce de résistance with over 100 entrées, all fresh and delicious daily. The selection embraces all kinds of meats and seafoods as well as frogs' legs, finnan haddie, bouillabaisse, sweetbreads, wienerschnitzel, baked rabbit, pigs' knuckles, and ox tongue. With its own bakery on the premises, Haussner's is also known for its desserts (over 30 varieties, from strawberry pie and apple strudel to honey almond cake).

OBRYCKI'S, 1727 E. Pratt St. Tel. 732-6399.

Cuisine: SEAFOOD. **Reservations:** Not accepted.
$ Prices: Appetizers $2.95–$8.95; main courses $11.95–$21.95; lunch $5.95–$9.95. AE, CB, DC, MC, V.
Open: Mon–Sat 11:30am–11pm, Sun 4–9:30pm. **Closed:** Apr–mid-Dec.

East of Little Italy is Fells Point, the waterfront neighborhood where Baltimore began—and one of the best areas for seafood. Without a doubt, the benchmark of all the eateries here is Obrycki's. Food connoisseurs Craig Claiborne and George Lang rave about this place—and so do we. The decor is particularly charming, with stained-glass windows, brick archways, and wainscotting along the walls.

But the big attraction at either location is the food, especially if you enjoy crabs. This is the quintessential crab house—where you can crack open steamed crabs in their shells and feast on the tender, succulent meat to your heart's content. There's crab soup, crab cocktail, crab balls, crab cakes, crab imperial, and soft-shell crabs.

The rest of the menu is just as tempting—shrimp, lobster, scallops, haddock, flounder, and steaks. Among the lunchtime choices are seafood salads and sandwiches. The service is extremely attentive.

SABATINO'S, 901 Fawn St. Tel. 727-9414.
   Cuisine: ITALIAN. **Reservations:** Recommended.
   $ Prices: Appetizers $4–$12; main courses $11–$22; lunch $5–$12. AE, MC, V.
   Open: Daily noon–3am.
Both northern and southern Italian cuisine are featured at this Little Italy restaurant with a plain stucco facade and a colorful interior. This is a particularly good late-night dining spot since it is open every day until 3am. Dinner entrées include veal francese, shrimp scampi, calamari marinara, beef pizzaiola, lobster fra diavolo, and two dozen pastas such as spaghetti with broccoli and anchovy sauce.

MODERATE

BERTHA'S, 734 S. Broadway. Tel. 327-5795.
   Cuisine: INTERNATIONAL. **Reservations:** Accepted only for party of six or more.
   $ Prices: Appetizers $2.95–$5.95; main courses $6.95–$18.95; lunch $4.95–$11.95. MC, V.
   Open: Sun–Thurs 11:30am–11pm; Fri–Sat 11:30am–midnight.
Don't miss this Fells Point landmark known for its mussels and music. The decor is a blend of yesteryear, with original brick walls, antique prints, old wine bottles, and nautical bric-a-brac. You'll also see musical instruments fashioned into chandeliers and wall hangings, a reminder that traditional and folk music or jazz are performed here on many weekend nights. Lunch includes shepherd's pie, seafood, salads, omelets, and fish cakes. Mussels are the featured dish at dinner (fixed almost a dozen different ways); other entrées range from paella or curried seafood to filet mignon, a vegetable platter with brown rice, and chicken staccato (boneless breast with kumquats and peanuts).

5. BALTIMORE ATTRACTIONS

Although much of Baltimore's business activity takes place along Charles Street, the focus of the city for visitors is on the Inner Harbor, home of the Baltimore Convention Center and Festival Hall Exhibit Center, the Baltimore Area Convention and Visitors office, the National Aquarium and other museums, and the Pier 6 Concert Pavilion.

It is also the site of historic and working ships, a host of major hotels, dozens of restaurants and shops, and, as of 1992, the new Orioles Baseball Stadium, in Camden Yards, downtown.

✪ And the centerpiece of it all is **Harborplace,** positioned right on the waterfront. It occupies a full two blocks along Light and Pratt Streets, and has been the keystone to the revitalization of Baltimore as a tourist mecca. Designed to duplicate the look of an early steamship pier headquarters, Harborplace is made up of two pavilions, named after the streets they occupy—the Light Street Pavilion and the Pratt Street Pavilion.

Built in 1981, Harborplace is to Baltimore what Station Square is to Pittsburgh, Faneuil Hall to Boston, South Street Seaport to New York, or Ghirardelli Square to San Francisco—a historic setting transformed into a contemporary, bright, and airy complex of restaurants, food markets, curiosity shops, and trendy boutiques, side-by-side in a milieu of music, camaraderie, and good times. Shops are open Monday through Saturday 10am to 10pm, Sunday noon to 6pm, with later hours for restaurants and entertainment.

Start your tour of Baltimore at Harborplace and then branch out to the many other varied attractions of this great city.

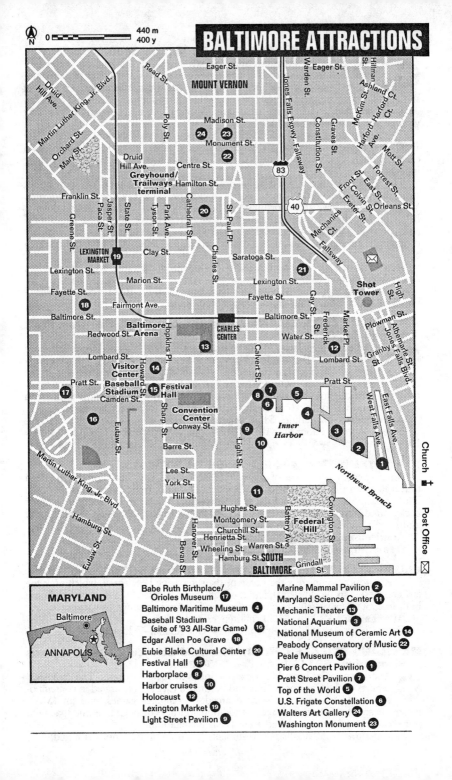

BALTIMORE ATTRACTIONS

0 — 440 m / 400 y

N

MOUNT VERNON

Eager St.
Read St.
Eager St.
Warden St.
Hillman St.
Ashland Ct.
McKim St.
Hartford Ct.
Harford Ave.
Madison St.
Monument St.
Graves St.
Constitution St.
Mott St.
Centre St.
Druid Hill Ave.
Front St.
East St.
Colvin St.
Forrest St.
83
Hamilton St.
Greyhound/ Trailways terminal
Exeter St.
Orleans St.
40
Mechanics Ct.
Franklin St.
Jasper St.
Paca St.
State St.
Park Ave.
Tyson St.
Cathedral St.
St. Paul Pl.
Fallsway
Greene St.
Saratoga St.
Clay St.
LEXINGTON MARKET
19
Charles St.
Lexington St.
Marion St.
Lexington St.
21
Fayette St.
Fayette St.
High St.
Shot Tower
Fairmont Ave.
18
Baltimore St.
Baltimore St.
Gay St.
Frederick St.
Plowman St.
Albemarle St.
Jones Falls Blvd.
Baltimore Arena
Redwood St.
CHARLES CENTER
Water St.
Market Pl.
Lombard St.
13
Lombard St.
12
Granby St.
Visitor Center
14
Pratt St.
Howard St.
Pratt St.
Baseball Stadium
17
15
Festival Hall
Camden St.
8
7
5
West Falls Ave.
East Falls Ave.
6
4
16
Convention Center
Sharp St.
Conway St.
9
Inner Harbor
3
10
2
Barre St.
Light St.
1
Lee St.
York St.
Hill St.
11
Northwest Branch
Martin Luther King, Jr. Blvd.
Eutaw St.
Hughes St.
Montgomery St.
Churchill St.
Henrietta St.
Wheeling St.
Warren St.
Hamburg St.
Federal Hill
Battery Ave.
Covington St.
Grindall St.
Hamburg St.
Hanover St.
Bevan St.
SOUTH BALTIMORE
Eutaw St.
Druid Hill Ave.
Martin Luther King, Jr. Blvd.
Orchard St.
Mary St.
Poly St.
Jones Falls Expwy - Fallsway

Church ✝
Post Office ✉

MARYLAND

Baltimore
ANNAPOLIS

Babe Ruth Birthplace/ Orioles Museum **17**
Baltimore Maritime Museum **4**
Baseball Stadium (site of '93 All-Star Game) **16**
Edgar Allen Poe Grave **18**
Eubie Blake Cultural Center **20**
Festival Hall **15**
Harborplace **8**
Harbor cruises **10**
Holocaust **12**
Lexington Market **19**
Light Street Pavilion **9**

Marine Mammal Pavilion **2**
Maryland Science Center **11**
Mechanic Theater **13**
National Aquarium **3**
National Museum of Ceramic Art **14**
Peabody Conservatory of Music **22**
Peale Museum **21**
Pier 6 Concert Pavilion **1**
Pratt Street Pavilion **7**
Top of the World **5**
U.S. Frigate Constellation **6**
Walters Art Gallery **24**
Washington Monument **23**

NATIONAL AQUARIUM, 501 E. Pratt St. Tel. 576-3800.

A spectacular five-level glass and steel structure, this aquarium is the center-piece of the Inner Harbor. It contains more than 5,000 specimens of mammals, fish, rare birds, reptiles, and amphibians. All the creatures are on view in settings that re-create their natural habitats, including a South American rain forest, an Atlantic coral reef, and an open-ocean tank. Moving belts and ramped bridges carry visitors from one exhibit level to the next.

The newest addition is the $35 million Marine Mammal Pavilion, opened in late 1990. It is home to three beluga whales and six Atlantic bottlenose dolphins, in a carefully controlled environment that enables visitors literally to go whale-watching indoors.

The mammals are housed in a 1.2-million-gallon complex of four pools, surrounded by the world's largest acrylic windows and a 1,300-seat amphitheater. Visitors not only have an opportunity for close-up observation of whale and dolphin behavior, but they also can attend an ongoing program of 30-minute educational talks, presented by aquarium trainers. In addition, there are nature films, plus a gallery of exhibits, an aquatic education resource center, and an animal care and research complex.

Admission: $10.75 for adults, $8.50 for students and seniors, $6.50 for children 3–11, free for children under 3.

Open: Mid-Sept–mid-May Sat–Thurs 10am–5pm, Fri 10am–8pm; mid-May–mid-Sept Mon–Thurs 9am–5pm, Fri–Sat 9am–8pm.

U.S. FRIGATE *CONSTELLATION,* Constellation Dock, Pier One, Pratt Street. Tel. 539-1797.

One of the Inner Harbor's biggest draws is this ship, launched from Baltimore in 1797, the first that the U.S. Navy put to sea and the first to defeat an enemy man-of-war. It has been continuously afloat longer than any other ship in the world. With a long history of travels to the Barbary Coast, England, France, and many other ports throughout the world, the *Constellation* is now permanently at home in Baltimore and welcomes 20th-century mates on board to inspect her decks.

Admission: $2.75 adults, $1.50 children 6–15.

Open: June 15–Labor Day, daily 10am–8pm; day after Labor Day–Oct 14 daily 10am–6pm; Oct 15–May 14 daily 10am–4pm; May 15–June 14 daily 10am–6pm.

TOP OF THE WORLD, 401 E. Pratt St. Tel. 837-4515.

For a sweeping overview of the whole harbor and city, head for this sky-high observatory on the 27th floor of the pentagonal World Trade Center, just opposite Harborplace. In addition to a look at the cityscapes below, you can acquire a bit of background about Baltimore from the sky-high exhibits, hands-on displays, and multimedia presentations at this facility.

Admission: $2 adults, $1 children 5–15.

Open: Mon–Sat 10am–5pm, Sun noon–5pm.

BALTIMORE MARITIME MUSEUM, Pier 4, Pratt St. Tel. 396-5528.

This outdoor complex is the home of the submarine USS *Torsk,* which sank the last enemy ship in World War II; and the Lightship *Chesapeake,* a floating lighthouse built in 1930. The vessels are moored to the dock and are open to visitors.

Admission: $3 adults, $1.50 children 12 and under.

Open: Nov–Apr 9:30am–4:30pm; May–Oct 9:30am–7:30pm.

MARYLAND SCIENCE CENTER, Maryland Science Center and Davis Planetarium, 601 Light St. Tel. 685-5225.

Another popular Inner Harbor attraction is this science center. The geological aspects of the Chesapeake Bay and Baltimore City are illustrated in contempo-rary hands-on displays, science arcades, computer games, and an IMAX theater, geared to visitors of all ages. In addition, journeys through time and space and star shows are featured in the adjacent Davis Planetarium.

Admission: $7.50 adults, $5.50 students (children under 5 not permitted).

Open: June–Sept Mon–Sat 10am–8pm, Sun noon–6pm; Oct–May Mon–Thurs 10am–5pm, Fri–Sat 10am–10pm, Sun noon–6pm.

BALTIMORE AND OHIO [B&O] RAILROAD MUSEUM, 901 W. Pratt St. Tel. 752-2490.

A trailblazer in American railroading, this city is also the setting of a fascinating railroad museum. Often called a railroad university, this museum has hundreds of exhibits, from double-decker stagecoaches on iron wheels and early diesels to steam locomotives and the 1830 Mount Clare Station, the nation's first passenger and freight station, as well as the 1844 roundhouse with the original B & O tracks and turntable. Peter Cooper built and tested his famous Tom Thumb on this site, and Samuel Morse strung his first telegraph wires through this depot. A visit here will chug you along on a 150-year round-trip through the annals of American train travel.

Open: Tues–Sun 10am–4pm. **Closed:** Mon and major holidays.
Admission: $5 adults, $3 youngsters 5–18; children 4 and under free.

CITY LIFE MUSEUMS, 800 E. Lombard St. Tel. 396-3523.

Collectively, these three attractions—the Carroll Mansion, the 1840 House, and the Center for Urban Archaeology—are part of the city's "Museum Row." The centerpiece building is the **Carroll Mansion**, one of Baltimore's great historic houses, dating back to 1812. Recently restored, it is primarily associated with Charles Carroll of Carrollton, a Maryland patriot who signed the Declaration of Independence. Carroll wintered here during the last 12 years of his life (1820–32), when he was the focus of much attention as the last surviving signer of the Declaration. Today the building is filled with Early American furniture, decorative arts, and paintings from the late 18th century through the 1840's.

The **1840 House** is a reconstructed 19th-century row house with reproduction furnishings, and the **Center for Urban Archaeology** is a working exhibit featuring recently excavated artifacts from the Baltimore area.

Admission: $3 for all three sites, $1.75 for each.
Open: Tues–Sat 10am–4pm, Sun noon–4pm.

LEXINGTON MARKET, 400 W. Lexington St. Tel. 685-6169.

Founded in 1782, this Baltimore landmark claims to be the oldest continuously operating market in the United States. It houses more than 140 merchants, selling ethnic foods, seafood, produce, meats, baked goods, sweets, and more. It's a real slice of Baltimore, well worth a visit—for the aromas, flavors, and sounds, as well as the sights.

Admission: Free.
Open: Mon–Sat 8:30am–6pm.

THE SHOT TOWER, 801 E. Fayette St. Tel. 396-5894.

A local landmark, this 215-foot-tall brick structure was built in 1828 for the production of lead shot ammunition and is one of the nation's few remaining shot towers. Visitors are not allowed to climb the 310 steps to the top, but exhibits show how shot was produced here until 1892, by pouring molten lead through perforated pans from "dropping stations" high up in the tower.

Admission: Free.
Open: Daily 10am–4pm.

WALTERS ART GALLERY, 600 N. Charles Street. Tel. 547-9000.

Designed in an Italianate Palazzo style, this is an internationally famous museum of more than 30,000 works of art spanning 5,000 years. The collection includes Egyptian, Greek, Roman, Byzantine, medieval, Renaissance, baroque, romantic, impressionist, and art-nouveau works. In addition, there are exhibits of historic jewelry, medieval armor, and illuminated manuscripts.

Admission: $3 adults, $2 seniors, free for persons 18 and under. Free admission to all on Wed.
Open: Tues–Sun 11am–5pm.

EDGAR ALLEN POE HOUSE, 203 N. Amity St. Tel. 396-7932.

The tiny house where Edgar Allan Poe wrote many of his great works is located in the heart of Baltimore. Poe lived here for three years (1832–35) while courting his cousin, whom he later married. The building contains Poe memorabilia plus period furniture, ever-changing exhibits, and a video presentation of leading Poe works.

Admission: $2 adults, $1 children under 12.

Open: Apr–July and Oct–mid-Dec, Wed–Sat noon–3:45pm; Aug–Sept, Sat noon–4pm. **Closed:** Mid-Dec–Mar 31.

FORT McHENRY NATIONAL MONUMENT AND HISTORIC SHRINE, E. Fort Ave. Tel. 962-4299.

One of the most visited landmarks in the city is this monument, birthplace of our national anthem. The sight of our flag flying over this star-shaped fort during the 1814 Battle of Baltimore inspired Francis Scott Key to write the words of "The Star-Spangled Banner." Not only was the song written, but the American forces were successful against the British and the fort never again came under attack. It remained an active military base for many years, however, until 1925, when it became a national park. To assist visitors in touring the fort, there are historical and military exhibits, a 15-minute film shown every half hour, explanatory maps; during the summer months, guided activities are regularly scheduled.

Admission: $1; visitors under 17 and over 62 admitted free.

Open: Day after Labor Day–mid-June daily 8am–5pm, mid-June–Labor Day daily 8am–8pm. **Closed:** Christmas Day and New Year's Day.

STAR-SPANGLED BANNER FLAG HOUSE AND 1812 MUSEUM, 844 E. Pratt St. Tel. 837-1793.

This is the home of Mary Pickersgill, the seamstress who made the 30-by-42-foot red, white, and blue Fort McHenry flag, the symbol that motivated Francis Scott Key. This Federal-style (1793) house is full of period furnishings and a collection of Early American art. Outside the building is an unusual garden featuring a map of the continental United States made of stones native to each state.

Admission: $2 adults, $1 students 13–18, 60¢ children 6–12.

Open: Mon–Sat 10am–4pm; last guided tour 3:30pm. **Closed:** Sun and major holidays.

BABE RUTH BIRTHPLACE AND MUSEUM/MARYLAND BASEBALL HALL OF FAME, 216 Emory St. Tel. 727-1539.

Baseball fans of all ages enjoy a visit to the house where the great player was born on February 6, 1895. This restored house and adjoining museum contain personal mementos of George Herman ("Babe") Ruth, otherwise known as the "sultan of swat." The exhibits, which focus on the Baltimore Orioles and Maryland baseball as well as the great Babe, include "touchable" items such as hats, bats, and gloves; there is also an audiovisual presentation on baseball, World Series film highlights, and a wall mural of famous baseball personalities.

Admission: $3 adults, $1.50 children 12 and under.

Open: Apr–Oct daily 10am–5pm; Nov 1–Mar 31 daily 10am–4pm. **Closed:** Easter, Thanksgiving Day, Christmas Eve and Christmas Day.

ORGANIZED TOURS

Good Time Tours, 3395 Main St., Manchester (tel. 539-3330), operates regularly scheduled half-day and full-day bus tours around Baltimore. There are two half-day tours, one a morning tour focusing on Baltimore's historical districts (Mt. Vernon Place and Fells Point), priced from $18 per person, and the other an afternoon trip covering Baltimore's history and attractions (Fort McHenry, the Star-Spangled Banner House, and more), priced from $20. In addition, you can take both tours on the same day for a combination price of $30. All tours operate on Wednesday and Saturday. Children pay half of the adult rate. Tour tickets are available at most hotels, and pickup points include the Hyatt Regency, Omni Inner Harbor, and Holiday Inn Hotels.

Baltimore-Rent-A-Tour, 3414 Philips Dr. (tel. 653-2998), designs tours to suit any request, from walking rambles to insomniac late-evening jaunts about town. Prices vary according to itinerary; reservations are necessary.

HARBOR CRUISES

See Baltimore from its harbor on board a variety of nautical craft. The twin-deck **Patriot II** and **Patriot III** offer 1½-hour narrated cruises from Constellation Dock, Pratt and Light Streets (tel. 685-4288). The schedule is April 15 through April 30, at 11am, 1 pm, and 3pm; from May through September, hourly departures from 11am through 4pm; and in October at 11am, 1pm, and 3pm. Additional evening cruises are also scheduled on some summer weekends. The cost is $6 for adults and $3.30 for children 2 to 11.

In addition, another company, **Harbor Cruises**, 301 Light St. (tel. 727-3113), operates more extensive excursions on board two 450-passenger cruise ships. The first, *Lady Baltimore*, departs Harborplace for scenic all-day trips as follows: to Annapolis, every Wednesday, 10am to noon, from mid-June through September, priced at $15 for adults and $7.60 for children 12 and under; and a 12-hour cruise to the Chesapeake and Delaware Canal for a fall foliage viewing, at 9:30am on selected weekends in October, at $25.95 for adults and $13 for children. The second ship, *Bay Lady*, offers a "showboat" experience with dining and entertainment in a cruise-ship setting, lunch or dinner with a full musical revue. Lunch cruises, which operate on Tuesday through Sunday, from noon to 2pm, are priced at $13.85 per person (reduced rates for children 12 and under); dinner cruises, from 7pm to 10pm, go out on Tuesday through Thursday and Sunday at $22.50 per person, on Friday and Saturday at $26.95 per person, and on Monday at $19.95 per person. In addition, special event and theme cruises are available throughout the year.

CATAMARAN CRUISES

The *Chesapeake Flyer*, a 110-passenger high-speed-powered catamaran offers daily cruises during June through September from the Constellation Dock of Baltimore's Inner Harbor to Rock Hall on Maryland's eastern shore and Annapolis (1- to 2-hour layovers are provided in each port for lunch/dinner or sightseeing). On Monday through Friday departures are at 9:30am and 6:30pm. On Saturday departures are at 9:30am and 6:15pm from Baltimore, and on Sunday there is one departure, at 10:30am from Baltimore. Prices are $29.25 for adults and $15.50 for children 3 to 12. Reservations are recommended and schedules/prices are subject to change; for more information, contact the Chesapeake Flyer (tel. 301/783-7500 or toll-free 800/869-7320.

SAILING CRUISES

The *Clipper City*, a 158-foot replica of an 1854 topsail schooner and the largest tall ship licensed to carry passengers in the United States, offers 3-hour sea excursions from the Inner Harbor in the summer months, at noon and 3pm daily (except Monday), with a sailing at 8pm on Friday and Saturday evenings and at 7pm on Sunday. Cost is $12 per person for adults and $2 for children 5 to 15. On Sunday a champagne brunch cruise is also operated, from 11am to 2pm, at a cost of $29 per person. To reserve a place, contact **Clipper City Inc.**, 720 Light St. (tel. 539-6277).

6. BALTIMORE SPECIAL/FREE EVENTS

HARBOR LIGHTS FESTIVAL

The highlight of the summer calendar in Baltimore is the **Harbor Lights Music Festival**, Pier Six Concert Pavilion, Pier 6 and Pratt St., Baltimore Inner Harbor (tel. 625-1400). Running from late June through August, this is a series of evening open-air concerts featuring big names in popular, folk, symphony, jazz, and bluegrass music. In recent years, the program has included Harry Belafonte; Tony Bennett; Ella Fitzgerald; Crystal Gayle; Peter, Paul and Mary; Pia Zadora; Ferrante and Teicher; and Rosemary Clooney. Reserved seats are priced from $15 to $25 and lawn tickets go for $8 to $15. Tickets can be purchased at the Pier 6 Box Office and at other outlets throughout the city.

PREAKNESS CELEBRATION

✪ Probably the best known of Baltimore's annual celebrations is the **Preakness Celebration,** held in mid-May. This citywide event pays tribute to the race called the "Preakness Stakes" at the Pimlico Race Course. The middle jewel in horse racing's Triple Crown, the Preakness is regarded as one of the prime sporting events in the world and annually adds more than $18 million to the local economy. The week-long hoopla surrounding the race begins on the previous weekend and includes hot-air-balloon races, a polo match, a golf tournament, a frog hop, boating races, food-eating contests, and other waterside activities, based mostly in the Inner Harbor area. On the eve of the race, there is also a Preakness Festival Parade of Lights, with lighted floats, equestrian teams, and marching bands. More than 80,000 people usually attend the race itself; post time is approximately 5:30pm. All seats are reserved at the **Pimlico Race Course** on Preakness Day (phone 301/542-9400 or toll-free 800/638-3811 for further information). For details on the entire Preakness Celebration, call 301/837-3030.

7. BALTIMORE SPORTS & RECREATION

WATER SPORTS

Several concessions along the Harborplace dock rent small craft for individual use (two people per vessel). Electric boats can be hired for $9.90 per half hour; and paddleboats are available at $4.50 per half hour, and $7.75 for a full hour's splash. For information, call 539-1837. Cruise vessels, sailboats, and water taxis also operate throughout the summer season (see "Getting Around," above).

HORSE RACING

Maryland's oldest thoroughbred track and the site of the annual Preakness Stakes is **Pimlico Race Course,** Park Heights and Belvedere Aves. (tel. 542-9400), about 5 miles from the Inner Harbor on the city's northwest side. The full racing season extends from mid-March to the end of May, mid-July to mid-August, and early September to early October. Post time is 1pm, and admission charges are $3 for the grandstand and $5 for the clubhouse, plus $1 per car for parking. Pimlico is also the home of the **National Jockey's Hall of Fame,** open from 9 to 11am during the racing season, free of charge.

BASEBALL

The Baltimore Orioles play their April-to-October season at **Memorial Stadium,** 33rd Street and Ellerslie Avenue (tel. 481-6000). Ticket prices range from $5 for adult general admission ($2.50 for children under 12) to $10 and up for a field box seat. In addition to the stadium, tickets are on sale at the **Baltimore Arena,** 201 W. Baltimore St. (tel. 347-2010). *Note:* In April 1992, a new Orioles Stadium will open four blocks west of the Inner Harbor, at Camden Street, off I-395. It will have a seating capacity of 47,000 and parking facilities for 5,000 cars.

8. BALTIMORE SAVVY SHOPPING

For visitors, Baltimore's prime shopping scene is centered around the Inner Harbor. **Harborplace,** Pratt and Light Streets (tel. 332-4191), is the benchmark of the city's quintessential shopping experiences. It is an attractive waterside complex of two glass-enclosed bilevel shopping malls, known as the **Light Street Pavilion** and the **Pratt Street Pavilion,** featuring over 135 shops, markets, craft vendors, restaurants, and cafés. You'll find everything from bonbons and books to scrimshaw and silks, as well as names such as Laura Ashley, Crabtree and Evelyn, and Pappagallo. To add to the ambience, from April through September free concerts are staged in the amphitheater in front of the pavilions. Open Monday through Saturday, from 10am to 10pm, and Sunday from noon to 6pm.

Across the street is the **Gallery at Harborplace,** Pratt and Light Streets (tel. 332-4191), an outgrowth of the original Pratt and Light Street pavilions. Opened in 1987, this is a six-level atrium of over 70 fine shops, including Brooks Brothers, Ann Taylor, Sharper Image, the Disney Store, and Williams-Sonoma. Open Monday through Saturday, from 10am to 10pm, and Sunday from noon to 6pm.

In a different vein, another important cluster of shops is **Antique Row,** N. Howard and Read Streets (tel. 462-2000), situated uptown two blocks west of Charles Street. At these 35 independent antique shops you'll find everything from clocks and lamps to jewelry, silver, fine art, china, curiosities, collectibles, statuary, furniture, and political memorabilia. Open Monday through Saturday from 10am to 5pm.

9. BALTIMORE EVENING ENTERTAINMENT

THE ENTERTAINMENT SCENE

Baltimore is the home of the Baltimore Symphony Orchestra, the Baltimore Opera Company, and many fine theaters. Check the arts/entertainment pages of the *Baltimore Sun* for daily listings and ticket information. Also, for latest developments check with the Baltimore Area Convention and Visitors Association at the time of your visit.

Morris Mechanic Theater, 25 Hopkins Plaza (tel. 625-1400), an ultramodern showplace in the heart of midtown's Charles Center, stages contemporary plays with original casts en route to or from the Great White Way; recent productions have included *Cats, The Tap Dance Kid,* and *Singin' in the Rain.* The curtain is at 8pm, Monday through Saturday, with matinees at 2pm on Wednesday and Saturday. The box office is open from 10am to 8:30pm. Ticket prices average $20 to $30 for most shows.

Among other leading theaters in the city are the **Center Stage,** 700 N. Calvert St. (tel. 322-0033), for classical and contemporary dramas, and **Arena Players,** 801 McCulloh St. (tel. 728-6500), a prominent black theater company. Prices and schedules vary with the productions.

In addition, the **Baltimore Arena,** 201 W. Baltimore St. (tel. 347-2010), is the setting for an ever-changing program of entertainment and sports events, including circuses, ice shows, and concerts.

DINNER THEATER

The **Fell's Point Cabaret Theater,** 723 S. Broadway, Fells Point (tel. toll-free 800/766-0028), features murder mysteries and comedies, along with a four-course dinner. Performances are scheduled Friday through Sunday at 7pm, with an additional late-night show on Saturday at 10:30pm and a Sunday matinee at 3pm. Prices range from $22.50 to $29.95, depending on production and time.

OPERA/CLASSICAL MUSIC

For classical music and concerts, head to **Meyerhoff Symphony Hall,** 1212 Cathedral St. (tel. 783-8000). This beautifully designed, 2,450-seat venue is the home of the Baltimore Symphony Orchestra and also hosts a varied program of renowned soloists and visiting artists. Nearby is the showcase for the Baltimore Opera at the **Lyric Opera House,** Mount Royal Avenue and Cathedral Street (tel. 685-5086).

POPULAR MUSIC

The showplace of the Inner Harbor is the **Pier Six Concert Pavilion,** Pier 6 and Pratt Street (tel. 625-1400). This is a 3,000-seat outdoor facility perched at the end of one of Baltimore's old-fashioned harbor piers. Pier Six is the setting for frequent open-air and covered concerts throughout the summertime, such as the annual 2-month Harbor Lights Festival. The *Quick City Guide* magazine is the best source of up-to-date program information.

PIANO BARS

Many of the city's leading hotels and restaurants have piano-bar lounges, including **Phillips** at Harborplace, 301 S. Light St. (tel. 685-6600), **Danny's,** 1201 N. Charles St. (tel. 539-1393), and Explorer's Lounge at the Harbor Court Hotel, 550 Light St. (tel. 234-0550).

JAZZ CLUBS

Among the list of ever-changing venues are **The Brokerage,** 34 Market Place (tel. 727-4822), **Hooters of Harborplace,** 301 S. Light St. (tel. 244-0367), and **Le Bistro** at La Provence, 9 Hopkins Plaza (tel. 837-6600).

CHAPTER 16
ANNAPOLIS

A gem of Colonial architecture, Annapolis is home to a historic district of more than 1,500 buildings. Situated at the confluence of the Chesapeake Bay and the Severn River, this picturesque port is also the capital of Maryland.

First settled in the mid-1600s, Annapolis was initially known as Providence, and later called Anne Arundel Town, after the wife of Cecilius Calvert, the second Lord Baltimore who sponsored the area's first English settlers. It was an Englishman, Francis Nicholson, who laid out the city's streets in 1695 according to a pattern of radiating thoroughfares. In 1694 the name of Annapolis was chosen, in honor of Princess Anne, who later became the Queen of England.

With all of its lofty connections, it is no wonder that Annapolis has led a charmed existence. A prosperous seaport due to the tobacco trade, Annapolis had its golden years from 1750 to 1790, as the commercial, political, and social center of Maryland. The first library in the colonies as well as the first theater are believed to have been founded in Annapolis during those years, as was St. John's College, one of the first public schools in America. Between November 1783 and August 1784, Annapolis was also the first peacetime capital of the United States. It was during that period that the city served as the site for the ratification of the Treaty of Paris, the document in which Great Britain formally recognized the independence of the United States, ending the Revolutionary War.

1. ORIENTATION

As you stroll down the streets of Annapolis today, you can't help thinking that not much has changed here since those glorious days. Except for the cars, it is almost as if time has stood still. The city is a vista of 18th-century mansions, churches, and public buildings. The original layout is still in place—narrow brick streets fanning out from two circular thoroughfares, State Circle and Church Circle. Colonial names are everywhere: King George Street, Duke of Gloucester Street, Compromise Street, and Shipwright Street, to cite a few.

This charming seaport city (pop. 35,000) does have newer claims to fame, of course. It is the home of the U.S. Naval Academy and the government of the state of Maryland. With 16 miles of waterfront, tiny Annapolis is also the pleasure-boating capital of the eastern United States and a tourism destination renowned for its landmark sights, historic inns and restaurants, convivial taverns, trendy shops, and relaxed atmosphere.

WHAT'S SPECIAL ABOUT ANNAPOLIS

Ace Attractions

☐ Annapolis Historic District, with more than 1,500 18th-century mansions, churches, and public buildings.

☐ U.S. Naval Academy, a national historic site spread over 300 acres.

☐ Maryland State House, the oldest U.S. state capitol in continuous use.

☐ City Dock and Marina, a yachting hub with hundreds of craft of all sizes

☐ Market House, a central farmers' market dating back to 1784.

Activities

☐ Take a guided tour of the U.S. Naval Academy.

☐ Enjoy a sightseeing cruise of Annapolis Harbor.

Events/Festivals

☐ Commissioning Week at the U.S. Naval Academy.

☐ U.S. Sailboat Show, the world's largest in-the-water boat show.

☐ U.S. Power Boat Show, the largest of its kind.

☐ Maryland Seafood Festival, 3 days of continuous entertainment and the best of Chesapeake Bay seafood.

Museums

☐ Shiplap House Museum, one of the oldest structures of Annapolis dating back to 1715 and focusing on Annapolis history.

☐ Banneker-Douglass Museum, with exhibits on the historical and cultural experiences of Afro-Americans in Maryland.

ARRIVING

BY AIR

Annapolis is served by **Baltimore-Washington International Airport.** More than 300 flights a day land at this northern Maryland gateway, located approximately 20 miles northwest of Annapolis. Minibus transfer services between the airport and the major hotels of Annapolis are operated by Limousines Unlimited (tel. 268-0094). The fare is $12 one way and $22 round-trip. Transfer by taxi is approximately $35 one way.

BY TRAIN OR BUS

If you want to arrive in Annapolis by train, the nearest stations are Baltimore, 20 miles to the north, and Washington, D.C., about 40 miles to the west.

BY CAR

Located in the center of Maryland's Chesapeake Bay coast, Annapolis is about 30 miles south of Baltimore (via Rte. 2), and 40 miles east of Washington, D.C. (via Rtes. 50 and 301). Annapolis is also accessible from the east via the William Preston Lane Memorial Bridge, locally known as the "Bay Bridge."

TOURIST INFORMATION

There are three main sources for tourist brochures and maps of Annapolis: the **Visitors Center,** Maryland State House, State Circle, Annapolis, MD 21401 (tel. 301/974-3400); the **Annapolis and Anne Arundel Conference and Visitors Bureau,** 1 Annapolis St., Annapolis, MD 21401 (tel. 301/280-0445 or 268-TOUR);

and the **Annapolis Public Information and Tourism Office,** City Hall, 160 Duke of Gloucester St., Annapolis, MD 21401 (tel. 301/263-7940).

CITY LAYOUT

The city layout is based on two central circles—State Circle and Church Circle. All other streets radiate from these two points. The U.S. Naval Academy is in its own enclave, east of State Circle.

2. GETTING AROUND

BY PUBLIC TRANSPORTATION

The city operates a shuttle-bus service using gasoline-powered trolleys between the historic/business district and the parking area of the Navy–Marine Corps Stadium. Shuttles operate every 20 minutes from 6:30am to 8pm, every day except Sundays; the one-way fare is 75¢. For up-to-date information on this shuttle service, call 263-7964.

BY TAXI

Once you are in town, if you need transport call **Arundel & Colonial Cab** (tel. 263-2555); **Blue Star Cab** (tel. 268-1323); or **Yellow Checker Cab** (tel. 266-8835 and 268-3737).

BY CAR

CAR RENTALS

Firms represented in Annapolis include **Budget,** 2001 West St. (tel. 266-5030); **Discount,** 1032 West St. (tel. 269-6645); and **Enterprise,** 1023 Spa Rd. (tel. 268-7751).

PARKING

True to its 18th-century style, midtown Annapolis is very compact, with lots of narrow streets; consequently, parking in the historic district is limited. Visitors are encouraged to leave their cars in a park-and-ride lot, located on the edge of town, off Rowe Boulevard, on the west side of the Navy–Marine Corps Stadium.

 ANNAPOLIS

Area Code   The area code of Annapolis is 301.
Baby-sitters   Inquire at your hotel or guesthouse.
Car Rentals   See "Getting Around," above.
Drugstores   Look under "Pharmacies" in the *Yellow Pages.* A downtown branch of the national chain **Rite Aid** is located at 179 Main St. (tel. 263-9895).
Emergencies   Dial 911 for fire, police, or ambulance.
Eyeglasses   Several national optical chains operate in the Annapolis area, including **Lens Crafters** and **Pearle Vision Center.**
Hairdressers/Barbers   Two downtown shops that cater to both men and women are **Annapolis Image Hair Studio,** 109 Main St. (tel. 268-9095) and **Hair Reflection,** 60 West St. (tel. 268-4439).
Hospitals   The nearest hospitals are located in Baltimore or the suburbs between Baltimore and Annapolis. Consult the *Yellow Pages,* under "Hospitals."
Information   See "Tourist Information," above.

Laundry/Dry Cleaning   Most hotels provide same-day laundry and dry-cleaning services. Convenient local firms include **Rainbow Cleaners,** 201 Main St. (tel. 626-1109) and **Norge Dry Cleaning and Laundry Village,** Roscoe Rowe Blvd. and Taylor Ave. (tel. 268-1008).

Library   The Anne Arundel County Library, West St. (tel. 280-1750).

Liquor Laws   Places serving alcoholic beverages may be open from 6am to 2am, except on Sunday and election days. The minimum age for buying or consuming alcohol is 21.

Newspapers/Magazines   Local daily newspapers include the *Annapolis Capital* and the *Anne Arundel County Sun.* The *Baltimore Sun* and the *Washington Post* are also widely available. The leading monthly magazine is *Annapolitan.*

Photographic Needs   Two convenient shops are **Miller's Camera Shop,** 2521 Riva Rd. (tel. 224-3808 or 261-8080) and **One-Hour Photo,** 112 Main St. (tel. 263-6919).

Police   See "Emergencies."

Post Office   The main branch is at Church Circle and N. West St. (tel. 263-9292).

Safety   Annapolis is generally safe. Nevertheless, there are precautions you should take whenever you are traveling in an unfamiliar city or country. Stay alert and be aware of your immediate surroundings. Wear a moneybelt and keep a close eye on your possessions. Be particularly careful with cameras, purses, and wallets, all favorite targets of thieves and pickpockets. Be especially careful when walking on dark streets and in parks after dark. Every society has its criminals. It's your responsibility to be aware and alert even in touristed areas.

Taxes   The local sales tax is 5%; the local hotel tax is 6%.

Taxis   See "Getting Around," above.

Telegrams/Telex   Check at your hotel.

Transit Information   Call the Annapolis Department of Public Transportation (tel. 263-7964).

3. ANNAPOLIS ACCOMMODATIONS

The main accommodation choices in Annapolis are concentrated in or near the downtown area. Consequently, most hotels and inns are within walking distance of the major attractions, shopping, and restaurants. Convenience is costly, however, and except for a few motels on the outskirts of town, it is hard to find a double-occupancy room in Annapolis under $100, and even more of a coup to find one under $75. To lessen the dent in your wallet, many properties offer packages at specially reduced rates; be sure to inquire if a package rate applies at the time you intend to visit.

VERY EXPENSIVE

ANNAPOLIS MARRIOTT WATERFRONT, 80 Compromise St., Annapolis, MD 21401. Tel. 301/268-7555 or toll-free 800/228-9290. Fax 301/269-5864. 150 rms, 1 suite. A/C TV TEL

$ Rates: $129–$279 single, $149–$279 double, $450 suite. AE, CB, DC, DISC, MC, V. **Parking:** $10.

Built of brick with a Colonial-Victorian exterior, this modern six-story hotel (formerly a Hilton), enjoys the best lodging location in town—right on the harbor—and many of the rooms have balconies overlooking either the water or the historic district. As we go to press, it is being thoroughly renovated under its new owners.

Dining/Entertainment: For meals or cocktails, it's hard to beat the views at the 5th-floor Penthouse restaurant and lounge. In the summer months, there is also a waterfront café on the ground level.

Services: Room service, valet laundry service.

Facilities: Outdoor swimming pool, sun deck, a 200-foot boardwalk, boat-docking slips.

EXPENSIVE

LOEWS ANNAPOLIS HOTEL, 126 West St., Annapolis, MD 21401. Tel. 301/263-7777 or toll-free 800/223-0888. Fax 301/263-0084. 210 rms, 7 suites. A/C MINIBAR TV TEL

$ Rates: $100–$150 single, $110–$160 double, $190–$300 suite. AE, CB, DC, MC, V. **Parking:** Self $4, valet $7.

Formerly a Radisson property, this hotel was acquired by Loews in 1990. As we go to press, all guest rooms, corridors, and public areas are being totally redecorated and updated, with new fabrics, furniture, window treatments, and floor coverings. The hotel has also recently acquired and restored an adjacent building, the historic Washington/Baltimore and Annapolis Power Substation, dating back to 1910, as a unique new meeting facility.

Dining/Entertainment: The Corinthian Restaurant (see "Where to Dine," below) offers full-service dining, and the Weather Rail Lounge serves light food and has nightly piano entertainment.

Services: 24-hour room service, valet/laundry service, concierge, nightly turndown, Federal Express drop-off in lobby, complimentary van transportation within local area.

Facilities: Gift shop, hair salon, conference center.

MODERATE

GIBSON'S LODGINGS, 110–114 Prince George St., Annapolis, MD 21401. Tel. 301/268-5555. 13 rms with shared baths, 5 with private bath, 2 suites with private bath. A/C TV TEL

$ Rates (include continental breakfast): $58–$75 single, $68–$85 double, $110–$120 suite. AE, MC, V. **Parking:** Free.

Operated by Claude and Jeanne Schrift, this three-building complex consists of two restored town houses and a modern three-story annex. The main building, the Patterson House (dating to 1760), is a Federal-Georgian house with a Victorian facade. It has five rooms, sharing three bathrooms, and two parlors where breakfast is served each morning. The adjacent Berman House, a trigable variation of a 19th-century stucco Homestead-style dwelling, has eight guest rooms with four adjoining baths and one room with private bath. The annex, harmoniously constructed, in 1988, of brick to blend in with the older buildings, has two suites and four guest rooms, all with private bath, plus meeting and seminar rooms.

The bedrooms are furnished with antiques. A central garden and courtyard serves as a common ground for all three buildings, and there is plenty of off-street parking for guests. It's an ideal location if you want to be within walking distance of the harbor, the historic district, and the Naval Academy.

COMFORT INN, 200 Revell Hwy., Annapolis, MD 21401. Tel. 301/757-8500 or toll-free 800/221-228-5150. Fax 301/757-1005. 60 rms. A/C TV TEL

$ Rates: $54–$75 single, $64–$85 double. AE, CB, DC, DISC, MC, V. **Parking:** Free.

Conveniently located midway between downtown and the Bay Bridge, this modern two-story motel is set back from the main road in a shady setting. The guest rooms, accessible by computer-card keys, offer a choice of one king-size or two queen-size beds, with a decor of light woods and pastel fabrics. The bathrooms are equipped with hairdryers; some units have pull-out couches or whirlpool baths. On-site facilities include a (seasonal) outdoor pool.

COURTYARD BY MARRIOTT, 2559 Riva Rd., Annapolis, MD 21401. Tel. 301/266-1555 or toll-free 800/321-2211. Fax 301/266-6376. 149 rms. A/C TV TEL

$ Rates: $68–$88 single, $78–$98 double. AE, CB, DC, MC, V. **Parking:** Free.

Nestled in a quiet setting outside of the historic district, this is a contemporary three-story facility. The rooms follow the usual Courtyard plan, with sliding glass windows and balconies or patios facing a central landscaped terrace. Guest units, most of which have king-size beds, are spacious, with a separate sitting area, sofa, desk, and coffee-making fixtures. Hotel facilities include a restaurant, indoor swimming pool, whirlpool, and exercise room.

PRINCE GEORGE INN, 232 Prince George St., Annapolis, MD 21401. Tel. 301/263-6418. 4 rms (2 with bath). A/C

$ Rates (including breakfast): $60–$75 single, $75–$85 double. AE, MC, V. **Parking:** On street.

A reasonably priced bed-and-breakfast choice is this 100-year-old Victorian town house in the heart of the city, just a block from State Circle. Converted into a guest home in the early 1980s, this three-story brick building offers comfortable rooms, a cozy parlor with a fireplace, and a pleasant side porch breakfast room. The rates include a full buffet breakfast.

HISTORIC INNS OF ANNAPOLIS

Thanks to the efforts of a local preservationist and developer, Paul Pearson, five of Annapolis's most historic buildings were purchased and saved from destruction over 20 years ago. With the guidance and encouragement of the nonprofit group Historic Annapolis Inc., Pearson has since turned the properties into **four elegant inns**. Clustered around Annapolis's two key city circles, these landmark buildings are now collectively known as the Historic Inns of Annapolis. To reserve a room at any one of the locations, contact the central office of the **Historic Inns of Annapolis**, 16 Church Circle, Annapolis, MD 21401 (tel. 301/263-2641 or toll-free 800/847-8882).

GOVERNOR CALVERT HOUSE, 58 State Circle. Tel. 301/263-2641 or toll-free 800/847-8882. 51 rms (all with bath). Fax 301/268-3813. A/C TV TEL

$ Rates: $90–$185 single, $100–$185 double. AE, CB, DC, MC, V. **Parking:** Free.

Both a conference center and a hotel, this lodging is composed of several restored and integrated Colonial and Victorian residences. Dating back to 1727, one of the public rooms, partially built on the site of the old Calvert family greenhouse, contains an original hypocaust (a warm-air heating system), now covered with a huge sheet of tempered glass and used as a museum display area. The bedrooms are furnished with antiques. Facilities include underground parking and a sunny ground-floor atrium.

MARYLAND INN, 16 Church Circle. Tel. 301/263-2641 or toll-free 800/847-8882. Fax 301/268-3813. 44 rms (all with bath). A/C TV TEL

$ Rates: $90–$185 single, $100–$185 double. AE, CB, DC, MC, V. **Parking:** Free.

Wedged into a busy triangular intersection, this impressive flatiron-shaped structure has been operating as an inn since the 1770s. It has been carefully restored and is now decorated in period furnishings ranging from antique fireplaces, rush-seated chairs, lantern fixtures, and country hunt prints to Queen Anne and Louis XIV pieces. Facilities include the Treaty of Paris restaurant (see "Annapolis Dining," below) and a tavern.

ROBERT JOHNSON HOUSE, 23 State Circle (1765). Tel. 301/263-2641 or toll-free 800/847-8882. Fax 301/268-3813. 30 rms (all with bath). A/C TV TEL

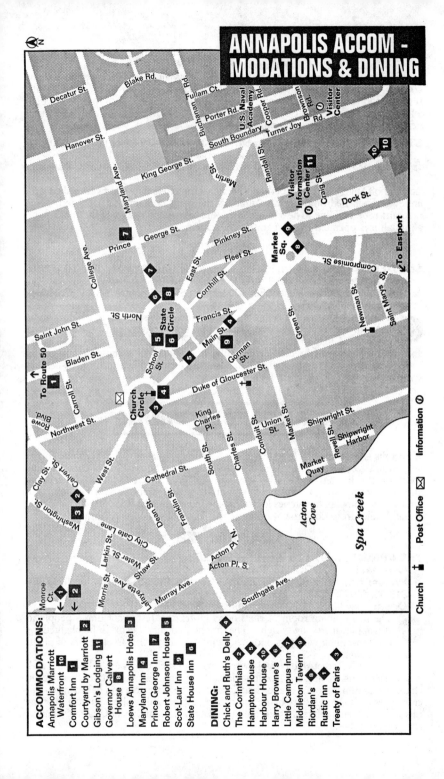

ANNAPOLIS ACCOM - MODATIONS & DINING

ACCOMMODATIONS:

Annapolis Marriott Waterfront **10**
Comfort Inn **1**
Courtyard by Marriott **2**
Gibson's Lodging **11**
Governor Calvert House **8**
Loews Annapolis Hotel **3**
Maryland Inn **4**
Prince George Inn **7**
Robert Johnson House **5**
Scot-Laur Inn **9**
State House Inn **6**

DINING:

Chick and Ruth's Delly **4**
The Corinthian **2**
Hampton House **5**
Harbour House **10**
Harry Browne's **6**
Little Campus Inn **7**
Middleton Tavern **9**
Riordan's **8**
Rustic Inn **1**
Treaty of Paris **3**

Church ✚ Post Office ⊠ Information ⑦

$ Rates (including continental breakfast): $90–$185 single, $100–$185 double. AE, CB, DC, MC, V. **Parking:** Free.

Overlooking the governor's mansion and the Maryland State House, this lodging consists of three adjoining Georgian homes, dating back to 1773. The artfully restored and furnished guest rooms are individually decorated with four-poster beds and antiques; each unit also has a private bath. A hearty continental breakfast is delivered to guest rooms each morning.

STATE HOUSE INN, 200 Main St. Tel. 301/263-2641 or toll-free 800/847-8882. Fax 301/268-3813. 9 rms (all with bath). A/C TV TEL

$ Rates: $90–$185 single, $100–$185 double. AE, CB, DC, MC, V. **Parking:** Free.

Located off State Circle, this bed-and-breakfast inn offers nine rooms furnished with antiques. Each bedroom key also unlocks the main door of this 1820 four-story, mansard-roof building. The Hampton House restaurant occupies the main floor, although it is operated by a separate management.

BUDGET

SCOT-LAUR INN, 165 Main St., Annapolis, MD 21401. Tel. 301/268-5665. 10 rms (all with bath). A/C TV TEL

$ Rates (including breakfast): $50–$70 single, $55–$75 double. MC, V. **Parking:** In adjacent public garage.

The best value in town is this inn, housed in a three-story brick building in the heart of the historic district. The ground floor belongs to Chick and Ruth's Delly, an Annapolis tradition for good food at reasonable prices. The eatery and the inn are owned by the Levitt family, who are full of enthusiasm and offer a warm welcome. The guest rooms are handsomely furnished in a turn-of-the-century style.

4. ANNAPOLIS DINING

Annapolis is well known for its excellent restaurants—from Colonial dining rooms and taverns to romantic bistros and waterside seafood houses. Many choice dining spots are also located in the city's hotels and restored inns. In addition, for families and travelers on the go, Annapolis is home to a Restaurant Park, a fast-food and family-style complex of eateries located at the intersection of Rtes. 50, 301, and 450, about 3 miles from downtown, opposite the Annapolis Shopping Plaza.

EXPENSIVE

THE CORINTHIAN, 126 West St. Tel. 263-7777.
   Cuisine: INTERNATIONAL. **Reservations:** Recommended.
$ Prices: Appetizers $3.95–$8.95; main courses $13.95–$19.95; lunch $5.95–$13.95. AE, CB, DC, MC, V.
   Open: Daily lunch 11:30–2pm, dinner 5–10pm.

The main dining room of the Loews Hotel, this restaurant draws people to Annapolis in its own right. The bright and airy decor is highlighted by floor-to-ceiling windows, indirect lighting, and colorful assortments of plants and dried flowers.

The menu is a creative blend of ingredients with such dishes as veal paillard with wild mushrooms, shallot, and hazelnut glace; shrimp in whisky cream; southern baked chicken with tomato, orange, and chocolate barbecue marinade; and baked angel-hair crab cakes with Dijon buerre blanc and orange zest; as well as filet mignon and prime ribs of beef. Lunch offers simpler fare, including salads, sandwiches, pastas, frittatas, and stir-fry dishes.

HAMPTON HOUSE, 200 Main St. Tel. 268-7898.
  Cuisine: FRENCH/HUNGARIAN. **Reservations:** Required.
  $ Prices: Appetizers $4.95–$9.95; main courses $16.95–$26.95; fixed-price dinners from $18.95 and up. AE, MC, V.
  Open: Mon–Thurs 5:30–10pm, Fri–Sat 5:30–11pm.
A touch of old Europe can be found at this small dining room in a restored 1820 town house right in the heart of midtown. Combining a selection of light French and Hungarian dishes, the menu features such entrées as medallions of pork and chicken in paprika and wienerschnitzel Modena (veal, cured ham, and cheese in pimiento sauce), as well as swordfish with crab imperial, capon with chestnut mousse, and steak au poivre. Starters average between $3.95 and $4.95 for such authentic treats as Hungarian gulyas soup and stuffed cabbage.

MIDDLETON TAVERN, 2 Market Space and Randall St. Tel. 263-3323.
  Cuisine: AMERICAN. **Reservations:** Recommended.
  $ Prices: Appetizers $3.95–$8.95; main courses $11.95–$23.95; lunch $3.95–$9.95. MC, V.
  Open: Daily lunch 11am–4pm; dinner Sun–Thurs 5–10pm, Fri–Sat 5–11pm.
Established by Horatio Middleton as an inn for seafaring men in 1750, this restaurant had many prominent patrons, including George Washington, Thomas Jefferson, and Benjamin Franklin. Today, restored and expanded, this City Dock landmark is enjoyed by men and women. The lunch menu includes chili, fish and chips, and barbecued seafood kebabs. Dinner entrées include crêpes Middleton (shrimp, scallops, and crab in a light Newburg sauce); lobster Luicci (lightly breaded lobster tails broiled in herbs and butter); filet of sole stuffed with crab, spinach, and mushrooms; as well as steak tartare and chateaubriand for two.

TREATY OF PARIS, 16 Church Circle. Tel. 263-2641.
  Cuisine: AMERICAN. **Reservations:** Recommended.
  $ Prices: Appetizers $3.95–$8.95; main courses $13.95–$22.95; lunch $5.95–$9.95. AE, CB, DC, MC, V.
  Open: Daily lunch 11:30am–3pm; dinner 6–9:30pm.
Centrally located in the Maryland Inn, this cozy dining room exudes an 18th-century ambience with a decor of brick walls, Colonial-style furnishings, and an open fireplace, all enhanced by the glow of candlelight. The eclectic menu offers such dishes as duck with cranberry and apple-honey glaze, crab imperial, rack of lamb, veal Oscar, seafood brochette, blackened steaks, and beef Wellington.

MODERATE

HARBOUR HOUSE, 87 Prince George St. Tel. 268-0771.
  Cuisine: SEAFOOD. **Reservations:** Recommended.
  $ Prices: Appetizers $3.95–$6.95; main courses $12.95–$19.95; lunch $5.95–$7.95. AE, CB, DC, MC, V.
  Open: Daily lunch 11:30am–2:30pm; dinner 5–10pm.
⭐ The place to go for maritime views while you dine is this nautical-style restaurant overlooking the city dock, run by two generations of the Phillips family. Seafood selections dominate the lunch menu with crab quiche, salmon strudel, and seafood pie, as well as sandwiches and burgers. Soups, such as cream of crab with sherry and crab vegetable, are popular any time of the day. Dinner entrées include a host of crab creations, prime rib, butterfly shrimp, lobster thermidor, and steaks. In the summer months, meals are also served on an outside terrace. An extensive wine list is offered (from $9 to $30 a bottle), which features labels from Maryland, California, and Europe, as well as "house" wines imported from France.

HARRY BROWNE'S, 66 State Circle. Tel. 263-4332.
  Cuisine: INTERNATIONAL. **Reservations:** Recommended.

$ Prices: Appetizers $3.95–$7.95; main courses $12.95–$19.95; lunch $4.95–$7.95. AE, CB, DC, MC, V.
Open: Lunch Mon–Sat 11am–3pm; dinner Sun–Thurs 5:30–10pm, Fri–Sat 5:30–11pm; brunch Sun 10am–3pm.
A favorite haunt of legislators is this midtown eatery with nautical chandeliers, globe lights, large framed mirrors, and an old-Maryland ambience. For a change of pace, there is also an art-deco cocktail lounge upstairs and an outdoor brick-floored courtyard café. Lunch includes an interesting array of salads, quiches, croissant-wiches, chili, and pâté and cheese platters. Entrées at dinner range from blackened swordfish, shrimp scampi, and seafood pasta to grilled duck breast and chicken breast with asparagus mousse.

RIORDAN'S, 26 Market Space. Tel. 263-5449.
Cuisine: AMERICAN. **Reservations:** Recommended.
$ Prices: Appetizers $2.95–$7.95; main courses $9.95–$19.95; lunch $3.95–$7.95. AE, MC, V.
Open: Lunch daily 11am–2pm; dinner Sun–Thurs 6–11pm, Fri–Sat 6pm–midnight.
An Irish ambience prevails at this early-American tavern, as evidenced by an illuminated shamrock at the entrance and an Irish flag on the ceiling. The eclectic decor also includes Tiffany lamps, ceiling fans, vintage pictures and posters, and colorful stained glass. Light choices (overstuffed sandwiches, burgers, pastas, and salads) are available at lunch. The regular dinner menu includes crab-stuffed flounder, prime ribs, steamed shrimp, broiled swordfish, and steaks.

RUSTIC INN, 1803 West St. Tel. 263-2626.
Cuisine: INTERNATIONAL. **Reservations:** Recommended.
$ Prices: Appetizers $3.95–$7.95; main courses $10.95–$21.95. AE, MC, V.
Open: Mon–Thurs 5pm–10pm, Fri–Sat 5–11pm.
With a suitably rustic decor, this restaurant is known for its fresh seafood, Iowa choice beef, and Provimi milk-fed veal. Entrées include scallops champignon (baked in Marsala wine with fresh mushrooms and grated Cheddar), oyster imperial and crab imperial, veal (marsala, piccata, or francese), chicken Divan, and steak béarnaise.

LITTLE CAMPUS INN, 61–63 Maryland Ave. Tel. 263-9250.
Cuisine: AMERICAN. **Reservations:** Recommended.
$ Prices: Appetizers $1.95–$5.95; main courses $7.95–$14.95; lunch $2.95–$7.95. AE, MC, V.
Open: Lunch Mon–Sat 11am–3pm; dinner Mon–Sat 5–10:30pm.
Conveniently situated, this midtown restaurant has been a favorite since 1924. The second generation of the Nichols family now runs the homey eatery, known for its hearty home-style food and decor of original brick, dark woods, and murals of early Annapolis. Lunch includes fried chicken, omelets, and breaded veal steak. Dinner selections range from beef or lamb shish kebab and spaghetti with meatballs to chicken Kiev and seafood samplers (crab, lobster, scallops, shrimp, crab claw, fish filet, and clams casino).

BUDGET

CHICK AND RUTH'S DELLY, 165 Main St. Tel. 269-6737.
Cuisine: AMERICAN. **Reservations:** Not required.
$ Prices: Main courses and lunch $2.50–$5.50. No credit cards.
Open: Daily 24 hours.
To sample an Annapolis tradition, stop in at this ma-and-pa establishment run by two generations of the Levitt family for more than 20 years. The small storefront deli-restaurant is famous for sandwiches named either after world political figures or after local attractions, as, for example, President Bush (ham, turkey,

and bacon on rye), Golda Meir (lox, cream cheese, onion, and tomato, on a bagel), and Main Street (corned beef and cole slaw). Platters and salads are also available.

5. ANNAPOLIS ATTRACTIONS

The entire midcity area of Annapolis is a National Historic District, with more than 1,500 restored and preserved buildings. Since the streets are narrow, the ideal way to see the sights is on foot. Several guided walking tours are described below; self-guided walking tour maps are also available free of charge from the various tourist offices.

Plan to spend some time around the City Dock along the Annapolis waterfront. This is a yachting hub, with hundreds of craft of all sizes in port. Various sightseeing cruises of the harbor are available in spring, summer, and fall. The City Dock is also home to fine seafood restaurants, lively bars, specialty shops, galleries, and a summer theater.

Other highlights of this area include **Market House,** a central farmers' produce station built in 1784 and again in 1858. Today it still retains much of the flavor of the open stalls, with a variety of foods, although the wares now fall mostly into the fast-food category (open Monday and Wednesday through Saturday from 9am to 6pm, and Sunday from 10am to 6pm).

MARITIME ANNAPOLIS, 77–79 Main St. Tel. 268-5576.

This historical triorama is housed in the Victualling Warehouse. The exhibit will give you an idea of what the waterfront looked like in 1751–91, when the port of Annapolis was in its heyday.

Admission: 50¢ adults, 25¢ children 6–18.

Open: Daily 11am–4:30pm. **Closed:** Thanksgiving Day and Christmas Day.

MARYLAND STATE HOUSE, on State Circle. Tel. 269-3400.

Located in the center of Annapolis, this is the oldest U.S. state capitol in continuous legislative use (built 1772–79). The building also served as the capital of our country from November 26, 1783, to August 13, 1784. As you step inside the Old Senate Chamber, you'll be in the historic spot where George Washington resigned his commission as commander-in-chief of the Continental armies. This was also the setting for the ratification of the Treaty of Paris, which ended the Revolutionary War. The dome of this building, the largest of its kind constructed entirely of wood, is made of cypress beams and is held together by wooden pegs. You can stroll throughout the State House on your own, examining the various exhibits that depict life in Annapolis in Colonial times, or you can make use of the free guided tours that depart on the hour, 10am to 4pm (except 1pm), from the Visitors Center on the first floor.

Admission: Free.

Open: Daily 9am–5pm. **Closed:** Thanksgiving Day, Christmas Day, and New Year's Day.

U.S. NAVAL ACADEMY, King George and Randall Streets. Tel. 263-6933.

Annapolis is known for this academy, founded in 1845; it is the U.S. Navy's undergraduate professional college and a national historic site spread over 300 acres along the Severn River on the eastern edge of town. Visitors are welcome to stroll the grounds at leisure and to see such sights as the chapel and crypt of John Paul Jones and the Preble Hall Museum, containing fascinating collections of nautical relics, paintings, ship models, and other historic items relating to the Navy's role in wars, global exploration, and space.

Commissioning Week, usually the third week in May, is a colorful time of full-dress parades; it is also a busy period for Annapolis hotels, as relatives and friends of the cadets pour into the city. Guided tours are available, departing daily from Ricketts Hall at Gate 1, March 1 through May 31, from 10am to 2pm on the hour; June 1 through the Labor Day weekend, from 9:30am to 4pm, every half hour; after Labor Day through the Thanksgiving weekend, from 10am to 3pm, on the hour. The charge for tours is $3 for adults and $1 for children under 12 (note, however, that tour prices are subject to change).

Admission: To grounds free.

Open: Mon–Sat 9:30am–5pm, Sun noon–5pm. **Closed:** New Year's Day, Christmas Day.

WILLIAM PACA HOUSE AND GARDEN, 186 Prince George St., at Martin Street. Tel. 263-5533.

⭐ Among the great historic residences in Annapolis is this former home of William Paca, a signer of the Declaration of Independence and a governor of Maryland during the Revolutionary period. Built in 1763–65 and restored by Historic Annapolis Inc. from 1965 to 1976, it is a five-part structure, with a stalwart central block, hyphens and wings, and a total of 37 rooms. Guided tours of the house are available.

Another attraction of the Paca estate is the adjacent two-acre pleasure garden. The layout includes five elegant terraces, a fish-shaped pond, a Chinese Chippendale bridge, a domed pavilion, and a wilderness garden. If you are not touring the house first, you can enter the garden directly through a Visitor Center at 1 Martin St. (tel. 269-0601). Combination packages, covering both the house and the garden, are $5 for adults and $3 for youngsters 6–18.

Admission: To tour house, $3.50 adults, $2.50 youngsters 6–18. To tour garden, $2 adults, $1 youngsters 6–18.

Open: House, Tues–Sat 10am–4pm, Sun and holidays noon–4pm. Garden, May–Oct Mon–Sat 10am–4:30pm, Sun noon–4:30pm; Nov–Apr daily noon–4pm.

HAMMOND-HARWOOD HOUSE, 19 Maryland Ave. Tel. 269-1714.

Built in 1774, this house is one of the finest examples of Georgian architecture in the United States. It is also an outstanding example of the Maryland five-part plan that connects the central section by hyphens to semi-octagonal wings. Famous for its center doorway of tall Ionic columns, the interior is a showcase of decorative ornamentation and wood carvings. The house is named for its first and its last owners: Mathias Hammond, a Maryland member of the Provincial Assembly, and the Harwood family, who owned the house in recent years before it became a museum.

Admission: $3.50 adults, $2.50 children 6–18.

Open: Apr–Oct Tues–Sat 10am–5pm, Sun 2–5pm; Nov–Mar Tues–Sat 10am–4pm, Sun 1–4pm. **Closed:** Monday, as well as New Year's Day, Thanksgiving Day, and Christmas Day.

SHIPLAP HOUSE MUSEUM, 18 Pinkney St. Tel. 626-1033.

One of the oldest surviving structures in Annapolis (dating back to 1715), this was a tavern serving a waterfront clientele in the 18th century. It is now a museum with exhibits highlighting the history of the building and the city of Annapolis. The facility includes a gift shop.

Admission: Free.

Open: Daily 11am–4pm.

BANNEKER-DOUGLASS MUSEUM, 84 Franklin St. Tel. 974-2894.

Named after two prominent local black residents, Benjamin Banneker and Frederick Douglass, this museum presents arts and crafts, exhibits, lectures, and films, all designed to portray the historical life and cultural experiences of African-Americans in Maryland.

Admission: Free.

Open: Tues–Fri 10am–3pm, Sat noon–4pm.

CHARLES CARROLL HOUSE, 109 Duke of Gloucester St. Tel. 263-2969.

Built in 1721–22 and enlarged in 1770, this is the birthplace and dwelling of

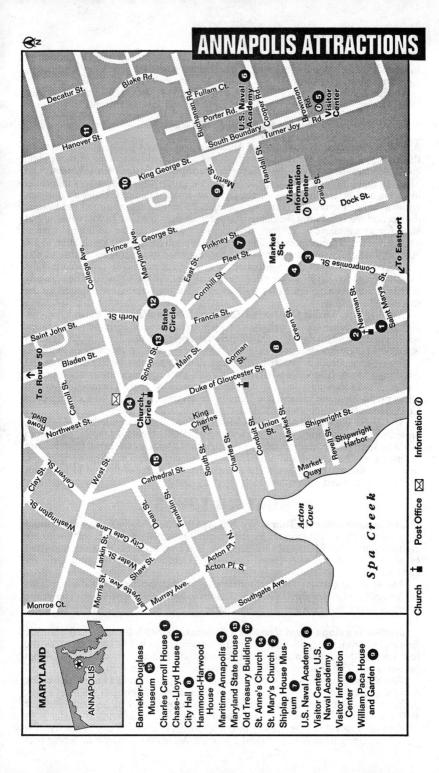

ANNAPOLIS ATTRACTIONS

Decatur St.
Blake Rd.
Hanover St.
King George St.
Prince George St.
Saint John St.
Bladen St.
College Ave.
Maryland Ave.
North St.
School St.
Main St.
Francis St.
State Circle
Church Circle
West St.
Cathedral St.
Northwest St.
Carroll St.
Rowe Blvd.
Clay St.
Calvert St.
Washington St.
Lafayette Ave.
Larkin St.
Water St.
Shaw St.
Dean St.
Franklin St.
City Gate Lane
Monroe Ct.
Murray Ave.
Acton Pl. S.
Acton Pl. N.
Southgate Ave.
South St.
Charles St.
King Charles Pl.
Gorman St.
Duke of Gloucester St.
Conduit St.
Union St.
Market St.
Shipwright St.
Revell St.
Shipwright Harbor
Market Quay
Market St.
Green St.
Newman St.
Saint Mary's St.
Compromise St.
Craig St.
Dock St.
Martin St.
Randall St.
Cooper Rd.
Brownson Rd.
Turner Joy
South Boundary
Porter Rd.
Fullam Ct.
Buchanan Rd.
U.S. Naval Academy
Visitor Center
Visitor Information Center
East St.
Pinkney St.
Fleet St.
Cornhill St.
Market Sq.
To Route 50
To Eastport
Acton Cove
Spa Creek

MARYLAND
ANNAPOLIS

Banneker-Douglass Museum 15
Charles Carroll House 1
Chase-Lloyd House 11
City Hall 8
Hammond-Harwood House 10
Maritime Annapolis 4
Maryland State House 13
Old Treasury Building 12
St. Anne's Church 14
St. Mary's Church 2
Shiplap House Museum 7
U.S. Naval Academy 6
Visitor Center, U.S. Naval Academy 5
Visitor Information Center 3
William Paca House and Garden 9

✝ Church   ⊠ Post Office   ⓘ Information

Charles Carroll of Carrollton, the only Roman Catholic to sign the Declaration of Independence. Although it is undergoing restoration, the site welcomes visitors.

Admission: Free to house and garden, $1 charge to tour wine cellar.

Open: 3rd Sat and Sun of each month 9:30am–4:30pm. (*Note:* As of August 1992, visiting days will be expanded to 6 a week; call for exact details.)

WALKING TOURS

Although you can easily walk around Annapolis, you'll enjoy twice the fun (and twice the history) if you put yourself in the hands of a qualified guide. One of the leading guide services is operated by **Historic Annapolis Foundation Tours,** Old Treasury Building, State Circle (tel. 267-8149), the group that has been very influential in saving and preserving many of the city's landmark buildings. Using a "museum without walls" theme, this company conducts 90-minute walks around the historic district and the U.S. Naval Academy. Tours depart from the Old Treasury Building at State Circle weekdays at 1:30pm, with daily departures and an additional tour at 11:30am in the summer months. The fee is $6 for adults and $3.50 for children 6–18. Historic Annapolis also has several excursions designed specifically for adults, such as a 3-hour exploration of the interiors of the city's great mansions. Tailor-made tours focusing on preservation and the decorative arts can also be arranged. The regularly scheduled tours are operated on a walk-in basis, but reservations are required for the specialized tours.

Another firm, **Three Centuries Tours of Annapolis,** 48 Maryland Ave. (tel. 263-5401), is known for its well-informed guides in Colonial costume. These tours, which cover the highlights of the historic district and the Naval Academy, are 2 hours in length and are operated on a turn-up-and-go basis, with no reservations required.

From April through October, there are daily departures at 9:30am from the Annapolis Marriott lobby, and at 1:30pm from the City Dock Information booth. The price is $5 for adults and $3.50 for youngsters 6–18. Three Centuries Tours also offers preplanned and tailor-made tours by reservation, focusing on such topics as Colonial life (for young visitors), historic mansions, and bay cruises.

The **U.S. Naval Academy Guide Service,** Ricketts Hall (tel. 267-3363), provides guided walking tours of the academy, March 1 through May 31, daily from 10am to 3pm, on the hour; from June through the Labor Day weekend, from 9:30am to 4pm, every half hour; and after Labor Day through the Thanksgiving weekend, from 10am to 3pm, on the hour. The current charge is $3 for adults and $1 for pupils in the 6th grade and under, but it is subject to change.

BOATING TOURS

✪ **Chesapeake Marine Tours,** Slip 20, City Dock (tel. 268-7600), operates various sightseeing cruises of Annapolis Harbor. Unless indicated otherwise, these trips are available daily from Memorial Day through Labor Day; on weekends from mid-April to Memorial Day and after Labor Day to mid-October. Children's rates apply for children 2 to 12.

The Harbor Queen offers a 40-minute narrated cruise that covers the highlights of Annapolis Harbor, the U.S. Naval Academy, and the Severn River. The cruise operates hourly from 11am to 5pm; the charge is $5 for adults and $3 for children 2 to 12.

Little Miss Anne I and II provide a 40-minute tour each focusing on the historic Annapolis harbor and residential waterfront along Spa Creek. The boats depart on the half hour, 2:30–8:30pm weekdays; at 15 minutes past and to the hour, 12:15–8:45pm on weekends. The charge is $5 for adults and $3 for children 2 to 12.

Providence provides a 90-minute outing, leaving Annapolis Harbor and sailing past the U.S. Naval Academy up the Severn River, considered one of the most scenic bodies of water of the Chesapeake Bay. The cruise operates Saturday and Sunday at 1:30 and 3:30pm. The charge is $9 for adults and $6 for children 2 to 12.

Annapolitan II, on Wednesday through Sunday, offers a full day on the bay (7½ hours), departing from Annapolis and cruising to St. Michaels, a historic fishing port on the eastern shore. The tour includes 3 hours of onshore sightseeing before the return trip to Annapolis. In all cases, boarding is at 9:30am; the return to the City Dock is at approximately 5:30pm. The price is $28 for adults and $18 for children 2 to 12.

6. ANNAPOLIS SPECIAL/FREE EVENTS

Various events might attract you to Annapolis at certain times of the year. Conversely, if you have no interest in a particular happening, avoid visiting during peak periods when hotel rooms will be hard to find and often subject to a surcharge. For example, in October the boating world converges on this city for the **U.S. Sailboat Show,** the world's largest in-the-water boat show, and the **U.S. Power Boat Show,** the largest show of its kind, with more than 300 boats on display in and out of the water. For information on either of these events, contact the **Annapolis and Anne Arundel Conference and Visitors Bureau,** Annapolis St., Annapolis, MD 21401 (tel. 301/280-0445 or 268-TOUR), or the **Annapolis Public Information and Tourism Office,** City Hall, 160 Duke of Gloucester St., Annapolis, MD 21401 (tel. 301/263-7940).

If you love seafood, plan ahead to come to Annapolis in early September for the **Maryland Seafood Festival.** Started in 1966, this event is held at Sandy Point State Park, about 8 miles from downtown. The program includes 3 days of continuous live entertainment and lots of good eating (steamed crabs, oysters, crab cakes, steamed shrimp, fried fish, and clam chowder).

Other leading events include the **Annapolis Bayfest** (May), the **Annapolis Wine Festival** (June), the **Chesapeake Appreciation Days** (October), and **Christmas in Annapolis** (December). For more information on all these events, contact the Annapolis Public Information and Tourist Office.

7. ANNAPOLIS SPORTS & RECREATION

With the Chesapeake at its doorstep, Annapolis is synonymous with sailing and home of the world-famous **Annapolis Sailing School,** P.O. Box 3334, Annapolis, MD 21403 (tel. 301/267-7205 or toll-free 800/638-9192). With over 120 boats and a huge support and teaching staff, this school offers a wide range of instructional programs for novice and veteran sailors. Courses range from a weekend beginner's course, priced from $180 to a 5-day advanced course for bareboat (skipperless) chartering for $525 and up.

Other boating activities in Annapolis are described under "Boating Tours," above.

8. ANNAPOLIS SAVVY SHOPPING

Annapolis is a good shopping and browsing town. The historic district is lined with boutiques and shops of international and local appeal. Below is a cross-section of some of the wares you can expect to find.

ANNAPOLIS COUNTRY STORE, 53 Maryland Ave. Tel. 269-6773.

Claiming to be the oldest and largest wicker shop in Maryland, this store also stocks pottery, mugs, jams, and kitchen accessories.

Open: Mon–Sat 10am–6pm, Sun noon–5pm.

ANNAPOLIS POTTERY, 61 Cornhill St. Tel. 268-6153.

As its name implies, this is a real working pottery studio, as well as a shop. The hand-designed items include vases, dishes, and plates, as well as artistic one-of-a-kind pieces. Many pieces can be personalized with names or logos on request.

Open: Mon–Sat 10am–6pm, Sun noon–5pm.

AVOCA HANDWEAVERS, 141–43 Main St. Tel. 263-1485.

This is the American branch of the Irish company of the same name, established in the Emerald Isle in 1723. As might be expected, soft and colorful Irish tweeds are the specialty here, with a wise selection of capes, coats, caps, suits, shawls, and sweaters, as well as Irish books, jewelry, glassware, and pottery.

Open: Mon–Thurs 10am–6pm, Fri–Sat 10am–8pm, Sun 11am–6pm.

CHARING CROSS BOOKS AND CARDS, 88 Maryland Ave. Tel. 268-1440.

This shop has a wide selection of volumes on Maryland and Annapolis history, as well as seafood cookbooks, greeting cards, and more.

Open: Mon–Sat 10:30am–5:30pm, Sun 9am–4pm.

THE GIFT HORSE, 77 Maryland Ave. Tel. 263-3737.

This is an emporium of unusual crafts, glass, brass, pewter, armetale, oil lamps, figurines, prisms, mobiles, and paper weights.

Open: Mon–Sat 10am–5:30pm, with added hours from noon–5pm on Sun in spring, summer, and fall.

THE PEWTER CHALICE, 140 Main St. Tel. 268-6246.

If you are fond of pewter, this is a great spot to browse or shop—for pewter goblets, bowls, tankards, candelabra, pitchers, flagons, plates, teapots, candlesticks, cutlery, flasks, inkwells, jewelry boxes, vases, and much more.

Open: Mon–Sat 10am–6pm, Sun noon–5pm.

THE SHIP AND SOLDIER SHOP, 55 Maryland Ave. Tel. 268-1141.

This is a good source for metal models and miniatures of the Army, Navy, and Marines (and the Canadian Mounted Police), as well as toy soldiers and models of cars, ships, trains, and planes.

Open: Mon–Sat 10am–5:30pm, Sun noon–5:30pm.

WALNUT LEAF ANTIQUES, 50 Maryland Ave. Tel. 263-4885.

This shop specializes in period and oak furniture, European and Asian porcelain, cut glass, linens, and vintage costume jewelry.

Open: Daily noon–5pm.

9. ANNAPOLIS EVENING ENTERTAINMENT

As the state capital, a college town, and a yachting center, Annapolis is a lively place at night. One of the top spots for music is the **King of France Tavern** in the Maryland Inn, 16 Church Circle (tel. 263-2641 or toll-free 800/847-8882). These former Colonial kitchens have been transformed into a jazz club, the home base of guitarist Charlie Byrd. In addition to jazz, the nightly program also offers occasional programs of folk, classical, and chamber music, and dinner/cabaret shows featuring songs of the 1930s and '40s.

For Broadway musicals, the place to go to is the **Annapolis Summer Garden Theater,** at the corner of Main Street and Compromise Street (tel. 268-0809), near the City Dock. Once a blacksmith shop, this theater was established in 1966, with productions ranging from *Carnival* to *Pajama Game.* Curtain time is at 8:45pm Thursday through Sunday, Memorial Day through Labor Day. Tickets are priced from $6 and up.

The **Annapolis Dinner Theater,** 339 Revell Hwy., Rte. 50, Annapolis (tel. 301/757-9450), offers a year-round program of entertainment, featuring Broadway-style musicals with a full dinner or brunch. Performances are scheduled Wednesday and Thursday at 8pm, Friday at 9pm, Saturday at 8pm, and Sunday at 2pm. In each case, the meal starts 2 hours prior to showtime. Prices range from $24 to $30.

Annapolis is also a town of trendy pubs, often featuring live music, entertainment, and dancing. Most of the in spots are clustered around the waterfront area, such as **McGarvey's Saloon,** City Dock (tel. 263-5700); **Riordan's Saloon,** City Dock (tel. 263-5449); **Armadillo's,** City Dock (tel. 268-6680); **Fran O'Brien's,** 113 Main St. (268-6288); **Mum's,** 136 Dock St. (tel. 263-3353); and **Marmaduke's,** 301 Severn Ave. (tel. 269-5420).

CHAPTER 17

MARYLAND'S EASTERN SHORE

A peninsula bordered on one side by the Atlantic and on the other by Chesapeake Bay, Maryland's eastern shore is almost an island. For centuries, this area was linked to the rest of Maryland's mainland only by a northeasterly spit of land closer to Wilmington than to Baltimore.

It wasn't until 1952, when the William Preston Lane Bridge was built from Annapolis over the Chesapeake Bay, that the eastern shore really became easily accessible to the rest of the state.

Back-to-back with Delaware and nudging Virginia's coastal strip, these eastern Maryland counties have developed a personality of their own, as part of the Delmarva peninsula. Much of James Michener's novel *Chesapeake* was inspired by the everyday lifestyle of these rural coastal communities.

Two of Maryland's most active ports, Cambridge and Salisbury, are located on the eastern shore, and some of the state's oldest towns and early shipbuilding centers are also here.

Most of all, this part of the world is known for its good eating. A haven for crabs, oysters, and other seafood, Crisfield is modestly called "The Seafood Capital of the World," and the Salisbury area, home of Perdue farms, is readily recognized as one of the nation's leading poultry producers. Top-class restaurants line the shore, in settings ranging from picturesque Victorian buildings and converted crab shacks to wide-windowed marina decks.

Added to all of this is Ocean City, the eastern shore's premier beach resort, with 10 miles of sandy beach, a 3-mile boardwalk, and hundreds of hotels, restaurants, and amusements. In contrast, this part of Maryland is also the home of the Blackwater National Wildlife Refuge, one of the chief resting areas for migrating wildfowl along the Atlantic Flyway.

The best way to reach the eastern shore from the west is via Rte. 50 and the bridge over the bay. Once you arrive, Rte. 50 will take you to Easton, Cambridge, Salisbury, and all the way over to Ocean City. If you are approaching from Delaware on the north or from the south via Virginia's coast, then Rte. 13 is the most direct road. Rte. 13 and its offshoot, Rte. 413, will also bring you to Crisfield.

---

1. EASTON

40 miles SE of Annapolis, 60 miles SE of Baltimore, 110 miles SW of Wilmington, 76 miles NW of Ocean City, 70 miles SW of Dover

GETTING THERE   By Air   Easton Municipal Airport (tel. 822-8560) is about 3 miles north of the city on Rte. 50. Among the carriers offering local charter

WHAT'S SPECIAL ABOUT MARYLAND'S EASTERN SHORE

Ace Attractions

☐ Easton's Historic District, the eastern shore's Colonial capital, with more than 40 preserved and restored buildings.

☐ St. Michaels Marina, attracting over 20,000 pleasure craft a year.

☐ Wye Oak, largest white oak in the United States and Maryland's official state tree.

☐ Blackwater National Wildlife Refuge, 17,000 acres of rich tidal marsh and a chief resting area for migrating wildfowl along the Atlantic Flyway.

Activities

☐ Ride the Oxford-Bellevue ferry across the Tred Avon River, America's oldest privately operated ferry, dating back to 1683.

☐ Cruise around St. Michaels on a "Patriot" boat, or to the offshore islands of Smith or Tangier from Crisfield.

☐ Fish the Chesapeake waters with Harrisons of Tilghman Island, the largest charter fleet on the bay.

Events/Festivals

☐ Waterfowl Festival, Easton, 3 days of waterfowl art, contests, auctions, workshops, and exhibits.

☐ Annual Hard Crab Derby and Fair, Crisfield, weekend of crab-themed feasting, frolic, and fun.

☐ PolkaMotion by the Ocean, continuous polka music and dancing at Ocean City.

Great Towns/Villages

☐ Crisfield, crabbing center and "seafood capital of the world."

☐ Berlin, an inland town with eye-catching Victorian buildings and a dozen antique shops.

Museums

☐ Chesapeake Bay Maritime Museum, a waterside showcase of seafaring history, with a 110-year-old lighthouse, a skipjack, and a bugeye.

☐ Historical Society of Talbot County, a museum complex of 18th- and 19th-century buildings depicting Easton's rich heritage.

Shopping

☐ Carvel Hall Factory Outlet, in Crisfield, for discounts on brand-name cutlery, glassware, pewter, and more.

---

service are **Maryland Airlines** (tel. 822-0400 or toll-free 800/451-5693), flying between Easton and Washington, D.C.

By Bus   Greyhound offers regular service into its depot at the junction of Rtes. 50 and 309 (tel. 822-0280).

By Car   The best way to get to the Easton area is by car, via Rte. 50 from all directions.

ESSENTIALS   For complete lodging and restaurant information, maps, and brochures about Easton and environs, contact the **Talbot County Chamber of Commerce,** 805 Goldsborough St., P.O. Box 1366, Easton, MD 21601. (tel. 301/822-4606). This helpful office is located at the junction of Rtes. 50 and 328.

SPECIAL EVENTS   One of Easton's most noteworthy gatherings is the annual **Waterfowl Festival,** held each mid-November since 1971. This 3-day event is attended by waterfowl artists, carvers, sculptors, photographers, collectors, and anyone with an interest in waterfowl. Activities include duck- and goose-calling contests, workshops, auctions of antique decoys, dog trials, and exhibits of waterfowl paintings, artifacts, books, carvings, duck stamps, and memorabilia. Admission charges are $8 for 1 day and $20 for 3 days; children under 14 with an adult are admitted free. There are small additional charges for auctions and calling contests; all proceeds go to wildlife conservation causes. For complete information, contact the Waterfowl Festival, P.O. Box 929, Easton, MD 21601 (tel. 301/822-4567).

Once known as the Colonial Capital of Maryland's eastern shore, Easton is today a quiet little community (pop. 8,500), closely tied to nearby waters. Directly facing the center of the Chesapeake Bay, yet sheltered by the many coves of the Miles River and the Tred Avon River, Easton and neighboring towns were an ideal locale for shipbuilding in the 18th century, and now the area is equally perfect as a haven for those who love to savor the sea or to sample seafood.

Easton is also the gateway to several neighboring maritime retreats. We like to picture Easton as the inner core or heart of the area, with two arms stretching out toward the Chesapeake. The upper (and longer) arm takes you to the village of St. Michaels on the Miles River and to Tilghman Island, dangling right on the Chesapeake. The lower arm goes straight to Oxford, a sheltered town nestled along the shores of the Tred Avon River.

Named after the archangel of the same name, St. Michaels was one of the oldest settlements along the Chesapeake and flourished in Colonial times as a shipbuilding center (the birthplace of the illustrious Baltimore clipper). Today it is an aesthetic delight—no billboards or fast-food chains; just quiet tree-lined streets, rows of boutiques housed in graceful old restored buildings, and a marina so clean that it seems to sparkle. At least 20,000 boats a year pull into this idyllic harbor just 11 miles outside of Easton (via Rte. 33). Another 15 miles will bring you to Tilghman Island, an important base for fishermen of oysters, crabs, clams, and fin fish—an enclave with great seafaring atmosphere.

Oxford, also one of the oldest towns in Maryland, was the Colonial home of Robert Morris, Jr., the man who befriended George Washington and then used his own savings to help finance the Revolution. The Morris family home is now a first-rate inn and restaurant, which in itself is worth the 10 miles from Easton to Oxford (via Rte. 333). The most enjoyable way to reach Oxford, however, is to take the Tred Avon ferry across from the Bellevue section of St. Michaels. No matter how you come, don't miss Oxford—it's a town that time has hardly touched, with a pervasive quiet charm and views of the water at every turn.

GETTING AROUND

BY RENTED CAR

If you haven't brought your own car to the Easton area, you can rent one from **Avis,** Easton Municipal Airport (tel. 822-5040), or **Hertz,** Goldsborough Rd. and Rte. 50 (tel. 822-1676).

BY TAXI

For local cab service, try **Rasin's Taxi** (tel. 822-1048); **Scotty's Taxi** (tel. 822-1475); or **Thomas's Yellow Top Cabs** (tel. 822-1121).

BY FERRY

For the trip between St. Michaels and Oxford or just for a scenic and satisfying experience, don't miss a ride on the **Oxford Bellevue Ferry** (tel. 745-9023). Established in 1683, this is America's oldest privately operated ferry. Crossing the Tred Avon River, the distance is just a mile, and 7 minutes in duration. You can catch the ferry either from Bellevue, off Rtes. 33 and 329, near St. Michaels, or at Oxford (off Rte. 333). Operating year round except from Christmas through February, with continuous service every 20 minutes, the ferry schedule is June 1 to Labor Day, on Monday through Friday from 7am to 9pm, and on weekends from 9am to 9pm; Labor Day to June 1, on Monday through Friday from 7am to sunset, and weekends from

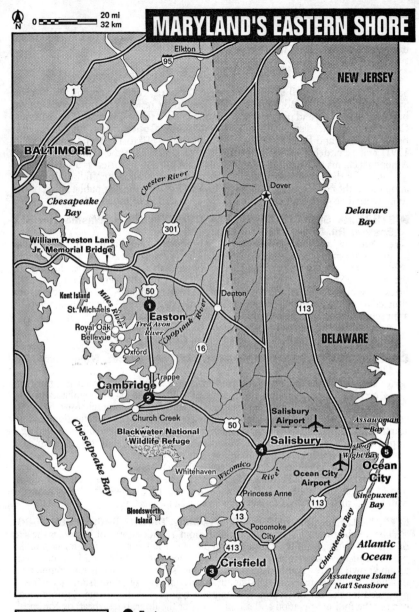

MARYLAND'S EASTERN SHORE

20 mi
0
32 km
N

Elkton

95

BALTIMORE

1

Chester River

Chesapeake
Bay

Dover

NEW JERSEY

Delaware
Bay

William Preston Lane
Jr. Memorial Bridge

301

Kent Island

St. Michaels

Royal Oak
Bellevue

Oxford

Miles River

Tred Avon
River

Choptank River

Denton

Easton

DELAWARE

113

50

16

Trappe

Cambridge

Church Creek

Blackwater National
Wildlife Refuge

50

Salisbury
Airport

Salisbury

Assawoman
Bay

Isle of
Wight Bay

Ocean
City

5

Whitehaven

Wicomico   River

Ocean City
Airport

Sinepuxent
Bay

Chesapeake Bay

Bloodsworth
Island

Princess Anne

13

Pocomoke
City

113

Chincoteague Bay

Atlantic
Ocean

413

Crisfield

3

Assateague Island
Nat'l Seashore

MARYLAND
Eastern Shore Area

ANNAPOLIS

1 Easton
2 Cambridge
3 Crisfield
4 Salisbury
5 Ocean City

9am to sunset. Rates for a car and two persons are $4 one way and $5.75 round-trip; extra car passenger, 25¢; walk-on passengers, 50¢.

WHAT TO SEE & DO

Start with a stroll around Easton's **Historic District,** centered around Washington Street. Here you will find more than 40 beautifully restored and preserved public buildings, churches, and private homes, all dating back to the 18th and 19th centuries. Centerpiece of the district is the **Talbot County Courthouse,** on Washington between Dover and Federal streets. First built from 1710 to 1712, and then again in 1791, and remodeled in 1958, this impressive structure is the symbol of Easton. Among its claims to fame is the fact that its main portion was used as a subcapital of Maryland for the eastern shore. In addition, a document called the "Talbot Reserves," adopted on the courthouse grounds in May of 1774, was the first public airing of the sentiments that were later embodied in the Declaration of Independence.

HISTORICAL SOCIETY OF TALBOT COUNTY, 25 S. Washington St., Easton. Tel. 822-0773.

A highlight of the historic district, the headquarters of this museum is housed in a renovated 19th-century building. The interior consists of a three-gallery modern museum with changing exhibitions, all depicting the rich heritage of the area. The Society also maintains a 1795 Quaker cabinetmaker's dwelling, an 1810 brick Federal town house, and a reconstructed 1670 building. All of the structures are situated around a Federal-style garden. In addition, a restored 1795 building serves as a museum shop with museum reproductions and unusual gifts.

Admission: $2 adult, 50¢ children 6–16.
Open: Tues–Sat 10am–4pm, Sun 1–4pm. **Closed:** Jan–Feb.

CHESAPEAKE BAY MARITIME MUSEUM, Mill Street, Navy Point, St. Michaels. Tel. 745-2916.

Dedicated to the preservation of maritime history, this waterside museum consists of 18 buildings on 6 acres of land. Some of the highlights are an authentic 110-year-old Chesapeake Bay lighthouse, a comprehensive bay-craft collection, a boat restoration shop, an extensive waterfowl decoy collection, and an aquarium featuring life from local waters. There are also floating exhibits, including a skipjack and a restored log-bottom bugeye. Guided tours of the museum are conducted at 10:30am and 1:30pm at no extra charge.

Admission: $5 adults, $2.50 children 6–17, seniors $4.50.
Open: Apr 1–Oct 31 daily 10am–5pm; Jan–mid-Mar Sat–Sun 10am–4pm; mid-Mar–Apr 1 daily 10am–4pm; Nov 1–Dec 30 daily 10am–4pm. **Directions:** At Mill Street, turn right, and follow signs to museum.

WYE MILL, Rte. 662, off Rte. 50, Wye Mills. Tel. 827-6909 or 685-2886.

The nearby town of Wye Mills, located about 12 miles north of Easton, is the site of this mill dating from the 17th century. Though the town is named for two mills, only one of these structures survives today. Owned and maintained by a nonprofit group known as Preservation Maryland, the mill is the earliest industrial-commercial building in continuous use in the state. In Revolutionary days, flour from this mill was produced for the use of George Washington's troops at Valley Forge. Visitors today can see the mill in operation and sample some of the flour, buckwheat, or cornmeal.

While in Wye Mills, stop to see the huge tree that dominates the town—the Wye Oak, the largest white oak in the United States and Maryland's official state tree. Measuring 4½ feet above its base, the Wye Oak is 37 feet in circumference and 95 feet high, with a crown spanning 165 feet, shading an area almost half an acre. The tree is believed to be over 400 years old.

Admission: Free, but donations welcome.
Open: Apr–Dec Sat–Sun 11am–4pm, and by appointment.

ORRELL'S BISCUITS, Main Street, P.O. Box 7, Wye Mills, MD 21679. Tel. 822-2065.

This tiny community is also the home of a family enterprise producing a uniquely eastern shore biscuit that has been a tradition for over 300 years. With their kitchen as a bakery, the Orrell family produces hundreds of biscuits every day. Following an original recipe that lacks baking powder or soda, the Orrells and their staff literally "beat" these doughy treats with the help of an electrically powered biscuit beater, and then shape each specimen by hand into the size of a walnut, producing a crusty biscuit with a soft center. Visitors are welcome to watch the baking process, sample the results, and purchase at the source, although the biscuits are also on sale throughout Maryland, including at the fashionable Harborplace shops in Baltimore.

Admission: Free.

Open: Normal business hours; phone for exact times.

GUIDED TOURS

With a couple of days' notice, you can arrange a guided walking tour of Easton's historic district. Make a reservation by contacting the **Historical Society of Talbot County,** 25 S. Washington St., P.O. Box 964, Easton, MD 21601 (tel. 301/822-0773). The prices are $2 for adults and 50¢ for students.

If you prefer a tour via an antique horse-drawn carriage, contact **San Domingo Surreys,** P.O. Box 42, St. Michaels (tel. 745-3115 or 822-6432). Drivers provide an interpretive historic tour of St. Michaels, departing from and returning to the grounds of the Maritime Museum. Price is $4 per person; reservations are not required, but it is wise to phone in advance for exact schedule.

HARBOR CRUISES

See the highlights of the area from the water on board the *Patriot*, a 65-foot and 150-passenger sightseeing vessel operated by **Patriot Cruises Inc.,** P.O. Box 1206, St. Michaels (tel. 745-3100). These 90-minute narrated cruises ply the waters of the Miles River and the shoreline off St. Michaels. The two-deck air-conditioned boat, which has snack and bar services, departs daily from the dock at the Chesapeake Bay Maritime Museum, St. Michaels. The schedule is April through mid-December, at 11am, 1, and 3pm; the cost is $7 for adults and $3.50 for children under 12.

SPORTS & ACTIVITIES

Much of the focus of outdoor life in the Easton–St. Michaels–Oxford area is in and around the water. Whether you have your own boat or not, you'll always find lots of activity at **St. Michaels Town Dock Marina,** 305 Mulberry St., St. Michaels (tel. 745-2400). You can rent runabouts with outboard engines for $75 for the first 2 hours, $125 for 4 hours, or $185 per day. Sailboats rent from $55 to $90 for 4 hours, and $80 to $135 for 8 hours, depending on the size of the craft. If you have your own craft, you can also dock it here. Overnight dockage charges are $1.30 per foot on weekdays and $1.70 per foot on weekends. Some smaller slips are also available, and there is hourly dockage, with a $5 minimum. If you prefer terra firma, you can also rent bikes here at $3 an hour, $5 for 2 hours, or $16 for a full day; tandems start at $6 an hour. Open April through November.

Eastern Shore Yacht Charters, Bachelor's Point, Oxford (tel. 226-5000), charters sailboats and powerboats from April to mid-November.

FISHING

Fishing excursions along the Chesapeake are the specialty of **Harrison's Sport Fishing Center,** Route 33, Tilghman (tel. 886-2121 or 886-2109). This is a family enterprise, dating back over 100 years, now comprising the largest charter fleet on the bay. Complete fishing packages are available, from $115 to $130 a day, including all fishing, tackle, boat transport, a room at the nautically themed Harrison's Chesapeake House Country Inn, and meals (a boxed lunch, plus a huge fisherman's breakfast and dinner at the Harrison's Chesapeake House restaurant). Depending on the time of year, the catch often includes sea trout, blues, striped bass, croakers, spot, or perch.

GOLF

There's plenty of room to swing at the **Hog Neck Golf Course,** Old Cordova Road, Easton (tel. 822-6079), rated among the top 25 public courses in the U.S. by *Golf Digest.* Situated north of town off Rte. 50, between Rte. 309 and Rabbit Hill Road, it offers a par-72, 18-hole championship course and a par-32, 9-hole executive course. Rates for nonresidents are $19 for 18 holes, $7 for 9 holes; cart rental is $18 and $9, respectively. Facilities also include a driving range, putting green, and a pro shop. Open February to December, weekdays from 7am to sunset, and weekends from 8am to sunset.

HUNTING

Maryland's eastern shore is considered by many to be the finest duck- and goose-hunting region on the Atlantic Flyway. Every year, over 500,000 migratory game birds winter on the fields, marshes, rivers, tidal flats, and waters of Maryland. More than 20 local organizations conduct regular guided waterfowl hunts for Canada geese (late November through late January), ducks (late November through mid-January), and sea ducks (early October through mid-January). Some quail and pheasant hunting is also available. Goose hunting for two people ranges from $300 to $400 a day plus licenses; and quail and pheasant rates are based on the number of birds caught. Four reliable sources of more information are **Richard D. Higgins,** Box 365, Neavitt, MD 21652 (tel. 301/745-2433); **Ray Marshall,** Rte. 5, Box 659, Easton, MD 21601 (tel. 301/745-2060); **Bob Ewing,** Rte. 1, Box 217, Easton, MD 21601 (tel. 301/822-0272); and **Jay W. Tarmon,** P.O. Box 1201, Easton, MD 21601 (tel. 301/822-9334).

BICYCLE RENTALS

In addition to bike rentals at St. Michaels Town Dock Marina, you can also get two-wheelers of all sorts (from three-speeds to tandems) at **Oxford Mews,** 105 Morris St., Oxford (tel. 820-8222) daily except Wednesday, from $3 an hour with a $6 minimum; $12 a day; or $69 a week.

SHOPPING

In this haven for waterfowl enthusiasts, a shop that really is in tune with the setting is **Goose Crossing,** 19 Harrison St., Easton (tel. 822-1127), located opposite the Tidewater Inn. It specializes in decoys and gift items with goose and duck motifs, from original art prints and glass miniatures to Christmas tree ornaments, statues, handbags, clothing, lamps, mailboxes, and key rings. It's open Monday to Saturday from 10am to 5pm.

Antique shops are also plentiful in this region; one particularly worth noting is **Dover Antiques,** 7 E. Dover St., Easton (tel. 822-9190). It's a fascinating emporium of period and country furnishings, fine art, pottery, and brass, as well as duck decoys and guns. Open from 9:30am to 4pm every day except Wednesday.

Seafaring clothes and collectibles are the specialty of the **Ship's Store,** 202 Bank St., Oxford (tel. 226-5113) and at 100 Talbot St., St. Michaels (tel. 745-9501). One of the best-stocked chandleries on the eastern shore, this shop's wares range from nautical necessities and yachting apparel to gifts and games. Open all year, daily from 8am to 6pm (closed Sundays in the winter).

Creative cooks flock to the **Tender Herb,** 201 Tilghman St., Oxford (tel. 226-5503) for all kinds of home-grown herbs and spices. This shop also stocks herb gifts, art, prints by regional artists, and carved duck decoys. Open daily from 10am to 5pm (except Wednesdays and January through mid-March).

The town of Preston, 11 miles east of Easton via Rte. 331, is considered an antique-hunters' haven. Two of the most interesting shops are **The Quaker Bonnet,**

202 Main St. (tel. 673-2322), for old coins, jewelry, and dollhouse collectibles; and **Country Treasures,** 202 Main St. (tel. 673-2603), a good source for home furnishings, from quilts to rolltop desks.

WHERE TO STAY

The Easton–St. Michaels–Oxford area offers a range of modern and old-world accommodations. Most of these fall into the moderate category, although suites and luxury rooms can be expensive. Rates on weekends are often subject to surcharges; summer prices are usually the highest. One exception to this is the waterfowl hunting season (October through January), when top rates can also apply at many places.

VERY EXPENSIVE

THE INN AT PERRY CABIN, 308 Watkins Lane, St. Michaels, MD 21663. Tel. 301/745-2200 or toll-free 800/722-2949. Fax 301/745-3348. 19 suites. A/C TV TEL
$ Rates (including full breakfast): $160–$385 single or double. AE, CB, DC, MC, V
Parking: Free.
Although it may seem out of place along the Chesapeake, this proper English country inn fits in well. Acquired by Sir Bernard Ashley of Laura Ashley Enterprises in 1990, it aims for the highest luxury standards and charges accordingly. No expense has been spared in the appointments or decor which, not surprisingly, are a showcase of Laura Ashley designs and furnishings. Pampering, too, sets this place apart—from a full-time concierge to turndown services, fresh flowers in every room, morning newspaper at your door, and a complete afternoon tea in the drawing room each day. Set on the Miles River, this Colonial Revival manor dates back to the early 19th century and was named after Commodore Oliver Hazard Perry, a friend of the original owner. Over the years, Perry Cabin served as a private home and a riding academy before first opening its doors as a inn in 1980. Facilities include a restaurant, outdoor terrace, rose and herb garden, boat docking, and helicopter pad.

EXPENSIVE

ROBERT MORRIS INN, N. Morris Street and The Strand, P.O. Box 70, Oxford, MD 21654. Tel. 301/226-5111. 34 rms (all with bath). A/C
$ Rates: $70–$180 single or double. MC, V. **Parking:** Free.
A star in this region is this inn, once the home of the man who financed the Continental Army during Revolutionary times, and now the focal point of one of Maryland's loveliest towns. Situated on the banks of the Tred Avon River, this historic (1710) building was constructed by ships' carpenters with wooden-pegged paneling, ships' nails, and hand-hewn beams, all of which remain today. The house still has much of its original flooring, fireplaces, and murals. The guest rooms of this renovated facility are spread out among the original house and nearby cottages and lodges. Many rooms have river views, private porches, and sitting rooms; many nonsmoking units are available.

ST. MICHAELS HARBOR INN, 101 N. Harbor Rd., St. Michaels, MD 21663. Tel. 301/745-9001. Fax 301/745-9150. 8 rms, 38 suites. A/C TV TEL **Directions:** From Rte. 33, turn right on Seymour St. or E. Chew St., left on Meadow St., to Harbor Rd.
$ Rates: $120 single or double; $159 suite. AE, DC, MC, V. **Parking:** Free.
If you enjoy views of the water and boats, then it's hard to beat this inn, one of the best in the area. Situated right along the marina, the modern hotel offers rooms and suites, all with sweeping views of the water and most with private balconies or terraces. Each room has a digital clock radio, plush wall-to-wall carpeting, and contemporary furnishings in soft pastel sea tones. The suites also have kitchenettes, wet bars, and sitting rooms.
Other amenities include short-term berthing for guest boats on a 60-slip marina,

an outdoor swimming pool, sun deck, an exercise room, bike rentals, guest laundry, a poolside bar, and a nautical-style restaurant overlooking the harbor. The restaurant is particularly romantic at dinner as the sun sets over the marina.

MODERATE

TIDEWATER INN, Dover and Harrison Streets, P.O. Box 359, Easton, MD 21601. Tel. 301/822-1300. Fax 301/820-8847. 112 rms, 7 suites. A/C TV TEL

$ Rates: $74–$94 single, $84–$94 double, $150–$175 suite. AE, D, MC, V. **Parking:** Free (valet).

If you want to stay right in the heart of Easton, the ideal place is this inn built in 1949 in the tradition of old public houses of Colonial days. The four-story hotel exudes an old-world feeling, with its decor of dark woods, arched doorways, hurricane lamps, electric candles, flagstone floors, open fireplaces, and paintings of 18th-century Easton. Bedrooms are furnished with an Early American–theme. Amenities include a swimming pool, valet service, entertainment on Saturday evenings, and a full-service restaurant.

WADES POINT INN ON THE BAY, Wades Point Road, P.O. Box 7, St. Michaels, MD 21663. Tel. 301/745-2500. 23 rms, 15 with private bath. A/C (new building only). **Directions:** Head 5 miles west of St. Michaels, off Rte. 33.

$ Rates (including continental breakfast): $60–$90 in main house; $95–$145 in new building, single or double. MC, V. **Parking:** Free.

A long country road leads to this grand old house (circa 1819), set on a curve of land overlooking Chesapeake Bay. Surrounded by a sprawling lawn and 120 acres of fields, woodlands, and nature trails, this inn offers seclusion, peace, and some of the best sunset views you'll ever see. Named after Zachary Wade who received a land grant here in 1657, the inn dates back to the early 19th century. It was erected by Thomas Kemp, a shipbuilder credited with creating the Baltimore Clipper ships, including the famous *Pride of Baltimore*. It is now owned by caring and cordial innkeepers Betsy and John Feiler.

The main house today offers varied guest rooms (with shared baths), furnished with antiques and cooled by the cross-ventilation of bay breezes whirling through ceiling fans and screened porches. For modern comforts mixed with reproduction furnishings and decor, request a room in the new adjacent Kemp Building; these rooms have private baths, air conditioning, and most have private porches or balconies; two have kitchens. Breakfast is served in a bright wicker-filled room in the main house overlooking the bay. A 2-night stay required for weekends and holidays in summer season. Discounts available for stays of 3 days or more.

HAMBLETON ON-THE-HARBOUR, 202 Cherry St., St. Michaels, MD 21663. Tel. 301/745-3350. 5 rms. A/C TV **Directions:** From Rte. 33, turn right on Cherry Street; the inn is on the right at end of street.

$ Rates (including breakfast): $95 single or double. MC, V. **Parking:** Free.

A turn-of-the-century atmosphere prevails at this lovely bed-and-breakfast inn facing the harbor. Innkeepers Aileen and Harry Arader have completely renovated this historic antique-filled retreat and furnished each guest room with an individual style and decor. All rooms have a view of the waterfront, private bath, and antique furnishings; some also have working fireplaces. A lovely enclosed porch is also available for guests as a relaxing lookout from which to watch the boats go by.

BUDGET

COMFORT INN, 310 N. Rte. 50, Easton, MD 21601. Tel. 301/820-8333 or toll-free 800/228-5150. Fax 301/820-8436. 84 rms. A/C TV TEL

$ Rates (including continental breakfast): $49–$69 single, $54–$76 double. AE, CB, DC, MC, V. **Parking:** Free.

One of the newest lodgings in this area, this two-story hacienda-style property is the best choice along the busy Rte. 50 corridor. Set back from the main road and surrounded by trees, it has a bright and airy lobby with lots of light woods and plants. The guest rooms, many of which surround a central courtyard, are furnished with pastel tones and waterfowl art. Facilities include an outdoor swimming pool and a small restaurant.

DAYS INN, Rte. 50, P.O. Box 968, Easton, MD 21601. Tel. 301/822-4600 or toll-free 800/325-2525. Fax 301/820-9723. 80 rms. A/C TV TEL
$ Rates: $42–$60 single, $52–$70 double. AE, CB, DC, DISC, MC, V. **Parking:** Free.

Set back from the main road in a shady setting between Easton and Oxford, this motel (formerly known as the Marinor Motor Lodge) has only recently become affiliated with Days Inns. The guest rooms offer a well-maintained contemporary decor with a choice of bed sizes and standard furnishings. Facilities include a restaurant, lounge, and an outdoor swimming pool.

WHERE TO DINE

Seafood lovers, rejoice, this is the place! The Easton area is the heart of Maryland's crab, oyster, and fish country. Crab is the prime attraction—whether it is served as "crab imperial" in a rich creamy sauce, rolled up in plump crab cakes, floating in crab chowder, as crab claws, soft-shell crabs, or the just plain hard-shell variety. Come and have your fill; the crab is plentiful and the price is right.

EXPENSIVE

CECILE'S, 42 E. Dover St., Easton. Tel. 822-2500.
   Cuisine: CONTINENTAL. **Reservations:** Recommended.
$ Prices: Appetizers $4.95–$11.95; main courses $14.95–$22.95; lunch $5.95–$8.95.
   Open: Lunch Mon–Fri 11:30am–2:30pm; dinner Tues–Sat 6–10pm. AE, MC, V.

Located on the second floor of the restored 1921 Avalon Theater complex, this is the most highly acclaimed of the three restaurants known as the "Trio at the Avalon." Originally the ballroom of the theater, this room is a formal French dining room that exudes the ambience of a country chateau, with huge crystal chandeliers, a fireplace, fine linens, and fresh flowers.

The dinner menu offers such dishes as poached lobster, shrimp, and scallops in pastry; over-roasted mahi mahi with leeks and lemon mango sauce; roast leg of Maryland-raised lamb with goat cheese, spinach, and fresh rosemary; Talbot County Muscovy Duck breast with fresh ginger, lingonberries, and scallion pancake; free-range veal scaloppine and duck confit with morels; and beef tenderloin in black pepper crust with truffled demi-glace. Lunch fare puts emphasis on fitness cuisines, sandwiches, salads, and stir-fries.

ROBERT MORRIS INN, N. Morris Street and The Strand, Oxford. Tel. 226-5111.
   Cuisine: AMERICAN/SEAFOOD. **Reservations:** Not accepted.
$ Prices: Appetizers $2.50–$8.50; main courses $14.95–$29.95; lunch $4.95–$11.95. MC, V.
   Open: Lunch Wed–Sun noon–3pm, dinner Wed–Sat 6–9pm. **Closed:** Mid-Jan–mid-Feb and Christmas.

Dating back to the early 18th century, the dining room and tavern of this old inn (see "Where to Stay," above) are attractions in themselves. The decor includes original woodwork, slate floors, fireplaces; the murals of the four seasons were made from wallpaper of 140 years ago, which was printed on a screw-type press using 1,600 woodcut blocks carved from orangewood.

Crab is the specialty here, with such entrées as crab cakes, crab Norfolk (crab sautéed with butter and sherry), crab imperial, and baked seafood au gratine cakes (crab and shrimp with Monterey Jack cheese, Cheddar, and seasonings). Other favorites include combination platters of various types of crab with scallops, clams, or fish filets, as well as filet mignon or prime rib. Lunch items range from sandwiches and salads to omelets, burgers, seafood platters, and hot entrées. Jackets are required for men in the main dining room except Memorial Day to Labor Day.

MODERATE

LONGFELLOWS, 125 Mulberry St., St. Michaels. Tel. 745-2624.
   Cuisine: AMERICAN. **Reservations:** Recommended. **Directions:** From Rte. 33, turn right on Mulberry Street.
$ Prices: Appetizers $3.95–$7.95; main courses $10.95–$19.95; lunch $4.95–$9.95. MC, V.
   Open: Lunch daily 11am–4pm; dinner daily 4–10pm. **Closed:** Mon–Tues Jan–mid-March.

⭐ If you'd like a view of the harbor when you feast on seafood, try this restaurant located in a gracious old home. There are two dining levels inside; meals are also served on a sheltered outdoor patio and on an adjacent deck. A lounge overlooking the water offers dancing on Saturday and Sunday. Salads, burgers, omelets, and sandwiches are featured at lunchtime. Dinner entrées focus on an ever-changing selection of crab dishes and seafood platters, as well as steaks, prime rib, chicken, and stir-fry choices.

PEACH BLOSSOMS, 6 N. Washington St., Easton. Tel. 822-5220.
   Cuisine: INTERNATIONAL. **Reservations:** Recommended.
$ Prices: Appetizers $3.25–$7.25; main courses $14.95–$19.95; lunch $6.95–$8.95. AE, MC, V.
   Open: Lunch Wed–Fri 11:30am–2pm; dinner Wed–Sat 5:30–9pm.
This is a bright café-style restaurant and wine bar, with a decor of leafy plants and light caned furniture. Everything is made on the premises, from tangy salad dressings to breads, pastries, and desserts. Lunch features salads, sandwiches, omelets, and pastas. Dinner choices include grilled duck breast with apple-raspberry chutney, seafood cannelloni, shrimp and scallops sauté, boneless beef fore-rib, veal Provençal, and grilled swordfish.

RUSTIC INN, Talbottown Shopping Center, Easton. Tel. 820-8212.
   Cuisine: INTERNATIONAL. **Reservations:** Recommended.
$ Prices: Appetizers $3.50–$7.95; main courses $10.95–$21.95; lunch $4.95–$9.95. AE, MC, V.
   Open: Lunch Tues–Fri 11:30am–1:30pm; dinner daily 5–10pm.
An affiliate of the restaurant of the same name in Annapolis, this eatery is situated in the midst of a string of shops. Although it can easily be overlooked, it is well worth finding, especially for families. The decor fits its name, with a fascinating display of early farm implements, fishing gear, tobacco-growing tools, and old newspapers, all surrounding a wood-burning fireplace. Entrées include surf-n-turf, oyster imperial and crab imperial; veal (marsala, piccata, or francese); chicken Divan; steak béarnaise; and "salty strip" (strip steak covered with freshly shucked sautéed oysters and mushrooms).

CHAMBERS PENTHOUSE, 42 E. Dover St., Easton. Tel. 822-2500.
   Cuisine: AMERICAN. **Reservations:** Recommended.
$ Prices: Appetizers $3.95–$5.95; main courses $11.95–$18.95; lunch $3.95–$7.95. AE, MC, V.
   Open: Daily 11:30am–midnight.
A nautically themed rooftop eatery, this is one of the "Trio at the Avalon" restaurants housed in a restored 1921 theater. The decor includes a 14-foot-high stained glass dome, a horseshoe-shaped bar, and wraparound windows, with seating either indoors or outside on a deck offering panoramic views of the Easton area. Dinner entrées include a range of seafood and meat dishes, such as stuffed shrimp, crab cakes,

surf-n-turf, barbecued leg of lamb, and steaks. Lunch items range from salads, sandwiches, and stir-fry dishes, to burgers and stuffed tortillas.

HARRISON'S CHESAPEAKE HOUSE, Rte. 33, Tilghman. Tel. 886-2123.

Cuisine: SEAFOOD. **Reservations:** Not required.

$ Prices: Appetizers $1.95–$5.95; main courses $9.95–$17.95; lunch $4.95–$10.95. MC, V.

Open: Daily lunch 11am–4pm, dinner 4–9pm.

A tradition on the eastern shore dating back to 1856, this nautically themed restaurant has been run by four generations of the Harrison family. It sits right on the water and the two dining rooms offer great views of the bay and fishing fleet. Fresh Chesapeake Bay seafood is the specialty and people drive from many miles away just to savor the local catch. The menu includes all types of crab, shrimp, oysters, scallops, and fish—prepared broiled, fried, au gratin, or sautéed. There is also pan-fried chicken, prime rib, and steaks. All dishes are cooked to order and served family-style with lots of vegetables (be sure to try the mashed potatoes topped with stewed tomatoes).

LEGAL SPIRITS, 42 E. Dover St., Easton. Tel. 822-2500.

Cuisine: AMERICAN/REGIONAL. **Reservations:** Not required.

$ Prices: Appetizers $3.95–$7.95; dinner $8.95–$14.95; lunch $3.95–$8.95. AE, MC, V.

Open: Lunch Mon–Sat 11:30am–2:30pm; dinner daily 5:30–10pm.

A former corner store and pharmacy, this ground-floor tavern-style eatery has the flavor of turn-of-the-century America, with a tin ceiling, stained glass windows, and brass fixtures. It is the least expensive and most informal of the "Trio at the Avalon" restaurants (see Cecile's, above). The eclectic menu features Maryland seafood favorites such as crab cakes and fried oysters, as well as regional dishes, ranging from blackened catfish and coconut shrimp to beef fajitas. There is also an option to "grill your own" meats and vegetables, with portable grills and appropriate dipping sauces brought to your table. Lunch items range from salads, sandwiches, and stir-fry dishes, to burgers and stuffed tortillas.

SALTY OYSTER, Rte. 33 and Peaneck Road, St. Michaels. Tel. 745-5151.

Cuisine: SEAFOOD. **Reservations:** Recommended.

$ Prices: Appetizers $3.95–$8.95; main courses $10.95–$19.95; lunch $4.95–$6.95. MC, V.

Open: Mon–Fri 11:30am–9:30pm; Sat–Sun 11:30am–10pm.

Although not perched right on the water, this restaurant is thoroughly nautical, with a decor of ship ropes, lanterns, model boats, divers' helmets, and fishing nets. There is seating both indoors and out, depending on the weather. Lunch choices feature sandwiches and crabwiches, burgers, seafood salads, and soups (crab vegetable and cream of crab are local favorites).

Crab is also the main focus at dinner; selections include an "all-you-can-eat crab feast," hard crab of all sizes (available April 15 to November 15 only), soft-shell crabs, king crab legs, crab imperial, Chesapeake surf-n-turf (two crab cakes and two pieces of fresh fried chicken), and oysters Chesapeake (stuffed with crab imperial). Different varieties of shrimp, scallop, and steak dishes are always also on the menu.

TOWN CREEK, Foot of Tilghman Street, Oxford. Tel. 226-5131.

Cuisine: SEAFOOD. **Reservations:** Recommended.

$ Prices: Appetizers $3.95–$7.95; main courses $10.95–$19.95; lunch $3.95–$9.95. MC, V.

Open: Sun–Thurs 11:30am–9pm, Fri–Sat 11:30am–10pm.

Situated right on the marina, this informal spot is understandably known for its fresh seafood. The decor is nautical but most of the focus is on the wide-windowed views of the water, with seating both indoors and on an outside deck. The menu changes daily, depending on the latest catch, but usually includes such choices as hot steamed crabs in season, lobster pasta, crab cakes, crab imperial, jumbo shrimp scampi, soft shell clams and crabs, mussels, and fried oysters, as well as steaks, prime rib, and barbecued or broiled breast of chicken.

TOWN DOCK RESTAURANT, 305 Mulberry St., St. Michaels. Tel. 745-5577.

Cuisine: SEAFOOD. **Reservations:** Recommended. **Directions:** From Rte. 33, turn right at Mulberry Street.

$ Prices: Appetizers $2–$6; main courses $11–$19; lunch $4–$9. AE, MC, V.

Open: Year-round lunch daily 11:30am–4pm; dinner daily 4–10pm.

This restaurant, located right on the marina, emphasizes casual dining, with a choice of indoor (air-conditioned) dining amid a nautical decor, and a large outdoor area lined with picnic tables and umbrellas. The building itself dates back to the 1830s, when it was an oyster-shucking shed; the patio bricks outside were kilned in St. Michaels during the late 1800s.

Lunch choices include oyster stew, shrimp and crab salads, crab and meat sandwiches, quiches, and seafood platters. An international flavor dominates the dinner menu, with such dishes as swordfish au gratin, cold-water lobster tails, parma (shrimp, scallops, and lobster in sherry cream sauce over fettuccine), rack of lamb, veal alla marsala, wienerschnitzel, chicken florentine, and veal Simone (with cream sauce and shrimp).

BUDGET

CRAB CLAW, Navy Point by Maritime Museum, St. Michaels. Tel. 745-2900.

Cuisine: SEAFOOD. **Reservations:** Recommended.

$ Prices: Appetizers $.95–$6.95; lunch and dinner $5.95–$16.95. No credit cards.

Open: Mar–Nov daily 11am–10pm.

Seafood in the rough is the specialty of this restaurant, a favorite for almost 25 years. There is no air conditioning, just ceiling fans and lots of bay breezes, in this casual indoor and outdoor eatery on the lower end of the waterfront. The emphasis on the all-day menu is on crabs, served from hot, steamed, and seasoned to fried hard crab, backfin crab cake, crab chowder, soft crab, "crab dogs" (on a stick), and crab imperial; other seafoods and fried chicken are also available.

NIGHTLIFE

Although sunsets, moonlit strolls, and seafood dining fill many nights in this area, there is also some fine entertainment. The **Avalon,** 42 E. Dover St., P.O. Box 2298, Easton (tel. 820-5775), a restored 430-seat art-deco theater, is the home of the nonprofit **Mid-Shore Center for the Performing Arts.** This company presents a regular year-round program of Broadway shows, dramas, and concerts by visiting artists. The box office is open Monday through Saturday, from 11am to 3pm. Tickets average $10 to $25 for most events.

2. CAMBRIDGE

55 miles SE of Annapolis, 75 miles SE of Baltimore, 15 miles S of Easton, 61 miles W of Ocean City, 61 miles SW of Dover

GETTING THERE   By Bus   Regular bus service is operated to Cambridge by **Greyhound/Trailways** into its depot at 216 Dorchester Ave. (tel. 228-4626).

By Car   You can take Rte. 50 to Cambridge from all directions.

ESSENTIALS   Maps, walking-tour folders, and brochures on Cambridge are available from the **Dorchester County Tourism Office,** 203 Sunburst Hwy. (Rte. 50), Cambridge, MD 21613 (tel. 301/228-1000) or from the **Chamber of Com-**

merce Office, 203 Sunburst Hwy. (Rte. 50), Cambridge, MD 21613 (tel. 301/228-3575).

Founded in 1684, Cambridge is situated on the Choptank River, just off Chesapeake Bay. As Maryland's second-largest deep-water port (after Baltimore), Cambridge today (pop. 11,700) has an active harbor, supplying ocean-going vessels and coastal freighters with grain and seafood cargo.

For visitors, the **Cambridge marina** provides opportunities to stroll in grassy bayfront public parks. The town is also known for its restored Victorian buildings downtown and its scenic drives along the river. Gracious old homes line the shoreline, including a house originally built for Annie Oakley.

Twelve miles southeast of Cambridge is the **Blackwater National Wildfowl Refuge,** one of the chief wintering areas for Canadian geese and ducks along the Atlantic Flyway.

GETTING AROUND
BY CAR

The best way to get around Cambridge is to bring your own car and then to walk the streets and the riverfront at your leisure. Walking-tour folders and driving routes are available from the tourist office and chamber of commerce.

BY RENTED CAR

Two major firms are represented in Cambridge, **Avis,** 324 Sunburst Hwy. (tel. 228-4088), and **Hertz,** 206 Cedar St. (tel. 228-1688).

BY TAXI

Reliable services are operated by **Bay Country Cab** (tel. 228-7177), **Blue's Cab** (tel. 228-1449), **City Taxi** (tel. 228-6354), and **Mills Taxi** (tel. 228-0985).

WHAT TO SEE & DO

Historic High Street is the focal point of Cambridge. This two-block area is lined with dozens of houses from the 18th and 19th centuries. Most were built as private homes, but some were inns, cottages, rectories, or meeting places. A free walking-tour brochure describing the history and architecture of these homes is available from the tourist office and the chamber of commerce.

DORCHESTER HERITAGE MUSEUM, 1904 Horn Point Rd., Cambridge. Tel. 228-1899.

Local country history is the focus of this working museum containing maritime, farming, natural resource, and Indian exhibits reflecting the development of the area.

Admission: Free.

Open: Mid-Apr to Oct Sat–Sun 1–4:30pm.

MEREDITH HOUSE, 902 Greenway Drive at Maryland Avenue, Cambridge. Tel. 228-7953.

This Georgian-style residence dating from 1760 was restored under the auspices of the Dorchester County Historical Society. The exhibits include a Governor's Room honoring governors of Maryland who are associated with the county. There is also an antique doll collection. The adjacent Neild Museum contains exhibits on local maritime and industrial development, and farm life including an original McCormick reaper (circa 1831) and an Indian implement collection. Other attractions on the property are an herb garden, a meat house, and an 18th-century stable.

Admission: Free, but guided group tours are $2 per person.

Open: Thurs–Sat 10am–4pm, and by appointment.

OLD TRINITY CHURCH, Rte. 16, Church Creek. Tel. 228-2940 or 228-3161.

Eight miles southwest of Cambridge is this landmark church built circa 1685 and meticulously restored in recent years. It is said to be one of the oldest Episcopal churches in active use in the United States.

Admission: Free.

Open: Mar–Dec Mon, Wed–Sat 9am–5pm, Sun noon–5pm; Jan–Feb Sun 11am–4pm, and by appointment.

BLACKWATER NATIONAL WILDLIFE REFUGE, Key Wallace Street, Church Creek. Tel. 228-2677.

More than 130,000 visitors a year visit this 17,000-acre site of rich tidal marsh, freshwater ponds, and woodlands. Located 12 miles southeast of Cambridge, the refuge serves as a resting and feeding area for migrant and wintering wildfowl, including huge flocks of Canadian geese (approximately 30,000) and ducks (exceeding 17,000) at the peak of fall migration, usually in November. The grounds are also the home of three endangered species: the bald eagle, the Delmarva fox squirrel, and the migrant peregrine falcon.

Facilities for visitors include an observation tower, a 5-mile wildlife drive, and walking and biking trails. Self-guided driving-tour leaflets are provided free of charge. A visitors center is open Monday through Friday from 8am to 4pm, and from 9am to 5pm on Saturday and Sunday (except for weekends during June, July, and August; Labor Day weekend; and all major holidays). The wildlife trail and other outdoor facilities are open daily, all year, dawn to dusk.

Admission: Entrance fee for the wildlife drive is $3 per vehicle and $1 for bicyclists and pedestrians.

Open: Daily, dawn to dusk.

WHERE TO STAY

Most of Cambridge's lodging facilities lie on the outskirts of the city, either along Sunburst Highway (U.S. 50) or eastward along the Choptank River.

MODERATE

GLASGOW-ON-THE-CHOPTANK, 1500 Hambrooks Blvd., Cambridge, MD 21613. Tel. 301/228-0575 or toll-free 800/225-0575. Fax 301/228-1321. 7 rms (3 with bath). A/C

$ Rates (including breakfast): $75–$80 midweek double; $90–$100 weekend double. MC, V. **Parking:** Free.

To experience the charm and comforts of early Cambridge, there's no place quite like this, in a quiet residential neighborhood bordered by the Choptank River. It is set back from the road on its own tree-shaded seven-acre estate, but within viewing distance of the river. Dating back to 1760, this gracious southern mansion was built by a Scotsman, hence its name. Today, listed on the National Register of Historic Places, it is operated as a bed-and-breakfast by Louise Lee Roche and Martha Ann Rayne, two native Marylanders and avid quilters.

The house is furnished with lovely handmade quilts as well as local antiques, Oriental rugs, and 18th-century reproductions. The guest rooms have either air conditioning or a ceiling fan. One guest room is on the ground floor and has its own screened-in porch. Open all year.

BUDGET

LODGECLIFFE, 103 Choptank Terrace, Cambridge, MD 21613. Tel. 301/228-1760. 2 rms (1 with bath). A/C

$ Rates (including continental breakfast): $50 single, $60 double. No credit cards. **Parking:** Free.

A smaller bed-and-breakfast choice is this lodging run by Mrs. F. W. Richardson, who welcomes guests to her gracious old Victorian-style home right on the river. The two rooms available have either twin or double beds, shared or private bath, and have air conditioning and ceiling fans. During the day, guests can enjoy a comfortable screened-in porch, the perfect spot to watch the sailboats breeze by. Open all year.

THE QUALITY INN, Rte. 50 and Crusader Road, P.O. Box 311, Cambridge, MD 21613. Tel. 301/228-6900 or toll-free 800/221-2222. Fax 301/228-4029. 60 rms. A/C TV TEL

$ Rates: $38–$45 single, $44–$55 double. AE, CB, DISC, MC, V. **Parking:** Free.
Located near major shopping areas and close to the historic district, this modern two-story motel is decorated in a Colonial motif. The guest rooms have a modern decor, with standard furnishings and a choice of one or two double beds or a queen-size bed. Facilities include a restaurant, The Shoals (see "Where to Dine," below), a coffee shop, and an outdoor swimming pool.

WHERE TO DINE
MODERATE

BLUE CRAB, 205 Trenton St. Tel. 228-8877.
   Cuisine: SEAFOOD. **Reservations:** Required on weekends.
$ Prices: Appetizers $2.95–$5.95; main courses $7.95–$17.95; lunch $4.95–$6.95. MC, V.
   Open: Lunch Mon–Sat 11:30am–3pm; dinner Wed–Sun 5pm–9pm or 10pm.
Another long-standing favorite is this restaurant housed in a restored 1906 grain warehouse beside the water. The informal restaurant started as a hot-dog stand and grew in menu and size over the years. It now has two nautically themed dining rooms seating 110 people, and an outdoor deck. Lunch items include seafood salads, quiches, sandwiches, and soups (house specials are cream of crab or a unique hamburger soup). Dinner entrées focus largely on local crab and other seafood dishes, as well as prime rib, ham steak, and fried chicken.

THE SHOALS, Rte. 50 and Crusader Road, Cambridge. Tel. 228-7599.
   Cuisine: AMERICAN. **Reservations:** Recommended.
$ Prices: Appetizers $2.95–$6.95; main courses $7.95–$19.95. AE, CB, DISC, MC, V.
   Open: Dinner only, Mon–Thurs 5–9pm, Fri–Sat 5–10pm, Sun 4–9pm.
Although it is right on the main highway, this restaurant has a rustic country atmosphere. There are no water views or unique ambience, but the food is dependable and fresh. Entrées include flounder stuffed with cheese, crab cakes, lobster tails, baked Virginia ham, and steaks.

---

3. CRISFIELD
64 miles SE of Cambridge, 32 miles SW of Salisbury,
54 miles SE of Ocean City, 79 miles SE of Easton

GETTING THERE   By Car   Crisfield is accessible from all directions via Rtes. 413 and 13.

ESSENTIALS   For brochures, maps, and all sorts of helpful information about Crisfield and the surrounding countryside, contact the **Somerset County Tourism Office,** Rte. 13 (Mile Marker 19 of southbound Rest Area), P.O. Box 243, Princess Anne, MD 21853 (tel. 301/651-2968 or toll-free 800/521-9189); or the **Crisfield Chamber of Commerce,** J. Millard Tawes Museum, Somers Cove Marina, P.O. Box 292, Crisfield, MD 21817 (tel. 301/968-2500).

SPECIAL EVENTS   Since 1947, the **Annual Hard Crab Derby and Fair** has been a major fixture on the Crisfield calendar (each Labor Day weekend). Highlight of this 3-day event is a crab race in which crustaceans from other states (as far as Hawaii)

try to match the speed of the eastern shore crabs. Other activities include crab-picking and crab-cooking competitions, a tennis tournament and a fishing tournament, a beauty contest, fireworks, and a parade. Daily admission charges are $3 for adults and $1 for children. For a full program and information, contact the **Crisfield Chamber of Commerce,** P.O. Box 215, Crisfield, MD 21817 (tel. 301/968-2682 or toll-free 800/782-3913).

Legend has it that Crisfield is built almost entirely on oyster shells. It's a likely story, considering that this tiny town (pop. 2,900) has long laid claim to the title of "seafood capital of the world."

Tucked into the most southerly corner of Maryland's eastern shore along the Chesapeake, Crisfield has relied on the sea for its livelihood for over 100 years.

Stroll the city dock or marina—you'll see everything from the fish-laden head boats to the crab-picking, oyster-shucking, and seafood-packing plants. Better still, breathe in the salty air and amble into one of the town's restaurants to taste the maritime bounty.

Although many types of seafood are caught in the waters off Crisfield, crab is unquestionably king in this port—there is even a crab derby festival staged here at the end of each summer.

WHAT TO SEE & DO

The **J. Millard Tawes Museum,** on the Somers Cove Marina (tel. 968-2501), was founded in 1982 to honor a Crisfield-born former governor of Maryland. The headquarters of the Chamber of Commerce offices, this museum is a good place to start a walk around the town. The exhibits will give you useful background about the history of Crisfield and the development of the city's seafood industry; there is also a fascinating wildfowl wood carving workshop on the premises. Open daily late May through September 10am to 4pm; and Tuesday through Saturday October to November and March to late May 10am to 4pm. Admission charge is $1 adults, 50¢ children.

About 15 miles north of Crisfield on Rte. 13 is **Princess Anne,** a well-preserved Colonial town created in 1733. The highlight is the **Teackle Mansion** (tel. 651-1705), built in 1801–03 and patterned after a Scottish manor house. This was the residence of Littleton Dennis Teackle, an associate of Thomas Jefferson and one of the principal transoceanic shipping magnates of the 18th century. He also is credited with establishing Maryland's first public school system and the first public commercial bank on the American continent. With two entrances, one fronting the Manokin River and one facing the town, this grand house measures nearly 200 feet in length and is symmetrically balanced throughout. The house is open for guided tours every Sunday from 2 to 4pm. Some of the things you will see include elaborate plaster ceilings, mirrored windows, a 7-foot fireplace and beehive oven, American Chippendale furniture, Della Robbia (fruit-designed) ceilings, a Tudor-Gothic pipe organ, an 1806 silk world map, and a 1712 family Bible. The admission and tour charge is $2 per person.

In addition, about 20 other houses in this charming town open their doors one weekend a year (in mid-October), as part of the **Olde Princess Anne Days' Celebration.** The structures, which are both private and public buildings, range from Federal, Victorian, Italianate, and Georgian mansions to cottages and the town's oldest inhabited dwelling (1705). Self-guided tour folders are provided to all visitors; fee for the day-long open-house event is $10 per person.

SPORTS & ACTIVITIES

The **Somers Cove Marina** (tel. 968-0925), a $30-million development built on the site of a farm started in 1663 by Benjamin Somers, is one of the largest facilities of its kind in Maryland. The marina is ultramodern, able to accommodate all types of vessels—from 10 feet to 150 feet. There are 272 boat slips, boat ramps, deluxe tiled showers, a laundry room, a swimming pool, boat storage, electricity and water, and a fuel dock.

Head boats leave from the marina and from the nearby town dock each day on **fishing trips** in pursuit of flounder, trout, spot, drum, and blues. For further information, walk along the waterfront and talk with the various boatmen on duty or call any of the following: **Captain Curtis Johns** (tel. 623-2035); **Captain James Landon** (tel. 968-0177); **Captain Joe Asanovich** (tel. 957-2562); and **Captain Lionel Daugherty** (tel. 968-0947).

Most visitors to Crisfield also take cruises to the nearby offshore islands of Smith and Tangier, featured in the 1986 *National Geographic* TV film, "Chesapeake Borne." Both are approximately 1 hour away by boat, and all vessels usually depart Crisfield's marina or town dock at 12:30pm, returning between 5 and 5:30pm. Reservations are not required, but are recommended in the busy summer months. Rates average $15 for a round-trip boat ride, and $25 for a trip that includes sightseeing on the islands and a bountiful lunch.

For a trip to Smith Island, contact **Captain Alan Tyler** at Somers Cove Marina (tel. 425-2771) or **Captain Jason** at the City Dock (tel. 425-5931 or 425-4471). Tangier Island Cruises can be arranged through **Captain Rudy Thomas** at the City Dock (tel. 968-2338).

SHOPPING

Besides its copious crab, this area's other claim to fame is that it is the home of the **Carvel Hall Factory Outlet,** Rte. 413, Crisfield (tel. 968-0500), a division of Towle Manufacturing Company. Carvel Hall was started in 1895 when a young blacksmith hammered out his first seafood-harvesting tools on a borrowed anvil. Today discounts of up to 50% are given on brand-name cutlery, made entirely in this Crisfield plant, plus hundreds of other nationally known gift items such as glassware, pewter, sterling silver, plated hollowware, brass, woodenware, and crystal. Open Monday through Saturday from 9am to 6pm (closed major holidays).

WHERE TO STAY

Choosing where to stay is easy in Crisfield. There are only three motels in town, all in the moderate category.

PADDLEWHEEL MOTEL, 701 W. Main St., Crisfield, MD 21817. Tel. 301/968-2220. 19 rms. A/C TV
$ Rates: $35–$55 single or double. MC, V. **Parking:** Free.
The newest property (opened in 1987), located in the heart of the town, is this modern two-story motel. Open all year, the Paddlewheel offers rooms equipped with two double beds and standard furnishings.

PINES MOTEL, N. Somerset Ave., P.O. Box 106, Crisfield, MD 21817. Tel. 301/968-0900. 40 rms. A/C TV
$ Rates: $35–$65 single, $40–$70 double. No credit cards. **Parking:** Free.
For almost 30 years, this motel has offered fine lodging in a quiet residential setting of tall pine trees. The modern ground-level units all have contemporary furnishings, two double beds, wall-to-wall carpeting, and views of the adjacent outdoor swimming pool and picnic area. Two efficiencies are available at $10 extra per room. Open all year.

SOMERS COVE MOTEL, Inc., R.R. Norris Drive, P.O. Box 387, Crisfield, MD 21817. Tel. 301/968-1900. 40 rms. A/C TV TEL
$ Rates: $45–$75 single or double. MC, V.
Views of the water add to the setting of this modern two-story facility. Opened in 1979, the motel offers rooms with one or two double beds; each room also has a balcony or patio. Guest amenities include an outdoor heated swimming pool, patios, picnic tables, barbecue grills, boat-docking facilities, and ramps. Open all year. Seven efficiencies are available for $10 extra per room.

WHERE TO DINE

The focus of attention here is simply seafood, plenty of it. From crab omelets for breakfast and crab soup and crabwiches for lunch, to crab cooked in a dozen different ways for dinner, this is the place to have your fill of this tasty and succulent crustacean. Most all restaurants in town serve breakfast, with choices usually priced from $2 to $5, starting between 5:30 and 6am to cater to the resident and visiting fishermen. Beer, wine, and cocktails are available at most restaurants, unless noted otherwise. Reservations are particularly necessary on weekends.

MODERATE

CAPTAIN'S GALLEY, W. Main Street at the City Dock. Tel. 968-1636.
  Cuisine: SEAFOOD. **Reservations:** Recommended.
$ Prices: Appetizers $1.95–$6.95; main courses $6.95–$17.95; lunch $2.95–$6.95. DISC, MC, V.
  Open: Lunch daily 11:30am–2:30pm; dinner 5–10pm.

The ideal place to watch the boats in the harbor is this bright, contemporary-style restaurant. The sweeping view is only the beginning; this is also the home of "the world's best crab cake." After tasting them (solid and succulent sweet crabmeat), we think you'll agree. This critically acclaimed dish is available at lunch or dinner, along with a host of other items from the sea.

Lunch choices include sandwiches (such as the illustrious crab cake, oyster fritter, crab imperial, soft crab, shrimp or tuna salad, as well as meats). The dinner entrées range from a gargantuan "eastern shore dinner" (soft crab, crab cake, fish filet, scallops, shrimp, and oysters) to the famous crab cakes, crab imperial, crab au gratin, plus steaks and fried chicken.

WATERMEN'S INN, 9th and Main Streets. Tel. 968-2119.
  Cuisine: AMERICAN. **Reservations:** Recommended.
$ Prices: Appetizers $3.50–$5.50; main courses $7.95–$17.95; lunch $2.95–$6.95. DISC, MC, V.
  Open: Lunch daily 11:30am–2:30pm; dinner Mon–Sat 5–10pm, Sun 5–9pm.
  Closed: Mon in winter.
Although this eatery does not boast water views, the food here is just as good as the other waterside restaurants. Dinnertime choices focus on baked stuffed jumbo soft crabs, crab cake fluff, regular crab cakes, baked stuffed flounder, jumbo fantail shrimp, crab au gratin, fried chicken, imported baby back ribs, charbroiled steaks, and a seafood sampler plate.

---

4. SALISBURY

106 miles SE of Baltimore, 60 miles SW of Dover,
30 miles W of Ocean City, 128 miles SW of Philadelphia,
96 miles SW of Wilmington, 119 miles SE of Washington D.C.

GETTING THERE By Air Salisbury/Wicomico County Airport, Airport Road (tel. 749-0633), is the second-largest airport in Maryland. It is a gateway for scheduled passenger flights operated by **USAir** (tel. toll-free 800/428-4322).

By Bus Greyhound/Trailways operates regular service into its Salisbury depot at 310 Cypress St. (tel. 749-4121).

By Car From north and south, take Rte. 13; from east or west, take Rte. 50.

ESSENTIALS Lodging and restaurant directories, brochures, and walking-tour maps are available from the **Wicomico County Convention and Visitors**

Bureau, Civic Center, Glen Avenue, Salisbury, MD 21801 (tel. 301/548-4914 or toll-free 800/332-TOUR).

Originally a settlement at the intersection of Indian trails, Salisbury has long been considered the crossroads of Chesapeake Country. Nestled on the banks of the Wicomico River, this "hub city" of today lies at the junction of Rtes. 13 and 50, equidistant from Cambridge and Ocean City.

In addition, Salisbury (pronounced *Salls*-berry) is the largest city (pop. 17,000) and second-largest port on Maryland's eastern shore, and it is also widely recognized as a major trade and transport center for the entire Delmarva Peninsula. An abundance of seafood and fresh produce of all kinds is part of everyday living in Salisbury.

As the business headquarters and home of Frank Perdue, Salisbury is also known as the "poultry capital of the world." No visit to this area is complete without a "down home"–style dinner of fried chicken, fresh crab, oyster fritters, hush puppies, and sweet-potato pie.

Equally positioned in the heart of wildfowl country, this bustling city is also home to the world's largest collection of contemporary and classic wildfowl art, the **Ward Museum of Wildfowl Carving and Art Museum.**

GETTING AROUND
BY RENTED CAR

Three major car-rental firms are represented in the Salisbury area, all with desks at the Salisbury-Wicomico Airport: **Avis** (tel. 742-8566), **Hertz** (tel. 749-2235), and **National** (tel. 749-2450).

BY TAXI

Reliable taxi services are operated by the following companies: **Allied Taxi** (tel. 749-4500), **Gene's Taxi** (tel. 742-4444), **Ideal Taxi** (tel. 742-3200), and **Salisbury Taxi** (tel. 742-6666).

WHAT TO SEE & DO

As a city chartered in 1732, Salisbury boasts two significant historic areas. The first is its two-block **Downtown Plaza,** located on Main Street in the heart of the city's business district. It is a picturesque open-air pedestrian walkway, lined with trees, fountains, and shops housed in Victorian buildings dating back to the 1880s.

Nearby is the six-block **Newtown Historic District,** Elizabeth Street and Poplar Hill Avenue, north of Salisbury Parkway (Rte. 50). The homes on these streets reflect architecture that spans two centuries, from Victorian and Queen Anne to Greek Revival, Colonial Revival, and Second Empire. A self-guided walking-tour leaflet, available free from the tourist office, describes 27 of these buildings.

One of the few buildings in the Newtown district that is opened to the public is the **Poplar Hill Mansion,** 117 Elizabeth St. (tel. 749-1776). This is said to be the oldest property in the city, circa 1805, and is built in the Georgian and Federal style of architecture. Its prime features are second-story Palladian windows, bull's-eye windows, cornice moldings, and a fan-shaped window over the front fluted pilaster doorway, as well as a fine collection of period furniture, original fireplaces and mantels, and large brass locks on the doors. Open free of charge on Sunday from 1 to 4pm, and other times by appointment. Closed in January.

Another great house to visit, **Pemberton Hall,** Pemberton Drive (tel. 548-4914), is located about 2 miles southwest of the downtown area, off Rte. 349. Built in 1741 and listed on the National Register of Historic Places, this is one of Maryland's earliest dated brick gambrel-roofed houses, typical of eastern shore plantation style. Currently under restoration, the house is surrounded by a park with nature trails, a picnic area, and pond. Open May through October on Sunday 2pm to 4pm and by appointment. There is no admission charge, but donations are welcome.

✪ Two miles south of the city on the campus of the Salisbury State University is the

Ward Museum of Wildfowl Art, Holloway Hall, 655 S. Salisbury Blvd. (tel. 742-4988), is a prime showcase for displays of duck and geese decoys and carvings of songbirds. The exhibits include an evolutionary history of decoy-making, antique hunting decoys, modern carved decoratives, paintings, and sculpture of wildfowl art, as well as prints of wild birds. The museum also sponsors an annual (October) exhibition for wood carvers; an on-premises shop also sells unique wildfowl-related gifts. Open Tuesday through Saturday from 10am to 5pm, and Sunday from 1 to 5pm. Admission is $2 for adults and free for children under 12.

SPORTS & ACTIVITIES

Outdoor activity in Salisbury is centered in **City Park** (tel. 548-3188), a delightful sylvan setting in the southwest corner of town near the Civic Center. Surrounded by shady ancient pines, the park winds around Beaver Creek Dam, part of the south prong of the Wicomico River. Facilities include an outdoor zoo, footbridges, a picnic island with gazebo, jogging and walking trails, duck ponds, and a horseshoe pavilion. There are four free tennis courts on the grounds. Paddleboats are also available on the waterways ($3 for a half hour and $5 for 1 hour), daily from June through Labor Day, and on weekends in the spring and fall. Music concerts are held every Sunday at 7pm.

Walkers and joggers also enjoy **Riverfront Walk,** the path that meanders along Salisbury's downtown district.

COOL FOR KIDS

The **Salisbury Zoological Park,** 755 S. Park Dr. (tel. 548-3188) is a 12-acre open-air zoo in the heart of City Park. Appealing to all ages, this zoo houses more than 200 mammals, birds, and reptiles in naturalistic habitats among shade trees and exotic plantings. Major exhibits include spectacled bears, monkeys, jaguars, bison, bald eagles, and waterfowl, all native to North, South, and Central America. There is no admission charge to the zoo, which is open from 8:30am to 7:30pm daily Memorial Day to Labor Day, and 8:30am to 4:30pm the rest of the year.

SHOPPING

One of the leading local crafts is **Salisbury Pewter,** Rte. 13 North, Salisbury (tel. 546-1188). This is both a factory and shop, allowing visitors to watch as each piece is hand-spun and transformed from a metal disc into goblets, platters, bowls, and other fine pewter products. Open Monday through Friday, 9am to 4:30pm, and Saturday 10am to 3pm.

With its proud Victorian heritage, Salisbury is also alive with good antique shops. One of the most interesting is **The Windfall,** on the Downtown Plaza (tel. 742-6681), a haven for antique silver, brass, china, crystal, furniture, prints, and paintings. Open Monday through Saturday from 10am to 5pm.

WHERE TO STAY

Most of Salisbury's hotels are located along Rte. 13 (known locally as Business Rte. 13 or Salisbury Boulevard), a commercial strip that runs north-south along the eastern edge of downtown.

MODERATE

SHERATON SALISBURY INN, 300 S. Salisbury Blvd. (Rte. 13), Salis-bury, MD 21801. Tel. 301/546-4400 or toll-free 800/325-3535. Fax 301/546-2528. 160 rms. A/C TV TEL
$ Rates: $74–$87 single or double. AE, CB, DC, DISC, MC, V. **Parking:** Free. This delightful lodging is located along the edge of Salisbury's Riverwalk Park and is the closest hotel to the Historic District and the midtown Plaza area. Renovated in 1987, the five-story property offers rooms furnished in contemporary style; some nonsmoking rooms are available.

Amenities include an indoor swimming pool, an exercise room and aerobic classes, a jogging trail, valet service, an entertainment lounge, and a three-tiered restaurant with a view of the water.

BUDGET

COMFORT INN, Rte. 13 North, Rte. 11, Box 235, Salisbury, MD 21801. Tel. 301/543-4666 or toll-free 800/221-2222. 72 rooms, 24 suites. A/C TV TEL
$ Rates (including continental breakfast): $37–$50 single, $43–$65 double, $75 suite. AE, DC, DISC, MC, V. **Parking:** Free.

One of the newest good-value lodgings in the area is this motel designed in a stylish motif of wood, brick, and brass. The modern two-story property sits in a well-landscaped grassy setting about 4 miles north of downtown and offers rooms furnished in a bright, contemporary style, with double or king-size beds. The suites have a refrigerator and wet bar, and a Jacuzzi bath.

HAMPTON INN, 1735 N. Salisbury Blvd., Salisbury, MD 21801. Tel. 301/546-1300 or toll-free 800/HAMPTON. Fax 301/546-0370. 102 rms. A/C TV TEL
$ Rates (including continental breakfast): $39–$50 single, $44–$55 double. AE, CB, DC, DISC, MC, V. **Parking:** Free.

Designed in the usual style of this chain, this is a sleek two-story property, both well maintained and well landscaped. The guest rooms are decorated in a bright contemporary style with nautical art and comfortable furniture, including lounge chairs and ottomans. Facilities include an outdoor swimming pool, exercise room, and free local phone calls.

WHERE TO DINE

In the heart of seafood, chicken, and farm country, Salisbury has many fine restaurants at all price levels. Rte. 13 is the location of most of the fast-food eating spots, while the more distinctive restaurants are spread out from the heart of downtown well into the suburbs.

EXPENSIVE

JOHNNY'S AND SAMMY'S, 670 S. Salisbury Blvd., Salisbury. Tel. 742-1116.
Cuisine: AMERICAN. **Reservations:** Not required.
$ Prices: Appetizers $1.95–$5.95, main courses $7.95–$18.95, lunch $3.95–$7.95. DISC, MC, V.
Open: Wed–Fri lunch 11am–2pm and dinner 5–10pm; Sat dinner 5–10pm, Sun buffet dinner noon–6pm.

Best described as a Salisbury tradition, this restaurant has been in business since 1946. The core of the enterprise is a dependable coffee shop-style eatery that offers exceptionally fine food at moderate prices in an informal atmosphere. The menu features sandwiches, burgers, and salads at lunchtime and a variety of entrées at dinner—from steamed shrimp, crab imperial, crab cakes, and lobster, to veal cutlet parmesan, fried chicken, baked ham, steaks, and prime rib of beef.

In addition, there is another dining area, the Mid-Ocean Room. It operates on a more limited schedule, but usually features the same seafood and beef specialties.

WEBSTER'S 1801, 1801 N. Salisbury Blvd., Salisbury. Tel. 742-8000.
Cuisine: INTERNATIONAL. **Reservations:** Recommended.
$ Prices: Appetizers $2.95–$7.95; main courses $12.95–$19.95; lunch $4.95–$7.95. AE, MC, V.
Open: Mon–Sat lunch and dinner 11am–10pm; Sun dinner only 4–9pm.

If you are staying at a motel along the northern stretch of Rte. 13, this is a good place to know—it is not only convenient, but also one of the few fine dining spots in this part of town. A bright and brassy structure with a cathedral-style ceiling and lots of plants, this modern restaurant offers an eclectic menu, with entrées such as chicken Cordon Bleu and veal alla marsala, as well as a variety of steaks and seafood. Lunch items concentrate on sandwiches, burgers, and salads.

MODERATE

TOLLEY POINT, 507 W. Salisbury Pkwy. Tel. 742-2193.
   Cuisine: SEAFOOD. **Reservations:** Recommended.
$ **Prices:** Appetizers $2.95–$8.95; main courses $8.95–$15.95; lunch $3.95–$6.95. AE, MC, V.
   Open: Lunch Mon–Sat 11:30am–3pm; dinner Mon–Thurs 5–9pm, Fri–Sat 5–9:30pm, Sun noon–9pm.

The top choice for seafood is this restaurant about 2 miles west of downtown on Rte. 50. With a facade and decor reminiscent of a Chesapeake Bay lighthouse, the eatery specializes in the best of the local catch, particularly crab. On the ground floor there is a seafood market and a deli-café for light meals or carry-out/picnic choices, while the second floor is devoted to a full-scale restaurant with bar service. Lunch items include crab cake platters, seafood salads, chowders, burgers, and sandwiches. Entrées feature crab imperial, steamed or stuffed shrimp, snow crab legs, stuffed flounder, chicken, and steaks.

BUDGET

ENGLISH'S FAMILY RESTAURANT, 735 S. Salisbury Blvd. Tel. 742-8182.
   Cuisine: AMERICAN. **Reservations:** Not required.
$ **Prices:** Appetizers $1.95–$4.95; main courses $5.95–$10.95; lunch $2.95–$5.95. MC, V.
   Open: Sun–Thurs 7am–10pm, Fri–Sat 7am–11pm.
The ideal spot to try kettle-fried chicken, hush puppies, and sweet-potato biscuits with apple butter is this restaurant founded in Salisbury in 1933; it is actually one of a chain of 10 restaurants of the same name along the eastern shore throughout Maryland. Lunch choices include salads, burgers, omelets, and an assortment of seafood and meat sandwiches. Dinner offers a half-dozen varieties of chicken, plus seafood, steaks, honey-glazed ham, and Maryland turkey. Sweet-potato pie is also on the menu.

NEARBY DINING

RED ROOST, Clara Road, Whitehaven. Tel. 546-5443.
   Cuisine: SEAFOOD. **Reservations:** Not accepted. **Directions:** About 16 miles southwest of town, take Rte. 50 west, then Rte. 349 south to Rte. 352.
$ **Prices:** Appetizers $.75–$3.50; main courses $6.95–$15.95. MC, V.
   Open: Late Mar–mid-May Thurs–Fri 5:30–10pm, Sat 5–10pm, Sun 4–9pm; mid-May–Labor Day Mon–Fri 5:30–10pm, Sat 5–10pm, Sun 4–9pm; Labor Day–late Oct Wed–Fri 5:30–10pm, Sat 5–10pm, Sun 4–9pm.

One of the most delicious (and enjoyable) dining experiences in Maryland is this restaurant about a half-hour's drive from Salisbury. It's well signposted, and so popular with the locals that you can usually just follow the patterns of traffic on this scenic country road, past the corn and soybean fields. Located in a refurbished (and now air-conditioned) Perdue chicken house, this restaurant was founded over a dozen years ago by the Palmer family, who are still enthusiastically in charge.

The menu includes whole steamed fish, steamed shrimp, fried chicken, porterhouse steak, and baby back ribs, but the overwhelming dinner choice is CRAB. Steamed in huge vats and dipped in a spicy blend of seasonings, crabs here are served with mallets and picks to crack and extract the succulent crab from its shell. The Palmers stroll around the restaurant and are eager to offer crab-cracking advice, as are most of the other more-experienced patrons. Beer, wine, and wine-based cocktails are also available.

---

5. OCEAN CITY

116 miles SE of Annapolis, 136 miles SE of Baltimore, 29 miles E of
Salisbury, 71 miles SE of Dover, 76 miles SE of Easton,
and 145 miles S of Philadelphia

GETTING THERE By Air The **Ocean City Municipal Airport,** Stephen Decatur Memorial Road, off Rte. 611 (tel. 289-0927), is located 3 miles west of town. This facility handles regularly scheduled commuter flights to and from Baltimore and other cities via **USAir Commuter** (tel. toll-free 800/428-4322).

By Bus **Greyhound/Trailways** has daily services into Ocean City from points north and south, stopping at 2nd St. and Philadelphia Ave. (tel. 289-9307).

By Car From the west, use Rte. 50; from north or south, take Rte. 13.

ESSENTIALS Ocean City has a very active and enthusiastic tourist office that stocks all kinds of helpful information, maps, and brochures. It is located right in the heart of town and is open daily all year, with extended evening hours on summer weekends. Be sure to head for the **Ocean City Visitors and Convention Bureau,** 4001 Coastal Hwy., Ocean City, MD 21842 (tel. 301/289-8181).

SPECIAL EVENTS Among its many claims to fame, Ocean City is known as the "white marlin capital of the world." Two summertime competitions draw white-marlin enthusiasts from far and wide: the annual **White Marlin Tournament** (started in 1958), on the last weekend of August, sponsored by the Ocean City Marlin Club, 201 S. St. Louis Ave. (tel. 289-6363); and the **White Marlin Open,** held in early or mid-August, offering $50,000 in prizes, and organized by Harbour Island Marina, 14th and the Bay (tel. 289-9229).

Other highlights of the Ocean City calendar include the annual **Sand Castle Fest** in late June; the **Antiques by the Sea Show** in August; **Sunfest,** a 4-day arts-and-crafts, music, and entertainment event in September; and **PolkaMotion by the Ocean,** a mid-September festival of continuous polka music, polka dance groups, free dance lessons, and merriment. Contact the Ocean City Visitors and Convention Bureau for complete details on these and other events.

The narrow peninsula known as Ocean City is Maryland's star attraction along the Atlantic. A 10-mile strip of white sandy beach, Ocean City is a lively and well-developed vacationland, sandwiched in between the "quiet" Delaware resorts of Fenwick Island and Bethany Beach to the north and the equally tranquil Assateague Island and the Virginia border to the south.

In addition to its seafront side to the east, Ocean City is also rimmed on its west by a series of picturesque bays with memorable names like Assawoman, Montego, Isle of Wight, and Sinepuxent. To add to its glories as a summer mecca, Ocean City's wide expanse of free beach is complemented by a 3-mile-long boardwalk, lined with hotels, restaurants, shops, and amusements. It's no wonder that the city's small resident population of 7,000 easily swells to over 200,000 on July and August weekends.

Like other destinations in Maryland, Ocean City also has a proud history. Officially opened as a beach resort on July 4, 1875, Ocean City was first reached by stagecoach from Salisbury, Philadelphia, and Baltimore. Turn-of-the-century sun-seekers thought nothing of long train journeys from as far away as Wilmington to reach Ocean City's shores. In 1910, when the first permanent boardwalk was laid, its length was just five blocks; today it spans 27 blocks.

The beach itself has been developed to a 145-block length. The lower section, which was the original Ocean City, is home to the boardwalk, the amusement parks, and most of the older hotels. The upper section, from about 40th St. to 145th St., is rich in modern motels and rows of towering condominiums.

One road, Rte. 1 (otherwise known as Coastal Highway), spans the entire length of the beach from north to south. This road divides Ocean City into two halves, the ocean front and the bay side. The city is connected to the Maryland mainland by two bridges, the Rte. 50 bridge (which crosses over into First Street at the southern tip of Ocean City) and the Rte. 90 bridge (which brings you midway into the city at 62nd St.).

GETTING AROUND
BY BUS

Regular daily bus services are operated up and down Coastal Hwy. (Rte. 1) by the **Ocean City Municipal Bus Service,** 65th St. and the Bay (tel. 723-1606 or 723-1607). In the summer months, the schedule is every 10 minutes, 24 hours a day. From October 1 until Memorial Day, buses run every half hour, except between 11pm and 7am, when service is hourly. The fare is 75¢ one way, and exact change is required.

BY BOARDWALK TRAIN

Starting at South First Street, a tram-type train runs along the boardwalk every 20 minutes up to 27th Street. The trip lasts about a half hour and is an ideal way to get an orientation to the hotels, restaurants, and shops along the boardwalk. You can also signal the conductor by raising your hand and then disembark at any point you wish before the end of the line. The fare is $1 and you pay as you board the train at the starting point. If there is room, the tram will also pick up new passengers along the route, but the fare remains the same. The train runs from Memorial Day through Labor Day.

BY CAR

Parking is difficult, particularly at the height of the season. Many public facilities, such as shopping centers and restaurants, usually offer ample free parking to patrons. There are also public parking lots in certain areas near the beach, such as the Inlet on South First St. Otherwise, parking is by meter on the streets. Most hotels and motels have their own parking lots or garages and supply their guests with parking permits that usually allow one free parking space per room.

BY RENTED CAR

The car-rental firms represented in this area include **Avis,** 106 Wicomico St. (tel. 289-6121), **Hertz,** Ocean City Airport (tel. 289-8355), and **National,** Rte. 50 (tel. 289-4522).

BY TAXI

If you need a ride, call **Ocean City Taxi** (tel. 289-8164) or **Resort Taxi** (tel. 524-9339).

WHAT TO SEE & DO

✪ To give yourself a proper feel for Ocean City, a stroll along the **boardwalk** is a must. You'll see lots of amusements and shops and some food concessions that have become traditions, like Dumser's Dairyland (since 1939); the Alaska Stands (since 1933); and Thrasher's French Fries (since 1929). Your eyes will also be drawn to the unique **Ocean Gallery World,** at 2nd St. and Boardwalk. Famous for its fine art at close-out prices, this colorful emporium is chock-full of art posters and original oil paintings.

At the southern tip of the boardwalk is the **Ocean City Life-Saving Station**

Museum (tel. 289-4991), founded in 1878. In addition to exhibits on the U.S. life-saving service from 1875 to 1914, this museum offers a fascinating display of dollhouse models depicting Ocean City in its early days, and a pictorial history of the fishing industry in Ocean City. There are also two 300-gallon saltwater aquariums that contain marine life indigenous to this area, and a unique collection of fossils and beachcomber finds. Hours of operation are June through September, daily from 11am to 10pm; May and October, daily from 11am to 4pm; and weekends only during the rest of the year, from noon to 4pm. Admission charge is $1.25 for adults and 50¢ for children under 12.

☉ Just south of Ocean City is **Assateague Island National Seashore and State Park**, a 32-mile-long island belonging jointly to Maryland and Virginia. The state of Maryland owns 680 acres that contain 2 miles of ocean frontage, divided into two equal sections, with a beautiful white sandy beach and dunes (ranging from 14 to 22 feet) on one side, and salt marsh on the other. There is a visitor center, a boardwalk, a bath house with changing rooms and lockers, a tackle shop, charcoal grills and tables, a picnic area, some primitive campsites, nature walks, and lots of room for swimming, surfing, and fishing. Assateague's greatest claim to fame, however, is its resident wild ponies that roam the island. Descended from domesticated stock that grazed here as early as the 17th century, these shaggy and sturdy ponies are smaller than horses, and well adapted to their harsh seashore environment, with the marsh and dune grasses supplying the bulk of their food. They are a thrill to see, but visitors are warned to keep a safe distance. For further information, contact the Park Manager, Assateague State Park, Rte. 2, P.O. Box 293, Berlin, MD 21811 (tel. 301/641-2120).

☉ If it happens to rain or you'd like a change of pace from the beach and the bay, try a drive in the nearby countryside. Head about 7 miles southwest of Ocean City to the town of Berlin, a historic inland enclave with a turn-of-the-century charm. Enjoy a stroll along Main St. and visit some of the many intriguing antique shops and gift boutiques, as well as the recently restored **Atlantic Hotel**, a Victorian gem dating back to 1895 and the centerpiece of the town (see "Where to Stay" and "Where to Dine," below). For more information, including a map of the shops, contact the **Berlin Chamber of Commerce**, P.O. Box 212, Berlin, MD 21811 (tel. 301/641-2770).

BAY CRUISING/FISHING

Since Ocean City is surrounded by the waters of the Atlantic Ocean and four different bays, sightseeing by boat is especially popular, as is fishing. From Memorial Day through September, most vessels double as fishing boats by day and sightseeing boats in the evening, but a few specialize in sightseeing or fishing only. Below is a sampling of what is available.

THE ANGLER, **Talbot St. and the Bay, Ocean City. Tel. 289-7424.**
This 97-passenger vessel offers 7-hour head-boat fishing excursions and 1-hour sightseeing cruises that go through the Inlet and north along the ocean coast.
Fishing Price: $24 adults, $12 children under 12; $4 rod rental.
Fishing Departure: Daily 7am.
Sightseeing Price: $4 adults, $2 children under 12.
Sightseeing Departures: Daily 7pm, 9pm.

THE BAY QUEEN, **Ocean City Fishing Center, Shantytown Pier, West Ocean City. Tel. 289-8121.**
Day and evening cruises are operated on this 60-passenger boat, covering the harbor as far south as Assateague Island.
Sightseeing Price: $6 adults, $3 children under 12.
Sightseeing Departures: Daily 10:30am, 12:30pm, 2pm, 3:30pm, 7pm.

THE CAPTAIN BUNTING, **307 Dorchester and the Bay, Ocean City. Tel. 289-6720.**

This 88-passenger boat offers 7-hour head-boat fishing by day and 1-hour evening cruises through the Inlet and north along the ocean coast as far as 65th Street.
Fishing Price: $24 adults, $12 children under 13; rod rental $4.
Fishing Departure: Daily 7am.
Sightseeing Price: $5 adults, $2.50 children under 13.
Sightseeing Departures: Daily 6pm, 7:30pm, 9pm.

JUDITH M., Bahia Marina, 21st St. and the Bay, Ocean City. Tel. 289-7438.
Four-hour deep-sea fishing is available to 75 fishermen each day, followed by scenic ocean cruises for up to 150 passengers each evening on this new vessel, equipped with all electronics.
Fishing Price: $18 adults, $15 children under 12.
Fishing Departures: Daily 8am, 1:30pm.
Sightseeing Price: $6 adults, $4 children under 12.
Sightseeing Departure: Daily 7:30pm.

THE MARINER, Talbot St. Pier, Talbot St. and the Bay, Ocean City. Tel. 289-3503.
This 95-passenger boat offers 7-hour head-boat fishing excursions each morning; evening cruises through the Inlet and along the ocean to 100th Street last 1¼ hours.
Fishing Price: $24 adults, $12 children under 12; $4 rod rental.
Fishing Departure: Daily 7am.
Sightseeing Price: $5 adults, $3 children under 12.
Sightseeing Departure: Daily 7:30pm.

MISS OCEAN CITY, N. 1st St. and the Bay, Ocean City. Tel. 289-8234.
Seven-hour head-boat fishing is available each morning on this 150-passenger vessel, followed by evening cruises from the Inlet to 60th Street.
Fishing Price: $24.50 adults, $12.25 children under 12; $4 rod rental.
Fishing Departure: Daily 7am.
Sightseeing Price: $4 adults, $2 children under 12.
Sightseeing Departures: Daily 6:25pm, 7:55pm, 9:25pm.

MISTY, Bahia Marina, 21st St. and the Bay, Ocean City. Tel. 289-7438.
Sightseeing is the specialty of this 25-passenger craft, with 2-hour excursions to Assateague Island to see the wild ponies, take a nature walk, or stroll the beach.
Sightseeing Price: $7.95 adults, $4 children under 12.
Sightseeing Departures: Daily 10:30am, 2pm, 4pm.

THE TAURUS, S. Harbor Rd., Rte. 1, West Ocean City. Tel. 289-2565.
This 75-passenger boat operates daytime 4-hour head-boat fishing excursions and evening 1-hour harbor cruises from West Ocean City through the Inlet and along the ocean coast to 45th Street.
Fishing Price: $16 adults, $8 children 10 and under; $4 rod rental.
Fishing Departures: Daily 8am, 1pm.
Sightseeing Price: $5 adults, $3 children under 10.
Sightseeing Departures: Mon, Wed, Fri 7:30pm.

THE THERAPY, Ocean City Fishing Center, Shantytown Marina, West Ocean City. Tel. 289-8818 or after 6pm 352-5192.
Cruise in bay and ocean waters for 3 hours aboard a 34-foot sailboat, accommodating a maximum of six persons. Reservations necessary.
Sightseeing Price: $30 per person.
Sightseeing Departures: Daily 9am, 1pm, 5:30pm.

THE TORTUGA, Bahia Marina, 21st St. and the Bay, Ocean City. Tel. 289-7438.

This 24-passenger boat offers 4-hour ocean bottom fishing trips for flounder in spring, summer, and fall.

Fishing Price: $16–$22 adults, $8–$11 children 12 and under; $4 rod rental.
Fishing Departures: Mon–Fri 8am, 1pm, 5pm; Sat 9am; Sun 11am.

SPORTS & RECREATION
WATER SPORTS

From April through October, Ocean City is a haven for all types of water activity, from jet skiing and parasailing to sailboarding and windsurfing, or you can take to the seas in a motor boat, catamaran, or pontoon. Prices depend on type of equipment and duration of rental, but many boats can be rented from $20 to $50 an hour. Water skis and smaller equipment start at about $10 an hour, jet skis from $50 an hour. For full information, contact one of the following: **Advanced Marina Boat Rentals,** 122 66th St. and Bay, Ocean City (tel. 723-2124; **Bahia Marina,** 21st St. and the Bay, Ocean City (tel. 289-7438); **Ocean City Parasail,** 54th St. and the Bay (tel. 723-1464); or **Watersports Unlimited,** 142nd St. and the Bay (tel. 250-2777).

GOLF

There are a half-dozen golf courses within easy driving reach of Ocean City. Two of the closest are **Pine Shore,** 11285 Beauchamp Rd., Berlin (tel. 641-5100) and the **Bay Club,** Libertytown Rd., Rte. 374, Berlin (tel. 641-4081). Call for latest details on starting times and fees.

SWIMMING

The entire 10-mile stretch of Ocean City beach is open to the public, free of charge. Numerous beachfront concessions rent various equipment such as chairs ($3 a day) and umbrellas ($5 a day).

BICYCLING

Ocean City is ideal for bicycling, particularly early in the morning before heavy traffic hours. Boardwalk biking is also allowed between 6 and 10am. Rates vary according to the type of bike, but you can expect to pay between $3 and $5 an hour for a two-wheeler, $8 an hour for a tandem, and $10 an hour for a tri-tandem. Some of the best sources are **Sunburst Bike Rental** at 16th St. and Coastal Hwy.; **Pedal Pusher,** 609 N. Boardwalk (tel. 289-6865); **Trimpers Cycle Center,** 603-A S. Baltimore Ave. (tel. 289-5442); and **Ocean Park Bike Rentals,** 17th St. and Boardwalk.

TENNIS

Local public courts, offering free tennis on a first-come basis, are located at 14th, 94th, and 136th Sts. Two other public courts, at 41st and 61st Sts., are operated on a reservation basis, at $5 per hour (tel. 524-8337).

HEALTH CLUB

Rain or shine, for a variety of activities, try the **Ocean City Health & Racquetball Club,** 6103 SeaBay Dr. (tel. 723-2323), at 61st St. on the Bay. For a daily fee of $15, you can use the whirlpool, saunas, tanning rooms, racquetball courts, indoor running track, gym and weight room, and heated indoor swimming pool. There are also aerobics and dance classes. Open 7am to 10pm, Monday through Friday, and from 7am to 9pm on Saturday and Sunday.

COOL FOR KIDS

Ocean City is home to several amusement parks and child-oriented activities. Some of the leading spots are listed below.

Trimper's Park, on the Boardwalk near the Inlet, between South Division and South First Sts. (tel. 289-8617), was established in 1887 and is the granddaddy of Ocean City's amusement areas. It has over 100 rides and attractions for the whole family, including a water flume and a 1902 merry-go-round with all hand-carved animals. Most rides are 30¢. The park is open daily, May through September, from 1pm to midnight, and weekends February to April and October to November.

Jolly Roger, 30th St. and Coastal Hwy. (tel. 289-3477), is home to Ocean City's largest roller coaster, mini-golf courses, a petting zoo, water slides, and magic shows. Admission is $2, plus $3.50 for golf; the water park is extra at $7 per hour or $12 a day. The entire park is open daily from noon to midnight, May through September.

Frontier Town and Rodeo, Rte. 1, West Ocean City (tel. 289-7877), is a western theme park. Set on 38 acres of woodland, this park includes a replica of a western town of the 1860s, genuine rodeos, cowboy- and dance-hall shows, stagecoach rides, riverboats, a steam train, and a giant water slide. Children can also go trail riding and panning for gold, and visit a petting zoo. Open every day from 10am to 6pm, mid-June through Labor Day, the admission charge is $10 for adults and $8 for children 13 and under. To aid customers, a free van service is operated each morning and afternoon between the park and downtown Ocean City.

WHERE TO STAY

With more than 9,000 hotel rooms (and 6,000 condo units), a description of Ocean City's lodgings could easily fill a fat guidebook on its own. It is impossible to do justice to all of the hotels and motels in this short section, but we'll give you some of the highlights. We'll tell you about some of the large and small, the old and new, and a few on the ocean and along the bay, to help you get your bearings. If you have never been here before, it might be best to pick a place by relying on your favorite hotel chain. (Best Western, Comfort, Days Inn, Econo, Holiday Inn, Howard Johnson, Quality, and Sheraton are all well represented here.)

Most properties depend on a 5-month season, and summer (especially July and August) commands the highest rates, often with supplements on weekend nights as well. In many cases, minimum stays of 2 or 3 nights may apply, so check the rates in advance. Reservations are certainly a must.

In almost all cases, the larger hotels offer money-saving package plans, particularly in the late-spring or early-autumn seasons, when Ocean City can be equally as lovely as at the peak of summer (and a lot less crowded). Although it is a great treat to overlook the ocean, rooms with partial or no views of the water often cost considerably less than those with "oceanfront" prices.

EXPENSIVE

BRIGHTON SUITES, 12500 Coastal Hwy., Ocean City, MD 19971. Tel. 301/524-1433 or toll-free 800/227-5788. Fax 301/250-7603. 57 suites. A/C TV TEL

$ Rates: $59–$139 weekdays, $69–$169 weekends, single or double occupancy. AE, DISC, MC, V. **Parking:** Free.

Situated on the main highway, but within easy walking distance of beach or bay, this is a five-story all-suite property, ideal for families or two couples traveling together. Each suite has a bedroom with two queen-size beds or a king-size bed with contemporary furnishings, and a large modern bathroom with hairdryer, plus a separate living room with pull-out couch, wet bar, refrigerator-freezer, and a personal safe. Most units also have a private balcony. Facilities include an indoor heated swimming pool and secure underground parking.

COCONUT MALORIE, Fager's Island, 201 60th St., Ocean City, MD 21842. Tel. 301/723-6100 or toll-free 800/767-6060. Fax 301/723-2055. 85 suites. A/C TV TEL

$ Rates: $75–$155 single or double; $140–$175 for top floor (penthouse level). AE, CB, DC, MC, V. **Parking:** Free.

★ This new hotel, with a British Colonial name and ambience, stands out on the bayfront. The lobby is palatial, with gushing fountains, brass and crystal chandeliers, marble floors, tree-size plants, and an eager staff attending to guests.

With such a dazzling reception area, however, it isn't surprising that the guest rooms are also very distinctive—all decorated with a Caribbean flavor, including a collection of Haitian art. Each unit is a suite, comprised of a bedroom (often dominated by a four-poster bed) and a marble bathroom with whirlpool Jacuzzi, lighted makeup-shaving mirror, and hairdryer; plus a sitting and dining area, private balcony, kitchen, wet bar, refrigerator, microwave oven, and coffee- and tea-maker. Facilities include an outdoor swimming pool and sun deck and a full-time concierge desk. This hotel is also connected by footbridge (and by the same ownership) to Fager's Island restaurant and lounge (see "Where to Dine," below).

DUNES MANOR, 28th St. and the Ocean, Ocean City, MD 21842. Tel. 301/289-1100 or toll-free 800/523-2888. Fax 301/289-4905. 160 rms, 10 suites. A/C TV TEL
$ Rates: $55–$180 single or double; $100–$230 suite. AE, CB, DC, DISC, MC, V. **Parking:** Free.

★ One of the newest hotels on the ocean is the Dunes Manor, situated on its own stretch of beach north of the boardwalk. The stylish 11-story property is designed with a Victorian facade, including a grand open porch (with rockers), rooftop cupolas, and a private mini-boardwalk facing the ocean. Each of the bedrooms and suites has an oceanfront view, with balcony, two double beds, a decor of light woods and floral fabrics, and a refrigerator. The guest amenities include an indoor/outdoor pool, a Jacuzzi, an exercise room, a sun deck, and a Victorian-style restaurant and lounge. Afternoon tea is served in the lobby each afternoon. Open year round.

LIGHTHOUSE CLUB, Fager's Island, 56th Street in the Bay, Ocean City, MD 21842. Tel. 301/524-5400 or toll-free 800/767-6060. Fax 301/723-2755. 23 suites. A/C TV TEL
$ Rates (including continental breakfast): $90–$150 single or double; $150–$180 with gas fireplace. **Parking:** Free.

Overlooking the Isle of Wight Bay and boasting an octagonal lighthouse exterior, this unique three-story inn sits on a patch of wetlands, surrounded by water. The library-style reception area has a homey atmosphere and the guest rooms are equally welcoming.

Each unit is a suite, comprised of a nautically themed bedroom and a marble-trimmed bathroom with Jacuzzi, hairdryer, and lighted makeup mirror. There is also a sitting area, decorated with soft sea-tone fabrics, light woods, and rattan furnishings. Eight of the suites have gas fireplaces and 15 have balconies. The suites are equipped with wet bar, refrigerator, ice maker, and coffee- and tea-maker. Services include in-room continental breakfast, evening turndown, and VCR rentals. The only drawback is that there is no elevator between the lobby floor and the two guest floors. Facilities include an outdoor swimming pool and footbridge access to Fager's Island restaurant (see "Where to Dine," below), under the same ownership.

SHERATON OCEAN CITY RESORT, 10100 Ocean Hwy., Ocean City, MD 21842. Tel. 301/524-3535 or toll-free 800/325-3535. 228 rooms, 22 suites. A/C TV TEL
$ Rates: $60–$185 single or double; $95–$190 studio; $250–$500 bilevel suite. AE, CB, DC, DISC, MC, V. **Parking:** Free.

Of all the hotel chains in this beachfront community, this one is in a class by itself. It is located right on the ocean, far from the boardwalk and in the midst of the residential high-rise condo section of Ocean City. Recently renovated, this 16-story tower offers oversized rooms and suites, all with views of the ocean and bay. Each room also has its own private balcony, contemporary furnishings, plush wall-to-wall carpeting, and refrigerator.

Amenities include the Horizon restaurant and lounges overlooking the ocean, evening entertainment, a beachside terrace, valet services, an arcade of shops, a convention center, a video game room, an indoor heated pool; and a complete spa with Jacuzzi, workout room, steam room, sauna, whirlpool, and sun rooms. As its name implies, this hotel is a complete resort in itself.

MODERATE

ATLANTIC HOTEL INN, 2 N. Main St., Berlin, MD 21811. Tel. 301/641-3589. Fax 301/641-4928. 16 rms, all with bath. A/C TEL **Directions:** From Ocean City, take Rte. 50 west to Rte. 113 (Main St.), a total of 7 miles.
$ Rates (including continental breakfast): $60–$120 single or double. MC, V. **Parking:** Free.

If you'd like to have access to the beach and boardwalk attractions of Ocean City but prefer the quiet setting of a nearby historic town, this is the place for you. Dating back to 1895 and listed on the National Register of Historic Places, this classic Victorian three-story hotel has been updated with modern amenities, while still retaining its original charm. The guest rooms are individually furnished with local antiques and are rich in Victorian tones of deep green and burgundy, or delicate rose and aqua, with mahogany furniture, and accessories of lace, crochet, tassels, and braids. TVs are not usual fixtures in guest rooms, but they are available on request. Facilities include a reading parlor, outdoor balcony, and highly acclaimed restaurant (see "Where to Dine," below) and lounge.

CASTLE IN THE SAND, Ocean Front at 37th St., P.O. Box 190, Ocean City, MD 21842. Tel. 301/289-6846 or toll-free 800/552-SAND. Fax 301/289-9446. 36 rms, 137 suites. A/C TV TEL
$ Rates: $111–$128 single or double; $129–$156 suites. AE, DISC, MC, V. **Closed:** Nov–Mar. **Parking:** Free.
Another modern property on the beach north of the boardwalk is this hotel with a striking mock-castle exterior complete with turrets. Standard hotel rooms with two double beds are offered, as well as oceanfront efficiencies with balconies; all units have modern furnishings. Outdoor amenities include an Olympic-size swimming pool, a private beach, and an oceanfront patio. Lower rates apply in April to June and September to October.

COMFORT INN GOLD COAST, 11201 Coastal Hwy., Ocean City, MD 21842. Tel. 301/524-3000 or toll-free 800/228-5150. Fax 301/524-8255. 202 rms. A/C TV TEL
$ Rates: Summer $74.95–$154.95 single or double; off-season $39.95–$104.95 single or double. AE, CB, DC, DISC, MC, V. **Parking:** Free.

Among the many chain properties, one of the best choices for good value and great location is this hotel set back from the main road on its own grounds overlooking the bay. Opened in 1988, the modern five-story lodging offers every up-to-the-minute amenity; each room has a microwave oven, a refrigerator, wet bar, and an ocean or bay view. Facilities include ample parking, a glass-enclosed indoor pool, a Jacuzzi, a sun deck, a lobby convenience store, a guest laundry, and a branch of Libby's restaurant, a local institution in nearby Fenwick Island, Del., plus a lounge and movie theater. Nonsmoking rooms and rooms for the disabled are also available.

ECONO LODGE/SEA BAY INN, 6007 Coastal Hwy., Ocean City, MD 21842. Tel. 301/524-6100 or toll-free 800/888-2229 or 800/446-6900. 92 rms. A/C TV TEL
$ Rates: $34–$95 single or double. AE, DC, DISC, MC, V.

On the bay side, this modern five-story property offers rooms with a balcony and at least a partial view of the bay. Each unit is equipped with a sitting area, table and chairs, sofa bed, refrigerator, microwave, and wet bar.

Facilities include an outdoor pool, elevator, ample parking, and a trendy eatery, The Coaches Corner, specializing in quick and healthy items in the moderate price range. Nonsmoking rooms are available, as are handicapped-accessible units on the ground floor. Open year round, the hotel is also adjacent to the Ocean City Health and Racquet Club and the popular O. C. Sneakers restaurant on the bay.

PHILLIPS BEACH PLAZA HOTEL, 13th St. and Boardwalk, P.O. Box K, Ocean City, MD 21842. Tel. 301/289-9121 or toll-free 800/492-5834. Fax 301/289-3041. 60 rms, 26 apts. A/C TV TEL
$ Rates: $40–$115 single or double; $55–$135 apts. **Parking:** Free.
With an old-world ambience, this boasts an elegant Victorian lobby with crystal chandeliers, wrought-iron fixtures, open fireplace, and graceful statuary, plus a long open porch overlooking the ocean, a top-notch on-premises seafood restaurant, Phillips by the Sea (see "Where to Dine," below), and a piano bar. The accommodations are housed in an attached modern four-story bedroom block with both rooms and apartments (with an elevator). The apartments have dining and/or living areas with full kitchens.

BUDGET

DAYS INN, 4201 Coastal Hwy., Ocean City, MD. 21842. Tel. 301/289-6488 or toll-free 800/325-2525. Fax 301/289-1617. 162 rms. A/C TV TEL
$ Rates: $39–$130 weekdays; $49–$140 weekends, single or double. AE, DC, DISC, MC, V. **Parking:** Free.
For good value and convenience, this new seven-story property is a good choice. It is situated on the bay side of the highway, and all rooms have balconies. The guest rooms, accessible by computer card keys, are decorated in soft pastel tones with light wood furnishings. Facilities include a fully equipped health center with indoor heated swimming pool, and a sun deck.

TAKA-A-MITSIA, 401 11th St., Ocean City, MD 21842. Tel. 301/289-3200. 9 rms, with bath. A/C TV
$ Rates: $27–$55 single or double. **Parking:** Free.
This small motel on the bay side of the highway is furnished with an Oriental decor. Each of the rooms enjoys an open view of the bay and a private terrace, as well as full kitchen facilities, two double beds, and wall-to-wall carpeting. Boat slips are available for motel guests who arrive by water ($10 a day). Open all year.

WHERE TO DINE

At last count, there were well over 100 restaurants in Ocean City, plus at least 60 fast-food establishments. Understandably, seafood is a favorite here and, for the most part, a casual atmosphere prevails, although it is always wise to make a reservation in the better restaurants and to check on the dress code.

During summer, restaurants are rarely closed. Some start as early as 5am, dishing up hearty breakfasts for fishermen, and continue serving meals right through until 10 or 11pm. Unless there are specific hours given, you can be fairly certain that lunch will start at 11 or 11:30am and continue throughout most of the afternoon, and then a dinner menu will be in effect from 5pm until closing.

Most restaurants have full-bar facilities. Just to be safe, obtain a copy of the Ocean City Visitor Bureau's guide to restaurants; it gives descriptions, hours of opening, and price guidelines for at least 50 of the best eateries.

EXPENSIVE

ATLANTIC HOTEL RESTAURANT, 2 N. Main St., Berlin. Tel. 641-3589.
Cuisine: INTERNATIONAL. **Reservations:** Recommended. **Directions:** From Ocean City, take Rte. 50 west to Rte. 113 (Main St.), a total of 7 miles.
$ Prices: Appetizers $3.95–$9.95; main courses $11.95–$23.95; lunch $5.95–$10.95. MC, V.
Open: Lunch Mon–Sat 11:30am–2pm, dinner Sun–Thurs 5–10pm and Fri–Sat 5–11pm, Sun brunch 11am–2pm.

⭐ One of Ocean City's best restaurants is not along the beach, boardwalk, or bay, but a short 15-minute drive inland to the historic town of Berlin. This Victorian-style dining room exudes a welcoming ambience, with eager and able waiters in black tie, classical music in the background, a decor of rich colored glass, plush velvet drapes, chandeliers with bell-shaped glass, and the creative cuisine of chef Stephen Jacques.

The dinner menu changes nightly, but often includes such specialties as chicken and scallops with orange almond cream, roast duckling with ligonberry sauce, salmon with basil sauce, Thai pork with peanut glaze, and rack of lamb chèvre. Lunch items focus mainly on creative salads and sandwiches. In case you wish to linger, you may want to check into one of the rooms upstairs at this charming inn (see "Where to Stay," above).

BONFIRE, 71st St. and Coastal Hwy. Tel. 524-7171.
   Cuisine: INTERNATIONAL. **Reservations:** Recommended.
$ Prices: Appetizers $2.95–$8.95; main courses $10.95–$24.95. AE, DC, MC, V.
   Open: Dinner 4:30–11pm, except Tues in off-season.
Although it is on the bay side of the road, it is delicious food that provides the draw at this large, elaborately decorated restaurant. Diners may choose from four different rooms and two totally different menus. There is a huge oval bar in the center of the complex; and the eclectic furnishings include captain's chairs, plush leather banquettes, leaded- and etched-glass windows, gas lanterns, original oil paintings, and tree-size plants. The BonFire has been known for over 15 years for its charcoal-broiled steaks, aged prime rib, and beef Wellington, as well as its baby back ribs, crab-stuffed chicken, duckling à l'orange, and veal dishes. A recent innovation is its additional menu of 25 Chinese dishes ranging from Szechuan shrimp and pepper steak to roast pork with snow peas and lobster Cantonese. The music of a live band is also featured 7 nights a week. Open year round.

FAGER'S ISLAND, 60th St. in the Bay. Tel. 524-5500.
   Cuisine: AMERICAN. **Reservations:** Recommended.
$ Prices: Appetizers $2.95–$8.95; main courses $15.50–$25; lunch $4.95–$12.95. AE, CB, DC, DISC, MC, V.
   Open: Lunch daily 11am–10pm; dinner 5:30–10pm.
Perched on the edge of the bay, this restaurant is surrounded by three outside decks, a pier, a pavilion, and a gazebo. With wide wraparound windows, Fager's Island is ideal for watching sunsets and is very popular at cocktail hour. Overstuffed sandwiches and heaping salads are available all day. The dinner menu ranges from blackened fish and blackened prime rib, to locally caught seafoods, shrimp, steaks, chops, and fowl. An award-winning wine cellar also offers more than 600 labels. Open year round.

HOBBIT, 81st St. and the Bay. Tel. 524-8100.
   Cuisine: SEAFOOD. **Reservations:** Recommended.
$ Prices: Appetizers $2.95–$7.95; main courses $14.95–$19.95; lunch $4.95–$8.95. MC, V. **Closed:** Christmas.
   Open: Lunch daily 11am–3pm, dinner daily 5–11pm.
⭐ One of the loveliest places to dine while watching the sun set is this restaurant right on the bay. The emphasis is on continental cuisine and there is seating for about 160 plus outside decks; lacy tablecloths dominate the decor. Lunch features seafood pasta, burgers, quiches, salads, stews, and crab-stuffed artichoke hearts. Dinner entrées include flounder stuffed with lobster, rainbow trout stuffed with shrimp and crab, duck à l'orange, and shrimp or scallops with angel-hair pasta.

PHILLIPS CRAB HOUSE, 2004 Philadelphia Ave. Tel. 289-6821.
   Cuisine: SEAFOOD. **Reservations:** Not accepted.
$ Prices: Appetizers $2.75–$5.95; main courses $8.95–$23.95; lunch $4.95–$7.95. AE, DISC, MC, V.

Open: Apr–Oct daily noon–11pm.

⭐ The Phillips seafood restaurants that are so famous in Baltimore, Norfolk, and Washington, D.C., all owe their origin to a small crab carry-out that was started here by Shirley and Brice Phillips in 1956. That family enterprise is today an Ⓢ Ocean City tradition and the town's largest restaurant, seating 1,300 people in 11 different dining rooms. As on the menu of 30 years ago, seafood is the focus and crab is still king. Lunchtime choices include crab sandwiches and salads. Dinner entrées offer an extensive crab repertoire, including crab au gratin and imperial, crab cakes, soft-shell crabs, crab with Smithfield ham, and all-you-can-eat crabs. Lovers of salmon, shrimp, flounder, scallops, oysters, and lobster will also find their favorites here, prepared in a variety of ways, as well as steaks, filet mignon, and fried chicken.

In recent years, Ocean City visitors have enjoyed the Phillips seafood cuisine so much that two additional restaurant locations were opened to serve the demand. In 1973 business began at **Phillips by the Sea,** in the Phillips Beach Plaza Hotel, Oceanfront at 13th St. and the Boardwalk (tel. 289-9121); and in 1977 came the addition of **Phillips Seafood House,** 141st St. and Coastal Hwy. (tel. 250-1200). Both restaurants are open year round and maintain similar menus (and prices) as the 21st St. landmark.

MODERATE

A. T. LANTIC'S FOOD & SPIRITS, 10 Talbot St. Tel. 289-1441.
Cuisine: SEAFOOD. **Reservations:** Recommended.
$ Prices: Appetizers $2.95–$6.95; main courses $8.95–$17.95. AE, DC, MC, V.
Open: Apr–Oct daily 4–10pm.

A lovingly restored, 100-year-old Victorian building, known locally as Mount Vernon, is the home of this seafood house located on a quiet side street, just off the boardwalk. There are no water views, but a gentle old-world ambience prevails both in the upstairs dining room and on the front porch open-air deck and back patio. The menu is rather simple, just crabs, scallops, shrimp, clams, oysters, and flounder, all prepared to suit your desires, whether it be au gratin, barbecued, with imperial sauce, or au natural. Chicken and steaks are also available for non–fish-eaters.

BAYSIDE SKILLET, 77th St. and Coastal Hwy. Tel. 524-7950.
Cuisine: INTERNATIONAL. **Reservations:** Not required.
$ Prices: Appetizers $2.95–$5.95; main courses $6.95–$15.95. MC, V.
Open: Daily 24 hours.

Ⓢ One of the most creative kitchens in Ocean City belongs to this restaurant, a place you would probably pass by unless you were in the mood for a crêpe or omelet. While it's true that crêpes, omelets, and light dishes are served throughout the day, this modern restaurant also offers a wide range of other dinner entrées, such as baked shrimp and ratatouille provençal, seafood mornay (flounder, scallops, shrimp, and crab), filet of flounder stuffed with crabmeat and avocado, prime rib, and shrimp scampi. The crêpes are also worth a try at any hour, with such fillings as coquilles St-Jacques; chicken with mushrooms in Madeira sauce; or bacon, spinach, and hollandaise. This wide-windowed eatery also features tall beamed ceilings, knotty-pine walls, pink linens, hanging plants, and some of the best sunset views along the bay. Open year round.

CAPT. BILL BUNTING'S ANGLER, Talbot St. and the Bay. Tel. 289-7424 and 289-6980.
Cuisine: AMERICAN. **Reservations:** Recommended.
$ Prices: Appetizers $2.95–$6.95; main courses $9.95–$22.95; lunch $3.95–$7.95. MC, V.
Open: Daily lunch 11am–2pm, dinner 4–10pm. **Closed:** Nov–Apr.

Since 1938 this has been a favorite eatery on the marina of Ocean City. With a rustic and nautical decor, this spacious restaurant features an air-conditioned main dining room plus an outdoor patio deck overlooking the bay. It's an ideal spot to see the boats sailing by or to watch the fishermen bring back their bounty. Lunch focuses on tempting raw bar selections, fishwiches, salads, and burgers. The extensive dinner menu includes coquilles St-Jacques, shrimp scampi, flounder francese, surf-n-turf, roast turkey, fried chicken, and a popular "admiral's feast" that features a little of everything (flounder, scallops, shrimp, crab cakes, oysters, and lobster). In addition, Captain Bill provides a free evening cruise of the bay at 7 or 9pm as part of the dinner price. *Note:* For early risers, this is one of the restaurants that opens its doors at 5am for breakfast.

HARRISON'S HARBOR WATCH, Boardwalk South overlooking Inlet. Tel. 289-5121.

Cuisine: SEAFOOD. **Reservations:** Recommended.

$ Prices: Appetizers $2.95–$6.95; main courses $8.95–$19.95; lunch $2.95–$7.95. AE, DISC, MC, V.

Open: Daily 11:30am–11pm. **Closed:** Mid-Oct–mid-May.

You'll get a spectacular full view of the ocean and nearby Assateague Island at this restaurant, situated at the boardwalk's southernmost point. It's a large complex (seating 400), with various levels of seating, tile floors, lots of leafy plants, and a Colonial-nautical decor. Lunch emphasizes light fare (sandwiches and salads). A bountiful raw bar is the focus of attention at dinner, followed by entrées such as hickory-barbecued shrimp, whole local lobster, lobster linguine, crab legs, swordfish with crab imperial, steaks, and fried chicken.

O. C. SNEAKERS, 6103 SeaBay Dr. Tel. 723-DINE.

Cuisine: INTERNATIONAL. **Reservations:** Recommended.

$ Prices: Appetizers $3.50–$6.50; main courses $10.95–$18.95. AE, DC, MC, V.

Open: Summer daily 4:30–10pm; off-season Tues–Sat 4:30–10pm.

Priceless sunsets and moderately priced dining are the hallmark of this restaurant overlooking the bay. With the restaurant's floor-to-ceiling windows and two-tier seating, every table enjoys an idyllic view. The dinner menu offers local crab and fish dishes as well as international favorites such as Florida grouper, New Zealand orange roughy, and African lobster tails. Other choices include fresh pastas and Italian dishes, Louisiana blackened prime rib, chicken chasseur, and veal piccata. To add to the ambience, there is nightly keyboard entertainment in the lounge area.

BUDGET

DUMSER'S DAIRYLAND, 12305 Coastal Hwy. Tel. 250-5543.

Cuisine: AMERICAN. **Reservations:** Not required.

$ Prices: Appetizers $1.95–$4.95; main courses $6.95–$13.95; lunch $1.95–$6.95. MC, V.

Open: Breakfast daily 7 or 8am–4pm; lunch 11am–4pm; dinner 4pm–10 or 11pm.

An Ocean City favorite since 1939, this eatery originally began as an ice-cream parlor but is now equally popular as a restaurant. Lunch choices include sandwiches, salads, subs, and soups. Dinner entrées range from steaks and prime rib to crab cakes, stuffed flounder, fried chicken, and Virginia ham. And make sure to save room for dessert, especially the ice cream, made on the premises. No liquor is served. A second location, **Dumser's Drive-In,** 49th and Coastal Highway (tel. 524-1588), is also open seasonally, with a more limited menu.

PAUL REVERE SMORGASBORD, 2nd St. and Boardwalk. Tel. 524-1776.

Cuisine: AMERICAN. **Reservations:** Not required.

$ Prices: Buffet $7.99. MC, V.

Open: Apr–mid-Sept daily 4:30–8:30pm. **Closed:** Mid-Sept–Mar.

With eight Colonial-style dining rooms, this huge restaurant can accommodate up to 700 diners. One price prevails here. The buffet array of more than 100 items ranges from soups, salads, roast beef, turkey, fried chicken, ribs, seafood, and pasta to a tempting dessert bar. Beer and wine are served.

EVENING ENTERTAINMENT

Many restaurants and dining spots feature live entertainment and dancing in the evenings; among the most popular are **Capt. Bill Bunting's Angler Restaurant,** Talbot St. and the Bay (tel. 289-7424); the **BonFire,** 71st St. and Coastal Hwy. (tel. 524-7171); and **Fager's Island,** 60th St. on the Bay (tel. 524-5500).

The **Ocean City Convention Center,** 40th St. and Coastal Hwy. (tel. 289-8311 or toll-free 800/OC-OCEAN), also presents a year-long program of top entertainers (from Bob Hope to Robert Palmer), big-name dance bands, and other live shows. Tickets usually range from $10 to $25. Check with the visitors' bureau for the latest schedule.

Broadway musicals such as *Ziegfeld Follies Revue* are presented in a dinner-theater format at the **Commander Boardwalk Cabaret,** 14th St. on the Boardwalk (tel. 289-6166). Staffed by young professionals who not only sing and dance but also serve the meal, this show is available during the 10 weeks of summer, Tuesday through Saturday, with dinner seating at 7:30pm. Total cost for the dinner and show is based on the price of dinner (entrées range from lobster, crab and shrimp Newburg, prime rib, and crab cakes to ham steak), with a $25 minimum. Depending on space, seating is sometimes available at 9pm for cocktails/show only, with a $10 minimum. Reservations are required.

CHAPTER 18

WESTERN MARYLAND

From the shores of the Potomac to the Alleghe-ny mountaintops, western Maryland is a pano-rama of fertile farmlands and historic hillsides. Jutting out like a panhandle beyond Baltimore and wedged in between Pennsylvania and West Virginia, this land was the westward gateway of our ancestors as they headed their covered wagons for Ohio and beyond.

Alternate Rte. 40, this country's first National Pike, still meanders over the entire length of this countryside, connecting Frederick to Hagerstown, Cumberland, and other points east and west. This area was also the path for the great feat of mid-19th-century ingenuity, the 184½-mile-long Chesapeake and Ohio Canal (the C&O) linking Georgetown to Cumberland.

Western Maryland is the home of Francis Scott Key and Barbara Fritchie; and the site of Antietam National Battlefield, Fort Cumberland, and Fort Frederick. It is also the setting for Lily Pons Water Gardens; the "antiques capital of Maryland" at historic New Market; Camp David, the retreat of U.S. presidents since Franklin Roosevelt; and the Western Maryland Scenic Railroad excursions between Cumberland and Frostburg.

With an elevation ranging from 490 feet to 3,650 feet, this 225-mile stretch of land extends from the rolling hills of Frederick's horse country to the dramatic ski slopes of Wisp Mountain in Garrett County.

In addition to the trusty pavements of old Alternate Rte. 40, a network of modern interstate highways will bring you to this relatively undiscovered corner of the Old Line State. I-70 runs from Baltimore to Frederick and Hagerstown before it crosses up into the Pennsylvania border toward Breezewood. I-270 connects Washington, D.C., to Frederick, I-81 skirts Hagerstown as it runs in a north-south direction between Pennsylvania and West Virginia, and the new I-68 traverses the western part of the state, from Hancock to the West Virginia border.

1. FREDERICK

33 miles S of Gettysburg, 148 miles SW of Philadelphia,
47 miles W of Baltimore, 45 miles NW of Washington D.C.

GETTING THERE **By Bus** **Greyhound** operates regular services to Frederick into its depot on East All Saints Street (tel. 663-3311), between South Market and Carroll Streets.

By Car From the south and east, use I-70 and I-270; from the north, I-95 and I-70; from the west, I-70 and I-68.

WHAT'S SPECIAL ABOUT WESTERN MARYLAND

Ace Attractions
☐ Western Maryland Scenic Railroad, a 34-mile, round-trip scenic steam-train ride between Cumberland and Frostburg.
☐ Antietam Battlefield, in Sharpsburg near Hagerstown, scene of the bloodiest day of the Civil War.
☐ Hager House, 18th-century German-style home of Jonathan Hager, founder of Hagerstown.
☐ Wisp Resort, Maryland's largest ski area.

Architectural Highlights
☐ Frederick Historic District, a 33-block showcase of 18th- and 19th-century mansions and town houses.

Events/Festivals
☐ Hagerstown Fair, 6-day country fair and agricultural show with big-name entertainment.

☐ Rocky Gap Bluegrass/Country Western Musical Festival, a summer highlight near Cumberland.

For the Kids
☐ Rose Hill Manor Children's Museum, a hands-on experience of Early American life.
☐ Catoctin Zoo Park, a wildlife and petting zoo in a forest setting.

Museums
☐ Barbara Fritchie House and Museum, replica of the home of Frederick's fabled Civil War heroine.
☐ History House of Cumberland, a museum of Victoriana.

Religious Shrines
☐ National Shrine of St. Elizabeth Ann Seton, in Emmitsburg, home of America's first canonized saint.

ESSENTIALS The **Tourism Council of Frederick County** operates an efficient, helpful visitor center at 19 E. Church St., Frederick, MD 21701 (tel. 301/663-8703). This office not only supplies maps, brochures, and listings of accommodations and restaurants, but will also arrange walking tours of the historic district. Tourist information booths are also located in the rest areas of the Frederick exits of I-70 East and U.S. 15 South. All of these facilities are open daily from 9am to 4:30pm.

The gateway to western Maryland, Frederick is just an hour's drive from Baltimore or Washington, D.C. It's in the heart of Maryland's prime horse country, the seat of one of America's richest agricultural counties.

Frederick is also a city of beautifully preserved 18th- and 19th-century town houses, landmark church spires, and gracious Victorian gardens. Perhaps Frederick is best known, however, as the birthplace of Francis Scott Key, the author of our national anthem, and Barbara Fritchie, legendary heroine of the Civil War. It also lies in the shadow of the Catoctin Mountains, the home of Camp David, the presidential retreat.

Named for Frederick Calvert, sixth Lord of Baltimore, this proud city was founded in 1745 by English and German settlers. Initially a frontier settlement en route to the west, then a Colonial crossroads on the National Pike, and later, during the Revolutionary and Civil Wars, Frederick always played a pivotal role in our nation's progress.

Today, with a population of 35,000, Frederick is a shining example of a prosperous 20th-century city that melds its history into everyday life. Horse-drawn carts still pass by Frederick's squares and courtyards; rows of craft shops and antique galleries line the streets. Old brick homes are enjoying a second life as trendy restaurants, and abandoned factories are being recycled into chic shopping boutiques.

GETTING AROUND
BY BUS

Locally, the **Frederick City Bus Transit Service** (tel. 694-1166) connects major downtown points to the various shopping malls for a flat fare of $1.

BY TAXI

Taxis do not cruise the city, but are available by phone; two reliable firms are **Citycab** (tel. 662-2250) and **Bowie's Taxi** (tel. 695-0333).

BY RENTED CAR

Budget Rent-a-Car has an office at 6001 Urbana Pike (tel. 663-8255), and **Hertz** is at 511 W. South St. (tel. 662-2626).

BY BICYCLE

Bicycle rentals are available from **The Wheel Base**, 229 N. Market St. (tel. 663-9288).

WHAT TO SEE & DO

✪ The focus of Frederick is its 33-block **Historic District.** Not only have many of the buildings been carefully restored, but the streetscape today is much as it was in the early days. With Court House Square and Old Frederick City Hall at its heart, this city is a showcase of stately mansions and elegant brick town houses. The vista also includes a panorama of 18th- and 19th-century church spires, graceful Victorian parks and gardens, and the oldest and largest ginkgo tree in the U.S. The Frederick Visitor Center distributes a map of the district and also coordinates a full program of walking and horse-drawn carriage tours.

BARBARA FRITCHIE HOUSE AND MUSEUM, 154 W. Patrick St. Tel. 663-3833.

This house is a replica of Frederick's premier heroine during the Civil War. At age 95 Barbara Fritchie bravely waved the Stars and Stripes in the path of Confederate soldiers and was immortalized in a poem by John Greenleaf Whittier as the "bravest of all in Frederick-town." A visit to the house includes a video presentation of her life and times; a first-hand look at a collection of mementos including quilts and linens made by Barbara; her caps, shawls, and dresses; and her desk, tables, chairs, and china.

Admission: $2 adults, $1.50 children under 12.

Open: Apr–Sept Mon, Thurs, Fri–Sat 10am–4pm, Sun 1–4pm; Oct–Nov Sat 10am–4pm, Sun 1–4pm. **Closed:** Dec–Mar.

FREDERICK COUNTY HISTORICAL SOCIETY MUSEUM, 24 E. Church St. Tel. 663-1188.

✪ With notable architectural details and furnishings from the 19th century, this Federal-style landmark (circa. 1799) is Frederick's official town mansion—and a good place to broaden your knowledge of area history. Main exhibits focus on local heroes, such as Roger B. Taney, Chief Justice of the U.S. Supreme Court and author of the Dredd Scott Decision; Francis Scott Key, author of the "Star-Spangled Banner"; Thomas Johnson, first governor of Maryland; and Barbara Fritchie, heroine of John Greenleaf Whittier's poem. There is also a genealogical library, gift shop, and formal garden.

Admission: Free, but donations are welcome.

Open: Mon–Sat 10am–4pm. Guided tours available mid-Apr–Oct, Wed–Sat.

SCHIFFERSTADT, 1110 Rosemont Avenue. Tel. 663-6225.

✪ On the western edge of town is the oldest house in Frederick, one of America's finest examples of German Colonial architecture. Built in 1756 by the Brunner family, who named it for their homeland in Germany, this house is made of

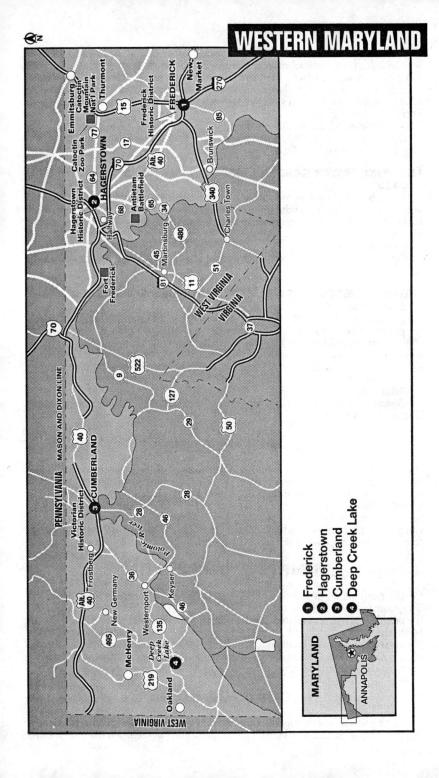

sandstone walls 2½ feet thick, and hand-hewn beams of native oak pinned together with wooden pegs. Unusual original features include an enclosed staircase, a vaulted cellar and chimney, a unique five-plate cast-iron stove, and a squirrel-tail bake oven.

A tour of the house includes a slide show and a self-guided tour leaflet. The adjacent gallery is an artisan's cooperative, selling crafts fashioned from clay, wood, fibers, metal, and glass.

Admission: $2 adults, 50¢ children.

Open: Apr–mid-Dec Mon–Sat 10am–4pm, Sun 1–4pm. **Closed:** Mon Dec–Feb, Easter, Thanksgiving Day.

LILY PONS WATER GARDENS, 6800 Lilypons Rd., Lilypons. Tel. 874-5133.

These beautiful gardens are named after the famous opera singer Lily Pons, who visited here in 1936. One of the largest suppliers of ornamental fish and aquatic plants in the world, this site has acres of water lilies and goldfish ponds. The lilies are at their blooming peak in July.

Admission: Free.

Open: Mar–Oct daily 10am–5pm, Nov–Feb Mon–Sat 10am–4:30pm. **Closed:** Easter.

NATIONAL SHRINE OF ST. ELIZABETH ANN SETON, 333 S. Seton Ave., Emmitsburg. Tel. 447-6606.

Less than a half-hour drive north of Frederick is the home of the United States' first canonized saint. The complex includes the Stone House, where Mother Seton established her religious community in 1809, and the White House, where she began the first parochial school in America. A visit here includes a 6-minute slide show of historical background and an opportunity to take a self-guided tour of the museum and grounds.

Admission: Free.

Open: May–Oct daily 10am–5pm; Nov–Apr Tues–Sun 10am–5pm. **Closed:** Christmas, Jan 18–31.

WALKING TOURS

If you prefer to see the sights on foot, walking tours of the Frederick Historic District are conducted by certified guides, April through December, at 1:30pm on weekends and holidays. All the 1½-hour tours depart from the Frederick Visitor Center at 19 E. Church St. and reservations and tickets may also be obtained there; the charge is $3.50 for adults and free for children under 12 with an adult. Tours at other times and days can also be arranged, with advance notice. In addition, the Visitor Center provides a free folder that maps out a self-guided walk around the city.

SPORTS & RECREATION

Of the many parks in the Frederick area, **Catoctin Mountain Park,** Rte. 77, Thurmont (tel. 663-9388), is the most famous, because it is adjacent to Camp David, the presidential retreat. Located 3 miles west of Thurmont and about 15 miles north of downtown Frederick, off Rte. 15, this 5,769-acre park is administered by the National Park Service. Facilities offered for visitors include hiking trails, fishing, cross-country skiing, camping, and picnic sites. A Visitors Information Center is operated daily, except holidays, from 10am to 4:30pm during the winter.

COOL FOR KIDS

A "touch and see" theme prevails at the **Rose Hill Manor Children's Museum,** 1611 N. Market St. (tel. 694-1646). Built in the 1790s, this Georgian mansion was the home of Maryland's first governor, Thomas Johnson. Now a museum of state and national heritage, it is designed to let children experience early-American life: combing unspun wool, throwing a shuttle on the loom, and adding a few stitches to a quilt. Other activities include soapmaking, candle-dipping, quilting bees, barn raisings, and apple-butter boiling.

More than 300 items are on display over 43 acres in the authentic settings of a manor house, a carriage museum, a blacksmith shop, a log cabin, herb and flower gardens, and a farm museum. Walk-in tours are conducted by costumed guides April through October from 10am to 4pm, Monday through Saturday; and from 1 to 4pm on Sundays. During March, November, and December, the museum is open only on weekends, and it is closed during January and February. Admission is $3 for those aged 18 to 64; children residing locally are admitted free; all nonresident children and seniors are charged $1.

Animal lovers of all ages enjoy the **Catoctin Zoo Park,** 13019 Catoctin Furnace Rd., Thurmont (tel. 271-7488), a wildlife, breeding, and petting zoo in a 30-acre woodland setting, and home to more than 500 animals, including big cats, monkeys, bears, and farmyard pets. Open daily from 9am to 6pm throughout the summer months, and from 9am to 5pm after September. Admission is $5.75 for adults and $4.25 for children 2 to 12; children under 2 are admitted free.

SHOPPING

For many years, **West Patrick Street** (Rte. 40) has been the "Golden Mile" because of its many shopping and commercial opportunities. The continuing restoration of downtown, however, has also led to a renewed shopping interest in city center streets.

Today Frederick is home to more than 30 antique shops in the midcity historic district and throughout the county. Merchandise ranges from furniture, diamonds, coins, baseball cards, vintage clothing, books, porcelains, clocks, and dollhouse miniatures to lamps and linens. A complete list of shops, with a map, addresses, and hours of business, is available from the Frederick Visitor Center.

Another pocket of good shopping is historic **Shab Row,** East Street (between 2nd and Church Sts.). This section is made up of 200-year-old buildings that were once the homes of local merchants and artisans. These small abandoned dwellings fell into disrepair until their recent restoration into specialty shops and craft centers.

✪ The most exciting shopping development of all is **Everedy Square,** a 2½-acre, nine-building complex between East Street and Patrick Street, originally the site of the Everedy Bottle Capping Company (founded in 1920 and one of the largest businesses in Frederick). More than $2 million was spent in the mid-1980s to transform these old industrial buildings into a cluster of courtyards, craft shops, boutiques, restaurants, and galleries.

WHERE TO STAY

The hotels and motels of Frederick are primarily located on major roads (Rtes. 40, 15, and 85) leading into the city, although there are plans in the next few years to restore old downtown buildings for use as up-to-date hotels.

MODERATE

HOLIDAY INN, I-270 at Rte. 85, at Francis Scott Key Mall, Frederick, MD 21701. Tel. 301/694-7500 or toll-free 800/HOLIDAY. Fax 301/694-0589. 155 rms. A/C TV TEL
$ Rates: $75–$97 single, $96–$115 double. AE, CB, DC, MC, V. **Parking:** Free.
Formerly a Sheraton, this hotel is in a landscaped garden setting. The modern two-story brick structure offers rooms with a double or king-size bed and modern

decor. Facilities include an indoor pool, a whirlpool, and a sauna, as well as a game room, and miniature golf.

Dining and entertainment facilities include Harrigan's restaurant and Mixers Lounge.

BUDGET

COZY MOTEL AND RESTAURANT, 103 Frederick Rd. (Rte. 806), Thurmont, MD 21788. Tel. 301/217-4301. 13 rms, 5 cottage units. A/C TV TEL

$ Rates: $35–$45 single or double for rooms, $40–$75 for cottage units. MC, V. **Parking:** Free.

A popular place with families is this motel in a country village setting at the base of the Catoctin Mountains. Founded in 1929, this bustling complex of motel and cottage units offers a restaurant with nine dining rooms, a pub, a bakery, and a village of shops. The motel rooms are furnished with one or two double beds and wall-to-wall carpeting. Deluxe cottages, each with two queen-size beds, a fireplace, and a small refrigerator, can accommodate up to four people. Weekend rates are slightly higher in all cases.

WHERE TO DINE

Downtown Frederick is a mecca for fine food; the area around Market and Patrick Streets alone boasts more than 20 good restaurants. Here are some of the best.

EXPENSIVE

THE RED HORSE RESTAURANT, 966 W. Patrick St., Frederick. Tel. 663-3030.
Cuisine: AMERICAN. **Reservations:** Recommended.
$ Prices: Appetizers $2.95–$7.95; main courses $13.95–$22.95, lobsters to $28.95. AE, CB, DC, MC, V.
Open: Mon–Sat 4:30–10:30pm, Sun 4–9pm.

Open for dinner only, this western-style restaurant has two large dining rooms, one with a glass-enclosed open kitchen where you can watch the chefs at work. Entrées focus on the best of beef and lamb and the freshest of seafood, with choices such as prime ribs, charbroiled steaks, lamb chops, crab cakes, whole lobsters, lobster tails, and surf-n-turf. If you crave a good cooked-to-order steak, this place is undisputedly the best in town.

MODERATE

BROWN PELICAN, 5 E. Church St., Tel. 695-5833.
Cuisine: INTERNATIONAL. **Reservations:** Recommended.
$ Prices: Appetizers $3.95–$7.95; main courses $10.95–$19.95; lunch $4.95–$9.95. AE, MC, V.
Open: Lunch Mon–Sat 11:30am–3pm; dinner Mon–Thurs 5:30–9:30pm, Fri–Sat 5:30–10pm, Sun 5–9:30pm.

This basement restaurant is decorated in a nautical style of vibrant sea tones, driftwood, and yachting collectibles. Dinner includes a variety of interesting dishes from walnut bourbon chicken, flounder amandine, chicken à l 'orange, stuffed shrimp with lobster imperial, and roast duckling to ever-popular steaks.

BUSHWALLERS SEAFOOD SALOON, 209 N. Market St. Tel. 694-5697.
Cuisine: INTERNATIONAL. **Reservations:** Recommended.
$ Prices: Appetizers $2.50–$5.50; main courses $9.95–$15.95; lunch $3.95–$6.95. MC, V.
Open: Lunch Mon–Sat 11:30am–3pm; dinner Mon–Sat 5–10pm, Sun dinner 3–10pm.

This restaurant is housed in an 1840s building that was used variously as a private home, a drugstore, and a dry-goods shop. Retaining its 19th-century atmosphere, the decor incorporates many Frederick family mementos as well as old pictures, newspaper front pages, and turn-of-the-century political cartoons. Lunch items include salads, pasta, chili, sandwiches, burgers, and raw-bar items. Dinner entrées focus on such seafood dishes as yellowtail flounder filets stuffed with lump crab; swordfish steak; crab cakes; and shrimp scampi; as well as meat choices ranging from veal scaloppine topped with imported Brie; chicken Bushwallers with garlic, mushrooms, and white wine; or steak Diane.

DI FRANCESCO'S, 26 N. Market St. Tel. 695-5499.

Cuisine: ITALIAN. **Reservations:** Recommended.
$ Prices: Appetizers $4.95–$14.95; main courses $11.95–$16.95; lunch $3.95–$6.95. AE, MC, V.
Open: Lunch Tues–Fri 11:30am–3pm; dinner daily 5:30–10pm; brunch Sun 11:30am–3pm.

Italian cuisine thrives in this restaurant decorated like a country villa, with white-washed walls and lots of leafy plants. Lunch features salads, omelets, pizzas, and pastas. Dinner is more elaborate, with over a dozen pastas available in full or half orders—fettuccine with smoked salmon, spaghetti with anchovies and garlic, cannelloni, and lasagne. Entrées include veal saltimbocca, shrimp marinara, seafood with linguine, veal alla marsala, chicken cacciatore, seafood and meat mixed grill, and filet mignon Christina (with basil, pine nuts, and garlic).

PROVINCE, 129 N. Market St. Tel. 663-1441.

Cuisine: INTERNATIONAL. **Reservations:** Recommended.
$ Prices: Appetizers $2.95–$5.95; main courses $11.95–$17.95; lunch $4.95–$7.95. AE, CB, DC, MC, V.
Open: Lunch Tues–Fri 11:30am–3pm; dinner Tues–Thurs 5:30–9pm, Fri–Sat 5:30–10pm, Sun 4–8pm; brunch Sat–Sun 11:30am–2:30pm.

Another old Frederick house, circa 1767, is the setting of this restaurant that consists of a small bistro-style front room and a bright brick-walled room in the rear. The latter overlooks the herb garden, which produces ingredients for the kitchen. The furnishings range from snowshoe chairs to handmade quilt hangings and paintings by local artists.

Lunchtime selections focus on salads, quiches, omelets, crab cakes, and "creative American" sandwiches (such as fried oyster and bacon, or country sausage and cheddar). Dinner entrées change daily but a few favorite dishes are lamb chops Dijon, Parisian poulet (chicken with mushrooms and dry sherry), scallops with Irish Mist, and herb-scented filet mignon. There is also a bake shop on the premises.

THE STARVING ARTIST, 137 N. Broad St., Frederick. Tel. 663-0073.

Cuisine: ECLECTIC. **Reservations:** Recommended for dinner.
$ Prices: Appetizers $2.75–$6.75; main courses $10.95–$14.95; lunch $2.75–$5.25. AE, MC, V.
Open: Lunch Tues–Sat 11:30am–3pm, Sun 11am–4pm; dinner Tues–Sat 6–9pm.

As its name implies, this place has an artsy ambience, with brick walls displaying paintings by Frederick area artists. The cheery decor also includes lots of flowers, hanging plants, and floral table linens. It's a good spot for an informal meal, and there is after-dinner entertainment (jazz, rock, and new music) on Thursday through Saturday, from 10pm to 1am. The eclectic menu ranges from veal piccata, chicken with sherry, and sole with fine herbs to pastas, steaks, and tenderloin of pork. Lunch items focus on fitness cuisine, with such choices as health club sandwiches, salads, and casseroles with fresh and natural ingredients.

TAURASO'S, 6 East St. at Everedy Square. Tel. 663-6600.

Cuisine: ITALIAN/AMERICAN. **Reservations:** Recommended.
$ Prices: Appetizers $3.95–$6.95; main courses $9.95–$21.95; lunch $4.25–$6.50. AE, CB, DC, MC, V.
Open: Lunch daily 11am–4pm; dinner Sun–Thurs 5–10pm, Fri–Sat 5–11pm.

Bright and busy, this restaurant is the main dining choice at the Everedy Square shopping complex. There are three settings—an indoor dining room, an outdoor patio, and a pub, but the menu is the same throughout. Entrées range from Italian choices such as pastas, Tauraso's original seafood sausage, and Italian bouillabaisse, to international favorites such as crab cakes, char-grilled chicken, steaks, and duck à l'orange. Lunch items focus on sandwiches, frittatas, pastas, and salads.

BUDGET

COZY RESTAURANT, 103 Frederick Rd. (Rte. 806), Thurmont. Tel. 271-7373.
   Cuisine: AMERICAN. **Reservations:** Not necessary, but helpful at busy times.
$ **Prices:** Appetizers included in entrée and buffet prices; main courses $7.79–$14.99; lunch smörgåsbords $4.99–$6.99; dinner buffets $8.99–$12.99. MC, V.
   Open: Lunch Mon–Sat 11am–4pm; dinner Mon–Thurs 4–8:45pm, Fri–Sat 4–9:15pm; Sun 11:45am–8:45pm.

Since 1929, this family-run enterprise has been a tradition in the Frederick area. Over the years, it has grown from a 12-stool lunch counter to a 675-seat full-service restaurant with a Victorian atmosphere. Known for its plentiful luncheon smörgåsbords and evening buffets, it also offers à la carte dining. Entrées include such items as country fried chicken, roast turkey, baked ham, fried shrimp, crab cakes, surf-n-turf, lobster tails, and seafood platters. All entrées entitle you to unlimited trips to the "groaning board," a hefty table of soups, salads, breads, relishes, desserts, and cheeses.

EVENING ENTERTAINMENT

In June, July, and August there are free open-air concerts at the **Baker Park Bandshell,** Second and Bentz Sts. (tel. 662-5161, ext. 247). Concerts are scheduled for 7:30pm on Sunday evenings, and feature a variety of local and military bands.

Throughout the year, the **Weinberg Center for the Arts,** 20 W. Patrick St. (tel. 694-8585), presents drama, dance, and concerts. This old-world theater is the home of the Fredericktowne Players and also welcomes visiting troupes. Tickets average $12 and can be obtained at the box office Tuesday through Friday from 10am to 5pm, Saturday from 10am to 2pm, and one hour before all shows.

EXCURSION TO NEW MARKET

Six miles east of Frederick is historic **New Market,** founded in 1793 as a stop for travelers on the National Pike. Today this beautifully preserved Federal-style town (pop. 300) is listed on the National Register of Historic Places and is also known as "the antiques capital of Maryland." More than 40 different antique shops line both sides of the half-mile-long main street. Unless noted otherwise, shop hours are usually Saturdays and Sundays from 1 to 5pm, and at other times by appointment. The New Market Antique Dealers Association publishes a free, handy guide/map that's available throughout the town. Below is a sampling of the shops and their wares:

MARIA'S CHALET ANTIQUES, 2 E. Main St. Tel. 865-5225.
   Maria's Chalet features German steins, teddy bears, old rugs, and clocks.

THOMAS' ANTIQUES, 60 W. Main St. Tel. 831-6622.
   This is the place for oak furniture, brass and copper items, and weather vanes.

FROMER'S ANTIQUES, 52 W. Main St. Tel. 831-6712.
   Antique and woodworking tools, Victorian furniture, prints, china, and glass are the attractions here.

SHAW'S OF NEW MARKET, 22 W. Main St. Tel. 831-6010.
   For vases, chandeliers, grandfather clocks, china dolls, and brass lamps.

NEW MARKET GENERAL STORE, 26 W. Main St. Tel. 831-6645.

This is the quintessential country store, with jars of rock candy, condiments, local honey and preserves, as well as potpourri, herbs, and baking meals and mixes. There is also a take-out food counter as well as a fine selection of antique toys.
Open: Tues–Sun 10am–6pm.

MYMANOR, 25 W. Main St. Tel. 865-3702.
Browse in Mymanor for 19th- and 20th-century sporting-art and antiques.

PARKSIDE ANTIQUES, 21 W. Main St. Tel. 831-6111.
For antique kitchen lamps and utensils.

MACNAIR'S CORNER SHOP, 1 W. Main St. Tel. 831-6882.
MacNair's offers country antiques, fine soaps and candles, and old chests.

THE HOUSE OF KINDNESS THISTLE STOP, 5 W. Main St. Tel. 865-3140.
In addition to the antique shops, New Market is also home to this top-class Scottish clothing import store. Housed in an 1840s building that was once a hotel, a stage office, a tavern, a post office, a library, and a general store, this shop stocks a wide range of Scottish kilts, skirts, sweaters, handknits, jewelry, and Prince Charles–type jackets.

WHERE TO STAY
MODERATE

NATIONAL PIKE INN, 9–11 Main St., P.O. Box 299, New Market, MD 21774. Tel. 301/865-5055. 4 rms (2 with private bath), 1 suite. A/C
Directions: Take exit 62 off I-70; 6 miles east of Frederick.
$ Rates (including continental breakfast): $70–$120 single or double, $120–$160 suite. MC, V. **Parking:** Free.

There's always a particularly warm welcome at this top-notch bed-and-breakfast named after the famous road that passes through the town. Meticulously restored and opened as a B&B in 1986 by Tom and Terry Rimel, this sturdy Federal house was built in the early 1800s; a unique widow's watch was added in 1900. The rooms are charmingly decorated with reproductions and local antiques. Guests also enjoy the use of the family rooms and a landscaped courtyard, as well as Terry's enthusiastic guidance about touring the local area.

STRAWBERRY INN, 17 Main St., P.O. Box 237, New Market, MD 21774. Tel. 301/865-3318. 5 rms (all with bath). A/C
$ Rates (including continental breakfast): $60–$90 single or double. No credit cards. **Parking:** Free.
Opened in 1973, this is a lovingly restored 120-year-old bed-and-breakfast home. Innkeepers Jane and Ed Rossig offer cheerful, antique-furnished rooms; each is individually decorated according to a special theme, such as the Strawberry or the 1776 Room. Ground-floor rooms are available. The complimentary continental breakfast is delivered to each room on a butler's tray.

WHERE TO DINE

MEALEY'S, 8 W. Main St. Tel. 865-5488.
Cuisine: AMERICAN. **Reservations:** Recommended.
$ Prices: Appetizers $1.75–$5.50; main courses $9.95–$19.95; lunch $2.95–$8.95. AE, MC, V.
Open: Lunch Fri–Sat 11:30am–3pm; dinner Tues–Sat 5–9pm; Sun noon–8pm.
Even if you can't stay in New Market, it's worth a trip just to dine at this restaurant tucked in a handsome two-story brick building dating back to 1793. Like a Colonial house, the restaurant offers several small parlor-size rooms as well as the Pump Room, a large main dining room built around a wooden water pump that dates back to 1800. The decor includes exposed brick walls, stone fireplaces, brass fixtures, lanterns, and candlelight.

The current owners have built a reputation for fine food as well as Colonial ambience. Dinner entrées feature a blend of Colonial and contemporary cuisine: chicken livers supreme (cooked in an old iron skillet), a half spring chicken country-style, crab imperial, jumbo fantail shrimp, crab cakes, prime ribs, and reef-and-beef (New York strip steak and a selection of seafood items).

2. HAGERSTOWN

25 miles W of Frederick, 72 miles W of Baltimore, 70 miles NW of Washington, D.C., 75 miles SW of Harrisburg, 70 miles east of Cumberland

GETTING THERE By Air The city is served by **Washington County Regional Airport,** Rte. 11 (tel. 733-5200), 5 miles north of downtown. Scheduled flights are operated by **USAir** (tel. toll-free 800/428-4322).

By Bus Greyhound Bus, 31 E. Antietam St. (tel. 739-7420) links Hagerstown to other cities and towns within Maryland and beyond.

By Car From east and north, take I-70; from the west, I-68; and from the south, I-81.

ESSENTIALS Information Brochures and maps detailing Hagerstown's attractions are available from the **Washington County Convention and Visitors Bureau,** 1826 Dual Hwy., Hagerstown, MD 21740 (tel. 301/791-3130 or toll-free 800/228-STAY). This office also operates a 24-hour information hotline (tel. 301/797-8800). Be sure to ask for a copy of the "Walking Tour of Downtown Hagerstown," a handy leaflet that describes the most significant public buildings, churches, and sights in the historic district.

SPECIAL EVENTS A major highlight each August is the **Great Hagerstown Fair** at the Hagerstown Fairgrounds, between Rtes. 11 and 70. This is a 6-day country fair and agricultural show with big-name entertainment nightly. Attractions include displays of antique steam and gas tractors and farmers' engines, parades, arts, and crafts. Admission is $4 per person and parking is $1. Further information can be obtained from the Hagerstown Fairgrounds, Mulberry Street, Box 1481, Hagerstown, MD 21740 (tel. 301/739-5550).

Known as the "hub" city of the Cumberland Valley, Hagerstown is at the crossroads between two major interstate highways (I-81 and I-70) and a half-dozen other state and local roads. It is not only at the center of Maryland, but it is also sandwiched in between Pennsylvania, Virginia, and West Virginia.

Hagerstown is consequently an ideal base—within an hour's drive of Gettysburg, Harper's Ferry, Antietam, Frederick, and other historic destinations, not to mention its own landmark attractions.

Hagerstown's annals go back to 1762 when it was founded by a German immigrant, Jonathan Hager, who courageously settled the area on his own in the 1730s. Hager also served in the French and Indian War under General Braddock and was later elected to the General Assembly in Annapolis in 1773. His house still stands and is one of the town's many buildings of significant heritage.

A city of 35,000 people, Hagerstown today is also a busy hub of agricultural and industrial activities.

GETTING AROUND
BY BUS

A local bus service, the **County Commuter,** connects Hagerstown to neighboring communities within the perimeter of Washington County, such as Boonsboro and Sharpsburg. For information, call 791-3047.

BY RENTED CAR

Rent-a-car offices are operated in the Hagerstown area by **Hertz,** Washington County Airport (tel. 739-6117) and 1735 Virginia Ave. (tel. 790-1840).

BY TAXI

A reliable local taxi service is **Turner's Taxi** (tel. 733-7788).

WHAT TO SEE & DO

⭐ To get your bearings in Hagerstown, take a walk around the **Historic District,** a 4-block square area of 18th- and 19th-century buildings, centered around Potomac Street and South Prospect Street. This downtown cluster, made up primarily of structures listed on the National Register of Historic Places, includes City Hall, the Washington County Court House, Federal-style homes, museums, churches, and the Maryland Theatre, a rococo landmark built in 1915. A descriptive walking-tour leaflet with map is available free of charge from the tourist office.

The next place to see is the **Hager House,** 19 Key St. (tel. 739-8393), the home of Jonathan Hager, the city's founder. Situated on the northern edge of Hagerstown's City Park, this 3½-story structure was built in 1739 by Hager himself, using uncut fieldstones, on a site over a cool-water spring. It is styled in the German tradition, with a large chimney at its center and 22-inch-thick walls. Now completely restored and outfitted with authentic furnishings of the period, this house is open to the public.

Next door is the **Hager Museum,** a collection of hundreds of farm implements, coins, household items, clothing, and other artifacts from the Hagerstown area. Admission to both the house and museum is $2 for adults and $1 for children under 12. Open April through December from 10am to 4pm on Tuesday through Saturday, and from 2 to 5pm on Sunday.

One of the state's oldest **markets,** the Hagerstown City Farmers' Market, also operates regularly here and is worth a look if you happen to be in town on a Saturday. More than 50 farmers, craftspeople, and exhibitors sell all kinds of local vegetables, fruits, meats, country crafts, and home-baked goods at this gathering, which has been a tradition since 1875, first at City Hall and in its present location since 1928. Look for the **Market House,** 11 W. Church St. (tel. 790-3200, ext. 118), year round on Saturday from 5 to 11am.

Fifteen miles southwest of Hagerstown along a winding country farm road is **Fort Frederick,** Rtes. 56 and 65, Big Pool (tel. 842-2155), the cornerstone of Maryland's frontier defense during the French and Indian War. This strong stone fortress, which was also used in the Revolutionary War and the Civil War, is a showcase of 18th-century military life. Some of the most interesting displays include the fort's massive stone wall, a garrison garden, cannons, barracks, bastions, and a wooden catwalk that originally spanned the entire inner perimeter of the fort wall. The fort and its surrounding parklands are open to the public year round, free of charge, from 8am to dusk; and the barracks and visitor center are open May 1 to October 1 from 8:30am to 5pm. In addition, from 9am to 5pm, Memorial Day through Labor Day, costumed guides are on duty to answer questions and explain the fort's layout. A free walking-tour brochure is also available.

☼ The **Antietam Battlefield,** scene of the bloodiest single day of the Civil War, is 12 miles south of Hagerstown near Sharpsburg along Rtes. 34 and 65 (tel. 432-5124). More than 23,000 men were killed or wounded on this site, where the Union forces met and stopped the first Southern invasion of the North on September 17, 1862. Clara Barton, who was to found the Red Cross 19 years later, attended to the wounded at a field hospital on the battlefield. Start your visit at the visitor center, located north of Sharpsburg on Rte. 65. Administered by the National Park Service and open daily except for major holidays, this office provides free information, literature, and suggested tours of the battlefield and cemetery. There are also helpful historical exhibits and an 18-minute audiovisual (shown every half hour). During May and September, musket and cannon demonstrations and historical talks are scheduled. Admission charge is $1 per person.

The Hagerstown area is also home to the **Ziem Vineyards,** Rte. 63, R.R. 1, Box 161, Fairplay (tel. 223-8352), a small award-winning Maryland winery. Owned and operated by Bob and Ruth Ziem, this eight-acre winery is set in a farmland complex that includes a 200-year-old stone house, spring house, and bank barn. It produces all of its wines (five whites and ten reds) from grape to bottle. Visitors are welcome to tour, taste, and to buy. Open Thursday through Sunday, 1 to 6pm, and by appointment. No charge for touring or tasting. Located about 6 miles southwest of Hagerstown, via Rte. 632 to Rte. 63.

SPORTS & ACTIVITIES

Hagerstown's outdoor life is centered in and around **City Park,** Virginia Avenue (tel. 739-4673), rated among the nation's most beautiful natural city parks. This idyllic 50-acre setting includes an artificial lake that is home to hundreds of ducks, swans, and geese; flower gardens; wooded picnic areas; softball fields; tennis courts; and an open-air bandshell, site of frequent summer concerts. For the last 10 years, a 2-day arts, crafts, and entertainment festival has also been staged here on the last weekend in June. Admission is free.

SHOPPING

Hagerstown is good territory for **antique-hunting.** There are two major clusters of antique dealers situated side-by-side, south of the downtown area on Rte. 40, just south of exit 32 of I-70. Both are open Thursday through Tuesday, from 9am to 5pm and both are housed in large air-conditioned complexes, with individual stalls for each dealer.

Antique Crossroads (tel. 739-0858) has 86 dealers, offering everything from furniture, glassware, statues, and spinning wheels, to tins, coins, magazines, stamps, postcards, books, and hand-embroidered linens. **Beaver Creek Antique Market** (tel. 739-8075) has over 150 dealers specializing in furniture, dinnerware, jewelry, glassware, and more.

COOL FOR KIDS

Corridors of limestone with jeweled stalactites and stalagmites are the unique underground attractions at the **Crystal Grottoes Caverns,** Rte. 34, Boonsboro (tel. 432-6336). Maryland's only commercial underground caverns, these formations were created by millions of years of chemical and mineral action beneath the earth's surface. Open daily, March through November, from 9am to 6pm; and on weekends in December, January, and February from 11am to 5pm. Admission, which includes the services of a well-informed guide, is $7 for adults, $3.50 for children 3 to 11, and free for those 2 and under.

WHERE TO STAY

EXPENSIVE

INN AT ANTIETAM, 220 E. Main St., P.O. Box 119, Sharpsburg, MD 21782. Tel. 301/432-6601. 4 rms and 1 suite, all with bath. A/C **Directions:** Take Alt. Rte. 40 to Rte. 34; inn is 6 miles west on Rte. 34 (Main Street). **$ Rates** (includes full breakfast): $65–$95 rooms, $130–$150 suite. AE. **Parking:** Free.

For a peaceful retreat in an historic setting, this three-story bed-and-breakfast inn is made to order. Built in 1908 in grand Victorian style, it sits on a hill amid a bucolic tree-shaded and well-landscaped setting overlooking the Antietam

National Battlefield. In the main house, there are two guest rooms and one two-bedroom suite (which is also made available as two separate bedrooms); all are individually decorated, with four-poster or brass beds, antique furnishings, graceful Victorian trim and accessories, and fresh flowers from the garden. There is also a fifth guest room in the adjacent smoke house, with country furnishings, loft bed, fireplace, and wet bar.

Facilities include a solarium, parlor, and an inviting wraparound porch with swing, rocking chairs, racks of magazines, and views of the surrounding farmlands, and an outdoor patio overlooking the Blue Ridge Mountains. The innkeeper is Betty Fairbourn.

MODERATE

BEST WESTERN VENICE INN, 431 Dual Hwy., Hagerstown, MD 21740. Tel. 301/733-0830 or toll-free 800/528-1234. Fax 301/733-4978. 228 rms, 12 suites. A/C TV TEL
$ Rates: $45–$60 single, $51–$70 double, $90–$150 suite. AE, CB, DC, MC, V. **Parking:** Free.

One of the most centrally located lodgings is this modern and recently expanded hotel. Rooms are either located in a high-rise tower or in a motel structure; each is decorated in a contemporary style, with one king-size or two double beds. King suites with whirlpools and rooms with kitchenettes are also available. Facilities include a restaurant (see "Where to Dine," below), beauty and gift shops, an outdoor Olympic swimming pool, and liquor store/wine cellar.

HOWARD JOHNSON PLAZA, 107 Underpass Way, Halfway Blvd. exit of I-81, Hagerstown, MD 21740. Tel. 301/797-2500 or toll free 800/654-2000. Fax 301/797-6209. 170 rms. A/C TV TEL
$ Rates: $55 single, $64–$80 double. AE, CB, DC, MC, V. **Parking:** Free.
The newest full-service hotel in the area is this six-story property situated in a quiet grassy setting opposite the Valley Mall. The sleek modern hotel offers rooms with contemporary furnishings, an in-room refrigerator, and a coffeemaker; nonsmoking rooms are also available. Amenities include a heated indoor pool with spa and sauna, a fitness room, and the cozy Fireside, a restaurant and lounge.

SHERATON INN, 1910 Dual Hwy., Hagerstown, MD 21740. Tel. 301/790-3010 or toll-free 800/325-3535. Fax 301/733-4559. 140 rms. A/C TV TEL
$ Rates: $54 single, $60 double. AE, CB, DC, MC, V. **Parking:** Free.
The closest hotel to I-70 is this modern motel in a leafy garden setting. Rooms have been newly renovated with bright contemporary furnishings. Facilities include a swimming pool, a health spa, a game room, and a lounge with evening entertainment.

This inn is also the home of Nicholas's, a restaurant/lounge associated with the original Nick's at the airport.

WHERE TO DINE

EXPENSIVE

NICK'S AIRPORT INN, Middleburg Pike (Rte. 11), Tel. 733-8560.
Cuisine: INTERNATIONAL. **Reservations:** Recommended, especially on weekends.
$ Prices: Appetizers $4.95–$7.95; main courses $15.95–$24.95; lunch $4.95–$10.95. AE, DC, MC, V.
Open: Lunch Mon–Fri 11am–2:30pm; dinner Mon–Fri 5–10pm, Sat 4:30–10:30pm.

This dining spot proves that airport restaurants can be outstanding in their own right. Recently renovated in a bright conservatory style, Nick's is such an institution in the area that it has produced a clone (in the Sheraton Inn). The lunch menu features hearty sandwiches and salads and crab imperial, fried shrimp, or prime rib of beef. The varied dinner menu focuses on seafood—crab au gratin, stuffed flounder, lobster tails, bay or sea scallops—a variety of steak cuts, rack of lamb, and veal and chicken dishes with an Italian or French finesse. There is an extensive wine list.

MODERATE

AVELLINO'S, 431 Dual Hwy., Hagerstown. Tel. 739-5700.

Cuisine: ITALIAN/AMERICAN. **Reservations:** Recommended.
$ Prices: Appetizers $2.75–$6.75; main courses $7.95–$20.95; lunch $5.95–$7.95. AE, CB, DC, DISC, MC, V.
Open: Daily lunch 11am–2pm, dinner 5–10:30pm.

Although it is housed in a hotel, this restaurant can stand on its own as a fine dining spot. Dinner choices range from pastas and cioppino to steaks, Maryland local crab dishes, stuffed shrimp, and veal prepared in a variety of ways. At lunchtime, the focus is on a buffet table of antipasto, soup, and Italian savories (select as many choices as you wish for $5.95), as well as a variety of light fare—from sandwiches and seafood omelets to vegetable and fruit salads.

DUTCH KITCHEN, 12 E. Washington St. Tel. 739-2252.

Cuisine: AMERICAN. **Reservations:** Recommended.
$ Prices: Appetizers $1.95–$5.95; main courses $9.95–$19.95; lunch $3.95–$7.95. AE, MC, V.
Open: Lunch daily 11:30am–2pm; dinner Sun–Thurs 4:30–9:30pm, Fri–Sat 4:30–10pm.

The top spot in the heart of the city is this restaurant, one of Maryland's oldest. It's a charming and classy candlelit enclave decorated in Old Williamsburg style—with stencilwork, crafts, and baskets decorating the walls, and a staff dressed in Colonial costumes. Lunch items include hot sandwich platters, burgers, salads, and pastas. Entrées at dinner feature apricot chicken, fried country ham, T-bone steaks, prime rib, veal Oscar, crab cakes, and whole baby flounder.

OLD SOUTH MOUNTAIN INN, Alt. Rte. 40, Boonsboro. Tel. 371-5400 and 432-6155.

Cuisine: AMERICAN. **Reservations:** Required.
$ Prices: Appetizers $3.95–$7.95; main courses $9.95–$21.95. AE, CB, DC, MC, V.
Open: Dinner Tues–Fri 5–9pm, Sat noon–10pm, Sun noon–8pm; brunch Sun 10:30am–2pm.

About a 20-minute drive southeast of Hagerstown is this restaurant perched atop Turner's Gap along the Appalachian Trail. Erected in 1732, this landmark building served variously as a wagon stand, a stagecoach stop, a wayside inn, a tavern, and a private residence; it was visited by several presidents and was a favorite stop of Henry Clay and Daniel Webster. Since 1981, it has been a Colonial-style restaurant in the hands of Russell and Judy Schwartz. The beautifully preserved stone building is augmented by an outdoor terrace, ancient trees, gardens, a wishing well, and panoramic mountain views.

The restaurant offers steak au poivre vert, prime rib, beef Wellington, chicken Cordon Bleu, cured country ham, fettuccine primavera, center-cut pork, and local seafood. There is also an extensive wine list, priced from $10 a bottle, including a few fine Maryland wines. A hearty country brunch, priced at $10.95, is also served on Sunday.

SCHMANKERL STUBE, 58 S. Potomac St., Hagerstown. Tel. 797-3354.

Cuisine: GERMAN. **Reservations:** Recommended.
$ Prices: Appetizers $2.95–$7.95; main courses $11.95–$19.95; lunch $2.95–$7.95. AE, DC, MC, V.
Open: Tues–Sun lunch 11:30am–4pm, dinner 4–10pm.

The name of this restaurant means literally "Delicacy Room"—and that's exactly what it is, offering a variety of specialties from Bavaria. The decor is rich in German influences, from wall pictures of Bavaria to steins and checkered tablecloths. In the summer months, seating is also available on an outdoor deck with a distinct *Biergarten* atmosphere.

Entrées include smoked pork loin with sauerkraut and bread dumplings; marinated beef in sweet-and-sour sauce and apple-flavored red cabbage; wienerschnitzel with noodles; steak roast with crispy onions; and nightly seafood selections. Save room for dessert, from buttercream tortes to black forest cake and apple streusels. Lunch items include salads, sandwiches, and cold-cut platters.

BUDGET

ANTRIM HOUSE II, 1905 Pennsylvania Ave., Hagerstown. Tel. 797-8111.
  Cuisine: AMERICAN. **Reservations:** Not required.
$ **Prices:** Appetizers $.95–$1.95; main courses $6.95–$13.95; lunch $1.95–$4.95. AE, MC, V.
  Open: Mon–Sat lunch 11am–2pm, dinner 6–9pm, Sun 11am–7pm.

A branch of the historic Antrim House of Greencastle, Pennsylvania, just over the state border, this restaurant is in the midst of a shopping center. The setting and decor may be more modern than the original premises, but the food is still homey and hearty and very good value. Entrées include steaks, prime ribs, and flounder stuffed with crab, as well as Pennsylvania Dutch cooking, with such items as creamed chipped beef, chicken pot pie, stuffed cabbage, and pan-fried chicken. No liquor or wine is served.

EVENING ENTERTAINMENT

No visit to Hagerstown is complete without a night at the magnificent **Maryland Theatre,** 21 S. Potomac St. (tel. 790-2000 or toll-free 800/34-SHOWS). Originally built in 1915 and rebuilt after a 1974 fire, this revered landmark has provided a stage for acrobats and opera, choirs and country-western concerts, and personalities ranging from Will Rogers and John Philip Sousa to Lowell Thomas and Anna Pavlova. Recent productions have included *Evita* and *A Chorus Line.* The Maryland Symphony Orchestra, under the direction of master French hornist Barry Tuckwell, is also headquartered here. The curtain is usually at 8pm, but exact schedules and prices vary with each production. Check at the box office, which is open Monday through Friday from 10am to 5pm.

For dinner-theater, you need only cross the street to the **Washington County Playhouse,** 44 N. Potomac St. (tel. 739-SHOW). With a repertoire that includes such productions as *Fiddler on the Roof, Little Shop of Horrors, 1776,* this theater presents a buffet on stage before each show. Performances are Thursday, Friday, and Saturday evenings ($19.95), and Sunday matinees ($19.95).

---

3. CUMBERLAND

70 miles W of Hagerstown, 140 miles W of Baltimore,
109 miles SE of Pittsburgh, and 134 miles SW of Harrisburg

GETTING THERE By Air Cumberland is served by the **Cumberland Regional Airport,** Rte. 28, Virginia Avenue, which is actually just over the border in West Virginia. Flights are operated by **USAir Commuter** (tel. toll-free 800/428-4322).

By Bus **Greyhound** operates regular bus service into Cumberland, stopping at 201 Glenn St. (tel. 722-6226).

By Train **Amtrak** operates limited passenger service through Cumberland from points east and west, stopping at a station on East Harrison Street. For full information, call 724-8890 or toll-free 800/872-7245.

ESSENTIALS   Walking-tour folders, maps, and brochures of Cumberland and the surrounding area are available from the **Allegany County Tourism and Public Relations Office,** Western Maryland Station Center, Canal Street, Cumberland, MD 21502 (tel. 301/777-5905). Open daily 8:30am–4:30pm.

SPECIAL EVENTS   Continuous country music and old-time cooking are the main features of the **C&O Canal Boat Festival,** in July each year. Held at the North Branch of the C&O Canal Park, 5 miles south of Cumberland on Rte. 51, this gathering also focuses on arts and crafts and American frontier life. Chief among the demonstrations is an encampment staged by the Wills Mountain Renegades, who erect teepees and wear authentic costumes. Other activities include walking tours of the canal by park rangers, guided tours of the canal boat, and horse and buggy rides. There is no admission charge, but a donation is expected. For more information, call 777-7563 or 729-3136.

Other annual Cumberland area events include the **Heritage Days Festival** (second weekend in June); **Allegany County Drumfest** (last weekend of July); **Rocky Gap Bluegrass/Country Western Music Festival** (first weekend of August); and the **Victorian Christmas at History House** (first 2 weeks of December). For complete details, contact the Allegany County Tourism and Public Relations Office (see above for address).

The most westerly of Maryland's big cities, Cumberland lies between West Virginia and Pennsylvania along the shores of the Potomac and in the heart of the Allegheny Mountains. First known as Fort Cumberland (after the English duke of the same name), this part of the state served as a western outpost in Colonial times for generals like George Washington and Edward Braddock.

In the 1800s Cumberland's importance grew as it became a gateway to the American West. Not only was it chosen as a terminus for the first National Pike (also known as the Cumberland Road and now Alternate Rte. 40), but it also became a focal point for the Western Maryland Railroad and the Chesapeake & Ohio Canal.

Today although the railroad and canal have diminished in commercial importance, they have re-emerged as tourism assets. In particular, the railroading era is now showcased in the new Western Maryland Scenic Railroad, a steam train ride through 17 miles of valley between Cumberland and Frostburg. This attraction is not only drawing more visitors to Cumberland, but it is also stirring up new enthusiasm for the surrounding Allegany County sights and the impressive historic highlights of neighboring Frostburg.

A city of 24,000 people, Cumberland is centered around a pedestrian downtown mall, lined with shops and commercial outlets, in a parklike setting of shade trees, flowers, benches, brick walks, and fountains.

WHAT TO SEE & DO

⭐ The highlight of a visit to Cumberland is a stroll through the **Victorian Historic District,** primarily along Washington Street on the western side of town. This area includes the site of the original Fort Cumberland (now the Emmanuel Episcopal Church) and more than 50 residential and public buildings, built primarily in the 1800s when Cumberland was at its economic peak. Placed on the National Register of Historic Places in 1973, this street is a showcase of homes with elaborate stained-glass windows, graceful cupolas, and sloping mansard roofs. You'll see architectural styles ranging from Federal, Romanesque, Queen Anne, Empire, Colonial Revival, Italianate, and English Country Gothic to Georgian Revival, Gothic Revival, and Greek Revival. Most of the houses are not open to the public, but a self-guided walking tour of the neighborhood has been plotted out and is described in a booklet available free from the tourist information office.

HISTORY HOUSE, 218 Washington St. Tel. 777-8678.

Originally built as a private residence in 1867 for the president of the C&O Canal, this house is now in the hands of the Allegany County Historical Society. The restored 18-room dwelling contains antique furnishings such as a Victorian courting couch and an 1840 square grand piano. Other features include a genealogical research room, an early 19th-century brick-walled garden, and a basement kitchen with authentic cooking utensils, fireplace, coal stove, dishes, and pottery.

Admission: $1 adults, 25¢ for children under 12.

Open: May–Oct Tues–Sat 11am–4pm, Sun 1:30–4pm; Nov–Apr Tues–Sat 11am–4pm.

WESTERN MARYLAND SCENIC RAILROAD, Western Maryland Station Center, Canal St. Tel. 759-4400 or toll-free 800/TRAIN 50.

★ It's worth a trip to western Maryland just to board this vintage steam train and ride the 34-mile round-trip between Cumberland and Frostburg. A genuine delight for young and old alike, this excursion—enhanced by an informative live commentary—follows a scenic mountain valley route through the Cumberland Narrows, Helmstetter's Horseshoe Curve, various tunnels, many panoramic vistas, and a 1,300-foot elevation change between the two destinations. All trains depart and terminate at Cumberland. The trip takes 3 hours, including a 1½-hour layover in Frostburg for local sightseeing, including the "Old Depot," which is composed of a complex of shops, a restaurant, and an active turntable where the train engine is turned in full view of the public, for the Cumberland-bound segment of the journey. Don't miss it!

Fare: May–Sept and Nov $12 adults, $7 children 2–12, and $10.50 seniors over age 60; Oct $14 adults, $8 children, and $13.50 seniors. Reservations are required.

Schedule: Early May–early June Tues–Sun 11:30am; early June–Sept Tues–Fri 11:30am, Sat–Sun 11:30am, 3:30pm; Oct Tues–Sun 11:30am, 3:30pm; Nov Sat–Sun 11:30am.

Directions: From I-68, take the Downtown Cumberland exit 43-C (westbound) or the Johnson Street exit 43-A (eastbound) and follow signs to Western Maryland Station Center.

GEORGE WASHINGTON'S HEADQUARTERS, in Riverside Park, Greene Street, at the junction of Wills Creek and the Potomac River.

This log cabin, believed to be the only remaining section of the original Fort Cumberland, was used by Washington as his official quarters during the French and Indian War. The cabin is not open to the public, but does have a viewing window and a tape-recorded description that plays when activated by a pushbutton.

Admission: Free.

Open: Open by appointment and on certain holidays. Exterior viewing at all times.

C&O CANAL BOAT, C&O Canal at North Branch off Rte. 51. Tel. 777-7563 or 729-3136.

A full-scale C&O canal boat like the ones that used to move along the 184-mile canal between Georgetown and Cumberland is on view near Cumberland. The boat features a captain's cabin with furnishings from the 1828–1924 canal era, a hay house where feed was stored for the mules, and an on-board mule stable. A restored log-cabin lock house is located nearby. Guided tours are conducted by volunteers on weekends.

Admission: Free, but donations are welcome.

Open: June–Aug Sat–Sun 1–5pm.

TOLL GATE HOUSE, Rte. 40A (the old National Road), at LaVale. Tel. 726-8538 or 729-1210.

Built in 1836, this historic toll gate house is the last of its kind to remain in Maryland. When this country's first national road was built, federal funds were used; ownership was then turned over to the states and tolls had to be collected.

Admission: Free.

Open: May, Sept, Oct Sun 1:30–4:30pm, June–Aug Fri–Sun 1:30–4:30pm, and by appointment.

SPORTS & ACTIVITIES

One of Cumberland's leading outdoor attractions is **Rocky Gap State Park,** Rte. 1, Box 90, Flintstone, MD 21530 (tel. 301/777-2138). Six miles east of the city off U.S. Alt. 40, this facility is a paradise for fishing, hiking, biking, and walking. There's a 243-acre lake with three beaches for swimming and a 278-unit campsite. Open year round, but hours vary seasonally. The entrance charge is $4 per car and $1 for walk-ins. Camping fees are $10 a night for regular sites, $12 to $15 for waterfront sites. Reservations are accepted.

Hoofprints, Old Depot at Depot Center, Frostburg (tel. 689-3461), offers horse-drawn carriage/sleigh rides departing from the Old Depot, traveling through the town of Frostburg or a nearby scenic wooded glen. Prices start at $5 per person, depending on the length and extent of ride. Hoofprints carriages and drivers also meet all the arriving trains of the Western Maryland Scenic Railroad. Rides can be arranged on the spot or by advance reservation.

WHERE TO STAY

The Cumberland-Frostburg area offers an inviting blend of historic inns, modern hotels and motels, and homey bed-and-breakfast lodgings. Take your pick—most fall into the moderate price category and offer very good value.

MODERATE

BEST WESTERN BRADDOCK MOTOR INN, 1268 National Hwy., LaVale, MD 21502. Tel. 301/729-3300 or toll-free 800/528-1234. Fax 301/729-3300, ext. 602. 108 rms. A/C TV TEL
$ Rates: $50–$72 single or double. AE, MC, V. **Parking:** Free.
A tree-shaded country setting adds to the rural atmosphere of this two-story inn, just east of the historic LaVale Toll Gate. The contemporary-style guest rooms are tastefully furnished and well maintained, with a choice of double or queen- or king-size beds. Facilities include a German-themed restaurant, lounge, indoor heated swimming pool, Jacuzzi, sauna, and exercise room.

FAILINGER'S HOTEL GUNTER, 11 W. Main St., Frostburg, MD 21532. Tel. 301/689-6511. 16 rms with bath. A/C TV TEL
$ Rates (including continental breakfast): $60 single, $80 double. AE, MC, V. **Parking:** Free.
Originally opened in 1897 as the Gladstone Hotel, this grand four-story landmark later came under the ownership and name of William Gunter, and it was for many decades the social center of Frostburg. After a stretch of lean times and disrepair, it was revived and restored several years ago by the present owners, the Kermit Failinger family. Although the work is not totally complete, the rooms that are open are masterfully done, as are the public areas and the main staircase, the centerpiece of the hotel. The restoration has added modern conveniences, like private baths in all rooms and an elevator, but it has not impinged on the hotel's magnificent Victorian style, nor its original oak doors and brass fixtures, claw-foot bathtubs, intricate wall trim, vintage pictures and prints, smoked glass lantern-style lamps, and delicate wall sconces.

The guest rooms are individually furnished, with canopy or four-poster beds, armoires, laces and frills, and pastel fabrics. The one exception is no. 307, decorated starkly in black and white, and named the Roy Clark Room, after the country-western entertainer who stayed in it during a 1990 visit. Throughout the corridors, there are one-of-a-kind collectibles, dried-flower assortments, and hanging plants. Facilities include a restaurant with wide-windowed views of the valley, a lounge, and a unique basement area that houses a sports bar (which was once a game-cock fighting arena), and the remnants of an old jail. Plans call for the restoration of a rooftop observatory.

HOLIDAY INN, 100 S. George St., Cumberland, MD 21502. Tel. 301/ 724-8800 or toll-free 800/HOLIDAY. Fax 301/724-4001. 130 rms. A/C TV TEL
$ Rates: $54–$66 single, $68–$80 double. AE, CB, DC, DISC, MC, V. **Parking:** Free.
Cumberland's only full-scale hotel is in the heart of town, adjacent to the train tracks—an ideal place for railroad buffs. Unbelievably long freight trains, many with rustic cabooses, pass through at all hours of the day and night. This can also be annoying at night for nonrail fans, but the reception desk staff readily obliges guests with earplugs, if needed. Ask for a room on the quieter front side of the house.

In addition to contemporary rooms typical of the Holiday Inn chain, this modern six-story property offers a restaurant, lounge, and outdoor swimming pool; in the summer months dinner-theater productions are staged on the premises.

INN AT WALNUT BOTTOM, 120 Greene St., Cumberland, MD 21502. Tel. 301/777-0003. 7 rms, 5 with private bath. A/C
$ Rates (including continental breakfast): $50–$65 double or single. MC, V. **Parking:** Free.
Located on a residential street in a quiet part of the city, this two-story Federal-style home is a stand-out in the bed-and-breakfast category. Dating back to the 1820s, it has been totally restored and furnished with antiques and period reproductions including four-poster and brass beds, tapestry rugs, and down comforters. The guest rooms are large and spacious, with high ceilings and large windows. There are three guest rooms on the ground level and four on the second floor. Facilities include a small restaurant, a garret TV and game room, and mountain bike rentals. The innkeeper is Sharon Ennis Kazary.

BUDGET

COMFORT INN, State Rte. 36 N., Frostburg Industrial Park, Frostburg, MD 21532. Tel. 301/689-2050 or toll-free 800/228-5150. 100 rms. A/C TV TEL
$ Rates (including continental breakfast): $44 single, $49 double. AE, DC, MC, V. **Parking:** Free.
Sitting on a hillside outside of town, with lovely views of the valley in all directions, this modern two-story inn is built in a hacienda style with a white brick exterior. Services are limited, but all the basics are here and are well maintained. Guest rooms have dark woods, pastel tone fabrics, separate sitting areas, and a choice of king- or queen-size beds. Facilities include a fitness center and sauna.

WHERE TO DINE
EXPENSIVE

AU PETIT PARIS, 86 E. Main St., Frostburg. Tel. 689-8946.
Cuisine: FRENCH. **Reservations:** Recommended.
$ Prices: Appetizers $3.95–$6.95; main courses $14–$19. AE, CB, DISC, MC, V.
Open: Tues–Sat 6–9:30pm.
Step into this restaurant and it's like strolling along a Parisian boulevard, thanks to a decor of French murals and posters and bistro-style furnishings. Established over 30 years ago, this restaurant is a local favorite for such dishes as trout with almonds, frogs' legs, duck à l'orange, coq au vin, filet of beef au poivre, chateaubriand, steak Diane, and veal Cordon Bleu.

MODERATE

GIUSEPPE'S, 11 Bowery St., Frostburg. Tel. 689-2220.
Cuisine: ITALIAN. **Reservations:** Recommended.

$ Prices: Appetizers $1.95–$4.95; main courses $6.95–$12.95. AE, MC, V.
Open: Mon–Sat 3pm–midnight, Sun 4–10pm.

In the heart of town and a block from the Frostburg State University campus, this is a popular dining spot for the college community and is staffed by many of the students. The decor is nondescript, but the food is first rate. Entrées include all the usual Italian favorites, such as pizza, pastas, chicken cacciatore, shrimp scampi, and sausage and peppers, and also a surprising array of nightly specials including fresh seafood, such as trout stuffed with crab imperial or orange roughy.

L'OSTERIA, Rte. 40/48, Cumberland. Tel. 777-3553.
Cuisine: ITALIAN/INTERNATIONAL. **Reservations:** Recommended.
$ Prices: Appetizers $3.50–$6; main courses $9–$15. AE, MC, V.
Open: Dinner Mon–Sat 5–9pm.

The ambience of "Old Cumberland" prevails at this mid-19th-century structure, said to have been erected as a tavern. The interior includes original woodwork and antiques, but the menu is thoroughly contemporary. Open for dinner only, the entrées include veal saltimbocca or picatta, filet of beef au poivre, shrimp parmesan, blackened red fish, chicken alla Romana with peppers and onions in tomato and wine sauce.

THE OLD DEPOT, 19 Depot St., Frostburg. Tel. 689-1221.
Cuisine: AMERICAN. **Reservations:** Not accepted.
$ Prices: Appetizers $2.95–$4.95; main courses $6.95–$15.95; lunch $2.95–$7.95. AE, MC, V.
Open: Daily lunch 11am–5pm, dinner 5–11pm.

Originally built in 1891 as the Cumberland and Pennsylvania Railroad Company passenger and freight station, this structure was abandoned after service was discontinued in 1973; it was then renovated and opened as a restaurant and lounge in 1989. With a decor and ambience that preserves the pace and din of a train station, it is a busy and informal dining spot, popular with students and faculty from the local university, as well as tourists who arrive via the excursion on the Western Maryland Scenic Railroad. Entrées range from Kansas City steaks to barbecued pork ribs, grilled shrimp, mixed grill seafood combo (mahi mahi, swordfish, and halibut), and barbecued chicken. Lunch items include sandwiches, burgers, omelets, pizzas, burritos, fajitas, wings, ribs, and other "finger foods."

BUDGET

MASON'S BARN, I-68, Cumberland. Tel. 722-6155.
Cuisine: AMERICAN. **Reservations:** Not required.
$ Prices: Appetizers $2.50–$3.95; main courses $7.95–$14.95; lunch $3.95–$6.95. AE, DISC, MC, V.
Open: Lunch daily 11am–4pm, dinner daily 4–11pm.

Established in 1954 as a small roadside diner, this dependable restaurant has been growing ever since, thanks to the friendly and attentive supervision of owners Ed Mason and his son Mike. As its name implies, it offers an authentic barnlike setting, with a decor of farming tools, local antiques, and an eclectic collection of Maryland memorabilia. There is also a casual saloon-style dining room downstairs. Entrées include steaks and seafood dishes as well as chicken, veal, and pasta items. Lunch choices range from salads and homemade soups to sandwiches (the crab cake sandwich is a standout).

4. DEEP CREEK LAKE

50 miles SW of Cumberland, 120 miles SW of Hagerstown,
190 miles W of Baltimore, 100 miles SE of Pittsburgh

GETTING THERE **By Car** You can reach Deep Creek Lake by heading westward along I-68 to Keyser's Ridge and then following Rte. 219 south. It's about an hour's drive from Cumberland.

ESSENTIALS   The **Deep Creek Lake–Garrett County Promotion Council** is in the Garrett County Courthouse, Oakland, MD 21550 (tel. 301/334-1948). From Memorial Day through Labor Day, an Information Booth is located on Rte. 219, at Deep Creek Lake, south of Deep Creek Lake Bridge (tel. 301/387-6171). In the winter, a telephone snow report service is operated (tel. 301/387-4000).

Maryland's largest freshwater lake is Deep Creek, nearly 12 miles in length, with a shoreline of 65 miles and covering nearly 3,900 acres. Located in the heart of Garrett County, on the state's western border, Deep Creek is completely artificial, a 1925 work project of the Youghiogheny Electric Company, which sold it to the Pennsylvania Electric Company in 1942. It is now leased to the Maryland Inland Fish and Game Commission for the nominal fee of $1 a year, and is managed by the Maryland Department of Natural Resources.

Nestled in the heart of the Allegheny Mountains, and with an elevation of 2,462 feet, Deep Creek Lake has long been a popular year-round recreational area. Summer temperatures average 65.9°F, ideal for boating and water sports. In the winter months, however, Deep Creek Lake really comes into its own, as Maryland's premier ski resort (with an average temperature of 28°F and a yearly snowfall of over 80 inches).

The two principal towns in the area are Oakland, the county seat of Garrett County, and McHenry, named for Col. James McHenry of Baltimore, who was an aide to General Washington during the Revolutionary War and a signer of the Constitution.

WHAT TO SEE & DO

A complete year-round resort, Deep Creek Lake is equally great in summer and winter.

BOATING

Summer activities focus on water sports, with every type of boat from sailboat to speedster on the lake. Nearly all marinas around the lake have craft for rent, 7 days a week. Pedal boats or canoes average $5 an hour; fishing boats, $10 an hour; pontoon boats, from $15 to $25 an hour; sailboats, $10 an hour; skiboats and runabouts, from $12 to $25 an hour, depending on horsepower. Some of the leading firms are **Echo Marina,** White Oak Drive, Swanton (tel. 387-5910); **Bill's Marine Service,** Rte. 219, Fox Den Rd., Oakland (tel. 387-5536); and **Crystal Waters,** Rte. 219, Oakland (tel. 387-5515).

GOLF

The **Golf Club at Wisp, Wisp Resort Golf Course,** Marsh Hill Road, P.O. Box 629, McHenry (tel. 387-4911 or toll-free 800/462-9477) is an 18-hole championship facility nestled between the Allegheny Mountains and Deep Creek Lake. Open from April through mid-October, the course welcomes guests 7 days a week. Greens fees and golf cart cost $40 per person for 18 holes and $25 for greens fees only. Rates are slightly lower after 3pm. There is a fully stocked pro shop on the grounds. In addition, the **Oakland Country Club,** Sang Run Road, Oakland (tel. 334-3883), invites visitors to play on its 18-hole championship course on weekdays. Greens fees are $7 to $20 for 18 holes. Golf carts are available for $12 for 9 holes and $18 for 18 holes.

SWIMMING

Deep Creek Lake State Park, south of McHenry on State Park Road, features a 700-foot sandy beach with lifeguards on duty.

SKIING

Deep Creek Lake is the home of Maryland's largest ski area. With an elevation of 3,080 feet and a vertical rise of 610 feet, the **Wisp Resort** offers 23 major ski runs and challenging trails on 80 acres of skiable terrain. The longest single run is 2 miles. Facilities include triple- and double-chair lifts, rope-tow, and poma lifts; snow-making; and night skiing. Slope fees range from $27 on weekdays to $32 on weekends, with reduced rates for night skiing, 2-day tickets, and children. The ski season opens at the end of November and closes in mid-March. The Wisp also operates an on-premises ski school, a rental service, and a ski shop. For full information, contact the Wisp Resort, P.O. Box 629, Marsh Hill Road, Deep Creek Lake, MD 21541 (tel. 301/387-4911 or toll-free 800/462-9477).

WHERE TO STAY
MODERATE

WISP RESORT, Marsh Hill Rd., Deep Creek Lake, MD 21541. Tel. 301/387-5581 or toll-free 800/462-9477. Fax 301/387-4127. 67 rms, 100 suites. A/C TV TEL
$ Rates: $65–$75 single or double; $125–$175 suite. AE, DC, DISC, MC, V. **Parking:** Free.

Deep Creek Lake's center of activity is this modern condo-hotel property. All regular bedrooms have a queen-size bed, a sofa bed, and a small refrigerator. Some units also have small kitchenettes or fireplaces. Amenities include an indoor swimming pool and whirlpool, a beauty salon, and an 18-hole championship golf course. The Wisp is also Maryland's largest ski area with major ski runs, lifts, and snow-making operations in the winter months. Future developments at the Wisp include tennis courts, a heated outdoor pool, and an indoor ice-skating rink. Golf and ski packages are also available at reduced rates.

Facilities include a lounge, a pizza parlor, a seasonal après-ski eatery, and a year-round restaurant, The Gathering (see "Where to Dine," below).

ALPINE VILLAGE INN, Glendale Rd., Rte. 6, Box 114, Oakland, MD 21550. Tel. 301/387-5534 or toll-free 800/343-5253. 29 rms, 14 chalets. A/C TV TEL
$ Rates: $50–$80 single or double; chalets $80–$150. AE, MC, V. **Parking:** Free.
Views of the lake and mountains are part of the charm at this inn nestled on 30 wooded acres. The facility offers a choice of lodge-style rooms and chalets. Rooms have queen-size beds and sun decks; many also have cathedral ceilings, fireplaces, and kitchenettes. The chalets, which have living rooms, patios, and complete kitchens, in addition to at least two bedrooms, can accommodate up to six people. Guests also enjoy docking facilities, beach swimming, and a heated outdoor pool (in summer).

POINT VIEW INN, Rte. 219, P.O. Box 100, McHenry, MD 21541. Tel. 301/387-5555. 22 rms. A/C TV TEL
$ Rates: $58–$90 double; efficiencies $60–$90. AE, MC, V. **Parking:** Free.
Right on the shores of Deep Creek Lake, this lodging offers motel-style rooms with two double beds or a king-size bed; many have porches or private terraces overlooking the lake, and most have charming Victorian or antique furnishings with individual flair, some with fireplaces. Facilities include a boat dock, a private beach, an informal café/lounge, and a full-service dining room that overlooks the lake.

WHERE TO DINE

Note: Garrett County liquor regulations prohibit restaurants from selling or serving any alcoholic beverages, including wine, on Sundays.

MODERATE

THE GATHERING, Marsh Hill Rd., Deep Creek Lake. Tel. 387-5581.

Cuisine: AMERICAN. **Reservations:** Recommended.
$ **Prices:** Appetizers $2.50–$5.50; main courses $9.95–$16.95; lunch $2.95–$6.95. AE, DC, DISC, MC, V.
Open: Daily lunch 11:30am–2pm, dinner daily 5:30–9:30pm.

A sporting lodge atmosphere prevails at this dining room located near the base of the Wisp skiing slopes and the golf course. Many of the entrées are named after sporting terms such as the "Hole in One" (a New York strip steak), the "Birdie" (a chicken breast stuffed with sage and topped with ham and mozzarella cheese), and the "Wedge" (sautéed calves' liver smothered with onions and Dusseldorf mustard). Other dishes include blackened Cajun-style fish of the day, crab cakes, and stir-fried beef with vegetables, as well as pastas and smoked barbecued ribs. Lunch items range from salads and sandwiches to quiches, pastas, and burgers.

SILVER TREE, Glendale Rd., Oakland. Tel. 387-4040.
Cuisine: ITALIAN. **Reservations:** Not accepted.
$ **Prices:** Appetizers $3.95–$5.95; main courses $8.95–$17.95. AE, MC, V.
Open: Mon–Thurs 5–10pm, Fri–Sat 5–11pm, Sun 4–10pm.

⭐ This lakefront restaurant and cocktail lounge has an 1890s decor of knotty-pine walls, beamed-ceilings, colored-glass lamps, and open fireplaces. Wide picture windows add a contemporary touch, framing views of the lake and surrounding woodlands. The specialty here is Italian food—veal parmigiana, spaghetti with a choice of sauces, lasagne, and manicotti.

In addition, there is a wide range of seafood entrées, ranging from crab imperial and crab soufflé to seafood Newburg and fish combination platters; prime rib and charbroiled steaks are also on the menu. In summer, lunch is served at a lakeside seafood bar on the restaurant grounds.

NEARBY DINING

PENN ALPS RESTAURANT AND CRAFT SHOP, Alternate Rte. 40, Grantsville. Tel. 895-5985.
Cuisine: PENNSYLVANIA DUTCH. **Reservations:** Not required.
$ **Prices:** Appetizers $1.25–$1.95; main courses $7.95–$13.95; lunch $3.95–$6.95. MC, V. **Open:** Mar–Dec Mon–Thurs 11am–7pm, Fri 11am–8pm, Sat 8am–8pm; brunch Sun 11am–2pm. **Closed:** Several days at Christmas, Jan–Feb.

⭐ Don't leave the mountainous countryside of western Maryland without a stop at this welcoming oasis. Situated between an 18th-century gristmill and an old stone arch bridge, this unique restaurant-cum-shop is housed in a remodeled log stagecoach inn dating back to 1818. There are five dining rooms, all with an old-world atmosphere, serving the best of Pennsylvania Dutch–style cooking such as roast pork and sauerkraut and hickory smoked ham, as well as roast beef, fried chicken, steaks, and seafood. Lighter items are also available, including sandwiches, soups, salads, and burgers.

The adjacent shop offers dozens of unique handcrafts and baked goods produced largely by the neighboring Amish-Mennonite community north of Grantsville. In the summer months, a half-dozen rustic buildings in the nearby Spruce Forest serve as studios for a group of local artisans, including a spinner, weaver, potter, stained-glass worker, wood sculptor, and bird carver. Visitors are welcome to watch the craftspeople at work. The hours for the shop are the same as the restaurant, but schedules for the working craftspeople vary.

CHAPTER 19

ATLANTIC CITY

The nation's most visited destination, Atlantic City welcomes over 33 million people a year. Although this beachfront resort has been a leading Jersey shore vacation spot for well over a century, the credit for the recent growth in tourism goes beyond beautiful beaches and a landmark boardwalk.

Atlantic City's official rebirth came on Election Day, November 1976, with the passage of the casino-gambling referendum. Since then, 12 high-rise casino hotels have sprouted up, over 1,300 gaming tables have been rolled in, more than 18,000 slot machines are in use, and 70,000 jobs have been created in the area. Now a city that never sleeps, Atlantic City is working hard to be the nation's "playground."

Located on Absecon Island, in a sheltered strip of land warmed by the Gulf Stream, Atlantic City is not the most accessible mecca for travelers. It is totally offshore, separated from the mainland by bays, inlets, and marshes, and connected only by artificial bridges and roadways. In spite of its location, Atlantic City has been attracting visitors to its white, wide sandy beaches since 1854, when it became an incorporated village. It gained worldwide fame in 1870 when the first ocean boardwalk was constructed here, and ever since then, this has been a city of firsts and foremosts.

The first salt-water taffy was introduced here in 1883, quickly followed by the first color picture postcards (1893). Other claims to fame include the world's first Ferris wheel (1869), the first amusement pier over water (1882), and the first Easter Parade (1876). The Miss America Pageant, synonymous with Atlantic City, took place here for the first time in 1921.

But life in this city-by-the-bay has not always been a celebration. The area began to decline in the mid-1960s and remained so until the casino law was passed. Consequently, not all of Atlantic City has been revived to unprecedented heights of glitter and glamour.

The **Boardwalk,** lined with the opulent casino hotels, may be a showplace, but just a few blocks away, you will find many neglected or abandoned buildings. Gradually, new housing is being built, as the profits from the casinos are being poured back into the municipal coffers. All casinos are required to pay 8% of gross gaming revenues to a Casino Revenue Fund, used exclusively for transportation, health, and housing for seniors and the disabled. Since 1978, more than $1.6 billion has been paid to this fund and nine social-service programs are in operation.

On the whole, Atlantic City (pop. 36,000) is making great strides toward a total renaissance. The casino hotels are expanding and reinvesting in their properties, and new noncasino hotels and motor inns are springing up within and near the city. The world's top stars appear here regularly in the showrooms and theaters; and cars and buses roll in by the thousands each day. Everywhere you look, people are placing their bets in favor of this magical city and its future.

WHAT'S SPECIAL ABOUT ATLANTIC CITY

Ace Attractions
☐ The casinos, with over 1,500 gaming tables and 20,000 slot machines.
☐ Atlantic City Convention Center, home of the world's largest pipe organ and the Miss America Pageant.
☐ Garden Pier, oceanfront setting for the New Jersey Art Center.
☐ Renault Winery, a leading producer of red, white, and blue (blueberry champagne) wines, open for touring.
☐ Pine Barrens, the largest tract of wilderness on mid-Atlantic coast.

After Dark
☐ Broadway-type shows, musical revues, comedy and cabaret acts, with big-name stars, at many of the casino hotels.

Events
☐ Miss America Pageant, the grande dame of beauty contests.

For the Kids
☐ Tivoli Pier, a two-acre indoor family amusement area.

Offbeat/Oddities
☐ Lucy, the Margate Elephant, a giant elephant-shaped building.

Regional Food
☐ Fralinger's Salt Water Taffy, an Atlantic City tradition, in 16 flavors.

Shopping
☐ Ocean One, a ship-shaped mall of 150 shops, extending 900 feet into the sea.
☐ Historic Towne of Smithville, a reconstructed 19th-century village with over 30 specialty shops and restaurants.

1. ORIENTATION

ARRIVING

BY AIR

There are two airports serving Atlantic City. Commuter flights via **Continental Express** (tel. toll-free 800/525-0280) and other local carriers arrive from nearby cities such as Newark and Washington, D.C., at **Bader Field Airport, 72** Albany Ave. (tel. 345-6402). Regularly scheduled commercial jet flights from most major east coast cities land at **Atlantic City International Airport,** Pomona (tel. 645-7895), about 10 miles west of town via the Atlantic City Expressway. Carriers currently include **USAir** and **USAir Express** (tel. toll-free 800/428-4322); **TWA Express** (tel. toll-free 800/221-2000; and **Trump Shuttle** (tel. toll-free 800/247-8786), connecting Detroit and Boston with Atlantic City.

Alternatively, you can fly into **Philadelphia International Airport** and take ground transport to Atlantic City. The following companies provide minibus or car service from Philadelphia's airport: **Casino Limousine Service** (tel. 646-5555) and **Rapid Rover Shuttle** (tel. 344-0100).

BY TRAIN

Amtrak operates "The Atlantic City Express," daily round-trip service from New York, Philadelphia, Washington, D.C., and other eastern corridor cities. The trains also provide connections to and from Amtrak's northeast corridor network. For more information, telephone toll-free 800/USA-RAIL.

New Jersey Transit also offers train service to Atlantic City from Lindenwold and other mid-Jersey communities such as Atco, Hammonton, and Egg Harbor. For information, call toll-free 800/AC-TRAIN or 201/935-2500.

BY BUS

Every day, more than 2,000 buses travel into the Atlantic City **Municipal Bus Terminal,** at Arkansas and Arctic Aves. The buses come from both the big cities and the small towns on the east coast, and are operated primarily by **New Jersey Transit** (tel. 344-8181) and **Greyhound-Trailways** (tel. 345-5403), although many other charter bus companies also run buses to Atlantic City. Many of the casino hotels also sponsor daily bus trips from New York, Philadelphia, Washington, D.C., and other cities within a 300-mile radius of the resort.

BY CAR

From the north, the best approach to Atlantic City is the Garden State Parkway to exit 38 and then the Atlantic City Expressway into the heart of the city near the Convention Center (Missouri Ave.). You can also get off the Garden State at exit 40N (the White Horse Pike, Rte. 30), which brings you into the north end of the city (Absecon Blvd.), or exit 36 (the Black Horse Pike, Rte. 40), which comes into town at Albany Avenue, on the city's southern edge.

From the west, via Philadelphia, take the Atlantic City Expressway directly into the heart of Atlantic City. From points south, the best route is via I-95 and Rte. 40 from Washington, D.C. (or Rtes. 13 and 9 from the Norfolk area via the Cape May–Lewes Ferry).

TOURIST INFORMATION

When planning your visit to this area, contact the **Greater Atlantic City Convention and Visitors Bureau,** 2314 Pacific Ave., Atlantic City, NJ 08401 (tel. 609/348-7100). This office can supply you with maps and brochures on lodgings, restaurants, and activities. When you arrive in the city, you can also visit the office to collect the latest data on shows and events scheduled during your stay. It's located in the Convention Center, between Mississippi and Georgia Aves.; the hours are Monday through Friday from 9am to 5pm. If you happen to be in town on a weekend, visitor information and brochures can be obtained at the Atlantic City Art Center on Garden Pier, New Jersey Ave. and Boardwalk; at the mall Ocean One, Arkansas Avenue and Boardwalk; in the Convention Center's Boardwalk lobby; and at the rail terminal as well as both airports.

CITY LAYOUT
MAIN ARTERIES & STREETS

If you ever played the board game Monopoly, you may feel a sense of déjà vu as you stroll around Atlantic City. This is because the game-board layout uses the street names of this seaside city. You'll see Boardwalk, Park Place, Mediterranean Avenue, and Baltic Avenue, but this time you'll be rolling the dice on the gaming tables, and not using play money!

As in the board game, all of Atlantic City's main streets are avenues, and all are named for bodies of water—Mediterranean, Baltic, Arctic, Atlantic, and Pacific. These main thoroughfares run parallel to the ocean. The cross streets running to and from the ocean are also called avenues and, for the most part, are named for states. However, they are not in alphabetical (or logical geographic) order, although Maine is in the northeast and California and Texas are in the city's southwest. Just to add to the confusion, not every state is represented and some state *capitals* are used in the lower part of the city. All streets are logically numbered, however, in blocks of hundreds. The best way to get around initially is to refer to the handy map supplied by the Greater Atlantic City Convention and Visitors Bureau.

DISTANCES

Atlantic City is 125 miles south of New York City, 60 miles east of Philadelphia, 175 miles north of Washington, D.C., and 40 miles north of Cape May.

2. GETTING AROUND

BY PUBLIC TRANSPORTATION

BUS

Municipal service is operated by the **New Jersey Transit,** Arkansas and Arctic Aves. (tel. toll-free 800/582-5946), covering the length of Absecon Island. You can board a bus at any corner along Atlantic Avenue. The fare depends on the distance traveled, but the minimum is $1, and exact change is required. Most bus routes operate 7 days a week, and some run 24 hours a day.

BY TAXI

As in most major cities, taxis line up at major hotels; they also cruise the streets, allowing people to hail a ride from curbside within Atlantic City. The local meter rate is $1.35 for the first ⅕ mile, plus 20¢ for each additional ⅕ mile, and 20¢ for each additional passenger. The average cab ride is $3 to $4 within the city. If you wish to order a cab, call **City Taxi** (tel. 345-3244); **Radio Cab** (tel. 345-1105); or **Yellow Cab** (tel. 344-1221).

BY CAR

See "Orientation" section, above, for directions for driving to Atlantic City.

CAR RENTALS

Among the car-rental companies based in Atlantic City and its environs are **Avis,** 114 S. New York Ave. (tel. 345-3350); **Budget,** Atlantic City Airport (tel. 383-0100); **Hertz,** 1400 Albany Ave., West Atlantic City (tel. 646-1212); **Jo-Lin Rent-a-Car,** Rte. 40, Pleasantville (tel. 645-2664); and **Thrifty,** 1406 Albany Ave., West Atlantic City (tel. 645-1901).

PARKING

If you bring your own car or rent one, you'll find that parking is moderately priced, and most hotels provide free parking. There are parking lots in various locations throughout the city, with day-long rates that range from $3 to $6 on weekdays and $4 to $7 on weekends. You'll find that rates are highest closer to the Boardwalk.

BY JITNEY

One of the best ways to get from casino to casino or among the restaurants is via the Atlantic City **jitneys.** These minibuses provide 24-hour service up and down Pacific Avenue, for the length of the city, in a north-south direction. They also travel from Park Place to Harrah's Marina and Trump's Castle, both located on the bay. Jitneys with a red sign in the windshield remain on Pacific Avenue only, and vehicles with a blue or green sign travel across to the bay. The one-way fare in either case is $1. For further information, call 344-8642.

BY ROLLING CHAIRS

Of all the forms of transport in this city, however, the most famous is the **"rolling chair."** Ever since 1887, these unique wicker chairs on wheels have been synonymous with the Atlantic City Boardwalk. Often topped by a surrey-style canopy, these mini-carriages are leisurely pushed along by attendants in 19th-century style.

Rolling chairs are available for set tours or as a link between casinos. Tour rates for two passengers are $15 per half hour or $25 per hour; the hourly rate for three persons is $30. Casino transfers (up to 10 blocks) cost $5 for two people and $7.50 for three people. During the summer season you can hire a chair (and pusher) between 9am and 4am daily; winter hours are 11am to 2am. You can board a rolling chair outside any of the casino hotels along the Boardwalk, from Bally's Grand at the south end to the Showboat on the north tip, a distance of 30 blocks. No reservations are necessary, but if you wish further information, call 347-7148.

FAST FACTS — ATLANTIC CITY

Area Code   The area code for all numbers in the Atlantic City area is 609.

Baby-sitters   Inquire at your hotel.

Car Rentals   See "Getting Around," above.

Climate   See "When to Go," in Chapter 2.

Drugstores   National chains that have pharmacies in Atlantic City include **CVS,** 1400 Atlantic Ave. (tel. 345-7418); **Rite Aid,** 1328 Atlantic Ave. (tel. 348-4206) and 1522 Atlantic Ave. (tel. 348-6828). **Parkway Pharmacy,** 3321 Atlantic Ave. (tel. 345-5105) offers radio-car delivery to casino hotels.

Emergencies   Dial 911 for police, fire department, and emergencies.

Eyeglasses   Consult the *Yellow Pages* under "Optical Goods–Retail." National chains that are represented in the Greater Atlantic City area are **Lens Crafters** and **Pearle Vision Center.**

Hairdressers/Barbers   Two casino hotels, Caesar's and Trump Plaza, both offer hairdressing salons on site. An independent shop for men and women convenient to the casino strip is **Cutting Cove,** 153 S. New York Ave. (tel. 345-5315).

Hospitals   24-hour hospital and medical services are offered by the **Atlantic City Medical Center,** Pacific Avenue, between Michigan and Ohio (tel. 344-4081).

Laundry/Dry Cleaning   Most hotels provide same-day laundry and dry cleaning services. Other alternatives in the downtown area include **Atlantic Cleaners,** 1222 Atlantic Ave. (tel. 345-6208), and **Brighton Cleaners,** 2903 Atlantic Ave. (tel. 348-0484).

Libraries   **Atlantic City Free Public Library,** Tennessee and Atlantic Avenues (tel. 345-2269), offers books, magazines, and newspapers as well as a collection on Atlantic City history.

Liquor Laws   Alcoholic beverages may be purchased 7 days a week by any person 21 years of age or over. Package stores are open from 9am to 10pm daily. Bar hours are unrestricted in Atlantic City, but hours vary by municipality.

Lost Property   If items are lost or found at a hotel or restaurant, consult the management. If lost or found in a public place, call the police.

Newspapers/Magazines   The city's daily newspaper is the *Atlantic City Press.* The monthly magazine is *Atlantic City.*

Photographic Needs   Photo shops convenient to the casino area include the **Camera Shop** at Ocean One Mall on the Boardwalk (tel. 344-4994), and the **Photo Center,** 1912 Atlantic Ave. (tel. 344-7646).

Police   Dial 911.

Post Office   The main Atlantic City Post Office is located at the corner of Pacific Avenue and Martin Luther King Jr. Boulevard (tel. 345-4212).

Radio/TV   Local **radio stations** include WFPG–FM 97 (CBS); **WJRZ** 100.1 FM (ABC); WUSS AM 1490, urban contemporary. **TV stations** are WMGM–TV (NBC) Channel 40; and WNJS–TV Channel 23, New Jersey Public Broadcasting.

Religious Services   There are dozens of choices in the Atlantic City area.

Check at your hotel or look in the *Yellow Pages* under "Churches," "Religious Organizations," or "Synagogues."

Restrooms All hotels, restaurants, and casinos have facilities available for customers.

Safety As resort areas go, Atlantic City is generally safe. Nevertheless, there are precautions you should take whenever you're traveling in an unfamiliar city or country. Stay alert and be aware of your immediate surroundings. Wear a moneybelt and keep a close eye on your possessions. Be particularly careful with cameras, purses, and wallets, all favorite targets of thieves and pickpockets. Be especially careful when walking on dark streets and in parks after dark. Every society has its criminals. It's your responsibility to be aware and alert even in the most heavily touristed areas.

Shoe Repairs Shops that are convenient to the casino/boardwalk area are **Ace Shoe Repairs**, 1704 Atlantic Ave. (tel. 345-0711), and **Atlantic Shoe Repair** at 2325 Atlantic Ave. (tel. 344-2404) and at 1 Chelsea Ave. (tel. 344-9128).

Taxes Sales tax is 7%; hotel occupancy tax is 6%.

Taxis See "Getting Around," above.

Telegrams/Telex You can use **Financial Exchange Company of N.J., Inc.,** 9 S. Tennessee Ave. (tel. 348-0714).

Transit Information See "Getting Around," above, or call **New Jersey Transit** (tel. toll-free 800/582-5946).

3. ATLANTIC CITY ACCOMMODATIONS

CASINO ACCOMMODATIONS

Atlantic City has 12 casino hotels, all of which are in the prime scenic spots; 10 line the Boardwalk, and 2 are located on the bay side. All of these casino properties have opened their doors in the last decade, since gambling was approved in 1976.

In addition to a casino, each hotel has at least 500 rooms, a variety of restaurants in various price categories, swimming pools, health facilities, and entertainment centers. With all of these amenities, it is not surprising that rooms are usually at least $100 a night. Furthermore, all hotels in Atlantic City quote one-price rates, single or double occupancy; and minimum stays of 2 nights sometimes apply on weekends.

However, that does not mean you have to be a big winner to stay in Atlantic City. There are bargains to be found, especially if you are willing to come during midweek in the October-through-March period. Most hotels offer special package plans, as low as $39 to $59 per person a night, which often include "welcome" cocktails, some meals, discounts, car parking, and special extras. So, if you request a hotel brochure, be sure to ask for any package rates that may apply at the time you plan to visit.

To avoid repetition, we'll point out only what is different in the casino hotels described below. Each property has one, two, or more cocktail lounges, often with live evening entertainment, and extensive gaming facilities.

With regard to meals, the casino hotels usually offer several coffee shop/deli/fast-food facilities that remain open for breakfast and lunch and sometimes 24 hours a day. Buffet-style restaurants are also popular, and these are normally available for lunch and dinner, from 11am to 11pm. The majority of these fall into the mostly moderate category.

Each casino also has at least one "gourmet" restaurant that is ordinarily open for dinner only (6 to 11pm or midnight). Some hotels have two or three of these top-class restaurants, usually with a theme decor and menu, offering either classically American, continental, French, Italian, or Oriental cuisines. The prices in these top restaurants can be classified as very expensive, with most entrées in the $20 to $30 bracket.

EXPENSIVE

BALLY'S GRAND HOTEL/CASINO, Boston and Pacific Ave., Atlantic City, NJ 08401. Tel. 609/347-7111 or toll-free 800/257-8677. Fax 609/340-7268. 522 rms. A/C TV TEL

$ Rates: $125–$175 mid-May–Sept; $100–$155 off-season. AE, CB, DC, MC, V. **Parking:** Free.

Opened in 1980, this 23-story property, formerly the Golden Nugget, is a glittering contemporary palace with lots of brass and crystal fixtures. The most southerly resort on the Boardwalk, the hotel's rooms offer ocean views and varying decors, from summer garden motifs to art deco or reproduction styles, some with semi-canopies over the beds.

Dining/Entertainment: Upper-bracket restaurants for dinner include Vanessa's, for continental cuisine in a room overlooking the ocean in a Victorian setting; and Mr. Ming's, for gourmet Cantonese dining. More moderate prices prevail at the Oaks Steak House (for lunch and dinner), and Caruso's, an Italian restaurant for dinner only. In addition, there is the Cornucopia Café (open 24 hours) and Cornucopia Buffet (for lunch and dinner); and the Sweetheart Café and the Creamery for fast food and exotic desserts. A 540-seat cabaret theater, the Opera House, offers musical and comedy revues, and top-name entertainment.

Facilities: Health club with indoor swimming pool, sun deck, and valet and self-parking for more than 1,900 cars.

BALLY'S PARK PLACE CASINO HOTEL AND TOWER, Park Place and Boardwalk, Atlantic City, NJ 08401. Tel. 609/340-2000 or toll-free 800/BALLYS-7. Fax 609/340-2595. 1,310 rms. A/C TV TEL

$ Rates: $115–$145 July to mid-Sept; $115–$135 off-season. AE, CB, DC, MC, V. **Parking:** Free.

Located on 8½ acres of oceanfront property, Bally's occupies the site of three historic hotels, the Dennis (built in 1860 and incorporated into the current structure), the Marlborough (1902), and the Blenheim (1906), in addition to a new contemporary 30-story tower. Many of the original ornaments and gargoyles of the older hotels were salvaged and blended into the current modern decor of raspberry and grape tones, brass columns, and mirrors. The guest rooms are furnished in contemporary style, some with round beds and mirrored ceilings.

Dining/Entertainment: The two premier dinner spots are By the Sea, an elegant seafood dining room that offers panoramic views of Atlantic City by candlelight; and Prime Place, a steakhouse also known for its wide-windowed views of the city and ocean. More moderate all-day meals can be enjoyed at Pickles—More Than a Deli, plus an oyster bar, coffee shop, Tex-Mex snack bar, and ice-cream parlor. And this is also the home of Atlantic City's longest-running show, *An Evening at La Cage*, a female impersonation revue.

Facilities: Indoor and outdoor pools, health spa, beauty salon, two video game rooms, a garage, and parking for over 1,000 cars.

CAESARS ATLANTIC CITY HOTEL/CASINO, Arkansas Ave. and Boardwalk, Atlantic City, NJ 08401. Tel. 609/348-4411 or toll-free 800/257-8555. Fax 609/348-8830. 645 rms. A/C TV TEL

$ Rates: $120 in June–Aug; $100 in Sept–May. AE, CB, DC, MC, V. **Parking:** Free.

A Roman atmosphere greets you here, complete with statues, fountains, and white columns, a showroom called Circus Maximus, and a shopping mall known as the Appian Way. The modern rooms located in 19 stories offer views of the city, pool, or ocean.

Dining/Entertainment: With a choice of nine restaurants and cafés, the upscale dinner venues are the Oriental Palace, for gourmet Chinese cuisine; the Prime

ATLANTIC CITY

Absecon Inlet

Maine Ave.
New Hampshire Ave.
Vermont Ave.
Rhode Island Ave.
Massachusetts Ave.
Connecticut Ave.
New Jersey Ave.
Delaware Ave.

Maryland Ave.
Virginia ave.
Pennsylvania Ave.
Adriatic Ave.
New York Ave.
Kentucky Ave.
Ohio Ave.
Michigan Ave.
Arkansas Ave.
Missouri Ave.
Mississippi Ave.
Georgia Ave.
Florida Ave.
Arizona Ave.   Texas Ave.
California Ave.
Iowa Ave.
Brighton Ave.
Morris Ave.
Chelsea Ave.
Montpelier Ave.
Sovereign Ave.
Boston Ave.
Providence Ave.
Hartford Ave.

N. Carolina Ave.
S. Carolina Ave.
Dr. Martin Luther King Jr. Blvd.

Atlantic Ave.
Pacific Ave.

Sen. Farley St. Marina

Atlantic City Municipal Airport (Bader Field)

Atlantic City Expressway

Thorofare

Beach

Trenton Ave.   Trenton Ave.
Roosevelt Ave.
Harrisburg Ave.   Harrisburg Ave.
Elberon Ave.   Dover Ave.
Annapolis Ave.   Annapolis Ave.
Richmond Ave.   Richmond Ave.
Raleigh Ave.   Raleigh Ave.
Delancy Pl.
Bartram Pl.
Kingston Ave.
Tallahassee Ave.
Montgomery Ave.
Jackson Ave.

Absecon Lighthouse
Art Center
Garden Pier
Steel Pier
Central Pier
Steeplechase Pier
Ocean Mall
Convention Center

Boardwalk

Atlantic Ocean

NEW JERSEY
Trenton
Atlantic City

Bally's Grand Hotel/Casino **1**
Bally's Park Place Casino Hotel and Tower **5**
Caesars Atlantic City Hotel/Casino **4**
Claridge Casino/Hotel **6**
Harrah's Marina Hotel Casino **12**
Merv Griffin's Resorts Casino Hotel **8**
Sands Hotel/Casino and Country Club **7**
Showboat Hotel and Casino **10**
TropWorld Casino and Entertainment Resort **2**
Trump Castle Casino Resort by the Bay **11**
Trump Plaza Hotel and Casino **3**
Trump Taj Mahal Casino Resort **9**

Rib Room, for fine beef; Primavera, for the specialties of northern and southern Italy; Hyakumi Japanese, featuring 7-course teppanyaki meals; and the Imperial Steakhouse for classically American steaks and seafood. More moderate meals throughout the day are on tap at the Boardwalk Café, which serves an all-day buffet; Café Roma; Ambrosia, a garden-style café; and Italian Festival, for light Italian dishes and antipasto bar.

Facilities: Two swimming pools, health spa, amusement arcade, beach club with canopied cabanas, volleyball courts, rooftop tennis and paddleball, free use of bicycles, and valet and self-parking for over 1,000 cars. Also, the ship-shaped Ocean One shopping and restaurant complex is at the Boardwalk doorstep of Caesar's.

CLARIDGE CASINO/HOTEL, Boardwalk and Park Place, Atlantic City, NJ 08401. Tel. 609/340-3400 or toll-free 800/257-8585). Fax 609/340-3867. 504 rms. A/C TV TEL
$ Rates: $80–$145 weekday; $115–$165 weekend. AE, CB, DC, MC, V. **Parking:** Free.
Set back slightly from the Boardwalk, this 24-story establishment is an expanded version of an earlier hotel built in 1930. The current appearance retains much of the original character, with a decor dominated by dark woods, rich reds, and crystal chandeliers. The hotel overlooks the gardens of Park Place while still enjoying unobstructed ocean views. Rooms are decorated with designer draperies and spreads, and sleek new furniture.

Dining/Entertainment: The finest restaurant is Martino's, which offers Italian specialties and homemade pastas in a gracious setting. In addition, there is the Twenties Supper Club for mesquite-grilled food; the Garden Room for 24-hour service; the Stadium Deli; Wally's, a coffee shop open for lunch and dinner; and the Great American Buffet, offering regional specialties from 11am to 11pm at moderate prices. At night, the Palace Theatre stages productions of hit Broadway shows, and the Claridge Comedy Club features new stars of humor.

Facilities: Indoor swimming pool, sun deck, health club, men's and women's spas, hair salon, and free valet parking for 831 cars.

HARRAH'S MARINA HOTEL/CASINO, 1725 Brigantine Blvd., Atlantic City, NJ 08401. Tel. 609/441-5000 or toll-free 800/2-HARRAH. Fax 609/344-7940. 760 rms. A/C TV TEL
$ Rates: $90–$150 single or double. AE, CB, DC, MC, V. **Parking:** Free.
Situated on a 14-acre site, this hotel has a 15-story and 16-story tower. Most guest rooms have bay views, and all have contemporary furnishings. A unique collection of antique slot machines and antique cars are on display in the hotel. For a change of pace, you can also board a jitney and travel over to the Boardwalk at any time of the day or night.

Dining/Entertainment: Top dinner spots include the Meadows, a gourmet French restaurant overlooking the harbor; Andreotti's, for northern Italian specialties; the Bay Wok, for Chinese cuisine; and the Steak House. More moderate meals are available at Reflections coffee shop, The Buffet (lunch, dinner, and Sunday brunch), the Deli, and the Food Bazaar for light snacks all day. In the evening, Harrah's offers the Broadway-by-the-Bay Theatre, featuring top stars and revues such as *Ziegfeld, A Night at the Follies*.

Facilities: Enclosed swimming pool, boardwalk along the bay, beauty salon, exercise room, deck tennis, and shuffleboard. For teens, there is a fun center arcade, and, for children 2 to 8, a supervised nursery. This is also the only United States gaming resort with a 107-ship marina (docking facilities are priced from $20 to $50 a day).

MERV GRIFFIN'S RESORTS CASINO HOTEL, Boardwalk at North Carolina Avenue, Atlantic City, NJ 08401. Tel. 609/344-6000 or toll-free GET-RICH. Fax 609/340-6284. 686 rms. A/C TV TEL
$ Rates: $120–$200 double. AE, CB, DC, MC, V. **Parking:** Free.
This 15-story property incorporates the facade of the former Chalfonte-Haddon Hall,

a Victorian hotel. Located at the north end of the Boardwalk by the old Steeplechase Pier, the hotel's rooms feature a modern decor and most have expansive views of the ocean or Boardwalk.

Dining/Entertainment: The top spots open for dinner only are Le Palais, for French haute and nouvelle cuisine; Camelot, which serves English specialties in a setting like a medieval baronial manor; and Capriccio, a gourmet enclave for northern Italian fare. For lunch and dinner, there is the House of Kyoto, an authentic Japanese eatery featuring everything from tempura to teriyaki. More moderate meals can be enjoyed throughout the day at the Café Casino, the Oyster Bar, the Celebrity Deli, and at a coffee shop and ice-cream parlor. In the evening, the Superstar Theater presents top stars or Las Vegas–style revues.

Facilities: Swimming pool, health club, separate men's and women's spas and saunas, whirlpools, squash courts, video arcade.

SANDS HOTEL/CASINO AND COUNTRY CLUB, Indiana Ave. and Brighton Park, Atlantic City, NJ 08401. Tel. 609/441-4000 or toll-free 800/257-8580. Fax 609/441-4457. 501 rms. A/C TV TEL
$ Rates: $110–$155 Apr–Oct; $99–$120 Nov–Mar. AE, CB, DC, MC, V.
Parking: Free.
Known as the Brighton when it originally opened in 1980, this 21-story property is decorated in one of four motifs—traditional, modern, French traditional, and Italian contemporary.

Dining/Entertainment: Mes Amis serves French haute cuisine. Moderate meals are offered at Rossi's Italian Buffet; and for lunch and dinner, try the Brighton Steak House, known not only for beef but also for its Turkish and Weight Watchers specials and Chinese dishes. A food court comprises a dozen fast-food eateries from Boston Pizza, Nathan's Famous (hot dogs), and Pat's Steaks to Bookbinder's Seafood and David's Cookies. Paradise Café is a coffee shop open 24 hours a day. In the evening, you can see top-name entertainment (from Rodney Dangerfield to Raquel Welch) at the Sands' Copa Room, an 850-seat theater.

Facilities: Indoor/outdoor swimming pool, tennis, racquetball, health club, boutiques, and valet parking for 450 cars. Registered guests also enjoy the use of the 18-hole championship golf course at the Sands Country Club in Somers Point.

SHOWBOAT HOTEL AND CASINO, 801 Boardwalk at Delaware Ave., Atlantic City, NJ 08401. Tel. 609/343-4000 or toll-free 800/621-0200). Fax 609/343-4532. 516 rms. A/C TV TEL
$ Rates: $125–$160 July–mid-Sept; $105–$130 off-season. AE, CB, DC, MC, V.
Parking: Free.
The northernmost property on the oceanfront strip, this 25-story hotel was launched in April of 1987. With a striking facade—shaped like a cruise ship—the hotel features a Victorian riverboat interior. Guest rooms have contemporary furnishings and most overlook the ocean.

Dining/Entertainment: Mr. Kelley's is an expensive American gourmet spot; other fine dining includes the Mississippi Steak and Seafood Co. for steak and seafood; Casa di Napoli for Italian cuisine; and the Emperor's Inn for Chinese dishes. For all-day dining in a more moderate range, there is a deli, pizzeria, snack bar, buffet room, coffee shop, and an ice-cream parlor. The Mardi Gras Lounge showcases top stars and revue-style entertainment.

Facilities: Outdoor swimming pool, sun deck, two whirlpools, family/youth-care center, video game center, and a huge state-of-the-art 60-lane bowling alley, open from 10am to midnight.

TROPWORLD CASINO AND ENTERTAINMENT RESORT, Brighton Ave. and Boardwalk, Atlantic City, NJ 08401. Tel. 609/340-4000 or toll-free 800/THE-TROP. Fax 609/340-4016. 714 rms, 300 suites. A/C TV TEL
$ Rates: $125–$175 rooms; $187.50–$250 suites. AE, CB, DC, MC, V. **Parking:** Free.
This huge multi-towered mega-facility is almost like a city unto itself, with its own indoor theme park as well as a 90,000-square-foot casino. Guest rooms feature all the

modern amenities with a variety of themes and furnishings, ranging from French and Italian to contemporary and art-deco designs. Suites range from apartmentlike, multi-room configurations to bilevel layouts. Approximately 200 units have a private whirlpool.

Dining/Entertainment: Among the 17 restaurants and lounges are Phoenix, for classic American cuisine; Il Verdi, a gourmet Italian dining room in an art-deco setting; Jade Beach, for Chinese cuisine; the Regent Court, serving prime steaks in a country-manor atmosphere; and Pier 7, primarily for seafood; A. C. Station, a fine dining room with a train station theme. In addition, the Carousel Coffee Shop features a mosaic tile mural of carousel horses and a light menu; Zim's Deli offers New York–style sandwiches; and the Miss American Food Court is a 70-seat fast-food emporium. Entertainment includes a show room, two lounges, a comedy club, and an indoor entertainment theme park, Tivoli Pier.

Facilities: Health club, tanning room, massage area, steam room, exercise room, two rooftop tennis courts, indoor and outdoor rooftop swimming pools, sun deck, jogging track, saunas, parking for 2,700 cars, and two shopping arcades.

TRUMP CASTLE CASINO RESORT BY THE BAY, Huron Avenue and Brigantine Blvd., Atlantic City, NJ 08401. Tel. 609/441-2000 or toll-free 800/441-5551. Fax 609/345-2021. 703 rms, 246 suites. A/C MINIBAR TV TEL
$ Rates: $95–$175 double; $200–$1,000 suites. AE, CB, DC, MC, V. **Parking:** Free.

This hotel sits on 14 acres and overlooks the bay's marina, providing an idyllic setting. Opened in 1985, it contains a 26-story main wing and a new $100-million addition, the Crystal Tower. All guest rooms offer panoramic views of the city skyline, the shoreline, or the marina; are decorated in an art-deco theme, with shades of brown, black, beige, or green; and have blond wood furnishings, brassy fixtures, and marble vanities.

Dining/Entertainment: The top dinner restaurant is Delfino's, for continental cuisine in Mediterranean villa style. The newest restaurant, overlooking the marina, is Harbor View, featuring gourmet seafood. For lunch and dinner, there is Portofino, serving Italian and American fare, and the Castle Steakhouse, a first-rate beef eatery in the upper price range; and the Food Fantasy Buffet for moderate meals. All-day dining is available at the Broadway Deli, the Coffee Shop, and the Ice Cream Parlor. The Crystal Ballroom presents top-name entertainment and sports stars, and the King's Court Showroom features variety shows, television show tapings, and dance bands.

Facilities: Health spa, swimming pool, five tennis courts, jogging track, pro shop, and shuffleboard courts.

TRUMP PLAZA HOTEL AND CASINO, Boardwalk and Mississippi Ave., Atlantic City, NJ 08401. Tel. 609/441-6000 or toll-free 800/677-7378. Fax 609/441-6249. 614 rms. A/C TV TEL
$ Rates: $175–$195 double; June–Aug; $110–$175 off-season. AE, CB, DC, MC, V. **Parking:** Free.

Adjoining the Convention Center, in the middle of the strip, is this 39-story tower with an adjacent 10-story transportation center called Central Park. The latter offers 2,700 parking spaces and 13 bus lanes, plus an assortment of boutiques and restaurants. The hotel's guest rooms all have ocean views.

Dining/Entertainment: Ivana's is the premier spot, offering east coast continental cuisine amid plush velvet furnishings, piano music, and orchids. Other upper-bracket dinner choices are Max's, for prime beef in a mahogany-and-marble setting; Roberto's, for Italian fare; Fortunes, for Oriental dishes; and the New Yorker, open 24 hours a day. More moderate prices can be found at the Broadway Buffet, Harvey's Deli, and Café 21. In addition, a 750-seat theater presents top-name entertainment.

Services: Nanny service.

Facilities: Two tennis courts, indoor swimming pool, health spa, beauty salon, and video arcade.

TRUMP TAJ MAHAL CASINO RESORT, 1000 Boardwalk at Virginia Ave., Atlantic City, NJ 08401. Tel. 609/449-1000 or toll-free 800/TAJ-TRUMP. Fax 609/449-6818. 1,013 rms and 237 suites. A/C TV TEL
$ Rates: $125–$175, double, June–Aug; $125–$150; off-season; $275–$400 suite. AE, CB, DC, MC, V. **Parking:** Free.

Touted as the largest casino hotel in the United States, this 42-story property stands out on its own 17-acre site along the boardwalk, and is presently the tallest building in New Jersey. The architecture owes its inspiration to a maharajah's palace, with 70 colorful minarets and onion-shaped domes, extending out into the ocean on the Steel Pier. In a similar vein, the decor of the public areas includes glittering chandeliers and bright neon colors, while the guest rooms are a bit more restful, decorated in muted colors, but with every modern amenity.

Dining/Entertainment: Top restaurants include the Scheherazade, the only Baccarat pit in the world where guests can dine overlooking the area where they play, for international cuisine; Dynasty, featuring a variety of dishes from the Far East; Sinbad's, a seafood restaurant with an open kitchen; Marco Polo, for upscale Italian fare; Safari Steak House, for fine beef amid a jungle theme; Sultan's Feast, an ocean-view buffet; Gobi Desert, a gourmet ice-cream parlor; New Delhi Deli, a high-tech place for sandwiches and fast food; and Rock and Rolls, an informal café with the music, menu, and decor of the 1950s. Shows and concerts are presented nightly at the 5,500-seat Mark G. Etess Arena, the Grand Ballroom, and the Casbah Nightclub.

Facilities: Health club, spa, four tennis courts, promenade deck, video arcade, and parking for over 5,000 cars.

NONCASINO ACCOMMODATIONS

Besides the casino hotels, Atlantic City has recently welcomed an array of new hotels and motor inns, located both in the city and on the many access roads. Usually providing shuttle transport to the casinos, these properties can offer more moderate rates and packages, and generally have ample free parking.

NEAR THE BOARDWALK & ENVIRONS
Moderate

MADISON HOUSE HOTEL, 123 S. Illinois Ave., P.O. Box 179, Atlantic City, NJ 08404. Tel. 609/345-1400 or toll-free 800/4-LUXURY. Fax 609/347-7265. 215 rms. A/C TV TEL
$ Rates: $65–$95 July–Aug; $30–$58 Sept–Jun. AE, CB, DC, MC, V. **Parking:** Free.

Old-world charm prevails at this 12-story hotel with a Georgian-style facade that dates back to the 1920s. Located a half-block from the Boardwalk and opposite the Sands Hotel, this property was completely restored and refurbished in 1986. The rooms, of varying sizes, are outfitted with reproduction furniture, floral fabrics, and light pastel tones.

Dining/Entertainment: Facilities include a restaurant and lounge.

QUALITY INN, South Carolina and Pacific Ave., Atlantic City, NJ 08401. Tel. 609/345-7070 or toll-free 800/228-5151. Fax 609/345-0633. 203 rms. A/C TV TEL
$ Rates: $72–$118 single or double, July–early Sept; $50–$110 single or double, off-season. AE, CB, DC, MC, V. **Parking:** Free.

This 16-story lodging, opened in July 1986, is located near the north end of the Boardwalk, two blocks from the casinos of Merv Griffin's Resorts, the Taj Mahal, and the Showboat, and four blocks from the Sands. Erected on the site of the historic Quaker Friends School and Meeting House, the hotel has preserved much of the original 1927 structure and masterfully incorporated it into the ground-floor public rooms, the multi-level Friends Restaurant, and the cozy Assembly Lounge.

The spacious guest rooms offer sweeping views of the ocean and the bay; furnishings are modern, featuring light woods and soft color schemes, with framed sea-scene prints on the walls.

NEARBY ACCOMMODATIONS

Moderate

COMFORT INN, 405 E. Absecon Blvd. (Rte. 30), Absecon, NJ 08201. Tel. 609/646-5000 or toll-free 800/228-5150. Fax 609/383-8744. 200 rms. A/C TV TEL
$ Rates: $69–$115 single or double, July–early Sept; $37–$115 single or double, off-season. AE, CB, DC, MC, V. **Parking:** Free.

⑤ Three miles from the Boardwalk, in an ideal setting overlooking the Atlantic City skyline on Absecon Bay, this five- and six-story hotel offers contemporary-style guest rooms, furnished in pastel tones and blond wood. Nonsmoking units are available. Amenities include free parking, a shuttle service to the casinos, an outdoor swimming pool, and an all-day coffee shop.

In addition, there is a three-story, 200-room Comfort Inn, Black Horse Pike (Rte. 40) at Dover Place, West Atlantic City, NJ 80232 (tel. 609/645-1818 or toll-free 800/228-5150). Located 3 miles west of the city, it overlooks Lakes Bay. Facilities are similar and the rates are comparable, with doubles from $75 to $125 in the summer and $39 to $105 at other times.

HOWARD JOHNSON, 539 Absecon Blvd., Absecon, NJ 08201. Tel. 609/641-7272 or toll-free 800/654-2677. Fax 609/646-3286. 208 rms. A/C TV TEL
$ Rates: $59–$175 double. AE, CB, DC, MC, V. **Parking:** Free.
This is a modern seven-story tower, and many of the rooms have views of Absecon Bay. Guest amenities include a free shuttle service to the casinos, free parking, and a sun deck. There is also an all-day garden-style restaurant and lounge with picturesque views of the bay and Atlantic City skyline.

BEST WESTERN WHITTIER INN, Black Horse Pike, Pleasantville, NJ 08232. Tel. 609/484-1500 or toll-free 800/528-1234. Fax 609/645-9657. 195 rms. A/C TV TEL
$ Rates (including continental breakfast): $65–$115 single or double, mid-June–mid-Sept; $55–$85 off-season. AE, CB, DC, MC, V. **Parking:** Free.
This inn is located in a quiet wooded setting near the Garden State Parkway (exit 37). The four-story Georgian-style lodging offers rooms decorated with pastel colors and furnishings reflecting a Queen Anne motif. Nonsmoking rooms are available. Amenities include a free shuttle bus, an all-day coffee shop/snackbar, guest laundry facilities, exercise room, and an outdoor swimming pool.

4. ATLANTIC CITY DINING

CASINO AREA

EXPENSIVE

CULMONE'S, 2437 Atlantic Ave. Tel. 348-5170.
Cuisine: INTERNATIONAL. **Reservations:** Recommended.
$ Prices: Appetizers $2.50–$9.50; main courses $15–$25. AE, CB, DC, MC, V.
Open: Dinner Mon, Wed–Thurs 5–11pm, Fri–Sun 4–11pm.

Established in 1964, this elegant old-world-style restaurant blends Italian, French, and American cuisines with flair. The entrées include chicken cacciatore, coquilles St-Jacques, sole Veronique, lobster tails, crab au gratin, rack of lamb, veal Oscar, and a unique surf-n-turf à la Giovanni (veal francese and shrimp scampi). The tuxedo-clad waiters are particularly attentive and helpful. It is open for dinner only.

DOCK'S OYSTER HOUSE, 2405 Atlantic Ave. Tel. 345-0092.

Cuisine: SEAFOOD. **Reservations:** Recommended.

$ Prices: Appetizers $2.95–$6.95; main courses $15–$21; up to $30 for lobster. AE, DC, MC, V.

Open: Tues–Sun 5–10pm. **Closed:** Dec–mid-Feb.

This is the oldest continuously operating seafood restaurant in Atlantic City, owned and operated by the Dougherty family since 1897. Dock's is a showcase of dark woods, etched and colored glass, brass chandeliers, and seafaring symbols such as lobster tanks. Entrée selections include crab imperial in puff pastry, shrimp scampi, scallops sauté, fried oysters, and lobster tails. Charbroiled steaks are also a specialty, and all baking is done on the premises. Main courses come with a selection of breads and pepper hash.

KNIFE AND FORK INN, Atlantic and Pacific Ave. Tel. 344-1133.

Cuisine: SEAFOOD/STEAKS. **Reservations:** Accepted for parties of 4 or more only.

$ Prices: Appetizers $3.75–$11.75; main courses $15–$25; lobster $21–$40. AE, DC, MC, V.

Open: Dinner Mon–Thurs 6–10:30pm, Fri–Sat 6–11pm.

At the southern end of the city, this landmark restaurant was built in 1912 and has been run by the Latz family since 1927. The establishment has a striking Tudor facade with a copper roof and an interior with a clubby and nautical style. The decor includes fish nets, duck decoys, and fish mobiles, as well as a vintage fireplace and lots of lush plants. The menu, known for its outstanding seafood, offers such choices as lobster tails and up to 4-pound lobsters, shore platters, bouillabaisse, whole baby flounder, swordfish, and soft shell crabs in season. Meat entrées include prime steaks and five-ribbed lamb chops. Even if you're a first-time visitor, don't be surprised if owner Mack Latz comes over to your table to check on how you like the food. Jackets are required for men.

MODERATE

ANGELONI'S II, 2400 Arctic Ave. Tel. 344-7875.

Cuisine: ITALIAN. **Reservations:** Recommended.

$ Prices: Appetizers $2.95–$10.95; main courses $10.95–$24.95. AE, CB, DC, MC, V.

Open: Dinner Mon–Sat 5pm–midnight, Sun 4pm–midnight.

An extensive wine list (more than 85 vintages) is the pride of this restaurant. The decor is dominated by a winery theme, with wine racks and cabinets, stone walls, and alcoves. The dinner menu offers pastas such as spinach ravioli, linguine, and lasagna; main courses range from veal sorrentino (with eggplant, ham, and mozzarella in red sauce), chicken francese, charbroiled steaks, pork chops pizzaiola, surf-n-turf, steak-and-tail, zuppa di pesce, and seafood Angeloni (mussels, shrimp, clams, and scallops over linguine).

AUBREY'S, 2024 Pacific Ave. Tel. 344-1632.

Cuisine: AMERICAN. **Reservations:** Recommended.

$ Prices: Appetizers $3.25–$5.75; main courses $9.95–$24.95; light fare $4.95–$7.95. AE, D, MC, V.

Open: Dinner daily 3pm–midnight, light snacks midnight to 6am.

This modern glass-enclosed bistro offers a patio garden setting and a menu of light dishes, as well as traditional American entrées at dinnertime. If you are not too hungry, you can choose croissantwiches, burgers, salads, omelets, quiches, and other light fare. Regular entrées include steaks, southern fried chicken, lobster tails, poached salmon, and stuffed flounder.

MAMA MOTT'S, 151 S. New York Ave. Tel. 345-8218.
   Cuisine: ITALIAN. **Reservations:** Recommended.
$ **Prices:** Appetizers $2.50–$8.50; main courses $11.95–$22.95. AE, DC, MC, V.
   Open: Dinner daily 4–11pm.
This popular restaurant has been a fixture for almost 20 years, in an area that is slowly feeling the prosperous effects of the nearby Boardwalk development. The small family-run dining room has a Victorian aura, with period furniture and floral wallpaper. The pasta courses include white or green ravioli; cheese or potato gnocchi; and manicotti stuffiti. Specialties are veal saltimbocca; steak pizzaiola; chicken florentine; flounder marinara; zuppa di pesce; lobster fra diavolo; and scampi cacciatore.

SCANNICCHIO'S, 119 S. California Ave. Tel. 348-6378.
   Cuisine: ITALIAN. **Reservations:** Recommended.
$ **Prices:** Appetizers $2.95–$7.95; main courses $11.95–$25.95. AE, DC, MC, V.
   Open: Dinner daily 5pm–midnight.
A wall mural map of Italy dominates the decor at this restaurant just half a block from the Boardwalk. This small and newly renovated establishment offers a varied menu of Italian specialties, including a wide range of pasta, such as cheese ravioli, ziti with asparagus, fettuccine, and gnocchi. Entrées include stuffed calamari, shrimp parmigiana, flounder florentine, lobster francese, chicken with sausage and peppers, steaks, and at least nine veal choices.

BUDGET

DELEGATE CAFE, 2301 Boardwalk. Tel. 348-7052.
   Cuisine: INTERNATIONAL. **Reservations:** Not required.
$ **Prices:** Lunch items $3.95–$6.95. No credit cards.
   Open: Lunch Mon–Sat 8:30am–4:30pm.
Located in the Convention Center, this café is an ideal place for light meals. Continental breakfast and lunch are served, with emphasis on bake-shop items and deli-style sandwiches, as well as salads, quiches, soups, and diet platters.

THE IRISH PUB, 164 St. James Place and the Boardwalk. Tel. 345-9613.
   Cuisine: AMERICAN. **Reservations:** Not required.
$ **Prices:** Appetizers $.95–$2.95; main courses $3.95–$6.95; lunch $1.95–$3.95. No credit cards.
   Open: Lunch Mon–Fri 11:30am–3pm; dinner Mon–Fri 3–11pm, Sat–Sun 11am–midnight.
   You don't have to be Irish to enjoy this special Atlantic City landmark. The decor reflects a turn-of-the-century atmosphere with stained-glass windows, bentwood chairs, mounted newspaper front pages, framed old posters, and business cards from previous patrons tacked up at every turn. There is even a Jack Dempsey Corner, filled with sporting memorabilia, and an old jukebox that most often plays "Danny Boy." Lunch items include hearty sandwiches, burgers, and salads. You can also have dinner here—Dublin beef stew, corned beef and cabbage, New England flounder, crab cakes, honey-dipped chicken, chili, and sandwiches. The jitney stops half a block away.

WHITE HOUSE SUB SHOP, 2301 Arctic Ave. Tel. 345-8599.
   Cuisine: AMERICAN. **Reservations:** Not required.
$ **Prices:** Sandwiches $2–$6. No credit cards.
   Open: Daily 10am–midnight.
Since 1946, visitors and locals alike have flocked here to try one of the famous Atlantic

City submarine-shaped overstuffed sandwiches. This busy restaurant claims to have sold over 15 million of its gigantic specialties in the past four decades, and, when you try one, you'll know why. Besides subs stuffed with everything from meatballs and ham cappacolla to provolone and salad, you can also order cheese steaks and burgers.

NEARBY DINING

The out-of-town choices all offer ample free parking (and are well worth the trip).

EXPENSIVE

RAM'S HEAD INN, 9 W. White Horse Pike, Absecon. Tel. 652-1700.
   Cuisine: INTERNATIONAL. **Reservations:** Required.
$ Prices: Appetizers $2.50–$8.50; main courses $14.95–$24.95; lobster $34–$38; lunch $6.95–$13.95. AE, CB, DC, MC, V.
   Open: Lunch Mon–Fri noon–3pm; dinner Mon–Fri 5–9:30pm, Sat 5–10pm, Sun 3:30–9:30pm.

A favorite with the stars who perform on the Atlantic City stages is this Colonial-style restaurant located in a grassy setting. The choice of dining areas ranges from a cozy early-American room with a piano accompanist to a skylit garden-style conservatory and an outdoor brick courtyard. The decor includes a gallery of original paintings by modern American artists, many of which are for sale.

Lunch items include salads, omelets, quiches, and light entrées such as boned breast of capon or seafood crêpes. Dinner focuses on seafood and traditional dishes such as crab imperial in pastry crust, lobster tails, chicken pot pie, crisp roasted duckling, stuffed pork loin, prime ribs, beef Wellington, and rack of lamb.

RESTAURANT ATOP THE WINERY, Renault Winery, 72 N. Bremen Ave., Egg Harbor City. Tel. 609/965-2111.
   Cuisine: INTERNATIONAL. **Reservations:** Required.
$ Prices: Appetizers included; main courses $23.95–$29.95. AE, MC, V.
   Open: Dinner Fri–Sat 5–9:30pm, Sun 4–7:30pm.

Located on the grounds of a 120-year-old working winery, this gourmet enclave is open only for dinner (although there's also a wine garden grill and bake shop open for lunch Monday to Saturday 11:30am to 3pm). You enter through a pathway enclosed by three century-old Redwood wine casks, via thick oak doors and beveled-glass-paneled windows, into the dining area, or Methode Champenoise Room, where champagne was once made. Much of the original room has been restored, including 100-year-old oaken casks that have been fashioned into seating booths.

Meals are composed of six courses, with a choice of five entrées that change weekly. On our most recent trip, the choices were Dover sole stuffed with king crab and Havarti cheese; lobster tail in pastry with orange butter and Grand Marnier sauce; sautéed veal topped with a mixture of spinach, tomato, and red onion; chicken stuffed with spinach, mushrooms, artichokes, and feta cheese; and prime rib of beef. The price of dinner includes red and white wine tastings plus a sampling of the winery's signature product, blueberry champagne. You can also order a full bottle of the wine of your choice to sip throughout the meal.

SMITHVILLE INN, Rte. 9, Smithville. Tel. 652-7777.
   Cuisine: AMERICAN. **Reservations:** Recommended.
$ Prices: Appetizers $3.95–$8.95; main courses $11.95–$22.95; lunch $5.95–$10.95. AE, CB, DC, MC, V.
   Open: Lunch Mon–Sat noon–3pm, dinner 4–9pm; Sun brunch 10am–2pm, dinner 2–9pm.

A Colonial theme prevails at this inn, in a reconstructed inland village. Established in 1787, and named for first owner John Smith, this much-expanded restaurant now has eight rooms, with all the trappings of early Americana, and a menu featuring authentic South Jersey cuisine. Lunch items include chicken shortcake, crab quiche, and salads. The dinner entrée selections usually comprise oyster pie, chicken pot pie,

Absecon duckling, coconut shrimp, stuffed pork chops, rack of lamb, and surf-n-turf. All main courses come with a crudite tray, traditional popovers and breads, preserves, and relishes.

5. ATLANTIC CITY ATTRACTIONS

Although the gambling casinos, high-rise resorts, star-studded shows, and white sandy beaches would probably be enough to make Atlantic City the nation's number-one destination, this ever-growing city has other notable attractions, not the least of which is the famous Boardwalk.

THE TOP ATTRACTIONS

Built in 1870 as an 8-foot-wide line of planks on the sand, the **Atlantic City Boardwalk** was the world's first oceanside walkway of its kind, built to allow vacationers to enjoy a stroll by the sea without tracking sand into the grand hotels. Today it is a much-expanded (now 60 feet wide) structure, built of herringbone-pattern wood, raised well above the sand and supported by steel and concrete. It is now the doorway to major casinos, hotels, amusements, shops, and snackeries. Take a stroll, breathe the sea air, and listen to the voices from all over the world. We think you'll agree that it is truly the benchmark of all boardwalks.

If you prefer to see the sights on wheels, you can be pushed around via a "rolling chair," this city's unique form of transport, which dates back to 1887.

For many years, the Boardwalk was also synonymous with a series of piers, jutting out into the ocean and lined by amusements, games, rides, and shops. Although most of the original piers have disappeared in recent years, you can still visit the **Garden Pier,** on the northern end of the Boardwalk at New Jersey Avenue. Today it is the home of the **Atlantic City Art Center,** which features new exhibitions each month. The former **Million Dollar Pier,** at Arkansas Avenue, is now a ship-shaped shopping mall called Ocean One.

Two blocks south of Ocean One is the **Convention Center,** 2301 Boardwalk (tel. 348-7000), home of the Miss America Pageant. Built in 1929, this recently restored building is also a meeting place for many businesses and conventions each year, and the venue for auto races, boat and flower shows, boxing matches, and other sports. In addition, the world's largest pipe organ is housed here.

THE CASINOS

Although the main Atlantic City **casino strip** covers about 3 miles of the total boardwalk distance, the complete structure stretches for 5 miles along the ocean and takes in the neighboring community of Ventnor. The best way to enjoy the sights, sounds, and smells of this oceanfront path is to walk, meandering at your leisure, dropping into a casino or two, shopping along the way, and perhaps sampling the saltwater taffy and other temptations.

Whether your favorite game is blackjack, big six, or baccarat, you'll find plenty of opportunities to play in Atlantic City. There are also ample tables for craps and roulette, not to mention almost 20,000 slot machines of all shapes, varieties, and payouts.

Each casino has pamphlets or booklets to acquaint you with the rules of the game. Be sure to ask for a copy when you arrive and study it before you try your luck at the tables.

Atlantic City's casinos are open from 10am to 4am on weekdays and from 10am to 6am on weekends and legal holidays. The legal age for entrance into a casino is 21. During daylight hours, attire should be casual and tasteful, but no shorts or T-shirts are allowed at any time. After 6pm, men are requested to wear jackets and women are expected to dress accordingly.

MORE ATTRACTIONS

TIVOLI PIER, TropWorld Casino and Entertainment Resort, Iowa Ave. and Boardwalk, Atlantic City. Tel. 340-4020.

A huge two-acre indoor family amusement area, designed to convey the atmosphere of the city's Boardwalk piers at the turn of the century, with an assortment of rides, including a four-story-high, neon-lit Ferris wheel, bumper cars, and rolling chairs, plus carnival-style games, a fun house, and musical shows.

Admission: $9.95 for unlimited access to all attractions and show; or $5 for general admission and show, plus $1.25 for each ride or attraction.

Open: June–Sept daily noon–8pm; Oct–May Sat–Sun noon–8pm.

LUCY, THE MARGATE ELEPHANT, 9200 Atlantic Ave., Margate. Tel. 823-6473.

This giant elephant-shaped building, located about 3 miles south of Atlantic City, is one of the most famous sights along the beach. Originally built of wood and tin in 1881, it has been used over the years to house a bazaar, a tavern, and as a gimmick by a real-estate developer to draw prospective buyers. Now fully restored, Lucy is a National Historic Landmark. Guided tours of the elephant allow visitors to walk inside and see various exhibits illustrating the giant animal's history.

Admission: $2 adults, $1 children 6 to 12.

Open: July–Labor Day daily 10am–8:30pm; Apr–June, Sept–Oct Sat–Sun 10am–4:30pm.

HARRAH'S BELLE BOAT SIGHTSEEING, Harrah's Marina, 1725 Brigantine Blvd. Tel. 441-5315.

This marina offers 1-hour sightseeing cruises of the Atlantic City coastline.

Admission: $5 per person. $3 for children under 6.

Open: Daily 11am–7pm, with departures every 90 minutes.

NEARBY ATTRACTIONS

HISTORIC TOWNE OF SMITHVILLE, Old New York Rd., Rte. 9, Smithville. Tel. 652-1756.

You can step back in time by visiting this reconstructed 1800s village, 12 miles north of Atlantic City. There are more than 30 specialty shops, cobblestone paths, a lake, and various Colonial buildings, including a gristmill and smokehouse. You'll probably be tempted by the craft shops and various restaurants.

Admission: Free.

Open: Summer daily 11am–9pm; fall–spring daily 9am–6pm.

BATSO VILLAGE, Rte. 542, Hammonton. Tel. 561-3262.

America's heritage thrives at Batso Village, in a remote part of the nearby Pine Barrens. Once the site of the Batso Furnace and Iron Works, this restored Colonial settlement dates back to 1766 and was the principal source of cannons and cannonballs during the Revolutionary War. It was also the home of the first American glass factory (1846), which produced flat glass for windowpanes and gas lamps.

Today you can tour the original furnace site as well as the ironmaster's mansion, gristmill, sawmill, and glassworks. Stroll around and watch craftspeople demonstrating early occupations, such as chair caning, potting, weaving, and basket-making. During the summer months, you can also traverse the grounds via stagecoach ($1 per person). From Memorial Day through Labor Day, there is a $5 parking fee.

Admission: Free admission to grounds; guided tours $2 adults, $1 children aged 6 to 11.

Open: Memorial Day–Labor Day 10am–4pm; off-season 11am–5pm.

RENAULT WINERY, 72 N. Bremen Ave., Egg Harbor City. Tel. 965-2111.

A landmark of another sort is this winery founded in 1864 by Louis Renault, from Reims, France. Now in the hands of the Joseph P. Milza family, the 1,400-acre vineyard has enjoyed more than 120 years of uninterrupted grape-growing, and has blossomed into a leading winery with its own gourmet restaurant (see "Where to Dine," above). Visitors are welcome to tour the facilities, including a look at the old and new methods of making wines and champagne. You'll also see a unique glass museum that houses antique champagne and wineglasses dating back to the 13th century. The tour concludes with tastings of award-winning Renault wines, which are red, white, and blue (a blueberry champagne).

Admission: $1 per person.

Open: Mon–Sat 10am–5pm, Sun noon–5pm.

Directions: From Atlantic City, take Rte. 30 west 16 miles to Bremen Avenue; turn right and follow signs for 2¼ miles to winery.

6. ATLANTIC CITY SPECIAL/ FREE EVENTS

"There she is! Miss America!" If you have heard that tune over the years and wished that someday you could see the Miss America Pageant for yourself, why not plan a visit to Atlantic City for the week after Labor Day? Started in 1921, and held without interruption since 1935, this glamorous annual event includes a host of varied activities, such as a Boardwalk parade, as well as the televised competitions, finals, and crowning of the new Miss America. Ticket prices range from $4 to $25 for most events. For ticket information and a full program, contact the Miss America Pageant, P.O. Box 119, Atlantic City, NJ 08404 (tel. 609/344-5278).

Other leading events include the **N.J. Fresh Seafood Festival** (June); **National Boardwalk Professional Art Show** (June); **Harvest Festival at Renault Winery of Egg Harbor** (September); and the **Annual Boardwalk Indian Summer Art Show** (September). For more information, contact the Greater Atlantic City Convention and Visitors Bureau.

7. ATLANTIC CITY SPORTS & RECREATION

With its location between the ocean and the bay, Atlantic City is ideal for swimming and water sports. All of the large casino hotels have indoor and outdoor swimming pools, sun decks, health centers, fitness tracks, tennis courts, and other sports facilities. The smaller inns and motor hotels usually also have outdoor swimming pools. Best of all, the 3-mile-long Atlantic City beach is free and open to everyone.

The Boardwalk is also available for walking, strolling, and jogging at all times. In addition, bicycling is permitted on the boardwalk from 6 to 10 am. If you haven't brought your own, you can rent a bike from AAAA Bike Shop, 8 S. Weymouth Ave., Ventnor City (tel. 487-0808). The rates average $6 an hour.

SPECTATOR SPORTS
HORSE RACING

If you tire of the tables or slots, you can always put your money on the horses. The thoroughbreds race at the **Atlantic City Race Course,** Black Horse Pike (Rte. 40), McKee City (tel. 641-2190), at Rte. 322, 14 miles from Atlantic City. Open daily from early June through August (except Monday, Tuesday, and Sunday), this track charges $2.50 for admission to the grandstand and $4 to the clubhouse. Post time is 7:15pm. There is year-round simulcasting from other tracks, and admission to this telebetting is free. Check with the track for details about what tracks are being simulcast.

RECREATION
BOATING

If you arrive in Atlantic City via your own craft, you can dock at the **Sen. Frank S. Farley State Marina,** 600 Huron Ave. (tel. 441-3600). Rates range from $30 to $95 a night for dockage.

BOWLING

You can bowl from 10am to midnight at the state-of-the-art **60-lane bowling center** in the Showboat Hotel, Delaware Avenue and Boardwalk (tel. 343-4000). This new bowling center features Brunswick automatic scoring, a spectator area, a pro shop, an arcade, and a beverage-snack bar. The bowling fee is $2.25 per game; shoe rental is $1.25.

FISHING

The waters off Atlantic City are known for good catches of striped bass, flounder, kingfish, snapper blues, and tautog. Deep-sea fishing also yields marlin, tuna, bonito, and albacore. A fleet of fishing boats that welcome visitors go out daily from Gardner's Basin Marina. A good choice is **Captain Applegate,** 800 N. New Hampshire Ave. (tel. 345-4077), who will set up 4-hour excursions at 8am and 1pm, priced at $15 for adults and $10 for children under 12; $2 extra for rod rental.

8. ATLANTIC CITY SAVVY SHOPPING

The most famous product on sale in Atlantic City is undoubtedly **Fralinger's Salt Water Taffy,** on the Boardwalk at Ocean One (tel. 344-0442) and Tennessee Avenue (tel. 344-0758). Established in 1885, this is the oldest name on the Boardwalk. Step inside any one of the shops and you'll find the fourth generation of Fralingers now serving 16 flavors of saltwater taffy, as well as almond macaroons, chocolates, and seafoam fudge.

New Jersey's first pedestrian mall is **Gordon's Alley,** Gordon's Alley and Atlantic Avenue (tel. 344-5000). A cluster of 30 shops in a two-block-square area, between Atlantic, Pacific, Virginia, and Pennsylvania Aves., this is Atlantic City's version of San Francisco's Ghirardelli Square or Boston's Faneuil Hall. You'll find everything from books and antiques to the latest designer fashions and fine arts.

The city's most unique shopping complex is **Ocean One,** the Boardwalk at Arkansas Ave. (tel. 347-8086). Shaped like an ocean liner on a pier that extends 900 feet over the sea, this is a complex of more than 150 boutiques, shops, and restaurants. There is also a video-game emporium, and facilities for mini-golf, shuffleboard, horseshoes, and boccie, as well as lounge chairs on the Top Deck.

9. ATLANTIC CITY EVENING ENTERTAINMENT

While it's true that much of the Atlantic City nightlife is centered around the casinos, you don't have to gamble to enjoy this town after dark.

Most of the casino hotels have large theaters and showrooms that offer a regular program of top-name entertainers, Broadway-style plays, or musical revues. The smaller lounges of these hotels also vie for attention with comedy acts and individual up-and-coming performers.

Shows and stars can change weekly, so if you are interested in top-name entertainment, it is best to check with the **Greater Atlantic City Convention and Visitors Bureau** in advance to see what will be scheduled during your visit.

Most tickets average $10 to $40, depending on the event, but some prices can go as high as $100 for top-name stars.

Here is a summary of the major venues, types of entertainment, and box office numbers:

Bally's Grand (tel. 340-7200), for big-name stars in concert.

Bally's Park Place (tel. 340-2709), known for its long-running female impersonation revue *An Evening at La Cage.*

Caesar's (tel. 343-2550), for Broadway-type shows with big-name stars.

Claridge (tel. 340-3700), features Broadway-style shows and a comedy club.

Harrah's Marina (tel. 242-7724), presents a variety of concerts by major stars, lavish Follies-style musical revues, and cabaret acts.

Merv Griffin's Resorts (tel. 340-6830), for concerts by big-name stars, musical revues, and comedy acts.

Sands (tel. 441-4591), for appearances by big-name stars.

Showboat (tel. 343-4003), for high-energy musical revues, concerts by big-name stars, and cabaret acts.

TropWorld (tel. toll-free 800/843-8767), for concerts by major stars, a comedy club, and saloon-style musical revues.

Trump Castle (tel. toll-free 800/284-8786), for concerts by major stars, variety shows with new acts, dance bands, and TV game shows.

Trump Plaza (tel. toll-free 800/759-8786), for concerts by major stars and Broadway-style shows.

Trump Taj Mahal (tel. toll-free 800/736-1420), for concerts by big-name stars, ice shows, musical revues, and boxing events.

CAPE MAY

At the southern tip of New Jersey, Cape May claims to be the nation's oldest (since 1761) seashore resort. Like dozens of other Jersey shore destinations, Cape May has expansive sandy beaches, a promenade, and a share of oceanfront motels and condos. But Cape May is a lot more than sea, sun, and surf.

Thanks to its preservation-minded citizens, Cape May is a stronghold of Victoriana. With more than 600 beautifully restored buildings, the entire city of Cape May has been declared a National Landmark.

Like many points along the east coast, Cape May was first discovered in 1609 by Henry Hudson, who claimed it for the Dutch. Credit for the founding of the town, however, goes to Captain Cornelius Jacobson Mey, a Hollander who arrived in 1620, and so enjoyed the area that he bestowed his name on it ("Mey" was anglicized to "May"). Captain Mey was the first of many who would sing the praises of this secluded spot. Jutting out into the sea, with the Atlantic Ocean on the east and Delaware Bay on the west, Cape May enjoys relatively cool summers and mild winters. It is one of the few vantage points in the mid-Atlantic states where both sunrise and sunset are visible over the water.

In the early 1800s, Cape May began to develop as a popular resort, even though it often took 2 or 3 days for vacationers from major east coast cities to journey here by horseback, stagecoach, or sailing vessel. Tourism really flourished by the mid-19th century, with the advent of the steamboat and locomotive. This was also the beginning of the Victorian era, a prosperous time during the reign of Queen Victoria (1837–1901), when a new ornate and showy style of architecture took hold on both sides of the Atlantic.

This Victorian influence brought new buildings with sloping mansard roofs, sweeping verandas, bright colors, and intricate flowery carvings that became known as "gingerbread" work because they resembled fanciful baking decorations. Cape May was lined with these whimsical structures, but, alas, a fire in 1878 leveled 30 acres in the heart of the city. The people of Cape May were quick to rebuild, however, and concentrated on the capricious gingerbread-style structures, each one trying to outdo the next. The results, of course, are the hundreds of Victorian buildings that we enjoy today.

Many visitors come to Cape May to walk the tree-lined streets and to see these buildings or perhaps to spend a night in one of the dozens of Victorian bed-and-breakfast inns. Thanks to an active preservationist group, the **Mid-Atlantic Center for the Arts,** visitors can also take guided walks around the historic district, tour the inside of many of these houses, or take a narrated sightseeing trip through the city via

WHAT'S SPECIAL ABOUT CAPE MAY

Ace Attractions
☐ Cape May Historic District, a Victorian enclave of over 600 buildings, homes, inns, and bed-and-breakfasts of national landmark status.
☐ Emlen Physick House, the benchmark of restored Victorian homes and headquarters for the Mid-Atlantic Center for the Arts, a local preservationist group.
☐ Cape May Point Lighthouse, dating back to 1859, one of the nation's most historic maritime sites.
☐ Historic Cold Spring Village, a prototype of a typical south Jersey 19th-century farm village.

Activities
☐ Narrated trolley tours of historic district.
☐ Fishing for more than 30 kinds of fish on board the head-boats plying the Atlantic waters off Cape May.
☐ Sailing the waters of Cape May on board the *Yankee Schooner*, 80-foot sailboat.

Beaches
☐ Sunset Beach at Cape May Point, a favorite with beachcombers in search of Cape May "diamonds," semiprecious pebbles of pure quartz.

Events
☐ Victorian Week, 10 days of Victorian-style shows, concerts, tours, lawn parties, craft demonstrations, workshops, and more.

Parks
☐ Cape May Point State Park, a 400-acre wildlife preserve popular with bird watchers

Shopping
☐ Washington Street Mall, a three-block pedestrian span with over 60 shops reminiscent of the Victorian era.

a motorized Victorian-style trolley. Other enterprising citizens also offer horse-and-carriage tours or antique-car jaunts, all in keeping with the spirit and style of a gracious era.

It's no wonder that the Cape May population (normally about 5,000) swells to 75,000 to 100,000 in the summer.

1. ORIENTATION

Cape May is located 150 miles south of New York City, 120 miles east of Washington, D.C., 80 miles southeast of Philadelphia, and 40 miles south of Atlantic City.

ARRIVING

BY AIR

The nearest air terminal is **Cape May County Airport,** Rte. 47, Erma (tel. 886-1500), about 5 miles northwest of the city. Regular service to this facility is operated by **USAir Commuter** (tel. toll-free 800/428-4253) from Bader Field in Atlantic City and Philadelphia International Airport.

CAPE MAY

Emlen Physick Estate ⑩
Farmers' Market ⑤
Mid-Atlantic Center fot the Arts ⑬
Seven Sisters ⑧
Stockton Place Row Houses ⑥
Washington Mall
Welcome Center

Cape May Firehouse Museum ⑦
Cape May Lighthouse ③
Cape May Point ①
Cape May Point State Park ④
Chalfonte Hotel ⑪
Christian Family Retreat House ⑨
Congress Hall ⑭

BY TRAIN

The nearest rail services arrive at Atlantic City, 40 miles north of Cape May.

BY BUS

Regular service into Cape May, from major cities such as Philadelphia and New York, is operated by the Cape May Line of **New Jersey Transit** (tel. 884-6139). Buses arrive and depart from the bus depot, 609 Lafayette Ave. (tel. 344-8181), in the center of the Cape May historic district.

For information in advance of your trip, contact New Jersey Transit, McCarter Highway and Market Street, P.O. Box 10009, Newark, NJ 07101 (tel. 215/569-3752 out of state or toll-free in southern New Jersey 800/582-5946).

BY CAR

Cape May is at the end (or, to be more accurate, the starting point) of the **Garden State Parkway.** As the parkway finishes, follow the signs into the heart of Cape May (Lafayette Street). If you prefer the local roads, you can also drive southward from any of the Jersey shore points via Rte. 9. From the west, you can use Rtes. 47 or 49 and the Atlantic City Expressway, and then southward via the Garden State or Rte. 9.

BY FERRY

If you are coming from points south, the most direct (and delightful) way to travel is via the **Cape May–Lewes Ferry,** a 70-minute minicruise on Delaware Bay from Lewes, in mid-Delaware, to Cape May.

In operation since 1964, this ferry service maintains a fleet of five vessels, each holding up to 800 passengers and 100 cars. Departures are operated daily year round, from early morning until evening, with almost hourly service in the summer months, starting at 7am until midnight.

Passenger rates begin at $4 per trip; vehicle fares, calculated by car length, range from $16 to $50, with reduced prices for motorcycles and bicycles. A drive-on, drive-off service is operated, so reservations are not necessary. The Cape May terminal is in West Cape May at the end of Rte. 9. Further information can be obtained by calling 609/886-2718 (in Cape May) or 302/645-6313 (in Lewes).

Note: This ferry ride can also be enjoyed as a round-trip sightseeing cruise. If you go for the day, plan to spend some time in Lewes on the other side. It's a charming seaport town with a bustling marina and a historic district with houses dating back to the 17th and 18th centuries (see Chapter 14, "The Delaware Beaches").

TOURIST INFORMATION

In advance of your visit, contact the **Chamber of Commerce of Greater Cape May,** P.O. Box 109, Cape May, NJ 08204 (tel. 609/884-5508). This office publishes a handy vacation directory, chock-full of facts about hotels, motels, bed-and-breakfast inns, restaurants, and activities.

Once you arrive in town, your first stop should be **The Welcome Center,** 405 Lafayette St., Cape May, NJ 08204 (tel. 609/884-9562), where you can obtain walking tour maps, brochures, tide tables, ferry schedules, and other helpful data. The staff here also stocks sample menus from restaurants in the city and operates a "hot line" service to help you find accommodations if you have not reserved a room in advance. The office is open Monday through Saturday from 9am to 4pm. When you are in town, you can also get on-the-spot advice at the Information Booth located in the Washington Street Mall, at the corner of Ocean Street. Another good source for walk-in data and brochures is the Cape May County Chamber of Commerce, Visitors

Information Center, Garden State Parkway (exit 11), Cape May Court House (tel. 465-7181). This office is open year round, Monday through Friday from 9am to 4:30pm, with extended hours including Saturday and Sunday, from mid-April through mid-October.

Last, but by no means least, is the **Mid-Atlantic Center for the Arts** (MAC), 1048 Washington St., P.O. Box 304, Cape May, NJ 08204 (tel. 609/884-5404). Since its founding in 1970, this organization has played a leading role in Cape May's revival by sponsoring tours and events that promote an interest in Victoriana. MAC administers the Emlen Physick House and Estate, which is an architectural focal point of the city, and conducts walking and trolley tours of the historic district. This not-for-profit organization also sponsors Victorian festivals, a concert series, music festivals, and summer theater. As a community service, MAC publishes "This Week in Cape May," a summary of all of its own activities and other leading happenings in the area.

RESORT LAYOUT

The best way to see and savor Cape May is to walk. The streets follow no particular grid or pattern, but, with a small map in hand, you'll find it easy to get to know this charming little city. The beautiful Victorian homes (over 600 of them) are on almost every street, so you'll be delighted at every turn. The oceanfront street, known as **Beach Drive,** is primarily a 20th-century strip, with a parade of modern motels, restaurants, and shops, although there are still some grand beachfront homes and buildings to be seen.

2. GETTING AROUND

BY TAXI

If you need a cab, radio-dispatched service is provided by **Jones Taxi** (tel. 884-5888).

BY CAR

If you have brought your car, you probably should leave it parked at your guesthouse or motel and do most of your sightseeing on foot. Parking spaces are at a premium in Cape May, and meters along the streets and at the beach offer very limited stays (usually 25¢ per half hour) and sometimes even metered parking is restricted to certain nonpeak hours. You'll get around a lot faster on foot, and if you get tired, there are many other ways to see the sights (from trolley rides to horse-drawn carriages).

BY BICYCLE

Cape May is also ideal biking territory, so, if you are so inclined, bring your own or rent one (see "Cape May Sports & Recreation," below).

FAST FACTS **CAPE MAY**

Area Code   All numbers in the Cape May area belong to the 609 area code.
Baby-sitters   Ask at your hotel or guesthouse.
Climate   See "When to Go," in Chapter 2.
Drugstores   Look under "Pharmacies" in the *Yellow Pages.* In the historic

district, a convenient choice is **Cape Pharmacy,** Acme Shopping Center, Lafayette Street (tel. 884-8553).

Emergencies   Dial "O" and stay on the line, or call 884-9500 for police, and 884-9510 for the fire department.

Eyeglasses   See "Optical Goods–Retail" in the *Yellow Pages.* The nearest choice is **Pearle Vision Center,** Cardiff Circle, Pleasantville (tel. 645-2100).

Hairdressers/Barbers   Two shops that cater to both male and female customers are **Angie's Beauty Shop,** 420 Washington St. Mall (tel. 884-4817) and **Hairloom,** 1002 Washington St. (tel. 884-7139). Consult the *Yellow Pages* under "Barbers" and "Beauty Salons."

Hospitals   **Burdette Tomlin Memorial Hospital,** Lincoln Avenue and Rte. 9, Cape May Court House (tel. 463-2000).

Information   See "Orientation," above.

Laundry/Dry Cleaning   **Model Dry Cleaners and Launderers Inc.** has three locations in the area: 1 Victorian Village Plaza, Cape May (tel. 884-8555), Bay Shore Road, N. Cape May (tel. 886-7544), and Rte. 9 and Dennisville Road, Cape May Court House (tel. 465-4101).

Library   The Cape May County Library is on Mechanic Street, Cape May Court House (tel. 465-1040).

Liquor Laws   Minimum drinking age is 21. Restaurants, bars, hotels, and other places serving alcoholic beverages are open from 10am to 2am. Visitors coming to New Jersey from another state can bring the following with them without a permit: 12 quarts of beer or ale, one gallon of wine, and two quarts of any other alcoholic beverage. Larger quantities require a permit.

Lost Property   If an article is lost at a hotel or restaurant, contact the manager; if lost or found in a public place, call the police.

Newspapers/Magazines   Local newspapers include the *Cape May County Herald,* and the *Cape May Star and Wave.*

Photographic Needs   Two convenient shops are **Harbour View Photo,** 1426 Texas Ave. (tel. 884-6779) and **The Photo Shop,** Rte. 9, Cape May Court House (tel. 465-3114).

Police   Tel. 884-9500.

Post Office   Cape May Post Office, 700 Washington St., Cape May (tel. 884-3578).

Religious Services   The Cape May area is home to about a dozen churches of various denominations. Inquire at the front desk of your hotel or guesthouse or consult the *Yellow Pages* under "Churches." The nearest temple is at Wildwood.

Restrooms   All hotels and restaurants have restrooms available for customers.

Safety   There are precautions you should take whenever you are traveling in an unfamiliar region or country. Stay alert and be aware of your immediate surroundings. Wear a moneybelt and keep a close eye on your possessions. Be particularly careful with cameras, purses, and wallets, all favorite targets of thieves and pickpockets. Be especially careful when walking on dark streets and in parks after dark. Every society has its criminals. It's your responsibility to be aware and alert even in touristed areas.

Shoe Repairs   **Young's Shoe Repair Shop,** 3 Mechanic St., Cape May Court House (tel. 465-5114).

Taxes   The New Jersey sales tax is 7%.

Taxis   See "Getting Around," above.

Telegrams/Telex   Check at a hotel, or the Chamber of Commerce.

3. CAPE MAY ACCOMMODATIONS

Accommodations in Cape May fall primarily into two main categories: Victorian bed-and-breakfast inns and modern motels. Inns such as the Mainstay and the Abbey have achieved widespread publicity over the last 10 years, and they are usually everyone's first lodging choice, but, between them, they have less than 20 rooms! Needless to say, these two are usually booked up a year in advance, so the Cape May Welcome Center, 405 Lafayette St., Cape May, NJ 08204 (tel. 609/884-9562), is quick to remind visitors that the city has dozens of excellent bed-and-breakfast choices. The office staff is always happy to assist visitors in finding available rooms.

BED-AND-BREAKFAST INNS

Before you race to book a B&B, we should warn you that these gingerbread-trimmed masterpieces are not for everyone. First of all, with their heirloom antiques and Victorian furnishings, these houses are really not suitable for children. Most inns require young guests to be at least 12 or 13.

In general, Victorian B&Bs do not have elevators, air conditioning, or in-room televisions and telephones; not all of the rooms in many houses have private baths. Rates quoted by innkeepers are usually for double occupancy; singles are usually $10 less per night. Minimum stays of 3 or 4 nights often apply in the summer months.

The majority of B&Bs do not accept credit cards, although some do take MasterCard and VISA, and all of them usually require a deposit of at least 1 night's charges in advance to confirm a reservation. Smoking is generally limited to verandas, and parking is not always provided.

As a rule, Cape May's B&Bs are open from April or May through October or November, although more and more are staying open all year. Rates in the off-season are often substantially less than summer.

The variety of B&Bs in Cape May is a feast for the eyes—all different shapes, sizes, and colors. Each house has its own distinctive personality, but, in the main, they all offer a wonderful opportunity to experience a gracious life-style of long ago. Whether you are sipping iced tea on the veranda or enjoying a country breakfast by candlelight, you'll treasure your Victorian vacation days at Cape May.

ABBEY, Columbia Avenue and Gurney Street, Cape May, NJ 08204. Tel. 609/884-4506. 14 rms (all with bath). A/C TEL

$ Rates (including breakfast): $80–$150 single or double, mid-June–Oct; $65–$115 single or double, Apr–mid-June and mid-Oct–Nov. MC, V. **Closed:** Dec–Mar.

One of the most photographed homes in Cape May is this Gothic gingerbread three-story inn with a steep mansard roof. Built in 1869 as a summer villa for John McCreary, a coal baron and U.S. senator, this delightful house was restored by its current owners, Jay and Marianne Schatz. It is painted in authentic Victorian colors, both inside and out, and its 60-foot tower offers panoramic views of the town and nearby sea. The typically Victorian decor includes stenciled and ruby-glass windows, gaslights, Oriental rugs, tufted velvet chairs and sofas, and 12-foot mirrors.

Guest rooms, available in the main house and an adjacent cottage, are furnished with tall walnut bedsteads, carved armoires, and ornate dressers. Seven additional rooms, all with bath, are also available in an adjacent cottage. The rates include on-site parking for main house guests and beach passes. Often featured in magazine and newspaper stories, the Abbey is often booked out up to a year or more in advance. For those who are not lucky enough to secure a reservation, the Schatzes conduct tours of the first floor on Thursdays through Sundays, April through October, at 5pm (the cost is $3 per person). Parking for cottage guests is at a lot several blocks away.

ABIGAIL ADAMS BED-AND-BREAKFAST BY THE SEA, 12 Jackson St., Cape May, NJ 08204. Tel. 609/884-1371. 5 rms (3 with bath).

$ Rates (including breakfast): $75–$125 single or double. AE, MC, V. **Parking:** Free.

Located just half a block from the beach, the architecture of this three-story country inn is a mixture of Victorian and Federal styles, with an open front porch and a festive front flower garden. With an eclectic all-American decor, this house is full of antiques, chintzes, quilts, and wicker, collected over the years by owner Kate Emerson. Besides breakfast, which is served in the hand-stenciled dining room, and ranges from scones and soufflés to quiches and cakes, the rates include afternoon tea, beach tags, and parking. Three rooms face the ocean.

ANGEL OF THE SEA, 5–7 Trenton Ave., Cape May, NJ 08204. Tel. 609/884-3369 or toll-free 800/848-3369. Fax 609/884-3331. 29 rms (all with private bath).

$ Rates (including breakfast): $125–$230 double in July–Aug; $62.50–$175 single or double off-season. AE, MC, V. **Parking:** Free.

Dating back to 1881, this fanciful three-story Victorian gem is actually two buildings joined together, restored and refurbished to the tune of $3.2 million, and opened as an inn in 1990. Situated in a mostly residential area, it is a good 20-minute walk from the historic district and the cluster of other Victorian B&Bs, but it is across the street from the ocean. Parking is no problem; bicycles are available for guest use and there are complimentary car rides to restaurants in the center of town.

The interior is rich in Victorian flourishes, wooden ceilings, wainscotting, brass chandeliers, floral wallpapers, and velvet upholstery. Guest rooms, all of which have ceiling fans, are individually decorated with either wicker or antique wood furniture, and have a variety of bed sizes and shapes, from four-posters and sleigh beds to canopied beds. Many of the bathrooms also have original fixtures, such as clawfoot tubs, pedestal sinks, or gooseneck commodes. Twenty rooms have ocean views, and 9 rooms are on ground-floor level (no elevator). Guests enjoy use of the oceanfront veranda, beach tags, chairs, and towels. Rates include a full hot breakfast, with choice of entrées, as well as afternoon tea and wine and cheese. Innkeepers are Barbara and John Girton.

BRASS BED INN, 719 Columbia Ave., Cape May, NJ 08204. Tel. 609/884-8075. 8 rms (6 with bath).

$ Rates (including breakfast): $95–$115 single or double, with bath, and $80–$100 single or double, with half or shared bath, mid-June–mid-Sept; $75–$95 single or double, with bath, and $55–$80, single or double, with shared bath, Jan–mid-June and mid-Sept–Dec. MC, V. **Parking:** Free.

This three-story Gothic revival cottage was built in 1872 and used as a guesthouse since 1930. The present owners bought the building in 1980 and completely restored it, using much of the original furniture, including the 19th-century brass beds that inspired a new name for the inn. Each bedroom is individually furnished and named after one of the city's great Victorian hotels of yesteryear; third-floor rooms also have air conditioning.

The decor includes lace curtains, Oriental carpets, elaborate brass gas lamps, and Queen Anne chairs; the wide enclosed front veranda is a comfortable oasis with large rockers and wicker chairs overlooking the gardens. Included in the price, besides breakfast, are afternoon tea served in the Victorian dining room, beach tags, and the use of a shower/changing area. Innkeepers are John and Donna Dunwoody.

CAPTAIN MEY'S INN, 202 Ocean St., Cape May, NJ 08204. Tel. 609/884-7793 or 609/884-9637. 9 rms (2 with bath).

$ Rates (including breakfast): $75–$145 single or double; off-season discounts of 15% available. MC, V. **Parking:** Free.

Built in 1890, this inn is named after the Dutch explorer who is credited with founding Cape May in the 1620s. Strikingly decorated in Victorian purples and browns, this 2½-story structure still conveys the heritage of Holland with its collection of Delft-blue china and Dutch artifacts. Even the breakfasts hark back to the days of Captain Mey—homemade breads, egg dishes, cheeses from Holland, fresh fruits, and jelly made from beach plums, all served by candlelight with classical music in the background. Thanks to the restoration and care of innkeepers Carin Feddermann and Milly LaCanfora, the inn is a showcase of European antiques, rich oaken woodwork, chestnut-oak Eastlake paneling, leaded-glass windows, and a fireplace with an intricately carved mantel.

The guest rooms, on the second and third floors, have marble-topped dressers, walnut high-back beds, carved vanities, handmade quilts, and Dutch lace curtains. Located two blocks from the beach, the inn also boasts a wraparound sun porch and shaded veranda with wicker furniture, hanging ferns, and Victorian wind curtains. Open all year, the rates include a full country breakfast, afternoon tea and sherry, parking, beach passes, and restaurant reservation service.

COLUMNS BY THE SEA, 1513 Beach Dr., Cape May, NJ 08204. Tel. 609/884-2228. 11 rms (all with bath). TV TEL
$ Rates (including breakfast): $95–$135 single, $105–$145 double. No credit cards accepted. **Closed:** Nov–Apr. **Parking:** Free.

This bed-and-breakfast overlooks the beachfront in a quiet residential area outside the historic district. Owned by Barry and Cathy Rein, this three-story 1905 Italian palazzo town house with Colonial revival accents was originally known as the "great cottage." As its name implies, the facade is dominated by grand fluted columns on its wraparound porch. The interior decor is equally striking, with 12-foot ceilings, hand-carved woodwork, and coffered ceilings.

Best of all, this house commands sweeping views of the Atlantic from most of its rooms and from the rockers on the front porch. The large and airy guest rooms have tall windows, Victorian antiques, and Chinese ivory carvings. Rates include a gourmet breakfast, afternoon refreshments, use of bikes, a hot tub, beach badges, and off-street parking.

GINGERBREAD HOUSE, 28 Gurney St., Cape May, NJ 08204. Tel. 609/884-0211. 6 rms (3 with bath).
$ Rates (including continental breakfast): $72–$130 double. MC, V. **Parking:** On street.

Elaborate Victorian woodwork is the hallmark of this establishment run by innkeepers Fred and Joan Echevarria. Dating back to 1869, it was one of eight "cottages" designed by Stephen Decatur Button and built in conjunction with the long-gone Stockton Hotel.

In addition to its Victorian antiques, original watercolors, seashells, and lush plants, this inn is enhanced with many photographs of the east coast taken by its owner. One of the guest rooms is a huge master bedroom with its own porch. Rates are reduced 20% to 30% in the off-season. The price includes an afternoon tea that features homemade baked goods, plus beach tags and the opportunity to sit back and relax on the wicker-filled front porch just a block away from the beach.

MAINSTAY INN, 635 Columbia Ave., Cape May, NJ 08204. Tel. 609/884-8690. 12 rms (all with bath). TEL
$ Rates (including breakfast): $75–$130 single, $85–$140 double. No credit cards accepted. **Closed:** Mid-Dec–Mar. **Parking:** Free.

✪ To many people, there is only one place to stay in town—the Mainstay Inn. Undoubtedly the best known Cape May bed-and-breakfast, this inn has certainly helped to put Cape May on the map as a showcase of Victoriana, and consequently is often booked out months in advance. If you can't get a reservation on your first or second try, don't be too disappointed. You can always visit the inn; tours are conducted at 4pm on Tuesday, Thursday, Saturday, and Sunday. The fee of $5 for adults and $4 for children includes afternoon tea.

And just what makes the Mainstay so popular? Built in 1872 as a clubhouse for wealthy gamblers, it is the creation of architect Steven Decatur Button, who was told to spare no expense. The result is a grand villa with ornate plaster moldings, elaborate chandeliers, a sweeping veranda, Italianate windows, and a cupola to top it all off. Now in the hands of devoted preservationists Tom and Sue Carroll, the Mainstay has been restored to its original grandeur and is furnished with richly ornamented Victorian pieces. Each bedroom is decorated with period antiques, quilted bedcovers, ornate headboards, 12-foot mirrors, and elaborate armoires. The stately wraparound porch beckons you to recline on a deep wicker seat or on a vintage chair-swing, while the gardens invite you to walk among their color and fragrance. The rates include a country breakfast (often featuring strawberry crêpes or quiche Lorraine), afternoon tea, and beach passes.

QUEEN VICTORIA, 102 Ocean St., Cape May, NJ 08204. Tel. 609/884-8702. 17 rooms and 7 suites (20 with bath). A/C TV

$ Rates (including breakfast): $55–$85 double with shared bath, $65–$140 double with bath, $99–$225 suite. MC, V. **Parking:** Free at nearby city lot.

⭐ Dating from 1881, the aptly named and frequently photographed Queen Victoria sits grandly one block from the beach. Opened as a bed-and-breakfast in 1981, this regal inn has grown over the years, and now offers accommodations in three adjacent restored Victorian homes and their carriage houses. Each guest room is different, but all are furnished with antiques and handmade quilts; most rooms have ceiling or window fans, and some are air-conditioned. Suites have air conditioning, color TV, whirlpool bath or fireplace, sitting room, minirefrigerator, and a private entrance.

During the day you can sit by the fireplace in the parlor and listen to classical music, relax in a rocker on one of the porches, meander in the colorful Victorian gardens, or browse in the well-stocked library. Rates include a buffet breakfast or breakfast in bed, afternoon tea, and the use of bicycles and beach passes. Smoking is permitted only in the library and on the porches. Innkeepers are Dane and Joan Wells.

SUMMER COTTAGE INN, 613 Columbia Ave., Cape May, NJ 08204. Tel. 609/884-4948. 9 rms (5 with bath). A/C

$ Rates (including breakfast): $75–$135 single or double. MC, V. **Parking:** Free nearby.

Another creation of architect Steven Decatur Button is this Italianate-style three-story house, built in 1867. The inn features large first-floor and second-floor wraparound verandas, tall windows, and a cupola on top of the building. Highlights of the interior include a three-story circular staircase, walnut and oak inlaid floors, Victorian furnishings, and lace curtains.

The guest rooms are decorated with a variety of Victorian furnishings. Rates include beach passes, afternoon tea, and creative country breakfasts (with such dishes as marinated melon with blueberry mousse, or sausage cheese crêpe, and savory quiches). Innkeeper is Nancy Risforth.

WILBRAHAM MANSION & INN, 133 Myrtle Ave., Cape May, NJ 08204. Tel. 609/884-2046. 6 rms, 2 suites (all with private bath). A/C

$ Rates (including full breakfast): mid-May–mid-Sept $85–$115 single or double, $135–$145 suite; rest of year $85–$115 single or double, $120–$125 suite. MC, V. **Parking:** Free.

Built in 1840 and enlarged in 1900, this imposing purple, yellow, and gray Victorian house was a private residence until the end of 1988 when it was acquired and opened as a B&B by innkeepers Pat and Rose Downes. It is a little off the beaten track, five blocks from the ocean and historic district, but it is in a lovely residential neighborhood overlooking a small park, and it has its own indoor heated swimming pool.

The interior is overwhelmingly Victorian—with many original furnishings, 100-year-old carpets, period reproduction wallpapers, wainscotting, stained-glass windows, floor-to-ceiling gilded mirrors, and a working Packard pump organ. The guest rooms are decorated in similar style with laces and frills and antique pieces; there is one ground-floor room. Breakfast is served by candlelight on the pool terrace or in the dining room. Rates include afternoon tea and beach badges; a 2-day minimum applies on weekends. Because of the pool, this property also offers spa/fitness packages.

HOTELS & MOTELS

In addition to the classic B&Bs, Cape May is home to some very fine hotels and motels, many located right on the oceanfront. For folks who like a modern decor, air conditioning, in-room TVs, and the privacy of their own bathroom, these properties are ideal.

EXPENSIVE

VIRGINIA HOTEL, 25 Jackson St., P.O. Box 557, Cape May, NJ 08204.
Tel. 609/884-5700. 24 rms (all with bath). A/C TV TEL
$ Rates: End of May–early Sept. $125–$205 single or double; rest of year $85–$175. AE, CB, MC, V. **Parking:** Free.

Dating back to 1879 and reopened in 1990, this three-story Victorian hotel blends the charms of a B&B with the full services and modern amenities of a hotel. The public areas include a dramatic stained-glass window, open fireplace, antique furnishings, and sweeping staircase. (True to its Victorian origins, it has no elevator, but ground-floor rooms are available.)

Guests rooms are contemporary, with blond woods or wicker furniture, pastel colors or sea tones, floral art, down comforters, modern tiled bathrooms, and VCR units. A few rooms have private porches overlooking the historic area. Dining and entertainment facilities include **The Ebbitt Room** restaurant, a lounge with live jazz or piano music on many evenings, and an outdoor rear garden. Complimentary morning newspapers are provided for guests and there is room service. Reduced rate packages are available in the spring and fall.

CHALFONTE, 301 Howard St., Cape May, NJ 08204. Tel. 609/884-8409. 77 rms (11 with bath).
$ Rates (including breakfast and dinner for two): $145 double with bath; $75–$135 double with shared bath. MC, V. **Closed:** Nov–Apr. **Parking:** On street.
Built in 1876, this is one of the few remaining great Victorian hotels in the city. With its gingerbread arches, verandas, balconies, and pillars, this three-story hotel was the work of Colonel Henry Sawyer, a Civil War hero who was released from a Confederate prison in exchange for Robert E. Lee's son, and it hasn't changed very much since. The Victorian-style guest rooms have neither air conditioning, telephone, nor TV, but this sprawling grande dame of a hotel does welcome children.

The Chalfonte is in a constant process of restoration, and guests are invited to pitch right in. The hotel has gained a lot of attention for its "work weekends" in May and late October, when architecture students, specialists, and interested tourists can exchange work for room and board. In addition, workshops and educational programs are also conducted in watercolor and oil painting, vintage dance, rug-hooking, quilting, journal-writing, and wine-tasting.

Dining/Entertainment: Helen Dickerson has been delighting guests with her down-home Southern cooking for 45 years, with country breakfasts including spoonbread, homemade biscuits, fresh fish, bacon, eggs, and kidney stew on Sundays. Dinners feature Virginia ham, roast turkey, fried chicken, deviled crab, and leg of lamb. There are special reduced rates for youngsters, plus a children's dining room and baby-sitting services. Breakfast is served from 8:30 to 10am daily; dinner is available Monday through Saturday at two seatings, 6:30 and 8pm, and on Sunday from 6:30 to 7:30pm, buffet-style only. Meals are open to people not registered at the hotel, for $7 for breakfast and $21 for dinner. Entertainment activities for adult guests include a classical music series, comedy shows, films, soap-opera theme parties, and other entertainments.

INN OF CAPE MAY, 601 Beach Drive, P.O. Box 71, Cape May, NJ 08204. Tel. 609/884-3500 or toll-free 800/257-0432. Fax 609/884-0669. 124 rooms, 23 suites. A/C TV TEL
$ Rates (including breakfast): Hotel $50–$140 single or double, $76–$200 suite; motel $44–$186 single or double, $52–$200 suite. AE, CB, DC, MC, V. **Closed:** Main building, Oct–April; motel wing, Dec–March. **Parking:** Free.
If you prefer a hotel with a more Victorian facade, then try this inn, owned by the same management as the Marquis de Lafayette Inn (see below). Formerly the Colonial Hotel, this is one of the city's oldest oceanfront landmarks, dating from 1894. It is a five-story feast of Victoriana—with "witch hunt" turrets, mansard roof, fish-scale shingles, etched-glass doors, and a huge wraparound porch overlooking the

beachfront. Years ago, this was the place to stay, and was also the first hotel in Cape May to have an elevator.

Purchased in 1987 by the Menz family, the hotel has undergone extensive renovations. Great care was taken to preserve the original architecture and ornamentation while updating the facilities. In addition, there is an adjacent wing with motel-style rooms, all with private bath and balconies. Only the motel rooms have air conditioning, TV, and telephone in each room. Facilities include a restaurant, lounge, an outdoor pool, free beach tags, and an antique shop.

LA MER MOTOR INN, Beach Dr. and Pittsburgh Ave., Cape May, NJ 08204. Tel. 609/884-9000. 68 rms (all with bath). A/C TV TEL

$ Rates: July–early Sept $80–$129 single or double; end of Apr–June and Sept–mid-Oct $42–$95 single or double. AE, DC, DISC, MC, V. **Parking:** Free. **Closed:** Mid-Oct–end of April.

Another good choice is this modern, two-story inn in a quiet neighborhood. There are five different types of rooms, from basic motel unit with one double bed to efficiencies with two double beds. Facilities include a restaurant, an outdoor swimming pool, a sun deck, a barbecue area, a launderette, bike rentals, and mini-golf.

MARQUIS DE LAFAYETTE INN, 501 Beach Dr., Cape May, NJ 08204. Tel. 609/884-3500 or toll-free 800/257-0432. Fax 609/884-0669. 73 rms, 43 suites (all with bath). A/C TV TEL

$ Rates (including breakfast): $34–$196 single or double, $42–$230 suites. AE, CB, DC, MC, V. **Parking:** Free.

If location is everything, then it's hard to beat this inn, right on the oceanfront in the heart of the historic district. Although the exterior is quite modern now, this hotel traces its roots to the original Lafayette Hotel built on the site in 1884. It has had various owners and affiliations over the years (including Best Western), but it is now in the hands of the Menz family, who are aiming to return a genuine Victorian decor and character to the hotel.

There is a choice of eight different room designs, many of which have antique furnishings and fixtures. All of the rooms face the beach and oceanfront, each has a balcony, and some have kitchenettes.

Dining/Entertainment: You'll find fine food at moderate prices at the Gold Whale, a ground-floor restaurant designed to recall an "old Cape May" ambience. For a special splurge, there is also a rooftop restaurant, The Top of the Marq, open only for dinner.

Facilities: Outdoor swimming pool and sun deck.

MODERATE

BLUE AMBER MOTEL, 605 Madison Ave., Cape May, NJ 08204. Tel. 609/884-8266. 40 rms (all with bath). A/C TV TEL

$ Rates: Mid-July–Aug $51–$89 single or double, May–early July and Sept $36–$51 single or double. AE, MC, V. **Closed:** Oct–Apr. **Parking:** Free.

This modern two-story property was completely renovated in 1986. All rooms have two double beds, and 10 of the rooms are efficiencies with kitchenettes (available at a $10 additional charge per night). Facilities include an outdoor heated swimming pool, off-street parking, barbecue grills, and picnic tables. Located seven blocks from the beach, it's just one block from the Emlen Physick Estate and other Victorian homes. In the summer months, there is usually a weekend minimum stay of 3 nights, and a per-night surcharge of $15 on weekends and $30 on holiday weekends.

MONTREAL INN, Beach Dr. at Madison Ave., Cape May, NJ 08204. Tel. 609/884-7011 or toll-free 800/525-7011. Fax 609/884-4559. 20 rooms, 50 suites (all with bath). A/C TV TEL

$ Rates: Mid-June–mid-Sept $64–$86 single or double, $86–$106 suite; off-season rates $28–$66 and $36–$85, respectively. AE, MC, V. **Parking:** Free. **Closed:** Dec–mid-Mar.

Of the many motels that line the beachfront, one of the best values is this modern property just three blocks from the heart of the Victorian inn district. Most rooms have two double beds, sea-toned furnishings, private balconies, and picture windows. Efficiency units with microwave ovens are also available at supplementary charges. In most cases, no minimum stay is required. Facilities include a restaurant, lounge, liquor store, heated outdoor swimming pool, a sauna, and miniature golf.

SEA BREEZE MOTEL, Pittsburgh and New York Aves., Cape May, NJ 08204. Tel. 609/884-3352. 12 rms (all with bath). A/C TV

$ Rates: July–Aug $80 double; mid-Mar–June and Sept–end of Nov $38–$75 double. MC, V. **Closed:** End of Nov–mid-Mar. **Parking:** Free.

One of the best bargains in town is this motel, two blocks from the beach in a residential neighborhood. There is a small sitting area, with lawn chairs, in front of each room. Parking is available on a small lot behind the motel and on a first-come basis on the street in front of the motel. Each room has standard furnishings and a tiled bathroom plus a refrigerator.

4. CAPE MAY DINING

Like the lodging choices of Cape May, many restaurants offer the ambience and setting of the Victorian era. In addition, you'll find some very fine seafood houses overlooking the water, and other ethnic specialty eateries.

Because so many people are on the beach or out touring during the day, quite a few Cape May restaurants serve dinner only. Some of the places that we describe below offer lunch. In addition, you'll find a number of cafés, taverns, and fast-food places near the beach and in the Washington Street Mall, the city's main shopping area.

Be advised that some of Cape May's best restaurants do not serve alcoholic beverages, but they usually let you bring your own bottle. They'll supply ice, wineglasses, and whatever set-ups you may need, sometimes at a nominal extra charge of $1 or so. It is always best to check in advance. For suggestions on where to buy wine, beer, or liquors in town, see "Cape May Savvy Shopping," below.

EXPENSIVE

AXELSSON'S BLUE CLAW, 991 Ocean Dr. Tel. 884-5878.
Cuisine: INTERNATIONAL. **Reservations:** Accepted. **Directions:** From Cape May, turn right after Harbor Bridge at the traffic light; restaurant is 1½ miles on the left.
$ Prices: Appetizers $3.95–$7.95; main courses $16.95–$28.95. MC, V.
Open: June–mid-Sept, dinner 5–10pm.
Closed: Mon–Thurs in off-season.

This restaurant is located on the water, north of downtown Cape May, overlooking the fishing fleet and the docks of the inlet. There are two dining rooms, seating about 125. The original room is full of hanging plants, ship's-wheel chandeliers, and hurricane candle lamps, while the newer room offers lovely views of the water in a setting of natural woods, paneled walls, and framed lithographs of tall ships. It also has a fireplace and a unique pitched and beamed ceiling finished in popcorn within glass, giving the illusion of dining under the stars.

Specialties include bass or snapper in parchment with tomato fondue; soft-shell crabs (in season); veal in a cream sauce with jumbo lump crabmeat; rack of lamb; duck with orange or plum sauce; and steak au poivre. Free parking.

410 BANK STREET, 410 Bank St. Tel. 884-2127.

Cuisine: INTERNATIONAL. **Reservations:** Recommended.

$ Prices: Appetizers $3.95–$6.95; main courses $18.95–$23.95. AE, MC, V.

Open: May–Oct, dinner daily 5:30–10pm.

A southern tropical atmosphere prevails at this restaurant housed in a restored 1840 drover house, across from the Victorian bandstand. Dinners are served on an outdoor deck and in a garden-style dining room with cane furniture, ceiling fans, and lots of flowering vines.

The menu focuses on the cuisines of France, New Orleans, and the Caribbean: Specialties include mesquite-grilled fish, Black Angus strip steaks, Cajun shellfish gumbo, barbecue-glazed chicken, blackened redfish, and soft-shell crabs with capers, hazelnut butter, and lemon sauce. You may bring your own alcoholic beverages.

RESTAURANT MAUREEN, 429 Beach Dr. at Decatur St. Tel. 884-3774.

Cuisine: AMERICAN. **Reservations:** Recommended.

$ Prices: Appetizers $4.95–$9.95; main courses $15.95–$23.95. AE, MC, V.

Open: Memorial Day–Sept 30 dinner daily 5–10pm; early May–Memorial Day, dinner Sat–Sun 5–10pm; mid-to-late Oct, dinner Wed–Sun 5–10pm.

This restaurant is the elegant creation of Maureen and Steve Horn, of Philadelphia culinary fame. Located on the second floor of a 110-year-old Victorian building, the restaurant overlooks the ocean from an enclosed glass veranda. It's a romantic candlelit setting, surpassed only by the innovative new American cuisine that Maureen presents each evening.

Entrées include veal au poivre; farm-raised pheasant in hunter sauce; cassoulet of lobster; filet of fish in parchment; flounder baked with a mixture of lobster, shrimp, and scallops; crab Versailles, with sherry, Dijon mustard, and Gruyere cheese, and filet mignon with a sauce of bourbon and fresh mushrooms.

WATSON'S MERION INN, 106 Decatur St. Tel. 884-8363.

Cuisine: AMERICAN. **Reservations:** Recommended.

$ Prices: Appetizers $3.95–$6.95; main courses $15.95–$28.95. MC, V.

Open: Dinner daily May–Oct 4:30–10pm; Fri–Sun 4:30–10pm in off-season.

One of the oldest restaurants in town is this inn, which has continuously served the public since 1885. Located one block from the water, the inn has a Victorian atmosphere, with candlelit tables, fresh flowers, antique bar, and gilt-framed paintings. The menu is classically American, with crab-stuffed flounder, lobster tails, surf-n-turf, honey-glazed ham steak, leg of veal with white wine and mushrooms, steak Dijon, sautéed and brandied chicken breast à l'orange, and Delaware Bay drumfish. If you are seated before 6pm, there's a 25% "early-bird" discount off any entrée.

FRESCOS, 412 Bank St. Tel. 884-0366.

Cuisine: AMERICAN. **Reservations:** Recommended.

$ Prices: Appetizers $3.95–$5.95; main courses $9.95–$21.95. MC, V.

Open: May–Oct, dinner daily 5:30–10pm.

Pasta lovers are flocking to this relative newcomer to the Cape May dining scene (1986). Under the same management as the adjacent 410 Bank Street restaurant, Frescos describes its decor and ever-changing menu as regional Italian. Open for dinner only, the entrées include such choices as rigatoni with wild mushrooms, fennel, and sausage; green noodle lasagne with four cheeses; tagliatelle with pesto and sun-dried tomatoes; veal chop with sage; filet mignon marsala; or Norwegian salmon with fresh green herb sauce. You may bring your own alcoholic beverages.

LOBSTER HOUSE, Fisherman's Wharf. Tel. 884-8296.

Cuisine: SEAFOOD. **Reservations:** Not accepted.

$ Prices: Appetizers $2.25–$7.75; main courses $11.95–$24.95; lunch $4.95–$10.95. AE, MC, V.

Open: Lunch Mon–Sat 11:30am–3pm; dinner Mon–Sat 4:30–10pm, Sun 4–10pm.

This top-notch seafood restaurant overlooks Cape May Harbor. The decor is decidedly nautical, and the menu focuses on the freshest of seafood. You know it has to be good, because the boats pull up right outside the door; and the restaurant maintains its own seafood store on the premises. Lunch items include chowders, fish stews, seafood salads, and sandwiches. Best of all, you can have your lunch in the main dining room and upstairs dining room with air-conditioned views of the wharf or on board the *Schooner America,* a tall ship docked beside the restaurant.

Entrée selections range from pan-blackened and herb-crusted redfish to locally caught bluefish, swordfish, and flounder, as well as lobster, crab au gratin, shrimp and scallops en papillote, fisherman's wharf platters (lobster tail, shrimp, scallops, crab cake, filet of local fish, and stuffed clams), and filet mignon. Throughout the day, a dockside takeout service also operates, with outdoor tables along the wharf.

MAD BATTER, 19 Jackson St. Tel. 884-5970.
   Cuisine: INTERNATIONAL. **Reservations:** Recommended.
$ **Prices:** Appetizers $4–$7.75; main courses $14–$23; lunch $5.95–$10.95. MC, V.
   Open: Mid-May–Sept breakfast and lunch Mon–Fri 9am–2:30pm, Sat–Sun 8am–2:30pm; dinner Mon–Fri 5:30–9:30pm, Sat–Sun 5:30–10pm. Mar–Apr and Oct–Dec Sat–Sun only, 5:30–10pm.

A fanciful three-story Victorian house complete with cupola is the setting for the Mad Batter, less than one block from the beach. This trendy restaurant offers a choice of dining al fresco on an ocean-view veranda or a shaded garden terrace, as well as indoors in a skylit Victorian dining room. Drawing raves from morning till night, the cooking here is totally eclectic, from Asian and Cajun dishes to eggs Benedict or bouillabaisse.

The constantly changing menu might offer such imaginative creations as cheese and fruit blinis, venezia pizza omelet, seafood frittata, sausage, vegetables, and cheese in phyllo pastry, and crêpes filled with cream cheese and smoked seafood, plus daily specials of quiche, pastas, salads, and seafood. Dinner choices include scallops and vegetables en brochette; honey-roasted duck; roasted rack of lamb with goat cheese and Chinese mustard; sugar-dipped chicken with raspberry vinegar, cream, and cracked cranberries; and sirloin of Colorado Black Angus beef. You may bring your own alcoholic beverages.

WASHINGTON INN, 801 Washington St. Tel. 884-5697.
   Cuisine: INTERNATIONAL. **Reservations:** Recommended.
$ **Prices:** Appetizers $4.50–$11.50; main courses $10.95–$20.95. AE, CB, DC, MC, V.
   Open: Early Mar–Mother's Day Sat–Sun 5–10pm; Mother's Day–late Sept daily 5–10pm, Oct Thurs–Sun 5–10pm, Nov–Dec Fri–Sun 5–10pm.

A restored 1856 plantation house is the location of this restaurant owned by the Craig family since 1979. Victorian decor dominates the main dining room as well as in the air-conditioned garden terrace, a newly added and delightful room of seasonal flowers, fountains, fans, wicker furniture, and flickering gaslights. The dinner menu blends new American and international cuisines—shrimp and scallops fettuccine, crab au gratiné, chicken in raspberry cream sauce, surf-n-turf, veal champignon, and veal Betsy (with cheese and wine sauce).

MODERATE

OCEAN VIEW, Beach Dr. and Grant Ave. Tel. 884-3772.
   Cuisine: AMERICAN. **Reservations:** Not required.
$ **Prices:** Appetizers $2.95–$5.95; main courses $9.95–$18.95; lunch $4.95–$6.95. AE, MC, V.
   Open: Summer daily 7am–10pm; off-season daily 7am–9pm. **Closed:** Dec–Feb.
Overlooking the beach, this modern ranch-style restaurant is particularly suitable for family dining. Lunch items include sandwiches, hoagies, burgers, and salad platters.

The dinner entrées feature veal parmigiana, honey-dipped fried chicken, roast turkey, Virginia ham steak, filet of bluefish, whole baby flounder, surf-n-turf, and steak. This restaurant also serves breakfast, with most items under $4.

BUDGET

THE FILLING STATION, 615 Lafayette St., Cape May. Tel. 884-2111.
  Cuisine: AMERICAN. **Reservations:** Not accepted.
$ **Prices:** Appetizers $2.95–$4.95; entrées $8.95–$14.95. AE, MC, V.
  Open: Apr and Oct Sat–Sun 4:30–9:30pm; June–Sept Tues–Sun 4:30–9:30pm.
  Closed: Nov–Mar.

As its name implies, this place is not very glamorous and it's not Victorian, but it is popular, particularly with families, for unadorned food and good value. There are three dining rooms, with a decor that can best be described as casual and comfortable. The menu offers fried chicken; barbecued ribs; steaks; seafood, including crab cakes; and a variety of pasta.

5. CAPE MAY ATTRACTIONS

Two buildings that are historically significant in Cape May are owned and administered as hotels by the Christian Beacon Press and the Cape May Bible Conference. The first of these, **Congress Hall,** Beach Drive and Perry Avenue (tel. 884-8421), was one of the earliest hotels (built in 1812), and was originally called the Big House. It was changed to its present name when the owner at the time, Tom Hughes, decided to run for Congress in 1828. The current building is actually the third structure built on this site, and it was erected after the disastrous fire of 1878. Declared a national landmark in 1974, Congress Hall is best known because it served as the Summer White House for President Benjamin Harrison. Free tours are sometimes conducted in the summer months, but you are welcome to walk around at any time and see the magnificent stencil work and restored furnishings.

The **Christian Admiral,** Beach Drive and Pittsburgh Avenue (tel. 884-8471), was originally called the Hotel Cape May when it was built in 1908. This building is significant for its marbled lobby, Tiffany glass dome in the front portico, and stained-glass windows on the staircase. It was used as a hospital by the Navy during World Wars I and II, and purchased in 1962 by the present owners, who conduct it as a Bible Conference hotel, but it is also open to the public in the summer months.

EMLEN PHYSICK HOUSE, 1048 Washington St. Tel. 884-5404.

This house is the benchmark of the restored Victorian homes of Cape May. Designed by Philadelphia architect Frank Furness and built in 1879, it is a fine example of stick-style architecture, with inverted chimneys and jerkin-head dormers. The interior contains an extensive collection of Victorian furniture, clothing, toys, tools, and artifacts. The house was saved from destruction in the early 1970s by the Mid-Atlantic Center for the Arts (MAC), the Cape May preservationist group. MAC has since opened its headquarters in a small building on the grounds of the estate, and conducts tours of the house on a regular basis. From this base, the organization also coordinates trolley tours of Cape May's historic district, gaslight tours to other outstanding homes in the area, Victorian Fairs, Christmas events, and an open-air summer theater series. (For further information on tours of other Victorian homes, see "Getting Around," above.)
  Admission: $4 adults, $1 children.
  Open: Year-round guided tours Sat–Thur every 45 minutes from 10:30am–3pm.

CAPE MAY COUNTY HISTORICAL MUSEUM, Shore Road, Cape May Court House. Tel. 465-3535.

This bastion of Cape May history is housed in the pre-Revolutionary home of John Holmes, an Irish immigrant who arrived in the area in 1773; the house remained in the Holmes family until 1935, and is now on the National Register of Historic Places. The exhibits include an 18th-century kitchen, bedroom, dining room, medical room, and collections of china, furniture, and glass. The barn of the house contains a mining exhibit, a decoy collection, whaling instruments, as well as Indian artifacts, a maritime display including some of the famous Cape May "diamonds," and the original flag from the *Merrimac*. This building is also the home of the Cape May County Historical and Genealogical Society, founded in 1927.

Admission: $2 per person, 50¢ children 2 to 12.

Open: Apr–mid-June, mid-Sept–Dec Tues–Sat 10am–4pm; mid-June–mid-Sept Mon–Sat 10am–4pm. Last tour at 3pm.

CAPE MAY POINT LIGHTHOUSE, Lighthouse Avenue. Tel. 884-5404.

Set on the spot where Delaware Bay meets the Atlantic Ocean, this lighthouse is one of the nation's most historic maritime sites. Dating from 1859, this vintage outpost is still an active aid to navigation, visible for up to 24 miles at sea. The entire structure has been recently restored by the Mid-Atlantic Center for the Arts (MAC) in conjunction with the New Jersey Department of Environmental Protection/Division of Parks and Forestry. Visitors can climb the 199 steps to the Watch Room Gallery, just below the lantern itself, for a panoramic view of the Cape May area.

Admission: Free admission to ground floor, which contains a display on the lighthouse's history. To climb the tower, price is $3 adults, $1 for children 3–12.

Open: Sat–Sun 10am–4pm. **Directions:** Follow Sunset Boulevard (Rte. 606) to Cape May Point.

LEAMING'S RUN GARDENS AND COLONIAL FARM, 1845 Rte. 9 North, Swainton. Tel. 465-5871.

The area's horticultural heritage is on display at this delightful open-air attraction 17 miles north of Cape May. The grounds encompass 25 separate gardens, each with a different theme, set amid 20 acres of lawns, ponds, and ferneries. In addition, there is a vegetable and herb garden, a cooperage, and a Colonial farm with tobacco and cotton fields growing much as they would have done in 1685.

Admission: $4 adults, $1 children 6–12.

Open: Mid-May–mid-Oct daily 9:30am–5pm.

HISTORIC COLD SPRING VILLAGE, 735 Seashore Rd., Cold Spring. Tel. 898-2300.

This is a re-creation of a provincial village just outside of Cape May. Although Cold Spring itself never existed, over a dozen buildings from all over Cape May County have been brought here to depict what a typical South Jersey 19th-century farm village would have been like. Set on 35 acres, this outdoor museum includes a blacksmith shop, a school, a train station, a jail, a nautical museum, an inn, and various shops. In the summer months, there are craft demonstrations, weekend entertainment, antique shows, and military encampments on the grounds.

Admission: $1.50 adults, 75¢ children 6–12.

Open: Memorial Day–early Oct, 10am–4pm.

WHEATON VILLAGE, 1501 Glasstown Rd, Millville. Tel. 825-6800.

About an hour's drive northwest of Cape May, this is a re-created Victorian glass-making community with a working glass factory dating back to 1888. Here you can watch glass-making demonstrations and tour the Museum of American Glass, a building with over 7,000 items on display, ranging from paperweights to fiber optics, mason jars to Tiffany masterpieces. Other attractions include a crafts and trades row, a print shop, a tinsmith, a paperweight shop, a general store, and a train ride.

Admission: $4 adults, $2 students.

Open: Apr–Dec 10am–5pm. **Closed:** Easter, Thanksgiving, Christmas, and New Year's Day.

ORGANIZED TOURS

WALKING TOURS

✪ Guided walking tours of the Cape May historic district are conducted by members of the **Mid-Atlantic Center for the Arts** (MAC), 1048 Washington St. (tel. 884-5404). Designed to provide insight into the customs and traditions of the Victorians and their ornate architecture, these tours last about 1½ hours and take in a cross-section of buildings and streets. Departure times vary with the season, but summer tours are usually at 10am daily, with some additional 7pm tours. The schedule in the spring and fall is 11am, operating on weekends and some weekdays, so it is best to check with MAC in advance or to consult "This Week in Cape May." The cost is $4 for adults and $1 for children. All tours assemble at the Information Booth of the Washington Street Mall, at the corner of Ocean Street.

MAC also organizes self-guided tours of historic Victorian homes and hotels, allowing participants to go inside four or five leading Victorian buildings, on an individual basis. These tours usually are offered in the evenings, by gaslight, from 7:30 to 10:30pm. Weekend tour departure points vary, and on Wednesday tours leave from the Emlen Physick House, 1048 Washington St. Tickets can be purchased prior to each tour at the respective starting points. The cost is $10 to $12 per person and $5 to $6 for children; the fare includes admissions to houses and transfers from place to place by continuous trolley bus service. For complete information, contact the Mid-Atlantic Center for the Arts, 1048 Washington St. (tel. 884-5404).

TROLLEY TOURS

An informative introduction to Cape May is provided by the open-air trolley-bus tour service. Narrated by knowledgeable guides, these tours depart from the Trolley Station at Beach Drive and Gurney Street during the summer (late June through August) and from Washington Street, opposite the Washington Street Mall, in the spring and fall months. Three different historic tour routes are offered: the east end, featuring Columbia Avenue, Hughes Street, and Ocean Street; the west end, around Congress Hall and its environs; and a beach drive, covering shorefront housing, from Victorian cottages to turn-of-the-century mansions.

Tours are scheduled daily from 10am to 7pm in the summer months, with additional "moonlight" rides at 8:30 and 9:30pm; in the spring and fall, the trolleys roll between 10am and 4pm only. Each tour lasts a half hour and costs $4 per person and $1 for children. Further information is available from the **Mid-Atlantic Center for the Arts,** 1048 Washington St. (tel. 884-5404).

CARRIAGE TOURS

If you'd like to see the sights from a surrey with a fringe on top, contact the **Cape May Carriage Co.,** 641 Sunset Blvd., Cape May (tel. 884-4466). This firm conducts half-hour horse-drawn carriage tours around the historic district, departing from the Washington Street Mall, at the corner of Ocean Street. Tours operate Tuesday through Sunday from mid-June through mid-September, 10am to 2pm and from 6 to 10pm; and in spring and fall from 11am to 3pm. The fare is $6 for adults and $3 for children 2–11; tickets can be purchased from the driver or at carriage stops.

NEARBY ATTRACTIONS

Another 15 miles will bring you to **Bridgeton,** a city of 19,000 people on the Cohansey Creek. Founded by Quakers in 1686, this town today comprises New Jersey's largest historic district. It is a mélange of 2,200 houses, taverns, and churches, embracing the Colonial, Federal, and Victorian periods. For self-guided walking-tour leaflets and further information, stop into the **tourist information center** at 50 E. Broad St. (tel. 451-4802).

6. CAPE MAY SPECIAL/FREE EVENTS

Cape May summers get off to a festive start each year with the **Victorian Fair,** held on the grounds of the Emlen Physick Estate, 1048 Washington St. (tel. 884-5404). Scheduled on the third Saturday of June, from 10am to 4pm, this festive open-air gathering features music and entertainment, craftspeople, and games of skill and chance. Admission is free. For complete information, contact the **Mid-Atlantic Center for the Arts,** P.O. Box 340, Cape May, NJ 08204 (tel. 609/884-5404).

The premier event of the year in Cape May is **Victorian Week,** held for 10 days in mid-October, including 2 weekends. The program includes antique shows, guided tours of the Victorian district, concerts, stained-glass tours, Victorian-style vaudeville, lawn parties, teas, craft demonstrations, fashion shows, workshops, and dinners. Many activities are free and others range in price from $5 to $50, depending on the event. For a complete program and ticket information, contact the Mid-Atlantic Center for the Arts (address above).

✪ **Christmas** is a special time at Cape May. Carolers stroll the streets, gaslit street lamps are bedecked with wreaths, and the Washington Street Mall merchants organize traditional "hospitality nights" for shoppers, with cider and cookies or wine and cheese. Other activities include a yuletide parade, a community tree-lighting ceremony, gingerbread house displays, and candlelight walks. Visitors can take tours in heated enclosed trolley cars to see Victorian homes bedecked in twinkling lights and holiday finery. For a Christmas calendar of events, write or phone the **Greater Cape May Chamber of Commerce,** P.O. Box 109, Cape May, NJ 08204 (tel. 609/884-5508).

7. CAPE MAY SPORTS & RECREATION

BICYCLING

If you haven't brought your own bicycle, you can hire one. The cost is $3.50 per hour ($9 for a full day) for a one-passenger vehicle or $32 per week. Hours are 7am to 9pm in the summer, with shorter hours during the rest of the year. The bike-rental shops with these rates are **La Mer Bike Rentals,** Beach Drive and Pittsburgh Avenue (tel. 884-2200) and **Village Bicycle Shop,** 2 Victorian Village Plaza (tel. 884-8500).

BIRD-WATCHING

Situated on the Eastern Flyway, Cape May has long been famous for its excellent bird-watching opportunities, especially in the spring and fall months when the great migrations take place. Most of this activity is concentrated in the vicinity of Cape May Point State Park and in the picturesque South Cape May Meadows along Sunset Boulevard, a 400-acre wildlife preserve. For further information, contact the **Cape May Bird Observatory,** 707 E. Lake Drive, Cape May Point (tel. 884-2736); there is also a 24-hour bird-sighting hotline (tel. 884-2626).

CAMPING

In the area surrounding Cape May, there are 26 campgrounds, catering to tent, trailer, or motor-home visitors, for weekends, by the week, or monthly. Most of these campgrounds have swimming pools, modern bath facilities, stores, laundromats, video arcades, and full hookups. For a complete listing, contact the **Cape May**

County Campgrounds Association, P.O. Box 175, Cape May Court House, NJ 08210.

FISHING

The waters around Cape May yield over 30 kinds of fish, including mackerel, flounder, cod, pollock, tautog, sea bass, fluke, sea trout, porgies, tuna, bluefish, bonito, albacore, and white and blue marlin. Deep-sea fishing trips can be arranged at the **Miss Chris Fishing Center,** 3rd Avenue and Wilson Drive (tel. 884-5445 or 886-8164). Boats go out every day from the end of March to November, and no reservations are required. Eight-hour day-fishing trips depart at 8am and cost $28 per person, with rod rental $5 extra. Half-day trips, priced at $17, are also available, pushing out at 8am or 1pm; and night fishing from 7pm to 3am, at $30. The craft used are 70-foot twin diesel boats, with the latest modern electronic fish-finding and safety equipment.

HORSEBACK RIDING

For travelers who enjoy seeing the sights from the saddle, horseback trail rides can be arranged through **Hidden Valley Ranch,** 4070 Bayshore Rd., Cold Spring, off Rtes. 641 and 607 (tel. 884-8205). Trails include the Cape May woods and fields. The cost ranges from $15 to $20, depending on time of day and the duration of the ride; lessons can also be arranged from $15 to $25 an hour. Open Monday through Saturday from 9am to dusk, and reservations are necessary.

SAILING/SIGHTSEEING

You can sail the waters around Cape May on board the 80-foot sailboat, **Yankee Schooner,** Ocean Highway Dock (tel. 884-1919). This boat offers 3-hour trips along the Intercoastal Waterway to Cape May Harbor and Inlet, and into the Atlantic Ocean along the South Jersey Cape. Sailings are scheduled daily mid-June through mid-September, at 11am and 4:30pm. The cost is $23 for adults, including snacks and beverages, $17 for children (on the morning cruise only). Tickets are available at the dock or in advance by reservation.

SWIMMING

Between Second and Philadelphia Avenues, Cape May has more than a dozen individually named beaches in a row along its Atlantic shoreline. With names like Broadway, Stockton, Grant, and Congress, these beaches usually take their names from the nearby streets that lead to the shore.

One of the city's most popular strands, **Sunset Beach,** is at the end of Sunset Boulevard, at nearby Cape May Point. At low tide, this beach is a favorite with beachcombers who wade out a quarter mile to search for sand dollars and "Cape May diamonds," semiprecious pebbles and stones of pure quartz that have been popular since early Victorian times. These "diamonds" come in various colors and sizes; when they are polished, cut, and set, they make most attractive jewelry.

Like many New Jersey beaches, Cape May requires beach tags, which can be purchased at the entrances to the beaches. The cost is $3 a day for adults and children over 12, or $8 a week. If you prefer not to get the sand in your shoes, most Cape May beaches are rimmed by a promenade.

8. CAPE MAY SAVVY SHOPPING

Shoppers and strollers alike enjoy the pedestrian area known as **Washington Street Mall.** Situated between Ocean and Perry Streets, this three-block span is Cape May's original downtown shopping district, restored and re-created to represent the commercial architecture of the Victorian era, with brick walks, benches, and lots of shrubs. Today there are over 60 shops, with wares ranging from pottery and prints to pastry, as well as fashions, antiques, stained glass, estate jewelry, needlepoint work, wicker, brass, nautical gifts, and the unique Cape May diamonds. If you work up an appetite, you'll also find ice-cream parlors, cafés, fudge kitchens, and fast-food shops. In the summer season most shops are open daily, from 10am to 10pm; hours vary at other times of the year.

The other major cluster of shops, called **Washington Square,** is located on a shady block between Ocean and Franklin Streets. These shops are primarily good for crafts, antiques, and Victorian-related items. One of our favorites is the **Baileywicke Leather Shop,** 656 Washington Square (tel. 884-2761), a good source of custom-made cowhide items, vests, hats, leather carvings, bags, wallets, luggage, made-to-measure boots and sandals, as well as solid brass hardware and antique leather restoration work. For Victorian furniture, vintage clothing, antiques, and collectibles, try **Midsummer Night's Dream,** 668 Washington St. (tel. 884-1380); while the **Victorian Sampler,** 680 Washington St. (tel. 884-3138), specializes in Victorian needlework kits and patterns.

One of the most elaborately decorated gingerbread-style cottages in Cape May is the **Victorian Pink House,** 33 Perry Street (tel. 884-7345), a photographer's dream (and a painter's challenge). The shop housed inside sells Victorian-era collectibles, antiques, cards, and prints.

As mentioned in the "Cape May Dining" section, above, many Cape May restaurants do not serve liquor, wine, or beer, but they welcome you to bring your own, to accompany your dinner. Two centrally located liquor stores are **Collier's,** Jackson and Lafayette Streets (tel. 884-8488), and the **Montreal Liquor Store,** Beach Drive and Madison Avenue (tel. 884-1186).

9. CAPE MAY EVENING ENTERTAINMENT

Compared to the dazzling nightlife of Atlantic City or other neighbors, like the Wildwoods, Cape May is relatively quiet after dark. If you are in town in the late-June-through-August period, however, you can enjoy indoor professional theater, performed by the **Cape May Stage Equity Theatre Company** and the **East Lynne Company,** an equity company devoted to Vintage American plays. Shows are sponsored by the Mid-Atlantic Center for the Arts (MAC), with performances usually slated Thursday through Sunday, at various venues, such as the Chalfonte Hotel, 301 Howard Street, or the Cape May Institute, 1511 New York Ave. Tickets average $10 and are available at the door. Schedules and information are available in advance from MAC, 1048 Washington St., P.O. Box 340, Cape May, NJ 08204 (tel. 609/884-5404).

In addition, free music concerts are held throughout the summer at the **Rotary Bandstand** on Lafayette Street, usually at 8pm, Wednesday and Sunday. No tickets required.

The summer months also bring music and entertainment to the **King Edward Bar** of the Chalfonte Hotel, 301 Howard St. (tel. 884-8409). The **Nite Club** of the Grand Hotels, Oceanfront at Philadelphia Ave. (tel. 884-5611), offers music and dancing nightly.

Live jazz, blues, reggae, and other music can be enjoyed nightly in the summer and in spring and fall on weekends at **The Shire,** 315 Washington Mall (tel. 884-4700). Another bar that often features live music is the **Ugly Mug,** 426 Washington Mall (tel. 884-3459).

CHAPTER 21

THE REST OF THE JERSEY SHORE

More than 50 beachside communities make up the 127-mile strip along the Atlantic Ocean collectively known as the Jersey shore.

These back-to-back beach towns stretch from Sandy Hook in the north to Cape May at the southern tip of the state, and include such well-known resorts as Atlantic City, Spring Lake, Long Beach Island, Ocean City, and the Wildwoods. Because of the interest in Atlantic City's gambling casinos and Cape May's Victorian architecture, we have devoted separate chapters to each of them.

Whether you seek tranquil beaches or busy ones, you are bound to find something of interest along the Jersey shore. Many of the resorts are famed for their boardwalk and amusement strips like Seaside Heights, Point Pleasant, or the Wildwoods. A family atmosphere prevails at Ocean City, while Victorian architecture draws folks to Ocean Grove or Spring Lake, and a bird sanctuary is the claim to fame of Stone Harbor. And the list goes on.

No matter what destination you choose, you'll usually have to pay for the privilege of swimming on the beach. Daily beach passes range from $2 to $8, although some beaches, like the Wildwoods, are free. The good news is that these fees are generally only charged from Memorial Day through Labor Day, so, if you plan a spring or autumn visit, you can enjoy the beaches for free. You can also save substantially on accommodations in the off-season months.

A note on shore restaurants: Most places are open 7 days a week, throughout the day and evening during the summer season. More limited hours are in effect in the spring and fall. Although we have tried to note hours of operation, these times are often subject to change, depending on the weather and the flow of business. We suggest you call in advance to check the days and times that restaurants are open, especially in the off-season.

GETTING THERE

BY TRAIN

Amtrak operates daily train services between Atlantic City and New York, Philadelphia, Washington, D.C., and other cities. For details, call toll-free 800/USA-RAIL. Rail service is also available via **New Jersey Transit** to major northern shore towns such as Red Bank and Long Branch. For complete information on schedules and fares, call toll-free 800/772-2222 (from northern New Jersey) and (in southern New Jersey) toll-free 800/582-5946.

WHAT'S SPECIAL ABOUT THE JERSEY SHORE

Ace Attractions

☐ The Spy House Museum, in Port Monmouth, a folk museum reflecting New Jersey's earliest days.

☐ Garden State Arts Center, in Holmdel, a 5,300-seat amphitheater for concerts, shows, and ethnic heritage festivals.

☐ Ocean City Music Pier, home of the Ocean City Pops, longest-running "pops" presentation in the east.

☐ Stone Harbor Bird Sanctuary, a National Landmark and prime resting place for herons.

Activities

☐ Spend a day rooting for the thoroughbreds at Monmouth Park, in Oceanport.

☐ Take a sightseeing cruise from Wildwood on board the *Delta Lady*, a Mississippi-style riverboat.

Beaches

☐ Point Pleasant, a wide sandy beach and a busy marina.

☐ Ocean City, an 8-mile "family-oriented" beach, with a 2½-mile boardwalk.

☐ Wildwood Beach, 3 miles long and 1,000 feet wide, with lots of amusements.

For the Kids

☐ Fantasy Island Amusement Park, in Beach Haven, a Victorian-style amusement center on Long Beach Island.

Parks

☐ Sandy Hook, part of the Gateway National Recreation Area, at Highlands, 6½ miles long, with seven beach areas.

☐ Monmouth Battlefield State Park, in Freehold, scene of one of the longest battles of the Revolutionary War.

BY BUS

New Jersey Transit provides daily bus service from New York, Philadelphia, and Newark to most points along the Jersey shore (see toll-free telephone numbers above).

BY CAR

The best way to get to the Jersey Shore, and to tour around, is by car. From points north, take the New Jersey Turnpike south to exit 11, and then get on the Garden State Parkway. The beach resorts start at exit 117 (for the Sandy Hook area) and continue southward, running parallel to the coastline, to exit 0 (Cape May). From the west, take the Atlantic City Expressway to the Garden State Parkway, and then go either north or south, depending on which resort is your destination. From the south, you can travel via Delaware and the Cape May–Lewes Ferry.

1. SANDY HOOK TO SPRING LAKE

The northernmost tip of the Jersey shore is Sandy Hook, part of the Gateway National Park, which also includes parts of New York (Staten Island and Long Island). Besides the Sandy Hook coast, the beaches in this area include Sea Bright, Monmouth, Long Branch (all on Rte. 36), and Asbury Park (off Rtes. 71 and 33).

In addition to the beaches, this area extends inland along the Navesink River (via Rte. 35) and includes the historic town of Red Bank, known as the "hub" of the northern shore. Nearby is Eatontown, famed for its thoroughbred racetrack.

SANDY HOOK

40 miles S of New York, 70 miles NE of Philadelphia,
100 miles SE of Newark

GETTING THERE **By Train** The New Jersey Transit provides service to north shore towns such as Red Bank and Long Branch. For information, call toll-free 800/772-2222 from northern New Jersey or 800/582-5946 from southern New Jersey.

By Bus The New Jersey Transit provides daily service from major cities to most shore points.

By Car Take the Garden State Parkway to exit 117.

ESSENTIALS **Information** Go first to the Sandy Hook, **Visitor Center,** Spermaceti Cove (tel. 872-0115) next to parking lot E, open daily in summer from 10am to 4pm; Wednesday through Sunday in spring, weekends in fall and winter. Here you can pick up self-guiding tour leaflets of the area and see exhibits and a 14-minute slide program. Although the beaches are technically free, there is a $4 parking fee on weekdays and $5 on weekends, from Memorial Day weekend through Labor Day. The mailing address for beach and other information is P.O. Box 530, Fort Hancock, NJ 07732.

Area Code Sandy Hook's area code is 908.

The highlight of this section of the shore is the Sandy Hook unit of the ✪ **Gateway National Recreation Area,** Rte. 36, Highlands (tel. 872-0115), within viewing distance of the World Trade Center and the rest of the New York City skyline. Administered by the National Park Service, this spit of beachland that juts upward into the Atlantic is 6½ miles long and ¾ of a mile wide at its widest point. There are seven different parking areas and beach sections. Besides the free beaches, highlights of the island include the **Sandy Hook Lighthouse,** built in 1764 and one of the oldest in the nation.

About 5 miles east of Sandy Hook along the coast is the **Spy House Museum,** 119 Port Monmouth Rd., Port Monmouth (tel. 787-1807). Overlooking lower New York Bay, this is a plantation house built in 1663 by Thomas Whitlock. It is said that this site was the earliest land grant in the state, and that Whitlock was the first permanent resident of New Jersey. The house was subsequently used as a base for Revolutionary soldiers who "spied" on the arriving British and often sank their ships. Now on the National Register of Historic Places, this folk museum is full of artifacts and furnishings from New Jersey's earliest days. Open Monday through Friday from 2 to 4pm; Saturday from 1 to 4pm; and Sunday from 2:30 to 5pm. Admission is free, but donations are welcomed.

RED BANK

5 miles SW of Sandy Hook, 45 miles S of New York,
70 miles NE of Philadelphia, 100 miles SE of Newark

GETTING THERE **By Train** New Jersey Transit provides daily service.

By Bus The New Jersey Transit provides daily service.

By Car Use exits 109–114 of the Garden State Parkway.

ESSENTIALS Information Contact or visit the **Chamber of Commerce of Red Bank,** 5 Broad St., Red Bank, NJ 07701 (tel. 201/741-0055). The office is open Monday through Friday, year round, from 9am to noon and from 1 to 5pm.

Area Code Red Bank's area code is 908.

Dating back to Colonial times, Red Bank is not a beach town but a river town, situated on the Navesink River, which flows into the Atlantic. It was a thriving shipping center in the early 19th century and a regular stopping point for stately masted schooners and paddlewheel steamers that plied the waters of the east coast.

Incorporated as a town in 1870 and a borough in 1908, Red Bank has grown into a commercial and social hub for the beach towns and other neighboring communities. Situated at exit 109 of the Garden State Parkway, Red Bank is also the gateway to a variety of attractions, as well as some of the shore's best hotels and restaurants, which, surprisingly, are not along the beach but inland.

WHAT TO SEE & DO

Among the area highlights are the **Monmouth Battlefield State Park,** Rte. 33, Freehold (tel. 462-9616), off Rte. 9, about 20 miles west of Red Bank. The scene of one of the longest battles of the Revolutionary War (1778), this is where the legendary Mary Ludwig Hays (more commonly known as Molly Pitcher) became a heroine by bringing pitchers of water to men in the field, and by taking up arms against the British when her own husband fell in battle. To learn the whole story, stop into the visitor center, open daily from 10am to 6pm in the summer and from 10am to 4pm the rest of the year. There are also picnic facilities and a nature center on the grounds. There is no admission charge.

✪ If you visit from mid-June through September, plan to spend at least one evening at the **Garden State Arts Center,** Telegraph Hill, Holmdel (tel. 442-9200), about 10 miles west of Red Bank and exit 116 of the Garden State Parkway. Set on a hillside on a 400-acre park, this 5,300-seat amphitheater offers a summertime program of evening open-air pop and classical concerts, musicals, ballets, and ethnic heritage festivals. Prices vary with events, but usually average between $15 and $25. For a schedule of upcoming events, write to the center at P.O. Box 116, Holmdel, NJ 07733.

✪ For sports fans, there is **Monmouth Park,** Oceanport Avenue, Oceanport (tel. 222-5100), about 5 miles south of Red Bank, off Rte. 36 or exit 105 of the Garden State Parkway. Ever since 1946, this has been a prime New Jersey venue for thoroughbred flat and turf racing. The season extends from the beginning of June through the first week in September, with racing daily except Monday and Thursday; post time is 1:30pm. General admission is $1.50, $4 for the clubhouse.

WHERE TO STAY

EXPENSIVE

OCEAN PLACE HILTON, One Ocean Blvd., Long Branch, NJ 07740. Tel. 908/571-4000 or toll-free 800/HILTONS. Fax 908/571-8974. 250 rms, 5 suites. A/C TV TEL **Directions:** Take exit 105 off Garden State Parkway, on Rte. 36.

$ Rates: May–Sept $134–$158 single or double, Oct–Apr $88–$138 single or double; $350–$1,000 suite. AE, CB, DC, MC, V. **Parking:** Free.

✪ Sitting right beside the ocean, this contemporary 15-story property is the newest full-service hotel along the northern Jersey Shore. Guest rooms, like the public areas, have furnishings that are rich in light woods and bright sea-toned fabrics. Each unit also has a balcony, and two phones with message alerts and data ports. Facilities include two restaurants, a lounge/piano bar, a nightclub, spa and fitness center, indoor and outdoor swimming pools, tennis courts, jogging paths, hair salon, gift shop, and an oceanfront promenade.

OYSTER POINT HOTEL, Bodman Place, Red Bank, NJ 07701. Tel. 908/530-8200 or toll-free 800/354-3484. Fax 908/747-1875. 52 rms. A/C MINIBAR TV TEL **Directions:** Take Garden State Parkway to exit 109 and go north on Rte. 35.

$ Rates: $95 single or double. AE, CB, DC, MC, V. **Parking:** Free.

This six-story hotel sits on a marina site overlooking the Navesink River. It's a grand European-style hotel, complete with marble lobby, atrium, and lots of glass, brass, and potted foliage. The rooms all have king-size or double beds, river views, private balconies, plus a sitting area.

Facilities include a spa with Jacuzzi, an exercise room, and a restaurant/lounge.

MODERATE

MOLLY PITCHER INN, 88 Riverside Ave., Red Bank, NJ 07701. Tel. 908/747-2500 or toll-free 800/221-1372. Fax 908/747-2713. 105 rms. A/C TV TEL

$ Rates: $59 single, $69–$85 double. AE, CB, DC, MC, V. **Parking:** Free.

Set on the Navesink River marina, this four-story inn is named for local heroine Molly Pitcher and dates back to 1928. With a brick Colonial-style facade, it offers 65 rooms in the old (and refurbished) inn and 40 in an adjoining motel-style wing. Facilities include a café-lounge and a gourmet restaurant, both overlooking the river, and an outdoor heated swimming pool.

BUDGET

CRYSTAL MOTOR LODGE, 170–171 Hwy. 35, Eatontown, NJ 07724. Tel. 908/542-4900 or toll-free 800/562-5290. Fax 908/542-1718. 77 rms. A/C TV TEL

$ Rates: $50 single, $60 double. AE, CB, DC, DISC, MC, V. **Parking:** Free.

Racing fans favor this two-story lodge located near the Monmouth Park Racetrack, and 3 miles from the beach. Guest rooms surround an outdoor pool in a secluded wooded setting. Each room is decorated in contemporary style, with two double beds, coffeemaker, and a refrigerator. In addition to the pool, facilities include a sun deck, shuffleboard court, two gazebos, and a playground.

WHERE TO DINE
EXPENSIVE

SHADOWBROOK, Rte. 35, Shrewsbury. Tel. 747-0200.
   Cuisine: INTERNATIONAL. **Reservations:** Recommended on weekends.
$ Prices: Appetizers $2.95–$7.95; main courses $15.95–$25.95. AE, CB, DC, MC, V.
   Open: Dinner Tues–Fri 5:30–9:30pm, Sat 5:30–11pm; Sun 3–9pm.

This restaurant has been a favorite in this area for almost 40 years. Owned and operated by the Zweben family, the two-story Georgian mansion is situated on 20 secluded acres of woods and rose gardens. The posh decor includes antiques, dark-wood paneling, crystal chandeliers, gilt-edge mirrors, and stone fireplaces. Dinner entrées feature Dover sole, chateaubriand, rack of lamb, flaming duckling à l'orange, caponette Kiev, heart of sirloin steaks, prime ribs, and "seafood trifecta" (king crab, Gulf shrimp, and scallops on pasta).

OLDE UNION HOUSE, 11 Wharf Ave., Red Bank. Tel. 842-7575.
   Cuisine: INTERNATIONAL. **Reservations:** Recommended.
$ Prices: Appetizers $2.95–$6.95; main courses $11.95–$22.95; lunch $5.95–$11.95. AE, CB, DC, MC, V.
   Open: Lunch Mon–Sat 11:30am–3pm; dinner Mon–Thurs 5–10pm, Fri–Sat 5–11pm, Sun 4:30–10pm; brunch Sun noon–3pm.

Nestled on the banks of the Navesink River is this restaurant that was established in 1791 as a Colonial inn. Restored and enlarged 25 years ago, the restaurant offers a cozy old tavern room with gas lights, antiques, and stained glass, and a modern section with a New Orleans atmosphere and wide windows overlooking the river. Lunch items include salads, burgers, seafood, pastas, diet dishes, and omelets. Entrées at dinner include veal Cordon Bleu, London broil, steaks, pastas, and a variety of seafood, including bouillabaisse.

THE OLD ORCHARD INN, 74 Monmouth Rd., Eatontown. Tel. 542-9300.
   Cuisine: INTERNATIONAL. **Reservations:** Recommended.
$ **Prices:** Appetizers $3.95–$7.95; main courses $11.95–$21.95; lunch $4.95–$11.95. AE, DC, MC, V.
   Open: Lunch daily 11:30am–3pm; dinner Mon–Sat 5–10pm; Sun 2–8pm.
   Closed: Mon–Tues Labor Day–March 1.

A country-club atmosphere prevails at this restaurant located on the grounds of the Old Orchard 18-hole public golf course. Incidentally, the greens fees range from $17 to $22, if you want to play a game before or after a meal (tel. 542-7666). There are four dining rooms, and an enclosed heated veranda overlooking the course.

Other rooms offer a clubby ambience with hunt scenes, tapestries, and a fireplace. Sandwiches, burgers, crêpes, omelets, light dishes, and cold platters make up the lunch menu. Dinner entrées include steaks, veal and lamb chops, lobster tails and other seafoods, and pastas.

SPRING LAKE

10 S. of Red Bank, 54 miles N of Atlantic City, 90 miles N of Cape May

GETTING THERE   By Train   The New Jersey Transit provides daily service.

By Bus   New Jersey Transit operates daily service.

By Car   Exit 98 of the Garden State Parkway.

ESSENTIALS   Information   Contact the **Greater Spring Lake Chamber of Commerce,** 1315 Third Ave., P.O. Box 694, Spring Lake, NJ 07762 (tel. 908/449-0577).

Area Code   The area code for all numbers in the Spring Lake region is 908.

Of all the resorts along the Jersey shore, Spring Lake is in a class by itself. Yes, it has a lovely beach and a 2-mile boardwalk, like many of the other resorts, and it boasts fine mansions and Victorian bed-and-breakfast inns like Cape May. But, as a unique feature, this tidy community also has the ambience of a lakefront enclave, with its namesake, Spring Lake, at its heart, surrounded by parklands, footbridges, and ancient shady trees.

Thanks to its natural endowments, Spring Lake is one of the most unspoiled and undercommercialized of the Jersey resorts, with a regular clientele that comes back year after year. There are no noisy amusements or arcades, no fast-food strips, and no nightclubs. Chic shops line its main thoroughfare, Third Avenue, and a motorized San Francisco–like trolley takes vacationers from shop to shop, and from inn to boardwalk or lakefront. (The trolley runs from Memorial Day to Labor Day and costs $1.)

You may wonder why so many Irish flags fly side by side here with the Stars and Stripes. That brings us to Spring Lake's other claim to fame. Over the years, thanks to an influx of devotees with Irish roots, Spring Lake has become known as the Irish Riviera. A focal point of the town is the **Irish Centre,** 1120 Third Ave. (tel. 449-6650), one of the mid-Atlantic's classiest import stores and a showcase of Irish crystal, linens, tweeds, knitwear, fashions, paintings, and gifts.

WHERE TO STAY

EXPENSIVE

BREAKERS, 1507 Ocean Ave., Spring Lake, NJ 07762. Tel. 908/449-7700. 70 rms. A/C TV TEL
$ Rates: $130–$180 single or double. AE, CB, DC, MC, V. **Parking:** Free.
If you'd like a room overlooking the beach, the best choice is this four-story Victorian landmark. A large wraparound porch beckons guests to sit on a rocker and enjoy the sea breezes, while a turn-of-the-century aura prevails in the public rooms, with their polished wood floors, antiques, and tones of royal blue and white. The guest rooms, each with a private bath, have all been modernized and all have refrigerators; some have whirlpool baths. Lower rates apply in the spring and fall months. Facilities include a restaurant, lounge, and outdoor swimming pool.

CHATEAU, 500 Warren Avenue, Spring Lake, NJ 07762. Tel. 908/974-2000. Fax 908/974-2000. 40 rms, 6 suites. A/C TV TEL
$ Rates (including continental breakfast): $44–$99 single, $49–$109 double, $65–$150 suite. AE, MC, V. **Parking:** Free.
⭐ The best of both worlds can be enjoyed at this charming country inn overlooking the lake and five blocks from the beach. Originally built in 1888, this property has been renovated and updated. The decor is bright and summery, with lots of wicker furniture, leafy plants, and pastel furnishings. Over the years, the guest list has included many celebrities, from Buster Keaton to Basil Rathbone, and many rooms are named and decorated in the style of the stars who stayed in them.

The inn is a combination of hotel rooms and parlor/suites; many rooms have private balconies, wet bars, brick patios, or sun decks. Each room has a refrigerator; suites have wet bars, and some have a fireplace. There are some ground-floor accommodations. Prices include beach and tennis privileges; reduced rates are in effect before mid-June and after early September. A minimum 3-night stay is required on summer weekends.

MODERATE

COMFORT INN, 1909 Rte. 35 South, P.O. Box 14, Spring Lake, NJ 07762. Tel. 908/449-6146 or toll-free 800/221-2222. 70 rms. A/C TV TEL
$ Rates (including continental breakfast): May–Sept $83–$105 single or double; off-season $48–$70 single or double. AE, CB, DC, DISC, MC, V. **Parking:** Free.
⑤ Tucked in a garden setting, this lodging is conveniently located on the main shore road, 1 mile from the center of town. The rooms of this modern two-story structure have a contemporary decor; nonsmoking rooms are available. Facilities include an Olympic-size outdoor swimming pool and a complete fitness center. There is a minimum 3-night stay on in-season holiday weekends.

CARRIAGE HOUSE, 208 Jersey Ave., Spring Lake, NJ 07762. Tel. 908/449-1332. 8 rms (6 with bath). A/C
$ Rates: $55 single, $65–$95 double. No credit cards. **Parking:** Free.
Two blocks from the ocean, this three-story Victorian bed-and-breakfast inn is located on a quiet, tree-lined street. Owned by Marie and Tom Bradley, this grand old house is furnished with family antiques and heirlooms and has a shady front porch

with rockers, gardens, and on-site parking. Most rooms have three to five windows, so there is a lovely cross-ventilation if you don't feel like using the air conditioner. The rates include complimentary morning coffee and Danish pastry, and there is a guest refrigerator on each floor.

STONE POST INN, 115 Washington Ave., Spring Lake, NJ 07762. Tel. 908/449-1212. 20 rms (8 with bath).

$ Rates (including continental breakfast): $55 single, $85–$110 double. AE, MC, V.
Parking: Free.

Relaxing in a rocking chair on the huge wraparound porch is one of the joys of staying at this inn. Located in a shady residential area, this three-story Victorian building dates back to 1882. It had a varied life as a hotel, restaurant, and private home until it was rejuvenated and opened as a bed-and-breakfast in 1988 by local residents Julia Paris and her daughters Janine and Connie. The Parises have filled the house with antiques and art, and have expanded the gardens outside. Each room has a ceiling fan and Victorian-style furnishings.

Rates include the use of beach passes and parking. There is a 2-night minimum stay on weekends and a 3-night minimum stay on holiday weekends; reduced rates are available during the rest of the year.

WHERE TO DINE

EXPENSIVE

OLD MILL INN, Old Mill Rd., Spring Lake Heights. Tel. 449-1800.
Cuisine: INTERNATIONAL. **Reservations:** Recommended.
$ Prices: Appetizers $2.95–$7.95; main courses $15.95–$22.95; lunch $5.95–$11.95. AE, CB, DC, MC, V.
Open: Lunch daily 11:30am–2:30pm; dinner Mon–Fri 2:30–9:30pm, Sat–Sun 2:30–10pm or 11pm; brunch Sun 11am–3pm.

The top dining choice in the area is this restaurant overlooking a lake in a countryside setting. Originally established in 1938, this popular, multilevel restaurant was expanded and updated in 1987. Not only are the views and the ambience delightful, but the food is top-notch. Entrées include prime ribs, roast duckling, grilled salmon, shrimp francese, veal béarnaise, and marinated roast chicken. Lobster dishes are also available, usually over $20. For a real bargain, early-bird dinners, priced from $9.95 and up for four courses, are served from 2:30 to 6pm on weekdays.

MODERATE

BEACH HOUSE, 901 Ocean Ave. Tel. 449-9646.
Cuisine: INTERNATIONAL. **Reservations:** Not accepted.
$ Prices: Appetizers $2.95–$6.95; main courses $12.50–$16.95; lunch $2.95–$5.95. AE, CB, DC, MC, V.
Open: Summer daily noon–10pm; off-season Sat–Sun noon–10pm.

Victorian towers and gables are the keynote of this restaurant opposite the Spring Lake oceanfront. You can dine on a screened-in wraparound porch or in one of three clubby old-world rooms lined with oak-framed prints depicting Spring Lake of yesteryear. The setting is casual and the food straightforward, but the views and ambience are the best in town.

Lunch offers burgers, sandwiches, quiches, and salads. Entrées at dinner include steaks, lamb chops, and seafoods such as flounder and scampi.

YANKEE CLIPPER, 1 Chicago Blvd., Sea Girt. Tel. 449-7200.
Cuisine: INTERNATIONAL. **Reservations:** Advised for weekends.

$ Prices: Appetizers $2.95–$6.95; main courses $11.95–$21.95; lunch $4.95–$7.95. AE, CB, DC, MC, V.
Open: Lunch Mon–Sat 11:30am–2:30pm; dinner 6–10pm.

This modern, elegant dining room with floor-to-ceiling windows overlooks the Atlantic. This spot is particularly popular at dusk, when birds gather at the shoreline. Dinner entrées include daily seafood specials, such as shrimp with lobster stuffing, or "fruits of the sea" with fettuccine, plus steaks, prime rib, veal, and poultry dishes. A champagne brunch is also featured on Sunday from 11am to 3pm, priced at $19.85.

2. POINT PLEASANT BEACH TO LONG BEACH ISLAND

The stretch of land from Point Pleasant Beach southward to the bottom of Long Beach Island takes in over 50 miles. These resorts are primarily barrier island beaches, with the Atlantic on one side and intracoastal waterways on the other. They are grouped on two slender land masses, the Barnegat Peninsula and Long Beach Island, and are connected to the mainland by bridges and causeways.

POINT PLEASANT BEACH

12 miles S of Spring Lake, 66 miles N of Atlantic City,
22 miles S of Red Bank, 51 miles SE of Philadelphia, 65 miles S of New York

GETTING THERE By Bus New Jersey Transit provides daily service.

By Car Take the Garden State Parkway to exits 98 through 88.

ESSENTIALS Information For specific brochures about this area, contact the **Greater Point Pleasant Chamber of Commerce,** 517 Arnold Ave., Point Pleasant, NJ 08742 (tel. 908/899-2424).

Area Code The area code for all numbers in the Point Pleasant region is 908.

If you follow Rte. 35 southward from Spring Lake, you'll cross over the Manasquan Inlet into Point Pleasant Beach. This is the start of a 22-mile island known as the Barnegat Peninsula. You can also enter the island from the more southerly points via Rtes. 88 and 37.

Point Pleasant is best known for its busy marina, fine sandy beaches, family-oriented boardwalk, seafood restaurants, and beachside bungalows. The communities that lie to the south are lined primarily with residential or rental properties, from the mansions of well-to-do Bay Head to the back-to-back cottages of Normandy, Chadwick, and Lavallette, and the summer bungalows of Seaside Heights and Seaside Park.

WHERE TO STAY

EXPENSIVE

WHITE SANDS MOTEL, 1106 Ocean Ave., Point Pleasant, NJ 08742. Tel. 908/899-3370. 60 rms. A/C TV TEL

$ Rates: Summer $95–$160 single or double; off-season $50–$80 single or double. AE, MC, V. **Parking:** Free.

This modern two-story property is located on the beachfront in a quiet section of the shoreline. Totally refurbished in 1990, each room has one or two double beds or a king-size bed and most have ocean views and terraces. Guest amenities include an outdoor pool, a snack bar, and private beach privileges.

MODERATE

MARINER'S COVE MOTOR LODGE, 50 Broadway, Point Pleasant Beach, NJ 08742. Tel. 908/899-0060. 24 rms. A/C TV TEL
$ Rates: $84–$90 single or double. AE, MC, V. **Parking:** Free.

This motor lodge is one block from the ocean and overlooks the marina. The two-story property has rooms with two double beds and standard furnishings; many rooms also have balconies. Outdoor facilities include a swimming pool and a sun deck. Rates are lower in the off-season.

WHERE TO DINE

LOBSTER SHANTY, 83 Channel Dr., Point Pleasant Beach. Tel. 908/899-6700.
Cuisine: INTERNATIONAL. **Reservations:** Not required.
$ Prices: Appetizers $2.95–$8.95; main courses $11.95–$21.95. AE, CB, DC, MC, V.
Open: Summer, dinner daily 5–9:30pm; off-season, Wed–Sat 5–9:30pm, Sun 1–9pm.

Since 1950, the Lobster Shanty has been synonymous with good seafood. Overlooking the Manasquan Inlet, the decor is understandably nautical. Open for dinner only, the menu includes various lobster dishes, Atlantic flounder, crab cakes, Cajun/Creole scampi, seafood samplers, chicken and shrimp stir-fry, and steaks. All main courses entitle you to unlimited helpings at the salad bar.

LONG BEACH ISLAND

40 miles S of Spring Lake, 37 miles N of Atlantic City, 71 miles N of Cape May, 65 miles SE of Philadelphia, 107 miles S of New York

GETTING THERE By Bus   The New Jersey Transit operates daily service.

By Car   Take the Garden State Parkway to exit 63.

ESSENTIALS Information   For complete information on this area, contact the **Long Beach Island/Southern Ocean County Chamber of Commerce,** 265 W. Ninth St., Ship Bottom, NJ 08008 (tel. 609/494-7211) or toll-free 800/292-6372), open from 10am to 4pm Monday through Saturday.

Area Code   Long Beach Island's area code is 609.

Long Beach Island is an 18-mile stretch of sand, quite different from its somewhat noisy neighbors to the north and to the south (Atlantic City). With only one connection to the mainland (the Rte. 72 causeway), Long Beach Island is the most remote of the Jersey shore resorts.

This slender isle, which is no more than three blocks wide in some places, was discovered by the Dutch in the 17th century and was a major whaling station in the years that followed. Officially named Long Beach Island in 1890, it grew into a fashionable resort at the turn of the century, particularly because it was said to be pollen free—a big inducement for hay-fever sufferers to this day.

Long Beach Island's main claim to fame, however, is the 172-foot **Barnegat Lighthouse** at the northern tip of the island. Known variously as the Grand Old Champion of the Tides and Old Barney, it was built in 1857–58 and played a key role on the Jersey coast in alerting approaching vessels to the dangers of the Barnegat shoals.

Long Beach Island consists of more than 20 separate towns and communities, with evocative and diverse names like Loveladies, Ship Bottom, Holly Lagoons, Harvey Cedars, Spray Beach, the Dunes, Beach Haven, and Surf City. One main artery, Long Beach Boulevard, extends the length of the island (although it sometimes changes its name simply to the Boulevard), and there is no boardwalk. In general, the northern communities of the island are primarily geared to residential or rental housing, and the majority of motels are concentrated on the southern stretch, below the causeway.

WHAT TO SEE & DO

Today the **Barnegat Lighthouse** is the central fixture in a small, 36-acre park. Visitors are welcome to climb the 217 steps to the top of Old Barney, and enjoy a panoramic view and picture-taking location. It's open from 9am to 5pm Memorial Day to Labor Day, and on weekends in May, September, and October. Admission is 50¢ for everyone over 12 and free for children under 12.

Swimming and sunning are undoubtedly the most popular pastimes, but fishing is also a favorite sport. If you'd like to join in, head for the **Beach Haven Fishing Center,** Centre St. and the Bay, Beach Haven (tel. 492-0333). From June through September, half-day fishing trips are available on the *Black Whale,* departing at 8am; the cost is $20 for adults and $15 for children under 12, including rod, bait, and tackle. This same company also operates 1-hour evening sightseeing cruises at 5, 6:30, and 8pm, with live entertainment, priced at $6 for adults and $4 for children under 12.

Another focal point on this strip is the **Fantasy Island Amusement Park,** 320 W. 7th St., Beach Haven (tel. 492-4000), a Victorian-style amusement center, with rides and video games for children and a casino arcade with "gambling" machines for adults. It's a pleasant setting, with brick walkways, oak benches, ornate lamp posts, and colored-glass fixtures. Admission is free, but rides are $1.50 to $2.50 each; on Friday, there is an all-inclusive price of $10 for unlimited rides, from 1 to 7pm.

WHERE TO STAY

EXPENSIVE

ENGLESIDE ON THE OCEAN, 30 Engleside Ave., Beach Haven, NJ 08008. Tel. 609/492-1251. 69 rms. A/C TV TEL
$ Rates: Mid-June–Aug $115–$145 single or double; off-season $61–$122 single or double; efficiencies $152–$189 and $64–$132, respectively. AE, MC, V. **Parking:** Free.
This modern, three-story motel is set right on the beach. Each guest room has two double beds, a refrigerator, a coffeemaker, a balcony, and contemporary furnishings. Facilities include a heated pool, a Jacuzzi, a health club, and a restaurant/lounge. East wing rooms have ocean views, and some units have small kitchenettes.

THE MARINER MOTOR INN, 33rd St. and Long Beach Blvd., Beach Haven Gardens, NJ 08008. Tel. 908/492-1235. 38 units. A/C TV TEL.
$ Rates: June–Aug $50–$100 single or double, Feb–May and Sept–Dec $40–$70 single or double; efficiencies $10 additional. MC, V. **Parking:** Free.
One of the newest properties in this area, this attractive, three-story brick motel is on the ocean side of the main thoroughfare but an easy walk to the beach. The contemporary guest rooms, each of which has sliding glass door/windows leading to a balcony, have standard furnishings plus a refrigerator. Some efficiencies are also

available. Facilities include an outdoor swimming pool, elevator, and complimentary morning coffee.

SPRAY BEACH MOTOR INN, 24th St. at Ocean Blvd., Spray Beach, NJ 08008. Tel. 609/492-1501. 88 rms. A/C TV TEL
$ Rates: July–Aug $99–$139 single or double; off-season $49–$129 single or double. MC, V. **Parking:** Free.

Located on the beach overlooking the Atlantic, this three-story property offers rooms with one or two double beds and a refrigerator; most rooms have private balconies or a deck. About a third of the rooms have ocean views. Minimum stays of 3 or 4 nights may apply during high season. Guest facilities include a heated outdoor pool, a restaurant, and a lounge.

WHERE TO DINE
EXPENSIVE

BAYBERRY INN, 13th St. and Long Beach Blvd., Ship Bottom. Tel. 494-8848.
    Cuisine: INTERNATIONAL. **Reservations:** Not accepted.
$ Prices: Appetizers $3.95–$7.95; main courses $10.95–$22.95; lunch $4.95–$9.95. AE, CB, DC, MC, V.
    Open: Lunch Mon–Sat 11:30am–3pm; dinner Mon–Sat 4–10pm, Sun 3–9pm; brunch Sun 10am–1:30pm.

    This restaurant has been in business since 1975, but it has a 1795 decor and ambience. Colonial-style furnishings and red, white, and blue table linens add to the atmosphere. Sandwiches, salads, and light entrées are featured at lunch. The menu at dinner includes Chesapeake oysters stuffed with crab, rock Cornish hen, red snapper, seafood crêpes, veal alla marsala, chicken Cordon Bleu, Grand Marnier duckling, daily local seafood specials, and steaks.

CHARLES' SEAFOOD GARDEN, 8611 Long Beach Blvd., Beach Haven Crest. Tel. 492-8340.
    Cuisine: INTERNATIONAL. **Reservations:** Not accepted.
$ Prices: Appetizers $2.95–$6.95; main courses $10.95–$20.95. AE, MC, V.
    Open: May–Oct dinner daily 5–10pm; off-season Sat–Sun 5–10pm. **Closed:** Winter.

Flowers and plants dominate the decor at this modern conservatory-style restaurant set back from the island's main road. Open for dinner only, the menu includes vegetarian specials and an imaginative blend of seafoods and pastas, such as clam tortellini, seafood pasta, fettuccine of the sea (with king crab), seafood florentine, as well as veal and lobster, seafood gumbo, and steaks. No liquor is served, but you can bring your own.

MORRISON'S SEAFOOD, 2nd St. and Bayfront, Beach Haven. Tel. 492-5111.
    Cuisine: SEAFOOD. **Reservations:** Not accepted.
$ Prices: Appetizers $2.95–$4.95; main courses $10–$20; lunch $3–$6. AE, MC, V.
    Open: May–Sept daily 11:30am–9pm; weekends Apr and Oct.

Located on the bay, this restaurant is a favorite for seafood, steaks, and chicken dishes. Featured dishes include french-fried lobster tails, Cajun catfish, Cajun rock shrimp, snow crab legs, and mahi mahi. You may bring your own alcoholic beverage.

PORT O' CALL, Engleside Ave. at the Bay, Beach Haven. Tel. 492-0715.
    Cuisine: INTERNATIONAL. **Reservations:** Recommended on weekends.
$ Prices: Appetizers $2.95–$6.95; main courses $9.95–$24.95; lunch $3.95–$7.95. AE, CB, DC, MC, V.
    Open: Lunch daily noon–2pm; dinner 5–9:30pm.

This contemporary restaurant overlooks the bay side of the island. Lunch items include salads, sandwiches, platters, quiches, and burgers. The menu at dinner is heavily slanted to seafood dishes, such as Jersey flounder, swordfish, scallops and shrimp. Other selections range from chicken florentine to steaks and prime rib. Entrées include a trip to the 20-item salad bar that is laid out on a miniature ship. In addition, "early-bird" dinners, priced from $9.95, are available to those who dine from 5 to 6pm, Monday through Saturday or 4 to 6pm on Sunday.

3. OCEAN CITY TO THE WILDWOODS

The remainder of the Jersey shore takes in the strip from Atlantic City to Cape May, both of which are covered in separate chapters. The purpose of this section will be to look at the major resorts in between, and, in particular, Ocean City, Stone Harbor, Avalon, and the Wildwoods—an area of about 35 miles and at least 150 small islands and 4 substantial barrier islands.

All of the resorts covered in this section are promoted by the **Cape May County Chamber of Commerce,** P.O. Box 74, Garden State Parkway (exit 11), Cape May Court House, NJ 08210 (tel. 609/465-7181). This office is open year round, daily from 9am to 5pm from mid-April to mid-October; and Monday through Friday from 10am to 4pm during the rest of the year.

All telephone numbers in this section belong to the 609 area code.

OCEAN CITY

47 miles S of Long Beach Island, 10 miles S of Atlantic City,
61 miles N of Cape May, 75 miles SE of Philadelphia,
117 miles S of New York

GETTING THERE   By Bus   The New Jersey Transit operates daily service.

By Car   Take the Garden State Parkway to exit 29 or 30 and follow Rte. 52 east.

ESSENTIALS   Information   For specific information about this resort, contact Ocean City Information Center, P.O. Box 157, Ocean City, NJ 08226 (tel. 609/391-0240 or toll-free 800/BEACH-NJ). Walk-in information centers are maintained at the Causeway Entrance to Ocean City, Rte. 52 (year round), and at the Music Pier, 8th Street and Boardwalk, in the summer months. The cost of a pass for Ocean City beaches is $2 a day or $5 a week.

❶f all the Jersey shore resorts, Ocean City prides itself as being the most family-oriented. Year after year, many of the same families come back, most often renting cottages and bungalows by the sea. Unlike its famous neighbor to the north, Atlantic City, this resort has no gambling, no nightclubs, and no liquor. It is a dry town and always has been, dating back to its founding as a Methodist retreat in 1879.

WHAT TO SEE & DO

Ocean City's main claims to fame are its 8-mile stretch of beach, 2½-mile **boardwalk,** and unique turn-of-the-century **Music Pier,** at 8th St. and Boardwalk, which is the scene of summertime open-air events. The premier attraction is the
✪ **Ocean City Pops Orchestra,** a tradition for over 60 years. These Pops concerts are held Sunday through Wednesday (admission is $1, except Sunday when it is free).

Visitors to Ocean City also come for the fishing, particularly bluefish, sea trout (weakfish), flounder, fluke, and black sea bass. If this is your sport, head for the **Ocean City Marina and Fishing Center,** 3rd St. and Bay Ave. (tel. 399-5011 or 399-5586). From late May through September you can take a 4-hour fishing trip for

$15 for adults or $8 for children under 10, with $2 rod rental. Trips leave the dock daily at 8am and 1pm.

In addition, this company offers 6-hour night bluefishing trips from $26 on Friday and Saturday nights. If the lures of Atlantic City tempt you instead, there are also nightly trips to the gaming capital, from June through September, and on weekends in spring and fall; departure times vary, so it is best to call in advance. The round-trip fare is $25, and reservations are required. For those who prefer a sightseeing cruise, this is also the place to come. Boats go out from mid-June through mid-September, Monday through Thursday, at 7pm for 1½-hour narrated cruises; the cost is $5 for adults and $3 for children 10 and under.

WHERE TO STAY
EXPENSIVE

FLANDERS, on the Boardwalk at 11th Street, Ocean City, NJ 08226. Tel. 609/399-1000 or toll-free 800/345-0211. Fax 609/399-0194. 220 rms. A/C TV TEL
$ Rates: Late June–Aug $114–$150 single or double; off-season $84–$120 single or double. AE, MC, V. **Parking:** $3.

Dominating the scene along the beach is this red-tile-roofed old-world hotel. Built in 1923, this grande dame was recently refurbished and updated, but it is still a favorite with Ocean City regulars. The guest rooms offer a choice of twin, double, or king-size beds. Guest amenities include a dining room, a full social program, a heated pool, a shuffleboard, miniature golf, entertainment, a shopping arcade, sauna and exercise room, and barber/beauty salons.

PORT-O-CALL HOTEL, 1510 Boardwalk, Ocean City, NJ 08226. Tel. 609/399-8812. Fax 609/399-0387. 98 rms. A/C TV TEL
$ Rates: High-season $146–$185 single or double; off-season $79–$95 single or double. AE, CB, DC, MC, V. **Parking:** Free.

This modern, nine-story beachfront property offers some rooms with ocean views and others facing the bay. Each room has a contemporary decor, a private balcony, a refrigerator, and complimentary in-room coffeemaker. Facilities include an outdoor beachfront pool, a terrace, and a sauna. There is also a moderately priced restaurant, the Portsider, overlooking the beach.

MODERATE

HARBOR HOUSE MOTOR INN, 200 Bay Ave., Box 582, Ocean City, NJ 08226. Tel. 609/399-8585. Fax 609/391-0769. 68 rms. A/C TV TEL
$ Rates: Mid-July–Aug $139 single or double; off-season $80 single or double. AE, DISC, MC, V. **Parking:** Free. **Closed:** Mid-Oct–Mar.

Located on the edge of Egg Harbor Bay, this motel/marina is on the bayfront. It is a three-story property, on a particularly good location if you want to be near the fishing fleets and boat rides. The guest rooms have contemporary light-wood furnishings, two double beds, and a balcony or terrace overlooking the marina. There is a 3-day minimum during high-season. Guest facilities include a coffee shop, a heated pool, a sun deck, marina, bike rentals, and jet-ski rentals.

WHERE TO DINE
MODERATE

BOOKER'S NEW ENGLAND SEAFOOD HOUSE, 9th St. and Wesley Ave. Tel. 339-4672.
Cuisine: AMERICAN. **Reservations:** Accepted for parties of 5 or more only.
$ Prices: Appetizers $2.95–$4.95; main courses $7.99–$19.99. AE, MC, V.
Open: Dinner daily 4:30–9:30pm.

Designed with a fishing-inn motif, this busy restaurant two blocks from the boardwalk is the top choice in the area. Open for dinner only, the menu combines fresh daily seafood specials with southern cooking, and includes such choices as stuffed flounder, lobster, deviled crab, Salisbury steak, Virginia baked ham, and fried chicken. There is free parking and a seafood take-out, in case you prefer a picnic by the sea.

STONE HARBOR & AVALON

17 miles S of Atlantic City, 23 miles N of Cape May,
90 miles SE of Philadelphia

GETTING THERE **By Bus** The New Jersey Transit provides daily service.

By Car Take the Garden State Parkway to exit 13 or 10.

ESSENTIALS **Information** For specific data and travel literature about this area, contact the **Chamber of Commerce of Stone Harbor,** 212 96th St., P.O. Box 422, Stone Harbor, NJ 08247 (tel. 609/368-6101).

These two resorts share an island called **Seven Mile Beach.** On the north end, Avalon is a relatively quiet town, appropriately named after the mythical resting place of King Arthur. Strong zoning ordinances have protected the beach and the high dunes from overdevelopment; consequently, there are relatively few motels or commercial enterprises. Avalon is further preserved by the fact that the World Wildlife Fund owns 1,000 acres of meadowland and has left it in its natural state.

On the southern end of Seven Mile Beach is **Stone Harbor,** a lagoon development of the Intracoastal Waterway and a haven for pleasure boaters. Dating back to 1892, Stone Harbor consists mainly of family homes and rental properties.

✪ The community is best known as the home of **The Stone Harbor Bird Sanctuary,** Ocean Drive (tel. 368-6101), a National Landmark and a prime nesting place for herons. Located at the southern end of Stone Harbor, between 111th and 116th Streets, this 21-acre facility is the only one of its kind in the United States that is sponsored by and located within a municipality. Established in 1947, it is home to more than 6,000 birds, including the American (common) egret, snowy egret, Louisiana heron, green heron, yellow-crowned and black-crowned night herons, cattle egrets, and glossy ibises. Visitors cannot enter the heronry, but can park in a special observation area and watch the birds flying in and out of this natural nesting site, generally in the March-through-October period. No charge.

✪ While in Stone Harbor, you should also visit the **Wetlands Institute,** Stone Harbor Blvd. (tel. 368-1211), a research facility located on the edge of a 6,000-acre salt marsh. Founded in 1969 to promote an understanding of the coastal and wetlands ecosystem, this attraction includes a visitor center with a wetlands "touch" museum, exhibits, a salt marsh trail, and an observation tower. Hours are 9am to 4pm, Monday through Saturday, and from 1 to 4pm on Sunday from mid-May to September; and 9am to 4pm Tuesday, Thursday, and Saturday during the rest of the year. Admission charge is $3 for adults, $1 for children under 12.

WHERE TO STAY
EXPENSIVE

GOLDEN INN, 78th St. and Dune Dr., Avalon, NJ 08202. Tel. 609/368-5155 or toll-free 800/426-4300. Fax 609/368-6112. 153 rms, 15 suites. A/C TV TEL

$ Rates: $62–$172 single or double; $97–$257 suites. AE, MC, V. **Parking:** Free.
An outstanding facility in the area is this lodging in the middle of Seven Mile Beach. Open year round, this property has contemporary rooms equipped with a refrigerator; all rooms have balconies. Reduced-rate package plans are available in the off-season.

Besides the views of the ocean, the facilities include an oceanfront restaurant, a well-landscaped setting with a rock garden, an outdoor heated swimming pool, and parking.

MODERATE

SEAWARD MOTEL, 9720 Second Avenue, Stone Harbor, NJ 08247. Tel. 609/368-5900. 17 rooms, 3 suites. A/C TV

$ Rates: $45–$90 single or double, $55–$110 suite. No credit cards. **Parking:** Free. **Closed:** Nov–Mar.

In the heart of Stone Harbor, one block from the beach, this three-story property offers rooms with two double beds, picture windows, and standard furnishings. Two-room efficiency units with kitchenettes are also available. Outdoor facilities include a heated swimming pool, a sun deck, a patio, and off-street parking.

WHERE TO DINE
MODERATE

HENNY'S, 97th St. and 3rd Ave. Tel. 368-2929.
  Cuisine: SEAFOOD. **Reservations:** Recommended.
$ Prices: Appetizers $2.95–$7.95; main courses $10.95–$21.95. AE, MC, V.
  Open: June–Sept dinner daily 5–10pm; off-season Fri–Sun 5–10pm. **Closed:** Dec.

For fine seafood, this restaurant is a tradition in Stone Harbor. There are no ocean views, but the decor is mostly nautical, with an elegant touch including linen tablecloths and a Steinway grand piano. Open for dinner only, Henny's offers seafood platters, filet of baby flounder, deviled crab, local sea scallops, Delaware Bay oysters with pepper hash, and stuffed soft-shell crabs, as well as prime rib, veal scaloppine, and steaks. Nightly entertainment adds to the atmosphere, and the Ship's Wheel lounge is a favorite with local boat owners.

WHITEBRIER INN, 260 20th St., Avalon. Tel. 967-5225.
  Cuisine: INTERNATIONAL. **Reservations:** Recommended.
$ Prices: Appetizers $2.95–$6.95; main courses $9.95–$22.95; lunch $5–$10. AE, MC, V.
  Open: Lunch Mon–Sat 11:30am–2:30pm; dinner Mon–Thurs 5–9pm, Fri–Sun 5–10pm; brunch Sun 10am–2pm.

This contemporary-style restaurant has a decor of pastel sea tones, pine woods, and skylights. Sandwiches, salads, and light fare are offered at lunch. The extensive dinner menu features lobster scampi, surf-n-turf, prime ribs, veal piccante, and at least four different local flounder choices. There is a reduced schedule from mid-September to mid-May.

THE WILDWOODS

32 miles S of Atlantic City, 8 miles N of Cape May

GETTING THERE   By Bus   The New Jersey Transit provides daily service.

By Car   Take the Garden State Parkway to exit 6 or 4.

ESSENTIALS   Information   Specific travel data about the area can be obtained by contacting the **Wildwoods Tourist Information Office,** Boardwalk and Schellenger Avenue, P.O. Box 823, Wildwood, NJ 08260 (tel. 609/729-4000 or toll-free 800/WW-BY-SEA).

An island known as **Five Mile Beach** is home to the Wildwood area of the Jersey shore. Wildwood is actually not one town but five. Known primarily as a place to party, the Greater Wildwoods attract a predominantly young crowd, although many families also return year after year. The beaches are clean, wide, and free of charge, and the 2½-mile-long boardwalk is lined with fast-food stands, amusements, and rides. Many of the bars are open until 5am and the horizon is crammed with back-to-back motels, at least 400 of them, offering more than 25,000 rooms.

WHAT TO SEE & DO

The focal point of this island is Wildwood, 3 miles long with a 1,000-foot wide beach, and the home of most of the boardwalk entertainment, arcades, and nightclubs. The other sections are designated as North Wildwood, West Wildwood, Wildwoods-by-the-Sea, and Wildwood Crest. The latter and southernmost portion of the Wildwoods is unique because it features two equally picturesque coasts, with the Atlantic to the east and Sunset Lake on the west.

The Wildwoods are also famous for water sports. If sightseeing on the water is your sport, try the **Delta Lady,** a Mississippi riverboat. It sails daily, June through August, from the **Wildwood Yacht Basin,** 508 W. Rio Grande Ave. (tel. 522-1919), at 10:30am, 2, 7, and 10pm (a banjo cruise). The 2-hour boat trip takes in the inland waterway, the bird sanctuary, and other harbor sights. The cost for adults is $6.95 and $3.50 for children under 12.

WHERE TO STAY

MODERATE

ADVENTURER MOTOR INN, 5401 Ocean Ave., Wildwood Crest, NJ 08260. Tel. 609/729-1200. 104 rms. A/C TV
$ Rates: $95–$110 single or double; off-season $45–$95 single or double. AE, MC, V. **Parking:** Free. **Closed:** Nov–Mar.
Located on the beach, this inn is next to the boardwalk. All of the rooms in this modern six-story property have ocean views and a refrigerator; most also have a private balcony. Two-room efficiency units are available from $140 a day. A 3-day minimum applies for all rooms in the peak season. Guest facilities include a parking garage under the building, a heated outdoor pool, a beachfront sun deck, a grill room, a guest laundry, and a game room.

BEACH TERRACE, 3400 Atlantic Ave., Wildwood, NJ 08260. Tel. 609/522-8100. 68 rms. A/C TV TEL
$ Rates: July–Aug $98–$120 double; off-season $36–$86 double. MC, V. **Parking:** Free. **Closed:** Mid-Oct–Mar.
One block from the beach, this modern six-story hotel offers guest rooms that have two double beds, standard furnishings, a small parlor, and a balcony. Guest facilities include an Olympic-size pool, a patio, a restaurant, and lounge.

NEWPORT MOTEL, 4900 Ocean Ave., Wildwood, NJ 08260. Tel. 609/522-4911. 15 rms, 20 suites. A/C TV TEL
$ Rates: $35–$95 single, $40–$98 double, $45–$117 suite. AE, CB, DC, DISC, MC, V. **Parking:** Free. **Closed:** Mid-Oct–mid-Apr.
This five-story property offers modern rooms equipped with dark wood furnishings, sea-toned fabrics, a refrigerator, and a private balcony. In addition, deluxe rooms and two-room efficiencies are available. Facilities include a swimming pool and a guest laundry.

SINGAPORE MOTEL, 515 E. Orchid Rd., Wildwood Crest, NJ 08260. Tel. 609/522-6961. Fax 609/522-6827. 56 rms. A/C TV TEL
$ Rates: Late-June–Sept $79–$149 single or double; off-season $39–$99 double. MC, V. **Parking:** Free. **Closed:** Mid-Nov–mid-Mar.
A pagoda-style facade fronts this modern property set on the beachfront. As its name implies, the motel is surrounded by Japanese gardens, pine trees, and fountains. The rooms all have a Far Eastern decor and a refrigerator, and the styles range from basic motel to efficiency; some rooms have views overlooking the oceanfront, and others,

the pool, street, and gardens. Facilities include a café, an outdoor swimming pool, a game room, a guest laundry room, an enclosed rooftop shuffleboard, and table tennis.

THUNDERBIRD INN, Surf Ave. at 24th St., North Wildwood, NJ 08260. Tel. 609/522-6901. 76 rms. A/C TV TEL

$ Rates: Mid-June–early Sept $89–$115 single or double; off-season $35–$79 single or double. AE, MC, V. **Parking:** Free.

Lush tropical gardens surround this inn situated one block from the beach. The modern two-story property has a driftwood motif and a Polynesian village atmosphere. The rooms have one or two double beds, a refrigerator, wall-to-wall carpeting, and a coffeemaker. Guest facilities include an outdoor swimming pool, a sun patio, a café, and a lounge.

WHERE TO DINE

EXPENSIVE/MODERATE

MARINER INN, 8100 Bayview Drive, Wildwood Crest. Tel. 522-1287.
   Cuisine: INTERNATIONAL. **Reservations:** Recommended.
$ Prices: Appetizers $2.95–$5.95; main courses $7.95–$25.95. AE, CB, DC, MC, V.
   Open: Dinner daily May–Sept 4:30–10pm.

The best place to watch the sun go down on Sunset Lake is at this lakefront restaurant in an idyllic setting. Open for dinner only, the selections include farm-fresh turkey, spring chicken, prime rib, surf-n-turf, steaks, and a wide variety of seafood, such as Jersey flounder, swordfish, scampi, and jumbo lobster tails. If you dine between 4:30 and 6pm, you can catch the early-bird specials, offering complete dinners from $6.95 to $12.95.

SEASONS, 222 E. Schellenger Ave., Wildwood. Tel. 522-4400.
   Cuisine: INTERNATIONAL. **Reservations:** Recommended.
$ Prices: Appetizers $2.95–$6.95; main courses $10.95–$23.95. AE, CB, DC, MC, V.
   Open: Dinner daily 4:30–10pm.

Cajun and Italian cuisines are featured at this restaurant located in midcity without a view, but with a yacht club ambience. The versatile menu emphasizes Cajun-blackened seafood and steaks, as well as such Italian specialties as flounder francese, scampi, lobster fra diavolo, and eight different veal dishes.

URIE'S REEF AND BEEF, 448 W. Rio Grande Ave., Wildwood. Tel. 522-7761.
   Cuisine: SEAFOOD. **Reservations:** Recommended.
$ Prices: Appetizers $2.95–$6.95; main courses $11.95–$24.95; lunch $5–$10. AE, CB, DC, MC, V.
   Open: Summer daily noon–10pm; off-season Sat–Sun dinner 4–9pm.

Situated beside the bay, this restaurant has a tropical garden atmosphere. Lunch items focus on sandwiches, salads, and light dishes. Dinner entrées include the namesake dish reef and beef (stuffed lobster tail and filet mignon), as well as lobster and shrimp marinara, jumbo shrimp and scallops mornay, crab au gratin, filet of flounder au gratin, lobster tails, fishermen's platters; prime rib, steaks, chicken, and veal.

THE AMERICAN SYSTEM OF MEASUREMENTS

LENGTH

1 inch (in.)			=	2.54cm			
1 foot (ft.)	=	12 in.	=	30.48cm	=	.305m	
1 yard (yd.)	=	3 ft.			=	.915m	
1 mile	=	5,280 ft.					= 1.609km

To convert miles to kilometers, multiply the number of miles by 1.61 (example: 50 mi. × 1.61 = 80.5km). Also use to convert speeds from miles per hour (m.p.h.) to kilometers per hour (kmph).

To convert kilometers to miles, multiply the number of kilometers by .62 (example: 25km × .62 = 15.5 mi.). Also use to convert kmph to m.p.h.

CAPACITY

1 fluid ounce (fl. oz.)			=	.03 liters
1 pint	=	16 fl. oz.	=	.47 liters
1 quart	=	2 pints	=	.94 liters
1 gallon (gal.)	=	4 quarts	=	3.79 liters
			=	.83 Imperial gal.

To convert U.S. gallons to liters, multiply the number of gallons by 3.79 (example: 12 gal. × 3.79 = 45.48 liters).

To convert liters to U.S. gallons, multiply the number of liters by .26 (example: 50 liters × .26 = 13 U.S. gal.).

To convert U.S. gallons to Imperial gallons, multiply the number of U.S. gallons by .83 (example: 12 U.S. gal. × .83 = 9.95 Imperial gal.).

To convert Imperial gallons to U.S. gallons, multiply the number of Imperial gallons by 1.2 (example: 8 Imperial gal. × 1.2 = 9.6 U.S. gal.).

WEIGHT

1 ounce (oz.)			=	28.35g		
1 pound (lb.)	=	16 oz.	=	453.6g	=	.45kg
1 ton			=	2,000 lb.	=	907kg
			=	.91 metric tons		

To convert pounds to kilograms, multiply the number of pounds by .45 (example: 90 lb. × .45 = 40.5kg).

To convert kilograms to pounds, multiply the number of kilograms by 2.2 (example: 75kg × 2.2 = 165 lb.).

AREA

1 acre			=	.41ha		
1 square mile	=	640 acres	=	259ha	=	2.6km^2

To convert acres to hectares, multiply the number of acres by .41 (example: 40 acres × .41 = 16.4ha).

To convert hectares to acres, multiply the number of hectares by 2.47 (example: 20ha × 2.47 = 49.4 acres).

To convert square miles to square kilometers, multiply the number of square miles by 2.6 (example: 80 square miles × 2.6 = 208km^2).

To convert square kilometers to square miles, multiply the number of square kilometers by .39 (example: 150km^2 × .39 = 58.5 square miles).

TEMPERATURE

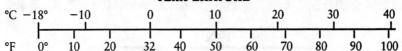

To convert degrees Fahrenheit to degrees Celsius, subtract 32 from °F, multiply by 5, then divide by 9 (example: $85°F - 32 \times 5/9 = 29.4°C$).

To convert degrees Celsius to degrees Fahrenheit, multiply °C by 9, divide by 5, and add 32 (example: $20°C \times 9/5 + 32 = 68°F$).

INDEX

GENERAL INFORMATION

DESTINATIONS

PENNSYLVANIA

KEY TO ABBREVIATIONS: *B* = budget; *E* = expensive; *I* = inexpensive; *M* = moderate; *VE* = very expensive; *$* = super-special value; * = one of authors' favorites.

DELAWARE

MARYLAND

NOW, SAVE MONEY ON ALL YOUR TRAVELS!
Join Frommer's™ Dollarwise® Travel Club

Saving money while traveling is never easy, which is why the **Dollarwise Travel Club** was formed 32 years ago to provide cost-cutting travel strategies, up-to-date travel information, and a sense of community for value-conscious travelers from all over the world.

In keeping with the money-saving concept, the annual membership fee is low—$20 for U.S. residents and $25 for residents of Canada, Mexico, and other countries—and is immediately exceeded by the value of your benefits, which include:

1. Any TWO books listed on the following pages;
2. Plus any ONE Frommer's City Guide;
3. A subscription to our quarterly newspaper, *The Dollarwise Traveler;*
4. A membership card that entitles you to purchase through the Club all Frommer's publications for 33% to 40% off their retail price.

The eight-page **Dollarwise Traveler** tells you about the latest developments in good-value travel worldwide and includes the following columns: **Hospitality Exchange** (for those offering and seeking hospitality in cities all over the world); and **Share-a-Trip** (for those looking for travel companions to share costs).

Aside from the various Frommer's Guides, the Gault Millau Guides, and the Real Guides you can also choose from our Special Editions, which include such titles as *Caribbean Hideaways* (the 100 most romantic places to stay in the Islands); and *Marilyn Wood's Wonderful Weekends* (a selection of the best mini-vacations within a 200-mile radius of New York City).

To join this Club, send the appropriate membership fee with your name and address to: Frommer's Dollarwise Travel Club, 15 Columbus Circle, New York, NY 10023. Remember to specify which single city guide and which two other guides you wish to receive in your initial package of member's benefits. Or tear out the pages, check off your choices, and send them to us with your membership fee.

FROMMER BOOKS
PRENTICE HALL TRAVEL   Date_____
15 COLUMBUS CIRCLE
NEW YORK, NY 10023

Friends: Please send me the books checked below.

FROMMER'S™ COMPREHENSIVE GUIDES
(Guides listing facilities from budget to deluxe, with emphasis on the medium-priced)

☐ Alaska $14.95	☐ Italy. $19.00
☐ Australia $14.95	☐ Japan & Hong Kong $17.00
☐ Austria & Hungary $14.95	☐ Morocco $18.00
☐ Belgium, Holland & Luxembourg $14.95	☐ Nepal. $18.00
☐ Bermuda & The Bahamas. $17.00	☐ New England. $17.00
☐ Brazil $14.95	☐ New Mexico $13.95
☐ California $18.00	☐ New York State $19.00
☐ Canada $16.00	☐ Northwest $16.95
☐ Caribbean. $17.00	☐ Puerta Vallarta (avail. Feb. '92). $14.00
☐ Carolinas & Georgia $17.00	☐ Portugal, Madeira & the Azores $14.95
☐ Colorado (avail. Jan '92) $14.00	☐ Scandinavia $18.95
☐ Cruises (incl. Alaska, Carib, Mex, Hawaii,	☐ Scotland (avail. Feb. '92) $17.00
Panama, Canada & US) $16.00	☐ South Pacific. $20.00
☐ Delaware, Maryland, Pennsylvania &	☐ Southeast Asia $14.95
the New Jersey Shore (avail. Jan. '92) . .$19.00	☐ Switzerland & Liechtenstein $19.00
☐ Egypt. $14.95	☐ Thailand. $20.00
☐ England $17.00	☐ Virginia (avail. Feb. '92). $14.00
☐ Florida $17.00	☐ Virgin Islands $13.00
☐ France $15.95	☐ USA. $16.95
☐ Germany $18.00	

0891492

FROMMER'S CITY GUIDES
(Pocket-size guides to sightseeing and tourist accommodations and facilities in all price ranges)

☐ Amsterdam/Holland	$8.95	☐ Minneapolis/St. Paul	$8.95
☐ Athens	$8.95	☐ Montréal/Québec City	$8.95
☐ Atlanta	$8.95	☐ New Orleans	$8.95
☐ Atlantic City/Cape May	$8.95	☐ New York	$12.00
☐ Bangkok	$12.00	☐ Orlando	$12.00
☐ Barcelona	$12.00	☐ Paris	$8.95
☐ Belgium	$7.95	☐ Philadelphia	$11.00
☐ Berlin	$10.00	☐ Rio	$8.95
☐ Boston	$8.95	☐ Rome	$8.95
☐ Cancún/Cozumel/Yucatán	$8.95	☐ Salt Lake City	$8.95
☐ Chicago	$9.95	☐ San Diego	$8.95
☐ Denver/Boulder/Colorado Springs	$8.95	☐ San Francisco	$12.00
☐ Dublin/Ireland	$10.00	☐ Santa Fe/Taos/Albuquerque	$10.95
☐ Hawaii	$12.00	☐ Seattle/Portland	$12.00
☐ Hong Kong	$7.95	☐ St. Louis/Kansas City	$9.95
☐ Las Vegas	$8.95	☐ Sydney	$8.95
☐ Lisbon/Madrid/Costa del Sol	$8.95	☐ Tampa/St. Petersburg	$8.95
☐ London	$12.00	☐ Tokyo	$8.95
☐ Los Angeles	$8.95	☐ Toronto	$8.95
☐ Mexico City/Acapulco	$8.95	☐ Vancouver/Victoria	$7.95
☐ Miami	$8.95	☐ Washington, D.C.	$12.00

FROMMER'S $-A-DAY® GUIDES
(Guides to low-cost tourist accommodations and facilities)

☐ Australia on $40 a Day	$13.95	☐ Israel on $40 a Day	$13.95
☐ Costa Rica, Guatemala & Belize on $35 a Day	$15.95	☐ Mexico on $45 a Day	$18.00
		☐ New York on $65 a Day	$15.00
☐ Eastern Europe on $25 a Day	$16.95	☐ New Zealand on $45 a Day	$16.00
☐ England on $50 a Day	$17.00	☐ Scotland & Wales on $40 a Day	$18.00
☐ Europe on $45 a Day	$19.00	☐ South America on $40 a Day	$15.95
☐ Greece on $35 a Day	$14.95	☐ Spain on $50 a Day	$15.95
☐ Hawaii on $70 a Day	$18.00	☐ Turkey on $40 a Day	$22.00
☐ India on $40 a Day	$20.00	☐ Washington, D.C., on $45 a Day	$17.00
☐ Ireland on $40 a Day	$17.00		

FROMMER'S CITY $-A-DAY GUIDES

☐ Berlin on $40 a Day	$12.00	☐ Madrid on $50 a Day (avail. Jan '92)	$13.00
☐ Copenhagen on $50 a Day	$12.00	☐ Paris on $45 a Day	$12.00
☐ London on $45 a Day	$12.00	☐ Stockholm on $50 a Day (avail. Dec. '91)	$13.00

FROMMER'S FAMILY GUIDES

☐ California with Kids	$16.95	☐ San Francisco with Kids	$17.00
☐ Los Angeles with Kids	$17.00	☐ Washington, D.C., with Kids (avail. Jan '92)	$17.00
☐ New York City with Kids (avail. Jan '92)	$18.00		

SPECIAL EDITIONS

☐ Beat the High Cost of Travel	$6.95	☐ Marilyn Wood's Wonderful Weekends (CT, DE, MA, NH, NJ, NY, PA, RI, VT)	$11.95
☐ Bed & Breakfast—N. America	$14.95		
☐ Caribbean Hideaways	$16.00	☐ Motorist's Phrase Book (Fr/Ger/Sp)	$4.95
☐ Honeymoon Destinations (US, Mex & Carib)	$14.95	☐ The New World of Travel (annual by Arthur Frommer for savvy travelers)	$16.95

(TURN PAGE FOR ADDITONAL BOOKS AND ORDER FORM)

0891492

☐ Paris Rendez-Vous . . . .$10.95   ☐ Travel Diary and Record Book. $5.95
☐ Swap and Go (Home Exchanging). . . . .$10.95   ☐ Where to Stay USA (from $3 to $30 a
                                                               night). $13.95

FROMMER'S TOURING GUIDES

(Color illustrated guides that include walking tours, cultural and historic sites, and practical information)

☐ Amsterdam. $10.95	☐ New York $10.95
☐ Australia $12.95	☐ Paris $8.95
☐ Brazil $10.95	☐ Rome. $10.95
☐ Egypt. $8.95	☐ Scotland. $9.95
☐ Florence. $8.95	☐ Thailand. $12.95
☐ Hong Kong $10.95	☐ Turkey $10.95
☐ London $12.95	☐ Venice $8.95

GAULT MILLAU

(The only guides that distinguish the truly superlative from the merely overrated)

☐ The Best of Chicago $15.95	☐ The Best of Los Angeles $16.95
☐ The Best of Florida $17.00	☐ The Best of New England $15.95
☐ The Best of France $16.95	☐ The Best of New Orleans. $16.95
☐ The Best of Germany $18.00	☐ The Best of New York $16.95
☐ The Best of Hawaii $16.95	☐ The Best of Paris $16.95
☐ The Best of Hong Kong. $16.95	☐ The Best of San Francisco $16.95
☐ The Best of Italy. $16.95	☐ The Best of Thailand. $17.95
☐ The Best of London $16.95	☐ The Best of Toronto $17.00

☐ The Best of Washington, D.C. $16.95

THE REAL GUIDES

(Opinionated, politically aware guides for youthful budget-minded travelers)

☐ Amsterdam $9.95	☐ Mexico. $11.95
☐ Berlin. $11.95	☐ Morocco $12.95
☐ Brazil $13.95	☐ New York $9.95
☐ California & the West Coast $11.95	☐ Paris $9.95
☐ Czechoslovakia $13.95	☐ Peru. $12.95
☐ France $12.95	☐ Poland $13.95
☐ Germany $13.95	☐ Portugal $10.95
☐ Greece. $13.95	☐ San Francisco $11.95
☐ Guatemala $13.95	☐ Scandinavia $14.95
☐ Hong Kong $11.95	☐ Spain $12.95
☐ Hungary. $12.95	☐ Turkey $12.95
☐ Ireland $12.95	☐ Venice $11.95
☐ Italy. $13.95	☐ Women Travel. $12.95
☐ Kenya. $12.95	☐ Yugoslavia $12.95

ORDER NOW!

In U.S. include $2 shipping UPS for 1st book; $1 ea. add'l book. Outside U.S. $3 and $1, respectively.

Allow four to six weeks for delivery in U.S., longer outside U.S. We discourage rush order service, but orders arriving with shipping fees plus a $15 surcharge will be handled as rush orders.

Enclosed is my check or money order for $_____

NAME _____

ADDRESS _____

CITY _____ STATE _____ ZIP _____